D1629473

Allen Curnow
Simply by Sailing
in a New Direction

Allen Curnow
Simply by Sailing
in a New Direction

A Biography

Terry Sturm

Edited by Linda Cassells

AUCKLAND
UNIVERSITY
PRESS

First published 2017
Auckland University Press
University of Auckland
Private Bag 92019
Auckland 1142
New Zealand
www.press.auckland.ac.nz

© Linda Cassells on behalf of the Literary Estate of Terry Sturm, 2017

ISBN 978 1 86940 852 7

Published with the assistance of

ARTS COUNCIL OF NEW ZEALAND TOI AOTEAROA

A catalogue record for this book is available from the National Library of New Zealand

Book design by Katrina Duncan & Carolyn Lewis
Typeset in Adobe Caslon
Jacket design by Sarah Maxey

Endpaper design by Betty Curnow. The design was commissioned by
Denis Glover of The Caxton Press for his book of poems *The Wind and
the Sand: Poems 1934–44* published in 1945 on his return from the war.

Printed in China by 1010 Printing International Ltd

for Terry

I owe a great deal to Allen Curnow, too. It was Allen who said . . . that a poem must be visceral. 'You can tell if it's alive by poking it with a stick.'

— *Elizabeth Smither*

CONTENTS

PREFACE AND ACKNOWLEDGEMENTS

Allen Curnow (1911–2001) was one of New Zealand's most eminent and influential writers and among the finest English language poets of his generation worldwide. Curnow was largely responsible for defining our literary nationalism in the 1940s, in an attempt to break away from the colonial dependence on English culture, and it was he who introduced modernist agendas into New Zealand writing.

During his seventy years of publishing, he dominated the New Zealand literary landscape at almost every stage, and from the 1960s onwards enjoyed an international reputation for his poetry. In 1989 he was awarded the prestigious Queen's Gold Medal for Poetry. His work has been published in translation, and continues to be widely anthologised.

By the time of his death at the age of ninety, he had completed a body of work which is unique in this country and increasingly recognised as significant in international terms. Remarkably, there has as yet been no full-length study of Curnow's work, taking into account the ways in which it makes sense of New Zealand's cultural history in the twentieth century. It is this significant lacuna that this project seeks to address.

These words, written by Terry Sturm, are drawn from his application for a Marsden Fund grant to research and write a literary biography of Allen Curnow. The subsequent Marsden endorsement of the project signalled it as a work of great significance to New Zealand's cultural history, and the panel's appraisal of Terry Sturm as researcher and writer was rated as outstanding. This book is the fruit of his research and writing, which spanned more than seven years.

The idea for this biography took firm shape over a dinner conversation at the French Café in Auckland in 2001 shortly after Allen Curnow's death. Curnow's widow, Jeny, had recognised the need for a literary biography of the poet's life, and Terry Sturm had the scholarly credentials and integrity befitting the task. He had long harboured an ambition to write such a book, and widow and writer quickly reached an understanding. Access would of course be granted to the Curnow archives. However, the route to publication was to be long and circuitous – much more so than any of us could have imagined that evening.

The ease and speed of their understanding rested on Terry's long-standing relationship with the Curnows and the trust and respect they had for each other. Terry's interest in Allen Curnow's writing stemmed from his student years – as an undergraduate at the University of Auckland he had studied Curnow's poetry, and it soon would form part of his doctoral thesis at the University of

Leeds on problems of cultural dependence. In 1973, while a lecturer at the University of Sydney, he began researching a book on Curnow's work as part of Twayne's World Authors Series, initiating a correspondence with Curnow and interviewing him at that time about his life and work. The project was aborted by the publishers for economic reasons, but Terry's notes and correspondence formed the basis of what was later to become an extensive archive on Curnow's life and writing, reflecting the many further years of painstaking research underpinning this biography.

Noted for his scrupulous research, Terry Sturm was uniquely qualified to write this literary biography, and it is a mark of his commitment to the subject that he continued to work on the manuscript throughout his final illness. When he died in 2009 he left a full first draft of the manuscript of some 460,000 words. He had known for many months that his time was limited, and had suggested a path for completion – which in the first instance would involve stringent structural editing. It would be a mammoth task for whoever was to undertake it, and the responsibility eventually fell to me, literary executor but also, as chance would have it, an editor and publisher by profession. The work required to bring the book to publication extended well beyond structural editing, however, and was far more expansive than I could have imagined when I first committed to ensuring the book would be published. The bibliographic notes had to be sourced and checked, copyright holders traced and permissions cleared, outstanding text queries resolved, photographs selected and captions written. While I have been actively involved in all these stages of preparation for publication, the work could not have been completed without the generous guidance of several Curnow scholars and publishing professionals.

The option, suggested by some after Terry's death, of publishing the first draft of the manuscript in two volumes was never seriously considered. Terry's modus operandi, which I had the privilege of observing at close hand with several of his previous publications, was to prepare an exhaustive first draft, and then to revise, cull and rework the material. Terry and I had detailed discussions during his last months as to how the draft biography could be cut and managed, weighing up the valuable feedback from key Curnow family members as well as scholarly colleagues who had read all or parts of the first draft.

The task of structural editing thus proceeded on carefully considered principles that had been agreed with Terry. For instance, multiple long quotations on a particular aspect of the narrative would be reduced to a single shortened one; plot summaries of the plays would be further condensed; direct quotations from the poems and long textual analyses would be contained and reserved for a range of key poems; the coverage given to Curnow's popular persona Whim Wham would be reduced because of the recently published edition of Whim Wham's poems,* and, more obviously, the inevitable repetitions of a first draft would be eliminated and a seamless narrative flow would need to be achieved.

I have no doubt that Terry would have carried out the structural editing differently and better, but I have done my best to ensure that justice has been done to the process we agreed.

A project of this scope would never have seen publication without the generous support of many institutions, academic and publishing colleagues, family and friends, to whom I express my thanks.

The Royal Society of New Zealand's Marsden Fund grant, awarded to Terry in 2002 for a three-year period, enabled him to devote his time fully to researching this project. The University of Auckland, where Terry had served as a professor since 1980, also supported the project in many practical ways during his tenure and after his retirement in 2006. I particularly acknowledge the encouragement given me by the then Dean of Arts John Morrow to complete the biography, and am grateful for the financial support from the Faculty of Arts towards the editing work.

I acknowledge the invaluable assistance of the librarians at the Alexander Turnbull Library and the Hocken Collections. Many individuals helped Terry in his research and writing, and he would no doubt have fulsomely acknowledged them here. Their generous contribution to this work is appreciated, and I regret any omissions below.

The Curnow family were unanimously helpful in making relevant material available during the research stages, particularly Allen's widow, Jeny Curnow, whose friendship and encouragement I valued deeply. Curnow's sons Wystan and Tim, his daughter Belinda and his brother Anthony were also generous in their support of the biography, making much family material available. Jeny, Wystan and Tim read the first draft of the manuscript while Terry was still alive and they were able to provide helpful feedback, verify facts and correct some misunderstandings and inadvertent errors. Wystan provided helpful advice in the early stages of structural editing to ensure that thematic weightings were balanced. Both Wystan and Tim mined the Curnow family photograph albums to provide a selection for reproduction in the book.

Tim Curnow had been Terry's literary agent for many years and continued in that role for me after Terry's death. His professional negotiation skills, knowledge of the subject and keen eye for detail have been invaluable, as have his prompt and encouraging communication and good humour throughout the eight years needed to bring this project to completion.

---

* *Whim Wham's New Zealand: The Best of Whim Wham 1937–1988*, ed. Terry Sturm, Vintage, Auckland, 2005.

In his final months Terry had recommended that I call on the judgement and skills of his friend and colleague Mac Jackson to reduce the manuscript to a publishable extent, and I am grateful for Mac's time and guidance. He had already read sections of the manuscript, and on Terry's death completed a detailed reading of the draft, providing useful input on the editing stages to follow. He later also read the final edited work, and helped clarify many queries in the text and references.

I am deeply grateful to my partner-in-editing Mike Wagg for his detailed attention, editorial skill and sensitivity to the subject matter. His input has been substantial and multi-layered, working directly with me and then under the auspices of my publisher Auckland University Press. He continued and refined the established editorial process of cutting and restructuring the draft manuscript, checking facts and highlighting inconsistencies. He later copyedited the manuscript and prepared an exhaustive list of permissions requirements. The incomplete and often cryptic state of the notes in Terry's first draft generated a laborious task of referencing them against Terry's 'matrix' and numerous, carefully filed boxes of materials. Mike met the challenging and painstaking assignment of compiling the notes and references with intelligence and level-headedness.

I owe special thanks also to Elizabeth Caffin, who proofread the edited manuscript and generously helped track down outstanding references, checking sources in the Alexander Turnbull Library. She also impressively helped resolve some queries where others had drawn a blank.

Sam Elworthy of Auckland University Press has endured the long process of bringing this biography to publication with patience and sound advice, and others on the AUP team, particularly Anna Hodge, Katrina Duncan, Katharina Bauer, Louisa Kasza, Sarah Maxey, Carolyn Lewis and Fiona Kirkcaldie contributed greatly to ensuring a high standard of publication. My thanks also to Robin Briggs for his indexing skills.

Many other people have supported and encouraged me in ways they may be unaware of, in particular my daughter Imogen Shephard, and friends Peter Bland, Angela Caughey, Anne de Lautour, Margaret Harris, Robin Hooper, Judith Huntsman, Jan Kemp, Caroline List, Jane Morgan, Peter Morgan, Judith Mollot, Karen Moloney, Sue Revell, the late Max Richards, Dieter Riemenschneider, Margaret Samuels, Elizabeth Smither, Joanne Wilkes and Margaret Wilson.

Finally, I am hugely grateful to Terry's three sons, Jonathan, Mark and Timothy Sturm, for the practical and moral support they have given me, and for keeping faith that this work of their father would finally see publication.

Tracing all copyright holders, 'the forensic end of editing' as Mike Wagg quipped, was challenging. I am grateful to Mike, who compiled the list of material to be cleared; to Anna Hodge, then of Auckland University Press, who shared the load and tapped into her network to help trace copyright holders; to Louisa Kasza, also of Auckland University Press, who prepared a shared tracking system without which we would have struggled to measure our progress; and to editor Kylan Luke-McKeen, who managed the permissions clearance process with terrific efficiency and good humour. I owe particular thanks to the many friends and contacts who helped trace copyright holders, including Elizabeth Alley, Rachel Barrowman, Chris Bourke, Bernard Brown, Elizabeth Caffin, Philippa Campbell, Euan Cant, Richard Cathie, Tim Curnow, Wystan Curnow, Brian Easton, Dinah Holman, Jenny Horne, Peter Lange, Robert Lee-Johnson, David Ling, Leslie McTurk, Siobhán Parkinson, Bill Sheat, Sarah Shieff, Peter Simpson and C.K. Stead. We have made every effort to trace copyright holders and to obtain their permission, but we apologise in advance for any errors or omissions and would be grateful to be notified of any corrections that should be incorporated in future reprints or editions of this book.

I am grateful to the following people and institutions for their kind permission to reproduce copyrighted material: Graeme Austin for extract from letter of William Austin; Peter-Paul Barker for extract from letter of Ronald Barker; Tim Bates for extract from letter; The James K. Baxter Trust for extracts from unpublished letters of James K. Baxter; Dr Anselm Kuhn of Finishing Publications Ltd (www.svenberlin.com) for extract from letter of Sven Berlin; Kay Malpass for extracts from letters of James Bertram; Alan Roddick for extracts from the journals and letters of Charles Brasch; Andrew Campbell for extracts from letters of Alistair Te Ariki Campbell; Judith Campion for extracts from letters of Richard Campion; Tim Curnow for extracts from unpublished letters, fragments, lectures, notes, drafts of poems, quotations from poetry and published prose of Allen Curnow, for information on the Le Cren family from 'The Le Cren Family, 1738–1988' by Denis Jaumaud Le Cren, for notes from a transcript of an interview of Belinda Curnow with Terry Sturm, for extracts from personal diaries and notes of Betty Curnow, for extracts of Jenifer Curnow from unpublished 'Biography of Allen Curnow', diaries and letters, for extracts of letters of Tremayne Curnow, for extracts from letters of Tim Curnow, from 'Eulogy for Mum' and from transcript of interview with Terry Sturm, for extracts from letters of Arnold (Ted) Wall; Simon Curnow on behalf of Elisabeth Curnow for extracts from letters and unpublished autobiography of Anthony Curnow; Wystan Curnow for extract from 'Eulogy for my Mother' and extracts from letters; Carcanet Press Ltd, Manchester, UK for extracts from letters of Donald Davie; Mark Horton and Sr de Pores of the Catholic Archdiocesan Archives for extracts from letters of Eileen Duggan; Dikkon Eberhart for extract from letter of Richard Eberhart; the A.R.D. Fairburn Literary Estate for extracts from letters; Penguin Random House UK for extracts from letters and cables of Eunice Frost and extract from letter of Richard Hollyer; Rupert Glover for extracts from letters of Denis Glover; Richard Goldsbrough for extract from interview of Diana Goldsbrough with Terry Sturm; Mike Heenan for extracts from letters of Joseph Heenan; Shirley Horrocks for extracts from interview with Allen Curnow towards the documentary *Early Days Yet* (Point of View Productions, 2001); Faber & Faber for extract from unpublished letter of Ted Hughes; Cecilia Johnson for extracts from letters of Louis Johnson; the Kinder Library Archives for extracts from letters of Canon E.H. Strong; Margaret Pope for extract from letter of David Lange; the Alexander Turnbull Library for extracts from letters of Douglas Lilburn; Vanya Lowry for extracts from letters of Robert Lowry; John Dacres-Mannings for extracts from letters of Ngaio Marsh; the Hocken Collections for extract from letter of R.A.K. Mason; Zoe Shine for extracts from letters of Richard Mayne; Rachel McAlpine for extract from letter; the late James McNeish for extracts from interview; Jane Collet for extracts from letters of Karl Miller; Gordon Ogilvie for extracts from letters and from *Denis Glover: His Life* (Godwit, Auckland, 1999); J.G.A. (John) Pocock for extracts from letters and from the unpublished manuscript 'Landscape as Ithaca: Island and History in Curnow's Earlier Poems'; Rogers, Coleridge & White for extract from letter of Peter Porter; Beverley Reeves for extracts from address of the Rt Rev. Sir Paul Reeves at funeral of Allen Curnow, 27 September 2001; Alan Roddick for extracts from letters; Joachim Sartorius for extract from letter; Michael Schmidt for extracts from letters; Mark Schroder for extracts from letters of J.H.E. (John) Schroder; Eric Sellin for extract from letter; C.K. Stead for extracts from letters and poem; Ben Tate for extract from letter of Allen Tate; Anthony Thwaite for extracts from letters; Sr Regina of Presentation Sisters Convent for extract from letter of Sr M. Vianney; Mary-Kay Wilmers for extracts from letters; Janet Wilson for extract from letter.

PART I

Chapter One

Family Ancestries

We all grow up with all kinds of psychic pressure-points, & have more
or less success at learning to live with them. . . . As with so many other
more obvious things, the surest healing has to be self-healing.[1]

Prologue: 'Self-Portrait'

In October 1945, during a visit Allen Curnow made to his parents' vicarage home
in Kaiapoi, near Christchurch, his mother Jessie showed him some early childhood photographs which had come to light while she and her husband Tremayne
were preparing to vacate the house and move to Auckland, where they planned
to retire. One photograph in particular caught Curnow's eye, of 'myself when
young (about 4 years old I think)':

> Surprised to see myself looking such a small creature, with a timid & imploring look
> – how I have covered over that surprised & timid little person, & never quite stopped
> feeling it. But *forward* one must go, however battered, & that child might have been
> a lot less lucky & happy.[2]

Curnow was born in 1911, so the photograph would have been taken in 1915,
when the family was living in the vicarage at Belfast, a freezing-works township
on the northern outskirts of Christchurch. The poem he wrote in 1945 about
the photograph – a sonnet entitled 'Self-Portrait' – reflects on the moment of
surprised self-awareness which the image of himself when young has given him:

The wistful camera caught this four-year-old
But could not stare him into wistfulness;
He holds the toy that he is given to hold:
A passionate failure or a staled success

Look back into their likeness while I look
With pity not self-pity at the plain
Mechanical image that I first mistook
For my own image; there, timid or vain,

Semblance of my own eyes my eyes discern
Casting on mine as I cast back on these
Regard not self-regard: till the toy turn
Into a lover clasped, into wide seas,

The salt or visionary wave, and the days heap
Sorrow upon sorrow for all he could not keep.

The image of the child which the poem constructs is more complex than Curnow's initial reaction to the photograph might suggest. The look is not only 'timid & imploring', but possibly 'vain'. There is a sense that the child is already learning to 'cover over' such feelings, as he clutches his toy, refuses to invite 'wistfulness', and 'stares' back obstinately at his older adult self. There is also a sense of self-containment about the child which masks resolute determination and desire as well as vulnerability, insecurity and self-protectiveness. It is as if the child-self is already aware that whatever personal or public failures and successes life holds in store for him, they will always carry with them dissatisfaction over what is not achieved and sorrow for what, inevitably, will be lost.

'Self-Portrait' was one of many poems which Curnow wrote from the mid-1940s onward – many of them appearing in the collections *Jack without Magic* (1946) and *At Dead Low Water* (1949) – in which, as he later put it, he 'turned away from questions which present themselves as public and answerable, towards the questions which are always private and unanswerable'[3]. A number of these poems also turned directly to childhood and family memories for their occasions. Indeed, from this point on – right through to poems in his last volume, *The Bells of Saint Babel's* (2001) – such memories provided one of the main sources of inspiration for many of his major poems. The poet's family background and childhood thus constitute an unusually important part of his literary biography. The figures introduced in this and the following chapter might be seen as the *dramatis personae* of what Curnow came to call his 'familial poems', figures who provided the vicarage-based young child with his first bearings on the wider world and remained influential on the kind of poet he was to become.

Maternal grandparents: the Allens and Gamblings

Allen's full name, Thomas Allen Monro Curnow, continued a strong family tradition of acknowledging forebears. Allen was the surname of a Norfolk-based English great-grandfather on his mother's side, Thomas Allen, while Monro was a family name with long-standing New Zealand connections, going back on his father's side through four generations to the 1830s. The Anglo–New Zealand heritage built into Curnow's name was strongly reinforced in the dynamics of his immediate family life. The 'tension' between English and New Zealand loyalties that found its way into a number of his poems in the late 1930s and early 1940s was not, he insisted, based on some 'South Island myth' but very personally and immediately experienced in his own family life – as it was, he imagined, in the lives of many New Zealanders of his generation:

> All the years of my childhood and youth, and pretty well until I was nineteen years old, our household consisted of my New Zealand father, my English-born mother and my English grandmother. All through those years a great share in my upbringing was taken by my grandmother. . . . Far from being 'myth', the actual tension was there under the very roof of every vicarage in which we lived between say 1913 and 1930. I grew up to my grandmother's sadness – her feeling of exile and the way she cut herself off almost from all social living outside the vicarage . . . .[4]

The reasons for the immigration of Curnow's grandmother with her young daughter to New Zealand are shrouded in mystery. Rose Letitia Maria Allen, the grandmother who was so much a part of his childhood, was born on 17 June 1854[5] in Norfolk, in the small English village of Caistor St Edmund near Norwich, and was brought up close by at 'Markshall', quite a large Georgian-style house on the farming estate leased by her father, Thomas Allen, who also owned farms nearby at Buxton Lammas and Cantley.[6] Rose was the oldest of six daughters and a son, and in the later 1870s married John Towler Gambling (born in 1855), one of numerous sons of a family living in the same area who owned a wherry fleet and a mill at Buxton Lammas.

Gambling became an accountant but otherwise very little is known about him. He was a great-grandnephew of the English rural clergyman poet George Crabbe (1754–1832), descended from Crabbe's sister,[7] and his and Rose's only child, Jessamine (Jessie) Towler Gambling (Curnow's mother), was born on 3 June 1880.

The marriage broke down in the 1880s and towards the end of that decade Rose left England with her young daughter and travelled to Australia, where for two or three years they were based in Sydney, before moving to Invercargill, New Zealand, in the early 1890s. In the mid-1890s Gambling himself moved to New Zealand, and the family was reunited in Invercargill for ten years,[8] after which Rose moved with her daughter to Timaru.*

Among her accomplishments Rose had been trained as a singer, and during her shifts of residence she survived by giving singing lessons and taking in lodgers, assisted by Jessie. Rose is likely also to have been supported by her family back in England, and to have had some inheritance money when her father died in the early 1900s.

It was in Timaru that Jessie met Curnow's father, Tremayne, who boarded with the family and from 1905 onwards was based in Timaru as assistant curate at St Mary's Church after his ordination as deacon at the end of 1904. Jessie and Tremayne were married at St John's Church, Invercargill, on 13 April 1909 and at this point both lived with Rose in Timaru.

Jessie's father, whom Curnow never met, remained a mysterious figure in the family's life. Speculation that the cause of John and Rose's marriage breakdown was alcoholism is largely based on Jessie's lifelong hostility to alcohol. However, there might have been some other reason, on which Curnow and his brothers later speculated: some kind of debility, illness or personality disorder. Curnow recalled that his grandmother continued to correspond with her husband, and on occasion referred to him as 'Dad-dad',[9] but her daughter never spoke of him, and neither Curnow nor his brothers ever felt able to ask her about him. Almost certainly Jessie would have felt a sense of abandonment by her father. Although she and Rose kept photographs and keepsakes of their Norwich connections,[†][10] there was no photograph of John Gambling.

In 1949, when Curnow visited England for the first time, he made contact with Willy Gambling, a younger brother of John, then living at Summer-Leyton (Fytton-de-Coy) on the Suffolk coast, but the conversation remained general and Willy volunteered no family stories. On the same trip Curnow did, however, seek

---

* The mystery of Gambling's life and of his on-again off-again relationship with Rose does not quite end there, however. When Jessie married Tremayne Curnow in 1909 the wedding took place not in Timaru, as might be expected, but in Invercargill, and Jessie's place of residence was given as Liffey Street, Invercargill, though there is no record that Gambling attended the wedding. Furthermore, around 1911, according to family tradition, Rose took her baby grandson, John (Curnow's older brother, born 1910), to Invercargill to meet Gambling and attempt yet another reconciliation, though without success. And on the 1914 Invercargill electoral roll, Rose again reappeared on the list with John Gambling, both of them described as living at Eye Street, Invercargill, and her occupation given as 'married' – a fact which suggests that a further brief (but again unsuccessful) attempt was made at a rapprochement in that year. The last reference to Gambling in official records is for the year 1915, when he was 60 years old and listed in Stone's Directory as a clerk living at Eye Street in Invercargill. After that he disappears without trace, assumed to have returned to England.
† Rose's room was 'a little shrine where she hung her pictures of places in Norwich, and in Markshall village'.

information from one of Rose's surviving sisters, Beatrice Goldingham, then a sprightly 89-year-old whom he visited in Edinburgh, but she too was unwilling to discuss what had happened, and died the following year. 'It was very sad and a long time ago', he recalled her as saying.* [11] It was not at all unusual for such silences about potentially embarrassing matters to have been maintained in families during the time of Curnow's childhood and youth, but for a child as observant and sensitive as he, the secrecy would surely have aroused his curiosity.

Curnow's most moving account of the influence of his grandmother in shaping the imaginary England of his childhood is contained in a radio broadcast he wrote after visiting Norfolk in November 1949, encountering in the Allen tombstones at Caistor St Edmund and the old farm and home at Markshall, 'places and people [who] were ghosts that haunted my New Zealand childhood':

> I knew the house the moment I saw it. An old yellow photograph of Markshall always hung on the wall of my grandmother's room – the room of her own that she had in all the New Zealand vicarages where our family lived. It was always part of the landscape of my imaginary England. As a child I could look at it, while I listened to stories of Norwich, and Caistor, and the old mill at Buxton Lammas.[12]

The encounter was especially poignant since the visit to Norfolk occurred in the immediate wake of Curnow's learning of his father's death in New Zealand, at the end of October 1949, and details of the trip to Norfolk are included in the powerful poetic tribute he wrote over the next few weeks, 'Elegy on My Father'. In his radio piece, Curnow sees the trip to Norwich as enabling him to substitute memories for ghosts, to test sentiment against reality. Contemplating the tombs of his ancestors, so surprisingly *recent* compared with the 700-year history of the Norman church where they are located, let alone compared with the Roman past contained in the name *Caistor* St Edmund: 'All I could think to say – and I did say it, aloud, was: "So there you are. You're real, after all."'[13] And that reality included not only their relative recentness, but their 'distance' or difference from himself: 'They seemed to be asking questions: "This is where we belong," they said. "Where do you belong? Where do you come from?"'[14] What is recorded here is a personal release from a disabling kind of sentimental identification with Englishness.

A similar kind of release is described in Curnow's moving and beautiful memorial sonnet to his grandmother Rose Gambling ('In Memoriam, R.L.M.G.'), which he wrote some fifteen years after her death in January 1931 at the age of 76.

---

* After his visit Beatrice asked her daughter Kathleen to jot down what she had told Curnow in case he forgot the details: 'The three sisters emigrated [sic] to Australia for various reasons; some of them too sad to rake up. Aunt Pets [?Rose] was adventurous. Mother cannot tell you anything about your grandfather John Gambling that you will not have heard from your mother.' Curnow's mother, however, had told him nothing.

Shortly before she died the family had shifted from West Lyttelton to the parish of New Brighton in Christchurch, and Curnow was about to embark on his own theological studies at St John's Theological College in Auckland. However, it was Rose's wish to be buried in the cemetery in the hills behind Lyttelton, where she had spent nine years in sight of the ships arriving and departing from the harbour below – ships which she had often watched from the window of the upstairs landing at the vicarage, occasionally weeping, as Curnow recalled, and longing to go home.[15] In the poem her sacrificial death, after an exile from England of more than 40 years, establishes a local past – a local 'ancestry' – for those who come after her and in so doing 'dismisses' them into the 'broad day' of the present. She is presented as a figure of courage, who deliberately chooses 'oblivion' for herself in order to allow the generations she nurtured to feel at home in a country which was always alien to her:

> The oldest of us burst into tears and cried
> Let me go home, but she stayed, watching
> At her staircase window ship after ship ride
> Like birds her grieving sunsets; there sat stitching
>
> Grandchildren's things. She died by the same sea.
> High over it she led us in the steepening heat
> To the yellow grave; her clay
> Chose that way home: dismissed, our feet
>
> Were seen to have stopped and turned again down hill;
> The street fell like an ink-blue river
> In the heat of the bay, the basking ships, this Isle
> Of her oblivion, our broad day. Heaped over
>
> So lightly, she stretched like time behind us, or
> Graven in cloud, our furthest ancestor.

In the companion sonnet to Grandmother Gambling's sister which Curnow wrote at the same time, 'To Fanny Rose May',* he praised his great-aunt (then living in Sydney) in similar terms, since, like her sister's, her 'blood sweetens

---

* Fanny Rose May was Rose's youngest sister, whose husband had died in the 1920s of complications from being gassed during the First World War. Curnow had great affection for her, and she attended his wedding in 1936, taking a special interest in his family and writing, sending gifts each Christmas, and occasionally hunting out overseas books and magazines at his request. After 1936 she immigrated permanently to Sydney, where she died in 1957.

the embittered seas between / Fabulous old England and these innovations /
My mountainous islands'.

Grandmother Gambling's role in the Curnow household introduced an
unusual dynamic. No doubt she was able to contribute something to the family
finances – which were never substantial – but her main role was a domestic one,
and she effaced herself socially. An older cousin, Arnold Wall (known as 'Ted'
to distinguish him from his father, who was professor of English and history
at Canterbury University College), remembered her 'dimly', on family visits to
the vicarage at West Lyttelton, as 'a kindly but rather anxious little personage
hovering in the background of Aunt Jessie, of whose ever-kindly personality I have
more vivid memories'.[16] She cooked most of the family meals until she was about
seventy. She also played a major role in the upbringing of the children, and was
especially protective of the eldest, John, who in his earliest years was often unwell.
Her domestic role was also helpful in freeing Jessie to assist Tremayne in the parish
duties expected of a clergyman's wife, but it did create occasional resentments in
Allen's childhood life: at what he felt to be favouritism towards his brother, and
at her being a 'substitute' for his 'real mother'.

Grandmother Gambling's unusual marital history in the 1880s is the subject
of an extended allusion in a memorable late poem, 'A South Island Night's
Entertainment', in which she is depicted as a member of the family trudging
home in darkness outside Sheffield (Curnow was eight or nine at the time), after
discovering that they had mistaken the evening on which a silent movie was to
be shown in a local barn. The starless night sky is as devoid of vivid entertainment
as the screen in the locked barn:

> What's visible here?
>
> Not the crab tropic's
> maidenliest stars
>
> twinkle-twinkling
> on my grandmother's
>
> East Anglian
> wedding night, swapped
>
> now, for a sphere
> *beyond the circuit*
>
> *of the shuddering Bear.*

The astronomical allusions here are obscure, but they evoke his grandmother's East Anglian wedding night as occurring under the 'crab tropic' (the northern constellation of Cancer) and her exile to New Zealand as an escape from the 'circuit of the shuddering Bear'. The italicised lines are from T.S. Eliot's 'Gerontion', where they offer a generalised image of a personality and world (by implication, in Curnow's poem, his grandmother's) which has been torn apart, 'in fractured atoms'. The lines also contain the phrase 'maidenliest stars', derived from the famous speech in *King Lear* in which the Duke of Gloucester's bastard son Edmund mocks his father's fervent belief in astrology:

> My father compounded with my mother under the dragon's tail, and my nativity was under *Ursa Major*, so that it follows I am rough and lecherous. Fut! I should have been that I am had the maidenliest star in the firmament twinkled on my bastardizing. [I. ii. 135–40]

At the very least the cluster of associations in the lines suggest that there may have been some profound sexual crisis in his grandmother's marriage which led to her decision to leave her husband, to immigrate to a sphere '*beyond the circuit of the shuddering Bear*'.* [17]

In another later poem, begun during his visit to Menton as the Katherine Mansfield Literary Fellow in 1983, Curnow attempted a different, much more personal, characterisation of Grandmother Gambling – neither the tragi-heroic figure of the early elegy nor the traumatised bride of 'A South Island Night's Entertainment'. Provisionally entitled 'Grm [grandmother] at the Piano, 1914–1916',[18] and based on some of his earliest memories from his Belfast vicarage years, the poem was never completed, containing a detailed description of his grandmother's piano, and of her soprano voice singing a musical arrangement of Tennyson's famous refrain in 'The Brook' as she played, as well as allusions to her 'casebound score of *The Messiah*' and to Tremayne's remembered quotations of the same Tennyson poem.

The reference to 'The Brook' contains a moving comparison between his grandmother's fate and that of Katie Willows, the young woman of Tennyson's poem who manages to overcome parental obstruction to marry James Willows, and *both* then immigrate to the Antipodes, 'By the long wash of Australasian seas / Far off': the marriage survives and both Katie and her husband eventually return to the farm in England, after 20 years, with a daughter. The effect

---

* In earlier versions of the poem, which evoke 'the night sky / of my granny's East / Anglian teens', and refer to his grandmother as having 'swapped / hemispheres, for / some sad . . ./ Victorian cause, / they never told me about', the sexual allusions are largely absent.

of the allusion, had Curnow been able to complete the poem, would have been a poignant contrast between the actual situation of Rose Gambling and the fate of the young woman about whom she sings. The notes to the poem indicate the continuing personal presence of Curnow's grandmother in his later memories, especially associated with his first experiences of music, as he wrote to Douglas Lilburn in 1998, after listening to an impressive performance of a Bartók Divertimento for Strings by the New Zealand Symphony Orchestra at the Auckland Town Hall:

> I think I've been more stirred – or nearly as much – as I was by the first little orchestra I ever heard, aged 14, in the old Christchurch Theatre Royal, striking up the overture to *The Gondoliers*. . . . Musically, of course, it's not exactly 'where I came in' – age 5 or six, hearing my grandmother (at her piano) singing that pastoral bit from The Messiah, as I believe she had sung it in Norwich.[19]

More broadly, she remained, always, the focal point of an Englishness he had *experienced* deeply and directly as a child, and grown away from. And Tennyson's famous line, 'By the long wash of Australasian seas' – epitomising the Victorian perception of the Antipodes as the realm of remoteness and exile – was to survive in a poem about the ending of the First World War ('Survivors') written shortly afterwards.

Paternal grandparents: John and Alice Curnow

On Curnow's father's side, there was nothing like the directness of English connection that existed through his mother and grandmother. Tremayne Curnow was born in Christchurch, New Zealand (in February 1881), and both of his parents, John Curnow and Alice Augusta Monro, were more strongly connected with an emerging New Zealand colonial history than with their English forebears overseas. As with Curnow's maternal side, however, it was the female line which remained most influential on his life: the Monro connection through his grandmother, rather than the Curnow connection through his grandfather.

Curnow never knew either of his grandfathers, and knew almost as little about John Curnow as he did about John Gambling, partly because he died so young. John Curnow was born in St Ives, Cornwall, in 1849, and immigrated with his parents in 1851 to Australia, where he later attended the University of Melbourne and gained BA and LLB degrees, at the time the youngest student ever to have graduated from that university. He taught at Scotch College before coming to New Zealand in 1874 to take up a teaching job at Auckland Grammar School, and married Alice Monro, daughter of Judge H.A.H. Monro, then serving on the Native Land Court, in Auckland in January 1876. He was an unusually committed and gifted educationist, publishing two textbooks in 1879, one on English history and the other on science.[20] The science textbook was co-authored with W.E.W. Morrison, who had married Alice Monro's older sister Ada, and it is likely that John met Alice in Auckland through Morrison.

In 1876 John and Alice moved to Christchurch where John – still only in his twenties – took up an appointment as headmaster of the newly established Christchurch Normal School. In 1879 he became headmaster of the East Christchurch Main and Side Schools, and shortly before his sudden death of typhoid disease, at the age of 33, in 1882, he was appointed as inspector to the Board of Education. Newspaper obituaries drew attention to his personal qualities as 'a genial friend and scholarly companion'[21] as well as to the loss to the education profession of so promising a career. Alice survived her husband by almost 40 years (until 1921), living in their Cambridge Terrace home in Christchurch where she brought up her three young children alone – Pendarves (born in 1877), Elsie (known as 'Gipsy', born in 1879) and Tremayne.

John Curnow makes no appearance in any of his grandson's poems, but on the same trip to England in 1949–50 in which he sought out his Allen and Gambling Norfolk connections, Curnow also sought to discover the Cornish connections inherited through his paternal grandfather. Basing himself at St Ives, John's birthplace, for several days in mid-January 1950, he walked across the Cornish moors to Zennor village, and beyond to Gurnard's Head. He discovered that the name Curnow, and variants on it, was common in the area (indeed, that the root of the name is the same as the word Cornwall itself):

> I looked out my bedroom window the first morning in St Ives, & there was T. CURNOW, Hairdresser, on a sign across the street. . . . A Curnow keeps an hotel (dry!), another Curnow keeps a restaurant, another is a men's outfitter & a member of St Ives Council, another has a little farm & grey stone house at Gurnard's head.[22]

Despite his efforts ('I spoke to a few Curnows & glanced at old marriage registers lent me by the Magistrate to see if some vague trace of my own original might not exist there'), he heard and found 'nothing that seemed worth following up'.[23] However, he was fascinated by the distinctive landscape, regional culture and dialect of Cornwall,* [24] and his discovery of these features of the place reinforced

---

*   It was not until the mid-1960s, when his friendship began with the historian A.L. (Leslie) Rowse, a Cornishman, that Curnow learnt that the likeliest location for his own branch of the family was Towednack, which he visited in 1974: 'it was the home village of most Curnows . . . to judge by the number of Curnows buried in the churchyard there'.

one of the driving impulses of his own work as a poet in New Zealand – to artic-ulate the country's distinctive culture and identity. He discovered a thriving art scene in St Ives, and on his return to London wrote two poems, under the general title 'Cornwall', which were published that year in the *Cornish Review*,[25] an act of personal identification with a magazine which was attractive to him precisely because of its regional focus and affiliations.

The first of the poems, entitled 'Sea Tryst', evoked his 'tribal' affiliations with the Cornwall Curnows and the local legend of the Zennor Maid, a changeling, Lilith-like, sea-maiden who tempted and lured men to their death. During the course of the poem the narrator takes the Maid on a remarkable undersea journey to the 'blind isles' of New Zealand where he was born, locating her as a magnetic, mythic force there, as in Cornwall.*[26] The second of the poems, 'Zennor Moors', published in the *Cornish Review* with the title 'A Walk',[27] described a long tramp over the rainswept, desolate coastal landscape between St Ives and Zennor village, attended by the ghost-like presences of abandoned tin-mine chimneys.†

Although the outcomes of his visits to maternal and paternal ancestral territories in England were different, the words which Curnow used when he discovered the Allen tombstones in the churchyard at Caistor St Edmund might equally be said of his encounter with Cornwall: 'So there you are. You're real, after all.' They signified a release from the 'ghosts' of his childhood into a realm, for the future, of actual memories of places and people.

Curnow did not see a great deal of his widowed grandmother Alice Curnow. Of her three children she remained closest to her daughter Elsie, who married Professor Arnold Wall, and she died, in August 1921, when Curnow was only ten years old. Like his maternal grandmother, Grandmother Alice was a person of great determination and strength of character. The memory of his stay with her towards the end of the First World War, when his older brother John had diphtheria and he himself was six or seven years old, remained extraordinarily powerful. At her Cambridge Terrace house he recalled her well-preserved furni-ture and china, including a brace of pistols on show on a table in her drawing room, which he believed had been passed down from her grandfather, Peter Monro. He also remembered Grandmother Alice at this time giving him a book of Ernest Rhys's versions of Cornish folk tales in which he discovered tales like 'Cherry of Zennor'.

----

* 'Sea Tryst' was also published in the *New Zealand Listener*, but was then substantially revised – indeed so wholly rewritten as to constitute a different poem – after Curnow's return to New Zealand, and republished under the title 'The Changeling'. All of the overt Cornish references in the poem were removed, and the action wholly located in the Lyttelton Harbour of his childhood.

† Despite the vividness of its imagery and the vigour of its conception, exploring the mythic ambiences of the Cornwall landscape, Curnow never reprinted this poem in book form, either.

Although Alice Curnow never appeared in any of Curnow's poems, her Cambridge Terrace location provided the imagined scene of a meeting between himself and his father in one of the most visionary of his later poems, 'An Evening Light':

> The sun on its way down torched the clouds and left
> them to burn themselves out on the ground:
>
> the north-west wind and the sun both drop at once
> behind the mountains. The foreground fills
>
> with a fallen light which lies about the true
> colours of absconded things,
>
> . . .
>
> The smallest leaf's alight where he looks
>
> at the riverside willows, the painted iron
> glows gold where he holds the garden gate.

Written in 1988, more than a hundred years after Tremayne's birth, the poem is, among other things, a kind of centennial memorial poem to his father, imagining him initially as a ten-year-old child in the home at Cambridge Terrace, and projecting onto that scene his persistent memory of the setting in a particular kind of falling light, a light in which time becomes concentrated in a visionary instant:

> My father was born in 1880 [sic]. So his tenth birthday was in 1890 [sic]. I have brought him into the scene of the poem – which is the *poem's* present time – or moved myself forward in time to be a contemporary of his. The two of us are walking hand in hand. We're keeping an appointment – and the appointed spot is one I know well, because when I was seven I stayed there with my grandmother Curnow in Christchurch, by the river near the corner of Cambridge Terrace and Manchester Street – and of course it's the scene of my father's childhood too. And the same evening light – you know what a nor'west sunset in Canterbury is like. . . . [I]t's that light which is all over what I'm calling the *poem's* present. It has always been present to me, and what it does to the nor'west clouds, unbelievably grand and glowing.* 28

---

* Curnow's overall datings are not strictly accurate, since he misremembered his father's birth date as 1880, instead of 1881, but close enough, also, for him to think of the date of writing of the poem itself as one hundred years after the visionary event he imagines occurring in 1890.

By this instantaneous light, in this particular location, the time – and history – that separates Curnow from his father collapses, so that he is able to meet with him as a ten-year-old, as well as relive his own childhood memory of meeting his father, and understand 'the extraordinary way he would talk to me about Christchurch':

> as if it were a place established from the beginning of time – a city which only 40 years earlier simply hadn't been there at all, hardly a stick or a stone of it, only streets and squares pegged out on a bare plain – as if there'd never been a time when it wasn't all there as he knew it in his childhood.[29]

Powerfully buried memories – powerful, perhaps, *because* buried – always required, for Curnow, some activating spark in the present, and in the case of 'An Evening Light' that was provided by a rare later visit he made to Christchurch the year before, in 1987:

> A couple of years ago there was a specially striking [sunset], & standing in Latimer Square, it occurred to me that granny Curnow's house was very near, just across the river (the house long gone by then, of course) where I stayed with her as a small boy. And that's where I 'place' my father, & where I'm to meet him, both of us children, or one & the same child. It's his 'tenth birthday', which makes it 1890 – close enough to a hundred years ago.[30]

The idea for the poem probably began at this point, though it took another fifteen months for it to issue *as* a poem.

The Monro connection

It was through Grandmother Alice Curnow that Tremayne and his family were directly connected with the long-established New Zealand family the Monros; and the presence of numerous branches of the Monro connection in Christchurch more than made up for the thinness of connections on the Curnow, Allen and Gambling sides. Curnow himself was fascinated by the questions about *personal* location, identity and motivation, and history which the connection prompted. If Tremayne knew little about his father's life and ancestry, he was certainly willing to share his knowledge about the Monros (he provided Curnow, in the 1940s, with his own detailed draft of the Monro family tree), and during Curnow's childhood strong bonds were forged with a number of Christchurch-based families and cousins descended from the original Monro colonist, Peter Monro, 'a native of Edinburgh, of Highland descent', Curnow's great-great-grandfather.

Curnow wrote two substantial later poems about the Hokianga life and times of Peter Monro, and their bearing on his own later life and times, based on prized documentary relics. In the early 1940s Arnold Wall gave him an 83-page scrapbook, perhaps belonging to Peter Monro's son Henry (Judge H.A.H. Monro), containing pages 'haphazardly occupied by sentimental verses, sketches, engravings of ships, houses, horses, clipped or copied from books or albums of the time',[31] covering the period of the Monros' life in the Hokianga, Northland, from the mid-1830s to the early 1840s, and afterwards. Curnow's 'The Scrap-book', written in 1989, was based on a single enigmatic page of comment and quoted verse – concerning two visits by a pious evangelical Wesleyan missionary, William Woon, to the remote Monro homestead in the Hokianga, the first during a severe storm in 1841, the second in 1844 – and the poem offered a kind of decoding of the palimpsest-like text for its piecemeal revelations about the history and culture of its time, as well as its relation to the present, including the poet's personal present, a century and a half later. The second surviving document, a copy of which was passed on to Curnow by Arnold Wall's son, Ted, was a longish letter which Judge Monro had written late in his life to his daughter, Ada Morrison (Grandmother Alice Curnow's older sister), in response to a request for information about *his* father, Peter Monro.

Judge Monro's narrative provides the main source of information about Peter Monro (1793–1863) and his wife Eliza Alcock. According to the letter, Peter Monro had been offered a grant of land in Tasmania as compensation for his 'loss of office' after the Napoleonic Wars.* He eventually took up a government post as superintendent of the Birch's Bay sawing station on the D'Entrecasteaux Channel facing Bruny Island, overseeing the extraction of timber by convicts; later continuing the business, not very successfully, under government lease. After he sailed to New Zealand, reconnoitring the Bay of Islands and the Hokianga, with its 'better class of Maoris and a number of highly respectable settlers', he decided on his return to Hobart to immigrate there. The family (there were now four children, including Henry (H.A.H.) Monro, born in 1824) arrived in the Hokianga in 1835. Land was purchased from the Maori, and Monro established a profitable export business purchasing timber and produce from local Maori and settlers and on-selling it to visiting ships. An economic depression in the early 1840s wreaked havoc in the Hokianga, and foreseeing the outcome, Monro shifted to Auckland before 'The War of the North' led by Hone Heke broke out in 1845.

---

* Editor's note: Subsequent research by Tim Curnow in Hobart in 2015 sheds doubt on the accuracy of some of Judge Monro's memories presented in the letter. His father Peter Monro was a hatter by profession and unlikely and perhaps too young to have held any office of significance during the Napoleonic Wars.

Something of the detached, considered method of a person used to weighing evidence and sifting fact from speculation characterises Henry Monro's style. However, there are two moments in his account of his father in which he allows himself a personal comment. The first occurs close to the start of his narrative, when he mentions that his father resisted *his* father's wish that he enter the navy: 'He did not like it, and I have often said that if his father had the same kind of temper that he had himself, I don't wonder that he did not like it.' The second moment interrupts his account of the youthful pleasures of growing up in the Hokianga, with 'a rough boat for rafting' and 'shooting and fishing galore': 'It was a pleasant life, and we could have been happy but for my father's abominable temper. He kept all his bad temper for home consumption; outside his own family he never quarrelled with anyone.'

It was this unusually personal intrusion into Henry's narrative that provided the spark for Curnow's long poem about his Monro forebears, 'An Abominable Temper'. He wrote it in 1972–73, though 'for a long time' prior to this he had 'had the idea, & some parts written'.[32] Based on Monro's letter to Ada, in ten sections, it stays close to the order of the main events of the narrative, and uses many of Monro's own words and sentences. Because the quotations are not identified as such, however, the whole of 'An Abominable Temper' gives the impression of a largely seamless, documentary representation of Henry Monro's text, except for occasional intrusions by the poet into the narrative – as in the final section, where Monro names 'Allen' as the prophet who shall predict the fate of Peter Monro's few surviving relics.

However, the documentary style of the poem is even more of an illusion than such moments suggest. Numerous details about Peter Monro's life are added, such as the fact that he died in San Francisco in 1863, and the speculation (based on a drawing in the scrapbook, and Curnow's own visit to the area in 1965) that the site of the original home was on the inner Hokianga Harbour, Horeke, near Mangungu, where the headstone of William Monro (the older of Peter Monro's sons, Henry's brother, who died in the 1860s) can be found. He also provides a listing of relics which went to Grandmother Curnow: duelling pistols, an 1812 edition of the poems of Burns, and a family Bible. Both the Burns volume and the Bible eventually came to Curnow, from his father Tremayne.

More importantly, the central character of 'An Abominable Temper' is perhaps less Peter Monro than Judge Henry Monro himself, the narrator of Peter Monro's story, and for these purposes there is a great deal of 'embroidery' masked by the documentary feel of the poem – and probably a great deal of Curnow himself. Henry Monro is an ageing man shadowed by death, 'dip[ping] and scratch[ing] like an old fowl' among his memories, aware of how little he knows or remembers and uncertain of his achievements in public life, puzzled about sexuality – the act of generation that produces the generations (his daughter and her children, and generations after that) in an ongoing process – for whom the act of writing is felt as a painful self-exposure in which the 'steel nib' searches 'wrist bone, skull bone, testicles'. Judge Monro also seems uncertain about the purpose or achievements of the enterprise of colonisation, and how and why Peter Monro became involved in it, a question Curnow also takes up in his later Hokianga poem, 'The Scrap-book':

> Blood sample of Peter Monro, where do I
> come in? The book doesn't say. Might as well ask
>
> this heart-murmur I've got, how Edinburgh rock,
> chipped like a golf ball cleared Arthur's Seat the day
> after Waterloo, first bounce Van Diemen's Land,
>
> holed up next and last a thousand sea miles more,
> Ngapuhi country, MacGulliver's last landfall.

However, the central mystery of the poem is the 'abominable temper' of Peter Monro himself, marking a dynasty founded – as Curnow puts it in the final section, using Old Testament imagery – in 'an angry father'. How much, in one's personal life, and in history itself, the poem seems soberingly to ask, is driven, motivated by anger, inherited and passed on?

> In the beginning was the four letter Word
> Tetragrammaton, an angry father.

Curnow himself was well aware of the boldness of the speculation:

> There's a high, not to say insufferable, conceit, in setting up one's great-great-grand-parent as the old Pentateuch god, his weapons (I think suitably) in a museum case, & his Book a poet's keepsake. But the allegorising is only for the more curious reader; I had to keep a tight rein on it. It ought to be readable in the first place, & there's nothing esoteric about the clues.[33]

In the mid-1990s Curnow contemplated, without completing, a more personal poem about Peter Monro, based on a surviving photograph in which he was intrigued by the absence of resemblance to his father Tremayne (Peter's great-grandson): 'too many genes / have baffled resemblances // inheritance is a heap'.[34]

Of course, whether Henry Monro (as distinct from Peter Monro) was remotely like the portrait his great-grandson drew of him in 'An Abominable Temper' is also hard to guess, though Curnow wrote to publisher Dan Davin at the time: 'I'm interviewing my great-grandparent, who would be startled by the result, I'm sure.'[35] Certainly, more than his father Peter, Henry Monro might be seen as the 'founding father' of the large New Zealand Monro-related dynasty. Although his role as judge of the Native Land Court was well known, his personal life appears only in glimpses. Ted Wall remembered how much his father enjoyed the company of Monro:

> He and mother [Elsie, Alice's daughter] made rendezvous with him at Rotorua when on their honeymoon [1902], and the old boy introduced them to many of his friends among the Maori elders. The latter made a great fuss of them and obviously regarded HAHM with great respect and affection; it interested Dad that they addressed him as 'Te Kooti' [Court of Law].[36]

Arnold Wall himself left a brief pen-portrait of Judge Monro in his autobiography, *Long and Happy* (1965),[37] and there is perhaps a hint of his great-grandson in Wall's comment that 'his judgments and comments on the notables of his prime were often very satirical and he pronounced them with great emphasis and much picturesque language'.[38]

Monro's narrative of his father ends in the mid-1840s, at the point where Peter and Eliza had brought their family to Auckland from the Hokianga. Peter Monro set up a general merchandise business, and Henry worked there for a time, before marrying Charlotte Coney in 1848. Henry got a job with the Native Office in Auckland in 1857 as an interpreter, and then transferred to the Native Land Court when the government was moved to Wellington. In 1865 he was appointed judge of that court, based in Auckland, and was later appointed judge of the Compensation Court for the adjudication of confiscated lands, retiring about 1886. For some years he held a special appointment as Commissioner of Native Land in Poverty Bay. Charlotte predeceased her husband by five years: she died in 1903, and Henry in 1908 aged 84.

Charlotte was born in London in 1828, and immigrated with her parents to New Zealand.* Charlotte and Henry had six children, two sons and four daughters: Clara [Ford], Henry (known as 'Harry', born in 1851), Ada [Morrison], Alice Augusta [Curnow] (born c. 1856), Laura [Cracroft Wilson], and the youngest, Arthur. The marriages of Clara, Alice and Laura took them to Christchurch,

---

* Her sister Emma married Edwin Fairburn, from whom the poet A.R.D. Fairburn was descended, establishing a family connection between Fairburn and Curnow.

and it was there that Curnow made connections with the immediate cousins descended through Alice, and the more distant cousinship descending from Alice's sister, Laura.

Apart from the connections with his grandmother Alice, and with Ada Morrison and Laura Cracroft Wilson, the other of Henry's six children whom Curnow was interested in was the older of the two sons, Harry, who married Harata Whareiahua, of Ngati Porou descent. Harata died at the age of 33, in 1894, after only nine years of marriage, but Curnow met her daughter, Helen [Monro] Neumann, in Auckland at the funeral of his uncle Pendarves in 1953, as well as, in 1980,[39] her granddaughter, Cora O'Dwyer, who rediscovered her Maori ancestry shortly before her death in 1985.

Harata was the only Maori connection in the Monro whakapapa. In the late 1980s Curnow worked at several drafts of a poem about her, based on his only personal experience of a connection with her. His father Tremayne kept a briar pipe, its bowl carved into the form of a tiki, which he claimed had belonged to Harata, and which Allen himself cleaned and used for a time before losing it in 1933, 'on the way', according to one of his drafts, 'to Arnold Wall's house'. In another draft he asks whether Harata herself had carved the tiki from the 'Loewe of London' bowl:

> Was it Harata's fine hand? Was carving
> a thing for a woman of the Ngati-porou?
> I've my father's word who was (I make it)
> fourteen when she died and whose advice was
> not to 'start' before eighteen
>
> a blip[40]

The poem was never completed but its aim seems to have been to recover and record what little is remembered of Harata, to resist the historical process of erasure, where 'nothing as distinct even as a blip' survives in any kind of family or public record.

Cousins: the Walls and Ronaldses

Of Curnow's immediate first cousins those he kept most in touch with were the children of his Aunt Elsie (Gipsy) and Arnold Wall – Hilary, Edith and Ted (Arnold junior) – all of them highly intelligent and lively figures who led interesting and varied lives. In later years he often recalled childhood visits with his father in the early 1920s to 'Lismore Lodge', the Walls' home in Christchurch, before Elsie's tragically early death in 1924, as well as a visit in 1923 to Monck's Bay, where the Walls were holidaying, during which Ted gave twelve-year-old Allen an old box camera (with which he 'took snaps of Patricia, Tennent [Patricia and Tennent Ronalds] ... and many ships').[41]

Hilary (Larry) married Norman Richmond, an important figure in the Workers' Educational Association (WEA) and adult education scene at Auckland University College in the 1930s. Both of them were active figures in left-wing politics in Auckland during that decade, and were hospitable and helpful to Curnow during his years there as a student, 1931–33, as well as in 1937 when he revisited Auckland after his marriage the year before. Writing to Faith Pinkney, their daughter, who in 1988 wrote a moving account of Norman's tragic mental collapse in the 1940s and 1950s in Australia, he remembered their 'kindness to a rather confused young cousin muddling his way through university and theological college':

> I admired them both tremendously. ... I owed Norman my first meetings with friends & contemporaries of his (all much my seniors) like John Beaglehole the historian & Willis Airey – a memorable bush tramp in the Waitakeres with him & Beaglehole, & the day he drove us to Piha beach, picking up Rex Fairburn on the way.[42]

Faith Pinkney's narrative of her family also included a delightful evocation of her Aunt Edith's sophisticated life as an artist with her architect-husband Oscar Bayne, based on a childhood visit to their waterfront home in Cremorne, Sydney, in 1948. At this time Edith was a 'satirical artist who work[ed] for a glossy Sydney magazine', and Faith was fascinated by the 'drollness' and wit of her conversation, as well as the unconventional bohemian circle in which she moved.[43] The age gap between Edith (born in 1905) and Curnow (1911) meant that they had little to do with each other during his childhood, but they caught up with each other in later life. Edith had even more of the remarkable stamina of her father, continuing to exhibit her work into the 1990s, and celebrating her hundredth birthday in 2005.*

Ted (Arnold junior), the youngest of the Wall cousins and three years older than Allen, had an equally distinguished career. He joined the RAF at Cranwell, England, in 1927, and lost an eye while patrolling the north-western border between India and Afghanistan in the late 1930s. He continued to serve in the RAF until 1951, attaining the rank of Group Captain as well as a military division OBE. In 1951 he returned to Christchurch, New Zealand, and became talks

---

* Editor's note: Edith Wall died in 2012, aged 107.

officer for the New Zealand Broadcasting Service, before shifting to Wellington in 1961 to the position of editor of the publishing house of A.H. and A.W. Reed, where he then became editorial director until his retirement in 1973.

From the time of Ted's return to New Zealand until his death in 1998, he and Curnow wrote lively letters to each other, mixing literary matters with family news and gossip, swapping information about the earlier family history that both were increasingly fascinated by, and (on at least one occasion) composing letters to each other in dog Latin. In one exchange in 1987 Ted was able to provide Curnow with detailed information about the aviation history and construction of the Avro 504K biplane in which, as an eight-year-old living in Sheffield, Curnow had flown for half an hour in 1919. The resulting poem, 'A Time of Day', was one of the richest of the later poems of childhood memory, and the first of his poems to appear in the *London Review of Books*.

Curnow's most complex relationship on the Wall side, however, was with his uncle-in-law, Arnold Wall – poet, academic, mountaineer, alpine botanist, philologist – who arrived in New Zealand in 1898 to begin a career as professor of English language, literature and history at Canterbury University College which lasted until his retirement at the end of 1931.[44] In the mid-1960s, at Ted's request, Curnow wrote a brief, carefully worded foreword to Wall's autobiography, *Long and Happy*, in which he alluded to the family connection. Curnow admired the man for his multi-sided achievements and his scholarly integrity, as well as for the absence of intellectual ostentation or ego in his personality: 'He is one of those rare, intellectual colonists of New Zealand, who may never perhaps be valued properly, because he made the country a free, unconditional gift of nothing less than all his interests in life, and demanded nothing in return.'[45] However, his admiration was complicated by his reaction to the verse, of which there was a huge amount, some ten volumes altogether, much of it written in an outmoded late nineteenth-century poetic style *against* which Curnow's own poetry and criticism was in revolt.

Nevertheless, he featured Wall's poetry quite strongly in his Caxton *Book of New Zealand Verse* (1945); and he retained four of Wall's poems in the *Penguin Book of New Zealand Verse* (1960), with a brief reference in his introduction to 'the fresh impact' of the country on Wall's verse. Perhaps in response to James K. Baxter's accusation that 'filial piety' had affected his literary judgement in including so much of Wall in both anthologies, he commented in his foreword to *Long and Happy* that '[the] best poems are hard to pick out from the mass of his notes in meticulous verse on so many occasions of his thought'. However, he remained loyal to Wall three decades later when he was asked to contribute a small selection of New Zealand poems to a Waterstone anthology of nineteenth-century verse in English chosen by poets, published by Carcanet Press (1997), selecting a piece by Wall alongside others by 'David Lowston', William Pember Reeves and Blanche Baughan. 'Wall remains for me', he wrote in a brief introduction, 'one of the very few who last century wrote verse of any distinction in this corner of the world.'[46]

Wall featured less as a poet, however, than as a family connection in a memorial poem Curnow wrote about him in 1980, entitled 'After Dinner'. The poem recalled a visit to Wall's home in Christchurch in 1964, where he was being looked after by his daughter Larry.[47] It was eighteen months before his death at the age of 96, and his uncle announced, in a dry, matter-of-fact way, 'I have been here long enough':

> Between him and his death's
> left foot the gangrene was
> no secret, already in the door
> and pressing hard, in a white fold freshly
> dressed for dinner.

As well as its aspect of sympathetic tribute to Wall's life, the poem is a study of a man's civility in the face of death, his refusal (as in life) to advertise or sentimentalise the fact.

The other main extended Monro family connection Curnow had in Christchurch was with the relatives descended from his grandmother Alice's younger sister, Laura May, married to Alex Cracroft Wilson, a son of Sir John Cracroft Wilson, who had been in the Indian Civil Service and created a wealthy estate in the hills near Christchurch, naming it Cashmere, after Kashmir in India,[48] as well as owning a sheep station in South Canterbury on the Rangitata River. Laura had six children – belonging to the same generation as Curnow's father, Tremayne – of whom three, Amcotts, Irene and Rita, were relatively familiar figures during Curnow's childhood. Amcotts' daughter, Audrey, married Guy Cotterill, both of whom were active in the repertory theatre movement in Christchurch in the 1930s and after. Curnow kept in touch with her over many years, though it was never an easy relationship. Audrey disliked her cousin's left-wing politics and unconventional family lifestyle in the 1930s and 1940s, and reacted against his criticism of the anglophile affiliations of the repertory theatre movement. He thought her bossy and opinionated, and disliked her controlling ways as a kind of self-appointed guardian of the extended family in Christchurch.

His cousin (once removed) Irene, however, who married Guy Ronalds, provided the warmest and closest of all Allen's childhood family connections, during his years at West Lyttelton and after. Irene and Guy Ronalds lived within easy walking distance of the vicarage in Lyttelton, their house was always open to visitors, 'adding a refreshing touch of frivolity to [. . .] life in West Lyttelton in the 1920s',[49] and two of their children – Patricia and Tennent – were among Curnow's closest childhood friends. Irene, in his later memories, was something of a 'surrogate mother', and Patricia, a year younger than Curnow, was his earliest adolescent love. The sonnet 'Children, Swimmers' evokes her lively, vital presence during summers spent swimming at Corsair Bay, Lyttelton, and comes as close to a remembered image of sheer, unalloyed childhood pleasure as any he ever wrote. Patricia is also, almost certainly, behind the portrait of the changeling, in the poem of that name, the 'girl kind of fish' who creates joyful, uninhibited mayhem among the puritans and moralists who dominate Lyttelton town, as well as figuring in the childhood and adolescent Eden – Corsair Bay with its 'summer come of sex' – momentarily evoked in 'Impromptu in a Low Key'.

Long after the family had shifted from the vicarage at Lyttelton, and Curnow had returned to Christchurch from Auckland and married, he continued to visit the Ronaldses, retaining a warm friendship with both Patricia and her husband, Tyndall Harman, as well as with her younger brother Tennent – all of them regular visitors to his own family home after his marriage to Elizabeth (Betty) Le Cren in 1936. Tennent's death in Tunisia, North Africa, during the Second World War, came as a deep personal shock, prompting an eloquent tribute ('In Memoriam: 2/Lieutenant T.C.F. Ronalds'), the first of numerous elegies that Curnow was to write during the course of his life:

> Weeping for bones in Africa, I turn
> Our youth over like a dead bird in my hand.
> This unexpected personal concern
> That what has character can simply end
>
> Is my unsoldierlike acknowledgement
> Cousin, to you, once gentle-tough, inert
> Now, after the death-flurry of that front
> Found finished too. And why should my report
>
> Cry one more hero, winking though its tears?
> I would say, you are cut off, and mourn for that;
> Because history where it destroys admires,
> But O if your blood's tongued it must recite
>
> South Island feats, those tall snow-country tales
> Among incredulous Tunisian hills.

When Curnow's first marriage broke down, Patricia and Tyndall Harman, and their daughter Angela, were the first members of the family to whom he introduced his new partner, Jeny Tole, and shortly before Patricia died in 1975, he wrote to his brother Tony: 'You know how close I've always been to *that* family, & specially to Pat – after Tennent, the only one I can think of with whom I never had a word or a feeling in disagreement.'[50]

Chapter Two

Early Childhood, 1911–21

Without names there are no places. Without places there is nowhere to come and nowhere to go.[1]

Tremayne

Curnow's parents, Tremayne Monro Curnow (born 4 February 1881) and Jessamine Towler Gambling (born 5 June 1880), were both 28 when they were married at St John's Church, Invercargill, in April 1909. Tremayne was in the fifth year of his appointment as assistant curate at St Mary's Church, Timaru, after being ordained as deacon in the Church of England in December 1904 and as priest in May 1907. He had already completed a BA in 1903 and an MA in History and French in 1904 at Canterbury University College, and it was in his early years at university that he began his theological training for the Church of England ministry at College House.

Highly intelligent and widely read, Tremayne possessed a prodigious memory (which Curnow would inherit), especially for the classics and the traditional English literature on which he was brought up. Like Curnow himself in later life, Tremayne enjoyed the cut and thrust of intellectual debate, both as a university student and later (in matters of theological disputation) at the annual meetings of the Anglican Synod in Christchurch. To his three sons he seemed a mine of information on all manner of people and places, all of it garnered from reading, since he never travelled overseas, and on only rare occasions travelled further afield than Canterbury.

During his student years Tremayne began writing verse. He was no doubt aware of his brother-in-law Arnold Wall's poems published regularly in newspapers and journals as well as in his own collections, and was perhaps also encouraged by W.F. (Fred) Alexander, a lifelong friend from his days at Christchurch Boys' High School. Alexander included one of Tremayne's poems, 'Pan',[2] in the anthology, *New Zealand Verse*, which he co-edited with A.E. Currie in 1906.

Curnow himself, when asked about his beginnings as a poet, spoke almost invariably of his father's verse interests, of growing up in a household where poetry was constantly part of his father's conversation, and of the books lining his father's study:

> I've not met a man since, and I've heard of very few, whose minds made so much *use* of poetry just in the ordinary day's march, whether odd lines coming to him, talking to us kids, or whole passages – anything from *Piers Plowman* or Chaucer to, shall we say, stanzas from Browning or Tennyson. . . . [H]is taste was Romantic in the oldest and perhaps the best sense – he must have read Malory's fifteenth-century prose version of the Arthurian stories at least a dozen times.[3]

To Naylor Hillary, literary editor of *The Press* in the 1980s, he later expanded on these comments:

> My beginnings as a poet were atypical. My father idolised verse, and wrote himself. All his life he was a parish priest, yet his head was full of poetry. His mind played a good deal; he remembered all the poetry he read. By eight or nine years old, I was being baffled by my father quoting obscure chunks to me. Like the last line of Browning's 'Popularity', the one that ends with 'What porridge had John Keats?' He would quote Coleridge, Tennyson, Arnold, or Piers the Plowman. I never thought there was anything unusual about poetry. It was all around me. I think I wrote my first verses when I was about nine, on the subject of a wet day.[4]

In notes Curnow made for the poem 'Early Days Yet', based on memories of his father doing his parish rounds at Sheffield in an old Model T Ford, Curnow listed the books (other than theological texts) he remembered in his father's library, toying with the idea of including a section on these in the poem. They included Tennyson's *Collected Poems*, Saintsbury's *A History of Elizabethan Literature*, and the works of Keats and Shelley. Others of Tremayne's books which Curnow encountered during his school years were an edition of Byron's collected poems, an anthology *From Blake to Arnold*, in which Blake's 'Songs of Innocence and of Experience' especially interested him, and the poetry and fiction of Edgar Allan Poe.[5]

However, Tremayne's tastes were not simply for 'serious' literature. He delighted in all forms of comic and light verse, knew much of Gilbert and Sullivan by heart as well as other nineteenth-century popular operas, and enjoyed the theatre and cinema, taking particular pleasure in pointing out errors of fact in historical or period dramas. In his only surviving letter to his son, written less than a fortnight before his death on 31 October 1949 while Curnow was in England, literary allusions are woven into his writing in precisely the way his son has described his conversation. He quotes at some length from Tennyson and Walter Scott on Edinburgh, which Curnow had recently visited, and from a popular song on Paris, which his youngest son Tony was currently visiting.[6]

It was as an author of light rather than serious verse that Tremayne excelled, publishing it regularly for most of his life. His friend Alexander encouraged and published much of it, first in the *Timaru Herald*,[7] where Alexander was editor between 1910 and 1920, then, after Alexander's shift to the editorship of the Dunedin *Evening Star* in 1920, in that newspaper, to which Tremayne contributed two topical pieces weekly under the pseudonym 'X.Y.' for more than 25 years. In 1945 the *Evening Star* published a selection of his contributions under the title *Bad King Wenceslas*, which received excellent reviews, most notably from Alan Mulgan,[8] who emphasised its 'metrical dexterity' and everyday humour as well as the kindliness of his satire, and from an anonymous reviewer in the *Southland Times* (possibly M.H. Holcroft) who commented, acutely, that despite the lightness of the themes, 'there is always a hint of the thinker in the background'.[9] Something of the sheer knowledge he brought to issues of versification is to be found in the only literary piece he ever wrote, entitled 'On Triolets and Training', in the Canterbury University College magazine *Canta* in 1933, which includes comments in passing on the vogue of 'vers libre':

> This 'verse libre' business, by the way, requires a good deal of sifting out and cleaning up. It is a style in which much good poetry has been written – and also a vast amount of stuff which is too amorphous to be called poetry, or even verse – just bad prose, cut into uneven lengths.... Most young writers of 'verse libre' could well be condemned to a year's hard labour on triolets, rondeaux, villanelles, ballades, and sestinas, to give them restraint, self-discipline, and a mastery of form. They – and the world at large – would thus be delivered from the publication of reams of untidy, shambling, incoherent, and shapeless stuff....[10]

For Curnow at this time, studying at St John's College in Auckland to become a clergyman like his father, and also interested in writing poetry, the sense of his father as a model to be emulated, but also an influence to be resisted, was inescapable. He later described his father's topical pieces as 'the most agreeable and least mischievous verses you could imagine. Not my kind of thing at all';[11] and a number of reviewers drew attention to his more serious 'wit' and satire as Whim Wham compared with his father's 'humour' as 'X.Y.' His own move to publish satirical verse, as Whim Wham, in 1937 owed a great deal to his admiration for his father's achievement, a desire to emulate his father's verbal dexterity and his ability to connect with a wide popular audience.

Although *Bad King Wenceslas* might give the impression that most of Tremayne's verse is on whimsical and domestic topics, a considerable amount of it traverses similar political and social territory to that of Whim Wham. Unlike Whim Wham, however, 'X.Y.' disagreed with many of the policies of the Labour Party, disliked trade unionism and socialism, and adopted a conservative stance on moral issues such as alcohol. Quite what Tremayne thought of his son's topical verse is unknown, but he is likely to have had mixed feelings about many of its attitudes, and he shared the negative view of many writers of his own generation towards the new poetic impulses of the 1930s.

Curnow always remembered his father as an affectionate presence during his early childhood and, as he grew up and got to know him better, as a tolerant and compassionate man. 'At Dead Low Water' evokes that sense of warmth in its central section – a vivid memory of a childhood walk with his father on the beach at Governor's Bay, Lyttelton Harbour, when he was about eleven or twelve years old – even as the scene, looked at in retrospect 20 years later, becomes a site of unbearable loss and decay:

> The father with the child came down
> First thing one morning, before any
> Dreamt of visiting the beach: it was
>
> Daylight but grey, midsummer; they
> Crossed high-water mark, dry-shod,
> Derelict shells, weed crisped or rotting,
>
> Down to the spongy rim, slowly
> Without fear, stepping hand in hand
> Within an inch of the harmless sea.

In later years, thinking about his father's tolerance of different viewpoints, Curnow often told the story of his reaction to his own decision not to enter the Anglican priesthood, after months of uncertainty following his return to Christchurch from St John's College at the end of 1933. It was a potentially difficult moment in their relationship, and an event that both might have felt as a personal failure. Tremayne, whatever his feelings of disappointment, reached for a metaphor, commenting that the Church gave its preferment to those whose matches 'strike directly on the box', who could be trusted, that is, never to rock the boat – a remark which allowed his son the freedom of his unorthodox opinions and at the same time released him from anxiety on his father's account. About his mother's response to her son's decision to abandon a career in the Church, Curnow always remained silent. She was deeply upset and troubled by what she saw as his seeming inability to settle into a steady career.

Jessie

Tremayne and Jessie, whose pet names to each other and to their children were always 'T' and 'Muz', had a warm marriage,[12] and worked very much as a team in the management of parish affairs. Curnow's younger brother Tony characterised his mother's life as one in which 'duty and faith came before everything else. Duty to her mother Rose Gambling, who was part of the domestic household, to the family, to the parish, and an unquestioning religious faith.'[13] Parish work was demanding for a clergyman's wife, involving visiting and assisting those who were ill or bereaved, as well as organising its social life. Curnow later recalled that 'Muz and T worked a lot with the sick in the 1918–19 influenza epidemic, giving food and company . . . T setting off with jars of soup on his bicycle, the soup in a carrier basket on the back'.[14]

The family was never well off, and Jessie looked after the finances, supplementing them by growing vegetables, keeping poultry, and even (in Sheffield) by making butter and cream from a cow the family acquired. She believed strongly in living within one's means, and disliked extravagance, though she was never mean. Gardening was one of her great passions, in all the vicarages in which the family lived during Tremayne's working life, and later at the home in Meadow Street, Papanui, to which they retired in 1948. After Tremayne's death in 1949, Jessie lived alone there for all except the last eighteen months of her life, dying at the age of 93 in 1974. Much as she always missed her husband after his death, she was a strong, resourceful woman, whose desire for independence Curnow understood and respected, when in later life some believed she should be moved to a nursing home. Self-reliance, stubborn determination, independence – these were key qualities in Curnow's personality which he inherited from his mother.

Jessie was also a woman 'of strong emotions, likes and dislikes',[15] who was warm and enjoyed chatting but could also be highly critical of behaviour she disapproved of, and forthright in expressing her opinions. She did not hesitate to complain to her grandson Tim when he grew a beard, or to Curnow himself when he grew sideboards in the 1960s, nor to point out bluntly when she saw a newspaper photograph of Curnow with the visiting American poet James Dickey in 1968, 'you look as if you dressed sort of carelessly, & one ear looks huge!'[16] According to Tony, she 'seemed to have a powerful capacity of resistance – moral as well as physical – and rarely gave way to her emotions'. She also wished she had had a daughter, and Curnow's daughter Belinda always remembered the special warmth and affection she received from her grandmother in the years before the family moved to Auckland in 1951.

Jessie's lifelong commitment to teetotalism meant that for her sons the prohibition on liquor in the house was absolute. She certainly disapproved of the unconventional lifestyle Allen and his first wife Betty led in Christchurch, and had probably hoped that Betty would be more of a conventional wife who would assist her husband to 'settle down'. She thought their purchases of books, records and alcohol, and the parties they regularly held, a sign of extravagance and living beyond their means, and tended to blame Betty for the untidiness of the house and for not providing adequate meals. Like Tony's first wife Ursula [Cooke], Betty was very fond of Tremayne, and tended to blame Jessie for Curnow's 'real or imagined' faults: his stubbornness, his determination to win an argument at all costs, his occasional withdrawals into himself.

Jessie also seems to have been aware, like her mother, that she was an outsider to the genteel Christchurch social networks to which Tremayne was connected through his Aunt Laura's marriage into the Cracroft Wilson family, and did not develop any close friendships with her husband's numerous Christchurch cousins. A great deal in Allen's own formation – his hostility towards Canterbury's ruling elites, his dislike of social pretension of any kind – might be seen to come from his awareness of his mother's socially marginal position in such circles. She developed friendships among parishioners, but the continual shifts of parish – eight over a period of 35 years until Tremayne's retirement at the end of 1945 – made sustained friendships difficult.

When Tremayne retired at the age of 65, he and Jessie moved to Auckland. Why they did so is unclear, though Tremayne's brother Pendarves and his wife Eva lived in Mt Eden, and at the very least the move suggested that they felt no strong connections with Christchurch and wished to make a clean break. The move did not work out – Tremayne's verses published in the Dunedin *Evening Star* during the eighteen months they lived in Auckland regularly make fun of the arrogance and pretentiousness of Aucklanders and the vagaries of its climate – and they returned to Christchurch in 1948, where they exchanged their Auckland house in south Epsom for a house at 18 Meadow Street, Papanui.

Tremayne lived for only another 18 months. However, Jessie, with remarkable resourcefulness and strength of purpose, set about making new friends in the local parish and tending her beloved garden, content to spend the rest of her life in Papanui. She remained a figure of considerable maternal, and moral, authority to all of her grown-up sons, whose feelings mattered much to both Tony and Allen when their marriages broke down. Given that Curnow wrote so many poems about remembered scenes from childhood, about his father, and about other family connections, it seems unusual that there are none dealing directly with his relationship with his mother, nor, among the numerous unfinished drafts of family poems in his papers, any which indicate an effort to write directly about her. She appears fleetingly in some of the published poems. At the end of 'A Raised Voice', his mother's scent is one of numerous remembered sensuous details in a scene dominated by his father, who is taking a Sunday service in St David's Church at Belfast. In 'A South Island Night's Entertainment' she is briefly glimpsed as a member of the family group trudging home in the dark from the empty barn, near Sheffield, in which they had hoped to see a movie. In 'A Facing Page' (also dating from Belfast days) there is an affectionate memory of his mother warming his nightgown by the fire, reading to him from a battered picture-book surviving from her own childhood, by Bram Stoker (the author of *Dracula*), before tucking him into bed, his eyes shut tight on a fearsome and never-to-be-forgotten illustration of a black-robed giant: 'Cruciform from full-stretched arms his black robe drops / the whole way to the city. His fingers point / down at our rooftops.'

His mother also appears in a strongly nurturing role in 'A Sight for Sore Eyes', a poem whose setting is the garden of the Belfast vicarage around 1917 when Allen was six, from which the child peers through a nail hole in the garden fence, aware of the mysterious mountains to the north-west and the dust-laden Canterbury nor'-west wind which has thawed the snow and flooded the Waimakariri River near the vicarage. The poem concludes with an image of his mother as a protective presence not only for the child but in the landscape itself, the garden which she struggles to build and defend against the destructive elements of wind, dust, flood and storm:

My mother

> bathes my eyes with boracic, she ties
> up torn dianthus, delphinium, phlox
> wasted on the alluvium the storm-
> waters have been scraping seaward since
> the sun mumbled the first implanted
> word. My mother grows it all from seed.

However, her absence may well be more significant than these relatively fleeting appearances. Curnow always needed to attain some distance in time and/or place from the family figures he wrote about (his father after his death, his grandmother Rose Gambling and great-aunt Fanny Rose May, Tennent and Patricia Ronalds, Arnold Wall, Peter and Henry Monro), and in each case they are catalysts for self-exploration. Perhaps his mother remained too close to him for this process to occur.

There may, however, be one exception, the poem 'What Was That?' which was written in the wake of a visit to Jessie in Calvary Hospital, Christchurch, towards the end of her life. Curnow regarded this as the best poem in his collection *An Abominable Temper*. For nearly two years before she died Jessie retreated entirely into herself, and rarely spoke to or recognised anyone. She is not mentioned in the poem, which is a powerful meditation on the universality and finality of death, accompanied not by the histrionics of a loud Last Trump but by an ongoing low 'murmur' or 'hum', absorbed like a sea or river into the poet's 'listening' blood. If the meditation is indeed sparked by his sense of his mother's approaching death it reveals a moving effort to identify with her silent withdrawal into herself, as if anticipating and accepting her absorption into a larger 'oceanic' rhythm which claims all lives.

Belfast, 1913–19

Curnow's earliest childhood memories belong to the parish of Belfast, some 10 kilometres north of Christchurch, to which his parents moved in June 1913 when he was two years old. The parish also took in Styx, Coutts Island and Tuahiwi, a Maori pa referred to in 'An Evening Light'. The family spent six and a half years at Belfast, until the end of 1919, their first reasonably settled period. Aside from Belfast, there were two other significant places in Curnow's childhood experience – Sheffield and West Lyttelton – each of which provided important memories for many of his later poems.

Belfast, as Curnow later spoke of it, wasn't then the suburb of Christchurch it was later to become:

> It was a freezing-works township of a few hundred souls, scattered along a mile of the Main North Road. . . . [It] lay between the little river Styx and the great river Waimakariri, the Cashmere Hills rose 1500 feet a few miles to the south-east, the Southern Alps 50 miles to the north-west. The nearest tram was Papanui, it took you to Colombo street and the Avon river.[17]

Initially the parish did not have its own vicarage, and for a year or so the family had to live in temporary premises while the new vicarage was being built.[18] Curnow

himself left one detailed memory of life in Belfast in a piece entitled 'A Colonial
At Home', which he wrote for radio broadcast in 1937:

> I remember the six-roomed wooden vicarage at Belfast – I have never quite rid
> myself of the impression that Belfast, Ireland, lies along a dusty road between Brown's
> Grocery Store and the hotel a mile away at the corner – and I remember the two
> cherry-plum trees by the sunny north side of the house. Almost at the back was the
> bleached wooden skeleton of a windmill wh pumped out water from a deep artesian
> well. On hot summer days my father would go with a great appearance of ceremony
> to the foot of the mill to draw off the ice-cold water from a tap below the pump; it
> was a ritual which delighted me; the bright water stood in a yellow Doulton jug on
> the dining-table, a rich, rare drink of our own special kind, because we had a tap at
> the bottom of the windmill. I have thought since that this fine luxury of drinking has
> carried over into habits of mine in which my father does not share my pleasure.
>
> On one side of the vicarage, in a ragged, rank-grown section, was the building
> wh I came to know as the Sunday School. It was the oldest thing I knew – to
> me far older than the antique monuments of England of wh I had been told,
> cathedrals mostly, for my father's books were mostly those proper to his pro-
> fession. The schoolroom had been the church of the township at one time, but as
> I knew it, it was the place where valiant attempts were made to instruct me in the
> faith of my fathers. Now I realize that I and others of my generation in this country
> have no fathers at Home, either in faith or any other element of living. Nothing
> that has been transplanted to this soil has flourished. We are a generation without
> inheritance – only the gift of reasonably fruitful earth and sound bodies. Literary
> traditions, the Churches, and our political institutions are incongruous beside
> the pagan happiness of the people; it is sad that in so many cases that happiness
> is cumbered by these intrusions from a civilization in escape from wh lies our
> only hope. I wonder if there is anything in the child-analogy, if New Zealand must
> suffer agonies and the defeats of growth to nationhood. I am afraid that it is true.
> But I know, none the less, that we are in revolt, spiritually, against the oppression of
> our self-appointed instructors.
>
> . . . I ask you to remember that these are the sentiments of a colonial of the colonies,
> one who has never narrowed his horizon by travel. . . . I shall never have a horizon more
> rich with mystery, of deeper majesty of receding blue, than from the back-door step of
> the vicarage in Belfast.* [19]

---

* In the later 1930s Curnow (and Denis Glover) often gave talks on Christchurch radio on literary topics
   and topics of general interest, and on some of these occasions Curnow drew on his own memories.

It was to be another half-century before some of these memories – the windmill, Gordon Brown and his grocery store, the immediate landscape and distant skyscape – were to find their way into the two poems, 'A Raised Voice' and 'A Sight for Sore Eyes', in which he explores his earliest childhood memories at Belfast. From the perspectives of 1937, Belfast is vividly remembered as a self-sufficient, richly sensuous, almost pagan world for the young child, and the sense of the child's remarkably acute powers of observation and sensuous alertness to everything going on around him remains strong in both the later poems.

The ideas provocatively broached in the radio piece, however, which use the child's experience to attack the alienness of the British political, literary and religious institutions imposed on the country, are different from those in the later poems. The anti-colonialist theme in fact provided the core of the poetic sequence *Not in Narrow Seas*, which Curnow was then working on, most of whose poems were published in the fortnightly magazine *Tomorrow*, during the months following the radio broadcast. Some of the piece's images and phrases – the 'child-analogy', 'suffering the agonies and the defeats of growth to nation-hood', and the notion of 'spiritual revolt' against colonial masters – reappear directly in *Not in Narrow Seas*.

Other late poems which return in memory to Curnow's Belfast years are 'An Evening Light', based on a stay with Grandmother Curnow in Christchurch around 1917, and 'Survivors', in which, lifted onto his father's shoulders, he recalls observing the scene of victory celebration in Hagley Park, Christchurch, at the end of the First World War.

However, there were some aspects of the family dynamic during these years to which the young child was unusually sensitive, and which are perhaps reflected in the photograph of the 'timid and imploring' four-year-old self the poet wrote about, 30 years later, in 'Self-Portrait', as well as in the later poem 'A Raised Voice'. 'The church [in "A Raised Voice"]', he wrote in explanation to the English poet and critic Donald Davie, 'is the little S. David's, Belfast (freezing works village a few miles out of Chch), my father's first parish, 1913–19. He used to say an office every weekday and "cause a bell to be tolled thereto" – I have an idea that nobody came, except on Sundays.'[20] The poem remembers his father preaching authoritatively from the pulpit at St David's, and ends on a note of anxiety, regis-tering a child's first inklings of loss – not so much loss of religious belief, though that is hinted at, as loss of the certainties and securities that parents provide for the young child:

> I'm looking into my thought
> of my father, my certainty, he'll

> be safe, but what about me? What else?
> A voice descends, feet scrape, we all
>
> stand up. The scent my mother wears is
> *vera violetta*. That can't be it.

Even his mother's reassuring scent does not satisfy the curious question, 'What else?' A poignant aspect of this poem is its sense that the child's deepest feelings and insecurities are entirely internalised: they remain unspoken, secret. The strength of this 'interior life' is central to any understanding of Curnow's personality, of his ways of engaging with others throughout his life, and of poetry's role and importance to him. Poetry was his means of releasing, though always with a sense of self-exposure and vulnerability, insights into what he was later to call 'questions which are private, and unanswerable',[21] the only questions, in the end, which mattered to him. His later memory-poems might be read as attempts to document key formative moments in the development of this sensibility during his childhood.

Curnow's somewhat marginal status within the family was reinforced by its domestic arrangements, in which the main responsibility for the upbringing of the children was carried by his grandmother, Rose Gambling, while Tremayne and Jessie were busy establishing the parish at Belfast. In Curnow's view it was John who was her particular favourite. She called him her 'little manny'; he was considered 'delicate', and she helped nurse him through two bouts of scarlet fever as well as diphtheria and 'shielded him from parental authority'.[22]

John was thought of by his parents, and certainly by his grandmother, as having bright career prospects, but perhaps because of the overprotectiveness of his upbringing, he was never able to settle to a career that fulfilled his intellectual potential. He was successful academically and eventually enrolled for a diploma in librarianship at the National Library, becoming librarian in the late 1960s at St John's Theological College in Auckland. His brother Tony's comment that 'he should have been there in the first place, in my view, as a student for the priesthood', is highly revealing.[23] Any parental expectation that John might pursue such a career, and chose not to, may have provided an added pressure on the younger Curnow to do so in the early 1930s.

Curnow's relationship with his older brother was never close. 'I never know where to plug into John', he once told Tony,[24] though in later years, when both were living in Auckland, they kept in touch at Christmas and on birthday occasions. Whereas Curnow developed a close relationship with his younger brother (they corresponded at length with each other, and their letters are a rich source of information about Curnow's literary life and intellectual interests as well as personal and family matters), he never seems to have felt able to talk openly to John, and there are no surviving letters between them.

As a child, Curnow seems to have been unusually self-possessed at a quite early age, and to have been uncommonly fascinated, anxious and occasionally guilty about what could not be spoken about in the family. The impression to be gleaned from his early family life is that the dominant aim of the parents, hardly unusual for its time, was to protect the children from unpleasant or unsettling knowledge, and to avoid discussing matters which might be personally upsetting or too self-revealing. Thus, Curnow never heard his father ever speak about his father or what his father's early death might have meant to him; nor was there any discussion about John Gambling: no questions asked or answered. To a sensitive child such silences could be as eloquent as any revelations.

Sheffield, 1920–21

In January 1920, when Curnow was eight, the family moved from Belfast to Sheffield, in the parish of Malvern, with its Mountfort-designed church of St Ambrose, 60 kilometres west of Christchurch on the Mid-Canterbury Plains. They made the trip in a small Model T Ford, its folded roof stacked with many of his mother's precious roses. In a lecture which he wrote in the later 1940s Curnow drew on his memories of this journey when seeking a parallel to Katherine Mansfield's account of her childhood journey to Picton, in her story 'The Voyage'. He recalled travelling in the back seat with his brother John in the heat of a nor'-wester:

> getting tired of the endless brown plain and the unchanging Torlesse range ahead [and] crouch[ing] down on the floor to shelter from the heat, the wind, and the dust. We were brought up, like many New Zealand children, on tales of an English countryside, and those images of populous scenes and farm nestling against farm, mixed with images of sentimental coaching and wayside scenes quite out of our time and country, were more real in our imaginations than what lay around us. . . .[25]

Curnow also began a fictionalised prose narrative about the trip (perhaps written in the late 1930s when Whim Wham wrote a number of such prose pieces for *The Press*), whose theme was the child's first encounter with the New Zealand countryside.[26]

Sheffield itself was a small, isolated settlement: 'my second vicarage', Curnow later commented, 'church, railway station and general store, Mt Torlesse on the west, Abner's Head south, Charing Cross to the south, a rural nowhere, Oxford a little to the north, hamlet among farms, not to be confused with Oxford, Mass.,

Oxford, Miss., Oxford N.C., Oxford Ohio, or Oxford Oxfordshire'.[27] The parish of Malvern also took in Darfield, Springfield and Kowhai Bush, en route to Arthur's Pass and the Otira Tunnel, linking Canterbury and Westland, which was in the final stages of construction during the 21 months the Curnows were based at Sheffield.

Tremayne asked Bishop Julius, head of the Christchurch diocese, whether he could also include the working men at Otira (100 kilometres west of Sheffield in the Southern Alps) in his pastoral duties, and made regular visits there, enjoying the company of the men and the change from the predominantly farming environment of the Malvern parish. Curnow later remembered his father's accounts of his Cobb & Co. coach journeys over the precariously steep, zig-zag Otira Gorge route to reach the tunnel workers, his delight in 'scrambling through the opening' when the two workfaces finally met, and his pleasure at being invited to attend the opening ceremony in 1923.[28]

Curnow attended the small primary school at Waddington, 2 kilometres east of Sheffield, walking the distance each day along the metalled main road parallel to which ran a railway line and a water race, and stored up (for a poem, 'A Balanced Bait in Handy Pellet Form', written 60 years later) a memory of a spectacular winter's morning sunrise, as light rose from the Pacific Ocean, gradually illuminating the snow-capped Torlesse mountain range to the north-west and creating a kaleidoscope of colours in the newly ploughed and mown fields along the roadside.

Although he skipped Standard Two, moving straight into Standard Three, his experience of school was marred by a traumatic incident in which he was falsely accused by an older boy of making an obscene phallic drawing on the lavatory wall. The boy blackmailed him over several weeks into stealing money from home to buy sweets, until his theft was eventually discovered when the local dairy store owner reported the blackmailer's excessive spending and the tale emerged. The scene which followed – his father's anger, his mother's efforts to console him, his sense of guilt, in which while admitting to theft he could not bring himself to mention the phallic graffito in the lavatory nor explain that he was being blackmailed – left an indelible impression on the young child.

In the later 1930s he attempted to write about the event in a short fictional sketch,[29] perhaps intended for publication in *Tomorrow*, to which he contributed a number of sketches at this time. Initially drafted in the first person, and then presented in the third person under the fictional name Joe, the sketch was never completed, but it is nevertheless highly revealing about the traumatic nature of the experience, especially the encounter with the sexual taboo at its centre. Bullied and threatened by the older boy, Charlie, whose lies he felt would be believed by the headmaster:

Joe had no thought of escape; no will to escape. A feeling was growing in him, a dreamlike sense of guilt, too strong for memory to overrule, compelling with fear, impelling with fascination, identifying [him] with the act of the drawing. Banned from the world of fact, denied with loathing in [his] world of home, the phallus was something that real memories had no power over.

After he gives Charlie his first penny, '[t]he phallus, the guilt, the above-all-not-to-be-discovered, joined them that moment in a kind of conspiracy', and they enjoy 'dawdling along the water-race that ran for miles between the railway and the road'. Then for what 'seemed a very long time' Joe regularly stole from the Sunday-school collection coins in 'a round tobacco box on his father's study mantelpiece', until one day he was called into his father's study:

> Have you been giving pennies to anyone, Joe?
> Father's voice sounded very quiet. Joe went red. He was more frightened than [he] had ever been before. Father seemed to move away.
> I gave Charlie Earnshaw some.
> Where did you get the pennies?
> Out of the brown box. But he wasn't thinking of the brown box. He was thinking of the dunnie, and the [headmaster's] strap.
> Charlie asked me.
> Then the crying began. He cried and cried. . . .
> Father was very angry.
> Mother took Joe in her arms. It was a long time before he stopped crying. . . .
> He told all about how he had taken the money, and then mother cried too. It was stealing, she explained. And they both cried some more till [he] had to be comforted, and allowed to take the black Pussy to bed.

There were two efforts to end the story, both of which focus in different ways on the issue of the 'above-all-not-to-be-discovered' image of the phallus ('denied with loathing in [the] world of home'), and on the deep-seated, permanent effect the events had on the child's later life. In the first, the emphasis is more on the child himself, and in the second, on the permanent change in his relations with his parents.

The country school in Curnow's poem 'Country School, North Canterbury' is not Waddington School, though the poem contains a number of elements transposed from the experience he had written about in the sketch. Like several others in the volume *Island and Time*, the poem records with surprise the swiftness with which time has transformed and eroded what seemed (and was) new at the time the speaker attended the school as a child. What loomed large in scale during his childhood now appears reduced and distant, evoking a mixture of nostalgic affection ('O sweet antiquity!') and sadness. However, the traumatic earlier event shadows allusions in the poem, transformed as they are into general images of mutability. A once 'scantling' '*Pinus*' (surely an unconscious Freudian slip) now 'stands mature', 'with rank tufts topping / The roof-ridge', and the poem concludes with a buried allusion to the drawing in the dunny:

> Look, the stone
> That skinned your knees. How small
> Are the terrible doors; how sad the dunny
> And the things you drew on the wall.

If Sheffield provided Curnow with the most traumatic experience of his life up to that time, it also provided him with the most exhilarating, the subject of a poem he wrote in 1987, entitled 'A Time of Day'. 'I'm trying to reconstruct in my mind's eye', he wrote to his cousin Ted Wall, seeking to draw on his specialist aviation knowledge, 'the very flying machine* in which I first flew – yes, I, your young cousin, at the age of eight, A.D. 1919, the present writer, in the second decade of Powered Flight, flew for some 30 minutes over Canterbury in an aeroplane of which I have clear memories.'[30] 'It was while T was Vicar at Malvern parish, and we lived at Sheffield', he went on:

> Some chaps – pilots with World War I service, I believe – took their aeroplane on a barnstorming tour in the country – using farm paddocks for airstrips, charging the locals to see the performance, and for short flights. I was one of a few children at Waddington school who sold tickets. The little girl who sold most tickets was too scared to take the free flight which was her reward. I pestered T and Muz to let me go up in her place. I did. T, bless him, climbed into the parish Model T and drove miles to pick me up at the farm where they parked the plane overnight.[31]

'Your memory is fantastic', Wall replied,[32] and although the poem's deeper resonances came from its wry comment on people's naive wish to believe in the miracle of a new age or a new start (such as seemed to be promised by the technological marvel of human flight), it is the richness of remembered and imagined detail – of the now-antiquated biplane itself, of the sights and smells of the scene – which carries its central meaning, that yesterday's new age is today's old hat and tomorrow's museum relic, that what remains constant is the 'load' of time-bound and place-bound 'things', unique and rich in their multiplicity in whatever so-called new age or new era, untranscendable.

---

* An Avro 504K biplane.

Sheffield was also the scene of one of Curnow's best-known late poems, the title poem of his last collected poems, 'Early Days Yet', written in February and March of 1994, an intimate, humorous and moving portrait of his father, as he fills the petrol tank of his Model T Ford with Big Tree 'spirit', goes through the elaborate ritual of crank-starting it, and drives with his son along a dusty road in 'a high / head wind, unhingeing / nor'west slammer' during one of his pastoral rounds of the Malvern parish, reciting snatches of poetry in tune with the motor's rhythms. The poem is a bold, virtuoso performance, 'driven' by its remarkable play on multiple senses of the word 'spirit'. Spirit not only fires the engine of the Ford, but contracts and expands to take in reflections on the liturgy (*'The Lord be with you . . . / And with thy spirit'*), on the spiritual or scientific origins and ending of the world ('with hey, ho, Bang!'), on the sheer vitality of his father's personality, and on the poetic act of memory itself, in which his father's 'spirit' survives the fact that 'I don't / see him any more / distinctly, for / dust of the earth, / his own'. 'I meant to make difficulties for myself with the tight little tercets', he wrote to his friend Bill Pearson, enclosing a copy of the completed draft, '& I did! – though not, I hope, for you.'[33] Its comically detailed account of the 'New Age' technology of the Model T Ford in 1919 also contained a pointed comment, as he explained to historian John Pocock, on 1990s millennial hype: 'I had in mind (1) current vulgar *fin de siècle* vapourings, (2) that New Age and Old Hat look alike, once you've seen more than one.'[34]

The writing of 'Early Days Yet' prompted the idea of yet another Sheffield-based poem, which Curnow described to Pocock as 'a companion or sequel' to it,[35] though its completion gave him a great deal of trouble. 'I do battle, almost daily, with another new poem', he wrote to Douglas Lilburn, '– as recalcitrant in content as it is in form.'[36] 'So many times', he wrote again to Lilburn, after it had been published almost immediately in the *London Review of Books*, 'I drove myself back to the beginning, wondering where (or how) it was ever going to end.'[37] The poem was 'A South Island Night's Entertainment'. Its aspect of 'companion or sequel' relates most directly to the theme of the New Age. Whereas in 'Early Days Yet' the New Age technology of the car made at least a stuttering entry into the child's world 'in reverse gear', in 'A South Island Night's Entertainment' a much-anticipated New Age silent movie fails to materialise in the remote back-country hall to which the family trudges on a starless night. This particular bit of the South Island, at least, remained beyond the reach of any New Age.

The poem's overwhelming feeling is of isolation and remoteness, as it is registered by the child in his 'ninth year'. Arriving at the 'shed of a hall' the family discover that they have mistaken the day and are 'shut out' of all the excitements promised by the technology of the Hollywood movie, just as the blackness of the night has locked them out of the cosmic dramas associated with the naming of the stars (Southern Cross, Pointers, the 'cartwheeling, hand- / standing giant / Orion'). The shed is padlocked and the gate leading to it is chained: 'nobody comes'. The atmosphere of the poem is permeated eerily with darkness and silence and emptiness, intensifying the sense of the family being entirely cut off and adrift, locked out of any meaningful relationship to the wider world – or, perhaps, with each other. The child feels his ninth year getting 'darker by the minute', and the poem concludes with an image of the family walking home in the darkness, each, it seems, entirely locked into his or her own thoughts:

> Only our feet go
> crunch-crunch in and out
>
> of step as they fall,
> all the way home.

Like 'A Raised Voice', the poem isolates a moment – with the lightest of references to a Fall – in which the child becomes aware of the world not only as a place where expectations are likely to be disappointed, but where he is essentially alone.

Chapter Three

The Lyttelton Years
and Adolescence, 1921–30

*Lyttelton was the one place we all liked unreservedly. We were together
there as a young family, there was the sea, the activity and constantly
changing scene of a busy port, a flourishing parish and a rich social
context. It was the only parish in which we had close relatives living
nearby.[1]*

West Lyttelton, 1921–30

Curnow was ten when the family moved to the parish of West Lyttelton, with
another Mountfort-designed church, St Saviour's, in September 1921. Tremayne's
parochial duties covered not only West Lyttelton, but Heathcote Valley on the
Christchurch side of the Port Hills, and included small churches at Governor's
Bay and Teddington, and ministering to settlements at Purau and Charteris Bay
and the small Maori community at Rapaki. St Saviour's was originally intended
also to be a seamen's church (the main Lyttelton Anglican church was Holy
Trinity, in the centre of the town), and Tremayne's responsibilities included being
chaplain to shore-based and visiting seamen. The vicarage, built in 1896, was in
Curnow's words 'a two-storey big box',[2] the living area (including Tremayne's
study) downstairs and the bedrooms upstairs. The third of Tremayne's and Jessie's
sons, Anthony (Tony), was born in 1923, two years after the move, and retained
vivid early memories of the vicarage and its surrounds:

We seemed to have fewer poor people than in the centre of town or perhaps just more of the local professional class. In a triangle of land, bounded by three roads, were the church, the parish hall and our house. This triangle was a stepped hollow in a valley gouged out of the steep hillside. Behind us were the Port Hills, which separate Lyttelton from Christchurch. High above and behind the house was the first of the Seven Sleepers, a series of sloping ridges which stretch away towards the far end of the harbour. . . . Turning the other way and looking down at the harbour, the water barely ruffled from the heads up to Teddington, ships arriving and leaving, yachts and motorized craft moving to and fro, and at the silent, rounded grassy hills and deeply folded valleys across the water, who would imagine that this was once the crater of an active volcano. . . .[3]

Curnow's world expanded hugely during the years he spent at Lyttelton. There was the fascination of the busy life around the wharves of the inner harbour below, the main South Island port of entry and departure for people (including visiting seamen from many different countries), and a hub of commercial activity, where cargoes of sheep and beef carcasses and wool were loaded for export. The port of Lyttelton provided 'a natural point from which to begin a study of the birth, life and growth of a nation', Curnow later wrote in the prose commentary to the first 'scene-setting' poem in his poetic sequence *Not in Narrow Seas* (1939), in which shrunken and derivative material aspirations are continually contrasted with the splendour and nobility of the South Island setting:

> The water is burred with rain.
> Men scrape rough iron, squatting
> On the slung plank, setting
> Knee and toe to the ship's flank.
>
> Rust and dust and the keen
> Wind strapping the ankle;
> Chips from the chisels sprinkle
> Down to the blue mud.
>
> There are five wharves.
> Today the port is quite full.
> They will load mutton and wool
> As soon as the rain stops.
>
> The Minister believes
> The price is sufficient to cover

Labour costs and something over
For a radio, perhaps a car.

There were the pleasures of swimming at Corsair Bay nearby, including the dangerous excitement for Curnow on one occasion of swimming from there to the inner harbour (while John returned on foot with his clothes), to the panic of his mother and the consternation of his father. He explored the bays further afield and the hills behind, sometimes on his own, sometimes with his closest friend of these Lyttelton years, Bob Crawford, and on occasion with his father, as evoked in the moving second section of 'At Dead Low Water', written in 1944, recalling their visit to Governor's Bay in 1923 or 1924. During these adolescent years he became interested in photography, taking many photographs with the box camera which his older cousin, Ted Wall, passed on to him, and hunted for rabbits with the .22 rifle also passed on to him by Ted before he left New Zealand to join the Royal Air Force in 1927.

In Lyttelton there was also, for the first time in Curnow's life, a close relation-ship with family relatives, his young cousins Patricia and Tennent Ronalds, whose mother Irene was a daughter of Laura [Monro] Cracroft Wilson, one of Tremayne's aunts. The Ronaldses lived only a short distance below the vicarage, close to the harbour, and the three cousins were constant playmates. Patricia, lively and spirited and uninhibited, was Curnow's first, youthful love, and in their innocent pre-adolescent games provided him with his first awareness of sexual difference, growing up as he had in a family of boys and in a protected vicarage environment in which sex was a taboo subject. She also brought out a mischievous streak in him, as when they raided St Saviour's in order to drink the communion wine:

> [A]s for vino I date my own preferences for the red variety to the early 1920s when ...a cousin and I took furtive swigs from a bottle kept in the W. Lyttelton church for the purposes of Holy Communion, not your Presbyterian unfermented grape, but the real stuff.[4]

'Children, Swimmers', a sonnet which Curnow wrote shortly after 'At Dead Low Water', vividly evokes the remembered sensuous presence of Patricia as a youthful fellow swimmer in the Lyttelton Harbour, and celebrates the sheer power of memory momentarily to transcend his anguished sense of time and loss:

> Oh but how under sea glitters no less
> Your flesh against time's fathoms, and not sunken

Ever, astonishes with a breath this drowned
Valley where tides are lost and love's dead found.

The image of Patricia, here, as an 'undersea' swimmer still capable of flooding the
poet's thoughts and taking his breath away, is likely to have sparked the image
of the changeling-mermaid in the strange, fantasy-like poem 'The Changeling',
which Curnow wrote in the early 1950s. Emerging from the waters of Lyttelton
Harbour one night, to create delightfully uninhibited sexual mayhem among the
staid citizens of the town before departing (by 'the town train'), the 'girl kind of
fish' leaves them mourning the loss of the anarchic energies she seemed to represent, which have momentarily offered them an image of a different kind of life
altogether. Perhaps the changeling's transformation into a young woman leaving
town by train, with 'her ticket in her hand', refers to her inevitable succumbing
to the pressures of normality and conformism. But the image of the changeling
as a vivacious, rebellious, anarchic figure remains, and the poem constructs her as
a figure of mythic potential, inhabiting the unconscious of a deeply conformist,
sexually repressed society. It was a theme Curnow returned to many times in
poems written during the 1950s.

Curnow returned to Lyttelton as a scene of deeply formative childhood experiences in a remarkable group of three 'Lyttelton' poems he wrote in the period
1988–91: 'A Busy Port', 'The Unclosed Door' and 'The Pug-mill', in which one of
the central themes is the child's almost voyeuristic discovery of 'taboo' moments,
having to do with death, violence, and secret access to a world outside that of
his parents. All of the poems record these crucial formative experiences in an
entirely inward way: they remain secret to the child himself, and remain especially
powerful because of that.

During his childhood Curnow sometimes accompanied his father, when, in
his role as port chaplain, he visited ships in the harbour. One such visit confirmed
his youthful taste for red wine:

[One] day my father, visiting a French warship's Commodore in his role as 'port
chaplain' took me aboard with him – now, how could any of that ship's company have
been Anglicans? – & the hospitable Commodore sent his steward to fetch wine, a full
glass of *vin ordinaire* for 'le petit garçon'.[5]

However, the occasion of 'A Busy Port' was a special one, the fulfilment of a
promise by his father to take him sailing for his eleventh birthday on the small
50-ton steamship (the SS *John Anderson*) which delivered supplies to remote
bays of Lyttelton Harbour and the peninsula. The event made an indelible impression for quite a different reason: as Curnow arrived at the wharf he was

shocked to eavesdrop unwittingly on the master of the boat, Bob Hempstalk, silently weeping, and to overhear subdued quayside voices referring to the reason for Hempstalk's grief – the death of his wife. In the final version of the poem this central incident is much more compressed than in earlier versions (and framed within a broader image of his father's and his own mortality, both walking down 'the steep gangplank' towards death):

> A man's tears, obscene to me
>
> caught looking. Too late now. The time-ball
> drops. Quayside voices (not for my ears)
> discuss the dead, bells repeat
>
> *ding-ding* across the wharf.

What happened during the process of revision was that the original, intensely personal focus on the details of the memory gradually shifted to a more impersonal focus on its interpretation and the way its deeply unsettling effects are resolved – or, at least, able to be accepted within a broader sense of bereavement as part of life – though the drama of the child's encounter with death and bereavement remains wholly internal, wholly unknown to the father accompanying him on his birthday outing.

Part Two of the poem, in which the steamship has left port and is under way, 'pitching like a beer-can' in heavy seas, was a later development during the process of composition. However, if the experience on the wharf continues in the second part to produce an upheaval in the child's world ('out of my depth, deeper yet . . .'), the poem concludes with the fact that Hempstalk survives the apparently traumatic nature of his grief, his identity merged with an image derived from T.S. Eliot's 'Eyes that last I saw in tears', as he expertly guides the ship towards the Heads:

> *Eyes that last I saw in tears* can read
> abstruse characters of waves, on course
> between them, our plunging bows.

Within a couple of months of completing 'A Busy Port' at the end of 1990 Curnow was at work on another poem from the time of his later primary school days (1922–23) at Lyttelton, asking his niece Faith [Richmond] Pinkney in Melbourne to tell his cousin Edith [Wall] Bayne that he had been 'hard at work finishing a new poem': '[It] happens to be about the old Abattoir at Lyttelton, not far from where her old friends the Morrises lived, at the time when she and I were children.'[6] The abattoir was located on the point between Corsair Bay and Cass Bay, discharging its waste over a cliff into the harbour, and the poem remembers an event in which Curnow with his school friend Bob Crawford, on an after-school cycling escapade, glimpse the activities inside the abattoir through a crack in an unclosed door at the precise moment when a slaughterman is cutting the throat of a lamb.*[7]

Curnow's first title for the poem was 'The Abattoir', but his revised title, 'The Unclosed Door', was more specific about the hidden nature of the shocking knowledge, of bloodshed and violence, to which the boys gain secret access. The door was not 'open'; it was a door that was meant to be closed. Again, in the early drafts of this poem, there is a strong emphasis on the secret, taboo nature of the knowledge the two boys gain, which leaves them fascinated, appalled and silent. Even stronger is the sense that what has been glimpsed is something that will never be spoken about, either to each other, or to parents. The final version, as in the final version of 'A Busy Port', is much less specific about the immediate thoughts and reactions of the children, much more concerned with interpreting the memory in the light of later reflection. The sense of shock the poem conveys is not simply the shock implied by the 'silence' of the two children during the course of the violent scene they witness (that is, it is not simply contained within their thoughts and feelings). It is also conveyed by the sheer vividness of the poem's description of the natural setting ('[f]reshened by any wind, sanitised / with pine and cypress'), the comparison of the slaughterhouse to a church, and the description of the act of killing itself in the disturbing musical metaphor of a base viol, 'the bowing hand slash[ing] / deep! *in blood stepped in so far* will up / to the eyes or the ears be enough?' The violence thus presented seems part of an 'incorrigible music', permanent and unchanging in human nature: 'Nothing', the poem concludes, 'alters this.'

Karl Miller, editor of the *London Review of Books*, accepted the poem with 'delight',[8] and fellow poet C.K. Stead was also enthusiastic, prompting Curnow to reply that there were 'possibilities for more "re-visit" poems': 'The trouble is that they only seem to come out of those occasions that have nagged one for years, & not all of those, either.'[9] The comment not only reveals how deep-seated and enduring such memories of childhood are for the poet, but an anxiety about that fact, as if the past is both deeply alluring and at the same time something to be resisted. 'Poems with too much past in them', he wrote in the wake of completing

---

* Bob Crawford was a son of the Lyttelton Harbourmaster, and he remained a close friend in the 1930s, when he was working in a solicitor's office in Christchurch, becoming the godfather of Curnow's first child, Wystan, before being killed in the Pacific during the Second World War.

one of his finest 're-visit' poems, 'An Evening Light', 'are like swimming against the undertow. It sucks one back, one swims harder, keeping head up and eyes on the beach.'[10] The processes of revision discernible in both 'A Busy Port' and 'The Unclosed Door' demonstrate the poet struggling against the undertow of the memory, removing or modifying or transforming those elements which might lock the poem into the specific parental and childhood traumas which generated them, and in this sense releasing him from their power to 'nag one for years'. It is in this sense that they function at a profound personal level, in the poem's (and the poet's) present.

Curnow's sense of the dangers of an 'undertow' from the past engulfing him probably also occurred in the wake of his work a few months earlier on 'The Pug-mill', which immediately preceded 'An Evening Light' and immediately followed the completion of his Sheffield-based poem 'A Time of Day' at the end of 1987. 'The Pug-mill' was another Lyttelton-based poem from the same time (1923) as 'A Busy Port' and 'The Unclosed Door', set in the same vicinity as the abattoir. Sending a copy to Stead, Curnow invoked Yeats's later forays into memory: 'I suppose this is my way of trying to climb Ben Bulben's back, without WBY's genius for splendour in nostalgia. I hope I haven't done it once too often, but at least it's a different scene & scenario.'[11]

The process by which Curnow's childhood memory became the central focus of the poem – watching Mr Prisk make bricks in his underground pug-mill dug out of the hillside above Governor's Bay – provides a remarkable example of the truth, at least for Curnow, that the process of writing a poem is a process of finding its true subject, or of waiting on the poem to declare its own true subject. In the early drafts Mr Prisk was a relatively minor presence in the poem, making an initial appearance in a rapidly written prose note:

> When Mr Prisk pulled on the cord the horse above us pulled on a beam & plodded around causing the clotted clay to extrude by an orifice over his bench reaching for a wooden mould he shaped another wet brick & another & another & pulled on the cord causing the horse to stand still.

At this point the poem's focus was quite different: on the rapidly changing Auckland city skyline during the spectacular expansion of high-rise building construction in the later 1980s. 'Will filling clouds with steel / improve our natures?' he asks, in one version. In other versions the meditation expands to include references to historic towers, now abandoned or in ruins – desert watchtowers, the Pharos, the tomb of Galla Placidia in Ravenna, Stonehenge – and, especially, the passage in the eleventh chapter of the Book of Genesis in which the descendants of Noah, all speaking one language, travelled to the plain of Shinar, discovered the technology of monumental brick architecture and began building the Tower of Babel to reach up to heaven. Interpreting this behaviour as an act of hubris, God intervened to 'confound their language' by creating many different tongues and scattering Noah's descendants across the earth. Reflecting on this archetypal story, Curnow suggests in one fragment that the ongoing 'instinct' to build towers is compulsive, 'pre-historical', having its roots primordially in the 'bone':

> (almost) as if in obedience to
> some purpose known to themselves
> scattered as they were they kept on building towers
> all over the face of the earth
>
> each a copy of a copy of the copy
> baked in the bone.

It took numerous further drafts, during which all these architectural motifs – the Auckland city skyline, the references to towers throughout history and across cultures, the Tower of Babel story – gradually receded and disappeared, for the poem to yield, as Curnow might have put it, its true subject, the memory of one of his visits to Mr Prisk at his pug-mill as a twelve-year-old.

At this point, refining the details of the memory – of Mr Prisk himself, of the way the pug-mill worked, and of himself as a child – also involved numerous further drafts. In one he lists buildings constructed out of Mr Prisk's bricks, including the town abattoir, 'in its grove of dark exotic macrocarpa / pouring blood and faeces / downhill to stain the sea where it bathes / the rock the slaughterhouse floor'. Although this description did not survive in 'The Pug-mill', it generated its own poem, 'The Unclosed Door', a few years later. However, although the broader historical and geographical perspectives of the poem disappear, they have clearly shaped the way in which Mr Prisk is presented. He is the primordial archetype of man-as-builder, his bricks the ur-types of all human building blocks (including the steel structures of high-rise towers). All such building blocks, whatever self-aggrandising high-rise aspirations are expressed through them, are subject, like the Tower of Babel, to decay and destruction. There is nothing outside 'the system we inhabit here', only the empty blue of the sky and sea, which at the end of the poem 'baffles' the steepening hillside as the child runs home.

Curnow emphasises the 'instinctive', almost 'unconscious', nature of Mr Prisk's brick-making (each brick doggedly patterned from 'the one / thought baked in the bones of his wrist'), as if defying time, though he is aware of his 'hands of clay' and the presence of 'a child looking on'. There is admiration for his persistence, despite the irony of the description of each brick as 'one more circle squared' and 'one more brick the desert will keep'. An unobtrusive connection is also made between the activity of the brick maker and the activity of the poet, whose building blocks are the components of language itself, a connection strongly built into the Tower of Babel story that appeared in earlier versions of the poem. Almost every detail of the poem carries an acute comment on the nature and motivation and purpose of poetry.

Curnow also took considerable pains with the poem's ending, which (like so many of his poems of childhood) involves the secret nature of the knowledge he has gained and his unwillingness or inability to share it with his parents. There is a suggestion, in his 'running barefoot home', that he will be in trouble for lateness, and the poem concludes with his effort to find a suitable excuse: 'They are asking *Where- / ever have you been?* I tell them *Helping Mr Prisk.*' In an earlier version he writes: 'when I get there they / will say *Wherever have you been?* I shall answer / *Helping Mr Prisk*, that's my story now.' In yet another: 'When I get home & they say / Wherever have you been I shall answer / *Helping Mr Prisk* – Will he help me now?' *'Helping Mr Prisk'* is delightfully apposite, functioning, at the child's level, as a hoped-for way of deflecting his parents' anxiety or censure, but, in terms of the broader concerns of the poem, identifying the poet with Mr Prisk, who 'helps' him in the sense that he is engaged, as a poet, in the same kind of enterprise.

Stead was intrigued by the suggestion of German mythology in Mr Prisk's gnome-like underground life. Curnow responded that for him 'the mythical shadows wouldn't have been northern, so far as they were conscious at all' and explained the biblical tale:

Of course when the Lord 'came down to see the city and the tower, which the children of men builded' he wasn't at all pleased with what he saw, & that was the end of that Development on a plain in the land of Shi-nar (Gen. ch. 11). My brick ought to be a sort of ur-brick or primal brick, a man-made original, hence 'in the bone', archetype & 'artefact', also a piece of mind, hence 'thought baked' – but the poem wasn't really prepense or 'programmed', it really did begin in & return to Mr Prisk's half underworld & what goes on there as well as not-there.[12]

The poems which Curnow later wrote about his years at West Lyttelton tell us a great deal about the expansion of his interests beyond the protected confines of vicarage life, about his growing sense of independence and insatiable curiosity about the broader world he lived in. The happiest years of his childhood were spent there, and Lyttelton always retained a special ambience for him, being a place to which he regularly returned on weekend visits or brief holidays with his young family during the 1940s. In Lyttelton he developed his first significant friendships outside the immediate circle of his family, and out of his fascinated encounters with unusual events and people in the port, the beaches and bays nearby, and the surrounding landscape of the Port Hills, some of the key pre-occupations which defined the kind of poet he was to become and the kind of poetry he was to write entered his maturing consciousness and imagination.

Christchurch Boys' High School, 1924–28

During his first two years in Lyttelton – 1922–23 – Curnow completed his primary schooling at West Lyttelton Primary School, and to the great pleasure of his parents was school dux in his final, Standard Six year. He received a medal for this achievement, which he later compared favourably with the 1990 sesquicen-tennial Commemoration Medals distributed by the New Zealand government to worthy individuals:

> Why do I have to remember that the Dux Medal I received for being top boy at the West Lyttelton Primary School was made of gold, a humble but durable 9ct? I expect Muz preserved it, but have no idea what became of it. The 1990 commemoration gong – I suspect widely distributed 'in recognition of services to NZ' – bears no mark or description of whatever aureate-looking substance was used by the *Australian Royal Mint*. It's positively morbid to dwell on these things.[13]

During his primary school years he was introduced to Thomas Bracken's 'Not Understood' and to 'a poem by Kipling beginning (I think), "Lord of our life, we pledge to thee …"': 'as far as I recall [it] set before us the noblest ideal that we should die for something or other, and hinted darkly that we had better keep our bodies fit and our minds clean for the event'.[14] The verse in the *School Journal* also did not especially interest him:

> Of the verse in the 'School Journal' (about 1917 to 1924 were my years) [I remember] only 'The Sea, The Sea', by Barry Cornwall, 'The Eve of Quatre Bras' (quite unintel-ligible to us at that age, though I liked the roll of the lines), a poem called 'The Blind Boy', and 'Abou Ben Adhem'.[15]

However, in his final year he had a teacher, Blake McKeown, whom he respected and liked, and who later recalled Curnow's recitation of Edgar Allan Poe's 'The Bells' as a wonderful performance: 'he remembered it for years afterwards, though for a long time I was not as grateful as I should have been'.[16]

In 1924 he enrolled at Christchurch Boys' High School, as had his older brother John the year before, and his father in 1890. For his first two years the school, with its 'small triple-arched Gothic porch', was still in its original building of grey stone in Worcester Street, and Curnow remembered it later in a piece, 'Notes for an Unwritten Poem', which he wrote for the school centenary publication in 1981:

> At least we were grey stone
> until 1926
> when red brick and Riccarton
> replaced all that
> early gothicolonial
> and the School moved on
> leaving the School standing
> where the School had stood
> fifty years
>   with Rolleston's
> effigy and avenue those words
> incised on the lintel of
> the Museum porch
>   *Lo*
> *these are parts of His ways*
> *but how little a portion is heard*
> *of Him*
>   the college clock
> striking as if time were
> an unheard-of novelty here
> and the First Four Ships not yet
> sighted* [17]

The return trip each day was a long one, and involved cycling to the Lyttelton train, followed by a tram trip to Worcester Street (this became two tram trips when the school shifted to its new 'red brick' premises in Straven Road, Riccarton, in 1926), arriving home at 5 p.m. The schedule limited Curnow's capacity to become involved in after-school activities, like sports, but – apart from swimming – these never particularly interested him. Although his friend Bob Crawford went to Christ's College, they both travelled on the same train between Lyttelton and Christchurch, and the friendship remained strong.

---

* The 'first four ships' (the *Randolph*, the *Cressy*, the *Sir George Seymour* and the *Charlotte Jane*) brought the Canterbury Association's first settlers to the new settlement of Christchurch in 1850.

Curnow began in Form 3A and remained in A forms throughout his five years at secondary school, taking English, mathematics, history, geography, science, Latin and French. He was not an especially ambitious student. In his Matriculation year his highest mark was English (70%) and the rest mainly middling, and he did not sit for a scholarship in his final year. He later remembered that during his secondary schooling in English 'we had no fiction later than Dickens. . . . I first read *Great Expectations* as a set book at high school.'[18] Although the curriculum 'did at least teach me that poetry was still being written':

> its enterprise ended (excusably, perhaps, for the time) with the little Methuen edition of 'Poems of Today'. But that day was then past or passing rapidly. Rupert Brooke accompanied me a certain distance, and Masefield; Flecker, Hodgson, W.H. Davies, and the ruck of Georgian asteroids made little or no impression on a boy living under the hard New Zealand light. But even then, I like to think, my first acquaintance with Yeats gave something I could connect, unrealising, with the few fixed stars of the great tradition by which I was trying to navigate – Shelley, Poe, Blake, Coleridge, Tennyson.[19]

He also remembered interested comments by one of his English teachers, A.C. Brassington, about a poem of 20 stanzas written when he was fifteen, 'which must have resulted from my first encounter with [Byron's] "Childe Harold"':

> What I remember about them – my only excuse for remembering them with any satisfaction – is that the [Spenserian] stanzas were properly shaped, the metre and rhyme scheme correct. I'm afraid that in most ways it was about what you would expect. It was all rather boyishly purple about an imaginary shipwreck.[20]

He also attempted a verse translation from Horace, and another of a passage from Tibullus which was published in the school magazine.[21]

Curnow won a number of prizes during his time at Christchurch Boys' High, though never any of the top aggregate prizes. On one occasion he took part in the annual debate between Christchurch Boys' and Waitaki Boys' on the subject 'Democracy is the best form of government for civilised nations'. The Waitaki team included two boys whose distinguished later academic literary careers intersected with his own at numerous times, James Bertram and Ian Milner.

John Schroder, who would become a mentor in later years, was a teacher at Christchurch Boys' High School and taught Latin to Curnow in Form Three. He remembered Allen as a 'quick and interesting boy with occasional "bright shoots of everlastingness"'. His reference to Henry Vaughan's phrase, from 'The Retreat',[22] was in response to a self-deprecating comment by Curnow himself about his 'muddled schoolboy soul' during the period he spent at the school. His time there suggests that although he was not especially interested in competing academically with other boys, and was uncertain about any future career, he took considerable pains with topics that interested him. He was also an acute observer of the habits and foibles of his teachers, and of the schoolroom environment.

> We smelt of ink powder
> acids damp waterproofs
> football boots urinals gun-oil
> oil of eucalyptus iodine
> chalk-dust
> the peculiar bouquet
> of the schoolbag blending
> smells of new books the raw
> new print the stale old
> bindings hand-me-down
> Inorganic Chemistry Caesar's
> Gallic Wars and Shakespeare's
> Julius Caesar with apples
> cakes lead pencils lacquer
> of the tin box containing
> 'instruments' item one pair
> brass compasses item set-squares
> item one celluloid protractor
> one pair dividers the whole kit
> for survival[23]

In a brief introductory prose section to these poem-notes, entitled 'Worcester Street, 1924', he recalled the original school and especially his first English teacher, R.M. [Pup] Laing, then one of the oldest members of the teaching staff, who had taught his father a quarter of a century before: 'I try to imagine, not very successfully, my schoolboy father sitting in one of those rows, waiting for the moving finger to point his way.'[24] In the poem which follows there are quirky portraits of the teachers he most remembered: Henry Dyer, his mathematics and science teacher; E.J.D. [Holy Joe] Hercus, his Latin teacher in the fifth form; George [Stump] Lancaster, the headmaster; A.C. [Brasso] Brassington, and others, including an affectionate tribute to his friend of later years, John Schroder:

Big Dick Doggy Holy Joe
Pup Tup and Krupp
50 years on would anyone know
If I'd made them up

Nicknames being tribal magic
for us one way
to master our masters and keep
those adversaries at bay

John Henry Erle Schroder
was Krupp for the obvious reason
World War One wit being not
yet out of season

but what could a name like that
have to do with JOHN
my teacher editor exemplar friend
50 years on

who forgave me my bad Latin
suffered me not ungladly
and for whom I tried and still try
not to write badly

Proofreading on the Christchurch *Sun*, 1929–30

Curnow seems not to have been thought of as 'university material' by his parents, and after he left school at the end of 1928, at the age of seventeen, he spent two years as a copyholder in the proofreading room of the afternoon daily newspaper, the Christchurch *Sun*, a job arranged by his father,[25] and perhaps facilitated by the support of John Schroder, who had left teaching and become associate editor of the *Sun* at this time: 'I was pitched into this as soon as I left high school because although my elder brother had a scholarship that took him to university I didn't have anything like that, and being a boy I had to earn my keep.'[26]

During this period he continued living at home with his parents, and shifted with them from West Lyttelton to the parish of New Brighton in May 1930. The job paid him 25 shillings a week in the first year and 30 shillings a week in the second, but he hated it: 'I learned to write verse but I felt inadequate and scared. I was scared of the whole town. I also felt inadequate in my job and scared of it.'[27]

He enrolled part-time at Canterbury University College, passing French I and English I in 1929, and Economics I in 1930. He made occasional visits to Lyttelton, to visit his cousin Irene Ronalds, commenting later that his child-hood sweetheart Patricia 'was always at the back of my mind; any other girl seemed handicapped',[28] though he was aware that nothing could come of the relationship.

In 1930 he was attracted for a time to Celia Twyneham, whom he met at university, and visited at her home. Celia later married the Reverend David Taylor, a friend whom Curnow came to know well during the course of his theo-logical studies, and after his own marriage to Betty Le Cren (who knew Celia from her own school days in Timaru) the Curnows and the Taylors kept in touch regularly during David's annual visits to Christchurch for synod meetings in the later 1930s and 1940s. One of the Taylors' six daughters was the poet and novelist Rachel McAlpine. She wrote to Allen in 1977, impressed by the 'intellectual power' of his *Collected Poems* (1974), reminding him of the Taylor family story that Celia had once been engaged to him ('for a fortnight. Was it?'), and comment-ing that through this brief connection she always felt that he had involuntarily played a role in her sense of herself as a poet, since none of her immediate family had literary interests.[29]

There was little writing of his own during these two years at the *Sun*, though enough to suggest that the impetus was stirring, if fitfully. In 1929 he wrote a poem 'about the idea of beauty' ('At the Brink') which was published in the quarterly *Art in New Zealand* in June 1932.[30] In 1929 or 1930 he also entered a poem for a competition run by the Auckland *Star*. The judge, Alan Mulgan, awarded first prize to A.R.D. Fairburn for his poem 'Odysseus', while Curnow's sonnet was 'very highly commended'. 'It was then', Curnow later commented, 'that I took the only good resolution which I've managed to keep, I think, that I would never again enter a poem for a literary competition.'[31]

Everything that can be gleaned about the two years Curnow spent with the *Sun* suggests uncertainty of purpose and drift. As the end of his apprentice-ship approached, he was also aware that continued employment was by no means certain:

> I knew a little of what it was to be a wage-earner with dismissal (in those years) possible for no other reason than that it was cheaper for the firm to hire a new boy at the bottom of the award scale: all fiercely competitive, and I was at best a weak & timid competitor.[32]

Towards the end of 1930 he made the first significant career decision in his life:

> By the end of two years in a newspaper office I decided the world was too wicked a
> place – or the world as I deduced it from a newspaper office was too wicked a place
> for me – and that the best thing to do was to follow my father into the Anglican
> ministry. So I did this, with the most serious of intentions at the time.[33]

In January 1931 he applied for and won a Marsh scholarship to St John's
Theological College, Auckland, which provided for two years' full-time university
study, followed by a year of theological studies intended to lead to ordination in
the Church of England. The following month he travelled to Auckland. He was
nineteen. It was not only his first break from home, but the first time he had moved
outside the Christchurch and Canterbury milieu in which he had grown up.

Chapter Four

Student Life in Auckland, 1931–33

[L]ooking back, I could diagnose my turning from the newspaper to the Church, as a fit of young poet's idealism and egotism: and three years later the fit returned, only it turned me from the Church and, ironically I suppose, back to journalism.[1]

New friends and networks, 1931

Curnow's Marsh scholarship included all necessary fees, accommodation in Selwyn House at St John's Theological College in Meadowbank, and some allowances,[2] and gave him his first opportunity for full-time university study. At Auckland University College in 1931 he passed English II, Economics II and Education I, and in 1932 English III and Philosophy I. In March 1933 he sat and passed Supplementary qualifying examinations in theology in order to enter Grade III of the qualifying system, run by the national Board of Theological Studies (BTS), and after passing all his examinations later in the year he was eligible to enter the first stage of ordination and be made a deacon.

During this period in Auckland, Curnow developed numerous friendships which were to remain important to him. His new life brought him into contact with three groups of people, whose lives often intersected: Auckland-based members of his extended family; the small community of fellow theological aspirants at St John's; and the youthful 'literary crowd' at Auckland University College – loosely affiliated writers, students, academics and radical intellectuals interested in new twentieth-century ideas about art, literature, politics, sexuality and culture, and disaffected with the pervasive conservatism and materialism of New Zealand.

Curnow's uncle and aunt, Pendarves and Eva Curnow, who had three daughters about his age – Nell, Elsie and Joan – were then living in Parnell, and offered warm hospitality on occasions when he visited, often bringing student friends from St John's. He was also made welcome by his cousin Larry (Hilary, daughter of his aunt Elsie and uncle Arnold Wall) and her husband Norman Richmond – then living in Owens Road, Epsom – whose politics were very different from those of his conservative Curnow connections in Christchurch and contributed strongly to the development of his own political interests. Richmond was a former Rhodes scholar and a pioneering figure in the WEA (Workers' Educational Association).[3] Both he and Larry were politically active in the left-wing movement that expanded during the Depression years, supporting other radical figures like the philosopher R.P. (Dick) Anschutz and the historian J.C. Beaglehole in their brushes with university authorities on the issue of free speech.[4] In 1933 Richmond engaged the poet R.A.K. Mason on his weekly WEA 1YA radio programme, in a series on 'The Development of Political Ideas'. The Richmonds were also friends of the poet A.R.D. (Rex) Fairburn, and introduced Curnow to him at the house of Rex's father, Arthur Fairburn, in New Lynn in 1932.[5] Fairburn had recently returned from an eighteen-month trip to England, and the young Curnow was invited to accompany Richmond and Fairburn on their tramps to Piha and Anawhata on Auckland's west coast.

Curnow also made a number of friendships among the small student community at St John's College. Wilfred (Wilt) Bool, whose first posting was to St Mary's in Timaru (like that of Allen's father Tremayne), remained a friend during Curnow's Christchurch years. So did Keith Harper, who was the son of Archdeacon Harper, the vicar at Timaru, and was later killed at Cassino in Italy during the Second World War. Another close friend, who enrolled in the same year as Curnow, was Paul Holmes, interested in music and the arts, 'with a fine voice and a talent for acting'.[6] He became active on the political left and went on to a career in teaching after going through a vocational crisis similar to Curnow's. Holmes, Curnow later wrote, was his 'one real friend ("friend" is a big word to me) [at St John's]', who stood by him 'in our troubles as rats in the Church trap'.[7] Holmes later stayed with the Curnows during visits to Christchurch. Fellow students R.H. (Dick) Toy and Neil Mowbray, who had distinguished academic careers in architecture and engineering, respectively, became close colleagues after Curnow shifted to the English Department at Auckland University College in 1951.

It was an older St John's student, T.P. (Tancred) Poole, who introduced Allen to R.P. (Dick) Anschutz, then a youthful lecturer in the Philosophy Department.

Anschutz was politically radical and also had interests in aesthetics and modernist literature, and became an influential intellectual mentor and friend of the youthful Curnow for many years. Hector Monro, himself influenced by Anschutz into a later academic career in philosophy, commented:

> [A]t one time Anschutz organised a series of informal meetings at which a selected group discussed various arts (poetry, painting, drama, architecture, etc.) in turn. James Bertram recalls 'Dicky Anschutz's "Aesthetics Club"', where a Thomist definition of Beauty straight out of James Joyce's Dublin was argued into the small hours to the music of Stravinsky's *Symphony of Psalms* or Gregorian chant from Solesmes Abbey .... [8]

Curnow would have been in his element with this intoxicating combination of modernist aesthetics, theology and music, and in 1932 felt confident enough to show Anschutz a long discourse he had written on poetry as '"pure communication" – not subject matter, style or words, but something abstracted from all of these'.[9] Anschutz was interested, though Curnow did not keep this first youthful foray into poetics.

Other older student contemporaries at St John's were Martin Sullivan (later to become Dean of St Paul's in London), who was active in student association politics and played a significant role in efforts to censor and control the magazine *Phoenix*, during the period in 1933 when it came under Mason's vigorous political editorship; and A.P. (Pat) Blair, who became a judge.[10] Blair remembered Curnow as a somewhat distant figure during his St John's days: '[he] formed close bonds with the literary crowd and, I think, felt somewhat superior to ordinary people'.[11] Curnow's body language in the college photograph for 1931 – his head slightly to one side, and an expression on his face which might suggest, 'I'm not sure what I'm doing here' – might confirm Pat Blair's observation.

There is no doubting the intensity and seriousness of Curnow's interest in the religious life at this time, nor the truth of his comment that he felt 'alone and strange'[12] during his first year in Auckland. In his next two years he became more involved in numerous social activities of the college, joining the tennis club and (in 1933) winning the annual college 'marathon', a long-distance handicap race of about 4 miles. In 1932 he led the St John's team in their annual debate with Auckland University College, arguing the negative on the proposition 'that convention does more harm than good'. (Robert (Bob) Lowry, who would become a renowned printer and typographer, was in the AUC team.)

At this time Curnow also contributed at least two poems to issues of the college's annual magazine, though contributions were not signed and there may have been others. An unsigned article of 1932, 'And Talking of Poetry –', a defence of modern poetry including quotations from T.S. Eliot and attacking the 'error' of judging poetry by 'looking to the subject-matter and the emotional attitude to subject-matter',[13] is likely to have been Curnow's, drawing on the ideas he had broached in the discourse on 'pure communication' he had shown to Anschutz.

In 1931, for the first time, he became seriously interested in writing poetry as a vehicle for his religious concerns, contributing no fewer than seven poems to the annual issue of the university literary magazine, *Kiwi*, then under the editorship of fellow student James Bertram. These poems all bear the mark of juvenile apprentice work – expressing vaguely romantic longings, spiritual idealism, and distaste for the shrunken aspirations of ordinary people. It may be that one or two of them had been written before Curnow went to Auckland. Though its setting is unnamed, the sonnet 'The Eyes Unseeing' appears to evoke a Christchurch sunset of the special, 'magical' kind which prompted 'An Evening Light' much later. The poem was awarded the magazine's prize for serious verse, for which the judge was Curnow's English professor, C.W. Egerton. An earlier version of 'The Eyes Unseeing' had appeared in the annual magazine of St John's College, entitled at this time *'Ye Kronikle' of the College of St. John*.[14]

Of these early *Kiwi* poems, only two survived into his first published collection, *Valley of Decision*, which appeared two years later in 1933, and only one of these ('The Agony') was retained, though very substantially revised, in his *Collected Poems* in 1974, perhaps because it was the only one of the group that showed an effort to move outside conventional verse forms. The exposure of so many of his poems in the one publication, the support of both Bertram and Egerton, and the reputation such publication gave him in the student literary circle of the time, boosted his confidence in the wake of his shift to Auckland. Lowry, enthusiastically promoting the idea of a new literary magazine, was also impressed, remarking to his printer friend Denis Glover that the young Christchurch import to Auckland was 'quite a cut above ours'.[15]

Curnow was also beginning to read more widely and intensively in contemporary literature, and was astonished to discover that R.A.K. Mason was a New Zealander living in Auckland. Without being aware of this fact, he had read and admired Mason's 'Latter-day Geography Lesson' and 'Body of John' (alongside work by T.S. Eliot, Edith Sitwell, D.H. Lawrence and the imagists) in Harold Monro's modern classic *Twentieth Century Poetry* (1929):

> It gave me great surprise and delight when a fellow student, hearing me mention these poems, said, 'Oh, R.A.K. Mason, yes, I saw him the other day – he's working in Queen Street.' . . . I went straight down to the little office in Queen Street where Mason's brother was doing some sort of business in foreign sweepstakes and there I found the poet sitting behind a little grille making out receipts on yellow paper. I introduced

myself, and after a little while he pushed under the grille a piece of office paper on which was typed a poem. Would I look at it? And it was 'Be Swift O Sun', a very beautiful poem I think.[16]

At the end of 1931 Curnow returned to Christchurch for the summer vacation. It was at this time that he first met the person who was to become his closest and longest-standing personal and literary friend, Denis Glover. He would have known of Glover, a year younger than himself, from Lowry, whose shared interest in printing and typography went back to an earlier period when both Lowry and Glover attended Auckland Grammar School. He may also have heard of Glover through his brother John, who knew him as a fellow student, and it was John who introduced Curnow to Glover in Christchurch.

It was during an Easter trip to Auckland in 1932 that Glover met the university 'literary crowd', admired the recently published first issue of the literary journal *Phoenix*, purchased a small hand-platen Kelsey printing machine through Lowry's contacts, and returned to Christchurch to establish the Caxton Club Press at the university with the aim, also, of establishing a lively new literary magazine.

Phoenix and the 'literary crowd', 1932

During his first summer vacation in Christchurch (1931–32) Curnow was contacted by Bertram with news of progress on the establishment of the new literary magazine whose first issue Glover was to see in Auckland at Easter the following year. Bertram was to be editor, but the idea for the magazine came from Lowry, who for the last six months of 1931 had enthusiastically promoted such a project to the Literary and Dramatic Committee of the AUC Students' Association as a means of 'encouraging New Zealand literature'. 'There are at least half a dozen men at A.U.C. capable of turning out excellent steady work', Lowry wrote to Denis Glover in July 1931.[17]

Bertram also discussed the project with his former Waitaki Boys' High School friends, Charles Brasch and Ian Milner. Modelled on John Middleton Murry's *New Adelphi*, the magazine was initially to be called *Farrago*, but this was then changed to *Phoenix* (derived from the device on a signet ring given to Murry by D.H. Lawrence), and the first issue came out in an edition of 250 copies in March 1932, printed by Lowry in Auckland on his press in a basement under the university's Old Choral Hall building. Curnow had been elected the previous November to a production committee,[18] but had little to do at any stage with either the editing or management of *Phoenix* over its spectacular 15-month career, during which four issues were published.

Shortly before the second issue appeared (a month late) in August 1932, Bertram left Auckland for Oxford on a Rhodes scholarship and asked Curnow to take over as acting editor, 'but the work was already done, and the copy in Lowry's hands',[19] and after Mason took over the editorship – determined, with Lowry's enthusiastic support, to radicalise and politicise the magazine – Curnow remained outside its editorial power centre, although (according to Lowry)[20] he had been interested in succeeding Bertram.

Phoenix was important to Curnow as a venue for his poems during the years 1932–33, when his ideas about poetry, politics and religion were undergoing intense reassessment. Equally important was the social and intellectual stimulation and excitement which his involvement with the 'literary crowd' at the university gave him. Among the men, he mixed with figures like Bertram, John Mulgan (who would write the classic New Zealand novel *Man Alone* (1939)), Hector Monro and Blackwood Paul (who would make his mark as a bookseller and publisher), as well as with Lowry, but they were never close personal friends, and in his later comments about this period he always resisted attempts to represent the people involved as a group with common purposes, 'when a little trouble to find out who they were and what they actually did might have shown what a heterogeneous bunch we were'.[21] Bertram and Mulgan were close friends with each other, as were Paul and Monro, Lowry and Glover, and Mason and Fairburn. Curnow knew and mixed with them all, but without the closeness of rapport that he later developed with Glover.

Numerous accounts and reminiscences of those years, however, suggest Curnow's growing social and personal confidence, despite his uncertainties about whether he was suited to a religious vocation. According to Jean Alison, who was also on the production committee of *Phoenix*,[22] he was a great talker who openly discussed these doubts with fellow students, as well as with Anschutz, who regularly invited the 'literary crowd' to his home in Ayr Street.

Like others of the *Phoenix* circle, Curnow also spent much of his time in Lowry's makeshift basement printery, where he would toss off squibs and rhymes, often with a theological twist to them, and pin them on the walls. Monro composed his own verses evoking the scene:

> His flowing tie in neat disorder set,
> The poet Curnow turns a triolet,
> While peering o'er his shoulder at each letter,
> A dozen others try to go one better.[23]

Clearly, 'the poet Curnow' (something of a nickname for him, invented by Lowry) was beginning to live *for* poetry at this time, as his literary and intellectual horizons expanded. He also contributed songs and parodies to Mulgan's *Jubilade*, a carnival play written to mark the university's fiftieth anniversary in 1933. To figures like Elsie Locke, who knew little of the personal insecurities behind the mask Curnow adopted in public, he seemed the epitome of enviably confident self-possession:

> He took himself very seriously as a poet and was not bashful about it either. He would declaim his latest poem at the drop of a hat. . . . To have an audience reaction is as useful for a poet as for a playwright, and Curnow knew it. So for that matter did Rex Fairburn, but it was easy to accept from him; he was already recognized, and not so demonstrably earnest.[24]

Curnow was also in and out of infatuations during this period with a number of the lively, independent women students who – though well outnumbered by the men – contributed actively to the university's literary and drama scene. There was romantic rivalry among both the male and female students,[25] and, according to Curnow remembering the scene later, 'sufficient tension', despite 'the social inhibition on sexual relationships'.[26] Rona Munro, a year older than Curnow, was for him 'a disturbing acquaintance because she was impassioned . . . pretty and very clever'.[27]

Jean Alison and Curnow were attracted to each other for a time, though both knew that nothing could come of it, as without money or prospects Curnow could not offer marriage to anybody.[28] She enjoyed his conversation, but also found him intense and self-absorbed.[29] In fact, there was a veritable merry-go-round of shifting student attachments among the 'literary crowd'. Alison was jealous to notice Allen sitting next to Rona Munro in a lecture the day after he had given Alison a love poem. Munro in turn was also in love with Mulgan,[30] and Lowry vied with Curnow for Alison's affections. Locke describes an occasion when she and other students, attempting a new track over the Waitakere Ranges to the hut at Anawhata, got lost and slept the night out in the open:

> Not having blankets we lay down in a long line, each body dovetailed into the next for warmth. Whenever somebody had to change position on that hard ground there was a shout of 'Turn!' and amid groans, cheers and laughter we all turned one by one.[31]

Alison also remembered the occasion. She ended up next to Curnow, much to the chagrin of Lowry,[32] who wrote about the event to Glover:

> And Curnow, blast him, is seriously in the offing. Strange thing about Curnow; when I first knew him I couldn't stomach him. But I've gradually worked into sympathy

with him. And queerer than queer is that when I first actively realized that I had
begun to appreciate him was the day he distinctly put it all over me one night when
a party of hikers, including us both and our feminine bone of contention, got bushed
and slept in the open. I rather fancy that my amazingly philosophical behaviour on
that occasion increased my appeal both to the feminine bone aforesaid and to the
poet Curnow.[33]

The small, remote two-roomed hut with nine bunks on a promontory at
Anawhata, overlooking White's Beach, provided a store of west-coast memories
from his student days which Curnow never forgot. He visited it many times on
weekends, in groups which might include Lowry, Monro, Paul, Holmes, Alison,
Locke, Edythe Matthews, and occasionally others like Anschutz and Mason.
A place for swimming, reading, tramping, conversation and debate well into the
night, it provided Curnow with the kind of relaxed social environment among
peers which had rarely (except at the Ronaldses' Lyttelton home) been available
to him during his vicarage upbringing.

The first issue of *Phoenix* appeared in March 1932 and included two poems by
Curnow. 'Egotism' was written on the pattern of a Hebrew poem, with the aim
of balancing the sense between each line of its couplets. He did not reprint it in
Valley of Decision, and later described it as 'rather a bad' poem,[34] but in its use of a
dramatic persona and its strong prose-like cadences it suggests a mood and tone
found in some of Ezra Pound's earlier poems. More justly, Curnow omitted the
sentimental second poem, 'Calm', from *Valley of Decision*, though it too seems to be
imitating Pound's imagist mode. The second issue of *Phoenix* (July 1932) contained
Curnow's 'The Spirit Shall Return', a strong, perhaps Mason-influenced statement
of religious struggle, and the following month *Kiwi* (1932) included 'The People
Perisheth', a portentously obscure attack on earthly vanities and materialism,
which survived into *Valley of Decision* (as 'The People Perish') but not into the
Collected Poems in 1974.

Both 'The Spirit Shall Return' and 'The People Perisheth' suggest that social
concerns – the ways in which the Christian spiritual life could be related to social
needs and arrangements – were tentatively beginning to enter the volatile mix
of personal and vocational questions relating to Curnow's theological studies.
Shortly after the first issue of *Phoenix* appeared, mounting social unrest at
increasingly widespread unemployment and poverty led to the Queen Street riot
in April 1932. In May, Sir George Fowlds (chancellor of the university) issued a
notorious memorandum to staff which placed dangerous limits on the extent to
which freedom of speech would be allowed; and in August, J.C. Beaglehole, who,
along with Anschutz and Richmond, had taken a strong stand on this issue, did
not have his contract in the History Department renewed.

Like Bertram, Mulgan and others, Curnow was one of the students recruited as 'special constables' in the aftermath of the riot. Unlike others, he offered no excuses, later, for his political ignorance and callowness at the time:

> . . . I doubt whether [Bertram's], any more than Mulgan's motives, for taking up the truncheon, were simple worthy aims 'to keep the peace', 'to protect property'. The sheer excitement of 20-year-olds with an opportunity to get into the action, no matter how, had a good deal to do with it. In my case, it got me a week's leave from St John's – without that truncheon I wld have been at nightly compline & morning chapels & nothing but the Herald to tell me anything. I cld as easily have been recruited to heave bricks into Milne & Choyce's plate glass – but who wld have given me leave for that? I really had no political or social ideas worth a damn – nothing but a callow revulsion from town rectitudes & people in swivel chairs.[35]

The political turmoils of 1932 affected Curnow deeply, but they did not produce the instant conversion to political rectitude that others (like Mason, Locke, Lowry and Alison) already possessed or later (like Mulgan) claimed to have achieved overnight. He remained out of sympathy with Marxist philosophy and with the analyses of class war which Mason, Clifton Firth (photographer and graphic designer) and others were to promote in the remaining two (1933) issues of *Phoenix*, while becoming increasingly hostile to what he saw as the complicity of institutional religion with capitalism and the reactionary political establishment.

'Free speech', in so far as his own poetry was concerned, was emerging as an issue for the authorities at St John's College. Pat Blair recalled that the line 'a body in a bag', from 'The Spirit Shall Return' in the second issue of *Phoenix*, was the butt of a tactless joke by Canon Edward Strong, appointed warden of the college in 1932, which went the rounds[36] – perhaps anticipating a major conflict Curnow was to have with the college authorities the following year. Curnow had to be careful on a Marsh scholarship, which could be withdrawn at any time 'for any serious breach of College Discipline such as would cause the expulsion of any other Student or Scholar',[37] in the panicky atmosphere generated by government and newspaper hostility to student communities supposedly as hotbeds of communism, revolution and sexual licence. It was a sign of this anxiety that he did not publish one of the liveliest of the poems he wrote in 1932, entitled 'Ethics', until 1934, and even then it appeared (in the *Canterbury College Review*, published by Denis Glover) under a pseudonym, 'Julian'.

'Ethics' offered a cynical account of Creation as a pact between God and the Devil. God is presented digging in a pit to create man out of the earth while the Devil looks on, holding a lantern (assisting in the creation of man), and grinning that his help is sought. At the moment of his birth the speaker is 'laid . . . in the devil's cart' whose 'scuttering wheels' transform themselves into 'life's tall hearse trundling to a start', while 'God hack'd his Chaos sullenly / and turned His thought to other clay.' No doubt Curnow guessed that had the church authorities known of the poem, they would hardly have judged its author a suitable candidate for holy orders.

Studying theology full-time, 1933

At the end of 1932, Curnow was still one subject short of completing his degree, and wrote to the St John's College Trust Board asking if he could have a further year of university study.[38] It was a long shot, and his request was rejected. Curnow had already been told that he was expected to complete his degree at the end of 1932 if he wished to keep his scholarship, and that in March 1933 he would be required to take a Supplementary (qualifying) examination in theology, condensing Grades I and II, prior to embarking on his full-time year in theology at Grade III level. This would lead to ordination into the diaconate, after which Grade IV (often completed during the initial period as a curate attached to a parish) would allow final ordination into the priesthood. The Supplementary examinations comprised topics in the Old Testament, the New Testament, the Book of Common Prayer, English Church History to 1714, Early Church History to 451 AD, and Dogmatics (including the Catechism and Articles I–VIII of the Church of England).

Curnow worked so frantically in Christchurch during the summer vacation to prepare himself for these Supplementary examinations in March that he made himself ill – effectively, he had to cover two years of courses in a little more than two months – but he sat the six papers, and scraped a pass, just above the minimum of 40 per cent needed for a Third Class result. The Board of Theological Studies expressed concern about the low marks to the St John's College Trust Board – the examiner of the paper on the Book of Common Prayer, for which Curnow had received 22 per cent, suggesting that he should be required to sit the paper again – but in this instance the trust board, advised by the warden, Canon Strong, took Curnow's side. He had passed on aggregate, even if only just, according to the rules, and should not be stopped from enrolling in his final full-time year of Grade III theological studies.[39]

There was nothing *inherently* conflicting in the idea of combining a career in the Church with a career as a poet. The English poetic tradition had produced numerous fine examples of such poetic/religious sensibilities, including John Donne, Thomas Traherne, Gerard Manley Hopkins and George Herbert (whose collected poems Curnow had received as a school prize). Closer to home were

the examples of his father, and of his distant forebear on his mother's side, the
Reverend George Crabbe. Despite Elsie Locke's retrospective comment that 'we'
(meaning fellow students at Auckland University College) never 'thought of him
as a future parson',[40] Curnow was wholly serious in preparing himself for the
prospect of a church career during this full-time year at St John's. He studied hard,
perhaps smarting from the narrow pass he had achieved in the Supplementary
examinations, and at the end of the year was the top student from St John's in the
national Grade III examinations, and second for the country as a whole.[41]

The conflicts which intensified during the year had little to do with theology
itself or with Christian belief per se, but rather with an increasing unease about
the behaviour of the modern church as a social institution (especially its alliance
with conservative and genteel forces in society), and with his increasing awareness that the church authorities were suspicious of, if not hostile to, the kind of
modern(ist) poetry he was interested in reading and writing.

Mason's first issue as editor of *Phoenix*[42] appeared a month late in April 1933,
with two of its pages blank (after the removal of an article promoting sexual
freedom), at the behest of Curnow's older fellow student at St John's, Martin
Sullivan, who was then also president of the AUC Students' Association.* At the
end of May, *New Zealand Truth* ran a banner front-page headline, 'N.Z. Hotbeds
of Revolution. Red Hot Gospels of Highbrows',[43] and in its accompanying article
pilloried the 'sneers, jeers, bellicose blasphemies, red rantings and sex-saturated
sophistries of young men and women who are graduating to become the leaders
of the community tomorrow'. Curnow himself later explained the absurd over-
reaction of the newspapers and the university authorities as follows:

> All of this has to be understood in a context of early 1930s Auckland. A much smaller
> city (and country). A university college with a total enrolment of about 1100. The years
> *before* the first Labour Government. A local press (*Herald* and *Star*) capable of
> believing that Mussolini was an enlightened leader who made trains run on time and
> dosed Communists with castor oil, and that Hitler's rise was a hopeful check to the
> Soviets. The clubs and the business leaders of Auckland regarded the university college
> with suspicion: *sinister forces* were at work there, teachers of radical, if not seditious
> doctrines. Politics were curiously confused in their prejudices with the Modern in
> literature and art. Of course, we young people were just as confused (and sure of
> ourselves): but we had some notion of how rapidly time was running out for what
> Auden (10 years later) called 'a low, dishonest decade'.[44]

---

* The story of the fuss it caused, along with Glover's *Oriflamme* (which was banned at Canterbury
University College in the same month), has been told in numerous places. See, for instance, *The Oxford
Companion to New Zealand Literature*, ed. R. Robinson and N. Wattie, Oxford University Press, 1998,
p. 416.

Curnow's contribution to Mason's first issue, a poem entitled 'Drawing-Room Window', was not directly in the public firing line, but it attracted a censorious comment about 'the use of indelicate epithets' from C.A. Marris in *Art in New Zealand*.[45] Perhaps in the wake of this censure, or *Truth*'s general condemnation of the magazine, the poem was pronounced 'immoral' (by Archbishop Averill of New Zealand, Bishop of Auckland) at the annual diocesan Anglican Synod a month later. Archdeacon Simkin, who oversaw finances and scholarships at St John's and chaired the St John's trust board, asked the warden to investigate:

> I was summoned to the Warden's study to explain myself. If the Warden, Canon 'Teddy' Strong, and the Archdeacon of Auckland [Bishop Simkin] who was Secretary of the St John's Trust Board hadn't cordially detested each other, the Church and I might well have parted then and there.[46]

Curnow then wrote what he thought was a disarming letter to Simkin, at the request of Canon Strong, saying that the poem was 'not intended to give offence',[47] and Strong sent it to the trust board, with tactfully phrased support:

> I enclose a full apology from T.A.M. Curnow for the poem by him which has recently engaged the Board's attention. I have every reason to believe that Curnow is sincere and means what he says, and I regard his action as a hopeful sign.[48]

Simkin then sent Strong a letter from the board to be passed on to Curnow, to which Strong replied equally tactfully:

> I have to thank you for your letter with enclosure for T.A.M. Curnow. In reply to your question, I should say that the letter is exactly what is wanted. It would spoil the effect to add anything. As it is it conveys precisely all that is needed to make him feel that the Board has generously overlooked something of which he clearly had not realized the seriousness.[49]

Although the matter appears to have been resolved at this point, Curnow clearly felt – correctly – that he was under the eye of the church authorities and suspected of 'unsoundness'.

He did not include 'Drawing-Room Window' in *Valley of Decision* (which he was beginning to assemble at this time), almost certainly in order to avoid further offence. It was in fact quite a lively poem, spoken by a sexually inhibited figure who hides the act of sex behind 'white blinds', its cynicism reminiscent of a mood in some of Mason's own poetry – which may explain why it appealed to Mason for *Phoenix*:

White blinds, and teeming Spring outside,
swelled breath of birth in bare green:
see – I have blinds about to hide
love's business that is best half seen.

The swell of breath is best half driven,
new life best calmly got within
where nothing's all and hotly given:
but half a rapture, half a sin.

... But, Lord, what poor brood of our whoring
we send the Spring's ecstatic prayer:
the vital green, and blue winds pouring
will drown them in an unknown air:

They shall lie husked as I am lying
sick for the fount unloosed in me,
failing whose blessing I am dying
in close white-blinded sanctuary.

In July 1933, three months after the banning of *Oriflamme* at Canterbury University College, Glover edited and published *Sirocco*, its appearance – albeit under a new name – a tribute to his diplomatic skills in persuading the CUC authorities to permit his Caxton Club Press to remain in operation under university auspices. The contents of *Sirocco* attracted numerous notices, but no one commented on a piece by 'Philo', entitled 'Christianity and Marxism', which occupied the magazine's opening pages. 'Philo' was a pseudonym of Curnow,[50] and the piece is significant, especially because it bears directly on the poetry he was then writing for his first collection, as well as on his attitudes to Christianity.

'Christianity and Marxism' is a lively piece of student polemic, a dual-pronged attack on the deficiencies of the 'materialist-atheist' thesis of Marxism, and on the failure of the contemporary Christian church to build on Marxist insights into the social order and acknowledge Marxists' use of the ethical concepts of equality, justice and brotherhood. Instead, Christianity is allowing itself to be 'exploited to its own destruction' by its identification with capitalism. 'Philo' is convinced that 'the present chaos must be resolved into some form of communal order'. However, while Marxism offers key insights into the current crisis, its historical materialist thesis is wholly inadequate because it 'cannot seek other grounds than those of the mechanistic conception of life in individual man', a conception undermined by 'all the puzzling phenomena of the human organism':

Accordingly it takes refuge in dogma. That is the final false step. Communist dogma is a far, far wilder thing than anything in mediaeval theology. . . . a fungoid spawn on the rotten carcase of nineteenth century mechanism.

However, it is the attack on the institutional church, turning its back on the momentous social forces revealed by Marxism, which concludes 'Philo's' polemic:

O you wretched Christian idealists, allowing a sour materialist taste to turn your stomachs against the greatest idea of centuries. The one way to settle the new Communal society which shall be, and preserve it from the mumbo-jumbo of artificial religion, sex-perversion and animality, is the Christian way. As it has risen on each wave of social progress and held the ground gained, so Christianity must rise on this next wave. It is strong enough, if it will only try its strength, to be in at the death of Capitalism.

As with the poems Curnow was preparing for *Valley of Decision*, there is nothing in the piece by 'Philo' to suggest that Curnow had any doubts about Christian belief, though it is clearly a radical form of Gospel-based Christianity which he espouses, centred on the notion of a residual 'Kingdom of God' working within and across history, 'riding its waves' in order to strengthen itself. The essay is an effort to *synthesise* his social and religious concerns, and the choice of the Jewish philosopher Philo of Alexandria (c. 20 BC–c. AD 50), a contemporary of Jesus, for his pseudonym, is particularly apt, given the effort to synthesise the best from two radically different systems. Philo was also a synthesiser, living in an era of momentous religious change, who drew widely on two opposed and divergent systems – Greek philosophical thought and the writings of the Old Testament – in an effort to reconcile revealed faith with philosophic reason.

Although there was nothing at all in 'Christianity and Marxism' to suggest doctrinal apostasy, its attack on the social inertia of the contemporary church and its alliance with capitalism clearly made Curnow nervous of further problems with the church authorities, especially since the article appeared at the time of his difficulties with 'Drawing-Room Window'. Writing to Glover about *Sirocco*, Curnow thanked him for 'the quite undeserved prominence given to my allowance of rant', adding, 'more and more I feel thankful for the *nom de plume*. Lucky for Philo he's dead this many a year.'[51]

Looking back from the 1970s, when he had completely forgotten the existence of the 'Philo' article, Curnow wrote that at the time 'the topic was hot, esp. for a student seriously preparing for Holy Orders, with whatever personal anxieties & confusions':

I expect I was trying to reconcile my Church discipline with ideas of a more practical redemption than the Church's? Wherever the Church is powerful, people worry about this. . . . But I suspect the article of being at best a bit juvenile & at worst puerile.[52]

As always, when looking back at the 1930s, Curnow emphasised the haphazard and eclectic nature of his own, and others', responses to the stresses and strains of the period, in which personal concerns were often mixed up with socio-political responses:

My 'Marxism' wasn't derived from any study of Marx, except that I believe I had read the Communist Manifesto and had the sense . . . of a society sharply polarised between labour & management. Later, I came to see myself as dreadfully ignorant & ill-equipped; a kind of sympathy and a bit of hero-worship caused me to identify myself with friends – or was it only Mason? – who were groping for some intellectual base for the much surer feeling that what we now call the Establishment was wrong. For me, at that time, Christian faith and doctrine had to be right. But the Church in its social (& implicitly political) positions, had little room for, patience with, inclinations which most clergy (I could name two bishops at least) felt to be godless and destructive. Looking back later, I could see what a mixed lot we were. Our problems were the same (mutatis mutandis) as those of the 'sixties – sexual, aesthetic, religious, political. How easily the sexual or aesthetic rebellion took on religious or political forms: and how easily the forms changed places.[53]

Valley of Decision, 1933

Despite Curnow's political differences with Mason, his respect for him as a poet was unqualified, and Mason in turn seems to have regarded Curnow as unusually promising. He included two of Curnow's poems ('Arcady' and 'Apocalyptic') in his second issue of *Phoenix*[54] which came out later in June. This last issue of *Phoenix* also advertised that 'it is intended to publish shortly a book of poems by Allen Curnow. Those interested should write to the Phoenix Secretary about the middle of July.'

Valley of Decision eventually appeared in an edition of 250 copies in September 1933, from Lowry's Auckland University College Students' Association Press, though its final stages of production were managed by Lowry's co-printer Ron Holloway,[55] after Lowry – under pressure from the university authorities (and the students' association) for his political activism and for financial problems in the AUCSA Press – suddenly left Auckland in September, for several months of 'time out' in Christchurch, where he made contact with and assisted his old friend Denis Glover at the Caxton Club Press. The volume contained 23 poems, eight of them reprinted from the fifteen poems Curnow had published up to that point in *Kiwi, Art in New Zealand* and *Phoenix*, the other fifteen consisting of new poems. The volume was dedicated to 'T.M.C.', his father Tremayne, and contained a brief foreword, cleverly worded in order to disarm criticism, insisting on the seriousness of the impulse behind the poems:

> Nobody who deprecates my conceit in permitting the publication of these first and no doubt ill-considered poems is likely to be convinced by any sort of apology I might make. I would say, however, that whatever conceit has led to their publication had no part at all in their writing.

The title of the volume was taken from the final chapter of the Old Testament Book of Joel – 'Multitudes, multitudes in the valley of decision; for the day of the LORD is near in the valley of decision'[56] – a somewhat obscure chapter full of apocalyptic imagery in which Joel both attacks Israelites for their backsliding and recalcitrance and prophetically imagines a confrontation between them and heathen nations in a Judgement Day which will see the destruction of Israel's enemies and the ushering in of a new era of peace and plenty. The nature of this reference to Joel might suggest that the primary implications of Curnow's title are political, bearing on a number of poems towards the end of the volume ('Apocalyptic', 'The Serpent', 'Host of the Air', 'Arcady', 'The People Perish' and 'Relief') which seem to share with the epigrammatic 'Status Quo' a strong sense of frustration at the spiritual failings of the contemporary church:

> If these stuck clods were blasted wide
> the rubble raked apart to give
> the sun below, they'd spill their pride
> and learn of worms the way to live.

In an article shadowed by the crisis of the Second World War which Curnow wrote for the Christchurch *Press* early in 1940, on the prophetic strain in modern poetry, he cited Joel's lines in this 'political' sense as a gloss on T.S. Eliot's *The Waste Land*, seeing both as sharing emphases on 'eschatology, "the last things" . . . and the sense of crisis and impending war'.[57]

However, the title poem itself, 'Valley of Decision', seems to use Joel's refer-ence in a more personal way, primarily as a metaphor for a moment of spiritual understanding and recognition. In the poem a tidal valley, observed from a cliff edge whose eroded base carries traces of the ceaseless ebb and flow of tides (perhaps a scene as observed from the cliff-top hut at Anawhata), offers a vision of the 'truth' that death, loss, disillusion and failure pervade all human experience of the world, even in its loveliest, most alluring and apparently satisfying moments. At the end the poet advocates turning away from ('disowning') such a world, embracing instead the idea of a spiritual world untainted by such forces:

> be naked in the highest place
> whence the fouled wave has fall'n away:
> you have that strong eternal grace
> which serves no time nor mark of day ...

It is this second, more personal, deployment of the biblical metaphor which seems most apposite to the volume as a whole, in which each poem might be seen as a spiritual exercise in a soul's pilgrimage of self-discovery. There is nothing in the poems to suggest religious indecision, or uncertainty of vocation, at this point in Curnow's life. While it is true that many of the poems emphasise the attractions of earthly beauty, the temptations of pride and self-will, and the difficulties of prayer itself, such emphases are thoroughly traditional devices of devotional poetry, to be worked through to a point of affirmation of the Christian message. At times the soul seems close to a dark night of despair, at other times confident in its address to weaknesses of will, at other times angered by the spectacle of secular and material power, and at yet other times, prophetically insistent in its wish for divine intervention in the affairs of the world.

But at the centre of all these stances is a clear affirmation of the Christian understanding of the world. 'Behold Now Behemoth' is one of the liveliest poems in the collection, a meditation on the biblical account of this mythical beast provided by Job,[58] and illustrates how vividly Curnow is able to evoke the gross physical particulars of the Leviathan-like monster himself, and his 'muddy truckling' with river weeds and mud holes – an image of sheer, mindless appetite – in order to assert more clearly the affirmation of Christ at the end, though this dimension is hinted at throughout the poem:

> See the wide-footed, pendant-bellied beast
> called Behemoth, burst loose the river weeds
> in cloudy mud-mist down the stream; he feeds
> grunting, suck-sucking Jordan with his feast
> of grass; slow swings his eyes to the east,
> blinks as the sun strikes, turns away; he needs
> no such clean light, shafting the trodden reeds;
> logs it in water-holes till day has ceased.

Drowse and be comfortable; lie, Behemoth
under the cross-stick shadow, trembling veil
heat-vibrant, quick in the slant-broken stems.
So has He made you; bone and sinew both
of iron, that His image man may quail
at sight of you, and clutch His garment's hems.

Valley of Decision hardly excited any public fanfare when it made its appearance. C.A. Marris, writing as 'Prester John' in *Art in New Zealand*, thought the poems showed promise, but attacked the obscurity of their style, '[perhaps] the outcome of too complete a surrender to the manner of the "Waste Land" school, and the manner of the Eliots, the McLeishs and the Aldingtons'. He also deplored 'the note of disillusion and discontent': 'the world is not such a hotch-potch of irremediable selfishness and bitter hopelessness as he conceives it to be'.[59] However, the volume was well received by people Curnow respected. Mason had encouraged its publication, Fairburn was impressed, Glover was to choose two of its poems ('Relief' and 'Renunciation') for the important small anthology, *New Poems*, which he edited with Ian Milner the following year, and Iris Wilkinson (Robin Hyde), searching at this time for a sense of spiritual direction in her life, felt a sense of kinship with the poet's struggle to explore spirit and matter, self and society. Significantly, too, Tremayne Curnow liked the poems, and for many years believed they were far better than any of the later poems his son wrote.[60] There was more than enough, in such responses, for Curnow to feel that the publication of the volume was justified, and to confirm his wish to keep writing poetry.

When *Valley of Decision* appeared, Curnow was in the midst of his Grade III examinations for the Board of Theological Studies. He had to sit eight papers, over a period of two weeks from the end of September. Whatever reservations the trust board may have had about his 'unsoundness' they could hardly complain about his performance in the examinations. New Zealand-wide there were seventeen candidates at Grade III level, and of the eleven who passed, seven came from St John's College. The top student overall was his friend David Taylor (at College House, Christchurch) who received a First Class pass, and Curnow was second, at the top of the Second Class list, leading the St John's contingent. In two of the papers he was the top student in the country: the Old Testament paper where the set texts were the Minor Prophets (including Joel, who provided the title for *Valley of Decision*), and perhaps most satisfying of all, in view of his Supplementary examination result earlier in the year, the Grade III paper on the Book of Common Prayer (its sources, history and meaning). He also performed well in the New Testament paper (on the Acts of the Apostles), in the Dogmatics paper on the Church of England Articles IX–XXXIX, and in the Apologetics paper. He did less well in papers on St Luke and St Augustine, which required knowledge of Greek and Latin.[61]

In November his time in Auckland was up. His formal qualifications for pursuing a career in the Church, at this stage, were excellent. 'The strength of the St John's training', the college's historian has written, 'lay in the way students were immersed in Anglican tradition, theology and worship through the daily experience of Prayer Book services in the Chapel and the encounter with aspects of the Anglican ethos through the BTS syllabus.'[62] Partly because of the leanings of the small number of staff there, the St John's ethos within the spectrum of Anglican thinking was High Church rather than Low Church, with a rigorous emphasis on intellectual tradition, on the ritual forms of worship, and on the regular practice of religious self-contemplation. The year of intensive study in which Curnow was immersed in this culture permanently affected his way of looking at and thinking about the world and himself, shaping the questions which remained important for him even after he rejected Christianity's explanation of them, providing him with a body of theological and biblical knowledge which he never forgot, and with a language of metaphor and allusion which enriched his poetry at every stage of its development. In the meantime he returned to Christchurch to live with his parents (whose parish since 1930 had been the industrial suburb of New Brighton), and to pursue the next stage in his ordination: appointment as a parish curate or assistant curate.

Chapter Five

Widening Horizons, 1934 to mid-1936

Don't forget I am (or was) a spoiled priest. No creek-jumper – I fell in,
& scrambled out with a mouthful of mud.[1]

Abandoning a career in the Church

To be ordained into the Anglican diaconate a candidate had to have an appointment as a curate or assistant curate. The process was largely controlled by the
diocesan bishops, who knew where vacancies were available. Several of Curnow's
fellow students were ordained in December 1933, but Curnow was not one of
these and when he returned to Christchurch at the end of the year he had yet to
find a position. He contacted the bishop of the Christchurch diocese, Campbell
West-Watson (who had supported his application for a scholarship to St John's).
West-Watson had little to offer and suggested that Curnow talk to Canon
Stephen Parr, at College House, Christchurch. Parr, who had been one of the
examiners who complained about Curnow's results in the Supplementary examinations earlier in 1933, seemed equally unimpressed by his credentials. 'I believe
you're a bit of a poet?' he commented. Curnow replied that he had written some
verse but wouldn't rate himself as a poet. Parr advised, 'Give it a bit of a rest.'[2]
It was a conversation, Curnow later commented, 'much funnier to recall than it
was at the time'.[3]

Despite this discouragement, Curnow was warmly supported by Canon
Charles Perry, vicar of St Michael's Church in central Christchurch, who 'took
my part at a time when the bishop (and others) viewed me as a young radical,

unsuitable for Holy Orders'.[4] Perry's leanings, like Curnow's own father's, were towards High Church Anglicanism, and he and his wife offered Curnow hospitality at their vicarage home, where he enjoyed their 'easy informality' and warmth, 'the liveliness and wit at their table',[5] and the company of their daughter, Claire. Mrs Perry was a sister of the Australian poet Hugh McCrae, so there was none of the hostility to his poetic interests that Curnow had encountered at St John's and from Parr and West-Watson.

In the early autumn (April) of 1934, and still without the offer of a position, Curnow decided to seek temporary work, and replied to an advertisement in *The Press* seeking 'a young man of standing, to teach three children, 11, 9, and 5, and also to do outdoor work'. 'For four months', he wrote later, 'I was tutor to a runholder's grandchildren, and my duties included feeding the pigs and mowing an acre of lawns.'[6] The Barkers were a well-connected South Canterbury family (consisting of the parents, their son and his wife, and three grandchildren) who lived in a homestead at Winchester, near Temuka, and owned a large run inland on the alpine foothills. Mr Barker was ill, and the job Curnow was appointed to (after satisfying Mrs Barker's strict requirements for a 'well-spoken young man' whose connections – with the Cracroft Wilsons and the Walls – also proved satisfactory) was to teach the children from 9 a.m. until lunchtime, and in the afternoon attend to such outdoor tasks as Mrs Barker found for him to do. At 6 p.m. he was expected to bathe and change into a suit for dinner. The job was not intended to be permanent, but it gave Curnow a taste of the formal rituals of the genteel South Canterbury social scene.

Following his return to Christchurch, Curnow had written to Iris Wilkinson at her office at *The New Zealand Observer* in Auckland, and shortly after his arrival at Winchester he received a reply from her, the first of a number of letters between them during the next nine months. Wilkinson was now living as a voluntary patient at The Lodge in Mt Albert, a residential convalescent clinic of the Auckland Mental Hospital at Avondale, after a breakdown and attempted suicide. What Curnow had said to her in his initial letter has to be inferred from her response, but it seems that he wanted to inform her of his return to Christchurch, of his career uncertainties, and of his hopes to continue writing poetry, and he may also have learnt of Wilkinson's illness and wished to express sympathy and support.

She wrote in detail about her own frustrated pilgrimage of the 'mind – or spirit? – . . . in looking, in a blind and futile sort of way, for what is called God', and about her interest in Curnow's concern to synthesise his religious beliefs with social awareness in his poetry, though as yet she had 'only had a bare glimpse of . . . your little scarlet and black book [*Valley of Decision*]'. Throughout, she kept coming back to their shared interest in writing poetry. 'No, you have not written your last, or even nearly your last, book for publication. Of that I am sure.' In her next letter she commented in detail on what was clearly a lengthy response by Curnow about his religious beliefs. She praised his 'braver belief in the Kingdom of the human heart as the secret Kingdom of God', his aspiration to a life of revolt 'against the great dead carcass of materialism', his belief in 'man as the instrument of beauty, the screen on which all the sound and colour are thrown', and his 'theory of eternal life, as contrasted with eternal existence'. She also asked him to send her some of his poems, and to describe his job at Winchester.

There was one further letter from Wilkinson while Curnow was staying at Winchester in which she enclosed half a dozen poems of her own and commented effusively on one poem in particular from a group that Curnow had sent her, entitled 'Unto Each His Labour', liking the way it shed 'light and shadow on a landscape altogether New Zealand', and 'because of its likeness to a Canterbury landscape I knew and loved seven years ago' – the landscape around Hanmer Springs where she spent several months, May to October 1927, recuperating from a breakdown after the stillbirth of her first child. Curnow never published the poem, but it appears to have been one of the earliest in which he turned directly to the landscape for inspiration, and Wilkinson was prescient in recognising how significant landscape would become in much of his later poetry.

The letter also revealed that the youthful Curnow had taken on a little more than he was able to cope with in initiating the correspondence. Wilkinson was only five years older but many years older in terms of her experience of life, and she replied to his letters with a length and intensity that he could not match, much as he seems to have tried. 'Don't ever write until you both can and will', she concluded. 'You are right, I do "make demands", and I'm rather glad you are honest and understanding enough to say so.'[7] There may have been further correspondence, but the last of her letters in reply to his occurred early in 1935, six months later.

Curnow later recalled his correspondence with Iris Wilkinson, in the context of criticism of himself and others in the 1930s, for 'anti-feminist bias':

I don't know how well Fairburn knew Iris Wilkinson, but they were both Old Believers of the Social Credit persuasion; .... during '34, when I was tutor-handyman for the Barkers of Winchester, she wrote long letters to me from the 'Grey Lodge' at the old Avondale Mental Hospital, where she was in some sort of care, but at the same time busy with the first of her novels. Feminism, pro- or anti- was hardly thought of at all. The newspaper people who admired the early 'Robin Hyde' in those dark patriarchal days, were as it happens, all of them men who thought her a gifted young poet – Marris, Schroder, Ian Donnelly (I think) – if anything, in those days her 'gender' was all in her favour....[8]

After four months at Winchester, Curnow's job came to an end. Barker's condition had deteriorated to the point where he needed full-time nursing care at home, and the family could not afford to employ Curnow as well. Back in Christchurch in July, jobless and still uncertain about the possibility of ordination and finding a position as a curate, he began casual work for the Christchurch *Press* doing university news reporting at the rate of 10s a column. At this time his parents had shifted from New Brighton to the Lincoln parish, and Curnow took a room at Florrie Pratt's boarding house in Gloucester Street in the centre of Christchurch. He worked hard at his new job. Reg Lund, chief deputy editor, liked his work, and the possibility of a permanent job on *The Press* opened up.

In the meantime, Canon Charles Perry had been working assiduously on Curnow's behalf to find him an opening, and, at last, arranged with the bishop of Waiapu for a possible appointment as curate in the parish of Tauranga. In late August, Curnow travelled to Auckland to meet the vicar of Tauranga and his wife. It was a difficult meeting, awkward (if polite) on both sides, and 'the whole thing suddenly became impossible for him',[9] reinforcing his sense that clerical life would demand a conformity of behaviour for the rest of his life that he was quite simply incapable of. His final decision to abandon holy orders was made 'in the middle of Cook Strait' on his way back to Christchurch.

In a witty poem written after Curnow's death, C.K. Stead (who would later become a university colleague of Curnow's and a close poet friend and neighbour) evoked the moment, melodramatically, as a critical point of rejection of belief in God, imagining Curnow throwing his Bible into the sea and resolving to be a poet and 'write his own' scriptures, since 'it came to him':

> ... that God
> wasn't there, was
>
> nowhere, a Word
> without reference or
> object.[10]

Although the question of belief in God was a factor in Curnow's rejection of a career in the Church, far more important was his inability to accept the institution of the Anglican Church at the time – its social and political conservatism, its hostility to intellectual enquiry, its decline into a system of genteel conventions to which he would be expected to conform in his day-to-day parish work, and its resistance to the life of the imagination. If he felt guilt at abandoning the Church, and failing to fulfil parental expectations, he also felt anger at being betrayed *by* the Church, which fell so short of *his* expectations, impractical and idealistic as they may have been. The one thing which his three years in Auckland had confirmed in him was the desire and ambition to write poetry, not as some kind of optional extra in his life, but as in some way central to his understanding of himself and the world.

More immediately, however, he had to deal, at the age of 23, with finding a way of living in the world, a career, which did not (in his view) limit and restrict the life of the imagination to which he was committed. The 'fit of young poet's idealism and egotism', which at the age of nineteen had taken him from journalism into a quest for religious answers, after four years returned to take him, 'ironically I suppose', back to the rat race he had earlier turned away from.[11] As he later explained:

> to my young eyes, nothing could seem less competitive or more secure (if ill-paid) than the life of a clergyman; looking back, I fancy it was as much fear of the World, i.e. the newspaper office! as religious vocation, that decided me to enter the Church. Though the latter was what I felt it to be. I was naive enough to be shocked, later on, to find that the Church, seen from the inside of a theological college, had a good deal in common with the World, seen from inside a newspaper office. It was taking me time (far too long) to find out what one must contrive to live with, if one is to have anything to live *on* or (in any and every ambiguous sense) live *for*.[12]

While figures like Bishop West-Watson and Canon Parr in Christchurch were no doubt relieved that 'the problem of Curnow' was resolved, it was more difficult to convey his decision to his parents and Charles Perry when he returned there early in September. Tremayne was disappointed, 'but made no reproaches'.[13] If Jessie was 'relieved',[14] the decision also reinforced her anxiety about what her son was going to do with his life. Charles Perry was also generous in his response.

Before he wrote to the vicar of Tauranga rejecting the curacy, Curnow asked Hugo Freeth, editor of *The Press*, whether there was a permanent job for him. The answer was 'yes', and in January 1935 Curnow started as a junior reporter.

Julian and *Tomorrow*

From September 1934, within weeks of Curnow's decision, a new, angry, and often bitterly satirical voice, under the pseudonym 'Julian', appeared in the *Canterbury College Review* and in *Tomorrow*, the radical weekly (later fortnightly) magazine which had begun a few months earlier in 1934, edited in Christchurch by Kennaway Henderson. For the next two and a half years almost every new poem Curnow published appeared first under this pseudonym. The pieces which appeared in the remaining months of 1934 – one poem under his own name,

six poems and a fictionalised autobiographical piece under the name of Julian –
also broke something of a drought. Although he had continued writing poems
after the publication of *Valley of Decision* a year earlier, he had published nothing
new. His only appearance in print since September 1933 had been in July 1934,
when Denis Glover and Ian Milner included two poems from that volume ('Relief'
and 'Renunciation') in *New Poems*, published by Glover under the Caxton Club
Press imprint.

Curnow's new pseudonym was derived from Julian the Apostate, the Roman
Emperor who during his brief rule (360–363 AD) began a vigorous political
campaign against the entrenched Christian institution with the aim of re-
establishing the old paganism of the Greeks and Romans. Curnow's adoption of
Julian was at least initially a self-protective device, a mask behind which he could
release his accumulated frustrations and anger at the institution of the Church,
delight in giving vent to outrageous or offensive opinions, and express radical
ideas (political and sexual), without fear of personal repercussions. If nothing
else, Curnow's experience of clerical displeasure at his poetry had made him
aware of the need to be careful, if he was not to earn the same reputation on the
Christchurch *Press*. He was aware that Glover had lost his job on the paper in
the wake of his printing of *Oriflamme*,[15] and that Oliver Duff had been sacked
as editor in 1932 'for printing parts of Cresswell's *Present Without Leave* which
offended the directors, and for being editorially soft on strikers'.[16]

For the *Canterbury College Review* (edited in 1934 by Glover and Reginald
Clarke and published by Glover in September that year) he resurrected the
blackly comic unpublished poem 'Ethics', from 1932, using his new pseudonym, and wrote a companion poem, 'Metaphysics', offering a comic image of
the Paraclete (the Holy Spirit) as a clumsy figure maddened by jealousy of the
sensuous freedom and vitality of the natural world. 'The Four Last Things',
chosen by the editors as the prize-winning contribution to the magazine, offered
an Eliot-derived parody of Hell, Heaven, Death and Judgement as dimensions of
a corrupt secular world divided between the pretentiously genteel and those who
lived in squalid poverty. Fairburn, to whom Glover sent everything he printed,
was extremely impressed:

> Curnow is really writing remarkably well. Those things of his in the 'Review' are
> amazingly good. He has a good head on his neck, you know, and is a much more *subtle*
> thinker than most of us boys: which is a help. His verse is very direct and compact,
> and firmly handled.[17]

In the same month that the *Canterbury College Review* appeared Curnow
published the first of more than 50 contributions to *Tomorrow* during the next four

years. Published under his own name, 'Lunar Prospect', with its Poundian title, developed a clever, anti-romantic description of the moon surrounded by wispy, diaphanous clouds as if it were participating in a fashion parade of lingerie before an imaginary audience. Together with the earlier 'Drawing-Room Window', it was subsequently attacked as obscene in *Tomorrow* by Barbara Leigh.[18] It was not until 1937 that he contributed any further poem to *Tomorrow* under his own name. Alongside 'Lunar Prospect', Curnow also published his first contribution as 'Julian', a brief satirical vignette lampooning a vicar at his 'Daily Office':

> Lord, save Thy people, sang the Vicar:
> I saw one altar-candle flicker.
> The fat flame wink'd, the parson whined,
> and in that instant I divined,
> full-faced between the candle-sconces,
> old Mammon mouthing the responses.

A month later Julian contributed a vigorous autobiographical piece, 'Per Ardua Ad – ?', to *Tomorrow*,[19] which revealed the extent to which Curnow's mind at the time was driven by personal and political conflicts, and in which Julian descants fiercely on Christ's words, 'in the world ye [poets and artists] shall have tribulation':

What Christ meant by 'the world' is simply the damned huckstering, grovelling, golfing, guzzling, indigestion-tablet-chewing world, that sits behind a desk doing 'business' with the brute concentration and unwavering determination of a pig nosing the last rotten apple out of the sty-floor slime. It is 'the world' which fancies that culture consists in separating man the consumer from the raw materials of the earth by as long and complex a chain of processes as possible, much as it is thought that modesty consists in separating the sexes by a reasonable textile opacity.... The general dissatisfaction with the teaching of Christ ... is of course due to man's having so greatly blessed himself that there is nothing for God to do but take his Goods off the market.

The piece concluded on a note of self-mockery. The only response to such a 'mad world' was to adopt a pose of 'calculated insanity' – though 'oddly enough', he added:

I have a notion even at this stage, that I shall remain sane. It will be hard to compromise with Mammon – the Church has tried for generations, and has, to my mind, never succeeded. But I have the hope away down that there may be a revolution by which sanity will swing to the top. For the present, I shall put straws in my mouth, foam a little (all in a manner of speaking) and trust to my good genius that the habit does not grow on me.

After his return to Christchurch from Winchester, Curnow began to develop a new circle of acquaintances on *The Press* and at the university, and his room at Gloucester Street gave him much greater freedom for socialising than he had had up to this time. He saw a good deal of his cousin Pat and her husband Tyndall Harman, as well as David Taylor, who was completing his theological studies in Christchurch and was shortly to marry Celia Twyneham (Curnow's girlfriend from his pre-St John's days). It was at the university that Curnow met Doris Craig, a nineteen-year-old first-year student who was studying for a BA in French and English, and interested in the university drama society, in which Curnow was also involved. Their relationship quickly became serious, and by the end of 1934 they were engaged.

Craig was flattered by the attention of a man who seemed so much older, though the age difference was only four years. She would wait for him to finish his day's work at *The Press*, and they would visit his friends – including Glover, the sculptor and art teacher Francis Shurrock and his wife, Professor and Mrs Frederick Sinclaire, and Douglas Lilburn. They also spent time walking in the Port Hills, and he wrote poems to her. On occasion Tremayne would pick them up after work and drive them to stay at the vicarage in Lincoln. Early in 1935 Iris Wilkinson wrote to congratulate Curnow on his engagement, adding 'I *am* so glad that you write poetry to "the woman I am about to take"'. The poems Wilkinson refers to were eventually to form a sequence of seven love lyrics entitled 'A Woman in Mind' published in *Enemies* (1937), and Craig was also the woman addressed in the most ambitious poem he wrote at this time, 'Aspect of Monism'. Wilkinson also counselled Curnow to be more relaxed in his attitudes to making a living in the world:

> You still accept society's demands with some distaste? Oh Allen, I don't know. I've come to the conclusion that social and business relations are only a fretful burden for our unfortunate flesh. They can't matter much one way or another – one is damned or saved quite alone....[20]

Her letter, the only one signed with her pen name, Robin Hyde, is infused with what she called 'a queer long mood of weariness', and its tone suggests that she had hoped their relationship might have developed more intimately.

Despite the anxieties leading up to and following Curnow's decision to abandon a clerical career in 1934, the year ended with positive prospects. He was,

as Iris Wilkinson put it, 'on the simultaneous brinks of journalism and matri-
mony'.[21] He had launched Julian on a vigorous publishing career in *Tomorrow*.
Furthermore, 1934 had also seen the beginning of two of the longest and most
important friendships in his life: with the poet and printer Denis Glover,
then in his third year of studies at Canterbury University College, and with
the composer Douglas Lilburn, then a youthful first-year student of music at the
same university.

Julian's alter ego: Curnow as romantic lyricist

The next eighteen months were busy, and for the first time Curnow's life began
to take on a sense of purpose and direction. He worked hard at learning the ropes
as a junior reporter, and before the end of 1935 had become a general reporter.
He began to read much more intensively in contemporary English poetry, in the
work of the 'established' moderns like Eliot and Yeats, as well as in the thirties
poetry of W.H. Auden, C. Day Lewis, Louis MacNeice and Stephen Spender.
He was especially interested in the poetry of Blake and Shelley, of D.H. Lawrence
and William Empson. He also began to read more widely in New Zealand history,
especially in the revisionist history produced in the 1930s by J.C. Beaglehole.

    Curnow wrote and published a considerable amount of poetry and prose
during the eighteen months to mid-1936. In addition to the love lyrics he wrote
for Doris Craig, he contributed fourteen pieces as 'Julian' to *Tomorrow*. In May
1935 Glover printed a small volume of Curnow's poetry, entitled *Three Poems*,
which contained two poems reprinted from *Tomorrow* ('Aspect of Monism'
and 'Restraint', printed there under the name Julian) and a new poem, 'The
Wilderness'. In August he contributed another new poem, one of the best he had
written up to this time, entitled 'Doom at Sunrise', to another of Glover's small
Caxton Club Press anthologies, *Another Argo*.

    Eight of the fourteen poems he contributed to *Tomorrow* during this period
were reprinted in the first *Verse Alive* anthology from this magazine that Glover
published at the Caxton Press (as it was now known) in March 1936, five of them
under his own name. The other contributors were Beaglehole, Fairburn, Glover
and Milner, but because Curnow's contributions appeared under two names,
the fact that his was the largest presence in the anthology remained unknown,
since none of *Tomorrow*'s readers seemed to notice the fact that Julian was his
pseudonym. Although the print runs of all these early Caxton publications
were small (50 copies of *Three Poems*, and 230 of *Verse Alive*), Curnow began to
establish himself as one of the 'up-and-coming' young avant-garde poets on the
New Zealand scene.

During this period Curnow began to engage polemically with literary, cultural and political issues that moved beyond the religiously focused interests of his earlier prose pieces. His article in *Canta* in March 1935, 'Pricking Some Intellectual Bubbles', caused controversy for its attack on what he saw as woolly thinking about Marxism promoted by the Friends of the Soviet Union and other 'well-intentioned spinners of social reforms'. The article is also especially revealing about his own aims as a poet at the time.

John Schroder, now literary editor of *The Press*, encouraged Curnow to write a number of feature articles for its Literary Page, whose titles all show his interest in general cultural issues relating to the writing and reading of poetry in New Zealand. In November 1935 Glover published Curnow's lively and opinionated *Poetry and Language*, a fourteen-page 'manifesto' about the nature of poetry, whose none-too-subtle subtext was a polemic against the bad verse and criticism practised by the literary establishment in New Zealand. If the lineaments of much that became a trademark of Curnow's mature poetry can be traced in the apprentice poetry of this period, the same can be said of the early impulse of his prose to write about poetry in ways that engaged with the country's culture as a whole.

When 'Aspect of Monism' was reprinted in *Three Poems* under his own name only a month after it had appeared under that of Julian in *Tomorrow* in April 1935, the change signified a clarification of how Curnow conceived the role and purpose of his pseudonym. Although the need for a protective device remained, that motive was now less important than the need to make an *aesthetic* distinction between two different kinds of writing, with different purposes. Asked later in life about the distinction, he attempted what he called 'a circumstantial reconstruction', since his memory of Julian was 'indistinct':

What I took then to be poems of my own (sgd. AC) were attempts to shape a 'poetic self' – if they did betray some religious or social disposition, that was incidental; after all, a 'poetic self' must be made out of something or somebody; one's headache is nobody else's and nobody else sees quite the same things out the window. A Julian piece . . . seemed different, polemic in character, raising one's voice to argue. Not making a thing about which there can or should be no argument (unless aesthetic, but that's another thing). The ideas, whatever they were, that a Julian piece expressed seemed extraneous to the main poetic work: I don't say they actually were, only that it would have seemed so to me at the time. – If anyone had asked me *then* what you justifiably ask me *now*, I wouldn't have answered at all like this; if the question hadn't grassed me completely, I might have said it was nobody's business but mine.[22]

'Aspect of Monism' was the most ambitious and substantial poem Curnow had written up to this time. In four sections and written from a strongly romantic perspective, it was a sequence of philosophical speculations, evoking the physical act of love as the supreme experience of the oneness of self and other, of the lovers and the world:

> Nothing passes, all is as one moment
> possessing richly world's breadth; and the clear
> succession, which is illusion, of jewelled hours
> is a burning peace in the eyes of one woman;
> and it is time there was an end of asking.

Not surprisingly, the unnamed woman (Doris Craig) to whom the poem addresses its Marvellian exhortation to make love appears to have remained unconvinced by the dense logic of the poem. However, there is no doubting the passionate romantic idealism that drives the poem, nor the intensity with which it strives to reconcile the vital, instinctive, bodily energies of the natural/human world with a notion of visionary understanding that transcends mere rationalism. The poem rejects the Cartesian theory of the duality of matter and mind; the sensuous bodily/natural world is known only as 'form of thought, weapon of will to do'.

In the poem's concluding section Curnow attempts to integrate the lovers' self-knowledge with a secular, Blakean vision of transformed humanity, extending the romantic nature symbolism he has used throughout:

> So with me you must come into certain places
> where the live blood of earth runs clear
> in a slim green plant and in a standing tree
> and there are no separate death-hardened faces
>
> dividing in a dream the shadow of man;
> then it may be life will look on life,
> eye into eye and see no difference,
> but earth, love, death, lost in a single span.

The likely immediate trigger for the poem was a long review by a Christchurch doctor, R.R.D. Milligan, of a book by the British scholar W.P.D. Wightman, entitled *Science and Monism*,[23] which appeared in the Literary Page of *The Press* a few weeks before Curnow wrote it.[24] Curnow was acquainted with Milligan, and his poem was an effort to provide precisely that view of monism, 'on the side of art and metaphysics' (if not of religion), that Milligan saw as lacking in Wightman's treatment of the subject.

Curnow's article, 'Pricking Some Intellectual Bubbles',[25] illuminates the poem's personal and political concerns. Opinionated and polemical, the article deplored the absence of intellectual rigour among the various groups who espoused the cause of social reform, and their reliance on abstract creeds and slogans and on easy, untested assumptions, and argued that 'any worthwhile enthusiasm for social reform must be preceded by an entirely personal exploration of satisfactory ways of living':

> After all, nobody has a shadow of right to dictate the conditions under which men shall live, unless he has some conception of reasonable living. And his only approach to such a conception is through his own personal experience, frankly accepted and honestly analysed. If we dig deep enough in this field of personal experience, we shall no doubt find the level of common human needs. But we shall never find it if we poke about in a rubbish-heap of second-hand and cast-off experiences, in the process which is vulgarly known as thinking. William Blake said (I hope I quote correctly) –
>
> > You are a man; God is no more –
> > Your own humanity learn to adore.

Anticipating that such a position might be criticised as 'self-centred and narrow', Curnow then expanded on the proposition, and makes numerous comments that might be read not only as notations of the poetry he was trying to write in a poem like 'Aspect of Monism', but as the beginnings of a poetics which remained with him for the rest of his life: that poems are first and foremost acts of self-exploration, aimed at 'digging deep' into personal experience to discover a substratum of 'common human need' which links the poet (and the poems, if they are good enough) to his fellow beings:

> Any effective motives we have must spring from our own deep instinctive needs, so deep that they are common to all – such needs as that for the perfection of sensuality which is true art, for the perfection of human relationship which has (unfortunately) no better name than love, and for a spiritual balance of social demands and individual integrity. . . . Motives come from within, from instinct; and they gain force and direction through experience. Our ideas do not live happily together, just because they are not really ours – they have no proper counterpart of human, individual, bodily-mental need. . . . Christianity is failing because for centuries it has tried to breed little theologians instead of little Christs. We will likewise fail if we try to build a social order out of brainstorms instead of human beings.

Despite the polemical nature of Curnow's piece, it reveals that he was thinking hard about the ways in which – given his disenchantment both with the institutional church and with current left-wing discourse about social reform and revolution – poetry might be described as having a distinctive social purpose, and about the kind of 'truth' it tells about the world. It also explains why Curnow began to make a distinction at this point between poems published under his own name, and the polemical, argumentative, satirical pieces of Julian. In some instances the distinction was fairly easy to make, even if it involved retrospective assessments of the nature of the poems.

However, the distinction remained unstable for a number of years. One of the most curious later examples occurred in relation to the earliest versions of the sequence about Canterbury history, which became *Not in Narrow Seas* (1939). Most of this sequence originally appeared in two substantial blocks in *Tomorrow* in 1937. The first block (of four poems), entitled 'Rats in the Bilge', was signed under his own name, but the second block (of seven poems), entitled 'The Potters' Field', appeared a few months later under his pseudonym, suggesting that what Curnow had originally conceived as a more 'serious sequence' had shifted into a more satirical and polemical mode. The completed sequence in fact contains political and satirical dimensions as well as romantic elements that suggest an emergent metaphysical interest in the nature of time, location and history in the psychic formation of New Zealand's settler inhabitants. It is not easy to demarcate clearly its 'Julian' and 'Allen Curnow' impulses.

Although 'Aspect of Monism' reveals a shift away from the Christian themes of his previous poetry, its perspective remains strongly idealist, closely linked to the romanticism of Blake and D.H. Lawrence, to the thirties poetry of C. Day Lewis, and among his New Zealand contemporaries, to the poetry of A.R.D. Fairburn. Traces of Christian belief *remain* in the strongly idealist cast of Curnow's romanticism, and in the religious or spiritual associations attached to his natural symbolism. A great deal of Curnow's earlier religious thinking is thus 'displaced' or 'transposed' into much of his poetry over the next few years, apparent in numerous of the poems of his next two volumes, *Enemies* (1937) and *Not in Narrow Seas*.

Engaging with the literary culture: early critical writings

Reviewers at the time struggled to come to terms with the difficulty of such poems. C.A. Marris, literary editor of *Art in New Zealand*, saw Curnow in *Three Poems* as less infected than in the past by the 'inflammation' of propagandist indignation at 'things social and economic', but as needing now to curtail his 'philosophic restlessness'.[26] *The Press*, commenting on the same volume, lamented the absence of 'a more plain and comprehensible form'.[27] Winston Rhodes (then a lecturer at Canterbury University College), writing in *Tomorrow*,[28] called for a 'body of intelligent and critical readers' for such work, 'otherwise it is to be feared that Mr Curnow may be pushed into a mannered obscurity'.

Curnow, however, had three strong supporters among people whose opinions he valued: Denis Glover, A.R.D. Fairburn and Douglas Lilburn. Glover's belief in Curnow's talent was unwavering (as was Curnow's in Glover's talent both as a poet and printer), and their friendship developed strongly after Glover's return from a four-month stint (December 1934 to March 1935) in Wellington as a temporary junior reporter on the *Dominion*. Curnow's *Three Poems* was the first of Glover's Caxton Club Press publications after his return, and Curnow often visited him at his room in Mrs Nanette Minogue's broken-down boarding house (where he later recollected 'beetroot swimming on the sideboard'),[29] at 903 Colombo Street. *Three Poems* was printed in the Colombo Street wash-house, 'set up by hand, using his own fount of type, and printing it on a little platen press on a bench at Mrs Minogue's'.[30] From this time on, Curnow began to show Glover everything he wrote. He trusted Glover's poetic intelligence and his instinct about whether a poem worked or didn't. They also became regular drinking companions.

Fairburn would have confirmed Glover in his judgement that Curnow was *the* most interesting and talented of the younger poets in New Zealand in the 1930s. He thought Curnow's *Three Poems* 'very good indeed', commenting that it was a pity 'the people who take it upon themselves to review his stuff don't give him the credit he deserves'.[31] Asked by Glover to contribute to his planned new anthology (*Another Argo*), Fairburn also admired Curnow's contributions to *Tomorrow*: 'I shall be more likely to be the coat-tails of the turnout if Curnow puts in any of those things he's been printing in 'Tomorrow.' They're very fine indeed. They are *poetry*. Can I say more?'[32]

Fairburn was intrigued to know whether *The Press* knew of Curnow's contributions to *Tomorrow*, especially after a squib by Julian ('Meditation on the Tenth Commandment') appeared in the issue for 4 September 1935: 'I see no earthly reason why / a lot of people should not die / because they're neither wise nor funny / and have such large amounts of money.' However, it was not until 1937, after the publication of Curnow's next collection, *Enemies*, that Fairburn was able to address publicly the deficiencies he observed in the reception of Curnow's work. His review of that volume in *Tomorrow* was the first substantial and considered criticism of Curnow's poetry to appear in print.

Douglas Lilburn was also fascinated by Curnow's poetry from the moment he encountered it, and despite the difference in their ages (he was four years younger than Curnow) they regularly socialised, discussing music and literature and playing each other's records, beginning at this time a friendship which lasted for the rest of their lives. These early years were formative in Lilburn's thinking about the nature and purposes of being a composer in New Zealand, as he generously acknowledged to Curnow on many occasions. 'It needs no ghost from the UK', he wrote to Curnow after being sent a copy of a favourable British review of his poetry in 1982, 'to tell me *that*, when I'd already picked it at CUC in 1934 – & as lodestar you've remained dear since then.'[33] For Curnow, Lilburn remained a kind of ideal reader: someone hugely talented in a different field of the arts, who instinctively picked up emotional tones, enjoyed and appreciated (because of his own experience in a different field) the technical accomplishment of the poetry, and where he was puzzled by obscurities – as he often was – did not immediately dismiss the poetry. Lilburn's letters to Curnow contain repeated references to phrases, lines and stanzas from the poetry – especially the earlier poetry – which functioned as touchstones for his aims as a New Zealand composer.

Perhaps because of his own experience of what Rhodes had referred to as the absence in New Zealand of 'a body of intelligent and critical readers' of the new poetry, Curnow himself began to engage – in articles in *The Press* – with various of the 'fallacies' behind much that passed for criticism. The first of these pieces[34] was occasioned by the appearance of an Australian anthology (*The Wide Brown Land*, edited by Joan and George Mackaness) which strongly featured the national tradition of bush balladry. Curnow attacked 'the fallacy of separate development' (from the English tradition), which he saw as sponsoring a parochial attitude to literature. He insisted that 'it is no more than an interesting aspect of a particular poem that it happens to embody impressions which could have been gained nowhere else but in Australia':

> Parochialism of the sort so often manifested in offhand statements about New Zealand or Australian literature is a fit enough attitude for tourist agencies and the authors of guide-books, but it is out of place among persons with any serious literary intentions. …The language is English; so the poetic values must be English; and there is no more to be said.

Curnow's assertions here were no doubt influenced by the reviewers' constant practice of bewailing the influence of the moderns – Eliot, Pound, the English thirties poets – on the new poets writing in New Zealand. But it certainly wasn't an issue about which there was 'no more to be said'. Curnow returned to it repeatedly over the next decades, developing increasingly sophisticated arguments about the relationship between New Zealand verse and the larger tradition of poetry in English.

A month later, in a piece entitled 'Poetry: Rough Sketch for an Aesthetic View',[35] Curnow addressed two other current fallacies: critical impressionism (the notion that poetic value is a matter of purely individual response); and critical moralism (the notion that poetic value resides in the truth of a poem's subject matter). Again, dismissals of the new poetry on both grounds were a staple of journalistic reviewing and editorial practice. As an alternative to such fallacies, Curnow invoked the notion of 'pure expression', a quality initially communicated through the sensation of pleasure evoked by the manner or form of the poem, whose expressive 'adequacy' is independent of *what* the poet may have chosen to express, and equally separate 'from the person to whom it may happen to be expressed'. Curnow's position, whatever its limitations, was essentially an argument for more complex *readings* of poetry, and for a more theoretically self-aware criticism.

Other pieces in 1935 reinforced these perspectives. 'Rural Writers: A Literary Daisy Chain'[36] attacked the factitious dilettantism of a book that yoked English poets of many different kinds into a nostalgic pastoralism. 'A Literary Heresy: Desire to Read Everything'[37] was aimed especially at the teaching profession, with a plea for reading in depth rather than simply to display erudition. But the most significant of his prose pieces in 1935 was a lively and opinionated piece about the language of poetry, a kind of manifesto disguised as a primer, directed sarcastically at 'professors of English, graduates, editors of newspaper columns and their satellites – who have not yet passed the elementary stages of a reasoned understanding of the art of poetry'. Glover published the piece, entitled *Poetry and Language*, as a slim Caxton Club Press booklet of 150 copies in November, hand-setting it in his recently acquired Gill sans serif typeface.

The piece was aphoristic in nature, set out loosely in eleven numbered blocks of varying lengths, reminiscent of Ezra Pound's assertive pedagogical style. Opening with a definition which emphasised that poetry is an artefact whose primary material is not 'content' (ideas or feelings) but language ('The skilful making of things with language, things which will please and stimulate the mind'), the main sections of the pamphlet repeatedly focused on the need for poetry to be rooted in the 'living language' of contemporary speech: 'Poetry must have its feet on the familiar earth of plain speech.'[38] Because written language by its very nature 'fixes' and 'systemises' the constantly changing flow of the living language, and thus has an inbuilt tendency to atrophy, it has to be constantly re-invented by poetry in the light of the changing nature of 'plain speech'. Poets need to be especially alert to the dangers of 'quasi-dead' language, fossilised language that survives in the present, but has lost any live contact with the language of 'plain speech' and 'ordinary conversation'. Poets also need to be especially aware of the 'quasi-dead' language that survives as 'poetical' language in the present, a chronic condition of much verse in New Zealand.

In case he should be misunderstood as promoting the notion that the language of poetry simply imitates or transcribes the contemporary language of plain speech or conversation – the criticism Wordsworth faced in developing a superficially similar argument in his famous preface to the *Lyrical Ballads* – Curnow concludes with a clear denial that such is his intention: 'I do not, most emphatically, intend to make a plea for what is vulgarly called "simplicity" or "clarity" in poetry.'[39]

Contemporary plain speech is the necessary *raw material* on which the poet works. The artefact he makes out of it might be 'simple' and 'clear', but equally it might be 'complex' and challenging (like, for example, 'Doom at Sunrise'), depending on the nature of the experience the poet wishes to communicate. Equally, also, the process by which the raw material is turned into an artefact may fail, and produce a botched product.

Reactions to the booklet were mixed. 'Mr Curnow's arrogance and dogmatism are not unpleasing', wrote the reviewer of *Poetry and Language* in *The Press*, but added:

> [H]e destroys the value of his pronouncements, many of which are largely true, by [his] too ample certainty. D.H. Lawrence, Julian Grenfell and Siegfried Sassoon were Georgians; but their language was hardly quasi-dead. A protestant should indeed protest, but not so emphatically as to ignore some of the facts.[40]

Rhodes, in *Tomorrow*, for whom the booklet was a statement of the obvious, adopted a tone of heavy irony:

> Putting it briefly I gather that Mr Curnow believes that poetry is made of language (in fact he says so), that poetry is written because the poet wants to communicate something to somebody and that therefore it should be written in a language that is not dead. The book is evidently intended for people like myself who are slowly beginning to agree with these elementary principles, and there is no need to beg Mr Curnow not to hasten too fast.[41]

Rhodes entirely missed the context in which the pamphlet was written. Curnow was the *only* critic in the 1930s to characterise the issues in the emergent conflict between the literary-journalistic establishment and the new poets as, centrally, issues to do with the nature and purposes of *language* in poetry. For others, name-calling on both sides of the conflict, the issues related to the ideas and beliefs expressed in poetry (about politics, religion, sex, economics) or to the emotions appropriate to poetry (pessimism or optimism, cheerfulness or gloom). Curnow, despite the naivety and dogmatism of this intervention, was trying to shift the terms of the debate altogether, beyond the 'fallacies' of impressionism, moralism, naive social realism, and belles lettres, and make a case for the importance of a poetics that theorised poetry as a unique and special way of understanding the world, irreducible to these other discourses. Furthermore, the issues he raised were to remain central to his own poetic practice for the rest of his life. No poem, he always believed, whatever the importance of its subject matter, attitudes, feelings and ideas, was worth writing unless the poem's language was 'adequate' to the task.

Fairburn, who had regularly crossed swords with Rhodes in the pages of *Tomorrow* ('he writes well as a rule, but there's a dash of priggishness now and then that I don't like'),[42] enjoyed the exchange between Curnow and Rhodes, commenting to Glover:

> Curnow's brochure is very sound, but I can well understand (without sympathising with) the rage of the Colossus. His annoyance will be no less now that Curnow has made it clear, in beautifully simple & direct & unmistakable terms, that the love-apple was in fact aimed at him. Rhodes, I think, is an ornament to *Tomorrow* on the whole: but occasionally he reminds me of something Elgarian – Pomp being over-ridden by circumstance. . . . My kind regards – & congratulations – to Curnow. Tell him he's too good to be a journalist. He ought to be given a job mending Rhodes.[43]

During 1935 and the early months of 1936, Curnow's sense of purpose developed strongly, both as a poet for whom poetry was an act of self-exploration in the fullest sense, and as a critic conscious (from his point of view) of the need to create an informed and intelligent readership for poetry in New Zealand. Moreover, for the first time in his life he had a reasonably secure job, as a journalist, and was beginning to develop a wide circle of like-minded friends among Christchurch's innovative arts scene and fellow journalists. His relationship with Doris Craig had generated personal love lyrics which were quite new to his poetry. Marriage was not to be contemplated until Curnow had established himself in a steady job and could offer reasonable financial security, and the engagement (as was common at the time) continued from the end of 1934 into 1936. However, this engagement would not last. In April 1936 Curnow's personal life changed dramatically. He met Elizabeth (Betty) Le Cren, and within four months they were married.

Chapter Six

Marriage, Journalism and *Enemies*, 1936–37

I wasn't a good journalist in the way successful journalists are. Every assignment remained a fright for me. Anyway, I never wanted that kind of success very much. I'll admit I rather despised myself as a journalist.[1]

Meeting Betty Le Cren, April 1936

Early in April 1936 Curnow was assigned to Timaru for three weeks to cover for the regular *Press* reporter who was on holiday, filing his news reports each day by the 4 p.m. express train to Christchurch. On 18 April he covered the annual St Saviour's fundraising fete for Anglican orphanages in the town. His friend David Taylor, now a curate there, was heavily involved in the organisation of the event, and introduced Curnow to Betty Le Cren, who was helping with the school's stall. There was an instant rapport, and by the time Curnow returned to Christchurch a week later, an understanding had been reached. Their engagement was announced a month later, on 26 May, and they were married three months after that, on 26 August.

Elizabeth (Betty) Jaumaud Le Cren came from a very well-connected, long-established South Canterbury family. Born in Geraldine on 31 October 1911, she was five months younger than Curnow, and both were 24 when they met. Betty was working as a reporter on social events for the *Christchurch Star-Sun* at the time. She was the second of three children of Charles John Le Cren and Daisy Roberts, and all three were given Jaumaud as a middle name, signalling the strength of earlier French connections on Betty's father's side – they were descended from a seventeenth-century Huguenot exile and a linen fibre manufacturer from Brittany. Betty's grandfather, Frederic Le Cren, arrived in Canterbury about 1855, where he established a number of prosperous businesses in the mercantile field (like his brother, Henry John, before him), as well as farming his own property, 'Strathallan'. Both brothers took an active part in Timaru's civic life, and lived close to each other in the stately homes 'Craighead' and 'Elmsdale', overlooking the sea.[2] Betty's father Charles (born in 1868) owned a sheep and agricultural station near Geraldine, which was lost in the slump before the First World War[3] and was later a wine merchant[4] as well as a stock and station agent, before his retirement when the family shifted to Timaru.

On her mother's side there were also significant social connections. Her maternal grandmother, Florence Sharland, came from an even longer-established family than the Le Crens, the original Sharland founding a prosperous pharmaceutical manufacturing company in New Zealand in 1843. The Sharlands also had French connections extending back to the time of William the Conqueror.[5]

Betty grew up according to the expectations of a well-connected family. She attended a private diocesan school and inherited from her family an interest and talent in painting and the allied arts, especially printmaking. She received her first encouragement to paint from her father and brother, 'both of whom drew outstandingly well'.[6] Betty's mother Daisy was equally accomplished and gave watercolour lessons to Colin McCahon when he was a young man, and in 1976 McCahon painted sixteen small landscapes in her honour.*[7]

After his return to Christchurch towards the end of April, Curnow had to face the difficult task of breaking his engagement with Doris Craig, whom he wrote to and arranged to see at Warner's Lounge in Cathedral Square in Christchurch. 'It was as cruel as I knew it would be', he wrote. 'She did make every sort of appeal to me .... Thank God she made it easier for me by trying to discuss the practical effects on herself, which showed me that she had the less concern at losing me.'[8] Recalling the episode 70 years later, Doris Craig herself did not see the break-up in quite such dramatic terms, regarding herself good-humouredly as having had a lucky escape. She had been fascinated by the intensity Curnow brought to the relationship as well as his talent as a poet and the circle of interesting friends he brought her into contact with. Nevertheless, like Jean Alison earlier, she had been put off by his youthful self-absorption.[9] Doris (later Diana) Craig married Guy Goldsbrough in the early 1940s. She and

---

* Editor's note: Wystan Curnow believes McCahon's connection with Daisy Le Cren belongs to the early 1950s.

Curnow met only once afterwards, in 1987, at the Readers' and Writers' Week festival in Wellington that year. When she approached him he did not recognise her ('Oh, oh, you have me at a great disadvantage. I'm terribly sorry.'), but both were able to enjoy her response, 'Well, of course, you were engaged to me for nearly two years!'[10]

During their courtship Curnow visited Betty in Timaru as often as his work schedule would allow, and she in turn visited Christchurch, staying with friends or relatives. In between visits they exchanged letters every day. Curnow introduced Betty to his family on her visits to Christchurch – to his brother John, and relatives Patricia and Tyndall Harman and Tennent Ronalds, all of them regular visitors to his boarding-house room at 57 Andover Street, to which he had moved in order to save money. He took Betty for drives and walks, to the Cashmere Hills (where he had presented her with the engagement ring the day before the formal announcement), to Lyttelton (his childhood stamping ground), and to the family home in Lincoln. They also went regularly together to concerts and films.

His letters to Betty reveal that his closest friends were the Glovers, Douglas Lilburn ('a youngster who tries to set verse to music'),[11] Francis Shurrock and Henry Thiele. Through the Glovers he also met Margaret Birkinshaw and her husband, Frank, a doctor active in socialist politics. The Birkinshaws had emigrated from England to New Zealand in 1929, then Margaret returned to England and re-emigrated in 1931, publishing under her maiden name, Margaret Jepson, a novel (*Via Panama*, 1934) based on the return journey. They had two daughters – Jane and Fay (who was to become well known as the English novelist Fay Weldon).*

In the months before the wedding Curnow initiated a correspondence with A.R.D. Fairburn – somewhat nervously and awkwardly, since he still thought of himself as very much Fairburn's junior, despite being aware (from Glover) of Fairburn's high opinion of his poems. 'I continue to write verses', he wrote, 'on an average, I shld say, once a week', though '[b]ut for a public of 2-3 heads, chief of which is Glover, I wld probably write no more'.[12] However, Curnow devoted most of his letter to an awkward defence of his job on *The Press*, aware of Fairburn's constant questions to Glover about it. 'Curnow ought to be ashamed of himself', Fairburn had written to Glover, '[b]ut I suppose he's shrewd enough to keep on good terms with both God and Mammon. Shrewd, schroder, schro – what's the superlative?'[13] In his letter to Fairburn, Curnow mentioned hearing (through Glover) of 'regrets that I am fallen on stony ground' and described his work on *The Press* as an 'experiment' ('I see no prospect of discontinuing my rather selfish and unprincipled experiment'):

---

* Fay Weldon's autobiography, *Auto da Fay* (Flamingo, 2002) discusses the lives of her parents and her own upbringing in New Zealand.

If my former associations are to take the form of a recall to Service, to Character, to unworldly ideals, I answer that a few years of hopeful endeavour in God's vineyard rather sickened me of such pursuits. And for the present at least, the game I am playing is my own. A dirty game – none knows better how dirty – so dirty that I don't feel inclined even to be funny about it.

You, and with you Glover, who have progressed so much further than I on the road of sincerity and social damnation, have earned a freedom in utterance which I envy at times. Still, I was always more of the idle aesthete in verse, than of the crusader.[14]

Fairburn's reply was typically direct, and probably not the response Curnow expected:

[Y]ou needn't trail your bleeding conscience across Cathedral Square for my benefit. Pull yourself together man! We all do a little whoring on the side, and it's no worse than getting your boots muddy. The folk I don't care for are the ones who actually eat mud – and like it.[15]

To Betty, Curnow quoted some more reassuring sentences from Fairburn's letter:

Please don't imagine me as peering down priggishly on your worldly ways. Having a wife and 3 kids I envy you your good fortune in having a decently paid job. Congratulations on your approaching marriage. Romantic fiddle faddle apart, it's the only way to live.[16]

Curnow began flat-hunting for better accommodation in July, eventually finding a suitable (if small) place for 32s 6d a week – one of two flats at 25 Gloucester Street, a short walk from the *Press* building in Cathedral Square. The approaching marriage also kept him busy, although the wedding arrangements were largely the job of Betty's parents. During her trips to Christchurch they purchased items for the flat (including having a bed built), and ten days before the wedding Curnow moved into it, commenting a few days later to Betty that 'it has definitely NOT got into a mess, in spite of the predictions of Mary [Glover] and others'.[17]

The wedding itself, on 26 August 1936, was a lavish affair, and created much local interest. It was held at St Mary's Church, Timaru, with a reception afterwards for the 150 guests at the Le Cren family home at 86 Grey Road. Tremayne officiated, in the church in which he had begun his career as a clergyman, and Curnow's brother John was best man.

The world that opened up to Betty when she shifted to Christchurch was an exciting one, though it required very considerable adjustments to the life she had lived up to this time. Curnow's hours as a journalist were irregular, and his wages poor, and she had to learn to make do with much less than she was used to. Often Betty would lunch with him in town, and when he was working late Curnow would come home for his evening meal, and drop in later for supper, and she also accompanied him to the films and plays he had to review.

The greatest pleasures were his days off work, when they visited friends, took day-long excursions, or simply read together. For much of the time, however, Betty's days and evenings were filled with the company of others, and from the start both determined to offer an 'open home' for visitors. She was fascinated by the burgeoning intellectual and arts scene in Christchurch – in literature, music, the theatre and the visual arts – and insatiably curious about the people at its centre and on its fringes. Above all she was excited by her husband's achievements as a writer, and began to keep a scrapbook of articles and reviews by and about him.

Curnow shared this excitement, but had his own adjustments to make. Financial worries were never far away, and he constantly sought ways of supplementing his income by casual writing and radio work. Although both smoked, and beer was an essential lubricant in the social world in which they moved, their only extravagances were books and records. In every other respect they learnt to live frugally. Above all, Curnow had to find time to pursue his serious writing. It was not easy.

Journalism, and new poems, 1936

With no savings, and a wife to support, Curnow redoubled his efforts to establish his credentials with the *Press* management as a valued reporter and sub-editor, and to supplement his earnings with paid reviews. The job involved often dreary tasks, such as attending and writing up court cases, sports and social events, and council and other meetings. Sometimes these reporting tasks meant tiring, day-long travel excursions outside Christchurch. At other times his assigned work was sub-editing. On these days he worked from 4.30 p.m. until late, turning national and overseas news cables into suitable items for publication. But there was interesting and challenging work as a roving reporter as well, which meant investigating promising stories and submitting them to the editor for consideration.

He also began to review films and plays regularly, encouraged by Ngaio Marsh's high praise of a review he wrote of her co-dramatisation with Dr Henry Jellett of her recently completed third detective novel, *The Nursing Home Murder*. Called *Exit Sir Derek*, it was the first full-length New Zealand play hosted at Canterbury University College's Little Theatre, in October 1935. On occasion, too, Curnow was asked (or volunteered) to write editorials. He was delighted when he heard that Fred Alexander, then editor of the Dunedin *Evening Star*, thought an editorial he wrote in mid-June on G.K. Chesterton's death had been written by Schroder.

Although he found the journalism stressful, and within a decade had come to heartily detest it, the stress was partly of his own making, since he set himself such high goals. In late June he succumbed to tonsillitis for a week, which he saw as a consequence of this competitive drive. However, the job was also rewarding in its way and he took great satisfaction when his stories were featured prominently in the paper – though he was also well aware of the simple pleasures that might be sacrificed to obsessive work routines.[18]

At about this time he had discovered that Schroder was taking a keen behind-the-scenes interest in his work. Just before he met Betty he had written a long review for *The Press* of a collection, *English Sonnets*, edited by Sir Arthur Quiller-Couch, in which he perversely asserted that 'sonnets are almost invariably remembered by their first lines'.[19] He was immediately taken up by a correspondent signed 'Cheesemonger', who provided a formidable list of much-remembered final lines of sonnets. Curnow blustered a lame reply, only to be challenged yet again.[20] Shortly afterwards, his friend Henry Thiele informed him that his adversary was none other than Schroder himself, then on leave, and that his motive was 'that he is very interested in my writings but thinks I need a "jolt"'. 'Well', Curnow wrote to Betty, 'I tried to feel "jolted" but didn't succeed, tho' Schroder's reply to me last Saturday was very effective.'[21] Curnow was not to know, of course, that his own best-known later sonnets were almost invariably to be remembered by their final lines – not least his sonnet about the skeleton of a giant moa in the Canterbury Museum, written half a dozen years later: 'Not I, some child, born in a marvellous year, / Will learn the trick of standing upright here.'

Above all, Curnow's newspaper work brought him into contact with a much wider range of people, from Canterbury's social elites to its working classes, than his relatively sheltered vicarage upbringing and time at St John's College had provided up to 1934. These contacts sharpened his sense of social and economic inequalities, and had an immediate impact on the poetry he was writing. On several occasions he commented on his experience of reporting court cases, on his inability to 'hate or despise the most brutal or unnatural criminal[s] … who seem more like trapped animals or terrified children':[22]

> Courts this morning, and courts again tomorrow. Pitiful people standing in the dock, wondering why they did it – thieves, vagrants, habitual criminals, all human souls. And I feel all the time that only a little of the fault is theirs. Day after day there are new creatures branded as criminals. The more you love the beauty of the world, the more terrible the ugliness appears.[23]

Around the middle of July 1936, Curnow's close friend and mentor Francis Shurrock had lent him a copy of Arthur Wragg's volume of black-and-white drawings entitled *Jesus Wept*. Wragg was an English radical Christian and offered bitter, compassionate and starkly stylised images of poverty, family and social breakdown, and unemployment, under the dark shadows of dehumanising urban industrial architecture, powerful political and military establishments, and the indifference of the institutional church. It was a heady brew for Curnow, given his own still recent break from the Church:

> Perhaps it was Wragg who put it into my head today to get a story about the wretched parts of Chch . . . . I went round Waltham & Sydenham . . . and walked close to the houses, glancing into the miserable yards & hallways. . . . That tour taught me something – just how trivial the discomforts of mine are, compared with those of these people.[24]

Curnow's story appeared (unsigned) in *The Press* under the title 'Growing Slums: The Darker Streets of Christchurch',[25] and began with a vivid descriptive account of the 'ranks of houses patched and blistered, ill-lighted and cramped' in Sydenham. It then traced the movements of an observer through various streets, whose observations include 'a tottering privy, apparently helped to its feet by the fence dividing it from the next house', and another, 'weatherboards moist and blackened . . . little more than six inches away', then houses with '[n]othing in front, no garden, not a tree in sight' where children 'play in the gutters', and others with bare verandahs where women sit knitting, 'their prospect . . . nothing but railways, smoke, brick and concrete stores and factories'.

A week or so later he wrote excitedly to Betty about two poems which had occurred in the wake of these events:

> What should happen but the finest poem, or two poems, I've done for many seasons. . . . I've been in an exhilarated state all day & all night because of them . . . Denis admires the new poems . . . [and] sd it was odd that as I became 'more respectable' my verse got 'more revolutionary' – it isn't odd, because outside appearances can't touch the real me, the same old rebellious spirit trying to break down the fusty walls & let in a little light & air.[26]

The longer poem was almost certainly 'Quasi-Slum' and the shorter one 'Enemies', which became the title poem of a slim volume of poems Glover published in February 1937. They were the first poems Curnow wrote in which (perhaps taking his cue from W.H. Auden) he assumed the voice of those he mocked – the political, economic and religious power brokers of the class society. The title 'Quasi-Slum' reflected the point Curnow had made at the conclusion of his newspaper story, that the people he had observed were not 'slum people' because they were conscious of the squalor of the environment in which they lived. The poem describes a Garden of Eden turned into an urban Gethsemane, mocking the Christian platitudes which attempt to explain away the existence of poverty:

> Walking in the garden one sees
> so many of our enemies,
> hearts fix'd strength undecay'd,
> that I wonder we are not afraid:
>
> but we are safe until the day
> our weapons show obvious decay.

'Enemies' is even fiercer in its characterisation of the contempt directed at the poor:

> Detestable gutter child, if you knew
> how we hate you, I and my kind,
> you would scramble bawling with terror
> to that refuge behind
> the sodden stinking privy at the back
> of the two rooms stuck by the railway track.

A number of other poems were written during the four-month period prior to the wedding. Several were published in *Tomorrow*, including one by Julian, 'Work and Pray',[27] which was subsequently included, revised, in *Enemies*, under the title 'Chief End'. 'Recall to Earth', a love poem originally written 'for Bets herself', also appeared later in *Enemies*, and was composed soon after he met her. However, his most ambitious poem at this time, written after one of the many evenings he spent with Glover and Lilburn listening to each other's collections of classical music recordings, was 'Mountain Rhapsody'. The poem was initially suggested by the different movements in Bach's Suite in B Minor for Flute and Strings,[28] though Curnow removed the musical subheadings for publication in *Enemies*, where it is subtitled 'A Symbolic Elegy'. The idea for the poem may also have been influenced by J.C. Beaglehole's 'Considerations on Certain Music of J.S. Bach', which Curnow liked and later included in his 1945 Caxton Press anthology, *A Book of New Zealand Verse*.

The poem extends the romantic themes first broached in 'Aspect of Monism' and 'Doom at Sunrise', imagining a spectacular alpine sunrise as if brought to birth, 'created', by the early-morning waking and soaring flight of a hawk.

As darkness falls, eclipsing the scene, the bird – perhaps symbolic of human consciousness – re-alights on its remote alpine ledge and settles back into its night-long, dreamless sleep of death. Perhaps it was partly in explanation of the mood of the poem that he wrote to Betty a few days later about another moment of intense identification with nature:

> [T]he sun and the river reminded me of a splendid thing written by a man named Traherne some hundreds of years ago – I've never forgotten it:
>
> > You never perceive the world aright till the sea
> > itself floweth in your veins, till you are clothed
> > with the heavens and crowned with the stars.
>
> We're not just spectators of all the loveliness and life in the world – we belong to it and we're part of it, moving in the same rhythm. And together we send out new life, or satisfy the life in us – so that there are always eyes to see and admire. So love is life, and fear and hate are death – the willows can't hate the earth, or fear the wind that blows the leaves away. . . . Sometimes I look at the sun and trees, and wonder if I've been blind all my life, and only just seen these things for the first time.[29]

Despite the romanticism of such a comment, and of 'Mountain Rhapsody' itself, the personal, self-exploratory impulses behind them remained central to Curnow's poetry throughout his life.

At this time also – partly in order to supplement his income – Curnow approached 3YA radio with a proposal to prepare three broadcasts, consisting of readings and commentary, on traditional English poets. The poets he chose were Robert Herrick, Andrew Marvell and Samuel Taylor Coleridge, and the broadcasts appeared fortnightly between early July and early August 1936. He put a huge amount of effort into preparing the texts and choosing the music for these broadcasts – they were the first such poetry programmes attempted on radio in Christchurch – and his brother John assisted him with rehearsals before they went to air live. They were reasonably well received, though one newspaper reviewer of his Marvell talk said that it would have been preferable for him to read his own poetry. But as Curnow wrote to Betty:

> they wouldn't let me say over the wireless some of the most important things the young poets think. . . . [F]or five years I have seen men like Mason, Fairburn, Glover, Beaglehole, & myself least of them all, trying to breathe life into the language of NZers, trying to say living things in living words.[30]

Nevertheless, these broadcasts broke the ice, as far as radio as a medium was concerned for Curnow, and he gave talks on a variety of topics over the next decades, though they became fewer after he shifted to an academic career at Auckland University College in 1951.

Enemies, February 1937

During the months following the wedding Curnow wrote a further five poems – sufficient, with those he had already written, to make a small volume, *Enemies*, for Glover to publish at the Caxton Press in February the following year. These included one of his most powerful, in the mode of 'Quasi-Slum', entitled 'New Zealand City', which took pride of place as the opening poem in the new volume. The pretensions of Christchurch, offered as a representative 'New Zealand' city, and the self-serving rhetoric of its power elites, are fiercely denounced. Here was a poetry of contemporary 'plain speech' indeed, energised by provocative metaphors and ironies:

> Small city your streets hold no particular legends,
> your brothels are inconspicuous as your churches,
> your potentates think in thousands not millions
> and the nations do not quote your newspapers.
>
> London has spawned. Here are banks in the egg,
> foetus Beaverbrooks, Edens and Baldwins,
> toy art and labour, the importance of children
> under an unstained sky.

The poem also contains some of Curnow's most often-quoted lines, including those in which he dismantles the national rhetoric of youthful promise ('This is the land of new hopes / joined with a thousand years' despair, / of children with senile faces'), and concludes with a savagely epigrammatic jibe at the country's willing subservience to overseas economic masters:

> Serf to them all
> for pleasure or pain;
> betrayed to the world's
> garret and gutter,
> bought at the export
> price of butter.

In the first two weeks of January 1937 Curnow took Betty on their deferred honeymoon trip to Auckland, where they stayed with his cousin Larry and Norman Richmond, and also met up with the family of his uncle, Pendarves Curnow. However, most of the time was spent socialising with friends and mentors of his earlier student days – with his St John's friends Holmes and Mowbray, with Anschutz, Neil Parton and Arthur Sewell from the university, with Lowry (now married to Irene) and Mason, and especially with Fairburn, his brother and his parents.

In the first week of their stay they spent several days at the Anawhata hut. It rained most of the time, and on one especially stormy night Betty was terrified that the hut would be blown off the cliff top into the sea. She enjoyed a later visit to the west coast better (to Piha, with Richmond, Parton, Fairburn and his brother),[31] but was struck by the perilous nature of the road and the violence of the surf. They also visited Frank Sargeson, now living in an army hut in Esmonde Road, Takapuna, and met up with Iris Wilkinson, in a 'large hat, flowery dress flowing to the ankles and [with] a walking stick', for coffee in Vulcan Lane.[32] Curnow was 'very disappointed' with the meeting – the first time in three years – writing to Alexander:

> I realize her difficulty in being solely dependent on free-lance work for a liveli-
> hood. What original genius she has is completely coloured by that necessity. She is
> compelled to write what the literary pages will print. That is quite salutary in prose
> work – but damnation to verse. Journalism demands compromise with the accepted.
> I don't mean that the finest poetry is necessarily excluded by the 'accepted' standard;
> only that a great deal of what is vivid and fresh must be so excluded.[33]

Betty liked meeting her husband's friends, but blamed Auckland's humid climate for bouts of illness during her stay. Fairburn in particular enjoyed their visit, and his friendship with Curnow deepened from this time on.

Back in Christchurch, Curnow finalised the selection of his new poems for *Enemies*, revising for inclusion a love poem ('Orbit') which had just appeared in *Tomorrow* under the pen name of Julian.[34] He also carefully constructed an 'Author's Note', which included a succinct restatement of ideas about poetry which he had been pursuing for a number of years – the need to learn from, without 'emulating', live contemporary poetic practice overseas, and the need to attend especially to language and form rather than to preconceived 'subject matter', especially of the sort which prompted speculation about 'a national literature':

> The only hope is in poetry written on a genuine impulse to present in expressive form
> the material which naturally suggests itself – suggests itself, that is, uninfluenced by

any notion of what is or is not fit subject matter for poetry. I have tried to avoid a
preconceived idea of what New Zealand poets should write about. And I have tried to
show the possibility of a technical development *pari passu* with that of recent English
poetry. Whatever may be said or written about a national literature for New Zealand,
England remains at the very least the 'technical research laboratory', where the finest
and most advanced work is done with that subtle material, the English language.

Enemies appeared on 22 February from the Caxton Press's premises situated at
152 Peterborough Street. It was a slim volume of 24 pages, consisting of fourteen
poems, with a small print run of 84 copies. Its subtitle, 'Poems 1934–36', was
strictly accurate but misleading, since only one poem, a fragment entitled 'Daily
Bread', belonged to 1934, and with the exception of some of the love lyrics in
the sequence 'A Woman in Mind', all of the poems post-dated his previous slim
collection (*Three Poems*) of May 1935. Nor did he include 'Doom at Sunrise', though
it deserved inclusion, presumably because it had already appeared in book form in
the small anthology *Another Argo* in August 1935. Most of the poems in *Enemies*,
including all of its important ones, were written in the second half of 1936 and
most had not previously been published. Given the rigorous nature of the selection,
Curnow looked forward anxiously to how the volume would be received.

The *Press* was quick off the mark in reviewing *Enemies* a fortnight after the
volume appeared,[35] its regular verse reviewer (R.G. McNab) producing, Curnow
felt, a 'highly flattering but not over-intelligent half-column'.[36] Fairburn's review
a month later in *Tomorrow* was the most considered Curnow had ever received.
It was a double-edged review, designed to praise Curnow's strengths and to
provoke those (like Glover) who admired Dylan Thomas and the 'pylon poetry'
of the English thirties poets (Auden, Spender, Day Lewis and MacNeice) by
suggesting that although Curnow was correct to acknowledge the technical
importance of their work for his own and others' poetry, his real strengths lay
elsewhere. 'Quasi-Slum', he argued, 'demonstrates convincingly that poetry can
make use of social criticism without degenerating into propaganda'.[37]

The review was successful on both fronts. In the next two issues of *Tomorrow*,
Rhodes, and then Glover, took Fairburn to task for his derogatory comments
on the English thirties poets, while Curnow, in correspondence, was happy to
concur with Fairburn's dissent from Rhodes's view of art as 'serving the masses'[38]
and agree with the gist of Fairburn's remarks on 'pylonese' ('just clever substitution'– of pylons for Wordsworthian daffodils).[39] However, he defended C. Day
Lewis, whom Fairburn had attacked as 'consistently meretricious',[40] describing
him as 'quite reasonable about death'.[41]

Apart from Fairburn, and later M.H. Holcroft – who admired 'New Zealand
City' and 'Enemies', and predicted, acutely, that 'Curnow's talent may be moving

towards a metaphysical verse'[42] – older-generation reviewers, like Alan Mulgan, struggled to come to terms with the poems, as did Curnow's father Tremayne, who refrained from direct comment, but preferred the style (and presumably the sentiments) of his son's *Valley of Decision* poems. 'Allen's verses puzzle me', he wrote to Alexander:

> [T]hey please a certain coterie – but he ought – by now – to have got out of the habit of regard[ing] verse as a way of expressing dislike, of everybody & everything he disagrees with. Also, too much of it is formless & obscure. I don't criticize it to him, because he is a creature of theories & he thinks mine out-of-date. I have told him, however, that some day a man will arise & rediscover the blueness of the sky, the greenness of the grass & the brightness of the sunshine, & announce this re-discovery in plain metrical English – & then we shall have a poet. But he still persists in giving an impersonation of Bunyan's Man with the Muck-rake.[43]

Alexander himself ventured a letter to Curnow criticising both *Enemies* and the 'coterie' of poets to which he belonged, and Curnow defended himself (as well as Glover, Fairburn and Mason) at length, apologising at the end for his 'long diatribe'. Alexander's objection to the line from 'New Zealand City', 'your brothels are inconspicuous as your churches', as 'arbitrary' and 'melodramatic' prompted an ingenious but not entirely convincing rebuttal of the notion that it was intended to shock which illustrates a personal characteristic that remained with Curnow all his life – perhaps formed or reinforced by his theological training – his delight in tenacious disputation on matters of small detail.[44]

Chapter Seven

A Turning Point in History:
Not in Narrow Seas, 1937–38

*In those few years between the Great Depression and World War 2,
there was any amount of facile optimism – almost up to the outbreak
of the war, any number of people who thought Hitler wasn't such a bad
guy – and in a world like that it was hard to feel optimistic about this
country, or patient with claptrap about its colonial past.*[1]

A turn to history: Canterbury Province

The twelve months from mid-1936 to mid-1937 – during the year, that is, after
Curnow first met Betty – were highly productive, as far as Curnow's poetry was
concerned, though that fact is somewhat disguised by the publication history
of *Enemies* and *Not in Narrow Seas* (the former subtitled 'Poems 1934–1936',
the latter published in 1939), which might suggest that the poems gradually
emerged over a five-year period. In fact, most of the poems in both volumes were
written in the period mid-1936 to mid-1937. This pattern – of concentrated bursts
of activity followed by long periods in which none of the drafts of his poems
seemed to reach what he thought of as 'finished', publishable versions – continued throughout his life.

The turn to historical questions in *Not in Narrow Seas*, in particular the history
of Canterbury Province as a paradigm of New Zealand's colonial and pioneering origins, followed quite quickly from his interrogation of the contemporary

scene in *Enemies*. Writing to Fairburn about his review of *Enemies* he referred in passing to a group of four new poems which had recently appeared in *Tomorrow* which he had 'stupidly' called 'Rats in the Bilge'.[2] 'Actually', he went on, 'it is the first instalment of a longish work which I have now dec'd to call the Secret Empire. Glover may print it as a booklet.'[3] Fairburn wrote back that the title Curnow now proposed had 'a too Chestertonian sound in my ears', adding that 'from the weight and texture' of the four poems in *Tomorrow*, 'it seemed to be like a thick rope about a foot long. It wanted the other 99ft to make it a rope, with all the qualities of a rope.'[4] Curnow interpreted Fairburn's comment as implying narrative deficiencies in the sequence, and when the next instalment of seven poems appeared in *Tomorrow* six weeks later (with yet another new title, 'The Potter's Field', and, oddly, reverting to his pseudonym of Julian), he added a prose commentary to each, forming a kind of contextual historical narrative for the poems.[5] It was his solution to the issue raised by Fairburn, in this first sequence of any length which he ever attempted, and one which he retained when the sequence – revised and expanded by a further four poems during the next twelve months – was eventually published by Glover in 1939.

However, the poem which most clearly signalled the shift to history in the immediate aftermath of *Enemies* was entitled 'Inheritance', a little-known poem, never reprinted, which appeared in another of Glover's small anthologies, *A Caxton Miscellany* (June 1937). Organised into three parts, it traces the gradual breaking of a child's spirit. Born in fear and guilt, he is 'taught backward-looking', grows up fearful of sexuality ('groping the entailed / estate of forebears'), and arrives at a 'maturity' of diminished material expectations, 'the swivel chair throne of benign success, / Caesar's sceptre a gold fountain-pen'. The poem invokes ironically 'the builders of this fame: / pale schoolmasters who broke the fine spirit, /employers preaching sound business methods', and concludes with a passionate, prophetic plea that such a figure might win 'harsh nobility' by remembering and confronting the ghosts of his inheritance:

> Pray for him now that he will not forget
> altogether the vast peaks and valleys of fear.
> If the heart is not dying yet,
> in that desolate country wandering among
> sudden horrors and impending despair,
> a harsh nobility may perhaps be won.

The impulse expressed in 'Inheritance' underpinned the turn to history in *Not in Narrow Seas*, with its opening address to a reader who 'knows hope more near / The straining heart's despair', and its introductory sestina ('Statement') which frames the episodes about colonial and pioneering history within a powerful metaphor of geographical isolation: two remote islands surrounded by vast oceans, their climate shaped by the ice-bound continent of Antarctica to the south: 'Therefore I sing your agonies, not upward, / For the two islands not in narrow seas / Cringe in a wind from the world's nether ice.'

Domestic, work and writing routines

After Curnow's return from his trip to Auckland with Betty in January 1937 the demands of journalism quickly reassumed their dominant role in his daily life. During the course of the year he found himself increasingly assigned to cable sub-editing late into the night, and special assignments involved work at any hour of the day or night. Often the meetings which he had to write up, or talks by civic dignitaries or politicians or overseas visitors, occurred in the evening, and once he had to write a story about the arrival of sheep at Addington between midnight and 3 a.m. for auction early in the morning. Assignments which took him further afield also often meant that he did not get home until very late (a trip to Rakaia, for example, usually meant a 1 a.m. return home), and he became proficient in writing stories in trains or buses or when accompanied by a driver in a *Press* car. In the second half of 1937 he worked hard to improve his shorthand rate, in order to meet the requirement for promotion to senior reporter. In December, Charles Williams, the chief of staff at *The Press*, took over the editorship of the Hawke's Bay *Daily Mail*, and thought highly enough of Curnow's talents to offer him the job of chief of staff there.[6] Curnow considered the offer, but in the end declined it. The attractions of cultural life in Christchurch, where he was beginning to make his name as a poet, had taken too strong a hold.

Because money was always scarce he continued to seek new ways to supplement his income. In 1938 he passed the final paper (in psychology) needed to complete his BA degree. He wrote many reviews of films for *The Press*, and in 1937 and 1938 gave numerous talks on 3YA radio, on topics of general interest. One such topic was travel, in which he criticised overseas travellers who on their return became instant pundits, a theme he would often come back to under the pseudonym of 'Whim Wham'. Early in 1938 he discussed the topic 'Are We a Nation?' and on another occasion reminisced about events from his own early vicarage childhood.

Around mid-1937, taking his lead from Glover, Curnow also tried his hand at fiction, contributing light, comic sketches to *Tomorrow*. 'A Bad Liver',[7] published under his own name, traced the misanthropic thoughts of a man walking home at the end of his working day in an office. 'Day of Wrath: A Tale',[8] published

under his pseudonym Julian, offered a comic political fantasy closely related to
the concerns of *Enemies* and *Not in Narrow Seas*, imagining Judgement Day as
an annual event in the British calendar celebrating the triumph of the status quo
and the eradication of 'subversive opinions'. Over the next two years he published
a further seven sketches in *The Press* (the first under the pseudonym Whim
Wham, the rest under his own initials), less heavy-handed than the *Tomorrow*
pieces, and modelled on the Canadian Stephen Leacock's *Sunshine Sketches of a
Little Town* (1912), a collection of stories about everyday life in the small fictional
town of Mariposa.

Whim Wham, the pen name under which Curnow was to contribute topical
satirical verses to *The Press* every Saturday, and later also to the *New Zealand
Herald*, for more than 50 years, first made his appearance at the end of 1937. At the
time the editor of the Literary Page, Schroder, was on holiday leave, and Curnow
was temporarily standing in for him. He wrote three pieces, in December, as
space-fillers. The first, 'Lament',[9] a gently mocking account of the ending of an
all-night sitting of Parliament, contained many of the trademarks for which
Whim Wham later became so popular – topical subject matter, humorous
portraiture (of Michael Savage, Walter Nash, and others), clever parody
(of Gray's 'Elegy'), and witty rhymes and wordplays. A week later he contributed
'A Square Deal',[10] a lively piece about council plans to alleviate traffic bottle-
necks in Christchurch's Cathedral Square; and at the end of the month 'New
Year Song', poking fun at the fuss made over a mere calendar change ('The best
of things that matter / (And plenty of the worst) / Don't happen with a clatter
/ On January the First').[11] *The Press* received numerous complimentary letters
about Whim Wham, though it was not until August the following year that the
verse became a regular weekly feature in the newspaper. Curnow was paid 10s for
each piece, a small but useful supplement to his weekly wage.

In November 1937 Curnow purchased his first car, an old 1926 Hupmobile
for which he paid £10, with a further £10 to be paid off. From the start it caused
trouble, but it lasted long enough – altered to allow for the seat to be let down for
sleeping in – for Curnow and Betty to make a two-week holiday camping trip
to Nelson in the second half of January 1938. They camped at the Conway River
north of Cheviot, after crossing the Waiau River, the location of one of Curnow's
most famous poems, 'House and Land',[12] as well as near Blenheim, and at Lake
Rotoiti, and later near Picton. In between they spent a week at Richmond, near
Nelson, staying with Betty's older brother Richard and his wife Maisie, and met up
with Curnow's brother John and his Aunt Fanny (recently arrived from England
for a three-month stay in Christchurch), who were also holidaying in Nelson.

Only one poem can be specifically identified with this trip – 'Dimensional',
a painterly depiction of a stagnant river scene near Picton which Curnow did not

publish until *Jack without Magic* (1946) – but the trip was important in extending his experience of the South Island landscape, which had until then been mainly confined to the Canterbury region. During the next couple of years there were other trips – to the Canterbury alpine hinterland, to Leithfield Beach north of Christchurch, and, especially, a tramping trip to the West Coast – all of them contributing to the sense of landscape which became increasingly important in the poems Curnow wrote from this time on.

The Hupmobile only just survived the trip to Nelson, and shortly after their return Curnow traded it in for an old Fiat, but had no better luck with it. On 20 March 1938 he had to be rushed suddenly to hospital with acute appendicitis. He was in hospital for eleven days, and had to take convalescent leave from *The Press* for a further month, not returning to work until early May. Perhaps because she panicked at the severity and suddenness of Curnow's collapse, Betty had taken him to a surgeon nearby, who operated on him in a private hospital. The hospital's and surgeon's bills (£55) were well beyond their means, and although Curnow was contributing to a sick-pay scheme with *The Press*, it by no means covered his loss of salary during the six weeks he was away. After the Fiat was sold they were still £30 in arrears, and it took many months to recover financially. From this time until the mid-1960s a car remained a luxury that Curnow could not afford.

Curnow's hospitalisation was distressing for Betty on another account – the barely disguised hostility directed towards her from Curnow's mother Jessie, who regarded their way of living as contributing to his illness, and blamed Betty for not keeping the house in better order and providing decent meals. The criticism was unfair. If Curnow was run down at this time, the main reason is likely to have been the intense pressure he put on himself in order to make ends meet while trying to sustain his serious writing projects, and the fact his hours of work often meant that he ate irregularly.[13]

As for domestic arrangements at Gloucester Street, neither Curnow nor Betty regarded domesticity as the norm by which they wanted to live. They had an expanding circle of friends, who in 1938 included Leo Bensemann, Rita Angus, the Birkinshaws, the Glovers and the Shurrocks, Curnow's journalist friends on *The Press*, and the relatives to whom they felt closest, Patricia and Tyndall Harman and Tennent Ronalds. Many of these visited regularly, and Betty learnt to make do with whatever food was in the house. When Curnow was not working they enjoyed visiting friends, going out to films and plays, and attending English Association evenings at Canterbury University College (in which Glover played a key organising role), playing tennis, taking picnic lunches on walks and tramps in the Cashmere Hills and to Lyttelton, and occasionally making longer excursions (including at this time a weekend ice-skating trip to Mt Harper, and a day trip inland to Lake Coleridge in a car hired by Aunt Fanny).

During 1938 the Curnows also met new people on the Christchurch drama scene, especially Owen Simmance, 'a recently erected pillar', Curnow wrote to Fairburn, 'of Leftism, Democracy, Freedom etc, whatever the current cant is – and a good man'.[14] Curnow wrote a glowing review[15] of Simmance's production of the Soviet play *Squaring the Circle*, a Left Book Club drama club production at the Radiant Hall in October, though some negative comments he made in passing about the 'rather narrow' range of amateur theatre brought him into conflict with his outspoken cousin Audrey Cotterill, who was strongly involved (with her husband, Guy) in repertory productions.

If Jessie disapproved of Betty's domestic shortcomings, Audrey Cotterill laid the blame firmly on Curnow himself, confronting him with his failings soon after the offending review appeared, at a family wedding reception she hosted. There was little in his behaviour of which she could approve – his politics, his social attitudes and opinions, the appalling shirt he was wearing, his drinking – all of these stemmed from the fact that he had got in with a bad lot and was disgracing the family (or, at least, the Cracroft Wilson side of the family from which she came).

Betty enjoyed socialising, and was certainly not a stay-at-home wife, though she sewed a great deal from oddments and reduced-price materials, and became adept at remodelling and recycling her own clothes and Curnow's. However, she also developed a degree of marital independence which Jessie no doubt thought was not what was expected of a wife. She developed her own friendship with the Glovers, the Shurrocks and others, and went to films three or four nights a week when Curnow was working at *The Press*. She also enjoyed reading fiction, and was encouraged by Francis Shurrock and Leo Bensemann (who joined Glover and John Drew at the Caxton Press in 1937) to develop her interest in painting, beginning tentatively in 1937 with drawings illustrating Curnow's 'The Potter's Field'. In May 1937 she met for the first time the painter Rita Angus, who was then working on her now well-known painting of the Birkinshaws' two daughters, Jane and Fay.

The Curnows' domestic circumstances changed in June 1938 when Betty discovered that she was pregnant, and since the one-bedroom upstairs flat at Gloucester Street was too small to accommodate a baby, they immediately began looking for a larger place to live, shifting on 8 August into a two-bedroom rented house on a quarter-acre block at 16 Nelson Street, Riccarton. This was to be their home for the next three and a half years. Though not in the centre of Christchurch, as the Gloucester Street flat was, it was within easy cycling distance of (or a tram ride across Hagley Park to) the *Press* office, and not too far from the Glovers, who were renting at Carlton Mill Road close to North Hagley Park.[16] The shift did, however, mean a significant increase in rent, from

30s weekly at Gloucester Street to £2 10s, and it is hardly a coincidence that the move coincided exactly with the resurrection of Whim Wham, after a seven-month gap. Half the increase in rent could be paid for by Whim Wham's weekly contributions from this time on.

By the end of the year what was to become a typical pattern of Whim Wham offerings had appeared – a mix of serious and light verses, on local and overseas topics, sparked by some absurd pronouncement or act of folly reported in the previous week's news. There were grim pieces on the growing threat of war in Europe, including lampoons of Hitler, Goebbels, Goering, and their apologists and appeasers; and lighter pieces on parliamentary politics and candidates as the 1938 election approached. A mock-Centennial Ode satirised the country's grandiose and costly plans to celebrate the centennial in 1940. (What was needed, he wrote to Fairburn, was 'a festival of penitence and humiliation, for our having been here 100 years and added more human shit than human wisdom to this soil'.)[17] Another piece ridiculed cultural rivalry between Wellington and Auckland over the number of emus that would be hatched in the zoos of each. There were also lighter pieces in which Whim Wham identified with the voice of the ordinary Kiwi: writing about the pleasures of suburban life, his disastrous attempts to play golf, his uncertainties where to go for his summer holiday. A prose piece, entitled 'A Pathetic Encounter', also represented Whim Wham in lighter vein, musing sentimentally about his encounter in the streets with a car he had once owned.

Readers were often interested in the origins of the pen name Whim Wham, but it was not until the 1950s that Curnow devoted a tongue-in-cheek piece, 'You May As Well Know', to its provenance. The Oxford Dictionary dates the use of the phrase to the sixteenth century, giving two meanings: 'a fanciful or fantastic object' and 'a fantastic or odd notion'. Curnow's piece quotes Wyld's similar dictionary definition ('a whimsical idea' or a 'toy, trifle, plaything'), and also remembers the name from his childhood, when his father, faced with persistent questioning from his 'inquisitive, idle' son, would reply, 'I'm making a WHIM WHAM for a Goose's Bridle'. Tremayne's proverbial phrase, of course, represents a deliberate recourse to nonsense in order to avoid giving a direct answer. The element of indirectness is essential to Whim Wham's social purposes, and in a typical example of such indirectness in the piece in which he discusses the pseudonym he plays on the metaphorical connection between geese (a docile New Zealand populace) under the bridle of state control.

Because Whim Wham's pieces were written in lighter vein (though they were full of inventive puns, and ingenious rhymes and allusions), and composed to meet deadlines in ways that were quite different from the demands he set himself in his serious poetry, Curnow always insisted on maintaining the anonymity of his pen name. But they were, or quickly became, something more than simply a means of earning extra money. Whim Wham brought Curnow into contact with a large popular readership for the first time, and the verse (despite its lightness) enabled him to voice particular ways of looking at the world, to express opinions and generate controversy about significant social, political and cultural issues that affected the country. Whim Wham also provided a kind of workshop in which Curnow could develop his skills of versification and exploit his talent for using vernacular New Zealand speech and idiom. Always serious and self-absorbed as far as his poetry was concerned ('One is searching oneself and searching the terms of one's very existence in an entirely different spirit'),[18] behind the mask of Whim Wham he could be more relaxed and simply enjoy the pleasures of constructing funny, whimsical verse. One of the most heavily annotated of Curnow's own books in the later 1930s was J.M. Cohen's Penguin selection *More Comic and Curious Verse* (1936), where he encountered many of the models (Lewis Carroll, Edward Lear, and others) for his own parodies and light satires.

In the wake of his own early ventures into the field of light verse Curnow also gained a new respect for his father's skill in the genre, and sought (unsuccess-fully) to have Tremayne's weekly verses in the Dunedin *Evening Star* syndicated to *The Press*. He and Glover also thought of publishing a selection of the verses at the Caxton Press, though the proposal came to nothing because of the cost.

During these early Christchurch years after his marriage, Curnow was writing light fiction and verse, film and drama reviews, radio talks, and occasion-ally contributed more serious critical items. One of these, in 1937, was a feature article in *The Press*,[19] 'Poets in New Zealand: Problems of Writing and Criticism', which offered a kind of defence of the poetry he had recently published in *Enemies*. Insisting – as he did throughout his life – that 'the production of good poetry cannot be assisted by the "national literature" sentiment', he argued that the crucial question poets in New Zealand had to address was whom they were writing for, and that the answer to such a question crucially affected the language they used, since 'language is the sole link between the poet and his reader'. Critics and poets, he went on, seldom stopped to think whether the language of most New Zealand verse (which took English literature up to the landing of the First Four Ships – which carried the Canterbury Association's first settlers – as its guide, producing 'highly local-coloured, impeccably rhymed and metrical' verses) was 'the natural property of any considerable body of readers into whose hands the work may fall'. 'At present', he concluded, 'New Zealand poets must *search the streets, as well as the classics* [author's italics] for a language which in purity and sincerity will compel the attention of the only public [a New Zealand public] able to receive them.' A 'national literature' might be the result of such effort, but it could not be its motive force: 'Practising artists do not belong among the foundations of the national culture, like so many illustrious corpses below the paving of Westminster Abbey.' Curnow was to return to this idea again and again over the next three decades, in his anthology introductions, reviews and lectures, and remained deeply puzzled that those who later accused him of being a prescriptive 'literary nationalist' could not understand what to him was a relatively straightforward distinction.

Curnow's most serious piece of critical writing the following year, a review of Fairburn's *Dominion* in *Tomorrow*,[20] reasserted his hostility to any 'national literature sentiment'. Fairburn's volume was, he began, 'an event of great importance to (the phrase must be used) New Zealand poetry'. The strength of the poem lay in its 'vision' of the 'here and now', of 'the strange half-nation New Zealand', and in the quality of 'sustained utterance by an artist who has mastered his material':

> The prophet on the housetops may tune into the Lord; but in these days (as indeed in those of Amos) it is necessary that he shall know what is going on beneath the housetops . . . he must know . . . what sort of books and papers are on the shelf, if any; what is the nature of the conversation; what work is done, and what things are made. Then he can go ahead and see visions, which in another context might be described as deductions.[21]

Quoting J.C. Beaglehole's comment (in his *New Zealand: A Short History*, 1936) that New Zealand 'is not . . . with any deep feeling, a nation' and that, in the twentieth century, 'it may be that the making of new nationalities is an anachronism, as it certainly is a danger', Curnow produced his own fierce gloss on the quality of nationhood New Zealand had produced, which he saw as the condition grasped by Fairburn in *Dominion*: 'a defeatism more cruel than could ever afflict one of the elder nations, and a hideous sub-human insolence and optimism which is (of course) that defeatism inverted'. For Curnow, the strength of Fairburn's poem lay in its New Zealand rather than its 'cosmopolitan' resonances, though as always he tried to distinguish between the absurdity of nationalism as a preconceived end to be aimed at by poets, and the idea of a nation as something which might be recognised in poems if they were good enough: 'Neither Mr Fairburn nor any honest man cares two straws about "New Zealand poetry" (leave it to the watery quarterly*); but if he will write so well, reference to it is unavoidable.'

It was in 1938 that Curnow first discussed with Glover the idea of a new anthology of New Zealand poetry. The idea arose from a visit to New Zealand by the English publisher Hugh Dent (publisher of the Everyman series), whom

---

* *Art in New Zealand.*

Curnow interviewed in Christchurch for *The Press* and took to visit Glover at the Caxton Press. Initially their interest in Dent was because he was a close personal friend of Eric Gill, an English artist and typographer whose work (as well as his politically radical, William Morris-influenced philosophy about the place of the arts in society) had been highly influential on both Lowry and Glover. Gill had also written warmly to Curnow about his pamphlet *Poetry and Language*, printed in Gill's own sans serif font, after Glover sent him a copy. Both Curnow and Glover were excited by their meeting with Dent, as Curnow wrote to Alexander – '[t]here is less of that cursed sense of isolation when one has a definite link with responsible minds in England'[22] – but the real reason for writing emerges almost casually at the end of his letter: he and Glover were planning a 'serious anthology' of contemporary New Zealand verse. 'Some day', he wrote offhandedly, they wished to produce a successor to Alexander's own *Treasury of New Zealand Verse* (co-edited with A.E. Currie in 1906 and 1926), but it is clear that they had already put sufficient thought into it to send a proposal to Dent, and that Curnow was anxious not to offend Alexander:

> Some day Glover and I want to follow [the Treasury], with a serious anthology which shall represent NZ verse today as well as the Treasury did in its day. We have written to Dents, but have not had a reply yet. Perhaps you could give me an idea, from your experience, what lies ahead of us. Making an anthology, we are beginning to realize, isn't quite so easy as it sounds. Of course, we would not touch the body of work from which collections have been made: the idea is to limit it to work published in the last 10 years.[23]

It was to be another seven years before the idea of an anthology was finally realised. War intervened, Glover went overseas on naval service, and Curnow did not get back to working seriously on it until 1943. And it was to be published, in the end, not by Dent or any overseas publisher, but by Glover himself at the Caxton Press.

Later contributions to *Tomorrow*, 1937–38

After the publication of *Enemies* in February 1937 Curnow's contributions as Julian to *Tomorrow* began to decline, and they ceased entirely the following year when Whim Wham appeared on the scene. In July 1937 a second *Verse Alive* anthology of verse from *Tomorrow* appeared from the Caxton Press, selected by Rhodes and Glover from the period up to the end of 1936. Curnow had three pieces in it under his own name, none under the name of Julian, and a fourth piece (a fierce polemic with the title 'The Rubbish Heap') under the pseudonym of 'Amen'.* [24]

Curnow contributed half a dozen poems to *Tomorrow* under his own name in the last months of 1937 and a further seven (two by Julian) in 1938. Except for three of these, which became part of the sequence *Not in Narrow Seas*, none were ever reprinted. 'Variations on a Theme'[25] was one of the best, an ingenious local political adaptation of the last stanza of Blake's famous lyric of unrequited love, 'Song', which Curnow later included as the 'Epilogue' to *Not in Narrow Seas*. Each line from Blake's stanza provides the first line of each of Curnow's quatrains:

> *Bring me an axe and spade*:
> For this is insolent country,
> James Cook's pig-farm
> Without rule or road.
>
> *Bring me a winding-sheet*:
> For the brown singing people
> Affront with death our triumph, an
> Unangry death without a fight.
>
> *When I my grave have made*
> I shall write to friends at Home,
> And with an English accent
> How shall I be afraid?
>
> *Let winds and tempests beat*
> On 1,000 bungalows,
> To our sad suburban funeral
> Drag followers on foot.
>
> *Down I'll lie*
> *As cold as clay*
> Thank God *true love*
> *Doth pass away,*
>
> The empire and the empty lands
> The iron and the golden sands

> Dredged and dumped
> With the wheezing sea clay.*

A number of the later *Tomorrow* poems show Curnow experimenting with different forms. In '"Can Ye Brew Poisons –?"',[26] attacking the ominous growth of the armaments industry in Europe, he introduced two voices in dramatic counterpoint. 'Sestina'[27] was a first effort at the difficult form of the sestina, a trial run for the more successful 'Statement' which he later wrote as a prologue to *Not in Narrow Seas*. Strongly influenced by Auden and heavily metaphysical in import, the poem invoked the idea of mountain-climbing as a spiritual quest for the unknown. The concluding stanza associates such spiritual knowledge or revelation with the split-second moment before violent death, a motif of victimhood or sacrifice which was to recur in his poetry of the next decade (including his most famous public poem of the decade, 'Landfall in Unknown Seas'):

> At Christmas or Easter consider the question,
> Bank-clerk and musician contemplating climb,
> Before road-map or meeting at railway stations:
> Do there exist tracks among the ranges
> Only the dead know, that on scree or glass
> Slipped, and were suddenly aware of mountains?

Another of these later poems, 'The Sword and the Bomb',[28] revealed Curnow's increasing interest in the poetry of W.B. Yeats. Curnow described the poem in a note as an 'imitation' of Yeats, sparked by Yeats's reference to fear of air bombardment in a late poem (presumably 'Lapis Lazuli'), but the 'imitation' here, which includes references to numerous of Yeats's later poems, anticipates the kind of heightened, lucid rhetoric which Curnow increasingly made his own in his poetry of the 1940s:

> That old man who raised ancient pageantry
> Now finds it in his heart to cast a bomb
> Boldly into a line. Maeve and Cuchulain
> Clutter old folios. That storm is past;
> Whoever conjured with the tight-strung wind
> And fought with heroes in the volleying rain,
> Hangs Sato's blade above the mantelshelf,

---

* Italics identifying Blake's lines (from 'Song: My silks and fine array', in *Poetical Sketches* (1783)) were introduced into the text by Curnow in his *Collected Poems* (1974).

Sweetens to tragedy with powerful rhyme
The formless horror of the modern wars.
What shelter has old age against the times
When Yeats can hear the siren and the shell
Beating about his tower of centuries?

'Defence Policy',[29] the last of Curnow's contributions to *Tomorrow*, was a mock-surrealist jeu d'esprit representing its subject in crumbling fragments of language and nonsense phrases.

For four years *Tomorrow* had provided the only significant journal outlet for Curnow's work. Despite the always wary though respectful relationship between Curnow and its literary editor, Winston Rhodes – Curnow distrusting Rhodes's proletarian sympathies, and Rhodes distrusting what he saw as Curnow's elitist tendencies – it is hard to imagine that Curnow would have kept writing poetry during those four crucial years, from the time of his rejection of a career in the Church to the emergence of the distinctive voice which appeared in *Not in Narrow Seas*, without the support of *Tomorrow*. Many of the poems Rhodes published there, from the time of 'Aspect of Monism' onwards, had no overt political bearing at all, and puzzled the journal's trades union readership. Furthermore, with that poem, as well as with the two large parts of the sequence which eventually became *Not in Narrow Seas*, Rhodes provided featured space in the magazine which no other poetry was ever given. Rhodes's practice, as literary editor, was much more liberal and accommodating towards poetry to which he was temperamentally opposed than Curnow gave him credit for.

Not in Narrow Seas, 1939

The two most significant of Curnow's late contributions to *Tomorrow* in 1938 were poems which completed the core sequence of twelve numbered poems in *Not in Narrow Seas*. 'A Loyal Show',[30] in four quatrains mocking New Zealand's obsequious reverence towards British royalty ('New land New Zealand / Dancing before the Throne'), provided the opening section of what became the eleventh poem in the final sequence. 'Predestination',[31] occasioned by a book of paintings by van Gogh which Betty had given Curnow for his birthday in 1937, became the final poem of the sequence, and addressed the issue of the role of the artist in New Zealand. It drew an analogy between the 'pain' and 'misery' suffered imaginatively by van Gogh as he painted the cornfields of Auvers, and the suffering of the artist in New Zealand as he struggled to depict 'the vertical ice, the dry / shriek of the kea' – the landscape, in each case, made to realise or symbolise dimensions of life which its inhabitants resist. This highly charged romantic/prophetic view of the artist, as sharing in the unacknowledged agonies of the people he speaks to and for, even their victim, seemed to be required by the disillusioned vision of New Zealand life in *Not in Narrow Seas*, if the artist was not to be accused of arrogantly exempting himself from the critique applied to everyone else. It was an anxiety which Curnow never completely lost, although in his Caxton Press anthology introduction written several years later, he addressed it in more tentative terms: 'Unless he is a new and altogether less passionate variety of "social man" – I wonder, is that possible? – the New Zealand poet is unlikely to escape wholly the character of prophet to his people'.[32]

By November 1938 Curnow was hard at work reshaping and revising the material which had appeared in *Tomorrow* over the previous eighteen months – the four poems of 'Rats in the Bilge', the seven poems of 'The Potter's Field', and the three later poems – into the final form of *Not in Narrow Seas*, writing to Fairburn: 'Between Bensemann and Glover, I hope in a few months to have on record my version of your "Dominion": a less melodious, less vehement, less exuberant "Dominion". Much of it has appeared in bits in Tomorrow.'[33] A considerable amount of revision to individual poems was involved, and in some instances blocks of material were shifted and combined into new poems. The prose commentaries which had been introduced into 'The Potter's Field' were also revised, and new commentaries written for the other poems in the sequence. Finally, a series of four quotations from Beaglehole's *New Zealand: A Short History* were selected as an epigraph, and two new poems were added: a brief 'Dedication' which functioned in lieu of an author's note, and 'Statement', a sestina whose opening line gave the volume its title.

The psychic dimensions of the vignettes of Canterbury's political and social history – from pilgrim dream to shrunken aspirations in the present – have been underemphasised in discussions of *Not in Narrow Seas*. The poems are in fact less directly concerned with the political and social manifestations of colonialism than with the internalised psychic conflicts – feelings, obsessions, frustrations, repressions and compensations – which sustain and reinforce the outward structures of colonial society. It is this approach to the social malaise of New Zealand in the 1930s (strongly apparent in the earliest of his 'social' poems, like 'Doom at Sunrise') which distinguished Curnow most clearly from other New Zealand thirties poets, and linked his poetry most closely to that of C. Day Lewis and Auden among the English poets of that decade. Fairburn touched on the theme occasionally, but even in *Dominion* his main concern is the characterisation of New Zealand's social and political and economic hegemonies and the debating of ideological issues, whereas Curnow's concern in *Not in Narrow Seas* is what might be called the 'psychic constitution' of colonial society.

The challenge Curnow set himself was ambitious and difficult, and it accounts for the sense of 'strain' which reviewers often detected in the verse, especially (though they were rarely specific about this) in the imagery. It was central to Curnow's understanding of colonialism that the generational shift – from the migrant dream of a new start to a mimic British society – was a result of profound shock in the new environment, and the mimicry was an outward expression of deeply repressed fear, anxiety and frustration. For Curnow such repression was most manifest in what had become most conventional in the behaviour of New Zealanders: in the obsessive drive for material acquisitions, in the obsession with sporting achievement, in the docile acceptance of nine-to-five work routines, and in the humourless hostility to anyone who rejected such norms. Curnow's imagery often works in an oxymoronic way to insist on such repressions: acts as simple as walking to or from work ('Doom at Sunrise') or driving a motor car are linked to fear and nightmare; iron, tarseal and concrete (the literal building blocks of the new society) are seen as hiding what is repressed; and what is repressed is symbolised in the threatening elemental forces of wind, ice, and the surrounding immensity of the oceans, a symbolism deeply rooted in the landscape and climate.

Responding later in life to a question from a school student who asked what Curnow meant by dedicating the poems to the reader 'who can distinguish / In an unfeigned anguish / What is general / From what is personal; / Who has heard optimism / Crash in the last chasm / And knows hope more near / The straining heart's despair', Curnow commented:

> I think I had to insist that the poem wasn't shamming, also that it mustn't be taken for a private ('personal') cry of distress, because it rose out of 'what is general'. In those few years between the Great Depression and World War 2, there was any amount of facile optimism – almost up to the outbreak of the war, any number of people who thought Hitler wasn't such a bad guy – and in a world like that it was hard to feel optimistic about this country, or patient with claptrap about its colonial past. A poet of the 'thirties couldn't escape conditioning by the times. . . . Everything happened in a very few years, didn't it? These days . . . I imagine one's optimisms can only be more personal, and short-term . . . moderated by the thought that, well, almost anything can happen, and probably will, and the only thing certain about it is that we shall not know why because we shall not be told.[34]

Perhaps the greatest strength of *Not in Narrow Seas* was the vivid directness and economy of utterance which Curnow achieved in many of the poems, as if fulfilling Pound's dicta to use 'no superfluous word, no adjective which does not reveal something', to 'go in fear of abstractions',[35] and to remember that good poetry must have the virtues of good prose: whether ironic prose, angry prose, eloquent prose or factual prose. It was perhaps no coincidence that in the poems' earlier life in *Tomorrow* the identities of Julian and Allen Curnow were blurred. In the final version it might be said that Curnow had found a way of absorbing Julian into a poetic self that was now more complex and subtle, able to accommodate descriptive, lyrical and satirical impulses, varieties of feeling and mood, within the same utterance. In *Not in Narrow Seas* what would always be henceforth recognisable as a distinctive Curnow voice, with its shifting, multiple registers, made its first appearance.

The year 1938 began and ended with a holiday. Because of Betty's approaching confinement Curnow arranged to take his annual holiday earlier than usual, in the weeks leading up to Christmas. 'The birth of an heir to the Curnow neuroses', he wrote to Fairburn,[36] was expected in February. A tramping and camping holiday, of the sort they had had at the start of the year in Nelson, was out of the question, and they arranged to rent a bach from 6 December at the holiday colony at Stewart's Gully, on the Waimakariri River just north of Christchurch. The place was also quite close to the vicarage at Kaiapoi where Tremayne and Jessie were now based. The holiday was largely uneventful, except for a strong nor'-wester. They visited the vicarage often, walked, were taken for drives in the family car as far as the Ashley River, and both Betty and Curnow tried their hands at painting local landscape scenes. Curnow's efforts don't seem to have prompted him, ever, to continue.

Chapter Eight

A Changing Christchurch, Dearth of Poems, and Whim Wham, 1939–40

I now enjoy a sort of nightmare local notoriety as a writer of funny verse: seem to have inherited the family curse of triviality in serious matters & great profundity in the trivial.[1]

Birth of Wystan, 1939

Wystan Tremayne Le Cren Curnow was born on 13 February 1939. The birth was difficult and Betty suffered severely from septicaemia, which kept her hospitalised for several weeks, during which time her mother and father stayed at the Curnows' home in Riccarton in order to assist the new parents. A Karitane nurse was then employed part-time for six weeks, and after that a live-in home help, Pearl Wardell, from May to September, when they could no longer afford the expense. Rita Angus stayed with the Curnows for about six weeks from December, and became an especially close friend, assisting Betty in the house and doing sketches in exchange for meals and accommodation. It was during this time she sketched Betty and began the first of two portraits of her.[2]

The extra help around the home meant that both Curnow and Betty could continue their involvement in Christchurch's intellectual and cultural life. Betty became a member of the progressive Women Today movement, and Curnow became more actively involved in the theatre scene. He took part in a reading

of *Power and Glory* (1937), an attack on political corruption by the Czech playwright Karel Čapec,[3] and his interest in writing for the stage seems to have
emerged at this time. The Curnows' cultural and intellectual interests involved
a number of different groups, whose members overlapped in different ways. The
Simmances' radical theatre activities were part of a left-wing movement associated with Winston Rhodes, connected to *Tomorrow* and the Left Book Club
whose Christchurch branch Rhodes had founded in 1937. There was a circle of
like-minded journalists which included Walter Brookes, Jim Caffin and others;
the Caxton Press circle which, in addition to Glover, included Leo Bensemann,
John Drew and Albion Wright; and the loose association of artists, including the
sculptor Francis Shurrock and painters like Rita Angus. Their lives would intersect
at each other's houses, at pubs and parties, at university events and public lectures,
at plays and concerts and exhibitions, and on winter ice-skating expeditions to
Lake Coleridge.

In 1939 this lively, moderately bohemian Christchurch intellectual and artistic
scene had been augmented by the arrival of numerous highly talented refugees
from Hitler's Europe, most notably Paul and Otti Binswanger, and Harry and
Margaret Lenk. The Lenks were refugees from Austria. Paul Binswanger was a
German Jew who had been lecturing in philosophy at the University of Florence;
Otti was of Anglo-German parentage (though one of her grandmothers had
been a New Zealander), and ran physical culture classes in Christchurch, which
Betty, Rita Angus and others regularly attended. Their presence, with others who
arrived throughout the 1940s, gave a distinctly cosmopolitan character to the
cultural scene in Christchurch.

Curnow's work as a journalist on *The Press* was helpful for all of these groups,
since he often wrote feature stories which publicised their work and activities,
and he ensured that overseas visitors were well reported and introduced into
Christchurch's intellectual and artistic circles. He saw such figures as providing the much-needed stimulus of new ideas – about the arts, politics and world
affairs – in the parochial local scene. In 1939, for example, he wrote key feature
articles on the refugees arriving in Christchurch and the work of the local
Refugee Committee, and on Tony McGillick, an Australian communist who
had spent time in the Soviet Union and whose lectures drew large audiences
in Christchurch and elsewhere. His interest in the remarkable life and work of
Rewi Alley in China also began at this time, when he interviewed Alley's mother
in Christchurch for a powerful, hard-hitting feature article in *The Press*. Drawing
on Alley's letters, Curnow vividly described the country's struggle for independence against the Japanese occupation through the organisation of industrial
co-operatives in the inland territories, and emphasised its need for economic
support from countries like New Zealand.

Not in Narrow Seas: Poems with Prose appeared in March 1939 in an edition of 120 copies, with a fine frontispiece by Leo Bensemann depicting a stern, square-jowled minister of religion standing behind a tattooed Maori male and holding a British flag across his face. Neither this image, nor sentiments like those expressed in 'The bishop boundary-rides his diocese', were likely to appeal to Tremayne, but he did not in any case read the book, having been put off – he wrote sarcastically to Alexander – by the snippets of it quoted in 'a little review in a corner of the "Press" Literary Page' which 'hails him as a Prophet':

> Judging by the gems quoted therefrom, the book seems to be the usual petulant diatribe against things & people who don't agree with him. He sees these things are all wrong & says so, – voila tout! . . . I wish he would get out of that way of writing – because it only represents a sort of surface-absorption of influences from Glover, R.A.K. Beaglehole [sic] & Co, & marks a decline from 'Valley of Decision'. I must admit that the damnable self-righteousness of these young satirists gives me a pain in the neck. Honestly, I prefer Gloria Rawlinson's 'Perfume Vendor' – immature as it is![4]

Curnow was himself surprised and delighted that the unsigned review had been written by J.C. Beaglehole, who praised his choice of 'the sure word, the right rhythm, and the revealing image' and described him as 'no weeping elegist, but a truth-teller, whose confidence in the power of the human spirit is his sole, great encouragement'.[5] This was praise, indeed, from an eminent historian, of a volume in which Curnow had for the first time ventured into history as a poetic subject.

Not in Narrow Seas was also reviewed enthusiastically in *Tomorrow* by F.G. [Frank Gadd], who described the poem as 'a lament that hopes have been unfulfilled: a lament that the ones who hoped were without vision; that they sought improvement by the elimination of minor evils and knew not how to create anew. So that what they built is nothing but a meaningless repetition of the land they sprang from.'[6] Winston Rhodes, however, in a later issue attacked Curnow's poem about van Gogh, taking him to task (as well as Charles Brasch and Fairburn) for emphasising, as he saw it, the exile and isolation of the artist in New Zealand, when the ills complained of were in fact a worldwide (capitalist) phenomenon:

> We are all exiles if you like, but it is the artistic exile who first loses his roots. . . . What I miss in the artistic exile is that fierce love of one's own native land, not the weak emotion that leads to flag-flapping and tourist hotels, but the deep indescribable affection which can no more be explained than it can be explained away. The moans of the exiles do not express this.[7]

Curnow did not respond to Rhodes's criticism, as he had done on occasion in the past. No doubt, he was buoyed by Eric Gill's response to the volume, a little later:

> I think it is first class and of course I agree entirely, completely and absolutely (etc) with the sentiments expressed, and I like their expression too. I cannot imagine that the book will be popular, but I hope you will go on writing. . . . I am handing the book round to various people.[8]

It was to be the last letter Curnow received from Gill, or the last that has survived. In response to a Christmas letter from Curnow in 1940, to which he attached Glover's recently published *Specimen Book of Printing Types*, Mrs Gill replied with news of her husband's recent death.

A dearth of poems, 1938–40

Most of the poems in *Not in Narrow Seas* had been written by mid-1937, and Curnow's next published volume did not appear until early in 1941, when he contributed nine poems to a four-handed Caxton Press anthology (with Fairburn, Glover and Mason) entitled *Recent Poems*, reprinting five of these a month later (March) in a collection of his own, *Island and Time*. With only one or two exceptions these later poems were written in a burst of activity that began during the second half of 1940, as he announced in August of that year to Lilburn, recently returned from London: 'In the last few weeks I've begun to break a long silence with some new work that is not without merit.'[9] In effect, for a period of nearly three years – mid-1937 until mid-1940 – he wrote very few poems that he regarded as publishable.

The suppression of *Tomorrow* in May 1940, under draconian censorship regulations introduced by the Labour government after the outbreak of war in September 1939, closed the only regular publishing venue that might have been possible. In any case Curnow had ceased contributing to it later in 1938, increasingly impatient – like Glover and others – with its shift of focus from broadly cultural issues to more narrowly political and economic ones. The only other places in which Curnow might have placed new poems were the ongoing quarterly *Art in New Zealand* and the annual *New Zealand Best Poems*, but they were hardly venues in which he would have wished to appear, even if he had been asked. The vacuum in poetry magazines was not filled until March 1941 (the month in which *Island and Time* appeared), when Glover launched a new literary magazine, *Book*, initially as a bi-monthly, from the Caxton Press. In any case, Curnow himself commented in retrospect,[10] in 1939–40 'the slow business of gathering credits by periodical publication would not have appealed much', even if there had been venues in which to place them: 'from the beginning I always thought first of a *book*, however small'. Glover's presence, with the Caxton Press, was thus always far more important for him than magazines.

The absence of periodical venues was not the main reason for the relatively small number of new poems published between 1937 and 1941, and nor was the fact that the business of earning a living consumed so much of his time. His career is full of gaps – often quite long ones like that between mid-1937 and 1941 – in which he published few or no new poems. Although he often came to be presented as a 'public' poet who could turn on poems at will, Curnow was never in control of the creative process, could never predict when a poem might 'announce' itself as completed, and was never entirely confident that his instinct about a poem's completion was right. He did not subscribe at all to the notion that poems were pure inspiration, and a gap in publication never meant that he stopped writing poems. There are numerous drafts of poems written in the two years or so after his shift to Riccarton in August 1938 – drafts which he never kept, but which Betty often rescued from the wastepaper bin each morning,[11] after he had worked at them on his return from work late at night. Some of these are quite substantial (involving the construction of sequences of poems), and some of them seem as finished as poems already published, but none of them reached a point of completion which satisfied Curnow himself.

He seems to have been guided, always, by two principles of composition. One was to keep writing poems, to keep working at them: the good poem would not write itself, even if its occasion was unpredictable. There is a special resonance, given Curnow's religious background, in the notion that an 'act of faith' is involved, the belief that good poems would eventuate, if one 'created the conditions' – patience and persistence – in which they might occur. Furthermore, the occasions were always inward. Particular events, observations, memories, dreams, from among the daily welter of such phenomena, persisted in the poet's 'unconscious', seeming to 'demand' or offering the possibility of a poem – and the process of exploration that the act of composition involved was correspondingly inward whether it resulted in a finished poem or not.

The second principle was perhaps more under the poet's control, since it involved, at least in part, critical, editorial judgements about what emerged during the process of composition. Poems needed to be 'new', not simply repeat what he had done before, or what others had done. One could not achieve this simply by changing the subject matter of poems (this could of course be controlled, but such a procedure, from Curnow's point of view, invariably cut the poetry off from its sources in the unconscious). In fact it could not be achieved by *any* kind of deliberate 'seeking', which was likely to produce superficial and meretricious novelty, a mere illusion of the new. 'Newness', in Curnow's understanding of it, involved a fundamental shift or reorientation in the way the world was perceived, as much a result of strenuous processes of reflection over time, as of sudden illumination. It also had a great deal to do with issues of style, form and language – the medium itself. Many of Curnow's working drafts reveal continual shifts in the form and shape of the poems – trying out different stanza sizes and rhyme arrangements, different line lengths, different orderings of the material, and these shifts would also generate new words and phrases and ideas. On occasion he would also try out different modes of utterance – first person presentation, dramatisation of the material in different voices, the introduction of choric voices, sequenced or counterpointed blocks of material. In later life Curnow almost invariably spoke of poems he thought of as 'complete', as poems which seemed to satisfy formally the obscure, nagging pressures from within which prompted the initial idea of starting them.

These principles lie at the core of Curnow's modernism, the quality of sensibility which most links his practice to that of Yeats, Eliot, Ezra Pound and others. The question Curnow's 'instinct' always needed to answer, as he worked patiently or impatiently on drafts of poems, was whether to jettison them, or to keep working on them. 'Completion' then came as a moment of triumph, exhilaration and exhaustion – followed by anxiety, once the poems were out in the world, or about to go out into the world, as to whether his instinct was right. The process also meant that fragments of discarded drafts – words, phrases, lines, images, ideas – often found their way, unconsciously, into other 'completed' poems whose locations and themes are ostensibly entirely different from their earlier contexts.

A number of the unpublished poems which Curnow wrote in 1939 indicate that the shift from Gloucester Street in the centre of the city to suburban Riccarton sparked his interest in the borough's local history. Much of Riccarton – its suburban streets and houses (including his own), and its recreation reserves like Hagley Park and Deans Bush (named after the original settlers, William and John Deans) – was built on what had once been a vast forest swamp. In one fragment he places himself within the lineage of such colonisers and settlers of the swamp; in another, entitled 'New Forest, Christchurch, New Zealand', he addresses a lone, surviving cabbage palm; and another, 'Park Lake', evokes the artificially constructed, 'park-coddled' lake in Hagley Park (Lake Victoria, built on drained swampland) as the poet cycles home from work at midnight.

These and other poems are often numbered into various forms of a sequence, suggesting an effort to continue the method of *Not in Narrow Seas*, but focusing less on the larger historical aspects of the founding of Canterbury Province than on the small-scale work of suburbanisation. In one poem he meditates on the tiny 10 acres of original kahikatea floodplain forest preserved as Deans Bush, surrounded by an 'exotic shelter belt' and 'misshapen oaks', which is 'Not too deep but that the cynical wink of / Streetlamp may signal through' and 'Not too wide / But that a shout is clear from side to side. And the by-laws at the gate.' What is particularly interesting in this poem, however, is its anticipation of an important theme of Curnow's late poetry – the notion that the failure and destructive cost of settlement is a manifestation of a failure of language, a failure to read the 'other' language of the swamp forest trees which, except for the mocking remnant of Deans Bush, were felled and destroyed wholesale. Put simply, that other language might simply have been the instruction: Keep Out, Do Not Disturb. The poem remarkably foreshadows the sense of the resistant 'otherness' of the natural world in a later volume like *Trees, Effigies, Moving Objects* (1972), its capacity to 'look back harder' at its observer and potential destroyer:

> Botanist, visitor,
> Resident of this borough, what do you say of
> This forest, bush, grove, reserve, assemblage,
> Kahikatea swamp-forest unique upon earth?
> This other Arden, un-secret Weald? I put it
> Fairly to you. Answer. You have no language,
> Or your language that should have grown like trees
> You felled like trees, sawed in your practical mills
> That made you easy lengths. 'Every effort is now being
> Made to preserve the bush as nearly as possible
> In its original condition'. Cleared, stumped, and
> Drained is your condition. You grow no trees.
> Dry lianes like bell-pulls in derelict homesteads
> Swing rope over beam in your equivocal scene.
> Construction-demolition, regeneration-decay:
> Can you credit actual doubt, a literal
> Nothing to say?

Such a poem also attempts a more flexible language closer to dramatic prose – unlike anything Curnow had written up to this time – and the same is true of a poem in which he imagines an early whaler's first, more distant but vividly realised view of the flat swampy plain stretching westwards from the vantage point of the Port Hills above Lyttelton Harbour:

> What the whaler saw from the hill
> In the middle distance at the far edge of the swamp, a blur, a cloud of foliage, 'An
> Assemblage of trees, plants and shrubs, of a special character.'

Three streams cross-hatched with rushes mazily draining
Smooth valleys, veining the grey slag over-clayed,
Streams relaxed, describing whorls on the flats
Between hills and sea. Looking, he was aware
Of the trenched sea behind, of where he came from
With that outward-looking habit. That was the easier
Attitude. After the first settler's children
Came, it was supposed, simply by calling it home,
That place looked at became place looked from.

It is a pity that these and other poems did not find their way into print, but it is likely that he saw them, quite simply, as insufficiently original to justify publication, too similar to the kind of poetry he had written in *Not in Narrow Seas*. Furthermore, from the time of his camping trip with Betty early in 1938 to the north of the South Island Curnow had begun to see a great deal more, at first hand, of the wider South Island landscape, visiting North Canterbury, revisiting his childhood environment at Sheffield, and travelling to Lake Coleridge. For his summer holiday in January 1940 he made a trip across the Southern Alps to the West Coast. He and Betty travelled by train to Hokitika (Curnow turned the difficulty he had in booking railway tickets into a comic sketch for *The Press* after his return, 'The Wheels Go Round'),[12] then tramped, bushwalked and hitchhiked from Ross to the Franz Josef Glacier and back, often riding in the cabs of large timber trucks. In the middle of this West Coast tour they stayed for almost a week with the Rev. Keith Harper (Curnow's friend from his St John's College days), who was now vicar at Harihari, and his wife Betty.

The new poems Curnow began to write in the middle of 1940 drew on these much broader experiences of landscape, outside Christchurch and its immediate environs. Occasionally they name the locations which prompted them: 'Country School, North Canterbury', 'House and Land' (Waiau in North Canterbury), 'Lake Mapourika' (on the West Coast), 'Crash at Leithfield'. Even where places are not identified – as in 'The Scene', or 'Time' or 'Wild Iron' – the sense of specific location in rural hinterland or coastal areas of the South Island is much stronger than in anything he had published earlier.

Even more importantly, world events began to displace the local emphasis on colonialism and British imperialism in Curnow's poetry of the later 1930s. It would be hard to underestimate the effect of the onset of the Second World War as a global phenomenon on his poetry, but it took the best part of a year for the trauma and continuing horrors of the war – and the shifts in his thinking which these generated – to begin to manifest themselves in his writing. Whatever fragile allegiance he had had to Marxist thought was finally abandoned, replaced by a renewed interest in metaphysics and in the poverty of scientific positivism, which seemed incapable of imagining, let alone intervening in, the new technologies of destruction its discoveries had made possible.

He began to read the philosopher Henri Bergson. Auden and C. Day Lewis – in fact, all of the English thirties generation except Louis MacNeice – were displaced by the urgencies and prophetic intensities he now began to see in the later work of W.B. Yeats. Eliot remained an important figure for him (especially *The Waste Land*), and the later poems – as the *Four Quartets* began to appear – exercised even greater, if always qualified, fascination. (Ezra Pound, detestably compromised with fascism, he ceased reading for the best part of two decades.) These new intellectual and poetic allegiances did not suddenly occur, and their effects on his thinking, and on the way the New Zealand scene and its people might be imagined – that is, the process by which they became internal urgencies seeming to demand poems – also took time. In the meantime, Whim Wham had become a regular fixture.

Whim Wham, 1939–40

In his letter to Lilburn after Lilburn's return from London, Curnow described the sudden burst of writing which began in mid-1940 as resulting 'mainly through tension caused by writing a weekly verse lampoon for the Press':

> I now enjoy a sort of nightmare local notoriety as a writer of funny verse: seem to have inherited the family curse of triviality in serious matters & great profundity in the trivial. Perhaps I shouldn't blame my ancestry – it's a very common Anglican trait.[13]

This is the first occasion on which Curnow himself broached the notion that the 'tension' between writing verse as Whim Wham and writing serious poetry might have created a productive dynamic for his poetry, not simply a distraction, despite his self-deprecating comments to Lilburn. Though it is tempting to describe the conditions under which Whim Wham pieces had to be produced each week as the polar opposite of the processes by which his serious poetry was written, that was never precisely the case. Of course, the topics had to be deliberately chosen each week, and were constrained by what had occurred in the previous week's news, and because of the weekly deadline he had little or no time for the kind of patient waiting on the poem to declare itself 'completed'. The 'tension' had much more to do with the fact that the composition process, in the case of Whim Wham, was speeded up, because of the time constraint: editing decisions during the process of composition had to be made much more quickly, as did decisions about the appropriateness of the stanza forms and rhyme schemes, about seriousness or lightness of tone, about the scope of literary allusion and parody in particular pieces. He deployed a huge variety of these, drawing widely on the great satirists of the English tradition (Pope and Byron especially), on well-known poems and passages from the English tradition which he knew most of his readers would be familiar with (Shakespeare, Wordsworth, Gray, Tennyson), as well as on nursery rhymes, on popular songs and ballads, and on the nonsense verse of Lewis Carroll and Edward Lear.

Once it became clear that there was a large popular readership for Whim Wham, as happened in 1939 and 1940 – the first years in which Whim Wham appeared weekly for the whole time – Curnow began to take them very seriously, and needed to find at least half a day each week to produce one. They were never simply 'tossed off'. Although Curnow sometimes gave the impression that they were, that was part of the persona he was creating as Whim Wham – someone who could think quickly and wittily on his feet and ask awkward questions. He constantly identified himself, in the verse, as an ordinary Kiwi who did all the ordinary things that Kiwis do – including possessing the do-it-yourself skill of being able to improvise verse at the drop of a hat. It was similar to the mask Byron created as the author of *Don Juan*. In Curnow's case, Whim Wham offered an idealised image of the average Kiwi – someone interested in local and world affairs, intelligent, literate and quick on the uptake. Many readers were quick to identify with it, whatever the mix of fantasy and truth such an image might have contained. It gave the lie to the notion that all New Zealanders were apathetic, materialistic and smug. It put question marks around any habit of generalising about New Zealanders with negative stereotypes, even though many aspects of New Zealand life were subject to satirical scrutiny.

Whim Wham cannot be wholly identified with the personality of Curnow. However, he was an important part of it, and the discovery that he could enjoy such a role and perform it successfully was also a significant moment of self-discovery for him. It was often his habit to complain about the demands Whim Wham made, to refer to it as a chore – on one occasion as an incubus which he would have to strangle before it strangled him.[14] But he enjoyed sending copies of pieces he regarded highly to friends who in later years were outside the orbit of *The Press* or the *New Zealand Herald* – like Glover and Lilburn in Wellington and Charles Brasch in Dunedin – and was pleased when the more controversial ones attracted debate in the correspondence columns.

Curnow never kept any drafts of his Whim Wham pieces, but one has survived by chance, from the time of the Vietnam War in the later 1960s. It is in longhand with crossings out, alternative words and phrases and lines, reordering of lines, though some parts of it went straight into the published version. This draft is not the poem's final version, though the remaining changes (including finding the title, 'Paying Guests') might have been made in the process of producing a final typescript from the longhand draft. This process clearly replicates the process by which the serious poems were written, though in a much more concentrated, speeded-up mode.

The Whim Wham pieces Curnow wrote in 1939 and 1940 confirmed the pattern of topics established during the second half of 1938. Almost half those written in 1939 were devoted to events in Europe up to and after the declaration of war by Great Britain in September, and of the rest several attacked the scale of wartime restrictions and censorship which were imposed almost immediately in New Zealand, while others were grimly comic reflections on history and the unpredictable future of the planet. In these the shift of preoccupation which occurred in his serious poetry can be traced.

When it was suggested in 1940 (presumably by Glover, and with the support of *The Press*) that a selection should be published Curnow was initially strongly opposed to the idea. However, he eventually went ahead, and advertised in *The Press* for readers who had kept any copies to send them, as he had never kept copies of them. He selected 48 from more than a hundred which had been published up to the end of September 1940, organising the pieces into six themes – A Present for Hitler, Himself, Public Life, Farms & Gardens, Domestic Bliss, and The March of Time – occasionally making small revisions and changing the titles. The Caxton Press published the selection, *A Present for Hitler & Other Verses*, with some of the original illustrated drawings by Josephine Mayo, in November in time for the Christmas market. It was probably the first book Curnow published for which sales were sufficient for him to receive a royalty payment, and two further selections were published in 1942 and 1943.

Chapter Nine

'The Shock of Another War':
Island and Time, 1940–41

These poems are an attempt to place New Zealand imaginatively in the widest possible context of Time and the current of history; but the poems have each their separate occasions springing from the natural scene, the history, and the life of New Zealanders.[1]

Response to the war

Although the creative 'tension' caused by Curnow's work as Whim Wham may have played some small part in the emergence of new poems in mid-1940, the particular event that triggered the shift of thinking which led to them was the outbreak of the Second World War nine months earlier. Even though its prospect had seemed inevitable for several years, and loomed large in Curnow's later 1937–38 pieces as Julian and in his pre-war 1938–39 Whim Wham pieces, its actuality came as a profound shock – the scale of the horrors it brought with it, the indiscriminate mass bombing and uprooting of civilian populations, genocide, and the general descent (on both sides) into lies and propaganda. On 1 September 1939, the day Hitler invaded Poland, he was summoned early into *The Press* to work on the overseas cables and arrived home the following day, exhausted, at 6 a.m.[2] This continued for a week until Chamberlain's inevitable declaration of war, on 8 September. From this time on the pattern of his work on *The Press* changed. It became the norm, when he was cable sub-editing, to finish work at 3 a.m., and as the war dragged on and *The Press* was hit by shortages of staff, he was manpowered onto the newspaper and became the sole overseas cable sub-editor. Norman Macbeth (then a night messenger who later became the paper's editor) recalled Curnow and his colleague 'Torchy' Webb:

> ... going into anxious consultation after the BBC news at 11.00 p.m., which usually meant 'faking' an NZPA cablegram (or at least anticipating a message which would be delivered from the Post Office by the night messenger an hour or two later).[3]

At the outset of the war Curnow became acutely aware of the scale of the contrast between the violence of events in Europe and the bland smugness of life in New Zealand, as if remote from the conflict, cocooned inside its own colonial illusions of safety and security. He was appalled by the speed and severity with which wartime restrictions and censorship were imposed in New Zealand (and as a reporter had to apply the censorship regulations himself in his editing of overseas and local war cables). He was also sympathetic to the pacifist cause, supported by his journalist friend John Drew, the artists Leo Bensemann and Rita Angus, and indeed Glover himself during the early part of the war. An early unpublished poem entitled 'Transmission',[4] written soon after the declaration of war in a style heavily indebted to Auden, bitterly invoked the insignificance and pettiness of New Zealand's internal 'warring', and of such 'smooth-fitting' sacrifices as might be at stake, compared with the magnitude of events in Europe, in which whole nations, like Poland, were sacrificed; and a piece by Whim Wham entitled 'Munich',[5] written in the wake of Hitler's occupation of Czechoslovakia, expressed the same feeling.

By early 1940, however, he had begun to engage much more directly with the implications of the war for New Zealand, and for poetry. In the longest and most important of the feature articles he had written for *The Press* up to this time, entitled 'Prophets of Their Time: Some Modern Poets',[6] he spoke of English poetry of the previous 20 years as 'a brief age already past, gone by, as it were, in a night', and characterised its 'distinctive accent' as prophetic. Citing the work of Eliot, Auden and Day Lewis, Gascoyne, and especially W.B. Yeats – work 'filled with warnings of impending disasters, with bitter indignation against human wrongs' – he drew parallels between their voices and those of Isaiah, Amos and Joel, emphasising that authentic prophecy like theirs was not 'a telescope for looking at the future' but was always 'couched in the terms of its own particular epoch' and grew from an irresistible compulsion to teach and warn about the trajectory of contemporary events.

Although the article praises the prophetic note in the work of the thirties poets, and their efforts to 'restore form as significant in poetry', its main arc is to elevate Yeats above them as 'the master singer . . . living and writing through poetry's seasons of decline, decay and restoration, and finally emerging as the greatest master in his time of beautiful form in verse'. Six months later Curnow repeated this view in a review of Yeats's *Last Poems* (1939) in *The Press*, emphasising that Yeats's poetic career – during the span of which 'ideas and values, both in literature and politics' had changed 'on a scale appropriate to centuries' – was a continuing effort '*not to escape history in flood, but to ride with it and search the horizon*'.[7] The earlier piece also reveals that for Curnow the crisis of the war had prompted a personal crisis of form for his own poetry – undoubtedly one of the reasons for his poetic silence at this time, and for his abandonment of the Riccarton sequence he had been working on:

> Will the ripening classicism of recent years, the restoration of form as significant in poetry, be continued? Or will both the classic form and the prophetic mood be swept away together by the storm of events? Will there be again the anguished incoherence of much poetry which followed the last war, poets torturing themselves with the deliberate denial of form.[8]

In his critique of colonialism in the 1930s Curnow had emphasised the effect of being cut off from time and history: it was as if, in the mental formation of New Zealand-born generations, the clock had stopped in the nineteenth century, producing a fixation on, or marooning in, the cultural values of a British-connected past, while global history in the twentieth century was sweeping the country (and the mother country) in quite different directions. Some of Curnow's most powerful images in his 1930s poems – like that of New Zealand's Depression-affected young as 'children with senile faces' – reflected this sense of the collapse of time, as if the normal processes of psychic growth had been arrested and distorted. With the advent of the Second World War it seemed as though the stopped clock of colonial history had begun, or might begin, ticking again, bringing New Zealand into active relation with the unfolding, unpredictable dynamic of contemporary history, bringing the marooned Island consciousness of the country for the first time into a potentially real relation with Time.

The possibilities for New Zealand of that awakening into Time, into the uncertainties and unpredictabilities of lived history, had little to do with the discovery of national identity, although the poems Curnow wrote at the time often came to be read that way. For Curnow, the war had in fact all but destroyed the value of the idea of the nation-state, as he wrote vehemently to Lilburn:

> Disparities seem obliterated in the general confusion, & the common preoccupation with lies and violence. . . . [Y]ou know how obsessed I am with the problem of the

rooted Dominion-ite vis a vis England. It's still my belief, though the hope is daily more tenuous, that NZ at least may fill some historic mission, i.e. in that it is a people without a nation; that it may be in the forefront of the certain revolution against the nation-idea, the beginnings of which I fancy I see. But I fear my hope is contradicted by the hard facts of local politics. With India, China, & others, we persist in ident-ifying freedom with the most destructive, most enslaving idea in history, the idea of nationality, of which fear is the father and murder the child.

For God's sake, never let them claim you as a 'N.Z.' composer. They are the great enemy, these publicists of 'national' arts & letters. That road begins with the ignorant patronage of newspapers & ends at a Rotary Club dinner.[9]

The direction that Curnow's thinking took at this time was not inwards, towards nationalism and national identity, but outwards. The sheer magnitude of the horrors of the war revealed a fundamental crisis for the future of the human race, demanding 'some imaginative reconstruction of the very idea of man itself'. That phrase occurs in a remarkable short article Curnow contributed to the first issue of *Book* in March 1941 – remarkable for the intensity of its response to the war, and for its prophetic, Yeatsian sense of the role of poetry in articulating that 'imaginative rehabilitation', now that man is to be measured 'in the half-discovered, half-forgotten dimension of Time'. The piece was originally written as a preface to the new collection of poems he was about to publish, *Island and Time*,[10] but was dropped from that book, perhaps because of its length. It was called, with deliberate understatement, 'A Job for Poetry', and its subtitle, 'Notes on an Impulse', belied the intensity of the self-reflection and self-questioning that had gone into the formation of its key ideas during the previous nine months.[11] They were, in effect, an extrapolation from the new poems he had written since mid-1940, which had been triggered, he wrote to Lilburn, by 'the new faith I have gained in poetry'[12] after 'almost 2 years' of silence.

'[T]he shock of another war', he wrote in the article, had shaken the 1930s poets (including himself) out of 'that tentative period of awakening' in which they discovered 'the inadequacy of their tradition'. '[S]omething analogous to a mutation of the intellect may well be in progress' – so momentous that 'the common categories of reasoning are proved inadequate', and 'we can no longer trust in some rearrangement of now-observable elements to bring us to some clearly desirable end'. Religions had lost 'even compulsive, let alone impulsive, power', and the 'mechanist confidence' of science in progress had been rendered absurd by the general collapse into anarchy. Events had confirmed once and for all that the scientific intellect was 'no substitute for belief', even though 'belief without knowledge is mere superstition':

The inarticulate faith and personal courage of millions may save them individually from the general wreck; but till such faith and courage become formulable in clearly understood terms, there will be no symbols on which a general will-to-live may be founded.

At the end of the article he returned to his opening theme, that poetry held a key to the 'act of faith' by which the 'idea of man' might be reconstructed:

The remaining hope is that the [scientific] intellect, like the religious drive, may become humbled by its vast communal failures. Humbled – I do not mean defeated. And in that self-humbling of the intellect poetry may play a considerable part: for poetry is the reconciling of reason and imagination – it has keys both to the intellectual order and to the real order, to the 'practical' prospect and to real Time.[13]

Time for Bergson

W.B. Yeats was clearly an influential *poetic* voice behind the argument of Curnow's article.*[14] However, the one figure whom Curnow directly named and quoted was the French philosopher Henri Bergson. 'We are faced', he wrote, 'with what Bergson calls "real duration, that duration which gnaws on things and leaves on them the mark of its tooth".'[15]

Bergson's metaphysics of process was the central influence on what might seem abstract and idiosyncratic in the concept of Time which Curnow adumbrated, and Bergson's traces are everywhere apparent in the poems of *Island and Time*. Time-as-duration, one of Bergson's central doctrines, was an experiential category, available only to intuition – not a homogeneous medium which can be divided into discrete linear periods, as in 'clock time' or in the analytical, 'spatialising' procedures of science or of positivist history (as if past, present and future were discrete, analysable and predictable entities on a linear continuum). Duration was 'time at its most timelike',[16] heterogeneous and 'ever-changing without repeating itself',[17] constituting the innermost reality and uniqueness of everything. For Bergson duration, or 'lived time', permeates our way of experiencing the world intuitively, and its importance had been obscured by the power of mechanistic science to control its heterogeneity, in the interest of controlling the environment in which we live. Bergson also argued that duration was not simply random in

---

* 'For some time past', he wrote to Lilburn in August 1940, 'I have neglected (except occasionally) all contemporaries bar Yeats, who looms in my perspective greater & greater as events expose the frailty of so much pre-war poetry.'

its operations: every unique, heterogeneous event carried within it traces of its past (and of the future), the process having an underlying organic unity and order which could be adumbrated only through symbols and images.

It is not difficult to see why Bergson's thinking was so attractive to Curnow, given his sense that war was plunging the globe into a crisis in which the past, as conventionally understood, was no longer relevant, the present uncertain and chaotic, and the future incalculable. In his article 'A Job for Poetry', and in many poems of *Island and Time*, Curnow's use of the notion of 'real Time' – prior to the analytical operations of the intellect – bears the unmistakeable traces of Bergson's notion of duration. In a footnote to 'A Job for Poetry' he described the 'underlying theme of all the poems' in his forthcoming volume as an 'attempt to assign to the New Zealander and the New Zealand scene some place in the larger current of history and Time', and he repeated, even more strongly, this connecting of the local with the global in a notice of the forthcoming volume included in *Recent Poems*:

> These poems are an attempt to place New Zealand imaginatively in the *widest possible context of Time and the current of history*; but the poems have each their separate occasions springing from the natural scene, the history, and the life of New Zealanders.[18]

'Time and the Child' addresses this wider theme directly:

> *Time:*   Island and continent
>   Roll in the sun through the minute and the event;
>   Man, his hour, his marvellous thought descend
>   Through perpetual beginning and perpetual end.
>   Boy, if you can make that teaching known
>   You shall have a house stronger than stone,
>   You shall have the Danube and the Mexique bay
>   And all the secular fury of Europe as well.
> *The Child:*   And what comes after that, Sir?
> *Time:*   Time will tell.

In the often anthologised poem 'Time', Curnow tries to convey the paradoxical doubleness of duration as analysed by Bergson: it has its own, unknowable order but suffuses the randomness of events. Personifying Time, Curnow offers a seemingly random catalogue of the events which it permeates:

> I am recurrent music the children hear
> I am level noises in the remembering ear
> I am the sawmill and the passionate second gear.

Such experiences-in-time, the poem continues, resist 'the measurable world'. The dimension of Time in which they occur is 'more than your conscious carrier', beyond the grasp of intellect, though such shapes as the events have may be conferred on 'the willing memory'. The Beginning and the End – order and shape – are contained within the ongoing process of Time thus conceived, even though they remain shrouded in mystery, unknowable.

'The Scene', one of the most formally complex of the poems in *Island and Time*, richly evokes a series of rural and coastal scenes in the South Island in which settlement and progress express the 'bare will' to subdue the land by measurement, while Time 'protracts forms of failure, instruments of collapse', but the poem ends with something like the Yeatsian 'heroic eloquence' Curnow invoked in his sonnet to Lilburn, 'Music for Words',* [19] imagining 'Man's shape' in the new country 'recast', given the imaginative order of sustaining myth. 'Sestina' expresses the same wish for an imaginative dimension of 'legend' which might flow from a true relationship with Time – Bergson's intuited order of time available only through image and symbol. 'On the wrong side of legend each man gropes / In the never-navigated currents of Time', a condition now shared with a world at war in which 'every sea has become a strange sea'. And in 'Dialogue of Island and Time' Curnow confronts the current public claptrap of nationality, much of it generated by the 1940 centennial celebrations.

If Bergson provided Curnow with his Time symbolism, the symbolic and metaphysical dimensions of the Island, in *Island and Time*, were very much his own.† [20] The Island, as Curnow used the symbol in *Island and Time*, carried a number of meanings – one of them being the 'island condition', which was precisely the opposite of the imagined communal/national entity that might be called a 'country' or a 'nation-state' and named 'New Zealand'.

The Island, for Curnow, also symbolised the condition of being outside time and history – the image of being 'marooned' or stranded recurs in the volume – while the immensities of surrounding oceans both separate and at the same time offer tantalising opportunities for reconnection with Time and History. The violent polar winds which sweep and envelop the Island, threatening its flimsy buildings and disturbing the dreams of its marooned inhabitants, carry something of the destructive and (potentially) creative social, political and psychic

---

* Written after learning that Lilburn's 'Prodigal Country' – a choral composition which set to music words from Robin Hyde's 'Journey from New Zealand', Whitman's 'Song of Myself' and Curnow's own 'New Zealand City' – had come first in its section in the Centennial Music Festival Composition competition, and enclosed in a letter from 1940.

† One literal-minded reviewer of the volume at the time, assuming that by 'Island' Curnow simply meant 'New Zealand', complained about Curnow's geographical ignorance, since New Zealand consisted of more than one island: '[T]he title would have us believe that we are situated on just one island. Or does Mr Curnow, who lives in Christchurch, suggest that the North Island doesn't matter?'

force of Shelley's West Wind, the violent sirocco that sweeps the Mediterranean Sea every autumn. Curnow's epigraph to *Island and Time*, taken from a passage in D'Arcy Cresswell's *Present Without Leave* which bore closely on the symbolism he was developing in his own volume, describes the 'violent sirocco' that results from the country's geographic and geological formation, while at the same time characterising the inhabitants as '[a]s yet [having] no future of their own'.[21]

The Island also symbolises – throughout the volume – that-which-is-to-be-discovered, new-knowledge-towards-which-one-voyages, if one is not to remain continent-bound, locked in the past. The Island, from this perspective, is a condition (or potential) of all humanity: 'all earth one island', he was to write in his next volume, adding 'and all our travel circumnavigation'.[22] The 'current of history' to which New Zealand might become related, in *Island and Time*, thus had a double aspect, in a world plunged into unprecedented crisis, repeating its own history of violence. The world itself needed to recover, or discover, an Island consciousness – in every sense in which Curnow developed the symbol – in order to understand its own crises of human and social identity. The reader imagined by the poet of *Island and Time*, from this perspective, was not simply a 'New Zealander' but a global citizen, needing to become the focus of 'some imaginative reconstruction of the very idea of man itself' if the planet were to survive.

Curnow pursued these philosophical speculations directly in numerous of the poems of *Island and Time* ('The Dance', 'Time', 'Time and the Child', 'Sestina', 'Second Song', 'Dialogue of Island and Time', and others), but in the better-known poems they are absorbed into the focus on particular scenes and events. The Bergsonian notion of time, for example, informs the two best-known of the poems, 'House and Land' and 'The Unhistoric Story', without being explicitly evoked. 'House and Land' offers a series of dramatic cameos of three 'types' of New Zealander who are alienated and marooned in different periods of clock time. Miss Wilson, the sole survivor of a once prosperous South Island sheep station, lives out a fantasy of aristocratic connection from her Anglo-colonial past, a cowman drifts purposelessly through life without any consciousness of time at all ('I just live here, he said'), and a positivist historian is obsessed with recovering facts in the belief that they can be neatly packaged into generalisations. What is tragically absent in the lives of these homeless 'souls' whose behaviour traces repetitive rituals, and what informs the Bergsonian perspective of the poem, is a sense of time and history as ongoing and dynamic. Because they are locked out of such 'real Time', they are deprived of the imaginative (and practical) possibilities and uncertainties of engaging with life as a 'present adventure'.

'The Unhistoric Story' offers a series of five vivid, stanza-length historical snapshots of key events in the discovery and settlement of New Zealand. All of them are presented as motivated by what Curnow a little later called our 'rational violence', the desire to exploit, measure and control, and all of them lead to unpredicted violent outcomes. Behind the unending, repetitive cycle of such failures, a choric voice articulates the Bergsonian notion of duration ('It was something different, something / Nobody counted on') in which events are always unpredictable, in which Time always subverts the hubristic 'mechanist confidence' in a future which can be planned and controlled. In the final stanza the deconstruction of triumphalist readings of New Zealand history is extended to take in all of human history – including humanity's dreams of island paradises like the fabled Atlantis, now sunken under the sea:

> After all re-ordering of old elements
> Time trips up all but the humblest of heart
> Stumbling after the fire, not in the smoke of events;
> For many are called, but many are left at the start,
>> And whatever islands may be
>> Under or over the sea,
>> It is something different, something
>> Nobody counted on.

How does one escape the unending cycle of violence bred of the desire to control events? In this final stanza of 'The Unhistoric Story', as in the final paragraph of his article 'A Job for Poetry', Curnow offers an escape route, not especially convincing, in the notion of the 'self-humbling of the intellect' in recognition of 'its vast communal failures'. 'Humbled', he adds, '– I do not mean defeated.'[23] Quite what the balance is between humility and defeat is unclear, and it points to a central difficulty Curnow had in articulating an ethical dimension in Bergson's philosophy of duration.

It is hard to escape the conclusion that Curnow brought a religious ethical impulse – never entirely abandoned – to Bergson's idealism at such moments. His phrase, in 'The Unhistoric Story', to describe those who might escape the cycle of violence draws on Christ's Sermon on the Mount. The 'humblest of heart' are a special few – since, ironically, 'many are called, but many are left at the start' – who stumble 'after the fire, not in the smoke of events'. Their imaginative acts of remembering, uncertain and faltering as they must be, are more 'faithful' (the ambiguity of this word – suggesting both *truer* to the record as well as expressing *faith* in the values of a record which includes loss and failure – was retained at the conclusion of 'Landfall in Unknown Seas'), since they include recognition of the violence of triumphalism – political, intellectual, scientific – and of its victims, the many who are 'left at the start'.

Such religious and biblical allusions recur throughout *Island and Time* to convey the poems' resolutions of the conflicts they deal with. Time, as the principle of order in duration, describes itself as 'the Beginning and the End', the Alpha and Omega of the God of the Old Testament. 'Pity and love', not 'plundering, possession of the land', are the resolving (or potentially resolving) terms in 'Dialogue of Island and Time'. The symbolism with which Curnow concludes 'The Scene', to indicate the sustaining imaginative possibilities of myth, is derived from the Old Testament Pillar of Fire, by which God led Moses to the Promised Land. In 'The Victim', Jan Tyssen, one of Abel Tasman's crew killed in the clash with Maori at Murderers' Bay in 1642, presents himself in Christian terms (as Curnow mentioned in a headnote to the poem) 'as a ritual sacrifice reconciling the unborn with Time'.*

The issues raised in such poems remained central in all of Curnow's poetry from this point on. Indeed his sense of the flux of events and phenomena (of duration in the Bergsonian sense) as heterogeneous, random, anarchic, intensified in the later poems. However, as he became more sceptical, resolving gestures towards some kind of transcendent order (ethical, religious or philosophical) ceased to be available to him, or at least became more difficult, though he continued to search for them. In the end, it might be said, he found no answers, and came to believe that there *were* no answers.

The new formal range of *Island and Time*

In the cover flap note which he wrote to *Island and Time* Curnow insisted on the differences between the new poems and those of his previous volume, *Not in Narrow Seas*. The need now, he wrote, was for 'legend rather than "realism"'. Although the 'time-images' represented no metaphysical system, as such, they gave 'a humanity & a tragic sense wanting in his earlier work'. He also emphasised an increase in the 'technical range' of the verse, in his search for 'a variety of forms and images to sustain the imagination in its thrust across the Pacific and through Time'. Writing to Lilburn in September the previous year, during the excitement of their composition, he emphasised the lyrical element in this new technical range – 'they have, I think, more of a singing quality than anything earlier'[24] – and promised to send him copies. By early December he had not done so, writing from Leithfield Beach, where he was holidaying, that

---

* Curnow removed this reference from the headnote, and changed the title to 'A Victim', in later selections of his poems, while retaining his acknowledgement to J.C. Beaglehole's *The Discovery of New Zealand* (1930) for the narrative detail of the poem. The effect of the revisions was to make the religious resonances of the poem less specifically Christian.

the poems were 'still at the stage when I must keep them by me in clear form – vital emendations keep on occurring, usually in the bath, at table, or at stool, being my only moments of real relaxation'.[25] However, by the end of December he had a 'collection of manuscript poems' – the core of the poems which made up *Island and Time* – ready to send.[26]

If it is true that Curnow's time-images in *Island and Time* 'represent no meta-physical system', there is certainly a distinction to be made between those poems which are more abstract and philosophical in their focus and those (like 'House and Land' and 'Country School, North Canterbury') which deal with specifically observed and imagined events and scenes. In fact one of Curnow's aims, in the organisation of the volume, seems to have been to intersperse the more abstract poems among the more concrete ones, as well as to suggest a loose structure of past, present and future. The volume begins, for example, with 'The Unhistoric Story' and ends with the grim future-oriented speculations of 'Dialogue of Island and Time' and 'No Second Coming'. For most readers at the time (and since) the most successful poems were those sparked by specific, often quite idiosyncratic, observations and events.

Three of these more localised poems occurred late in the piece, during and after a fortnight's summer holiday in December 1940, when he and Betty rented a bach at Leithfield Beach, north of Christchurch.* 'Quick One in Summer' is set in a coastal pub 'slammed by the Pacific-lurching gale' where a 'timeless sea clocks in', though the drinkers at closing time are oblivious to the strange-ness of the dimension – 'where Time and Island cross' – in which they 'lean and laugh'. 'Crash at Leithfield' is an elegy for two pilots pointlessly killed nearby on a training mission, capturing vividly the minutes before the crash in the gusty nor'-wester, the split second in which control is lost to 'the downthrust of Time', the uncanny quietness of the actual crash, and the silence afterwards.[†][27]

The holiday at Leithfield remained memorable particularly for a visit from the Glovers, and Curnow recalled it to Glover in 1943, while Glover was overseas on naval service, after hearing Ian Gordon read 'The Magpies' on radio:

> Of you he read the Quardle=ardle=doodle … poem, which I remember most lovingly on account of the Leithfield holiday: scratching at verses in the evening, with the scraggy topped pines behind & the sea in front of the bach, the harvesting & cooking of pipis, & walking north along the beach towards Amberley.[28]

---

* As well as the poems, Curnow wrote two Whim Wham pieces about Leithfield, 'Change of Air' (*The Press*, 14 Dec. 1940) and 'The Call of the Sea' (*The Press*, 21 Dec. 1940).

† The accident occurred on 11 December 1940, and its details (many of them with an interesting bearing on the poem itself) taken from the Court of Inquiry were written up, together with a reprint of the poem, by Cliff Jenks in the *Journal of the Aviation Historical Society of New Zealand*.

Glover arrived during a wild nor'wester. On the way he had stopped to relieve himself, amidst squawking magpies, and when he arrived at the bach said nothing at all except the words 'quardle oodle ardle wardle doodle'.[29] While he composed his most famous poem (choosing the names 'Tom and Elizabeth' for the small, heavily indebted farmers as an amusing reference to his hosts, whose first names were Thomas and Elizabeth), Curnow was writing 'Wild Iron'. Glover described the results:

> And then when we'd finished, Curnow read his 'Wild Iron' to me and I said, 'My God, Allen, I'm wasting my time trying to scribble verse. This is a brilliant, curious piece of Gothic verse.' And then I said, 'I'll read you mine.' I read that, and he said, 'What? I wish I could have written that.'[30]

'Wild Iron' was a purely impressionistic piece – 'there was some corrugated iron banging about somewhere, though I don't think it was on the bach', Curnow elaborated to Gordon Ogilvie later – and he had not planned to include the poem in *Island and Time*:

> When we were putting together the poems at the Caxton Press for *Island and Time* . . .
> [Glover] said at one stage, 'Where's that "Wild Iron"?'
> 'For God's sake, Denis, not that one,' I said. I hadn't taken this little poem very seriously. It had in some ways taken me by surprise. In fact I'd taken a special dislike to it.
> 'Don't be a bloody fool!' replied Denis. 'In twenty years it will be in every school anthology in the world.' And he was, of course, right. He did have that kind of judgement. And he had the immediate sense of a flaw or an infelicity. It was a quite remarkable intuitive gift.[31]

After many years, during which 'Wild Iron' was reprinted on scores of occasions in New Zealand and international anthologies, set to music, choreographed for dance performance, and (on one occasion) toured Europe in an exhibition of prizewinning entries from a British calligraphy competition, his opinion had not changed, though the poem – all ten lines of it – probably earned him more in royalties than any other single poem he ever wrote.

Few of the 29 new poems in *Recent Poems* and *Island and Time* can be dated with the precision of 'Music for Words' and the three Leithfield poems – other than that most were written between mid-1940 and early 1941. The last was the brief eight-line epigraph 'Sentence', written in early February, which he discussed with the German refugee poet Karl Wolfskehl, during Wolfskehl's first trip to the South Island in February and March 1941.[32] Curnow's own later efforts to date the poems were uncertain and confused, partly because he misremembered the dates of his trips to the West Coast (January 1940, not early 1938) and to Leithfield (December 1940, not 1939).[33]

What the three late Leithfield poems suggested, however, with their more particular focus on individual human beings and scenes, is that Curnow had already begun to move beyond the philosophical abstractions of Island and Time, and beyond the social and political stereotypes populating his 1930s poems. Curnow himself on the dustjacket of the volume had claimed for the poems 'a humanity and a tragic sense wanting in the earlier work'. These qualities were most apparent in the poems which reflected on particular scenes and individuals – Jan Tyssen in 'The Victim', the characters of 'House and Land', the dead airmen of 'Crash at Leithfield', even the idiosyncratic personal fantasy of 'Fantasy on a Hillside' – in which ideas were *implied* through the complexity of metaphors and images rather than explicitly stated. The complex, meditative lyric remained a staple form in his writing from this time on.

Chapter Ten

Pacific Outreach,
the Mid-war Years, 1941–42

*We, if the difference may be put so crudely, more often take our land for a
part of the seascape. The sea, if our poets are true witnesses, is everpresent
in imagination, another and larger republic than the land, now
friendly, now hostile, with which our relations are of first importance.*[1]

The reception of *Island and Time*

Island and Time was reviewed more widely than anything Curnow had written
previously, and was generally well received. J.C. Beaglehole, writing in *The Press*, was
even more impressed than he had been with *Not in Narrow Seas*, commenting that
'[Curnow's] clarity has, on page after page, the power and vehemence of real poetry':

> He does in fact show us the spectacle of a poet and a highly intelligent man approach-
> ing and rendering New Zealand and the history of New Zealand really imaginatively,
> with strength and with pity. Nothing like his 'Unhistoric Story' or 'The Victim' or
> 'Country School' or 'House and Land' has, as far as I know, ever been done here
> before. And it is not perhaps too lavish praise to suggest that as Mr Curnow finds
> himself we may find ourselves.[2]

M.H. Holcroft in the *Southland Times* described the volume as 'a pioneer effort to
bring perspective to a poet's environment', and W.F. Alexander in the Dunedin

Evening Star was impressed, in spite of his dislike of the 'prevailing note' of 'futility', arguing that the 'fine verse and fine description', throughout, were 'worth much more than their mood'.[3]

Island and Time exposed Curnow to an overseas readership for the first time. In August 1941 the English editor and critic John Lehmann reprinted 'The Unhistoric Story' in *Folios of New Writing*,[4] and Curnow was contacted by the prestigious American quarterly *Poetry*, of Chicago, informing him that *Recent Poems* and *Island and Time* (as well as Glover's *Cold Tongue*) were being reviewed in a forthcoming issue, and inviting him to submit any new poems.[5] *Poetry* was receptive to the new work he sent, and included three new poems – 'Discovery', 'In Summer Sheeted Under' and 'Rite of Spring' – in the same issue in which the review appeared in March 1942. In fact of the dozen poems in his next volume, *Sailing or Drowning* (1944), which were first published in magazines, more than half (including the title poem) were first published in *Poetry*.

Poetry and history – J.G.A. (John) Pocock

The poems of *Island and Time* also fascinated an eighteen-year-old student reader, John Pocock, son of the professor of classics at Canterbury University College, who arrived in 1942 at the university, where he began to specialise in history and political theory. Pocock was to become one of New Zealand's most distinguished international historians and political philosophers, a seminal figure in revisionist British historiography in the 1970s and after. On numerous occasions later he would recall his first encounter with Curnow's poetry, as well as the deeply formative influence of Curnow's 1940s work (and that of others like Glover and Brasch) on his thinking about the nature of history. 'There is a stubborn association in my mind', he recalled, 'between reading *Island and Time* and the north quadrangle of the old university buildings after dark':[6]

> What I learned from these poems – and I see everything Curnow wrote in those years as about this – was a poet's way of seeing history, first as the unpredicted –
>
>> It was something different, something
>> Nobody counted on
>
> – and second as that which occurred at a distance, so that we had to understand ourselves as part of it by distancing ourselves from it and bridging the distances which separated/united it and ourselves.[7]

It took some time for him to arrive at this understanding of Curnow's relevance to the practice of a new kind of history. What fascinated Pocock in Curnow's poetry was how 'expressly and decisively it *rejects* history'[8] in poems like 'The Unhistoric Story' and 'House and Land'. Pocock saw poets like Curnow as offering a challenge to historians to begin interpreting imaginatively 'the actual life of the people' in New Zealand. If the metaphysical or spiritual dimensions of that life were the necessary and legitimate province of poets, historians ought to complement that endeavour and in so doing bring 'historian and poet' into a relationship where their different approaches and ends might intersect. Curnow's poetry was never far from the processes by which Pocock continued to think through this early conception of the historian's role.

For Pocock the notion of the 'antipodean condition', where 'landfalls are neither utopias nor destinations, and all travel may end as circumnavigation',[9] was an immensely rich *imagined* construct in Curnow's poetry, richer than anything which might be described as 'nationalist', though it was rooted in the geographical facts of the country's remote oceanic and near-Antarctic island environment. It embodied the collapse of the positivist, Enlightenment conception of the voyage as a progressive, linear act of discovery moving towards some rationally conceived 'final' knowledge of the world, driven by the myth of discovering a final (usually utopian) destination. However, Curnow's dismantling of the construct did not carry anything like the 'futility' and 'gloom' which critics like Alexander read into the poems.[10] Rather, Pocock read their tone as an effort to turn the 'great gloom' of homelessness 'into some kind of joy':

> Curnow's poems were speaking not just of the colonial, but of the historical and even the human condition; we are none of us tangata whenua, but a biological species of voyagers and settlers. The poems taught us the irony and the tragedy, but also the oceanic joy of never being quite at home. And in their implicit capacity to tell us how to look at both sides of the world began an education in history.[11]

Whatever national bearing the poems might have, for Pocock they offered an immensely suggestive way of thinking about a universal (or at least Western) twentieth-century condition. They enabled the idea of history itself to be *re-thought*, in exciting if difficult ways, by substituting for the teleological thinking of the Enlightenment a powerful and dynamic metaphor of voyaging as an act of continual re-tracing, re-enacting, re-connecting across oceanic distances that are no longer thought of as pathways to a perfected future, but carriers for good or ill of the ongoing tides of history past and unpredictably present.

The 'antipodean condition', as Pocock saw it adumbrated in Curnow's poetry, also carried with it an awareness of the collapse of existing myths or (as in Butler's

Erewhon) the displacement of utopia by anti-utopia, and called for the construction of new myths embodying that awareness. 'Here is the world's end where wonders cease', Curnow was shortly to write in his most famous public poem, 'Landfall in Unknown Seas', speaking from the perspective of Abel Tasman's disillusionment at the outcome of his voyaging. Pocock also described the condition colourfully:

> To be at the antipodean point, where the voyage necessarily repeated turns back into itself, is to be on the far side of myth, where the landfalls remain undreamed and may be as horrifying as the statues Butler's traveller saw at the summit of the Whitcombe Pass before he began his descent into anti-utopia.[12]

Mythlessness in Curnow's poetry of the 1940s is not simply a bleak assertion of lack but a challenge to the imagination:

> [Curnow] presented an imagination which could never be fully at home where it was, could never fully return to where it might have come from, and had travelled too far to fly off and live anywhere else. The poems written in the first half of his long life developed this theme – 'Whole-hearted he can't move from where he is, nor love whole-hearted that place'– with a crispness and energy of language that made it clear that his was not an unhappy or impotent condition, but one intensely stimulating to the imagination it challenged.[13]

Re-thinking New Zealand verse, 1941

Although Curnow wrote a number of poems later in 1941 (including the three he sent to *Poetry*, and a sequence of four 'Pacific Sonnets' which later appeared in the fifth issue of *Book* early in 1942), only one new poem was published that year after the publication of *Recent Poems* and *Island and Time*. The new poem, which appeared in the first issue of *Book* in March 1941, was untitled, beginning 'Horizon's hatred smites Magellan, / Parched in Pacific, scurvy-swollen'. It was a historical poem on a similar theme to 'The Victim', written in couplets and experimenting with the Anglo-Saxon alliterative mode, perhaps in an effort to suggest something of the epic scale of the first European Pacific voyagings. But what was new was the broader Pacific perspective it introduced into the poetry, and this provided a distinctive new dimension in many of the poems of his next volume, *Sailing or Drowning*, as well as in his first full-length verse play, *The Axe*, set on the Pacific island of Mangaia, which began its long gestation in 1943. However, Curnow never reprinted the poem, perhaps because by the time he came to put *Sailing or Drowning* together two years later it had come to seem too thin a piece beside the eloquent sonorities of 'Landfall in Unknown Seas'.

Curnow wrote a considered piece on the poetry of R.A.K. Mason in the second issue of *Book* (May 1941). A follow-up on his article 'A Job for Poetry', it was written to mark the appearance from the Caxton Press of *This Dark Will Lighten*, which brought much of Mason's long-out-of-print work before Caxton's readership for the first time. In retrospect this article, along with numerous of Curnow's reviews in *The Press* during the previous year or so – and an article he wrote the following year, 'Aspects of New Zealand Poetry', for *Meanjin Papers* in Australia – can be seen as laying the groundwork for his long-contemplated intervention in critical discourse about New Zealand poetry, his edition of the Caxton *Book of New Zealand Verse*. The anthology appeared in 1945, but he began intensive work on it in 1943.

The key feature pieces Curnow had written in *The Press* the previous year about the English thirties poets and Yeats ('Prophets of Their Time' and 'The Last of Yeats'),[14] offered revised notions of the live contemporary tradition of poetry in English overseas, and these revisions were central to his reassessment of New Zealand poetry for the Caxton anthology. They also 'cleared the decks' for a revised, distinctly qualified view of his own and other New Zealand poets' thirties-influenced verse in the 1930s, which he advanced in the introduction to the Caxton anthology. Other reviews laid the groundwork for what would prove to be more controversial in the Caxton anthology's assessments. Despite struggling to be fair to C.A. Marris's 1939 edition of *New Zealand Best Poems*, and to 'Mr Marris's sincere and (it must be admitted) valuable work', Curnow remained largely unsympathetic:

> Why are the results so meagre, so unstimulating? The answer is perhaps that feeling, imagination, and command of language are not enough. The lack is intellectual. That is why most of these poems are sensitive and vivid, yet empty. Their intellectual content is stereotyped, so that one might suppose (unjustly) that they are all derivative in the most slavish sense. There is a limit to the imagery and the conceits which may be heaped upon a trite sentiment, however admirable the imagery and the conceits may be.[15]

The exceptions were Robin Hyde, whose 'Journey from New Zealand', he felt, stood head and shoulders above everything else in the selection, and poems by J.R. Hervey and Arnold Wall. All three poets were to be included in the Caxton anthology.

Curnow's review of Eileen Duggan's *New Zealand Poems* (1940) earned him her lifelong hostility and distrust. He praised her positive merits as 'feminine' – 'the preoccupation with the immediate perception direct and childlike, the uncomplicated, earthy emotion' – but argued that other aspects of her poetry, especially her 'deliberate and liberal' use of local colour (flora, fauna and legend), remained purely private because the body of myth and legend on which she drew had no 'real place in the lives and thoughts of New Zealanders'. Curnow's concluding sentences attempt to balance Duggan's strengths and weaknesses, but were hardly likely to mollify a poet accustomed to unqualified approbation:

> In spite of the praise she has enjoyed, some of it deserved, it is arguable that Miss Duggan's best contribution to New Zealand poetry is that she has proved the futility of 'local colour' writing and the danger of a too energetic will-to-poetry. Paradoxically, to have done so is a poet's achievement, and no slight one.[16]

Schroder, a friend of Duggan's and a warm admirer of her verse, had asked Curnow to write the review, and worked hard to mollify her. 'I think [the review] may have hurt you', he wrote, anxious after he had not heard from her for some months:

> When he turned his review in, I disliked it & regretted it; but . . . . I felt no more entitled to suppress it than a letter expressing political views I reject. . . . I am sorry . . . most sorry if Curnow's criticism gave you any pain. If you can tell me that it did not, I shall be greatly relieved.[17]

Duggan was *not* able to reassure him. She had a significant reputation among Catholic writers (especially Walter de la Mare) and readers in England and the United States, as well as in New Zealand, and among the older generation of men of letters was seen as carrying the flame of poetic succession to Jessie Mackay. Although she always protested her 'reticence' and vulnerability, Curnow's comments – the first to attempt a considered assessment of her achievement – appear to have affected her deeply. She wrote to Alexander thanking him for his favourable review in the Dunedin *Evening Star*, and briefly passed on to him her opinion of Curnow's review and that of C.R. Allen in the *Otago Daily Times*: 'I am easily cowed and Curnow and Allen had wiped out the comfort I felt that the "London Times" gave two notices to such a misprinted little book.'[18]

If Duggan's 'willed' interest in local colour and legend did not connect with the 'real' lives of New Zealanders, what kind of poetry could make such a connection? In his article on the poetry of R.A.K. Mason, Curnow set himself the challenging task of explaining why a poetry which offered so little by way of 'local colour', by way of explicit reference to the New Zealand scene and people, should nevertheless connect, in his view, so profoundly with the country, *'realise'* (as he put it in italics) the 'Pacific habitation' of 'this island community'.

The article was Curnow's first fuller-length critical discussion of a single poet, and his starting point was the poetry's awareness – far more vivid, direct and vigorous than in any other poetry ever written in the country, either earlier or among his contemporaries – of 'the elemental immediacy of birth, life, pain, and death . . . and of the problem of evil'.[19] The discourse Curnow used to connect such 'universal' themes to New Zealand was, essentially, psychoanalytical – an extension of his own long engagement in the 1930s with the psychic effects of colonisation on the behaviour of settlers. In his opening paragraph he offered an eloquent first statement, for critical purposes, of the idea of a psychic dislocation, a dissociation of sensibility, as the historical condition of settlement in the new country – an idea which was to become central in the introductions to his Caxton and Penguin anthologies:

> In bitterness and joy [the settlers] learnt just how much of the western life they in-herited could belong in the South Pacific. Above all, they learnt to know birth, life, pain, and death with a new immediacy. Yet in their poetry nothing of this immediacy is suggested. It might be said that they lived sagas but wrote only polite verse. While their limbs and senses perforce accepted the new environment, their hearts and minds denied it.[20]

Mason's poetry, often uncompromisingly bleak in its portrayal of loss, death, sexuality, suffering, gave voice precisely to that 'new immediacy' of what was lived but 'communally repressed' in hearts and minds as a result of the 'shock of translation' across ocean distances to the new environment; it offered a 'glimpse into the *unconscious mind* of this island community; perhaps something of that repressed yet living past'.[21] Liberally documented with quotations from the poems, Curnow's argument was bold and tendentious, an adaptation of modern-ist poetic principles to the problems of writing in a location as far distant as might be imagined from modernism's source: it required Mason's poems to be read as complex lyric utterances, driven by conflicts and uncertainties, reaching into the unconscious.

Nothing quite like it had appeared in New Zealand criticism up to this time, and the fact that critical discourse later in the century (often extending his arguments or resisting them) developed a comparable sophistication has almost entirely obscured the remarkable originality of such early critical pieces. They were built on extensive reading of modernist critical writings overseas, highly self-conscious thinking about how these might be relevant to the New Zealand/Pacific location, intensive close reading of the New Zealand poets and poems he wished to talk about, and the development of a supple and subtle style of critical writing.

Curnow did this work of reading and thinking and writing almost entirely *on his own*. Even his closest contemporaries – those he most admired, like Mason, Fairburn and Glover – lacked the interest (or, perhaps, the ability) to undertake such work. Although his reading of Mason was later to come under attack, at the time it reinforced the sense that Curnow was not only a poet of great promise but by far the country's most intelligent, subtle critic. For the next two decades he was to pursue with the utmost seriousness the project of transforming critical discourse about the literature of the country.

Glover's departure, Lilburn's return, 1941

In later 1941 the sudden decision by Glover to volunteer for war service and join the Royal Navy overseas came as a profound personal shock to Curnow, re-inforcing his sense of isolation in the Christchurch cultural scene. It was 'a great solitude which you made a society for me', he later wrote feelingly to him,[22] as he struggled to come to terms with Glover's absence in his day-to-day life, and with the possibility that he might never see him again. There was one compensation, however – Douglas Lilburn's return to Christchurch early in September, where he hoped to make a living as a freelance composer and musician.[23]

They had exchanged letters regularly during the previous year, which Lilburn had spent in his home town of Taihape, then on a short-term contract conduct-ing the National Broadcasting Service (NBS) String Orchestra in Wellington, and their personal friendship deepened from this time onwards. Its basis was their shared passion and seriousness as creative artists, which both believed was an essentially solitary occupation, and about which they were able to speak to each other without reserve. When Lilburn sent Curnow a copy of the second of T.S. Eliot's *Four Quartets*, 'East Coker' (1940), it prompted a passionately self-revealing letter about the conflict between dogmatic Christianity and poetry in which he revealed how hostile he was to Eliot's Christian dogmatics in *After Strange Gods: A Primer of Modern Heresy* (1934) and how irreconcilable the poetic insights of 'East Coker' seemed to be with such dogmatics:

> Poetry (or music) is a way of life which cuts across religious prescriptions. What could be more un-Catholic, more opposite to dogmatic theology, than
>
> ....and every attempt
> Is a wholly new start and a different kind of failure
> Because one has only learnt to get the better of words
> For the thing one no longer has to say. . . .

And so each venture
Is a new beginning, a raid on the inarticulate
With shabby equipment always deteriorating
In the general mass of imprecision of feeling . . . .

I can't square this with his saying in AFTER STRANGE GODS that he 'naturally
believes' that accepting of his sense of the terms Tradition and Orthodoxy 'should lead
one to dogmatic theology'. Because I was reared in the kind of dogmatic theology
he means, & I once tried to become one of its priests; & I now know that 'a raid
on the inarticulate' means nothing to it. He may persuade himself that this accords
with some 'true & ineffably orthodox spirit of Anglicanism' – but he won't persuade
the Houses of Convocation to issue a new Liturgy every year, composed by Eliot.
Orthodoxy is no spirit. God is a Spirit, & moves Bets to put out crumbs for the
sparrows every day. But Orthodoxy is a thing people burn each other for, and spy on
each other for – supremely, it is Totalitarianism. . . . But the greater the man the more
obviously the antinomies of thought and belief appear in him, & perhaps poet Eliot
& churchman Eliot are necessary complements. . . .

I hadn't meant to cast such offensive matter at you; but I can't bear posting away a few
scrappy sentences.[24]

On his arrival in Christchurch, Lilburn stayed with the Curnows in Riccarton
for ten days, and in November was able to move back into the room he had
rented in Cambridge Terrace before moving to London in 1937. It was only a
short walk from *The Press*, and he and Curnow, when not visiting each other,
would often meet for coffee and conversation. Rita Angus was also a frequent
visitor to the Curnows' house at this time, when her friendship with Lilburn
flourished, and towards the end of the year Angus became pregnant, though the
baby miscarried early in 1942. Although the affair came to an end, largely it seems
because Lilburn felt that the relationship would be compromised by his homosexuality, she and Lilburn remained close friends.

Throughout these months the Curnows saw a great deal of Angus and
Lilburn, and Betty especially was a confidante to both. For a month during
December and January, Angus came to stay with the Curnows at Riccarton,
and began sketching Betty for a new oil portrait, though this famous painting
was not to be exhibited for nearly two years, in The Group show in November
1943. At this time she also did a second sketch of Wystan and one of Curnow
himself, which was reproduced in the fifth issue of *Book* soon afterwards. There
was not the least trace of idealism in the portrait of Betty, as can be glimpsed in
her portraits of male figures like Bensemann and Lawrence Baigent, and indeed

Lilburn himself, and the direct gaze with which Betty's face confronted viewers suggested reserves of determination, self-control and independence, amid the domestic objects that surround her.* [25]

It was the imminent departure overseas of his closest friend, Denis Glover, that most affected Curnow in the later months of 1941, and the prospect of a Christchurch without their often daily meetings at the Caxton Press, or in pubs, or in each other's homes, increased the restlessness he felt, about his job, and perhaps also about his marriage, which had become at this time, as he put it later, 'a marriage like any other'.[26] On both sides, it seems, the initial excitements had long cooled, but there remained many moments of affection and pleasure in each other's company, especially (as Betty described them in her diaries) in the walks and tramps they often did together on Curnow's days off. Although Curnow was attracted to other women (and they to him), there was never any question that the obligation to keep the marriage going was paramount, and this was strongly reinforced by his religious upbringing. During the next few years in Christchurch there were a small number of episodes with other women, and though none could be described as protracted extramarital affairs, they were clearly a sign of a marriage in trouble.

Although Curnow enjoyed the social world in which they moved, his detach-ment, usually masked by well-lubricated talk and argumentativeness at social gatherings, was often interpreted as arrogance. He was well aware of this trait in his character, complaining to Glover overseas about the time it took for their letters to reach each other: 'My itch to be heard – normally issuing in interrupting and shouting people down – becomes a torment when I think of the travel time of these letters.'[27] His great preference (and need) was for close, trusted personal friendships, and there were not a great many of these in his life: Glover, Lilburn from this time on, and later his brother Tony and W.H. (Bill) Pearson, his colleague at the University of Auckland. He could always talk and write to these friends without reserve, assured that whatever confidences he revealed would be respected, and his loyalty to them in turn throughout his life was absolute. His relationship with Karl Stead, later, was more complex. It was primarily a literary relationship, based on Curnow's side on unstinting respect for the quality of Stead's literary judgements, but there was always an element of reserve in personal matters, a sense (perhaps unfair, since Stead's letters to Curnow were always open and direct) of never being quite sure that confidences might not be turned against him. What the pattern of Curnow's relationships reveals, in fact,

---

* The portrait was later to take on an iconic status in the development of New Zealand painting, somewhat to Angus's exasperation ('I do not wish to be known by this work continually'), because she felt it deflected attention from other, later work.

is a deep-seated insecurity and anxiety about betrayal which seems to have its origins in childhood: these feelings both drove his desire to succeed, and were intensified (such was the force of his early religious training in self-questioning and self-analysis) when he failed or felt that he had failed. Indeed, on occasion he acted impulsively in ways which seemed to *invite* such feelings.

As if to underline the fragility of Curnow's sense of connection with the Christchurch world in which he moved, within little more than a month of Glover's decision to go overseas he decided to apply for a job in the Workers' Educational Association at Auckland, and on 26 November travelled up there to be interviewed. He returned to Christchurch a week later after being offered the job, but after a long discussion with Betty, for whom Auckland was never an attractive prospect, he wrote declining the offer.

During the early months of 1942 Curnow resigned himself to the likelihood that he would be drafted for military service in the army. Although he was sympathetic to the cause of conscientious objection, and hostile to the pervasive culture of patriotism promoted by the country's political and bureaucratic establishment, the expansion of the war into the Pacific strongly reinforced his personal sense of investment in the outcome. 'I shall not be an unwilling soldier', he wrote to Glover, 'though probably a bad one',[28] adding that he had nominated signallers as his preferred field – 'why, I haven't the least idea'.[29] However, after being passed as medically fit, he found that events were taken out of his hands by *The Press*, which won an appeal for exemption (for himself and others) on the grounds of the essential service to the country of their newspaper work reporting the war. It was a 'home front' contribution to the New Zealand war effort – alongside his poetry and other writings – which he continued to regard with a sense of high purpose and seriousness. He settled back into Christchurch at least for the duration, though Auckland retained its attraction to him as a place where he might eventually live.

At the time Glover departed he had brought out four issues of *Book*, and he left Curnow with copy for the fifth issue, to see through the Caxton Press, now largely in the capable hands of Bensemann, though the exigencies of the wartime economy (and Glover's absence) meant that its survival was now almost wholly dependent on jobbing work. For the next three years Glover came to rely on Curnow's letters for information about the Christchurch scene and the people they knew, and they are by far the richest source of information about Curnow's activities and feelings during this time. Glover himself provided long accounts of his meetings with writers in London and his efforts to promote New Zealand writing there, as well as (as far as wartime censorship would allow) describing his activities in the Royal Navy.

New poems, 1942: imagination's thrust across the Pacific

At the beginning of 1942 the Curnows took their first annual holiday in Wellington, where they stayed with Philip and Inga Smithells, whom they had met in Christchurch the previous year.* They also met up with others, including the historian Professor F.L.W. (Fred) Wood, his wife Joan, and Wood's colleague at Victoria University College, J.C. Beaglehole, who was now advisor to the recently established Historical Branch of the Department of Internal Affairs. Others they saw during their stay included Joseph Heenan, under-secretary in the Department of Internal Affairs, E.H. (Eric) McCormick, whose *Letters and Art in New Zealand* had recently appeared in the government's centennial publications series, and the young artist and photographer Theo Schoon, a recent refugee immigrant from Dutch Java. Rita Angus continued to stay in the house at Riccarton while they were away, and Wystan spent time with his Le Cren and Curnow grandparents. When Curnow arrived back in Christchurch on 13 January he found himself heavily committed to night work on overseas cables at *The Press*. The staff was now much smaller, thinned, with the departure on war service of many colleagues.

Before he left Wellington, Curnow had begun work on a new sonnet, 'Musical Criticism', after meeting Ernst Plischke, an Austrian-born architect who had immigrated with his Jewish wife Anna (a landscape designer) to New Zealand in 1939 to escape the Nazi occupation, and was at this time an architectural draughtsman for the Department of Housing Construction.† The poem was the result of a memorable evening in which Curnow listened to a recording of a Beethoven string quartet in a house which Plischke had designed for Joachim Khan (a political science lecturer at Victoria College, Hungarian-born and a wartime refugee from Munich), looking out through the large glass walls to the receding horizons on all sides.

Curnow's poem is a tribute to the power of music (like his sonnet to Lilburn written eighteen months earlier), but it is also a tribute to the architecture of the house – open to its surrounding environment rather than walled off from it – that enables an imaginative connection to be made with Beethoven's music. '[Y]our room', he wrote, with its 'glass wall' withstanding the southerly gales:

---

* Smithells had moved to New Zealand from England in 1939 to become superintendent of physical education in the Department of Education.
† A brilliant, innovative architect, trained in the modernist school, Plischke brought wholly new ideas to the design of domestic and public buildings and to town planning in New Zealand (though he was never accepted by the architectural establishment) before eventually returning to a professorship in Vienna in 1963.

> contains controls
> To track in dazed skies an invisible wake
> And pull his signals down just where you like,
> It happens, among these unconnected hills.

In this environment open to the horizons and the weather, Beethoven 'makes the whole sea his base' (as his early version put it).* His music has the capacity to break down distance, enabling listeners in the 'stone-deaf islands', 'on these tuned Strings' to 'ride gales to patience; or, to cross / Motionless horizons as if not marooned.' The poem anticipates the window-framed visual perspective of one of Curnow's best-known poems of the 1950s, 'A Small Room with Large Windows', a perspective which retains its power in many of the later poems, though it becomes increasingly complex, since the window both connects and divides the observer from what is outside it. It is hardly surprising, however, that Plischke's modernist architectural imagination should seem so consonant with Curnow's modernist poetic imagination. Curnow 'read' Plischke in the same way as he 'read' Lilburn, seeking connections with his own poetic practice.[30]

In February 1942 the fifth issue of *Book* appeared. Glover had selected all the material in it before he went overseas and there was little for Curnow to do beyond general oversight of its production at the Caxton Press. The issue included a sketch by Rita Angus of a 30-year-old Curnow in an armchair reading a book, in a very Yeatsian, dandified pose, wearing a silk dressing gown and cravat. It also included a new sequence entitled 'Four Pacific Sonnets', which Glover thought very highly of, though only one of them was ever reprinted (much revised and given the title 'The Navigators'), in *Sailing or Drowning*. The 'Four Pacific Sonnets' might be seen in retrospect as anticipating the concerns – and even the structural perspectives – of 'Landfall in Unknown Seas', which Beaglehole and Heenan were shortly to commission him to write for the tercentenary of Abel Janszoon Tasman's discovery of New Zealand in December 1642.

The first sonnet (like the opening section of 'Landfall') evoked the heroic scale of Tasman's enterprise, as well as the shock of the 'sheer loss' which is seen as the very condition of discovery, and even as more significant than the geographical discovery itself. In the poem's ironic concluding words, Tasman ('the flying Dutchman') is imagined as endlessly driven by his paradoxical desire to 'discover', beyond the antipodean end point.[31]

The second sonnet – the only one Curnow ever reprinted – focuses on the rationality underpinning the Enlightenment optimism that motivated the voyages

---

* The sonnet was printed in the first issue of Ian Gordon's *New Zealand New Writing* at the end of the year (Dec. 1942), and appeared, much revised, in *Sailing or Drowning* under the new title 'At Joachim Khan's'.

of discovery, soberly linking it with exploitation, the deployment of violence, and a contemporary legacy of Lady Macbeth-like guilt:

> Here in the vague
> Currents where cables mumble murder has slept
>
> And sleeps, but dreams, hands that will not come clean
> In perpetual dumbshow utter what they did.
> Because it was a rational violence
> To think discharge of cannon could add
> Island upon island, that the wide sea would fence
> And Time confirm them, in a change of scene.

The third sonnet (beginning 'You had not heard that we still eat each other?') turns, like the second section of 'Landfall in Unknown Seas', to the perspective of the indigenous people, playing on the myth of the 'Cannibal Isles'. But the turn is only a seeming one. The cannibalism which survives into this 'third, almost fourth generation' is the 'self-devouring' cannibalism of the colonial-settler generations who (in a travesty-reversal of the myth) reserve 'devotion' (instead of cannibalism!) for 'strangers', unable to live with the experience of rejection by visitors, like Tasman, who 'screaming "Horrible" fled, afraid to land'. It is a witty poem, perhaps altogether too ingenious and obscure, but its central conceit – the application of the metaphor of cannibalism ('Figuratively, figuratively you understand', the poem concludes) to the behaviour of Pakeha, unable to live with themselves – would have been irresistible to Glover.

The fourth sonnet – the most vivid of the sequence – is the voice of the Pacific Ocean itself, presented as a Leviathan-like figure endlessly sweeping between the northern and southern hemispheres, receptacle of all the history that has flowed between them. Only a few of Curnow's earlier poems convey the feeling of the 'oceanic' – its remote depths, its spatial sweep traversing vast astral maps, its surface tides, its huge surfs and smallest eddies where it washes against islands – as such a powerful agency in human history. However, he never lost a sense of this antipodean, insular perception of the oceanic: a sense of the globe not as a vast, fixed land mass fringed by oceans (the perspective of those whose lives are contained within continents), but as a vast, ever-present, shifting oceanic mass in which even the largest continents might be seen as unstable 'islands'. In the introduction to the Caxton *Book of New Zealand Verse*, written two years later, Curnow drew a distinction between English poetry's habit of imagining the sea as a feature of the landscape, and the very different habit of antipodean poets:

Above left: Curnow's father, Rev. Tremayne Curnow (1881–1949), as the young deacon of St Mary's Church in Timaru, where he boarded with Mrs Rose Gambling. He married Rose's daughter Jessie in 1909, when they were both 28. (*Privately held*)

Above right: Curnow's mother, Jessie, née Gambling (1880–1974), in the 1940s. She survived her husband for eighteen years, living to the age of 93. Known to each other and to their children as 'T' and 'Muz', Curnow's parents enjoyed a warm and long marriage. (*Privately held*)

Below: Curnow's paternal grandparents were strongly connected with an emerging New Zealand colonial history. This photo, taken in 1903, shows Curnow's paternal grandmother, Alice, née Monro, standing left. Her father, H.A.H. Monro (1814–1908), 'sometime Judge of the Native Land Court', is seated right. Curnow had a long fascination with his Monro ancestry, prompting poems such as 'An Abominable Temper' and 'The Scrap-book'. Far right is Professor Arnold Wall, who married Tremayne's sister Elsie (Gipsy), seated left with their baby daughter Hilary (Larry). (*Privately held*)

Opposite: Curnow's maternal grandmother, Rose Gambling, née Allen, lived with the Curnow family and was closely involved in bringing up the children. She is pictured here with the young Allen, left, and older brother John. Rose Gambling is the subject of Curnow's moving sonnet 'In Memoriam R.L.M.G.'. (*Privately held*)

Left: In 1945 Curnow wrote the sonnet 'Self-Portrait' about this early childhood photograph, reflecting on the moment of surprised self-awareness captured here. Memories provide one of the main sources of inspiration for many of Curnow's major poems. (*Privately held*)

Below: In 1924 Curnow enrolled at Christchurch Boys' High School, as had his older brother the year before and his father in 1890. Allen is standing fourth left, with his brother John beside him, fourth right. (*Privately held*)

Right: At nineteen Curnow left Christchurch to take up a scholarship to St John's Theological College in Auckland, his first break from home and the Canterbury milieu in which he grew up. Shown here with the family dog. (*Privately held*)

Below: At St John's Theological College, 1931, second row from the back, third right. Curnow formed close bonds with the literary crowd in Auckland. His body language here might suggest a certain distance from his fellow theology students. (*Privately held*)

Curnow on a tramping trip to the West Coast of the South Island, mid-1930s. This was one of several trips in the South Island that contributed to Curnow's sense of landscape – something that became increasingly important in the poems he wrote from this time on. (*Denis Glover, courtesy of Rupert and Pia Glover*)

The remote hut at Anawhata on Auckland's wild west coast, which Curnow first visited as a student at St John's Theological College. This landscape would become a source of inspiration for many of Curnow's poems, most famously 'The Loop in Lone Kauri Road'. (*Privately held*)

Above left and right: After Curnow's marriage to Elizabeth (Betty) Le Cren, the couple spent several days at the Anawhata hut as part of their honeymoon trip to Auckland in January 1937. (*Privately held*)

Left: Curnow with his great-aunt Fanny Rose May, photographed here with him at the time of his first marriage in 1936. She was the youngest sister of his maternal grandmother Rose Gambling. His sonnet 'To Fanny Rose May', written in 1947, was later published with a sonnet about his grandmother, 'In Memoriam R.L.M.G.', under the collective title of 'Tomb of an Ancestor'. These poems were often chosen by Curnow for public readings, including a television appearance in the United States in 1961, and were later translated into German. (*Privately held*)

Below: The Curnows spent a quiet summer holiday in 1938–39 at Stewart's Gully, on the Waimakariri River. Their first child was due in February 1939. Betty and Curnow tried their hand at painting local landscape scenes. Curnow's efforts apparently did not prompt him to continue. (*Privately held*)

Curnow in Kaikoura, January 1938. He and Betty were en route to Nelson on a two-week camping trip in their recently purchased 1926 Hupmobile, which was altered to allow for the seat to be let down for sleeping in. (*Privately held*)

We, if the difference may be put so crudely, more often take our land for a part of the seascape. The sea, if our poets are true witnesses, is everpresent in imagination, *another and larger republic than the land*, now friendly, now hostile, with which our relations are of first importance.[32]

The central premise of Curnow's play *The Axe*, about the momentous clash of indigenous and Christian world views on the Cook Island of Mangaia in the 1820s – which he worked on intermittently between 1943 and 1948 – was powerfully premised on a Pacific island perception of 'the world we know' as 'a swaying disc of ocean / With a scrap of green ground at the hub';[33] while his later sequence, *An Incorrigible Music* (1979), is only one instance of the persistence of the oceanic perspective in his poetry, which in this volume links histories, times and spaces as diverse as Auckland's west coast, Renaissance Florence, and terrorist-afflicted contemporary Italy in the era of Aldo Moro: 'All the seas are one sea, / The blood one blood / and the hands one hand.'[34]

In the following month, March 1942, *Poetry* published its first poems by Curnow, written and submitted sometime after July the previous year. Of the three poems, two contain traces of his location in the reclaimed swamp that became the suburb of Riccarton, and both gesture somewhat obviously towards T.S. Eliot's mythic concerns in *The Waste Land*. 'Rite of Spring' is a wry reflection on the absence of myth and legend as sustaining forces in this contemporary suburban setting, the poet digging in his garden describing himself moodily as a 'weekly tenant of the swamp', unable to conceive this mundane annual ritual occurring 'between famous seas' in the mythic dimensions either of optimistic rebirth and renewal, or of tragedy and loss, as in Eliot's *Waste Land*. 'The gilt is off my Golden Bough', he concludes.* 'In Summer Sheeted Under' also invokes the 'drained estate', reclaimed from swampland, on which iron-roofed suburban houses have sprouted, their inhabitants living private domestic lives, 'sheeted under' as if reduced to corpses, or 'walk[ing] fast, wordless' in the streets, oblivious to the summer season of 'exotic growth, / Fleshy of limb and leaf' beyond.

However, the most important of the three poems in *Poetry* was 'Discovery', which provided a template for all Curnow's poems about the early Pacific voyagers at this time. 'How shall I compare the discovery of islands?' he asks in the opening stanza, emphasising that all explanations of historical processes have to be conceived now (since we live in a post-Freudian age of self-analysis, in which whatever innocent trust might once have been placed on history as an

---

* The association of a 'swamp' with the absence of tragic or heroic possibilities recurs in one of Curnow's best-known poems of this period, 'The Skeleton of the Great Moa', its bones discovered in a 'private swamp', and which 'broods over no great waste'.

instinctive process is no longer available) as framed within 'master-narratives'. Because they are imagined constructs they are fragile, subject inexorably to decay and re-invention or replacement. The poem then offers, in four stanzas, a series of vivid, deeply ironic characterisations of historical master-narratives informing the voyages of discovery: a biblical narrative of discovery as serving merely to expand knowledge of the pervasiveness of the Fall, encompassing the whole globe; a Renaissance narrative driven by a belief in the illimitable capacity of the mind to free itself from ignorance; an eighteenth-century Enlightenment narrative of belief in Reason combined with the practice of exploiting indigenous peoples believed to be childlike in their lack of Reason; until finally, at the farthest antipodean point, no further lands remain to dazzle the 'discoverer's eye' in his *retreating* mirror, no 'Landfall undreamed or anchorage unsure'.

For every narrative the end result is 'something different, something nobody counted on'. In his concluding stanza Curnow offers his own bleak but challenging master-narrative, an antipodean perspective in which 'all earth' is to be re-imagined as 'one island', 'lost again' because the earlier narratives have lost whatever purchase they might have had, in their time, as truth:

> Compare, compare. Now horrible untruth
> Rings true in our obliterating season:
> Our islands lost again, all earth one island,
> And all our travel circumnavigation.

Curnow spent some time revising this final stanza from its original format ('And here among the latest islands sunk / In shrunken Time's obliterating season, / Comparing, I know the round earth is one island / And all our journeys circumnavigation.'), and Pocock is surely right to insist that whatever disillusion underpins the perception – whatever scepticism that all teleologically conceived voyagings after truth are doomed to self-defeating circularity – a counter-statement and a counter-feeling, intensely stimulating to the imagination, are also implicit in the lines. The words with which Milton ended *Paradise Lost* as Adam and Eve were expelled from their Eden paradise – 'The World was all before them' – might also be relevant. What is 'lost' might stimulate new attempts at discovery, in different terms, informed by knowledge of what has ceased to serve its turn.

Pacific war poems, 1942

Curnow sent a copy of the Joachim Khan sonnet to Glover, as well as another poem, 'The Seascape' ('a most poignant Pantoum'),[35] he had written earlier in the year, in January, the first of his poems to respond to the new global Japanese threat – the rapid thrust of Japanese military forces through south-east Asia and into the Pacific Ocean after the bombing of Pearl Harbor in December 1941 – and that reflects grimly on the collapse of scale and proportion with which the momentous events of the Pacific war are filtered through propaganda and censorship to the New Zealand public ('The casualties were few, the damage nil'), based on the need to maintain morale. However, by far the most impressive of the Pacific war poems Curnow wrote in 1942 was the sonnet 'Sailing or Drowning', which appeared in the July issue of *Poetry* and became the title poem of his next collection:

> In terms of some green myth, sailing or drowning,
> Each day makes clear a statement to the next;
> But to make out our tomorrow from its motives
> Is pure guessing, yesterday's were so mixed.
>
> Papa, Atea, parents of gods or islands,
> Quickly forgave the treacherous beaches, none
> So bloodily furrowed that the secret tides
> Could not make the evening and the morning one.
>
> Ambition has annulled that constitution;
> In the solid sea and the space over the sea
> Explosions of a complex origin
> Shock, rock and split the memory.
>
> Sailing or drowning, the living and the dead,
> Less than the gist of what has just been said.

It might be seen as the foundational text for the essentially locally based, antipodean and Pacific mythopoeic impulses of all the poetry Curnow wrote at this time, making the allusive, narrowly classical gestures towards Eliot's *The Waste Land* in poems like 'Rite of Spring' and 'In Summer Sheeted Under' seem thin and exclusive. 'Sailing or Drowning' was clearly the product of Curnow's increasing interest in the anthropology of the Pacific, especially the accounts of the Polynesian oceanic migrations and the mythic narratives these generated, by scholars like Te Rangi Hiroa (Sir Peter Buck) in *Vikings of the Sunrise* (1938) and *Anthropology and Religion* (1939). The poem evokes an older Polynesian 'constitution' of 'green myth', a master cosmic narrative of origins sponsored by the earth mother (Papa) and the sky father (Atea), which functioned effectively to make sense of even the most violent historical events – tribal conflicts which left 'bloodily furrowed', treacherous beaches – enabling such catastrophic events to be contained, even forgiven, within a pattern of history and time seen as spiritually sponsored, purposeful, unbroken, unifying, remembered. In the present, however, that 'constitution' has been 'annulled' by 'ambition' – the unprecedented hubris of a humanism which has spawned the global horrors and the power-driven violences of totalitarianism – creating an absolute fracture in the psyche, an inability to 'make out our tomorrow from its motives' except by guesswork, since 'yesterday's were so mixed':

> In the solid sea and the space over the sea
> Explosions of a complex origin
> Shock, rock, and split the memory.

The 'explosions' which, like massive subterranean earthquake-generated tsunamis, fracture the sense of solid space and of the distance of violent events 'over the sea', are military-political – the destructive violences occurring on an unprecedented scale in the Pacific theatre of war – but, perhaps more importantly, they manifest a fundamental psychic fracture within the self. Like the words 'constitution', 'ambition' and 'explosion' in the poem, 'complex' is multiple in its meanings, one of which is certainly a Freudian allusion to the psychopathological discontents of contemporary civilisation, describing a condition in which the memory is split, cut off radically from anything in its past which might enable the self to understand, even accept, what is happening in the present. In the opening quatrain this splitting of the memory fractures the possibility of explaining events from one day to the next; in the second quatrain the time scale is broader; in the concluding, grimly ironic couplet the fracture is as immediate, and terrifying, as that between word – the utterance of the poem itself – and its meaning:

> Sailing or drowning, the living and the dead,
> Less than the gist of what has just been said.

In one of its earlier versions, Curnow prefaced the poem with a quotation from his favourite among Eliot's *Four Quartets*, 'The Dry Salvages', which had only recently been published:

> We cannot think of a time that is oceanless
> Or of an ocean not littered with wastage
> Or of a future that is not liable
> Like the past, to have no destination.

The opening line of the passage he quotes would have been irresistible. It is precisely the possibility of a 'time that is oceanless' – ungrounded in the solidities of oceanic space and distance – and a future with 'no destination', which the poem asks us to contemplate as a contemporary condition. Curnow's sonnet is dense, economic, its argument brilliantly conducted. Its roots are in modernism – loss of meaningfulness, psychic fracture and the divided self, and an apocalyptic sense of impending political and social disaster – but it is remarkable for its translation of that modernism into the context of a Pacific habitation and history.

Chapter Eleven

'Landfall in Unknown Seas': 1942–43

The music thrilled me as never before . . . so clear & purposeful – doing everything for the poem that it can't do for itself, but nothing that the poem doesn't mean to do with all its heart. . . . I can hardly think of the poem except as a first stage in the creation of 'Landfall in Unknown Seas' now that it has been performed . . . as it deserves to be.[1]

Leinster Road, May 1942

In April 1942 Curnow's domestic circumstances changed again, with news of Betty's second pregnancy and a due date for the baby of December later in the year. In order to economise on rent and meet the expenses of supporting the expanding family they decided to shift to a house at 41 Leinster Road, Merivale, owned by Winifred Buchanan. The house was already known to the Curnows (and the Glovers). Buchanan and her husband (before his death) had lived there with their daughter Ina, who was also a friend of Douglas Lilburn.[2] The relocation meant settling for smaller premises – and sharing the house with Maisie Kilkelly, a music teacher who rented a small self-contained flat at the rear. However, although the move, in May, was made in pouring rain, and Wystan was ill with mumps, they soon felt at home and settled there.[3]

The house, a little to the north-west of the city centre, was further from the *Press* offices in Cathedral Square than the Riccarton house, but was still conveniently close and well serviced by buses and trams along the main Papanui Road or Rossall Street, a short walk away. Otti and Paul Binswanger also lived nearby. Otti had become one of Betty's closest friends, as was Marjory Mitchell, who lived with the Binswangers: her small daughter, Juliet (who would later become a professor at the University of Cambridge and a well-known writer), was one of Wystan's childhood playmates.

During the winter months Curnow worked on getting the sixth issue of *Book* ready for Bensemann at the Caxton Press, eventually deciding to feature M.H. Holcroft, with a short story ('Dangerous Turning') and an extract from the manuscript of 'The Waiting Hills', a sequel to Holcroft's centennial prizewinning reflective essay on New Zealand's history and culture, *The Deepening Stream*, which Glover had published in 1940. At the time, the sequel was languishing for want of a publisher, and until the essay opportunely arrived, Curnow was worried that incoming copy for the issue 'lamentably lacks criticism', and tried himself 'to compose some little critical tract for the times' along lines suggested by Spender's recently published *Life and the Poet*, 'easily the best discourse on poet, poetry & society I have read'.[4] After trying for weeks, he wrote to Glover, he 'failed utterly' to produce anything satisfactory.

Though he was later to qualify his views about Holcroft's cultural thinking, at this time he was as impressed by much that he read in the new manuscript as he had been by parts of *The Deepening Stream*. The passage he chose – hardly surprisingly, perhaps, given the thrust of so much of his recent poetry into the Pacific Ocean – was from a section headed 'Memory of a Voyage', in which Holcroft argued eloquently for the persistence of such memory as an enduring experience of New Zealanders (both Pakeha and Maori). Writing to Holcroft at the time, Curnow described the essays as a 'new kind of writing' which came from 'the impulse to write our own anthropology', and compared his work favourably with the work of New Zealand's historians:

> With all respect to our historians . . . I feel that their work does not constitute a native record and testament . . . . From your approach, I think there is a chance of New Zealanders learning what they are, instead of what they look like to a sympathetic and intelligent, but detached observer.

> What is written about New Zealand does matter so much – in fact I believe that what we write IS New Zealand – that I find myself getting quite angry with the historians and commentators, passing off their truth as the whole truth & nothing but the truth.[5]

As always, he was careful to differentiate the 'New Zealand' he mentions here, from the idea of nationalism, adding: 'but I am always looking for some view that by-passes the nationalist idea. Nationalism, as NZ seems to have it, is an odd thing.'[6]

Curnow kept Glover informed about progress on *Book*, including Glover's own 'Leaving for Overseas' and also poems by Rosemary Seymour and Fairburn, as well as hoping ('if shortened space permits') to include 'a new sonnet of mine'.[7] The sonnet was 'The Old Provincial Council Chamber, Christchurch', about one of the city's earliest examples of Victorian gothic architecture in the grand manner, an excellent example of Curnow's skill in selecting details from a closely observed scene in order to generate an ironic reflection: in this case on the brevity and the shallowness of the history of the 'children of those who suffered a sea change', despite the seeming solidity of the building itself, with its intricate carved details suggestive of a history stretching back into the European architectural past. That brevity, and perhaps the dawning awareness of it among contemporary New Zealanders, is conveyed at the end of the poem in an image of the building's 'stopped clock', from which those observing the fact get back 'their own surprise'.

The third quatrain, in particular, went through many changes before it found its eloquent final shape:

> Children of those who suffered a sea change
> May wonder how much history was quarried
> And carted, hoisted, carved; and find it strange
> How shallow here their unworn age lies buried . . .

It is this present generation, 'wondering' about the past, noticing a sense of strangeness and a feeling of surprise in themselves as they contemplate the signs of decay in the building with its stopped clock, who have the beginnings, perhaps, of an awareness of living in real time, an awareness of change and loss, brevity and fragility.

By mid-1942 Curnow and Glover had heard from each other at least two or three times, though letters were erratic because of the bombing of merchant shipping, and Curnow's to Glover often followed him around to different places where his naval postings took him. The letters are highly revealing of their strength of feeling for each other, and (at least on Glover's side) for their glimpses into Curnow's character. In a long letter of 30 and 31 May, in reply to a letter of early March from Curnow which included his Joachim Kahn sonnet and the pantoum, Glover gave a wonderfully detailed, slightly acerbic account of his meetings with John Lehmann, C. Day Lewis, Stephen Spender and others, while in London, remarking on an Englishness of reserve in their manner which was quite the opposite of the South African William Plomer, whom he took to immediately. Spender struck him as 'a young pukeko', who became animated when ideas were discussed, though in a different way from Curnow:

[W]hen an abstract idea crops up, his mind seizes on it in a spider-like way &
proceeds to spin. He has your facility for analysing the subjective & the metaphysical,
though I should call you a crab rather than a spider, from your more direct tenacity
of approach.[8]

On 3 September Glover wrote again, delighted to hear of the impending arrival
of the new baby, 'this second string to your bow', and commenting: 'It's a most
important creative act, especially now, & rather easier than a sestina.' The feeling
for the loss of companionship with Curnow is strong:

> There are so many things I want to talk about with you. I miss your robust pugnacity
> & humour (the English are so pale) and it's small consolation to rehearse old scenes
> in my hammock and kindle happy memories with damp tinder. I do not regret this
> journey etc, but it has its unutterable sadnesses.[9]

Curnow for his part filled his long letters, apart from their references to his
anxieties about Glover's fate in naval engagements, with accounts of their
literary and artistic acquaintances in Christchurch and elsewhere, the activities
of the Caxton Press, his own ideas and poetic activities, and (with a special
tact and unspoken awareness of what Glover wanted to hear) descriptions of
weather and season and of the rituals of companionship they had long become
accustomed to.

Soon after Glover left New Zealand, Curnow tried drafting verse letters
to him, but it was not until November 1942 that he sent one off, though he
commented to Glover in his next letter that having indulged this 'one strong
impulse' he was unlikely to do it again, since 'it's too self-assertive an engine of
communication'.[10] The coda to this verse letter (an eloquent meditation on the
state of the nation and the world as he travels from Merivale to the office by bus)
was later salvaged, under the title 'Spring, 1942', for *Sailing or Drowning*. But this
self-contained coda, in short lines of three stresses, was preceded by more than
200 lines, in an informal pentameter measure, in which he spoke casually and
at length about people and places they both knew. One section rehearses their
Saturday ritual of visiting the pub, offering familiar memories of people, places
and weather which he knew Glover would enjoy:

> Saturday. At five o'clock to the Carlton,
> Rossall street, Rugby, Naseby, Merivale Lane,
> Winchester, Andover, Salisbury, Carlton Mill,
> With the grey rucsac and the jar against my elbow,
> Walking under the nor'west quilt that is tucked

Round every visible edge; the thick, still, stage
Of the nor'wester, contemplating rain.
Out by the Park and the humped willows.
A few cars behind the Mecca; I cross
Somebody's bumpers & enter, turn right
Towards the glass doors; through into the buzzing bar.
There are still sportscoats among the battledresses,
But fewer and older.
                    Times and coats may change,
But not Charlie in the grey cardigan, he
Serves them all. Come in khaki, come in flannels,
Come spats and sweaty caps, he serves them all,
Bends, strides, and pulls a pump, and fills a handle,
Pushes the bottle over, wipes, rakes up
Silver and notes and bangs down your change.
He serves them all. First come, first served.
This handle – is it the one? bears many washings
And is no different from your drinking from it
When we leaned here under the wicked neons
And introduced unpopular Poetry
Into the congress of the hole-in-one,
The double[?s] chart and the young girl of Madras;
Though we too could admire that famous lady
And her vivacious Finger.
                    The jar is filled,
Half a gallon for three-and-nine (it's sevenpence
A handle now – I can't say, 'Sevenpence in').
I come up into the muggy afternoon
And look along for trams.[11]

He also spoke of regular visits with Betty to Glover's wife Mary, to catch up with
correspondence to her from Glover, and of his own domestic life. 'All goes with
me much as ever', he wrote in July, 'except that Curnow II has now travelled five
months towards being born, so far without causing trouble to anyone.'[12]

   The most significant literary event in Curnow's life at this time, though he was
not aware of it when he mentioned it in his letters to Glover, was the commission
to compose a poem for the tercentenary of Tasman's discovery of New Zealand,
which would occur on 13 December 1942. The most widely known, widely published

and performed of all his poems,* it had 'a more deliberately planned beginning than anything I've ever written', he commented later to MacDonald P. Jackson.[13]

Interlude: the making of a poem, 'Landfall in Unknown Seas', 1942

Curnow was first approached formally about this commission in a letter from Beaglehole in early April 1942.[14] The commemorative book in which it was proposed that Curnow's poem appear was to be published by the Department of Internal Affairs with Whitcombe & Tombs, including an essay on Tasman by Beaglehole, together with a new translation of relevant sections of Tasman's log of the voyage made by Vigeno, the Dutch Consul-General to Australia and New Zealand. It was almost certainly Beaglehole's idea to approach Curnow, but the project also had to be approved by the head of Internal Affairs, Joseph Heenan,[15] as well as by the Prime Minister, Peter Fraser, and his Cabinet.

Mason and Fairburn were also considered as poets who might be approached, and if there were official anxieties attaching to Curnow's appointment they were that he would produce something too obscure for public acceptance. Heenan was a man of literary interests, but his tastes had been formed in the Georgian period, and he had to overcome a degree of scepticism about the value of the work being done by the new generation of New Zealand writers. Curnow accepted the commission readily, though quite what its specific terms were, if there were any, is unknown. The poem had to be produced by October, in order to meet the publication deadline for the commemorative book, timed to coincide with the tercentenary date of 13 December, and the finished product had to be acceptable. At the end of July, Curnow wrote to Glover that although the poem was 'officially sanctioned', its acceptance was by no means a foregone conclusion:

> I have had a note from Beaglehole passing on dire threats from Heenan 'if Curnow poem should prove incomprehensible'. I am adjured to 'lead the Muse cautiously forth'. How I shall manage to conform to these strange instructions I have no idea. Probably I shall not.[16]

Curnow spent at least six months thinking about and working assiduously on the poem, reading intensively in the historical background and making notes, and attempting many drafts – 'throwing away thousands of words' he later said,[17]

---

* Probably no poem in New Zealand has proved so quotable, or been so extensively mined for titles of books. It also provided the title for Charles Brasch's influential literary quarterly *Landfall*, when it first appeared in 1947, supplanting an earlier idea that the magazine might be called *Tuatara*.

though many of them were retrieved by Betty from his wastepaper basket and stored away. He was already familiar with Beaglehole's own books on the subject of Pacific exploration, *The Exploration of the Pacific* (1934) and *The Discovery of New Zealand* (1939), and re-read the anthropological writings of Te Rangi Hiroa (Sir Peter Buck), especially *Vikings of the Sunrise*, whose writings lay behind the Polynesian mythic references of 'Sailing or Drowning' and were to inform other poems which he wrote soon afterwards. Volume II of R.G. McNab's *Historical Records of New Zealand* (1914) provided invaluable access to important historical documents relating to Tasman's expedition, and the same author's *From Tasman to Marsden* (1914) offered a useful general account. Curnow also studied early maps of the globe, depicting Marco Polo's 'Land of Beach', or the Great South Land (Terra Australis), a vast undiscovered continent presumed to exist at the antipodes of the then-known world, between Africa and South America – as well as Tasman's (and other explorers') own early maps of the coastlines they discovered.[18]

There was one particularly serendipitous discovery at the time, in a Christchurch bookshop:

> One item that made a great difference to the poem I think was a rather beautiful quarterly published in the late thirties in Shanghai called I think *T'en Hsia* where I found a translation of a late sixteenth- or early seventeenth-century account of the Portuguese island of Macao and the whole of that region. This somehow oriented me towards Batavia from which Tasman set out and in fact some of the earlier lines of that poem – where I speak of 'the dogs of bronze and iron barking from Timor to the straits' and so on – really came direct from reading a few accounts like this.[19]

The article added invaluably to his understanding of the motivations of the Dutch in the East India Company at the time, which he came to see as an important perspective to include in the poem.

By the end of July, Curnow had begun and discarded numerous drafts, and wrote to Holcroft: 'So far I have only experimented, finding out all the forms etc. that *won't* do. My hopes are still high, of producing a Public Work which will be fit to last.'[20]

The poem's structure eventually consisted of three vividly contrasting parts. Part One, with its famous opening lines, 'Simply by sailing in a new direction / You could enlarge the world', used a flexible, mainly four-stressed blank verse line which could shift between tones of heightened eloquence and ironic understate-ment, set the scene, and evoke the background and motivations of the expedition from the perspective of the Dutch imperial hegemony based in the East Indies – in which the wish to expand the frontiers of knowledge and the determination to discover new opportunities for the commercial exploitation of the new world were inextricably mixed. Part Two evoked the moment of discovery and its immediate aftermath in the violent encounter with Maori, using a shorter, much more urgent and dramatic three-stressed line, with occasional strong rhymes (and vigorous alliterative patternings similar to those he had deployed in the earlier poems about Jan Tyssen and Magellan). It conveyed the excitement of arrival, the suddenness and violence of the clash with Maori at what is now called Golden Bay (but which Tasman named Murderers' Bay), and the irony of the sense of 'failure' recorded by Tasman as the expedition 'sailed away'. In another of the poem's famous moments, Curnow turned in this section to the perspective of the Maori – 'Always to islanders danger / Is what comes over the sea' – anticipating the concerns of the poem's final section, before describing the death of four of Tasman's crew:

> Death discovered the Sailor
> O in a flash, in a flat calm,
> A clash of boats in the bay
> And the day marred with murder.

In the final part the poem turns to the present, offering a powerful meditation, of extraordinary technical virtuosity, on the significance for contemporary New Zealanders of the failure at the centre of the Tasman story and of official, public pronouncements which ignore or sanitise the violence in the country's past. Even more, however, the concluding section offers the poem's own discovery of the nature of discovery, Curnow's most eloquent statement of the theme of so many of his poems in the preceding years. Since there are 'no more islands to be found', he writes (as he had in 'Discovery'), the 'eye scans risky horizons of its own': humanity has been cast adrift from the Enlightenment optimism and confidence in the voyage of knowledge as a steady outward progression towards a goal of complete illumination, and cannot predict what 'unknown / But not improbable provinces' lie in the future. As Pocock later insisted,[21] this condition is not seen as a matter for despair or gloom:

> O not the self-important celebration
> Or most painstaking history, can release
> The current of a discoverer's elation
>   And silence voices saying,
> 'Here is the world's end where wonders cease'.

> Only by a more faithful memory, laying
> On him the half-light of a diffident glory,
> The Sailor lives, and stands beside us, paying

Out into our time's wave
The stain of blood that writes an island story.

Curnow's feeling here for the new adventure of discovery he articulates in this section – freed of the dogmas of scientific rationalism, historical positivism, political or religious utopianism, even of those Jeremiahs whose voices prophesy the end of knowledge ('"Here is the world's end where wonders cease"') – is, quite simply, 'elation'. Furthermore, the 'island story' with which the poem concludes is not simply New Zealand's, though New Zealand is included in that story, and the poem is misread if it is seen (as it so often has been) as simply a civic proclamation about national identity. The message of the 'island story' is of an antipodean condition with a new twentieth-century global relevance, in which knowledge of the past and present (and of the violences contained in them) is always a matter of imaginative invention and self-understanding. Every country, from this perspective, has its own antipodes, offering the challenge to new kinds of self-understanding. We may well believe that we have discovered all there is to know about the physical world; but we have hardly begun to articulate imaginatively the human discoveries made excitingly possible by the collapse of no longer tenable epistemologies.

Towards the end of September Curnow completed the poem – which required extensive experiment and revision to reach its final shape – and sent it off nervously to Beaglehole, suggesting a number of titles, including 'Unknown Seas' and 'Landfall'. Beaglehole combined these and suggested 'Landfall in Seas Unknown'. Curnow did not like the inversion, and Beaglehole agreed to the form it finally took.[22] As was habitually the case, however, Curnow felt unsure about its quality, and certainly had reservations about whether he had sacrificed too much in the interests of 'popular comprehensibility', as he wrote to Glover:

> I have completed, & send a copy of, my poem for the Internal Aff. Dept. on the Tasman centennial (I mean ter-). Beaglehole has seen and admired, [Eric] McCormick too, but I have not yet heard whether Heenan agrees. Holcroft, here the other night, said he thought it the best thing I had done so far; which I am inclined to doubt; the range & depth of the symbols & images seems to me very limited; had to be, to meet the demand of popular comprehensibility.[23]

Glover's reaction, when the poem arrived three months later, was similarly qualified, picking up on the comments Curnow had made. It provides an excellent example of his way of speaking directly and honestly, yet sympathetically, to Curnow about his poems:

I thought it lost some of your knotty characteristics in the desire to make things clear to Mr Heenan: it was, therefore, not what I expected. I noticed a certain flat clarity in the images more typical of Eliot than you, images however which may grow powerfully on the mind in certain cases or fail to impress at all. There was certainly little of the Auden touch, that I can remember. The cohesion was good. Taken by itself, I don't think it shares the unique quality of the Pacific sonnets. Taken with your Pacific poems as a bulk installation, yes. There are few writers, my lad, who manage such a collective impressiveness as you do with a number of poems on some central idea. This is your own gift, I think, enriched by close appreciation of Yeats. But he reverts to a favourite line of thought, where you succeed in revolving round it.[24]

Glover's reference to Auden was more than coincidental. It responded to Curnow's telling him – in the same letter in which he enclosed the poem – of a dream he had had in which he met Louis MacNeice in the Masonic pub in Christchurch and talked about poetry. MacNeice, he wrote, 'reproved me a little for fearing the influence of Auden'. Curnow did not make any connection between the dream and the Tasman poem, but Glover, astutely, did, and aimed to reassure Curnow on that score. Early versions of the poem often strongly suggested Auden, and the revisions, at least partly, seemed to have aimed to remove these associations. Auden's strongest remaining traces belong to the final section, in the intricacy of the verse form, in lines like 'that is a chapter / In a schoolbook, a relevant yesterday / We thought we knew all about', and in the homely image of the child underpinning, and saving from over-inflation, the lines 'Who reaches / A future down for us from the high shelf / Of spiritual daring?'

In October 1942 the sole extent of Curnow's commission was for a poem which was to be published in a commemorative booklet, and its fate might have been very different if Curnow, acting on an instinct which had developed during the course of writing it – though only after Beaglehole had approved the poem – had not dropped in on Douglas Lilburn at his room in Cambridge Terrace, 'full of misgivings',[25] leaving him with a copy to read over and think about for a possible setting to music. 'I thought it was pretty good and Douglas was feeling pretty neglected – he had good reason to be – and was pining for work. I offered it to him in fear and trepidation that it wouldn't strike him as something he could do music for.'[26] The poem took a new direction at this point, and events moved quickly. Lilburn was hugely impressed by the poem and within a few weeks had drafted two parts of a score to accompany it. Curnow then approached Beaglehole again to propose a performance of the poem on radio, with Lilburn's music, on the anniversary day itself. Lilburn completed the score, and it was sent to Sir James Shelley, director of the National Broadcasting Service, in Wellington. Plans were in hand for a broadcast performance from radio 2YA.

The work – completed too recently for advance publicity of it to appear in the *New Zealand Listener* – was broadcast on the YA network on the afternoon of Sunday 13 December, with the NBS String Orchestra conducted by Anderson Tyrer, and a Wellington lawyer, A. Eaton Hurley, as the narrator of the poem. Hurley tried hard but did not read the poem very well, and one disgruntled correspondent to the *Listener* ('E.M.D.') complained that he 'marred all' by 'elocuting' to such purpose 'that I did not catch one sentence. The senseless rise and fall of the voice robbed the words of all meaning.'[27] Antony Alpers, writing as 'Marsyas' in the same issue, confined himself to mentioning the 'high level of excitement' with which the poem was read, but warmly welcomed the performance as 'an important event in the story of our arts', and spoke rhapsodically about the excellence of Lilburn's effects, especially the 'stilled hush' he achieved 'through the movement of sounds' immediately after the violent events at the end of the second part. For Curnow himself, hearing Lilburn's music for the first time, it was the beginning of a new sense of 'Landfall' as primarily a poem-for-performance, whatever its effect might be on the printed page. He gave his own account of the radio performance to Glover, after meeting Hurley in Wellington early in 1943:

> I . . . spent an evening with a lawyer named Hurley, who read the Tasman poem from 2YA; read it far better than I feared, but very badly none the less. He obliterated line-endings & mistook rhythms, & used one word that wasn't in the text at all. But a fine serious man. . . . He and his wife persuaded me to deliver the poem there and then, after dinner. Though embarrassed I did so . . . with careful attention to verse structure. The poem and Lilburn's music have been recorded, and will be broadcast again soon. . . . Of the music, I believe Lilburn surpassed himself; both in its own right and as a heightening setting for the poem, his music is superb. It doesn't, of course, strictly 'accompany' the reading. It is: music, then first part of poem; music, second part; music, third part; and then a finale.[28]

His feelings about Lilburn's music intensified when the poem received its first concert performance on 29 September 1943 in Christchurch at the Canterbury College Hall. This remarkable event was the first all-Lilburn concert, with Lilburn as conductor, and it was Curnow himself who gave this first concert reading of the poem. Though the work was to be performed with many different readers on scores of occasions afterwards, this was the only occasion in which both Lilburn and Curnow ever appeared on stage together. The performance in Christchurch was highly successful, despite Curnow's nervousness. 'I rather wish I knew', he wrote beforehand to Heenan, 'what W.B. Yeats meant when he told someone that he read his poems as "all the great poets since Homer" had done it.'[29]

The critics were also impressed. 'F.J.P.' (Frederick Page) in *The Press* recognised that the concert was a historic occasion and was largely won over by 'Landfall in Unknown Seas':

> Music and words fitted happily until perhaps the final section, where one would rather that the poet had had the last word, or perhaps that the music had rounded off the affair more briefly, but the excitement of the first, the expectancy of the second, the searching questions of the third, and slow, movement, were best achieved. As to Mr Curnow's poem, one can but diffidently say that one listener listened to it with some excitement, that lines caught the ear and the imagination, and the whole work rings true.[30] * [31]

'Marsyas', in the *New Zealand Listener*, was even more complimentary than he had been about the first radio performance, asking of Lilburn, 'If he can do this already, what may he not do in time?' and commenting on 'Landfall':

> As a work for an occasion it is truly remarkable when we think of the great ugly graveyard of such things . . . what spontaneous inspiration could produce anything more fresh and adventurous than the bold tune that opens the first Tasman piece? – Mr Lilburn's way of saying 'On a fine morning, the best time of the year.'[32]

However, the most important moment in Curnow's understanding of how the words and music related to each other – perhaps, also, the moment when he could finally acknowledge to himself the lasting quality of what he had written – occurred more than ten years later, in the wake of a reading he gave of the poem, on 27 March 1954, in the Wellington Town Hall with the Alex Lindsay String Orchestra, in a concert devised to reciprocate musical greetings between Wellington and the city of Birmingham in Alabama. The programme included contemporary American and New Zealand compositions, and this was the first concert performance of the Tasman poem since the premiere in Christchurch in 1943. The reviews were unanimous that it was the highlight of the concert, and from this time on 'Landfall in Unknown Seas' became part of New Zealand's classical music repertoire as well as Lilburn's best-known composition. Before the concert Curnow spent a few memorable days in Wellington with Lilburn, preparing and rehearsing for the reading, and wrote revealingly and movingly to

---

* Alex Lindsay, whose string orchestra performed the poem on several occasions in the 1950s, was later moved to suggest to Lilburn that he rewrite the last movement, but Lilburn remained adamant: 'He at least considered it, but eventually said to me, "I can't do it and that's that." I had thought it sounded too inconclusive. "Well, that's how it's supposed to sound," he said. "The poem's inconclusive. It leaves a question in the mind."'

him from Auckland after listening to the radio broadcast of the concert on the 2YC programme on 28 April:

> The music thrilled me as never before; all the distances, colours, & *enlargings* of what the poem says. And the design from beginning to end, so clear & purposeful – doing everything for the poem that it can't do for itself, but nothing that the poem doesn't mean to do with all its heart. . . . I can hardly think of the poem except as a first stage in the creation of 'Landfall in Unknown Seas' now that it has been performed – I'm in a fix, I can't help but praise my own share! – as it deserves to be. I listened with one self-doubting ear cocked for the falsities I always catch when I hear myself played back, but soon found myself deep in both words & music, as if someone else were speaking. . . .
>
> Now I think I understand the work, which I thought so long I did understand. I had sometimes thought the poem belonged to some 'phase' of my own. What egotism![33]

These feelings remained with Curnow for the rest of his life. 'I tend to think of the music first and then the poem. I can't easily think of the two separately', he commented to Jackson two decades later.[34]

Chapter Twelve

Family Expansion,
Sailing or Drowning, and
the Caxton Anthology, 1943–44

I would leave the Press at 2.30am, come home, brew a cup of coffee and
get down to it. The anthology was the centre of my life for some time.
I don't know how many words I wrote for the Introduction and then
threw away. I do recall ripping up about 10,000 words on one occasion.[1]

Belinda's birth, year's end, 1942

By sheer coincidence, Sunday 13 December 1942, the day of the radio performance of 'Landfall in Unknown Seas' to celebrate the tercentennial, marked
a more important event for Curnow – the birth of his second child, Belinda
Elizabeth Allen. A delighted Curnow described the day's events in detail to
Glover:

> On Sunday, December 13, the day Tasman sighted the 'great land uplifted high', the
> second Curnow was born. In the afternoon, about 2pm, we listened to my Tasman
> poem being read on 2YA, with the NBS strings playing the music Lilburn wrote
> for it. A bit later I made some coffee, Bets then feeling a few twinges; taxi at 5pm to
> Lewisham, and all was accomplished by 10.30pm. Bets tells me she knew nothing of
> the real labour at all; no miserable after-effect this time, and Belinda is declared by all
> the experts to be a perfect child.[2]

Curnow's family responsibilities took up a great deal of his time. In December 1942 he was finally promoted to senior sub-editor, and welcomed the bit extra it provided for the family budget. He also decided, after many years, to pay the fee required to take out his BA degree (which he had completed in 1938) at Canterbury University College – looking to improve his employment prospects.

After completing the Tasman poem, Curnow continued to be busy on new writing projects in the last two months of 1942. Writing to Glover in early October he broached for the first time (with a diffidence that matched the doubts he felt about the Tasman poem) the idea of putting together a collection of new poems:

> With what brief and scrappy time remains, I want to make myself a better poet if I can; every new line set down seems to measure an enormous falling short. If I can scrape up a few pounds, I hope nevertheless to have Leo [Bensemann] print in some unambitious format the few poems since Island & Time, probably grouped around the Tasman poem; just in booklet style, the way Eliot had East Coker & Burnt Norton done.[3]

Curnow was working on another group of sonnets at this time. One of these, 'The Skeleton of the Great Moa' – sparked by a visit with Wystan to the Canterbury Museum, where they observed the exhibit of a giant moa (*Dinornis maximus*), its skeleton, held upright by iron rods, reconstructed from bones discovered in a swampy area of a private farm in South Canterbury, together with the fragments of a huge egg which had also been painstakingly pieced together* – was to become the best known and most often quoted of all his sonnets. Its famous final lines, 'Not I, some child, born in a marvellous year, / Will learn the trick of standing upright here.' – encapsulating the poet's identification with the ungainly skeleton propped up on 'iron crutches', the image of a generation's 'failure to adapt on islands' – came almost as an afterthought. In earlier drafts the final lines focused on a quite different idea, on the absence of any connection between the moa and the poet: 'And I have found† no tragic parallel, / Staring among children across a varnished rail.'

Commentators on this poem have almost invariably read it as Curnow's definitive statement about New Zealand identity in the 1940s. It isn't. It was the third of three sonnets Curnow wrote at the time under the general title 'Attitudes for a New Zealand Poet', and he was careful to preserve the sense that it was part of a larger poem from the time of the sequence's earliest publication in *Poetry* in November 1943 to the appearance of his *Collected Poems* in 1974. The other

---

* The whole exhibit, in an enclosure artificially lit to suggest a night sky, was arranged to give some idea of the bird in its original nocturnal habitat.
† Also 'can find' and 'can trace'.

two sonnets offer quite different 'attitudes'. The most that one can say about the Moa sonnet, from this perspective, is that it is offered as one among several possible ways of thinking about the purposes and conditions of being a poet in New Zealand at the time.

The first sonnet, which originally had the title 'New Zealand Decade', presents an 'attitude' altogether unlike that of 'The Skeleton of the Great Moa', exploring the idea of being more accepting of the world as it is, less inclined to project a gloomy personal or apocalyptic drama onto its events, as Curnow seems to suggest his poetry had done in the 1930s:

> That part of you the world offended so
> Has atrophied, or else your strategy has changed,
> Or else you have so much to do
> The simplest way is seeming to agree.

Although the ironies in the sonnet's subsequent references to war undermine any simple notion of celebrating the world as it is, the 'attitude' invoked here is less angst-driven, more impersonal, more aware that human experience contains an inextricable mix of pleasures and pains, positive and negative feelings, and that life goes on, despite the 'horrible age' in which the poet lives:

> Come world, poor Jack-world, and let us reason
> Together, settle down and take our time.
> We shall have bomber and bud in the same season,
> Music and malice both in the one rhyme.
>
> Thunder and tears; committed at this stage
> Neither to horror nor a horrible age.

Of the three sonnets, the most complex and moving was the second, perhaps suggesting an 'attitude' somewhere between the casualness of the first and the sense of his generation as a grotesque museum piece in the third. The second, untitled ('World, up to now we've heard your hungers wail'), deals with the new meanings and feelings that can be dimly discerned through the country's experiences of war. The poem's starting point – the subject of an extended allusion in the second quatrain – seems to have been the remarkable scene in Webster's Jacobean play *The Duchess of Malfi*, in which the 'great sad Duchess' is tricked by a waxworks display into believing that she sees the dead bodies of her husband and children. Curnow saw the Webster play at New Brighton in November 1942, where he and Betty holidayed for a few days as Belinda's birth approached. The poem develops a contrast between the *artifice* of these deaths and the grief they arouse in the Duchess, and the country's awakening to 'the *natural* body of our grief' [author's italics], 'farther off, darker than in a glass', in the nation's collective experience of the actual death and maiming of thousands of New Zealanders on overseas service, and in the reticence of those returning. The poem gives full weight to the biblical metaphor of 'seeing through a glass darkly', which it opposes to the 'trick' in Webster's play, implying the distant possibility of new self-knowledge. Its accompanying emotions – *real* because rooted in actual experience, becoming part of the 'natural body of our grief' – would have the lineaments ('if the shapes would show') of pride and pity: a sense of national identity which is neither spurious nor narrow nor self-congratulating, but generated *through* the country's connection with the sufferings of the wider world.

The 'attitudes' explored in the three sonnets do not exclude the possibility of others. The collective title is simply 'Attitudes', not 'The attitudes'. Nor are they presented as prescriptive for all New Zealand poetry. They are attitudes for '*a* New Zealand poet', not '*the* New Zealand poet'. Nor is any one 'attitude' privileged over the others, though each almost certainly reflects an aspect of Curnow's thinking (and feeling) at the time. Collectively, they reveal a poet absorbed in questions about the nature and purpose of poetry, driven by conflicting, unresolved feelings about how it might be made relevant to the life of his time.

Another Whim Wham

In the latter part of 1942 Curnow also began preparing a second volume of Whim Wham verses for the Christmas market. He was most reluctant to embark on the second venture, and so little had he thought of ever repeating the exercise that he had to go through the same laborious process, with Betty, of advertising in *The Press* for readers to send in any copies they had kept. The publication was undertaken wholly by the Caxton Press, although the idea had come originally from Harold Fenton of the Progressive Publishing Society. By mid-November, in his verse letter to Glover, Curnow was able to report that copy was ready, though still awaiting permission from the censors ('the Factory Controller') in Wellington.[4]

Whim-Wham: verses 1941–1942 went on the market in an edition of 600 copies, just a week before Christmas. Curnow thought it looked well, although it contained no illustrations this time, and 'the verses [were] laid head to tail throughout to save paper'.[5] By the end of January 1943 he reported to Glover that sales were very good ('Whitcombes here disposed of more than 100 in the first week, just before Christmas'),[6] and Glover was impressed with the volume when his copy arrived months later.[7]

Curnow chose 42 pieces for the new selection from more than a hundred which had appeared since *A Present for Hitler*, and they were organised loosely along much the same lines: a dozen war-related pieces followed by a similar number of light, whimsical pieces, then a section entitled 'Home Front' dealing with the effects of the war on different aspects of New Zealand life, and finally a section, 'Public Works', dealing with issues of broader political, cultural and economic significance. The volume contains some of Whim Wham's most delightful lighter pieces, including 'Inside the Shell', speaking out, half tongue-in-cheek, for the rights of Bluff oysters (traditionally, tight-lipped, but revealed as having 'bivalvular feelings') in an industrial dispute. Its allusion to *Alice in Wonderland* at the end reveals how well he had mastered the art of witty allusiveness as a way of entertaining his wide readership:

> 'A Loaf of Bread, the Walrus said,
> > Is what we chiefly need' –
> But all the same the Oysters came,
> > And he began to feed;
>
> But I prefer the Carpenter,
> > Whose honest Eyes were wet.
> Who can reveal what Oysters feel?
> > They have not spoken yet![8]

However, the years during which the pieces in this volume were written were grim ones for the Allied war effort – they included the entry of Japan as an Axis power, bringing with it an extension of the war into the Pacific – years during which, for Curnow, the outcome became less and less certain, and its implications for the future, as these were explored in his serious poetry, profoundly unpredictable. Numerous of Whim Wham's pieces dwelt on the sanitisation of official Allied reporting of the war – reports which Curnow encountered nightly in his work on cables for *The Press*, with the official government handbook of what he might or might not report under war regulations at his side. The issue of truth, in official reporting of the war, found its way directly into poems like 'Pantoum' (originally titled 'The Seascape'), but more generally into the poems' scepticism about public pronouncements of any kind – like 'decorations for merit that congratulate themselves', as he put it in 'Landfall in Unknown Seas' – aimed at reinforcing sanitised versions of the country's past.

Perhaps a piece like 'After All That', satirising easy assumptions about the world that might emerge in the wake of post-war reconstruction, most expresses the mood behind poems like 'The Unhistoric Story', 'Sailing or Drowning' or

'Landfall in Unknown Seas', with their underlying scepticism about predicting the future, or believing that in some way a utopian destiny might be shaped by the human will out of the wreckage and carnage of the war:

> We, who inherit evil Days
> When Nations starve and Cities blaze,
> Are much addicted to the Phrase,
>   'After the War.'
> We have a better World in View,
> Completely overhauled, like new,
> That's what we're looking forward to,
>   'After the War.'
>
> It's only natural and right
> To keep that high Ideal in Sight,
> That Brave New World for which we fight,
>   'After the War'–
> I would not have it otherwise.
> But Words are apt to hypnotise.
> Will Peace be such an easy Prize,
>   'After the War'?
>
> Does Bloodshed of itself presage
> A self-supporting Golden Age?
> Shall we have no more Wars to wage
>   'After the War'?
> That is to say, when we have won,
> Can we declare, 'The Job is done'?
> Or will it be but half begun,
>   'After the War'?
>
> To preach in Verse may be a Crime.
> ('How vilely doth this Cynic rhyme!')
> I'll finish this another Time,
>   'After the War':
> Like Others, I postpone my great
> Conclusions to some future Date,
> Trusting it will not be too late
>   'After the War'![9]

Shifting impulses and interests, 1943

Curnow did not write a great many poems in 1943 – perhaps four or five – and all of them were sonnets. He had been pleased and surprised when *Poetry* accepted 'Sailing or Drowning' the previous year,[10] and no doubt felt challenged to attempt more poems in the same form. Among those he wrote in 1943 were a memorial sonnet for his cousin, Tennent Ronalds, killed on the North African front that year; 'Polynesia', based on Sir Peter Buck's description of a Polynesian ritual in *Vikings of the Sunrise*; and a ground-breaking sonnet for his later development, entitled 'Out of Sleep'. A sonnet to M.H. Holcroft, written after he had read Holcroft's recently published *The Waiting Hills*, seems altogether less effective than the others, more a personal gesture than an opening up of new poetic territory.

'Polynesia' was published under the title 'South Pacific' in the Melbourne quarterly *Meanjin Papers* in its winter issue of 1943.[11] Like 'Sailing or Drowning', it revealed Curnow's fascination with the ways in which Polynesian myth and ritual indicated a unique way of looking at the world, containing a body of knowledge which might assist his thinking about the contemporary world. The poem was based on a Polynesian ritual relating to sea voyaging, in which small gods dressed in 'shawls of bark', but 'blind, numb, and deaf', were cast into the sea to ensure a safe voyage. This association of oceanic migration with sensory deprivation – as Curnow read the mimicry of the ritual – fascinated him, and the sonnet imagines the long sea voyages of the discoverers and settlers (not only Polynesians but Europeans, later) as leaving behind a sensuously rich 'cold or sweltering' world (the northern or tropical climates from which they emigrated), in order to traverse a '*resonant* hades' [author's italics], plunging into an oceanic environment of relentless, repetitive, deafening ('drumming, drumming, drumming') sound.

'Surf is a partial deafness islanders / All suffer from, committed to the land', the sonnet begins. It is as if this deafening oceanic experience, mingling the 'salt of tears within' (grief for what has been left behind) and 'spray without', has permanently entered not only the memory but the sensory economy of later island-dwellers, pervading the way in which the world is seen and felt, even atrophying the senses of sight and touch. At the *sight* of land 'the glove of blindness clapped / On trusting eyes'. Lilburn, who so often sought to explore landscape musically in terms of pervading sea-rhythms, would have understood wholly the impulse behind this remarkable sonnet.

The death on the Allied front in Tunisia of Second Lieutenant Tennent Ronalds, Curnow's cousin, childhood playmate, and friend and regular visitor during the pre-war Christchurch years, affected Curnow deeply. The sonnet he wrote in his memory, 'In Memoriam, 2/Lt. T.C.F. Ronalds', conveys this depth of feeling more keenly because of the restraint with which it avoids inflated rhetoric about those killed in war:

And why should my report

Cry one more hero, winking through its tears?
I would say, you are cut off, and mourn for that.

From its opening lines, in which the poet's weeping for distant 'bones in Africa' suddenly generates the contrasting and intimate image of 'turn[ing] / Our youth over like a dead bird in my hand' – where 'Our youth' is specific to his cousin, as well as invoking their shared childhood closeness – the poem modulates its tones beautifully, avoiding any rhetoric of heroic glorification, and leading to an imaginative reclaiming of his cousin as the voice of the South Island alpine landscape in which so much of his active life was led.

The sonnet to Holcroft, completed in August 1943, was a late addition to the manuscript of *Sailing or Drowning*, and was the last poem Curnow would write for quite some time. In fact, nearly two years were to elapse before any new poem appeared in print. A remarkable three-year period of creativity, from mid-1940 to mid-1943, had drawn to a close, though many of the poems lived on, definitive of their time and speaking freshly to new generations. For Curnow himself, however, it was as if the historical and metaphysical impulses which he had been exploring had exhausted themselves, at least as far as his poetry was concerned, and when *Sailing or Drowning* appeared six months later he described it, self-deprecatingly, as 'mainly transitional'.[12] On the face of it this was an odd phrase for a volume that included so many seemingly achieved poems, but was a clear sign that he was seeking new directions.

One direction was signalled by his reaction to Tennent Ronalds's death, and by the personal implications of a phrase which had appeared in that most public of his poems, 'Landfall in Unknown Seas': 'the eye scans risky horizons of its own'. This direction, that is, took him, for the first time, into his personal past, into personal memory, and into immediate personal experience, as material for poetic exploration. A second new direction was signalled by one of the last of the 1943 sonnets he completed for *Sailing or Drowning*, entitled 'Out of Sleep'. It explores an intimate, internalised moment – a moment between sleep and waking, in which sounds from the outside world are registered with preternatural clarity, but as if in a mist, since consciousness is not yet fully active.

The driving impulse behind the poem is epistemological anxiety: a scepticism about the very possibility of knowledge or meaning – about the world or the self – as something which might be either intuited or 'grasped' by consciousness.

In the half-sleeping, half-awake state distinct sounds are registered, but because full consciousness has not returned and time still remains in suspension, they are 'Noises the mind may finger, but no meaning'. The elusiveness of the 'real', and the provisional nature of any attempts to characterise it, let alone define and discern in it an order and pattern, provided an essential underpinning to all the poetry Curnow subsequently wrote. The poem does not represent a break from the metaphysical and historical preoccupations of *Island and Time* and *Sailing or Drowning*. Curnow's term, 'transitional', better describes the shift. His reflections on the 'oceanic imagination', on the nature of time and history, had defined for him at least one of the directions a twentieth-century voyage of discovery might take. As that journey unfolded over succeeding decades it brought his work into fascinating relation with broader philosophical, intellectual and aesthetic movements of thought in the second half of the century.

Putting poetry on the stage, 1943

Later in 1943 Curnow began work on two major new projects: a play, which was eventually given a public reading, then performed and published, under the title *The Axe*, and his long-contemplated anthology of contemporary New Zealand poetry. Although his wartime workload as a cable sub-editor left him with no time to write theatre reviews, his interest in the theatre remained as strong as ever. He had been considering writing a play himself, occasionally drafting dramatic fragments of different kinds. In a draft of 'Dialogue of Island and Time' which he showed to Glover in 1940 he added a long marginal note, indicating his continuing interest in the possibility of putting formal verse on the stage,[13] and in a long aside in his verse letter to Glover in November 1942 the idea of writing verse plays was still in his mind, particularly the example of W.B. Yeats, even though he joked about his ambitions:[14]

> (God knows whether this is any more intelligible
> Or any less prosy than my prose correspondence:
> I only hope it's a change; you may find patches
> Enough to make the rest worth while. Blank verse
> Isn't after all suited to the gossip column:
> Octosyllabics would have been better perhaps:
> But partly you are suffering from my insistence
> On hammering out a measure of sorts – blank verse,
> With my own impatience stirring in it:
> One day I shall write plays as a result of this,

Dreadful verse drama, and everyone will say,
What a pity he didn't leave it alone; but probably
No-one will even print them. Not quite relevant:
But I recall that Eliot in an address on Yeats
Suggested that what Yeats did with the Drama
Might in the long run have more influence
Than Ibsen or Shaw. But very few seem to agree.)

In 1942 a number of verse drama fragments were written during the course of Curnow's background reading for 'Landfall in Unknown Seas', and in October of that year he discussed with Lilburn (who was then working on the music to accompany the poem) ideas for a possible verse play, with music by Lilburn, which the Canterbury University College Drama Society was interested in producing the following year.[15] He was particularly struck by the dramatic potential of Buck's narrative of the destruction of the complex polytheistic religious system which had evolved on the island of Mangaia with the advent of Christianity, in the third of his Terry Lectures given at Yale University in 1938, which were published as *Anthropology and Religion* in 1939.[16]

Nothing came of it until Lilburn, in August 1943, again prompted Curnow to go back to these fragments and seriously commit himself to the writing of a verse play. At this time Lilburn had recently written music for Ngaio Marsh's production of '*Hamlet* in Modern Dress' by the CUC Drama Society at its Little Theatre, which Curnow reviewed warmly in the *New Zealand Listener*,[17] and had also been struggling unsuccessfully to compose music for a play about New Zealanders on Crete by Anton Vogt, which was intended to launch a new national drama group. Lilburn and Rita Angus met Curnow over lunch at the university, 'both in v. good spirits' according to Curnow, in a letter he wrote to Betty, who had just gone to Craigieburn with Wystan and Belinda for a ten-day holiday on a high-country farm:

We had lunch at the College, though I suppose I shld have gone home to bed – but the weather was bad & the thought of the empty house wasn't cheerful just then . . . . Gordon [i.e. Lilburn] opened a blitz to get me started on a verse play, which he didn't stop till I left them by the library an hour later. He wants a verse play with some music from him & a décor by Rita. If amiable bullying cld make a man write a verse play, I wld be starting one at this moment.[18]

The attraction of poetry in a performance on stage was reinforced by his own involvement as narrator in the first concert performance of 'Landfall in Unknown Seas', and by the impression Maria Dronke made on him as a reader of poetry on stage.[19] A refugee from Germany, Dronke was an actor and voice teacher and Curnow had first met her and heard her read when he was in Wellington at the beginning of 1943, when he wrote excitedly to Glover:

> She is a refugee woman, most beautiful in a large style, and was Elisabeth Bergner's understudy in Berlin. I have heard her read Donne, Shelley, Hopkins, and Eliot; often over-dramatising, but with magnificent grasp of verse structure. . . . [I] think the dramatics can be modified; and if they are we shall have a reader of poetry Willie Yeats might have envied, when he scoured the London stage and found no actor who knew the difference between poetry and prose.[20]

On 7 August, Dronke gave a warmly received poetry recital in Christchurch. Curnow had introduced her to New Zealand poetry and assisted her to prepare for the readings, and the Curnows provided a supper party for her afterwards at Leinster Road, capping what Curnow described to Holcroft as 'a good week', which had begun with the performance of 'Hamlet in Modern Dress'.[21]

By March the following year, 1944, Curnow had made considerable progress in drafting the play. Ngaio Marsh visited for an afternoon, and they discussed progress and plans for its production. Soon afterwards he described it to Glover as 'a short and unambitious verse play [on] the religious-political-military crisis on Mangaia, in the Cook Islands, which led to the triumph of Jahweh & the final confusion of Rongo, Te A'aia, & other oceanic godheads':

> Most of it is there now: Lilburn is keen to do the music, & Ngaio Marsh to produce or help with the stage trickery which she really knows pretty well. . . . It needs another short play with it, so I have pushed Yeats's 'The Resurrection' into Ngaio's hands, & shall think my own venture worth while if it is a lever for getting the Yeats play staged here.[22]

However, the play – which at this stage was called 'The Island and the Kingdom' – still had a great deal more revision and rewriting in store, and it was a long time before it received a full-scale production. In July or August 1943 Curnow asked a few friends around to Leinster Road for an informal reading, including Owen Simmance, Eric Ramsden (a specialist in missionary history who had helped him with the material), Margaret Birkinshaw, and one or two from the college drama group, in order to 'check for false notes'.[23] Ngaio Marsh had previously been consulted about the viability of the climactic battle scene in the play, and was ill and unable to attend the informal reading, but she wrote to Curnow at this time saying how 'very much indeed' she liked the play, and offering detailed advice for what was obviously a production planned at this time.[24]

This production did not eventuate. Its earliest 'completed' form was still significantly shorter than the final version, and was renamed *The Axe*. It received a formal reading two years later in August 1946 at the Little Theatre (the readers included Marsh, who read the chorus, and John Pocock), alongside a one-act play, 'The Land of Heart's Desire', by W.B. Yeats. The play was then revised and extended by the addition of a third act, before receiving its first full-scale stage production, directed by John Pocock, in the Little Theatre in April 1948.

Making an anthology, the Caxton *Book of New Zealand Verse*

In the last few months of 1943, while he began serious writing on the play, Curnow decided to start work on the anthology of contemporary New Zealand poetry which he and Glover had long had in view, announcing his decision to Glover in a letter in October: 'I'm making an anthology of N.Z. verse since 1920 & hope I may draw on yours at will.'[25] Before this, however, he worked on a third collection of Whim Wham pieces, at the request of Harold Fenton. Once again he had to go through the ritual of advertising in *The Press* for readers to send any they had kept, and because the selection covered only a year, *Verses by Whim-Wham, 1943* contained almost all the pieces he had written during that time, and did not quite sustain the liveliness of the previous two collections. Nevertheless it sold well – 950 copies according to one Progressive Publishing Society report – perhaps because of the broader market provided by the *New Zealand Listener* readership,* [26] and it was as warmly reviewed as the earlier collections. It was the last Whim Wham collection he was to make for more than fifteen years.

By the end of October Curnow was buried in the editorial work of the anthology, discovering not only how much reading he had to do but how much correspondence he had to enter into with poets he wished to include, explaining the project and seeking permission to draw from their work. It was a slim anthology, containing sixteen poets whose work had appeared between 1923 and 1945, but within these constraints aimed to present the more significant poets in better than token fashion. Indeed, given the smallness of the print runs of many of the volumes from which the poems were selected, and the fact that many (like Mason's) were out of print, he regarded the volume as effectively making many of the poets and their poems available in print to a substantial readership for the first time.[27]

---

* Editor's note: One hundred Whim Wham verses appeared in the *New Zealand Listener* between 30 January 1942 and 21 December 1945.

The volume was also designed as a counter-statement to the kind of late colonial, sentimental album verse selected in Quentin Pope's *Kowhai Gold* anthology of 1930, and to the persistence of that sensibility in much that Charles Marris published in the annual *New Zealand Best Poems* and in *Art in New Zealand*, of which he was literary editor. However, four of the sixteen poets – Arnold Wall, J.C. Beaglehole, Robin Hyde and Douglas Stewart – were primarily associated with those publications, as would have been Eileen Duggan, if she had agreed to be included in the anthology. That group of five was a generous selection, and showed careful discernment, and certainly nothing like the fixed prejudice he was later accused of bringing to Marris's publications.

The poet given most space in the 1945 anthology was Ursula Bethell (with fifteen pages), slightly ahead of Fairburn, Mason and Curnow himself, and in the middle range (six to ten pages) were Cresswell, Beaglehole, Hyde, Brasch, Glover and (a discovery at a late stage) the verse of the youthful prodigy James K. Baxter. There were only two women poets among the chosen sixteen, though it is hard to think of any others who might have been included, apart from Eileen Duggan, and perhaps Eve Langley. Curnow was particularly severe on his own thirties work, including only two poems: a revised version of the sestina ('Statement') from *Not in Narrow Seas*, and the first poem from its following sequence, 'The water is burred with rain'.

Because Glover was overseas there was no opportunity for any significant discussion with him about the selection, and though Curnow regularly kept him in touch with progress, he felt his absence deeply at this time: 'The task of sole poet militant in the country is an exacting one but I do my best.'[28] Nevertheless, Glover provided an important point of contact with both Brasch and Cresswell in England, and offered what support he could.

Brasch was pleased that the project was going ahead, and concerned that the selection should be rigorous and maintain high standards, but as Curnow commented to Glover, 'his anxiety about the "standard" of the anthology only gave my own intention back to me'.[29] Fairburn was the poet with whom Curnow had most discussion about the contents of the selection,[30] and both Fairburn and Glover insisted that Curnow should not allow false modesty, as editor, to under-represent the presentation of his own poems.

Curnow had doubts about the inclusion of Douglas Stewart and Beaglehole,[31] and also expressed reservations about some aspects of Duggan's poetry. He liked those poems that revealed vividness of observation and imagery, but disliked what he saw as a factitious, decorative use of Maori and New Zealand reference in others, and her (Catholic) religious lyrics did not appeal to him.[32] Although there was never any question of not wishing to include her in the anthology, his efforts to persuade her to be included were to no avail. Duggan wrote to

W.F. Alexander at the time, 'Curnow is getting out an anthology but I stand out of it. Their New Zealand is not mine', explaining in the same letter that she had also refused repeated requests from Ian Gordon to contribute to *New Zealand New Writing*.[33]

Alexander passed on her comment to Curnow, who explained what had happened:

> . . . I approached her through the [Progressive] Publishing Society [the anthology's planned publisher] & her own publishers in England, & also by personal letter, & received in reply a refusal that was curt to the point of rudeness. I had to wait some time for a reply to my own letter to her, & it only came after I had recd the refusal through the publishers & had written to her again, saying that I wld not like to take this as final till I had direct word from her. So, in effect, I asked twice; & my own self-respect forbade any further importuning . . . . I do want you to know that Miss D. is not in my book, by her own wish, not mine: & I do not ask a third time.[34]

Although he was frustrated by Duggan's refusal, he respected her decision, and despite his note in the introduction that he wished to include poems by Duggan but had been refused permission,[35] Curnow was later subject to regular attacks that he had deliberately left Duggan out of the anthology, as part of a conspiracy against women poets.

Duggan is to be admired for the stand she took, which was to challenge the anthology on the grounds of her astute reading of its literary politics. She had a much larger following than any of the Caxton poets, not only in New Zealand, but also in England, where her verse had been admired by numerous of the Georgians, especially Walter de la Mare. But if she hoped that her absence from the anthology would confine its readership to the 'coterie' who read the Caxton publications, she badly misjudged its reception. The Caxton *Book of New Zealand Verse* – and its successor, the *Penguin Book of New Zealand Verse* (1960), from which Duggan also excluded herself – were to exercise a powerful influence on the shape of discourse about New Zealand poetry for at least the next three decades.

The introduction to the Caxton anthology

Curnow put a great deal of effort into the writing of the introduction to the Caxton anthology, and if it had not been for its persuasive critical force and Curnow's eloquence and stylistic panache, the anthology might well have been forgotten after a flurry of interest on publication. The article he had written in mid-1943, 'Aspects of New Zealand Poetry', for Clem Christesen, editor of *Meanjin Papers*, might be seen as a precursor of the introduction. However, he quickly became unhappy with it, in the wake of his reading for the anthology. With most of the selections decided, Curnow drafted his first effort at an introduction during a late annual holiday in South Brighton, where he stayed for three weeks with Betty and the family in March 1944, renting a place on the Esplanade. However, little of what he wrote at that time survived ('he threw most of this away').[36] 'Writing an introduction to the anthology is crazing me', he wrote to Glover a month later, 'thank heaven there are but 14 poets, & too scattered to form a lynching party.'* [37] He kept working at the introduction intermittently for the rest of the year. Two sections primarily dealing with the poetry of Ursula Bethell were published in *The Press* on 18 November, in a gesture of respect to Bethell, who was terminally ill with cancer and died two months later.

As late as December, however, Curnow was drafting new sections, including the late addition of a brief section on Baxter. The selection had been largely complete later in 1944, when Curnow met Lawrence Baigent at the Caxton Press, who was preparing Baxter's first, youthful collection of poems, *Beyond the Palisade*. Curnow's excitement when he read the poems in proof is evident in the paragraphs he wrote about him, and they were important in establishing Baxter as the most promising poet of a new generation. He asked to have as many poems as he could, aware that he could not dismember the individual volume, and eventually selected six.[38]

Although the introduction was later read as a manifesto of literary nationalism, offering prescriptions for how New Zealand poetry should be written, it was considerably more subtle than that, though – perhaps more than anything Curnow had written up to this time – it claimed to identify distinctive imaginative preoccupations emerging in New Zealand poetry, which made it different from poetry written in English elsewhere. Throughout, the introduction insisted that it was not forcing the poems into a preconceived pattern, but retrospectively discerning common themes and concerns that were 'plainly there', in the poetry. Alex Calder's term, 'critical nationalism', is more serviceable, since it captures two key dimensions of the introduction.[39] One was its running attack on earlier forms of national sentiment in verse – signalled by sentimental and decorative references to local flora and fauna and Maori legend, framed within a colonial nostalgia for Home (meaning England) – to be expected in verse written by the immigrant generation, but increasingly a sign of psychic dislocation in later generations of feeble, imitative poets. The other was its emergent sense that the 'fresh impulses' he discerned offered an explicit or

---

* The fourteen poets referred to here did not include Baxter, whose work he had not seen at this stage, and of course he did not discuss his own work in the introduction.

implicit critique of the kind of society New Zealand had become – dependent, materialist, hostile to the life of the mind and spirit.

What has been less emphasised in later commentary on the introduction is its application of modernist aesthetic principles to the issues it was dealing with: for example, the drive to dislodge the traditional canon of New Zealand verse and replace it with another; or the construction of New Zealand's cultural history in terms of psychic breakdown and dislocation – a local variant of the notion of a contemporary 'dissociation of sensibility' advanced in a number of forms by Eliot, Yeats, Pound and other high modernists. The language Curnow used to describe his favoured poets drew heavily on a modernist vocabulary of sensibility – their movements towards the recovery of 'wholeness' or a 'whole' self, through questioning of their relationship to 'land and people', to history, and to contemporary events. Above all, the test of such 'wholeness' of response was sought in the language and form of the poetry: in its complexity, its capacity to integrate emotional and intellectual impulses, its vivid, explanatory, non-decorative use of metaphor, imagery and symbolism. Although the Caxton introduction lacked the brilliance of modernist formal analysis which Curnow brought to his Penguin introduction fifteen years later (he did not have the space to demonstrate its utility as he had in his earlier article on Mason),[40] it was nevertheless premised throughout on the desirability of bringing modernist reading practices to New Zealand.

Birth of Tim, October 1944

The work routine which Curnow demanded of himself when he embarked on the play and the anthology in the latter part of 1943 was exhausting, and continued throughout 1944. If anything, his responsibilities as a senior sub-editor on *The Press* increased his nightly workload, and probably few except his closest friends and family were aware of the irregular hours he led. His letters to Betty, on the occasions when she took the children for brief holidays with members of her family, were invariably written after 3 a.m., when he had arrived home from the paper and before he settled in to working on his own projects for several hours until dawn. His days off from *The Press* (which occurred irregularly at this time) provided the only times when he could enjoy 'normal' daytime outings and recreations with Betty and the children, or visit his parents, to try to make up for the time he could not otherwise spend with them.

His younger brother Tony, who had left school in 1940, and was now in training for the air force, often visited and stayed overnight. On one occasion early in 1944 these daytime outings took them to Governor's Bay in Lyttelton

Harbour, and Betty noted in her diary that they reflected sadly on the changes that had occurred since their previous visit: including the deaths on war service of Tennent Ronalds and Curnow's childhood school friend Bob Crawford, and 'the vicarage no longer a vicarage Church not used'.[41] The seeds of one of Curnow's major poems about the erosions of time, 'At Dead Low Water' – eventually completed and dated 'Governor's Bay, December 1944' – can be seen in this visit to Lyttelton earlier in the year.

Betty's interest in painting and engraving, and her connections in the world of the visual arts, developed strongly during 1943 and 1944, and she spent a great deal of time encouraging Wystan (who started school in 1944) to develop his childhood talent for drawing. Among her productions was the design of a book plate for Curnow, whose elements summed up his life at this time. Betty also designed a commemorative wood engraving of Curnow's 'Landfall in Unknown Seas' in 1943,[42] which they presented to Lilburn at the time of its premiere performance that year, and in the same year she designed a woodcut with a Polynesian theme as a title-page illustration for *Sailing or Drowning*. She also completed a small oil painting of Curnow, seated at a table with a typewriter and manuscript.

Early in March 1944 Betty discovered that she was unexpectedly pregnant again, and Timothy Charles Monro (Tim) was born on 18 October that year. Fairburn and Tony were his godfathers, and Winifred Buchanan his godmother. Despite the pleasure he took in his children, his anxieties about his capacity to support his enlarged family, and about his imagined inadequacies as a father, clearly emerge in Curnow's correspondence during the course of the year. He had already exhausted the possibilities of increasing his income, and for much of the year, as he struggled to complete the play and the anthology to his satisfaction, he seems to have kept going by sheer force of will. To Alexander, three weeks after Tim's birth, he commented, 'I wonder sometimes what I am doing with a family of 3, & whether I ought to be trusted with them. Perhaps not; but all are thriving.'[43] A week later, in another letter to Alexander – written 'at this dead hour of 3am, after a night's work' – the symptoms of exhaustion are clearly apparent:

> I hardly like to mention that I have a notion of coming to Dunedin in January for one or two weeks – because it may seem like a hint, & you have entertained a Curnow often enough. But come I probably shall, & find some room or lodging house; besides yourself, there are few people I have a fancy to look up, & I am too tired for the inevitable hurly burly of a Wellington visit, & too hard up for a spell in Auck'd. And I have to have a spell – by myself & free of family.[44]

Ursula Bethell, whom Curnow visited on a number of occasions during the winter of 1944, offered an acute outsider's view of him at this time. He had first

met her in April 1943, through Maria Dronke, who had known Bethell from
the time of her first arrival in Wellington as a refugee in 1939. At that time
Bethell did not know quite what she thought of the Caxton poets, commenting
to Holcroft that she had not found Mason, Fairburn or Curnow 'easy' to read
and doubted their 'sincerity'.[45] However, she enjoyed her meetings with him, was
impressed by his verse epistle to Glover ('September, 1942') when Dronke read
it in Christchurch, and her first impressions of *Sailing or Drowning* were very
favourable. Later in 1943 Curnow introduced her to Lilburn and kept in touch
with her from then on about his plans for the anthology. She was both impressed
by his sensitivity as a critic and intrigued by his selections from her own work,
especially his receptiveness to her religious poems, which she imagined he would
not like.

In April 1944 she responded at some length to questions about Curnow from
Brasch (who had never met Curnow) in England, offering a portrait derived
from a mixture of gossip and her own meetings with him. She was clearly interested to learn of his Anglican background ('Allen says he's been driven to church
from 5 years old & the rhythms & phrases of the prayer-book remain, as they
do with me'), but she also felt that although he had 'outgrown . . . the anger &
bitterness of the revolt from his beginnings' he remained unsure, now, 'what to
stand on':

> [I]n his talk with me he was sympathetic with & in agreement with one's ideas, but
> its [sic] mostly negative I feel. He's not a 'virile' person – I think he's below par physi-
> cally & always overtired by the nature of his work – but that lack of conviction is not
> characteristic of his type alone – all these young N.Z.ers are afraid of committing
> themselves, giving themselves away. They wrap themselves around with phrases &
> catchwords they hear at the university – they don't take a stand on anything. . . .
> I like Allen – perhaps 'if I'm spared' I shall get to know him better. He's a really
> sensitive critic of verse I think – at any rate I saw the justice of what he said about
> mine! I think making this anthology will 'buck him up quite a lot' (as I hear them
> say). His domestic arrangements, as related to me by others, don't sound very helpful
> – a sort of slovenly bohemianism I greatly dislike. But now I am getting into the
> region of gossip. He's fond of his children! And perhaps that's all I can say about
> Allen Curnow.[46]

Bethell, of course, from her own position of fixed religious commitment
(although Curnow read her poems differently), misunderstood what she could only
see as a 'lack of conviction', an absence of 'virility' and commitment, in Curnow's
intellectual strivings, but her glimpses of his personal situation at this point ring
true, even if they express the censoriousness of her own generation: the toll on

his physical stamina from the nature of his job, and the strain of his 'bohemian' domestic arrangements – in which the house was constantly open to friends and visitors (local and overseas), and a regular venue for parties and gatherings after plays and concerts, though Curnow himself, unless these occurred on one of his days off, might often be only a fleeting presence at them, during a break from work at mid-evening or after an earlier-than-usual finish to his work at *The Press*.

Equally revealing is Bethell's comment, 'He's fond of his children!' It was in the nature of the Curnows' domestic arrangements (because of Curnow's job that Betty had by far the largest part in the children's early upbringing, and she provided a rich, supportive environment for them. But it was perhaps not until the 1960s and after, following the break-up of the marriage to Betty, when the children were grown up and pursuing their own careers and families and Curnow himself had achieved some security and stability in his marriage with Jeny Tole, that he was able to establish and enjoy independent relations with each of them.

Curnow had first made contact with Charles Brasch in August 1943, when he wrote to him in England seeking permission to draw on poems from his Caxton Press volume *The Land and the People* (1939), and from subsequent poems published in England, for his planned anthology.[47] Brasch replied at length, giving Curnow permission to draw on any of his work, and suggesting that the anthology, unlike 'omnibus anthologies like Kowhai Gold', be 'small & select':

> It is so easy to fall into the habit of applying a special standard in one's own country; so difficult, & often so discouraging, to stick to what one knows to be an absolute standard; & it wd. be very valuable to have in NZ a small 'model' anthology in wh. nothing fell below a certain level & from wh. the merely competent & clever & the merely local were jealously excluded.[48]

He also added a more personal comment, intrigued to know more about the personality behind the poetry (which he admired, but – like Bethell – had some reservations about) and aware of the close friendship between Curnow and Glover:

> I am really very glad to have to write to you now. I've wanted to do so many times before, to say something about your work, & always regret that Denis did not introduce us when I was in Chch in 1938. I have read yr. poems as they came out for the last 10 yrs or more (was Valley of Decision your first book?) & always with expectancy & surprise, admiring your restlessness & urge to experiment & wondering where you wd. be led next. . . . Denis tells me that the Caxton Press is soon bringing out a book of your more personal poems, such as the sonnet (Words for Music), wh. I thought fine, & so I look forward to seeing it.[49]

One of the pleasures Curnow looked forward to, towards the end of 1944, was the prospect of Glover's return to New Zealand for a period of leave from the navy. Though he had been pleased with the generally warm reception of *Sailing or Drowning* in the early months of 1944, it was Glover's response, and the circumstances in which it was written, that most moved him. Glover did not receive his copy until June, and it was delivered to him a week into his involvement in the D-Day invasion of Normandy while the craft he was captaining was beached on the French coast with bent rudders waiting anxiously and somewhat helplessly for the incoming tide to try to float it off, amid 'explosions, ours & theirs, [which] go on all the time'. The scene was one of 'murder, & the violence of cold enmity, and ships and bodies on the embattled beach', and – even as he wrote – German aircraft attacked overhead: 'Oh dear, here comes Jerry again – he dashes in, drops a stick of bombs, & out of it like hell.'[50] The scene could hardly have been more appallingly appropriate to the wartime content of so many of the poems. Glover's two airgraphs were brief, and welcoming, and alluded, in a line taken from Curnow's verse letter to him,[51] to his own, immediate 'amphibious hauntings of beaches', but it is astonishing that he wrote them at all, given the danger of his situation. 'May it be a short war here', he concluded:

> I'm sick for home & the rebuilding of my evaporated mana. And I need silence & seclusion. . . . This is written waiting for the tide to float me off. It's all waiting, but tides are predictable. Greenwich Mean Time – 10, time ticks me Back someday.[52]

Glover arrived back on 20 October 1944, two days after Tim's birth, and within days was back at the Caxton Press and enthusiastically involved in the planned anthology. Early in December he visited the Progressive Publishing Society in Wellington, which at that time had undertaken to publish the book (with the Caxton Press as printer), to try to resolve the financial arrangements so that he could at least get started on the production before his leave expired on 2 January.[53] On that day, an hour before he was due to depart, he was given a reprieve, and a week later heard that he had been granted a further six months' leave. The way was clear, at this point, for Glover to take over the entire publishing project at the Caxton Press.

Towards the end of 1944 Fairburn wrote to Curnow with two requests.[54] The first was for any poems that might be printed in *The Arts in New Zealand*, a revamped bi-monthly version of Marris's *Art in New Zealand*, of which Fairburn was now literary editor. Curnow replied that he had nothing to offer apart from a possible section from his verse play, but that further work would be needed on the versification of the chorus in the piece he wanted to send. It was not until April the following year[55] that the drought of poems was broken when he sent

Fairburn the first he had completed for nearly two years – 'At Dead Low Water' – which appeared in the April–May issue that year. Unfortunately, transposed lines made the third section of the poem unintelligible, and Curnow was extremely angry, writing to Fairburn: 'the result is grotesque'.* [56] The excerpt from *The Axe* had to wait longer, until the end of 1946.

Fairburn's second request was for biographical information and if possible a 'Credo', to be included in a piece on Curnow which he wished to write for the monthly magazine *Action*, as one of a series of 'New Zealanders You Should Know' that he was contributing. Curnow's reply provides a revealing insight into the way he saw his literary career up to this point. Apart from a list of facts and dates about his birth, schooling, St John's College studies, and career in journalism, and about his publications, the tone is constantly self-effacing, perhaps illuminating Bethell's not-quite-accurate comment a few months earlier about his 'lack of conviction'. Perhaps 'diffidence' or 'uncertainty' would have been better words. The chronology of his life, he wrote to Fairburn, 'isn't very impressive, & I can't see much being made of it'. About his 1930s publications he was equally diffident, remarking that 'Poetry & Language' was 'pretty callow as aesthetic but did lead to a correspondence with Eric Gill till his death'. He did, however, emphasise being 'more or less continuously in touch with Glover & the Caxton Press, & [I] like to think I was helpful in projection & selection of some of the verse he published'. He declined to offer a 'Credo' and suggested that there might be 'a scrap or scraps' that could be quoted from his more recent volumes, 'if any such catch your eye & seem to serve the purpose'.

On a number of issues he was more forthright, however, devoting a paragraph to his Monro ancestry and his status as a fourth-generation New Zealander, asking that mention also be made of his 'debt' to his father's 'grounding in poetic tradition, his skill (too little applied) in verse, & perhaps his poem in Alexander & Currie's *Treasury of N.Z. Verse*', and emphasising that he would like to be seen as placing 'far more significance' on his New Zealand reception than on any 'bouquets from overseas'. The Tasman poem, he added, 'I don't between ourselves set much store by'. He also sent Fairburn a copy of his *Meanjin* article on New Zealand poetry, which he 'felt apologetic about . . . . the balance is all wrong', and concluded his summation with the instruction, 'NOT A WORD ABOUT WHIM-WHAM'.[57]

Fairburn replied that the 'dope' Curnow had sent was 'ideal for the purpose'.[58] He used all of Curnow's factual material in his article,[59] but added his own commentary on a poet whom he presented as 'of the very first importance', who had already, at the age of 33, 'written some of the poetry that will be in

---

* The error was noted and corrected in the next (June–July) issue of the magazine.

New Zealand anthologies a hundred years hence'. He also detected in the poetry – especially in Curnow's distrust of 'synthetic glory masquerading under the name of history' – a strong Christian influence:

> Curnow is, I think, a Christian poet, in that he asserts the basic values of Christianity. But, living in an age of doubt and uncertainty, and feeling that he is involved in the chaos about him, he lacks the presumption to assert any dogmas. 'Time trips up even the humblest heart [sic],' he says, and that thought forms an undercurrent to much of his poetry.* [60]

Above all, as if by way of answer to those who regarded the poetry as obscure and difficult, Fairburn emphasised the *intelligence* Curnow brought to poetry:

> To say that he has written 'intelligently' may sound patronising. But intelligence is something that has been foreign to most New Zealand poetry in the past, and I regard Curnow's insistence on using his brain as being of great importance. Poetry apart – or rather, through the power of poetry – it helps to define an attitude. It helps us to break with that tradition of calculated nit-wittedness that has been the bane, not only of poetry written in New Zealand, but of much else that has been done here. For Curnow, poetry is something more than a chocolate confection to please the palate. It is a way of thinking and feeling, and of giving form and meaning to our lives.[61]

---

* Editor's note: 'Time trips up all but the humblest of heart' is the line Fairburn misquotes from Curnow's 'The Unhistoric Story'.

Chapter Thirteen

Restless Years, 1945–46

All these last weeks I have been more alone than I have ever been, a
discipline for the soul perhaps, but knowing an operation is necessary
doesn't make it less painful. . . . We are wife & husband, & every
marriage is a unique thing, two entirely unique personalities closely
related; no-one can predict the result, & someone (being very wise after
the event) might easily blame us both & say we made a mistake together
10 years ago; but we didn't, we simply made the same act of faith that
everyone makes in marrying . . . . No-one can say we have done badly
in our situation, because no-one has ever been in just our situation.[1]

Changing family circumstances

After Tim's birth in October 1944, Curnow arranged a live-in home help for four
months, and in January 1945 he had some time away on his own, which he desperately needed. It was his first proper break for two years, as the previous year's holiday
in March at New Brighton had been swallowed up by work on the anthology and
on his play. He stayed for a fortnight at 'Uplands' farm at Kakahu (inland from
Geraldine, in South Canterbury), which was owned by a Le Cren cousin, Betty, and
her husband, Douglas. His letters home every second day are full of the relaxing
pleasures of this holiday. He enjoyed the company of his hosts, tramped the hills
behind the farm and explored the Kakahu Bush, which was part of the farm.

He especially enjoyed rabbit-shooting. 'This letter seems to be nothing but
bloodlust', he wrote,[2] after providing an account of an expedition in which he shot

a hare, which he mistook for a large rabbit. The memory of this event remained buried for nearly forty years, when it resurfaced in the last section of the poem 'Dialogue with Four Rocks', remarkable for its dispassionate recall of the event, its empathy with the wounded hare as he crawls through blackberry trying to reach it, and for the irony of his blindly aimed 'shot in the dark' which ricochets off the rock under which the hare is trapped and kills it, but which might have killed himself. Hunter and quarry, hound and hare, 'under the one skin', are both subject to the randomness with which death strikes.

Curnow did not take on any major new projects during 1945, but he was nevertheless busy and, despite the relaxations of his holiday, was restless about his life in Christchurch and especially his job as a journalist. In March he wrote to the Press Association in London about a job it was advertising, and in September he applied for a lectureship in English at Auckland University College. Writing confidently to Betty,[3] he thought his application 'the most effective personal salesmanship I have ever done', but he was overlooked in favour of M.K. Joseph, and had to come to terms with this 'setback in one's self-conceit'.[4] At the end of the year he enquired about yet another job, again unsuccessfully, as successor to Alan Mulgan in Wellington in his position as supervisor of talks on the National Broadcasting Service.

At least part of his reason for applying for these jobs was to try to improve his financial circumstances, which were extremely tight with his expanded family. He had exhausted the options to increase his income on *The Press*, though he improved his weekly payment for Whim Wham from £1 to £1/10/- (after applying for £2). But by mid-1945 he was three months behind on rent. Friends and family tried to assist. David and Celia Taylor had Betty and Tim to stay for a week (in their vicarage at Akaroa) at the end of July, while Wystan and Belinda stayed with Jessie and Tremayne at Kaiapoi.

By this time no love was lost between Curnow and Betty's mother Daisy and sister Margaret, whom he regarded as interfering pests, nor between Betty and Curnow's mother Jessie, who made her disapproval of Betty (and of her son) known in no uncertain terms. Curnow himself, by no means innocent in these difficult family dynamics, nevertheless delighted in his children. Belinda's earliest memory of her father, at the age of three, dates from July of this year, when, returning from work at 4 a.m., he carried her outside to see the garden during Christchurch's heaviest recorded snowfall, and in the week afterwards built toboggans and snowmen for the children. His extended work hours at *The Press* did not begin to ease until the capitulation of Japan in August. He was especially commended by *The Press* management for his reporting of the war, largely on his own, for three years, and on the evening of Japan's surrender allowed himself, for the first time, to be carried home thoroughly drunk by his *Press* colleagues.

Jessie's impatience with Betty's domestic arrangements was not unconnected with her own anxieties at this time, with Tremayne's retirement from the ministry looming in February 1946, when they would have to vacate the vicarage in Kaiapoi where they had spent their last nine years, and make a decision about where to live. In the end they chose to uproot themselves entirely from Christchurch and retire to Auckland, and during the later months of 1945 began the business of sorting and packing their belongings, in preparation for their departure the following March. Perhaps they looked forward to re-establishing connections with Tremayne's older brother Pendarves and his wife Eva, who had lived in Auckland for many years. Perhaps they could also see that the years of close-knit family relationships in Christchurch were coming to an end. Although Allen and Betty and their grandchildren still lived there, they would have been aware of Allen's restlessness and wish to live elsewhere. Their elder son John had become a male nurse at Nelson Hospital, after spending much of the war as a medical orderly in an army hospital near Blenheim, and Tony, their youngest, was also living away from Christchurch. After he was called up for military service, he spent periods as a bandsman and stretcher-bearer at army and air-force bases in New Zealand, and in 1945 was based at Air Force Headquarters in Wellington.

Curnow was himself concerned at this time about how his parents would cope with retirement, and wrote to Fairburn immediately after they moved to Auckland, asking him to contact them:

> I know they wld appreciate a call from you. My father is half crippled with arthritis in one leg, & is feeling badly the loss of mobility with his motor-car – it was like the Arab's Farewell. I can't guess how you & he wld get on; but I hope you will be able to give tactful support to my promptings & persuadings.*⁵

Tremayne and Jessie purchased a house at Greenwoods Corner in Epsom, but, perhaps predictably, the move to Auckland was a disaster. They disliked the people and the climate, and two years later (in April 1948) they returned to Christchurch, where they arranged the exchange of their Auckland house for one in Papanui.

Reception of the Caxton anthology, 1945

In mid-1945 the Caxton anthology appeared, and Curnow was delighted with the substantial reviews it received, not only in New Zealand but overseas in the

---

* Editor's note: Curnow is referring to the well-known poem 'The Arab's Farewell to his Horse' by Caroline Norton (1808–1877).

Times Literary Supplement[6] and in *Poetry*.[7] By the end of the year it had sold 1000 copies, and Fairburn, Holcroft, Baxter and others had written to him at length about the book.

The New Zealand review which most pleased him was by Eric McCormick in his own newspaper, the Christchurch *Press*.[8] A postscript in a letter he wrote to Holcroft reveals how insecure he still felt in having to prove himself to others in Christchurch: 'Simply because he praises me so, at home in Christchurch, I more than "almost wept" for a moment when I read it.'[9] McCormick's praise was high indeed, comparing the force of Curnow's criticism (written 'with the authority of a practising poet') to the early criticism of T.S. Eliot, and describing the intro-duction as containing 'the most sustained and penetrating critical estimate yet given of New Zealand verse'.[10]

Fairburn thought the anthology 'a Landmark in NZ Literary history',[11] but he also felt that Curnow's critical position gave too much liberty to 'Romanticism' and 'Bardism', though he did not include Curnow's poems in his comments: 'I don't consider the romantic element in your work overdone; the tautness and sometimes the astringency you inject into it prevent excess, anyway – provide the extra dimension of irony.'[12]

For Brasch in London the book's inclusion of eleven of his poems, including the iconic 'In These Islands' and 'A View of Rangitoto', provided crucial personal recognition, confirming him in his decision (much discussed with Glover) to return to New Zealand to establish a literary periodical.

Baxter, then just nineteen years old, was also extremely impressed by the anthology, writing enthusiastically to Curnow:

> Dear Allen,
>
> Excuse the Christian name: but I have just bought and read your N.Z. anthology, and feel the mutual solidarity too strong for conventional titles. You have indeed created something sturdy and lasting; something long-needed; something of a classic nature. Your INTRODUCTION is essentially pithy and true, full of insight and a right balance between the opposing powers of our 'provincial' heritage and our new growth which is rank, raw maybe, but actual. Believe me, I have seen and recognized most of the trends and symptoms you mention, but not so clearly nor with so deep a probing.[13]

The letter is also interesting for Baxter's early assessments of the poets Curnow had included. Like McCormick he was not impressed by Arnold Wall's 'tang of the *Kowhai Gold* insipidity', but particularly liked Cresswell's 'great verse and strong poetry'. He had reservations about Bethell, and in Robin Hyde's work 'the emotion just breaks through, no more', but particularly liked Fairburn ('a miraculous perfection in poems like "The Cave"') and Mason ('easy water over fanged rocks'), and offered acute comments on Curnow's own poetry:

> *House and Land* always struck me as perfect of its kind. The best are the most subjective. *Wild Iron* for instance superb technically but gets its strength only from a sense of underlying subjective stress. Intellectual subtlety very apparent: epigrammatic mingled with emotion the best, as IN MEMORIAM ...*[14]

Shortly afterwards Curnow wrote a poem, 'Dunedin', which he dedicated to Baxter, sending it to Fairburn in September with the comment that it was 'a brief & slightly bardic piece, about sonnet size',[15] and it appeared in the first issue of Harold Wadman's *Yearbook of the Arts in New Zealand* at the end of the year alongside 'Self-Portrait'. Both poems, in different ways, questioned the process of perception itself, sceptical about the reliability of any representation of the self or the world. Whereas in 'Self-Portrait' the self behind the photographic image of the poet as a four-year-old child remains enigmatic and impenetrable, in 'Dunedin' the inability to separate the 'truth' of what is observed from the self-absorbed dreams, desires and anxieties of the observer-inhabitants provides the subject of the poem.†

Curnow was especially interested in Alexander's review of the anthology in the Dunedin *Evening Star*. He had taken care to keep him informed about the progress of the anthology, insisting on his high regard for Alexander's earlier anthology, *A Treasury of New Zealand Verse*.[16] Alexander's review was a small masterpiece in struggling to be fair to poetry with which he was basically out of sympathy. He gave some emphasis to its 'omissions' – the most 'weakening' of which was Eileen Duggan, though he acknowledged that she had 'refused permission' – but described it as 'a memorable book', with a 'thoughtful and most stimulating' introduction to 'a body of poetry which could not be ignored'. His lack of sympathy with much of the poetry was carefully phrased:

> Poetry, said Milton, and it has been generally agreed, should be simple, sensuous, and passionate. Here is poetry, in the most pronounced, predominant examples, that is none of the three. Ursula Bethell does not come into that type. She has passion. Above all this new poetry is not simple. Is it the new rhythms and broken metres, still imposing a strain despite their general effect of sameness in most of the writers,

---

* 'In Memoriam, 2/Lt. T.C.F. Ronalds'.

† The poem concludes with images of the antipodean 'doubleness' of Dunedin's location, as both a 'mirage of the cracked Antarctic' and a piece of 'the original dazed stone / Pitched out of Scotland to the opposite Pole', and is itself in the form of an 'inverted' sonnet – beginning with the sestet and concluding with the octet – as if miming this antipodean inversion.

or their profounder 'intellectual content' that makes these poems harder to read than almost all English poetry down to and including Housman? ... One can imagine one of these new poets reading Wordsworth's odes or sonnets, much more the 'Golden Treasury', and murmuring, 'How childish!'[17]

Curnow appreciated the effort Alexander had made, though he insisted that with the addition of two or three poems from Eileen Duggan 'the book would, without qualification, represent my own notion of what a representative & critical anthology of the period shld be'. 'Please do not think of any of my chosen poets despising Wordsworth or "The Golden Treasury"', he went on, rejecting Alexander's way of dividing the traditional and the modern, and suggesting (perhaps somewhat tongue-in-cheek) that it might have been the 'excellent education' in Alexander's time that made him and others think that all poetry before Housman is 'effortlessly lucid':

> In their day, Hazlitt had to defend Wordsworth against those who made him out a scurrilous and theory-ridden innovator – one of them said no-one but Mr W. wld have formed so 'arbitrary & capricious an association' as betw laughter & daffodils![18]

Curnow finished his letter in response to Alexander's review of the anthology on a personal note, alluding to pressures in his life:

> For me, the time of gestation of the book has been crowded enough. I have had the cables desk for nearly two years, with a succession of assistants, good and not-so-good; & three delightful but time-taking children. At the moment I am looking forward to a week's quiet 'baching': with the elder two at Kaiapoi [that is, staying with Muz and T], & my wife & the youngest at Akaroa.[19]

The week's baching seems to have been anything but quiet. When Betty returned from Akaroa, where she had been invited to stay by the Taylors, she noted ironically in her diary, 'Denis [Glover] made great use of the house while I was away', and spent the afternoon cleaning it.[20]

Charles Brasch meets Curnow, February 1946

Later in September 1945 Betty's parents drove her and the children to Nelson, where they stayed for ten weeks with her brother and sister-in-law, Richard and Maisie Le Cren, near Richmond, seeing a great deal of other Le Cren relatives (including Betty's sister Margaret) who lived in the area, as well as John and Averil Curnow. It was the longest time Curnow and Betty had been apart up to this time, and a generous gesture especially on the part of Richard and Maisie, who were aware of the Curnows' struggles to cope with a young family in Christchurch.

Curnow's letters to Betty, usually written at the *Press* office in the early hours of the morning, provided detailed accounts of his daily activities. In September he worked on an interview he had done with Ngaio Marsh for the first issue of the *Yearbook of the Arts in New Zealand*:

> .... rewrote nearly all Ngaio's parts & have passed it back to her: it looks now a much solider piece, except that the ideas are nearly all mine & Ngaio's part is rather like the ventriloquist's doll's. However, I think she'll be grateful.[21]

He saw a great deal of the painter Douglas MacDiarmid at this time, interested him in the poetry of Yeats, and gave detailed accounts of the progress of a painting he greatly admired (*Allegory*) which MacDiarmid was working on for the 1945 Group Show. There were occasional comments about Whim Wham, including a meeting with a woman 'who is another of the lunatic tribe who cut out all the Whim Whams & paste them into books',[22] and about the difficulties of writing them:

> Yesterday ... tried to write Whim Wham at the office ... but ... the sort of nerve-tension I use for Whim Wham just wouldn't come. So after two hours' trying, I went to the Caxton P – where all the rest of the anthology, bound, arrived for the Xmas market.[23]

He also gave a detailed account of his mother's discovery of a bundle of early childhood photographs, and of the particular one which sparked his poetic interest, sending an early draft of 'Self-Portrait' to her, and shortly before she returned in December described a letter from James Bertram in Auckland, recently returned from the Far East, with news that Charles Brasch was on his way to New Zealand:

> The last paragraph is typical Bertram of 'Phoenix' days: '. . . . everything, in fact (he says) seems to point to a literary renascence. Can't we start a new magazine or something?' Well – I wonder if 'we' can. Brasch, who has the money, does want to start a magazine, & with Bertram at his elbow it wld stand some chance of success. I've written my views on this to James B.[24]

Throughout 1946, after his arrival in Dunedin in February that year, Brasch travelled the country familiarising himself with the New Zealand artistic and intellectual scene and consulting key figures about the aims and shape the new periodical might take. Despite his doubts about his own capacities as editor, 'because of my insufficient knowledge, my limited interests, laziness, impatience, lack of energy and ideas',[25] Glover, Curnow and Lilburn were strongly supportive, emphasising to him that 'the aim of the quarterly shd. not seem to be to present NZ to the world, to explain & obtrude it as they say has been done ad nauseam'.[26] Brasch's first meeting with Curnow occurred in February at the Caxton Press:

> Curnow's appearance was unexpected: older, more set than I looked for (though at 34 he no doubt shd. look mature), very much the type of an English intellectual, robust in build, wearing glasses & a tweed jacket, smoking a pipe. I thought of Day Lewis, even Priestley. He did not attract me; I felt, or thought I did, something heavy, hard, slightly coarse in his features & expression, & was at first sight a little repelled. We kept gazing at each other as we talked; he was, if anything, more master of the situation than I.[27]

A few months later Brasch met Lilburn, the figure who alongside Curnow most interested him for his creative achievements, and immediately contrasted him with Curnow:

> When we had thawed somewhat towards each other he spoke a little of his aims as a composer, & I felt him to be single minded & of high solitary purpose, not worldly although enjoying the world. Very different in this he seemed from Curnow, who is indeed possessed by poetry & (with Lilburn, I think) by NZ, but whom I feel to be in some way unspiritual, though I have little enough to go on; we are already on good terms & I like him, yet I do not think I shd. ever wish to be intimate with him, except on literary grounds. In Lilburn I thought I divined a kindred spirit, & was drawn to him more than to anyone else in NZ yet.[28]

Behind such reactions was Brasch's fundamental disaffection with New Zealanders' inability (as he saw it) to 'live alone', to attend to their inner spiritual development. 'In New Zealand', he confided to his journal, 'most people try to live together without living alone – or try to avoid living alone by living together (Denis [Glover] is an example of this).'[29] He particularly detested the pub culture which both Glover and Curnow enjoyed, describing on a later occasion the 'mercilessly ugly' pubs 'in which I have spent two days drinking with [Glover] & Allen Curnow in the last few days – may it be a long time before I have to enter one again'.[30] In another entry he went so far as to link his reservations about aspects of Curnow's poetry to a mismatch between the poet's public and private life:

Allen Curnow's poetry is – as I find it – narrow & somewhat barren for all its accomplishment because he allows himself to lead too much of his life in common & keeps too small a part of it private. It may well be that his public life is a kind of defence about his private life: Douglas & I, being single & independent, can go our own ways regardless of other people & are not faced with the same kind of difficulties as Curnow. But even for us some stubbornness is needed; & Douglas certainly has it.[31]

Brasch half-glimpsed that Curnow's 'public life' might have been a 'defence' to protect his inner life, but was nevertheless somewhat jolted by Maria Dronke's analysis of Curnow in a conversation in which Brasch had disparaged Curnow for his scorn of Basil Dowling's spiritual 'emanations':

Maria has strong views about Allen's marriage & blames Betty severely for making no attempt to help him as a poet & being completely selfish. She has a high regard for Allen & feels that his outward hardness & coldness conceal a tender & shrinking nature, a strong religious sense & sense of goodness – I had mentioned Allen's remark about Basil, & she thought that was Allen defending himself against what he ought to be himself. . . . I had not seen this insight in Maria before – or not applied to people I knew much myself.[32]

Brasch's reactions to Curnow were complex, a mixture of curiosity and frustration that he could never get close enough to understand the inner workings of Curnow's personality, always a touchstone in his reactions to other males, alongside his reaction to their physical attractiveness. It may be that the personal distance Curnow preserved, on his side, in his relations with Brasch, was itself a reaction to the intense, somewhat possessive demands too close a relationship with him would entail.

Jack without Magic, 1946

In January 1946 Curnow had a second rabbit-shooting holiday, of a fortnight, at Betty's cousin's farm at Kakahu, enjoying the scene again, which he described as 'full of beauties', although 'there aren't nearly so many [rabbits] about as there were last year'.[33] Soon after his return to work Betty spent three weeks with the children at the cottage of Frederick and Evelyn Page in Governor's Bay while the Leinster Road house had major plumbing repairs done, and Curnow visited on weekends. While they were away Curnow arranged for an article about Ezra Pound, recently indicted in the United States for treason in the wake of his pro-fascist activities in Italy during the war, to be reprinted in *The Press* from the American *Saturday Review*.[34] The article, deeply hostile to Pound, was written by Henry Seidel Canby, an academic from the English Department of Yale University whom Curnow had interviewed and greatly liked during Canby's lecture tour of New Zealand the previous year, in which he drew comparisons between the national cultures of the two countries.*

A week later in *The Press* Curnow followed Canby's article up with his own angry indictment of Pound, in the form of a sonnet, 'Ezra Pound', alluding to many lines and phrases from Pound's earlier poems and focusing especially on his fascist politics as a betrayal of his claim to be a poet. In his sonnet he subjects Pound to the same scorn Pound himself poured on others in numerous of his early poems:

> Ezra, the game is up; all up, poor Pound.
> Short weight, deranged. Poising a case for treason,
> The law's contempt, not pity, weighed and found
> Your state unfit, wanting both rhyme and reason.
>
> You whose amusement was 'the public taste',
> Messer Pound, what have we to do with you?
> How is the 'strange rare name' you boasted based?
> Greek howlers in your verse, translations too
>
> Held suspect, came to judgment long before
> A few sad insolent lines escape this doom.
> 'Goldish weft', mutterings behind the door
> Of Smart in Bedlam, Hoelderlin's high room
>
> A flattery, that, after your own vain heart!
> 'Yet I am a poet' – there let judgment start.[35]

Curnow did not include this poem in a small collection of poems, *Jack without Magic*, he assembled at this time for Glover, who had discovered a small amount of high-quality paper stashed away at the Caxton Press and wished to experiment with a setting in 12-point Blado font.

Curnow had published only three poems since mid-1943 – 'At Dead Low Water', 'Dunedin' and 'Self-Portrait' – and struggled to find others to make up a

---

* Curnow wrote two articles about Canby in *The Press*, entitled 'Comparison of Literatures: Development of New Cultures' and 'Methods of National Expression', in June 1945. Canby's visit coincided quite fortuitously with the publication of Curnow's own anthology that month, whose introduction was highly relevant to the argument of the lectures.

slim volume of sixteen pages. Eventually he managed to assemble eleven poems. Two were retrieved from earlier years – 'Dimensional', a Picton-based landscape piece dated 1938, and a short poem, 'To D.G. Overseas', written during the war – and another brief poem, 'Darkness, Patience', seems to belong to the mood of 'Rite of Spring' and 'In Summer Sheeted Under' composed in 1941. The title poem, a quatrain with a witty, epigrammatic quality, was written as an epigraph for the collection, a defence of poetry against crusading scientific materialism, and it might also be seen as an epigraph for much in Curnow's later poetry. 'Jack without magic', hostile to the life of art and the imagination and the values of the heart, unable to accept the magic of nature, believes that his 'atom brain' makes him totally self-sufficient:

> Cleverer than ever O atom brain,
> Nature you dread, and next to nature, art:
> Jack without magic springs his traps in vain
> Against these giants and genii of the heart.

However, there were four other new poems, all sonnets – 'Children, Swimmers', 'Paradise Revisited', 'Unhurt, There is No Help' and 'The Waking Bird Refutes' – which were more than simply makeweights for the collection. 'Children, Swimmers', though slighter than 'At Dead Low Water', might be seen as a companion piece, based on a vivid memory of his lively childhood cousin Patricia Ronalds swimming at Corsair Bay in Lyttelton Harbour. Although it is suffused with a similar sense of the erosions wrought by time, the sonnet moves to a different, richly affirmative conclusion:

> O but how under sea glitters no less
> Your flesh against time's fathoms, and not sunken
>
> Ever, astonishes with a breath this drowned
> Valley where tides hinge and love's dead are found.

'Paradise Revisited' reimagines the Fall as a darkly charged sexual drama, in which the 'formidable' Eve ('no shy deer') deliberately mixes the pleasures she offers with intimations of their transience and of death. 'Unhurt, There is No Help' offers a similarly intense sexual drama, rejecting the idea of love as possession or ownership of the other ('Love, be your own / And stay the far side of that Tree / Whose seed struck earth between us'). 'The Waking Bird Refutes' offered a different kind of mythic reimagining – the steady downfall of rain at night ('listened to at windows by / The sleepless') invokes the beginning of Noah's Flood, in which the 'bright, waste repossessive element' reduces everything to silence as it accomplishes the destruction of the world – though again with strongly personal overtones, exposing such apocalyptic thinking as a grandiose delusion of the self in the final line: 'But the waking bird refutes: world will not end.'

Poems like these represented a distinct personal turn in Curnow's poetry, away from the public themes of his earlier volumes, based on sensuously observed scenes from which an intense and heightened natural symbolism is developed. Betty noted in her diary, reflecting a comment made to her by Curnow at the time, that there was 'something of Allen's "At Dead Low Water" in Dylan Thomas' *Map of Love*',[36] a comment which might also be applied to 'Children, Swimmers' and many of the poems Curnow wrote, on love themes, in the later 1940s.

By early April,[37] Glover had finished hand-setting the poems and *Jack without Magic* appeared the following month. To some among the older generation the volume simply confirmed Curnow's waste of his talents. 'As to Curnow Jr's last book', A.E. Currie wrote to Alexander, 'it's simply what Mulgan calls "coterie-potery". With a vocabulary like that, the man ought to be able to do something decent, but he won't.'[38] However, it had a notably welcoming reception from Baxter in the *Otago Daily Times*,[39] though Curnow – writing to Fairburn about Baxter as a possible author of a critical article for the second *Yearbook of the Arts in New Zealand* – felt that his praise was overstated:

> You want an opinion on B.? I think his criticism would be readable, sensible, but much more likely to betray his youth than his poems are; he's liable to undisciplined enthusiasm, e.g. a review of my 'Jack without Magic' in the 'Otago Daily Times', where he rather spoilt his case by overstating – from memory, I think he hailed me as 'a master of the sonnet form', which says far too much and means far too little.[40]

For Baxter, 'At Dead Low Water' – especially its concluding sonnet – remained a touchstone by which he assessed all of Curnow's poetry, the poem which above all others placed him 'in the first rank of modern poets'. Describing Curnow as 'the best New Zealand intellectual poet', he praised the poet's 'return to simple Biblical imagery, more deep-rooted and spontaneous than philosophical discourses on the nature of island time'.[41]

Lili Kraus

The Christchurch arts scene was greatly enlivened in July 1946 when the world-famous Hungarian-born pianist Lili Kraus gave her first concert there, headlined the day after in *The Press* as 'One of the Concerts of a Lifetime'.[42] She had been released the previous year from a Japanese prisoner-of-war camp in Java where she had been captured and interned for much of the war, and her performance had already taken Auckland by storm, prompting a long and enthusiastic article in the *New Zealand Listener*, as well as a letter from Fairburn claiming that 'no greater artist has been heard in this Dominion' and that she was 'an interpreter of music . . . of such luminous power that it is difficult to find words to speak about her – a pianist of quite transcendent genius'.[43] She in turn became enamoured of the country, staying for almost a year with her husband Otto Mandl and daughter Ruth, and returning again in 1948 before travelling back to England and Europe.

The country had been starved of overseas musical talent during the war years, and Kraus's experience of internment in Java perhaps linked her more immediately, in the minds of artists and intellectuals, with the Pacific theatre of the war rather than the more remote European theatre. Indeed, this sense of identification was hinted at in the *Listener* article:

> Nobody who had heard all that Lili Kraus played in Auckland in one week could imagine that her vitality, her technique, her repertoire – those things that her internment might have taken from her – are less than they were before. As a human being, as a musician, she cannot have stood still during this time. The excitement of the Town Hall concert was unique – perhaps we heard a new Lili Kraus, one that the other side of the world does not know yet.[44]

Kraus also had remarkable personal qualities, enjoying the social events organised for her and her family in the main cities (especially in Christchurch), remaining quite unaffected by the publicity she received, and involving herself in the cultural life of the country. Numerous entries in Betty's diaries convey something of the excitement which her presence aroused. After a concert given in her second major series, in 1947, Betty wrote:

> Last night a memorable night. We sat upstairs in seats provided for us by Lili with Denis & Mary & Rita [Angus]. I took Mary round after [sic], then we all went to Eunoe Smith's flat. Claude [Raines, music critic for *The Press*] was in raptures having lessons from Lili. She played bits to all of us for hours. Then we all sat on the floor chatting for ages. Lili did not leave till after 3 & we were home about 4. Ngaio Marsh, Mrs Schroder, Mrs Ballantyne, Claude, Ruth Mandl, Charles Brasch, Denis & Mary Glover, Lawrence Baigent, Rita Cook [Angus], Dr Norrie Rogers . . . . Gordon [Douglas] Lilburn, Ursula Cook, Pat Courage. After the older people had left we all sat on the floor on the landing. Lili next to Allen, Rita, Gordon, Ruth.[45]

In the last of her Christchurch concerts in this second series Kraus played a sonatina specially written for her by Lilburn, and praised it highly to him in a radio hook-up to Wellington at the end of the concert. However, it was the poets who seem to have been most inspired by Kraus's musicianship – so much so that, as early as July 1946, Bertram (who had himself suffered internment by the Japanese during the war) and Brasch planned a book about her, which never eventuated.

Curnow wrote two poems inspired by the music Kraus performed. 'Lili Kraus Playing at Christchurch' appeared in *The Press* on 6 July 1946, only two days after the first concert. The second, 'A Sonata of Schubert', was a much more considered poem, inspired by Kraus's main offering at the concert, in March 1947, whose social aftermath Betty described so animatedly. Curnow was initially unsure about the first one, commenting to Fairburn that 'it was done too hurriedly, to push into print and please her while she was in the town',[46] though he eventually agreed to send both poems to Brasch for publication in the second issue of *Landfall* in June the following year.* In later volumes Curnow always printed the two Lili Kraus sonnets together, conceiving them as companion pieces, the first dated 'July 1946' and the second, 'A Sonata of Schubert', dated 'March 1947'. 'I think', he wrote to Brasch, '– don't you? – that the dates are part of the story.'[47]

'Lili Kraus Playing at Christchurch' was a graceful tribute to Kraus, on the theme of the untranslatability of music into words. It is the marvellously dexterous *hands* of the pianist which through the medium of physical performance create music with the power to 'unburn Troy', quicken insight into 'the beautiful / Coast where seas and mountains dazzling turn / Their face of thirst', and reach into the dull heart of the forlorn Wanderer with a message of love. The reference to the Wanderer was a graceful allusion to the Schubert song on which the composer's Phantasy in C Major was based, a highlight of the concert.

The particular sonata Kraus performed in the March concert, Schubert's posthumous Sonata in A Major, composed shortly before his death, was also very much part of the story of the second sonnet. The mystery at the heart of Schubert's sonata, in Curnow's moving poem, is the music's capacity to confront and transcend death, both the particular death of the composer himself which was the occasion of his sonata, and death as an ongoing fact of the world in which his audiences, made 'strange' to themselves in their experience of the music, confront that which they 'most fear' and achieve a 'transfiguring' moment of understanding of 'the mortal marvel' of the 'joy and pain' of existence:

---

* Brasch began the second issue with a group of five 'Poems for Lili Kraus' – Curnow's two, together with poems by Bertram, Fairburn and Glover.

You move to the piano. What is it we know?
You have taught your hands to die;
All that we have to and most fear to do
Now to be done, sufficingly,

O and here, calling the lapsed soul again*
With music's trumpet-silences to witness
The mortal marvel of its joy and pain.
It is the falling brightness

From keen unusual skies, omen of birds,
Day breaking at the beach of sacrifice.
We are strange to ourselves. Who is it applauds
His own transfiguring? Who plays?

Not you, not we – this, we had never dreamt,
Those hands between us and the heavens' contempt.

'What is it we know?' the poet asks in the opening line. It is the *knowledge* of mortality (the condition of the 'lapsed soul') evoked through the performance. The phrase 'lapsed soul' comes from the introductory poem to Blake's 'Songs of Experience', set in Eden at the time of the Fall, and it is a Blakean idea of the transformative possibilities of *knowledge* of one's fallen state in the condition of 'experience' which informs Curnow's sonnet. The 'trumpet-silences', in this context, evoke the trumpet of the Archangel Gabriel as he stands guard over re-entry to Eden. Another Fall (in addition to Blake's reference, in the same poem, to 'fallen light') is also invoked in the reference to 'falling brightness', Milton's words in *Paradise Lost* to describe Lucifer after his expulsion from heaven.

The extraordinary cluster of images which Schubert's music aroused in Curnow remained unusually important in many of his later poems. Reference to 'the beach of sacrifice' not only evokes earlier poems like 'Sailing or Drowning' or 'Landfall in Unknown Seas' (and his play *The Axe*), where it provides scenes of violent cross-cultural encounter, but looks forward to one of his most famous poems of the 1950s, 'Spectacular Blossom', whose subject (similar to that of the Schubert sonnet) is the attempt to understand and accept mutability, the fact of death, as a condition of our experience of both beauty and its transience. The 'lapsed soul', and its Blakean context, reappears in 'Friendship Heights', in which the fallibility and unpredictability of memory is explored as a dimension of mutability. The glance at

---

* Curnow revised this line in his *Collected Poems* (1974) to 'If hands could call the lapsed soul again'.

Milton, combined with an allusion to Thomas Nashe's '[b]rightness falls from the air',[48] recurs in 'Narita', whose occasion, a horrific jumbo jet plane crash, evokes mutability – the unpredictability and randomness of individual death – in one of its extremest forms, providing yet another poem which attempts to do what 'we most fear to do' – confront the fact of death – 'sufficingly'.

Public reading of *The Axe*, 1946

Curnow's play, originally 'The Island and the Kingdom', had only recently acquired the title *The Axe*, and in the month after Kraus's triumphant first concert series, it finally achieved a public reading at the Little Theatre, by the Canterbury University College Drama Society, on 17 August 1946. As Curnow originally wrote the play – and as it was read in 1946 – it was a longish one-acter, consisting of eleven consecutive scenes. Its central event was derived from the third of the three Terry Lectures, published under the title *Anthropology and Religion* in 1939, which the Pacific anthropologist Sir Peter Buck delivered at Yale University in 1938. The lecture was entitled 'The Death of the Gods', and used the events of 1824 on the island of Mangaia in the Cook Islands to illustrate how abandoning indigenous gods in favour of Christianity had destructive ramifications for Polynesian social and cultural structures.

In 1824, after an abortive attempt the previous year, the Tahitian Christian missionary Davida succeeded in converting the king and chief priest of the ruling tribes, Numangatini, to Christianity. Numangatini's wholesale torching of indigenous gods and sacred places of worship provoked an uprising from the subject tribes, led by their chief priest, Tereavai, who also saw it as a means of regaining the political power they had lost. In the ensuing battle, on a plain observed from opposing hilltop vantage points by Davida and Tereavai, Tereavai's forces, fighting for the old order, were comprehensively routed, and the new Western political, moral and technological order of Christianity achieved control of the whole island.

When he first read Buck's narrative in 1942 Curnow was struck by the inherently dramatic possibilities of these tragic central events for a verse play, and of their contemporary relevance, both to New Zealand – a country with its own conflict between new and old orders – and to the wider context of world war in the Pacific, in which islands had been 'set adrift' from older certainties, and become the scene of a momentous (and as yet unresolved) conflict of ideologies. The events on Mangaia suggested, Curnow wrote later in his preface to the published play (1949):

> a tragedy of situations, encounter and conflict between the modern West and the Stone Age; the scene, a remote obscure island, therefore congenial to the theme of much verse

I had written and to much of my thought about New Zealand; the action, battle, victory and defeat, therefore morally implicating a modern audience. It was the modern, rather than the historical relevance to New Zealand which seemed important.[49]

In the preface to his *Four Plays* (1972) Curnow equally emphasised 'the shadow of a world war' as part of the modern relevance of the play:

The state of war, which the whole world was in, while we were commemorating what we *had* to commemorate, was a constant (and conscious) concern while I was writing *The Axe* . . . . I wanted to place New Zealand at the centre, the only possible place. Never mind the provincial cold shudder at the thought that this is not the place at all, and never can be; that here is a centre of sorts, but not *the* centre, wherever that may be. The islander, even while he shudders, is feeling something at his own centre. By shifting the scene to another island, I might mirror New Zealand . . . .[50]

Curnow realised from the outset that a realistic treatment of events or characters was impossible, even if he had the theatrical skill or knowledge to manage such a treatment. For a start, the characters had to speak English. He retained the central events and characters of Buck's narrative, aiming for a streamlined, dramatic, scene-by-scene momentum leading inexorably to the climax of the war between the converted tribes and the 'pagans', and the apparent triumph of Christianity, but built into the process and its immediate aftermath a series of destabilising questions. What he aimed for was thus a symbolic play of ideas, energised by the dramatic possibilities of its central events, and the richness of its poetic speech. The models for such a poetic treatment of history, in which the fate of myths and belief systems was at stake, were Eliot's *Murder in the Cathedral* and W.B. Yeats's plays.

The triumph of Christianity in the play was an equivocal one. This was partly because much of the audience's emotional identification naturally fell on the outcast and eventually finally defeated 'pagan' Ngativara tribe, who were given scenes strongly balancing those of the converts as well as a poetry full of lively, authentic Polynesian imagery which Curnow was at pains to learn from books and articles recommended to him by historian Eric Ramsden and ethnologist Roger Duff, especially Teuira Henry's work incorporating translations of Polynesian myths and legends and chants. One of the two choric voices incorporated into the play comments in the immediate aftermath of the battle, 'I think the defeated dead are happier / Than the red-handed victor striding home, / Haunted by images of defeat and death'; and the 'red-handed victor', the converted king Numangatini, is himself killed at the end by an ostensible follower who hates him and under the new Christian dispensation sees him in any case as having been stripped of the sacred authority as chief priest which he held prior to his conversion.

Equivocation was thus an intentional aspect of the play, as Curnow stated in his 1949 preface:

> The play, if it could be written, would display inevitable, irreconcilable conflict, and would have no opinion upon the balance of gain or loss in the end. It would make audible, in our modern terror, the reverberation of one irretrievable step in history: the motion of the hour-hand would be perceptible.[51]

Such were the sensitivities of audiences at the time, however, that Curnow felt drawn to address possible accusations of anti-missionary bias, in his programme note for the 1948 stage production:

> It has been suggested to me that this play may be taken for an attack upon the early missionaries in Polynesia. I hope I shall be forgiven the expedient of a Note, in which to say explicitly that nothing of the kind is intended. It would not have occurred to me to attempt a play for such a purpose. I do not think, myself, that there is anything to give offence, unless perhaps to some particularly tender or defensive religious sentiment.[52]

However, the equivocal, questioning aspect of the play puzzled some reviewers, who felt that its meaning needed to be more clearly stated. Curnow's concern, however (familiar from many of his earlier poems), was to destabilise the notion of stability itself. As events tragically unfold, the second choric voice comments (echoing the choric voice which speaks at the end of each stanza of 'The Unhistoric Story'):

> Not on this island
> Is the colour of tomorrow's dawn determined:
> Traversing the mountain, treading the sea beaches,
> We felt the ground grow brittle; a stiff wind blew;
> Cloud lost lustre, land shuddered in the sea;
> Rocks toppled like water. Everything was turning
> Into something different, something we never expected.[53]

And the axe itself – symbol of the superior Western technology accompanying the introduction of Christianity – also functions as a metaphor for the general destabilisation of all old certainties:

                    A hand is fumbling
        At the roots of this island. The hand grasps an axe.
        The axe will cut away the ropes that bind
        The island to the sea's bed.[54]

    Curnow retained the three central historical figures from Buck's account
(Numangatini, Davida and Tereavai), but, as with the events themselves, introduced his own variations in order to reduce the conflict to stark symbolic outlines
– presenting them as type-figures who articulate particular points of view in the
unfolding struggle for power. 'Beyond three main characters who are historical in
the usual sense, and the large events which govern their action', Curnow added in
his 1948 programme note, 'it is all – character, incident, and plot – invention for
the stage.'[55] For example, Tereavai is blind, and carries something of the ambience
of the Greek prophet Tiresias, articulating a prophecy associated with a broken,
whirlwind-struck tree (one of the few stage properties in the pared-down, simplified *mise-en-scène*), that a new dispensation of gods from across the seas will
at some time supersede the established one. There is a genuine tragic irony in the
fact that he remains unaware until the end that he is *himself* enacting that violent
displacement and is its victim.*
    Around the three central characters Curnow introduces three minor charac-
ters, lesser priests, one a follower of Numangatini and Davida, the other two
followers of Tereavai, who function primarily at a political level in the action
of the play (acting as spies in enemy territory, carrying out orders), variously
committed to the absolute beliefs espoused by the main characters. However,
his two main inventions are a chorus, consisting of two voices (one male and
one female), and a subplot involving two young lovers, Hema and Hina, both of
them providing a counterweight to the abstract issues embodied in the conflict
between Numangatini / Davida and Tereavai.
    Described in the 1948 stage production as 'Ancestral Voices of the Island', the
choric voices speak most of the richest poetry in the play (with the exception,
perhaps, of Tereavai), drawing on a compelling, elemental symbolism of earth
and sea, storm and fire. They are not a chorus in the Greek sense, understanding
and foreknowing and judging events as they unfold. In fact, they are precisely the
opposite. They articulate, helpless to change events, feelings of terror and torment
at being cast adrift from stability, at the fundamental changes sweeping over the
island, at the sheer unpredictability of what the future might hold. At the climax

---

*   This same image, in a different context, was to recur in the core poem – 'A Four Letter Word' – of
    Curnow's later poetic sequence, *Trees, Effigies, Moving Objects*, though in that poem the broken tree,
    symbolising the collapse of theogonies, is 'Tane Mahuta', the decaying, lightning-struck giant kauri tree
    in the Waipoua Forest, in northern New Zealand.

of the play, on the eve before the battle, they deploy a typical oceanic symbolism to express an impending catastrophic shift in the order of things. And their voices conclude the play with the poignant image of *both* the dead and the living cast adrift on the ocean.

The chorus was Curnow's riskiest dramatic invention in *The Axe* – risky in the sense that they take no part in the stage action, and rely solely on the vividness and force of the poetry they speak. An act of faith was involved on Curnow's part that the verse was sufficiently strong and dramatic in itself to hold the audience's attention.

The second main invention which Curnow added to the broad historical events of the play, the introduction of the subplot involving two young lovers, Hema and Hina, also functions as a foil – if not 'realistic', at least personal and human in its bearings – to the large impersonal abstractions represented by Davida, Numangatini and Tereavai. Hema is fascinated by the power of the new technology represented by the axe, but detests Numangatini, who invokes the moral order of Christianity to forbid Hema and Hina their sexual freedom. Hema regards Numangatini, now deprived of his original sacred priestly powers, as a cynical political manipulator, concerned as king merely to retain worldly power. His resentment festers, and when Hina is killed at the hands of one of the Ngativara priests with the axe which he had earlier stolen from Hema, in a state of demented distraction he recalls Davida's biblical words, 'Vengeance is mine, saith the Lord' – used to justify or at least excuse the bloody massacre of the retreating Ngativara after their defeat in battle – and identifies *himself* as the agent of divine vengeance. In the final scene of the play, breaking in upon the triumphal scene of Christian victory, he murders Numangatini with the axe, and is himself killed at the command of the missionary priest, Davida.

In his revision of the play for the reading in 1946 Curnow was initially uncertain whether to pursue this conclusion, which leaves the stage littered with four murdered corpses – Tereavai and Hine, as well as Numangatini and Hema – though he knew the effect he wanted to create, the casting adrift of the present towards an unpredictable future, despite the seeming triumph of the new order.

The play, as it was finally given its first public reading at the Little Theatre in 1946, had been a long time in the making. Many of the earlier revisions had focused on what Curnow felt to be weaknesses in the *verse* of the play, but there were also matters of stagecraft about which he felt entirely ignorant, especially the extent to which action could be allowed to occur offstage. Ngaio Marsh's advice and support in this respect was invaluable – especially in relation to the climactic battle scene – as he later recalled:

> Where she came in – I was working on a part of the play where there has to be a battle and the battle can't be on stage (as in *Henry the Fifth*, for instance), and it has

to be observed, like some of the action and the fighting around Troy in *Troilus and Cressida*. I needed people on either side (from the unconverted side of the Mangaia people and from the Christianized people), and they would as it were be reporting the battle to the audience as it comes to them. I just did not know whether this wasn't some bizarre notion of my own which just would not work at all on stage. And I rang Ngai (it was some time early in the afternoon; I was working at *The Press* late at nights) and Ngai said: 'Would you like me to come down? I'll come down – I'd like to have a look at it,' so she drove all the way down from Cashmere to Leinster Road and sat in with me and assured me that she thought it would work. If she hadn't said that I would have been perhaps too dubious or too timid to press on with it, and there wasn't anybody else around I would have asked.[56]

In 1946, after showing the play to Brasch, Curnow returned to it yet again, 'rather in a fright' now that it would definitely receive a public reading in August, since he felt 'a good deal must be done to the piece'.[57] He worked intensively on the play for five weeks in April and May, restructuring the scenes in the light of Brasch's comments, and sent Brasch a scene-by-scene synopsis of the revised play, explaining his efforts to build more characterisation into it, as well as his reasons for changing the order of scenes, cutting some material and introducing new episodes, especially the late scene in which Hema, possessed by 'religious mania', assumes the role of an agent of vengeance against Numangatini.

At its first reading, on 17 August, the attendance was small and the programme was not reviewed in the newspapers, though *Canta*, the student magazine, welcomed the play warmly and at some length, praising especially the reading of Hema's role by Alan de Malmanche. Betty wrote briefly in her diary: 'I was very excited with it, very clear. Some parts read very well indeed.'[58] For Ngaio Marsh and John Pocock, who read the choric roles, the reading confirmed their instinct that the play deserved a full-scale production, and Pocock was very keen to direct it. During the following year, while he was touring New Zealand as an actor in Ngaio Marsh's production of *The Alchemist*, he mapped out the production he had in mind. Curnow himself, given his typical misgivings about the quality of what he had achieved, was sufficiently encouraged to persist with the play, and during the 20 months before the full stage performance in April 1948, revised it yet again in the light of what he had learnt from the public reading.

Marital crisis

Shortly after the play reading in 1946 Betty slipped on the floor at Leinster Road while carrying Tim and suffered a bad fall on the base of her spine. Improvement

was slow, and in later September her doctor – Dr Kraal, a war refugee – diagnosed general physical and mental exhaustion and sent her for two weeks to a
convalescent hospital in the Cashmere Hills, recommending also that she have
a complete break from her family after this for at least six weeks. Betty's mother
Daisy, who had recently returned from Nelson to Christchurch to live, took the
initiative in making suitable arrangements. In early October she arranged for
Betty to stay at Eastbourne in Wellington with a nurse friend of the family, while
she herself undertook to look after the house at Leinster Road.

Betty stayed at Eastbourne for a fortnight, where she chafed at being
'bossed around and treated like a child',[59] and in mid-October[60] her friend
Eva Christeller arranged for her to move to York Bay, where she stayed with
Hal and Molly Atkinson for a further month. She later remembered her stay
at York Bay, among a small community of artists, as a 'most happy time'* and
also visited many Wellington friends and acquaintances – Heenan, Beaglehole
and McCormick, Antony Alpers, Ramsden, the Woods, Maria Dronke, Plischke
and Joachim Khan, and numerous others.

Dr Kraal's understanding of Betty's need for a break on her own was astute,
since during the later months of 1946 the Curnows' marital difficulties – their
constant arguments over matters small and large – had reached a point of crisis.
In September during a visit to Auckland with Glover, Curnow met a woman
called Norah College and seriously considered leaving the marriage. Betty's
distress at this prospect – as well as her ill health – shocked Curnow, and forced
both to reassess their relationship after ten years together. In his letters to Betty
in Wellington, Curnow struggled to reappraise what had gone wrong (and right)
in the marriage, understand his own failings, and affirm their future together.
'Just now', he wrote soon after she left, 'getting back to you, all the way back,
seems what I want most.'[61] Much to Betty's distress, Norah College came to
Christchurch to see Curnow, and he tried to reassure Betty that the relationship
was at an end while reaffirming his love: 'I told her all I felt & thought about you
& me as one can't possibly tell things by letter', he wrote.[62]

Shortly before Betty returned to Christchurch in mid-November he wrote
at length again about what he saw love and marriage as meaning, as well as the
particular weaknesses (his own especially) which had led to the current crisis in
their own relationship. The sense of painful self-scrutiny is intense, and seems
to express itself naturally in a language – of 'penance', and soul-searching –
reaching back to his religious formation and training. Such self-analysis is also
deeply revealing of the sense of personal crisis which underlies so many of the

---

* 'Got all my spirits back, energy & found real joy of living', she added in a note made in 1974 to her 1946
  diary.

poems which he wrote in the second half of the 1940s, with their anguished sense of the erosions of time on all human relationships and of love itself as a scene of conflicting impulses and consequences:

All these last weeks I have been more alone than I have ever been, a discipline for the soul perhaps, but knowing an operation is necessary doesn't make it less painful. I'm not being sorry for myself. My own Betty, is it too much to say that I shall need aid & comfort from you – if you will only treat me as a thing you love, and a thing not any bigger than yourself, because it's a very lonely life being a god, especially when a man has some talent for worshipping on his own account. When I think it over, I think this has nothing at all to do with how often I get my way & how often you get yours. I'm always liable to get my own way, but that isn't always an advantage to me, & it needn't worry you how often I get it. But it's disastrous for me and for you too, when you are so worried about not crossing me that you can hardly act or speak without anxiety over whether it will be what I want. And half the time, of course, I don't really care a curse & don't even know what I want before it happens, in day-to-day things. That's how we got to a stage where small things, which it didn't matter whether we agreed or disagreed about, swelled up into matters for tense & weighty discussions. Nobody's nerves & feelings will bear the strain of a dozen little collisions & debates a day. Did it begin with the fears you had of me in the very first years – and my failure to see that you were afraid – till they became an invisible wall against which love beat itself till it turned resentful & went very near its opposite, hatred? Love & hate, very close together always ('ambivalent', the psychology people say). We shouldn't be afraid to admit now that there have been times when we have hated each other. Because of that wall in between we have tried to get closer to each other by talking, watching each other, brooding about each other, closer to each other than any two can bear to be without fighting. Love keeps people just a little apart, so they can see each other & each keep his individual part, soul or self, free. If you try, or I try – we've both tried – to take another's soul & change or make use of it, we'll only find that we are tampering with the thing we love, & making it part of our own self-love. You can only love another person, & if you try to swallow them up into yourself, you can only hate them . . . . All this is for me, & I think for you too, but only you can see where my explanation means something for you & where it stops. It's really an old story, it has happened to many people, & we're by no means peculiar except that I think we are more successful than many have been. I don't think I shall ever preach like this to you again, & I'm putting my thoughts in order as much to discipline myself as to let you know what they are. It would be as silly for me to blame myself as it would be monstrous to blame you. We are wife & husband, & every marriage is a unique thing, two entirely unique personalities closely related; no-one can predict the result, & someone (being very wise after the event) might easily blame us both & say we

made a mistake together 10 years ago; but we didn't, we simply made the same act of
faith that everyone makes in marrying, though there were problems in both of us that
neither of us suspected, neither of us very well-adjusted creatures. No-one can say we
have done badly in our situation, because no-one has ever been in just our situation.[63]

A kind of accommodation was reached, in the aftermath of Betty's time away
in Wellington, and for the next few years their relationship resumed the more
even tenor of what Curnow described as 'a marriage like any other'.[64] There were
fewer arguments, an acceptance of compromise on both sides, but whatever spark
had survived in the marriage up to this time had gone – a loss felt more strongly
by Curnow than by Betty. Betty seemed to take less interest in her husband's
literary activities and intellectual interests from this time on. She continued to
develop her own interests in the visual arts, meeting Colin McCahon in the later
1940s, and devoted much of her time to bringing up her growing family. Curnow,
in turn, seemed less interested in sharing his literary and intellectual interests
with his wife, and looked, increasingly, for an opportunity to change his career
from journalism and to leave what seemed to him an increasingly stultifying and
jaded cultural scene in Christchurch.

Chapter Fourteen

Last Years in Christchurch, 1947–49

If we are concerned with nationality it is because we recognize certain physical and social realities; that the poet, while his aims are universal, is yet the creature of a time and a place, even the creature of the audience he addresses. Yet he is creative as well as creature. He has other resources.[1]

New poems, 1947

In the aftermath of the marital crisis of the later months of 1946 Curnow wrote a sequence of poems under the general title 'Four Descriptions and a Picture', to which Brasch gave pride of place in the first issue of his new periodical, *Landfall*, in March 1947. The four 'descriptions' were in fact sonnets, tracing the vicissitudes of an intense love affair. 'Genesis', the first, associates the birth of love with stages in the creation of the world itself. The title of the second, 'With How Mad Steps', invokes Philip Sidney's sonnet of unrequited love from his 'Astrophil to Stella' sequence (No. 31, 'With how sad steps, O moon, thou climb'st the skies'). However, whereas Sidney's identification with the moon expresses sadness and resignation, Curnow's expresses feelings of frustration and madness at being 'tossed into space to cool / From my earth's body', locked out of the sensuous pleasures of closeness and intimacy. 'She Sits with Her Two Children', the third sonnet in the sequence, frames the woman's awakening to love within fairy tale and legend, intimating at the end that such an awakening carries with it a Fall into the world of time and death. The last of the sonnets, 'Then If This Dies', offers a 'description' of the decline of passion as a tormented and self-tormenting process of dying by degrees ('death finds him in a waiting torment / Lancing a straw hope against that steel / Night's disappointment'). Given the association of love with death throughout the sequence, the agonised final line of this fourth sonnet, 'death has not finished with us yet', quite simply implies the *persistence* of love, hopeless and futile as that love is.

Curnow concludes this sequence of sonnets with what he calls a 'picture', entitled 'All Darkens but Her Image', perhaps seeking in the idea of the 'picture' or 'image' of the loved one a consoling or sustaining idea which releases him from the torments of his relationship with the flesh-and-blood woman. The image is of a woman whose presence, like that of the female figure in Wallace Stevens's 'The Idea of Order at Key West', transcends the natural environment, of sea, mountains and sky, in terms of which and against which she is invoked:

> The door stood wide, she stood
> Between those pillars of the sea:
> She leaned against the evening light,
> Mountains no taller than her knee.
> The first star at her breast, her eyes
> Turned where the top of heaven should be.

Curnow wrote four further sonnets during 1947 – the last poems he was to write for two years – sending three of them ('In Memoriam R.L.M.G.', 'Eden Gate' and 'Old Hand of the Sea') to Fairburn in August for the third *Yearbook of the Arts in New Zealand* later that year. 'In Memoriam R.L.M.G.' paid moving tribute to his grandmother Rose Gambling's life as one of colonial self-sacrifice for the sake of following generations. A companion sonnet on the same theme, dedicated to her sister, Fanny Rose May, was later included alongside the memorial sonnet under the collective title 'Tomb of an Ancestor'. The other two sonnets, like so many others written at this time, were located in the Lyttelton of Curnow's childhood. 'Old Hand of the Sea' develops a familiar opposition between the 'blind', 'sightless', ongoing ('immemorial'), 'inhuman' depths of the oceanic – the ultimate purpose or end of its blindly searching hand unknown, as it reaches tidally into the harbour – and the vivid, transient, unpredictable energies of life at the littoral, in the harbour and on its beaches:

> Horizons bloomed here on the globes of eyes,
> Here grieving fog fastened those lids with tears
> Disfiguring, transfiguring; holidays
> Nested like bird or girl. All disappears

> But the salt searching hand.

'Eden Gate' reinterprets the Fall as an existential quality in the growing child's daily experience of events, in which the seemingly permanent, 'innocent' domestic garden of childhood becomes permeated with evidences of time and change, and turns into a site of desire and anxiety, as the child grows old enough to leave home each day and travel by train to school in Christchurch. The natural scene in this poem takes on all the qualities of human feeling, sexuality, guilt, panic. The sonnet concludes with an especially powerful image of 'God's one blue eye' looking down on 'the damaged / Boy tied by the string of a toy', as if the child struggles to retain his innocence in the face of the inevitability of growing up, becoming part of the universal, repetitive, daily pattern of the Fall in which God 'saw him off at the gate and the train / All over again.'

These poems, and the others which Curnow wrote in the years immediately after the Second World War – eventually collected in *At Dead Low Water and Sonnets* and published by Glover in 1949 – were difficult and challenging, very different from his earlier work. John Pocock, a great admirer of the earlier work, was puzzled by them, commenting on 'Four Descriptions and a Picture', in a review of the first number of *Landfall*:

> Mr Curnow . . . continues in the vein of 'Jack without Magic', and this reviewer does not wish to be taken as repeating the old and stale cry about 'obscurity' when he says that the particular imaginative route which Mr Curnow is at present following, at present escapes him.[2]

The impersonality of the poems, whether their theme is the failure of love or the corrosive effect of time on human relationships, in fact masks a deep-seated personal insecurity, loss of confidence and direction. Self-questioning and self-analysis recur in poem after poem, from the time of the first, 'Self-Portrait', with its image of the poet as a 'passionate failure' or a 'staled success', to the last, 'Eden Gate', with its image of the 'damaged boy' clutching the string of his kite. 'This way I went', he writes of his earlier poetic self in 'The Waking Bird Refutes', 'to pull our histories down', accusing the heavens of 'rainbowed guile' and inviting 'penal rains' to descend on the world, as if playing at being God. If there is any connection between these and earlier poems it is in fact with the introspective, self-questioning impulses of the *very* earliest, the poems of *Valley of Decision*, except that the later poems lack the consolations of religious belief, employing religious imagery in a purely secular way to emphasise human existence in a fallen, time-bound world without hope of redemption or transcendence.

Glover, Brasch, Fairburn, Schroder, Holcroft and others seem to have sensed Curnow's deep-seated restlessness, his disillusionment with his career in journalism, his increasing sense of frustration and entrapment in a Christchurch cultural scene in which everyone knew everyone else, and in which conversation, debate, tastes had become entirely predictable. For someone with Curnow's need for intellectual stimulation, for the challenge of new ideas, his life seemed to have fallen into a rut, a stultifying 'dry-rot' producing 'an ominous creaking at the back of the brain', as he later described the feeling to Schroder.[3]

Later in 1947, Glover and the others proposed to Heenan at the Department of Internal Affairs that an amount be set aside in the recently established New Zealand Literary Fund to support writers to travel abroad, suggesting that Curnow was at a point of crossroads in his creative career when he might benefit substantially from such travel. At this time he was in his later thirties, and unlike most of his contemporaries – including Fairburn, Brasch, Glover, Holcroft and Lilburn – had never been outside the country. Given this fact it was remarkable that he had played so formative a role in introducing contemporary overseas poetic impulses and critical thinking to New Zealand. His knowledge of these was entirely 'second-hand', derived from intensive reading in current poetry and critical writing as they appeared in the latest overseas books, poetry magazines, and journals devoted to current literature.

Curnow was excited by the prospect of travel to England, and also to the United States, and by the middle of the following year it looked as if a trip might be feasible, though the amount of funding that might be made available caused anxiety, since Curnow had a growing family to support during the year he would be away. In the meantime he continued to be active as a reviewer and commentator in *The Press* and elsewhere. Brasch was keen to engage him as a contributor to *Landfall*, and for the second issue (June 1947) Curnow wrote a long review of H.M. Green's anthology *Modern Australian Poetry* (1947), a volume which paralleled his own Caxton anthology.

'The neglected middle distance': Curnow's trans-Tasman perspective

Curnow had had some small connection with the Australian poetry scene since the early 1940s, mainly through Clem Christesen, the editor of *Meanjin*, who published Curnow's 'Aspects of New Zealand Poetry' in 1943 as well as his sonnets 'Polynesia' (in 1943) and 'Dunedin' (in 1946). In 1945, and again in 1946, Christesen enlisted Curnow to assist with putting together a special issue devoted to New Zealand poetry, but on both occasions the project fell through – in 1945 because Curnow could not get a sufficient number of poems together in the time required, and in 1946 because Christesen felt that the verse Curnow assembled was 'not up to standard'.[4] Curnow had gone to some trouble on this second occasion, liaising closely with Fairburn, who at this time was poetry editor for the revamped quarterly *The Arts in New Zealand*, as well as for Wadman's new annual *Yearbook of the Arts in New Zealand*. The selection he sent to Christesen included new poems by Baxter, Brasch, Fairburn, Witheford (and perhaps himself), though he commented to Fairburn that he would 'have none of Smithyman', whose work seemed to him at this time to be 'all unassimilated borrowings'. Although he felt that the verse he sent to Christesen *was* uneven, he was nevertheless annoyed by Christesen's response. 'One could say the same', he said to Fairburn, 'about 50 per cent of the prose in *Meanjin* and 90 per cent of the verse.'[5]

Curnow used his review of Green's anthology in *Landfall* as an opportunity to address 'the neglected middle distance of our outward scene' at some length for the first time, acknowledging that the time had long passed when 'the Sydney *Bulletin* provided something like a matriculation test for writers in the country it called Maoriland'.[6] What he read, among the hundred poems Green had chosen to represent the previous 30 years, nevertheless shocked him. 'I am staggered by the barrenness of the book', he wrote to Fairburn, 'the unrelieved badness of 75% of the verse', and described the writing of his review as 'a grisly job'.[7]

Only two poets, Christopher Brennan and Hugh McCrae, of the 54 represented in Green's volume ('at least half' of whom 'could have been dropped with advantage')[8] survived Curnow's scrutiny, and the two contemporary poets with the highest reputation in Australia at the time, R.D. FitzGerald and Kenneth Slessor, were savagely dealt to.* [9] Effectively, though Curnow does not use the term, he saw Australian poetry as falling short in terms of the modernist principles which had informed his judgement of New Zealand poetry in the introduction to the Caxton anthology, and his general summing up of the deficiencies of Australian poetry implies that the values of the modernist movement have either not reached that country's poets, or passed them by:

> [T]here is (with the few exceptions indicated) abundant invention without imaginative synthesis; abundant energy without understanding; ready versification without form; a verbal excitability constantly mistaking its object; everywhere a rawness of the intellect. Too much is written, not enough read.[10]

Curnow's review raised eyebrows in Australia and was remembered for many years. It also excited the hostility of the older literary generation in New Zealand (figures like P.A. (Pat) Lawlor[11] and A.E. Currie), who still maintained the old literary connection with the *Bulletin*. Lawlor, always hostile to Curnow in any

---

* Brasch himself seems to have been surprised by the review's ferocity, commenting 'I only hope the Australian libraries etc subscribe before LF2 comes out; for they won't afterwards!'

case, was also administrative secretary of the Literary Fund to whom application was soon to be made on Curnow's behalf, and Currie, writing to Alexander, was equally unimpressed.[12]

Curnow reviewed a considerable amount of Australian poetry in *The Press* during the following eighteen months, struggling to find strengths among much with which he was out of sympathy, and disparaging of the absence (as he had seen it in Green's anthology) of critical standards. The annual *Australian Poetry 1946*, selected by T. Inglis Moore, would have been strengthened in his view by focusing on seven or eight poets (including Judith Wright) and omitting the remaining thirty:

> These Australians at their best can make startling and brilliant pictures of their extraordinary landscapes. Their best gifts seem pictorial, and they remain curiously remote from the subjects they colour with so little depth or intellectual substance.[13]

At the conclusion of his comments on Francis Webb's historical poem *A Drum for Ben Boyd* (which opened promisingly but 'collapses lamentably', its protagonist failing to achieve the legendary aura aimed at, remaining 'a dimly seen scarecrow upon whom the poet's rhetoric flaps in a wind of uncertain direction') Curnow generalised, again, about the 'Australian tendency, perhaps less evident than it was, to admire loud shouting in verse without considering whether there is anything to shout about'[14] – a modernist criticism premised on the absence of a *synthesis* of what is observed with inward sources of thought and feeling.

Early in 1948, during this period of reading and thinking about Australian poetry, Curnow was approached by Alan Mulgan to consent to having poems included in a revised edition of *The Oxford Book of Australasian Verse*, for which Mulgan had been asked to select the New Zealand poems. This book, edited by the Australian Walter Murdoch, had first appeared in 1918 and been reprinted on several occasions since, most recently in 1945, by which time it was out of date (at least as far as New Zealand was concerned). Curnow was deeply sceptical about the whole project, and initially refused permission for his poems to appear in the new edition. He acknowledged that the anthology had served a purpose, two or three decades earlier, 'when there was less to distinguish poets in the two countries', but he doubted, now, 'whether it means anything whatever to call ourselves Australasians', and felt very strongly about having 'the O.U.P. imprint sanctioning [the] view of New Zealand verse as a kind of annexe [sic] to Australia'. In his letter to Curnow, Mulgan had used the unfortunate phrase 'lumped together' to describe the presentation of New Zealand poets in the new edition (that is, as distinct from submerging them indistinguishably among the Australian poets as was the case in the earlier editions), and Curnow seized on the phrase:

I cannot agree that it is any improvement to have the New Zealand poets 'lumped together', presumably at the back of the book. If it were simply a question of getting New Zealand verse better known in Australia – and they have something to learn from this country – it would be foolish to quarrel with the project. But I do not think it is worth it, at the price of subordinate representation in a book like this . . . . I would hardly suppose that our 'standing' is to be served by appending ourselves to this Terra Australis Incognita inhabited by Professor Murdoch. We may cheerfully and properly sink our identity in English poetry at large; but this, now, would be trading our birth-right for an Australasian mess with a famous imprint stuck on the outside.[15]

In the end Curnow withdrew his objections. Fairburn and others did not feel as strongly as he that the book's influence would be overtly 'harmful', and Mulgan himself worked hard to reassure Curnow about the issues he had raised, including arranging for the phrase 'Australasian Verse' to be removed from the title and 'Australian and New Zealand Verse' substituted.

Curnow was, however, grateful to Mulgan for raising a grammatical question about his own 'Self-Portrait', one of the poems Mulgan proposed to include. Should not, Mulgan politely asked, the verb 'Look back' in the lines 'A passionate failure or a staled success / Look back into their likeness' be singular ('Looks back'), and the pronoun 'their' be adjusted accordingly to 'its'? It was the kind of question which might seem like pedantry to some but which Curnow always enjoyed and took seriously. He replied appreciatively and at length:

I was on the point of conceding a grammatical fall to you: then weighed the alternative – 'looks . . . its' – & found that it disordered my intention in the lines, & cld not *feel* the construction to be wrong, or that there cld be so inflexible a rule as we assume for most purposes. I find my case clearly provided for in the Shorter Oxford, so, for your interest: 'When singular subjects (sb. or pron.) are coordinated by *or*, the tendency is for the vb. and the *fllg* [following] pronouns to be *plural*, when the mutual exclusion of the singular subjects is not *emphasised* '. To which are added these examples: 'If Tintoret or Giorgione are at hand.' – Ruskin. 'Mr Darwin or Barnum wld claim him as their own.' It's exactly that *emphasis* on the mutual exclusion (which I don't intend, certainly) which made me think twice about shifting to the *singular*. As for the meaning, the punctuation is correct in the book, & it is the 'passionate failure or a staled success' which 'Look back into their likeness'. Both *may* be present; I don't mean to assert this with an 'and', or to exclude it with a singular verb. I shld be grateful to you for raising the point; some day it might have struck me in the same way, & been a worry.[16]

Although he eventually agreed to be included, Curnow was quite correct in his view that the days of such an anthology were numbered. The book very quickly fell out of print, and within a few years Oxford had embarked on the quite new project of two separate Australian and New Zealand anthologies, the former with Judith Wright as editor, the latter with Jonathan Bennett and Robert Chapman as editors. It remained for Curnow to dispose finally (from his point of view) of the 'capacious term "Australasia"', and of the notion that any local cultural renaissance could be detected in the 'New Zealand poesy' patronised by the Sydney *Bulletin* at the end of the nineteenth century,[17] in his introduction to *The Penguin Book of New Zealand Verse* (1960).

A rush of reviews

Curnow wrote numerous other money-earning reviews for *The Press* during the later 1940s, often longish pieces on anything up to eight or ten volumes at a time of undistinguished poetry issuing mainly from British presses, but on occasion he devoted significant space to books which particularly interested him. He praised collections by Edith Sitwell,[18] and the American Deep South 'Fugitive' poet Allen Tate,[19] whose influential critical writings he was already familiar with. He warmly reviewed a collection of critical articles on T.S. Eliot, edited by B. Rajan, praising especially Cleanth Brooks's elucidation of *The Waste Land* and Helen Gardner's essay on the *Four Quartets*, and comparing Eliot and Dylan Thomas as poets who, in contrasting ways, have 'wrought true poetic forms out of the language that clashes and screeches in their ears, the Babel of specialized or corrupt dictions'. In an elegant phrasing he described the danger for Thomas's language as 'too convulsive a struggle with the past' and for Eliot's as 'too osten- tatious an alliance with it'.[20]

New Zealand poets did not feature very often in the reviews he wrote at this time, perhaps because he felt a degree of exhaustion in the wake of his work on the introduction to the Caxton *Book of New Zealand Verse*, or, more simply, because he felt that he had said all that he had to say, at least in the meantime. In 1947, in anticipation of a visit by Fairburn to Christchurch – Fairburn's first visit ever to the South Island – he wrote a feature piece in *The Press* which was an example of his journalism at its very best, combining essential biographical information about Fairburn for *The Press's* readership with acute comments about his poetry and its development, about the variety of his talents, and – perhaps with an edged sense of the parochialism of Christchurch culture – about the need for cultural commerce between different cities and regions in a country as small as New Zealand:

> No creative writer in New Zealand is a conspicuous public figure. His numerically small audience, once he is known at all, is thinly spread over the whole country. There

is no one centre of urban taste and intellect where an audience may be concentrated and serve the poet as a microcosm of the whole; and any writer must gain by direct contacts outside the centre to which he is tied by sentiment or economic pressures. New Zealand is not so large and various a milieu, culturally, that his actual, physical acquaintance with it can be limited without loss.[21]

He also reviewed Brasch's *Disputed Ground*,[22] a review which Brasch later wrote 'always stuck in my mind' because of its 'apparent dislike' of his verse.[23] However, the review was a much more balanced (and positive) assessment of strengths and limitations than Brasch's reaction suggests. For Curnow, Brasch was primarily an intellectual poet of 'aloof and somewhat abstract contemplation', whose 'abstract symbolism', deeply embedded in the personality of the poet, required patience from the reader in order to allow its unsuspected strengths to emerge. 'It is not only sentiment that betrays', he wrote, but 'the too-selective, too-supervising intellect may also mislead a poet'. In the poems which Curnow praised unreservedly – including 'A View of Rangitoto', 'Waitaki Revisited', 'Photograph of a Baby' and 'Great Sea' – the tendency to intellectual abstraction was tempered by the imaginative use of concrete imagery. Furthermore, in the same review, which also included Baxter's second volume, *Blow, Wind of Fruitfulness*, Curnow described the 'deliberate processes' of Brasch's art, and his 'discipline of thought', as qualities which Baxter's work might learn and profit from, though he was warm in his praise of Baxter as 'the most original [poet] now writing in this country and its sheerest poet by nature'. 'There could hardly be a greater contrast between two poets', he wrote, 'both New Zealanders, both having a common regional inheritance in the Otago landscapes'. Each, however, at their best, offered a 'distinctive gift ... for the reader's imagination'.

Curnow expanded his comments on Baxter in a much longer review he wrote shortly afterwards for *Landfall*,[24] emphasising the remarkable inventiveness, energy, passion and 'natural eloquence' of the poems, but hinting that such qualities tended to reside in 'the intense light of the phrase or fragment' rather than in the form of the whole. The review looks forward to a development in Baxter's work in which 'steadiness' might be integrated with the poet's raw, natural intensity, in which there might be 'a welcome gain in irony and detachment'.[25] The review also devoted considerable space to Baxter's poetic antecedents within New Zealand, the first substantial sign, perhaps, 'of the ability of New Zealand verse to draw strength from within itself'. This is not simply a matter of individual influences on Baxter, though Curnow mentions Fairburn and Mason in particular, as well as M.H. Holcroft's 'thought about New Zealand'. More interestingly, for Curnow, though he insists on the tentativeness of his reflections, the older poets still living and writing – now 'seeking a way back to more personal and universal themes' – may have established 'the first vestiges of a poetic tradition' in their earlier 'New Zealand' poems, noticeable in '[t]he way in which certain conceptions of his country haunt the background of Mr Baxter's poetry, having receded from the positive foreground of older poets'.[26] One effect of the achievement of the earlier poets may be that 'poets may now begin by crossing on a bridge the gulf which faced our imaginations even twenty years ago'.[27] The issues raised in this review were to become formative, and highly controversial, in discussion of New Zealand poetry in the 1950s – quite how controversial, Curnow did not discover until after his return from more than a year overseas, in 1950.

The Axe on stage, 1948

By early April 1948 Curnow was attending rehearsals for the full stage production of *The Axe*, scheduled for three performances at the Little Theatre of Canterbury University College on 24, 26 and 27 April. He was still tinkering incorrigibly with bits of the play, whose scenes were now divided and revised into two acts, and had written his own notes about matters of costuming, drawing on information from John Williams's *Missionary Enterprises* (1838) and E.H. Lamont's *Wild Life Among the Pacific Islanders* (1867). As with the play reading which had occurred 20 months previously, Curnow was anxious to have Brasch's opinion, and sent him a copy of the new stage version borrowed from a member of the cast.[28]

At the time of a second full production of the play in Auckland in 1953 Pocock evoked the excitement of being involved as director of the first production, at a time when he was shortly to depart overseas to pursue postgraduate studies in politics and history at the University of Cambridge. Pocock recalled 'the bare, strongly-lit stage', as well as his own role – as Tereavai – 'crouching on the stage in a nine-degree frost, dressed only in two lengths of hessian and some brown woad, and peering between the shivering legs of his fellow-tribesmen at an audience only less cold than we were'. Above all, for Pocock, the strength of the play lay in the dramatic power of much of its verse:

> Writing poetry for the stage was a new departure for Mr Curnow in those days. He had to broaden the condensed style of the verse he was then writing, and give his actors lines that could be delivered with the strength of high tragedy, in which the verse must move, not according to its own rhythm only, but in sympathy with the action developing on the stage.

The chorus that records the progress of the battle was in our production almost a dance. There could be more than one judgment of the play as a whole, but the verse was intensely satisfying for the actors to speak; its words filled the theatre and held the audience.[29]

Baxter was deeply impressed by the play – 'the best play to come out of New Zealand' – and was especially interested that a poet whose work was 'in the main symbolic and deeply introspective' could make the transition to the stage, which required a 'range of mood and capacity for making situations real'.[30] For Baxter the play touched 'more than a raw nerve of history', since 'most of us are at heart pagan, smarting under a half-comprehended Law':

> One gathers the impression that Mr Curnow, accepting the inevitability of its destruction, is fascinated by the old animistic paganism and prefers it to the new paganism that missionaries unwittingly carried with them – the Axe, symbol of sterile power.[31]

'When one considers', Baxter added, referring to the pressures Curnow's career placed on his creative work, 'that [the play] was made in the brief leisure snatched from fulltime occupation, one can only marvel at his creative powers.'[32]

Writing at the end of 1948 in the *Yearbook of the Arts in New Zealand* James Caffin was equally enthusiastic, describing the play as 'the first full-length dramatic work of a New Zealand poet of established name', and also mentioned that a number of 'uncertainties of construction' in the first act had led the author to make considerable revisions.[33] It was quite typical of Curnow's constant self-discipline, his wish always to learn from the reactions of others, that within a week he had begun revising this already much-revised play yet again, and it was again to Brasch that he confided his aims.[34]

By July he had largely completed the revisions – spurred, no doubt, by Glover's decision to publish the play the following year (1949) at the Caxton Press, though it did not actually appear until after Curnow's return from overseas in 1950 – and wrote to Eric Ramsden that he had rebuilt it considerably since the production: '[I]t has 3 acts instead of two: revision & the wording of stage directions (very few of these) has been a nightmare.'[35] Curnow dated his preface to this revised, published version of the play 'August 1948', and spent much of it discussing the 1948 production, and explaining his revisions – focusing especially on his conversion of the first act into two acts, with the addition of a new opening scene (the second act, largely unchanged, became the new third act), and on his efforts to incorporate the chorus more actively into the structure of the play. The preface was clearly aimed at encouraging and assisting further productions of the play, and included discussion about costuming and about the possibilities of different stage sets.[36] Curnow also addressed the issue of the historical licence he had allowed himself in the play, about which he also wrote to Ramsden, having recently discovered – through Sir Peter Buck – that Tereavai, the chief priest who led the resistance to Christianity, had not in fact been killed in battle, but survived and become a Christian convert:

> I have had moments of compunction about the way I have taken persons out of history & remoulded them for the dramatic purpose: but as we know, most often a historical truth can only be conveyed in the theatre by adaptation of historical facts. I have killed Tereavai (the anti-Christian High Priest) because in the play he must symbolise the death of the old Stone Age civilization: let no true historian complain that this is 'untrue' because the man did in fact embrace Christianity and became in God's good time (I am told) a Deacon. Because that is not the subject of my tragedy.[37]

Symbolic poetic drama of the kind Curnow attempted in *The Axe* had ceased to be fashionable by the later 1950s, when new impulses – realistic, expressionist, absurdist – began to dominate the English-speaking theatre, but Pocock was moved to protest vigorously in the 1990s at 'unhistorical' readings of Curnow's play which regarded both the subject matter and the style as an evasion of issues of culture, identity and race in New Zealand:

> . . . I read with incredulity, in the *Oxford History of New Zealand Literature* published in 1991, that there still are those who find it remarkable that Curnow, whose 'poetry had been much concerned with New Zealand's nationhood and social identity, should choose a dramatic subject that was geographically and historically distant from his Christchurch audience of 1948; the dramatic world seemed to some theatre-goers as remote as that of Greek tragedy.'

> I stare at these words. If there is one thing I know, and that Curnow and others had been achieving with their poems, it is that there existed a Christchurch audience in 1948 that knew geographical and historical distance to be its subject, and knew that confronting distance could be matter of tragedy.
>
> . . .
>
> . . . *The Axe*. . . . puts at the centre of a theatre the poet's view of island, time and ocean I have been trying to present as Curnow's central statement of the 1940s, in which an island is the world where one is never less at home than when at home, and forces can come out of the sea to sweep whole island worlds away.[38]

Much later Curnow was asked, 'Why did you start writing plays?' He replied:

> I think from the feeling that many poets experience; that somehow one wants to get out of the closed walls of one's literary room, and out of the covers of a book – into a more open space where one addresses people more directly. The ways of one's getting out always turn out to be much more difficult than one supposes.[39]

Despite the challenges, Curnow's first experience of writing for the stage, of addressing people more directly, was sufficiently positive for him to wish to continue writing plays – there were to be five more – during the next two decades.

A grant from the Literary Fund Advisory Committee

Throughout his life Curnow was deeply suspicious of bureaucratic interference in the arts, no matter how well meaning the aims of state patronage were, as was the case with the slowness with which the wheels turned in the case of the application made on his behalf by Glover (who emphasised, perhaps strategically, Curnow's stature as a literary critic rather than as a poet), and strongly supported by Brasch, Holcroft, Fairburn and others. There were a few on the New Zealand Literary Fund Advisory Committee (established by Peter Fraser's Labour Government in 1946), including Ngaio Marsh, John Schroder and Ian Gordon, whom he respected, but in general he felt that the Committee's membership and aims (especially its emphasis on supporting the publication of scholarly historical works) were conservative, 'safe', insufficiently interested in contemporary writing or in taking risks with new or experimental creative work. His disappointment at the absence of any progress on his own application is clear in a satiric comment to Fairburn early in 1948:

> I have in my possession the diaries and other private papers (ticket of leave, etc) of Arthur Hogget, first station cook at Mount Merino some time in the Sixties, including correspondence with his sister-in-law Martha Twottlewick, then pantry maid to Lord Tennyson, a former Poet Laureate. I am forwarding these papers to you in the hope that you may be able to interest the State Literary Fund Committee in their publication. I am sure you will agree that the Hogget-Twottlewick letters are not without literary interest, quite apart from their obvious historical importance. I might mention that Mr William Hogget, grandson of Arthur Hogget, served in the Home Guard in Merino County during World War II, and is a financial member of the county branch of the Labour Party.[40]

In May he wrote to Brasch that plans for a trip to England were still 'up in the air',[41] and in July, at Schroder's behest, wrote to the Committee, emphasising his critical and dramatic interests, and hoping that the trip 'would enlarge the scope of whatever I may do in the future for writing in New Zealand'.[42] The Committee, believing at the time that an offer of £300 from Joseph Heenan (from the Prime Minister's Special Fund in the Department of Internal Affairs, where the Literary Fund was administered) was to supplement whatever they provided, voted £625 from the Literary Fund at their October meeting, 'to enable Allen Curnow to spend one year's study in Great Britain'.[43] The total Curnow would thus receive, they thought, to cover his expenses overseas and at home, was £925. Unfortunately the £300 was a kind of contingency amount held in reserve, to be offered to Curnow from the Special Fund *only* if the Literary Fund did not agree to support the trip. It was not available once the Committee had, as it were, taken the proposal over.

The financial practicalities of the trip were not easy for Curnow, and impossible on £625, except by working overseas to supplement his grant – a prospect quite at odds with the reasons for its offer. He had no savings of his own, and a wife and three growing children to support while he was away. The three children were all 'healthy, noisy, & ebullient', he wrote to Ramsden, 'elder two both at school, & Wystan, now nine, already playing regular football – which I don't think he takes too seriously, not being, thank Heaven, physically aggressive, though mentally as tough as I could wish'.[44] He needed to leave £450 to £500 for Betty and the family to manage on while he was away, equivalent to his own weekly salary at *The Press* (about £7 10s per week at this time) together with his earnings from Whim Wham and his paid casual feature journalism. The cost of a one-way tourist-class fare by ship to London was £66.

In fact his situation was somewhat worse than this, since he had debts of £75 that would need to be paid before he left New Zealand. In effect, the grant of £625 meant that he would arrive in London penniless. By this time, however, he was determined to make the trip, and before his departure in March 1949 wrote many more reviews than usual and accepted commissions for radio (including, in February 1949, chairing the ZB Book Review programme). Unknown to Curnow, the chief reporter on *The Press*, Bert Kane, asked the editor Hugo Freeth to offer Curnow half-pay while he was away, but the newspaper's board refused Freeth's request. John Rhodes, then chairman of the board, did, however, much to Curnow's discomfort, agree to pay his itemised list of outstanding bills. *The Press* also agreed to give Curnow unpaid leave for a year, and were later happy to extend this by three months, until the end of May 1950, in order to enable him to spend time in the United States before returning to New Zealand.

Heenan, who remained entirely unsympathetic to any supplementation of the Literary Fund's grant, suggested that Curnow seek funds from the British Council. The Council, through its New Zealand representative, John Bostock, did what it could, paying Curnow's one-way fare to London, but although it also assisted with complimentary tickets enabling Curnow to attend events and performances at the Stratford and Edinburgh festivals, and later paid his passage from London to New York, its immediate assistance fell substantially short of the £200 in cash which Heenan anticipated it would be able to provide.

Although he continued to write warmly and politely to Heenan, Curnow was justifiably aggrieved at what he felt was shabby treatment from him, and was unlikely to have known (though he may have suspected) quite how unsympathetic, even hostile, Heenan was to his situation. Curnow, Heenan wrote to Schroder, had been given 'a thumping grant' from the Literary Fund, and had received 'far more consideration than anyone else'. On his calculations, Curnow would have £200 to live on for a year in England, and 'should have no difficulty whatever while in England in turning over at least £3 a week with his pen even as a free lance, and putting aside any possibility whatever of his being able to do special articles for New Zealand papers while in England'.[45]

It is also apparent that in the circles in which Heenan moved there was still a degree of residual hostility and resentment towards Curnow for his critical treatment of the older literary establishment, especially figures like Eileen Duggan – and difficult to escape the conclusion that a politically well-connected, Catholic-based, Wellington literary mafia deeply resented Curnow as an outsider.* If Curnow never knew quite how unsympathetic some in the Wellington bureaucracy were to his trip he also never discovered, perhaps, quite what an outspoken champion he had in Schroder. It was Schroder who raised, and kept pursuing, the issue of how Curnow could properly benefit as a creative writer from his time away when 'the visible margin [of funds remaining to him] . . . . is just hopeless for a year's serious work',[46] and who took Heenan to task for his suggestion that Curnow should be able to earn his own keep.

He's a writer and should be able to beat out enough to keep comfortable! – Oh hell, I wonder why even so wise and understanding a bloke as you can't ever grasp the real fact about 'writing a few articles' – that it's *hard work*. Curnow might, if he were

---

* The Literary Fund's historian, Andrew Mason, commented that the grant not only 'caused agitation among committee members' but 'consternation in official circles'. The author is indebted to Andrew Mason for access to the manuscript of his history of the Literary Fund, and for a number of details about its internal workings and the role of the Prime Minister, Peter Fraser. [Editor's note: *The Deepening Stream: A History of the New Zealand Literary Fund* by Elizabeth Caffin and Andrew Mason was published by Victoria University Press in 2015.]

financially free, occasionally write something while in England; because he had to get it off his chest there and then. But he ought NOT to be under the necessity. He's not there to write *but to feed*. If he writes, he should be writing raw material: filling his diary, notebooks, commonplace-books – not writing end-products. I feel this aspect of the matter is all-important. Send Curnow to England on conditions that compel him to pay his way, in part, by writing articles, and you destroy the whole proper foundation of the plan and its purpose. . . . . Take only this point. If he has to reap a few guineas every week, he has to consider, all the time, what to do and where to go, whom to see, and so on and so forth, with that end in view. And that's not consistent with the planning of his movements, his activities, his personal contacts, and so on, for the longer and larger purposes of his journey.[47]

Heenan remained unconvinced, merely repeating that Curnow 'is not to be wrapped in cotton wool, and I cannot see that a little money-making effort from his writing will interfere with the main object of his tour abroad'. 'All told', he added, 'I think Curnow has done better than any other beneficiary of either the Literary Fund or our Special Funds.'[48]

By this time Curnow was, as he wrote to Brasch, 'utterly sickened . . . of [sic] all the haggling over my head for sums of money', and resolved simply to accept that he would have to seek employment to support himself when he got to London and try to make time and space for literary activities around his work. 'I have had to make my preparations long in advance', he added, 'get work cleared up & make purchases I can't afford, & shall sail on March 18 whatever happens.'[49] News of the grant was announced in *The Press* early in December, and a week later he had booked his passage to London on the *Empire Star*, sailing via the Panama Canal, on 18 March 1949.

A new volume of poetry and a new edition of the anthology

Curnow had two further literary projects to complete before his departure. The more important of these was finalising the manuscript of a volume of poems, *At Dead Low Water and Sonnets*, which Glover published in July 1949 (while Curnow was away) as the fifth volume in his 'Caxton Poets' series. Apart from the title poem the volume was basically a 'collected sonnets' from all of Curnow's volumes of the 1940s, though one sonnet ('Dunedin', dedicated to James K. Baxter) was inexplicably omitted, and did not appear in book form until Curnow's next collection, *Poems 1949–1957*, in 1958. Of the 28 sonnets only ten, written in 1946 and 1947, had not previously appeared in book form, though they were familiar to readers of *Landfall* and the annual *New Zealand Yearbook of the Arts*. Perhaps for this reason the book was less widely reviewed, and reviewed at less length, than earlier collections, though it contained some of Curnow's most memorable poems.

Curnow had written no new poems, by this time, for eighteen months. The fact that the volume was not published until the end of the 1940s, and that the previous slim 1946 collection, *Jack without Magic*, had such a small print run and was so little known, has tended to obscure the extent to which *At Dead Low Water and Sonnets* was a retrospective collection, and to give a misleading impression that its new work belongs to the late 1940s. In the late 1930s the publication history of *Not in Narrow Seas* had obscured a significant hiatus in the writing of new poems, giving a similar misapprehension of steady and regular productivity. Curnow published no new poems between 1947 and 1949 (and the two poems of 1949, slight, descriptive travel poems from his voyage overseas, were not reprinted until 1958), a considerable gap, but not unusual throughout his career.

The ordering of the poems in *At Dead Low Water* is also unusual, in the sense that it does not appear to follow any obvious thematic or chronological sequence at all, though there are indications that he may have placed some poems beside each other in order to suggest links between them. A number of the Lyttelton-based family poems appear early in the volume, for example. Apart from inviting readers to consider the volume as an achievement in the sonnet form itself, the presentation rather seems designed to break down the idea of sequential development in the poetry of the 1940s, especially in the way it disperses the earlier 'historical' sonnets throughout, as if inviting readers to rethink the relationships among the poems. 'At Dead Low Water', for example, is followed immediately by one of the most 'public' of Curnow's earlier poems, 'Sailing or Drowning'. *At Dead Low Water*, in fact, is the earliest instance of a practice Curnow regularly experimented with in the ordering of his later selections and collections: displacing chronology in favour of other kinds of organisation, as if to invite the poems to be read differently from the time of their first appearance.

By mid-February 1949 Glover was able to send Curnow proofs of *The Axe*, and Curnow sought Brasch's advice yet again about the preface he had written for it, which Glover thought too long, 'but it is all so naturally what I am inclined to say that I don't care to change it'. [50] However, with Glover's affairs in relation to the Caxton Press in turmoil at this time, there was a long delay – until after Curnow's return from abroad – before the play finally appeared. A much more urgent and immediately demanding task for Curnow during the months before he departed was the preparation of a new, expanded edition of the Caxton *Book of New Zealand Verse*, since the first edition had almost completely sold out, and demand for it continued to be steady.* [51] He explained his aims for the new edition in a letter to Brasch which sought permission to use his 'Waitaki Revisited', mentioned that he also wanted to re-read Brasch's *Disputed Ground* with the anthology in mind, and also sought the addresses of younger poets (Keith Sinclair, Kendrick Smithyman, P.J. Wilson, Hubert Witheford, '& perhaps Louis Johnson') whom he was considering:

> The idea is more to supplement, than to expand, the original book, with, say, no more than 25 new poems all told; it wld strengthen the 1945 end of the period, which at present rests upon the few very early Baxter poems. . . . The new section must be entirely self-contained. I see no way out of this.[52]

In February he wrote to Fairburn seeking permission for three additional poems, commenting also on his reading among the younger poets:

> Have you been paying much attention to the new young poets? I have been all over LANDFALL, & the YEAR BOOK. My new boys are Sinclair, Smithyman, Barker (his trans. of a piece by G. Duhamel), Charles Spear, Ruth Dallas – perhaps Rewi Alley. Brasch draws my attention to W.H. Oliver, who seems to me corney [sic], though complex; so do Louis Johnson & P. Wilson – all these three are from Wellington. I've put in two scraps by Hart-Smith. The other two Ruths – France & Gilbert – I've meditated upon & discarded; can't find a piece by either that I really want to see in the book.[53]

Curnow had also approached Eileen Duggan again. 'I wonder if you feel able to reconsider your [earlier] refusal, and permit me to include some of your poems?' he wrote, adding, 'I hope you will forgive me, at this stage, for not naming the poems I would like to have; I cannot do this until I have re-read.'[54] She did not change her mind, and again refused permission.

By the time he left New Zealand Curnow had finalised the manuscript, completing an introductory note to the second edition on 5 March, and Schroder promised to proofread it 'if it comes to printing, as it should, while I'm away'.[55] In the end his selection of additional poems, extending the 22 years covered by the first edition by a mere four years (1945–48), was much more generous than he had originally proposed: the first edition's 116 poems were supplemented not by an additional 25 new poems but by 40 (more than a third as many again as in the first edition), and the sixteen contributors to the first edition were

---

*   Whitcombe & Tombs had ordered 200 copies for the Christmas market in 1948 which could not be supplied.

supplemented by a further seven, nearly twice as many as in the first edition – Rewi Alley, Ruth Dallas, William Hart-Smith, Arthur Barker (tr.), Keith Sinclair, Kendrick Smithyman and Charles Spear.

Though brief, the note also contained some of Curnow's most eloquent restatements of his critical position, carefully formulated as always to avoid any suggestion of a narrow, prescriptive nationalism:

> Much of the [original] introduction to this book is an attempt to show how the dilemma of our 'New Zealandness' arose with that long refusal or inability to engage in poetry as a present adventure, so that outworn fashions were mistaken for traditional values, and the paraphrasing of scenery for a native poetry.[56]

In a memorable sentence – 'Symbol and theme had wider relevance in a world everywhere brooding upon its insecurities' – he linked the anxieties about identity and location in New Zealand poetry written during the war to the wider anxieties of a world at war. He looked forward to poetic advances in the 'alert and passionate scrutiny of self or landscape' which might now be possible in a poetic soil 'already broken and tenanted', though at this stage the idea of a 'tradition' was scarcely at issue, since '[w]e are dealing in fractional perspectives, nothing resembling history'. Towards the end of the note he introduced a qualified notion of 'nationality', emphasising that the poet is not simply the *creature* of his time and place, but *creative*, able to draw on other resources:

> If we are concerned with nationality it is because we recognize certain physical and social realities; that the poet, while his aims are universal, is yet the creature of a time and a place, even the creature of the audience he addresses. Yet he is creative as well as creature. He has other resources.[57]

And his instances of such 'other resources' are the poems of Charles Spear, which 'come direct from a mind withdrawn upon itself, nourished by nothing we would call indigenous', and the three China-located poems of Rewi Alley, which have been selected in preference to poems of remembered New Zealand because 'These three from China, where his heart is, are better poems'.

Like *The Axe*, the new anthology was subject to publication delays, and did not appear until 1951 – long after Curnow's return from abroad. It never crossed his mind, given his sense that if anything he had been overgenerous towards recent poetry and the inclusion of new poets in the second edition, and given the carefulness with which he had presented his understanding of location in the poems, that during the next decade the new edition would be seen by some as both ungenerous and prescriptive in its approach to New Zealand poetry.

Preparing for departure overseas

There were many more personal matters to attend to in the last months before Curnow's departure. There were precious outings with Betty and the children, whom he would not be seeing for a year, and visiting and hosting family and friends. There were also family visits to David and Celia Taylor (with their six daughters) at Belfast, to Patricia and Tyndall Harman, and to Arnold Wall. Writers and artists who visited regularly during 1948 included Colin McCahon, Bill Pearson and Charles Brasch, James and Jacquie Baxter, as well as Curnow's long-standing friends Glover and Lilburn, the latter now based with Frederick Page in the Music Department at Victoria University College but visiting Christchurch during vacations. At the end of September, Ron Mason visited Christchurch and stayed with the Curnows for a week. Brasch and Glover were generous with advice and support for literary contacts in London, and Brasch arranged for Curnow to stay for his first fortnight in London with his cousins Esmond and Mary de Beer.

A shadow was cast over Curnow's departure when, just before Christmas, he was informed by the family doctor that Tremayne had a very weak heart, in addition to the extreme pain he suffered from arthritis in his hips. Curnow immediately told his mother and took her to see Dr Kraal the next day. Tremayne himself was not informed about how serious his medical condition was, and (despite the absence of Tony and his wife Ursula, who had sailed for England a fortnight after their wedding earlier in the year) Christmas 1948 was an enjoyable extended-family affair, with John and Averil attending as well. Allen hired a car for the Christmas period, took Wystan to the Cathedral on Christmas morning, and took his parents on picnic outings to the Ashley River and elsewhere. From his mother he collected all the addresses she could muster of Allen and Gambling relatives living in England; on his father's side all family connections had been lost, though he was determined to visit Cornwall during his time abroad.

This was the last extended period of time Curnow was to have with his father. During January and February 1949 he was frantically busy finishing his literary projects and making arrangements for his trip. However, the *Empire Star*'s sailing date was delayed for the better part of a week, and eventually left Lyttelton on 22 March. 'Exit, Pursued by a Cliché', the title of his last Whim Wham piece for fifteen months, was published in *The Press* the previous day. It concluded:

> Here's a Health to all Readers who drink before Six, and
>   An End to this vain valedictory Verse:
> He'll be back in a Year with a Bag of new Tricks, and

> If he's not better, he can't be much Worse –
> He'll be just the same Bore over all the wide Ocean,
>> If he writes you some More across all the wide sea;
> If he doesn't you'll just have to wait till he's back again,
>> And Back, whether welcome or not, he will be.[58]

A new phase in Curnow's life and literary career was about to open up. His Christchurch days – except for six months after his return the following year – were at an end.

PART II

Chapter Fifteen

United Kingdom, March 1949–January 1950

What is so liberating & stimulating about London? Simply that no-one knows or cares, in all these millions, who or what the person next him is; people don't watch each other, stare at each other. You've got to be just yourself – there's nothing else to be![1]

Arrival in London: the first weeks

Allen Curnow was to make numerous trips overseas in later years, but he never lost the sense of excitement at the prospect of seeing new places and people which accompanied his first. 'Simply by sailing in a new direction / You could enlarge the world'. It is hardly surprising that for an imagination which produced so empathetic a sense of the exhilarating moment of Tasman's first sighting of New Zealand, travel to the other side of the world should be a matter of such constant curiosity and anticipation, with its unpredictable pleasures, discoveries and disappointments.

There were no huge or sudden revelations – about self or country – in this or later encounters by Curnow with *his* antipodes, the northern 'other side', with a *there* always imagined to be different from the *here* where the poet started; but nor did such physical journeyings, when they became assimilated into the imagination, simply provide self-satisfied or nostalgic confirmations of the location from which the poet had started. The comfortable cliché often used to describe the travel experiences of the 'late-expatriate' generation of Curnow's contemporaries – that they discovered, overseas, that they were 'really' New Zealanders and had to come back – is only a half-truth as far as Curnow was concerned. What he discovered – or confirmed, through the experience of travel – was that he was *both* New Zealander *and* 'citizen of the world', and that 'the world' was neither quite as 'exotic' or 'other', nor New Zealand quite as commonplace and familiar, as might be supposed.

Within days of his departure from Lyttelton, Curnow began sending back detailed diary-like accounts of his shipboard experiences to Betty, and after little more than three weeks enclosed two poems ('Cristobal' and 'Curacao', dated 14 April 1949) written immediately after the ship's traversing of the Panama Canal. He also sent copies to John Schroder, who published them on the Literary Page of *The Press* on 14 May. Both were atmospheric companion pieces based on brief sorties ashore at Cristobal, at the Caribbean end of the Canal, and at the island of Curaçao, once colonised by the Dutch, off the coast of Venezuela, where the ship stopped overnight for refuelling. 'Cristobal' evokes the town's debilitating tropical heat, garish colours, and hints of violence just beneath the surface, its mixed-race inhabitants presided over by American 'Zone Troops' striking 'MacArthurian attitudes'. 'Curacao' carries equally unromantic overtones, its port, at Willemstad, serviced from the Venezuelan interior by 200 tankers daily, 'up the foul stream and down', with a refinery which 'mimes / Hell'. Curnow later gave them the collective title 'Intimations in Kodachrome' but changed it, at Glover's prompting, for *Poems 1949–57*, to 'Idylls in Colour Film'.

Curnow arrived in London on 24 April and was met at Tilbury by Tony and Ursula, spending the rest of the day with them. He stayed for a fortnight with Brasch's cousins, Esmond and Mary de Beer, in their comfortable eighteenth-century four-storey house near Regent's Park, before moving to Notting Hill Gate, where Tony and Ursula shared a house with acquaintances from Christchurch, Lyall and Helen Holmes, whom Curnow also knew. He boarded here until mid-October, before shifting for the last three and a half months of his stay in London to a small bedsitter, with a divan bed and a gas ring for cooking, at Paddington.

Curnow was not quite penniless when he arrived, but he had little enough – about £50 – and it was imperative that he make plans to support himself. During his two weeks at the de Beers he set a hectic pace in seeing London, meeting people, and seeking to attend to his financial needs. The day after his arrival – Anzac Day – by a combination of sheer luck and an act of brazen desperation (though Curnow used the phrase 'considerable thrust'),[2] he managed to have an interview with the New Zealand Prime Minister, Peter Fraser, who happened to be staying at the Savoy Hotel, near New Zealand House in the Strand. Curnow had visited New Zealand House early on that day to see Tony, who was employed there as an information officer. He then visited the British Council where he learnt, to his frustration, that there was no prospect of any additional cash resources being made available, as Heenan had assumed. Returning to New Zealand House later in the day, Curnow heard that Fraser was in London, and decided immediately to try to see him.

> I put on my formidable style & swept past the Daimler in the courtyard [of the Savoy] into an immense vestibule, & told a clerk I wished to see the Prime Minster of NZ: was at once shown up to Pete's suite by a bell boy. The first face I saw was Ken Sleight's, the PM's private secy, who knew me at once. I said, 'You'd hate to know what I've come for,' & Sleight said, 'So long as it isn't to see the PM.' I said, 'That's what it is, & I rather think he [will] see me.' I'd only just finished telling Sleight the facts, when Pete himself came in, & the introductions were made. . . . In five minutes I was in Pete's reception room, with the Savoy's fine view of the river, drinking tea & giving him the facts: i.e., that here was my programme, here was I, & that if the money wasn't there the programme couldn't be carried out – though I personally might manage to look after myself. Pete said at the start that he had thought the whole thing was properly provided for; was inclined to be indignant with the State Lit Fund for bungling it; insisted that as 'one of our Noo Zillun poets' I must *not* be reduced to earning my keep in England; & promised to do his best as soon as he got back to NZ, in a week or two. . . . I did touch on the mysterious lapse of Joe Heenan's promised £300; it seemed quite clear that Pete had not been consulted about this, if indeed he had heard of it at all. So I went my way back to dinner, & Pete to No 10 Downing Street. I still hardly dare hope that the amount will be made up, but at least I can feel that I've done the utmost to get it.[3]

Curnow wrote immediately about the meeting to Schroder, who once again took up the cudgels on his behalf. Fraser had 'expressed *horror*', he wrote to Heenan, 'at the idea that C. shld be obliged or expected to eke out his grant from the inkpot'.[4] In fact it was only at this point that Schroder realised that Heenan's offer of £300 was a contingency only. He wrote at length to Fraser[5] explaining the 'extraordinary misunderstanding' which had led him to *include* the £300 in the notional budget he had personally prepared for the Literary Fund, and proposed to Fraser that the Special Fund contribute £30 per month to Curnow for the rest of his stay in England. Fraser was as good as his word to Curnow in London, and in mid-June Heenan wrote to Schroder that the Prime Minister had decided on a 'straight-out grant' of £250.[6]

In the meantime, since he could not assume that any further funding was assured, Curnow looked ahead to the possibilities of employment and kept up a frantic pace of activities, exploring much of central London, which seemed so different from the claustrophobic atmosphere of Christchurch:

> What is so liberating & stimulating about London? Simply that *no-one* knows or cares, in all these millions, *who* or *what* the person next him is; people don't watch each other, stare at each other. You've got to be just *yourself* – there's nothing else to be! Before you find this out, you imagine it will be distressing, a sort of loneliness. It's nothing of the kind: though I've had enough even in two days to guess what kind of hell it can be to one person alone, needing a job or a place to live. For me, merely to travel in a tube – yes, even in a rush hour, as I did tonight – or stand in a bar, produces a kind of contentment of mind I had hardly counted on, & quite unlike anything I've felt at home, unless it was in my youth when Auckland seemed a big city.[7]

By the time his fortnight at the de Beers was up, he had had the first of numerous meetings with John Pocock (then a postgraduate student at Cambridge University, who came up to London to see him), met John Lehmann for drinks at the Café Royal, and attended a party at Lehmann's place where he particularly warmed to the poet Laurie Lee, about to travel to Italy, and met novelists Rose Macaulay and Rex Warner. With an introduction and message from Lilburn, he had also met D.G. (Geoffrey) Bridson at the BBC, who had taken him to the Stag's Head pub near Broadcasting House, a regular meeting place for BBC journalists and poets. Here he had his first meeting with Louis MacNeice, then busy on his translation of Goethe's *Faust*, and his fellow Irish author, Patrick Kavanagh.

An interview about a job with the Australian Associated Press at this time was promising if inconclusive. However, he was shortly to meet the New Zealand war historian and journalist Geoffrey Cox and his wife Cicely (whom he had known in New Zealand) at their Hampstead home. Cox was political correspondent for the *News Chronicle*, and arranged for Curnow to see the assistant editor, Noel Joseph, on 19 May, who introduced him to the editor, Robin Cruikshank. He was offered a sub-editorship for three months – until 22 August[8] – at 12 guineas a week, the starting date put off until 6 June so that he would not miss a British Council-sponsored trip to Stratford to see productions of *Macbeth*, *Cymbeline* and *Much Ado About Nothing*. By that time his own funds would be exhausted, and his aim was to make the three months' income (June to August) last for six months, and thus cover the rest of his time in England, with at least some time to attend to literary projects of his own.

Curnow continued to maintain his contacts with the BBC, hoping to attract the interest of its Third Programme in a talk on New Zealand poetry. W.R. Rodgers (the Northern Irish poet) and Terence Tiller (a Cornish poet) worked for the BBC, and Curnow found both sympathetic friends – especially Rodgers, who at the time was working on a feature on Yeats, but hoping to interest the Third Programme in a programme on Northern Ireland. However, the script Curnow prepared on New Zealand poets did not find favour at this time, though Rodgers liked it, and passed it on for consideration. The BBC was a hard world to break into.

However, the offer of a job on the *News Chronicle*, a daily that commanded 'intelligent respect',[9] was something of a coup. Fleet Street, Curnow wrote to Betty, was 'haunted by journalists looking for jobs, & one is considered very lucky indeed to get in as I have done'.[10] 'I am of course', he also wrote, 'in a state of invisible panic about my power to cope with the work.'[11] For the next three months his life took on an all-too-familiar pattern, the job beginning at 5.15 p.m. and often requiring him to work late into the night. After three weeks on the foreign news desk he was assigned a mix of foreign and home news subbing. Although he found the job, and the life, 'more exacting & more *crippling* of other writing one does, than anything possible in NZ',[12] there were compensations, and he came to agree with Cox's observation that 'the way to learn London is to *work* in it'.[13]

Meeting Dylan Thomas

Although the night work on the *News Chronicle* was tiring and limited his capacity to socialise with people in the evening and to attend plays and concerts, Curnow was free to meet people from late morning through the afternoon. On one of these occasions, on 14 June, when he had arranged to take the completed draft of his Third Programme talk to W.R. Rodgers at the BBC (Rothwell House), he discovered that Rodgers had arranged a lunchtime meeting with the Welsh poet Dylan Thomas at the George Hotel nearby, another haunt of BBC journalists and writers. The time Curnow spent with Thomas – his stay with the Thomas family at Laugharne, Carmarthenshire, for four days in September, and their meetings, again, during Thomas's first reading tour of the United States in February and March the following year – was one of the highlights of his trip abroad.

He was asked on numerous occasions, later, to write up for publication the story of his relationship with Thomas in 1949–50, but – except for one piece, 'Images of Dylan', which he contributed to the *New Zealand Listener* in 1982,[14] Curnow was never able to complete an account which satisfied him. The insoluble problem was one of proportion and scale. He could not present the story (especially for overseas readers) without too much *self*-explanation – about how and why he came to be in England and later the United States, and about why Thomas was a significant figure for *New Zealand* literature and for himself as a *New Zealand* poet at the time – so that what (in the context of Thomas's life) were quite minor events could only be given significance at the cost of seeming to promote Curnow himself. Curnow had too acute a sense of literary integrity not to see the dangers of inflating the events themselves or inflating his own role in them.

It came as a relief to him late in 1953, as he struggled to write a prose reminiscence of Thomas for *Landfall*, at Brasch's request, in the wake of Thomas's death in the United States in November of that year, that an elegy, 'In Memory of Dylan Thomas', should emerge instead. Even in the later 1980s, when Curnow was anything but the unknown literary figure he was in London in 1949, and Richard Mayne, literary editor of *Encounter*, sensed the interest Curnow's reminiscences of Thomas would have for the magazine's international readership, Curnow eventually had to write apologetically to Mayne admitting defeat. His papers contain the numerous drafts in which, as he put it to Mayne, 'I tried every way I can think of, straight line, medias res, round & round, London, Laugharne, Manhattan, Harvard, till the picture I'm looking for is as blurry as the snaps Caitlin took of us both with my old box camera.'[15] He went on:

> It's absurd, like so many other feelings, but all these weeks I've felt too close to the man, in his desperation over what to do next about *poetry*, to write about him plainly. It hit him very early, like everything else in his frighteningly precocious career. When he told me I was a 'late developer' he meant to be nice, but also that it wasn't such wonderful luck to be an early one.[16]

Not quite 'absurd'. It is Curnow's *own* poetic self, his anxieties about 'what to do next about *poetry*', four decades later, which create so strong an identification with Thomas, and which threaten to make his discussion of the poet so much more a discussion of himself than his ostensible subject.

Curnow nevertheless came to believe, strongly, that despite the relative brevity of their contact he understood Thomas, as a man and poet, much more accurately and profoundly than those who profited by the marketing of Thomas myths in the decades after his early death. By far the fullest and most sustained account of his memories of Thomas was written in 1967 for William Latham, a boyhood friend and youthful newspaper colleague (in the 1930s) of Thomas, who wrote to Curnow in April that year seeking his memories for a planned biographical sketch, saying that he wished to emphasise Thomas's 'workmanlike devotion to his poetry, the one thing that mattered'.[17] This intention greatly appealed to Curnow.

He spent several months drafting this 12,000-word manuscript, and even asked Evelyn Segal (an American acquaintance from 1950 with whom he had kept in touch) for any memories she had of an evening when they took Thomas to visit E.E. Cummings in New York.[18] He sent what he had written about Thomas to Latham in December, asking that it be referred to as 'an unpublished article' since 'I am in fact thinking of re-working the material into publishable form'.[19]

However, this project never came to fruition either, for the familiar reasons which he provided in an earlier letter about his progress to Latham:

> I am afraid my recollections are going to seem long-winded, self-centred: a very small vein of your all-important subject, in a mass of more or less irrelevant stuff.

> This is the only way I can manage, & the result may be a clumsy frame & mount for a miniature of Dylan, more a private keepsake than portrait of the poet he was.[20]

Nor, it seems, did Latham's project ever come to fruition.

At the time of writing his piece for Latham in 1967, Curnow did not have access to the letters he had written to Betty during his first trip (and may not have known that they still existed), so that his memory for dates and people is sometimes inaccurate.*[21] Its great value and interest, however, is its attempt to understand Thomas the person, and its attack on images or myths of Thomas, propagated after his death, which were 'as much the product of local or temporary obsessions with the artist as social outlaw or psychological type, as of what he actually was and did'.[22] He was especially appalled by the 'grossly disfiguring simplifications' of J.M. [John Malcolm] Brinnin's *Dylan Thomas in America* (1956):

> Dyl as witchmaster at some endlessly moveable *Sabbat*, – Dyl as randy, roaring boyo, – Dyl as hell-raiser and ringleader of hell-raisers, – Dyl as dionysian wrecker of decorums and maidenheads, – Dyl possessed of some daimon of surpassing eloquence, written or spoken, – Dyl as roistering disturber of the peace, – Dyl as reckless spender of others' time, affection and patience, – none of this answers to my own recollection, as I scrutinise it.[23]

Curnow actually owed his first meeting with Dylan Thomas at the George pub to a food parcel sent to Thomas by an Auckland admirer, Patricia Heslop, in which she had enclosed a copy of his anthology, the Caxton *Book of New Zealand Verse*.†[24] Thomas had been much struck by the 'high standard' of the verse,[25] especially that of R.A.K. Mason, whose 'Judas Iscariot' he had read to an audience of students at Oxford. When Rodgers mentioned Curnow's name to him, Thomas immediately made the connection with the anthology, and was interested to meet him. Curnow always remembered the discussion of 'Judas Iscariot' at this first meeting (and

---

* Curnow reread the main letters to Betty relating to Thomas, including all his letters from the USA, when he was trying to draft his piece for *Landfall* in 1954, but by 1967 had forgotten or mislaid the typed-out relevant passages which have survived in his papers.
† Later Curnow completely forgot that Thomas had identified his benefactress at this first meeting.

of how moved he was to listen to Thomas reciting much of the poem by heart), and told the story on a number of occasions, including in his introduction to *The Penguin Book of New Zealand Verse*:

> 'Didn't that poem shock people in New Zealand?' I had to explain that the shock, if any, had been anything but immediate: several years had passed before any New Zealand public for that poem, or its author, existed. There was no place for Mason's verse in the New Zealand of the 1920s.[26]

However, they also discussed other things. Thomas was interested to review the second edition of the Caxton anthology, or arrange for someone else to review it. Clearly impressed by Curnow's quality as an anthologist, he thought Curnow should 'try an English anthology on the lines of the NZ one', though Curnow hastened to point out his 'ignorance of the big field'. When Thomas mentioned his planned trip to the USA the following year Curnow was quick to ask about the possibilities of a New Zealand tour, and discussion moved on to the travel difficulties they both shared because of family responsibilities: in Thomas's case the difficulties of 'leaving wife & 2 children (another on the way) for some time, & can't afford to provide for them for very long'.[27] They seem to have talked easily, and Curnow later speculated:

> I think we liked each other pretty well. I have had the afterthought that he welcomed the company of an 'outsider' in that place; & that this may have answered to some 'outsider' feeling of his own. This didn't occur to me at the time. I expect I imagined him thoroughly at home in a place where I felt utterly strange.[28]

Before they departed the George, Thomas invited Curnow to meet at the Tavern at Lord's cricket ground the next afternoon, adding – when he noticed Curnow's hesitation (since he wasn't sure of his *News Chronicle* commitments) – that Louis MacNeice would be there. Curnow later read this as a sign of Thomas's lack of ego, his un-English unaffectedness, anything but the image of him as ego-driven promoted by the myth-makers: if he wanted to see Curnow again, he did not assume that Curnow would want to see him, and referring to MacNeice's presence might be a way in which another meeting could occur.[29]

Curnow did make sure he went to Lord's next afternoon, and stayed for several hours before heading off to Fleet Street. Rodgers was there, as well as MacNeice and his wife. Little of consequence was said that Curnow remembered, but he hardly could not be affected by the heady ambience of the occasion, less than two months after his arrival in London. The meetings with Thomas and MacNeice prompted him to send a polite letter to Heenan, reporting on his visit to Lord's and congratulating him on his recent knighthood. Heenan, not to be outdone, replied:

> I was very ticked [sic] with the circumstances under which you foregathered with MacNeice, Thomas and Rodgers. . . . The occasion would almost seem one for celebration by a poem by Allen Curnow or a delightful touch of Whim-Wham.[30]

Heenan also took the opportunity to congratulate Curnow on 'the extra grant the Prime Minister has made you', though he was unable to resist an edged comment – 'to pursue your studies, *shall I call them*' [author's italics]. It is hard to know if Curnow picked up the edge in Heenan's comment, but his letter may have had the effect for which it may have been intended: a cheque for £250 from the Department of Internal Affairs arrived a fortnight later.[31]

Working for the *News Chronicle*, visiting Edinburgh and Laugharne

A week or so after these meetings with Thomas in June, Curnow wrote to Betty that Thomas had invited him to his place in South Wales, at Laugharne in Carmarthenshire.[32] In the immediate future, however, such a visit was impossible, because of Curnow's *News Chronicle* commitments. Throughout July and most of August 1949, in one of the hottest English summers on record, his work as a journalist took up most of his time, though he saw a good deal of Pocock, who spent much of his summer vacation in London, frequenting the company of Tony and Ursula and other Christchurch friends living in Notting Hill 'during Allen's long London sojourn', and who remembered 'talking with him about Blake and Yeats on escalators and hot underground platforms'.[33] They also talked a great deal about theatre, and became involved in plans, sponsored by Ngaio Marsh, to establish a National Theatre enterprise in New Zealand.[34]

Curnow also enjoyed the company of Vivian (Vie) Lee, whom he met at Tony and Ursula's, and they would often go to concerts and plays together. She was a buyer's secretary in British Home Stores and had been briefly married after the war, during which she and her husband had both been in the Fleet Air Arm. Curnow was strongly attracted to her, and thought that she was fond of him as well, but his family situation meant that there was never any possibility of the relationship developing beyond an affair, and that was understood between them. They saw each other, on and off, for the rest of Curnow's time in London.

Early in August, Thomas wrote to Curnow confirming plans for a visit to Laugharne the following month. Curnow copied the letter (the original of which has not survived) into a letter to Betty:

Boathouse
Laugharne
Carmarthenshire, August 5

Dear Alan [sic], Very sorry not to have written long before. I've been away from here, in various debts and troubles. I have one job to finish, & then I'll do that N.Z. 2,000 words.

You said you could come down and see us in September some time. I hope that still stands, & that it won't be raining *all* the time. Let me know when to expect you and I'll send travelling details. It's really quite easy to reach here.

Sorry the 3rd programme don't want your N.Z. script. Much too coarse and colonial, or aren't you a colony?

I was in London for a few days last week, but can remember very little.

Write soon, Yrs, Dylan Thomas.[35]

The job Thomas had to finish was a big one, a film script of *Vanity Fair*, and he never got around to writing his New Zealand piece, which Curnow had arranged to appear in the *New Zealand Listener*. He followed up Thomas's letter and confirmed the arrangement to visit him in September, after his return from a visit to the annual Edinburgh Festival, sponsored by the British Council, which paid his fares and admission tickets but not his accommodation or other incidental costs. He left London for Edinburgh on 21 August, immediately after he had finished his three-month stint at the *News Chronicle*, and spent nearly two weeks there, staying at the Playfair Hostel.

Vivian Lee also travelled to Edinburgh with friends while Curnow was there and accompanied him to some of the performances. He limited himself to 'one, at most two, events on each day', fearing 'indigestion or bewilderment',[36] and found the place overwhelmed with tourists.[37] The theatrical draw card of the festival this year was the premiere production of T.S. Eliot's new play, *The Cocktail Party*, which Curnow saw twice (once with Pocock), though he was disappointed by it, much preferring Tyrone Guthrie's production of Sir David Lindsay's sixteenth-century Scottish play *The Three Estaits* (c. 1540). The undoubted highlight for him, however, was one of Verdi's less known operas, *Un Ballo in Maschera* (*A Masked Ball*), which he saw three times.

While in Edinburgh, Curnow made contact there with a great-aunt, Beatrice Goldingham, and her two daughters. Beatrice was a surviving sister of his grandmother, Rose Gambling, 89 years old but with 'a head that would do credit to a 50-year-old',[38] and the family made him welcome. He was interested in information, especially, about his grandfather John Gambling, and the reasons for Rose's immigration to New Zealand in the 1880s, but Beatrice politely evaded his questions.

Soon after his return from Edinburgh early in September, Curnow set out on his four-day trip to Laugharne.* Thomas had given him instructions to catch the Great Western line train to the village of St Clears, a seven-hour journey, where they would meet at the pub, and take the bus to Laugharne.

The visit was memorable to Curnow for many reasons. They enjoyed each other's company, and visited one or other of the two local pubs most days. Curnow had a room right at the top of the narrow boathouse (with primitive facilities) overlooking the estuary of the River Taf. He met and liked Caitlin, Thomas's wife, who took him swimming one day while Thomas got on unwillingly with the chore of writing his film script of *Vanity Fair*, and he enjoyed the company of their eldest child, Llewelyn, the same age as Wystan, who took him over Sir John's Hill and hitchhiked with him into Carmarthen. Not only the people he met (including Thomas's father and others encountered in the daily visits to the pubs), but the ambience of the *location* itself, and its relation to Thomas's poems, remained indelibly imprinted on Curnow's mind:

> From Sir John's Hill, on one side, where I climbed up one afternoon with 10-year-old Llewelyn Thomas, you see Carmarthen Bay, very wide beyond the tidal flats of the estuary: and on the right the long yellowish Pendine Sands – the beach once used by Sir Malcolm Campbell (?) for his motor speed records. It's the 'heron-priested shore' which Dylan mentions in one of his poems. I looked out from the sea wall at the Boathouse, & saw cormorants swimming and diving for eels almost under the back door; & a tall black heron knee-deep in the water fishing for his breakfast. I *think* I heard a curlew.[39]

Although never deliberately discussed, poetry cropped up occasionally in Thomas's conversation with Curnow. 'The craze for me is over', he said, when Curnow asked when his next volume of poems (the previous one had been *Deaths and Entrances*, 1946) would appear, '[t]hey won't like what I'm doing now'.[40] Thomas worked in a shed further up the steep hill above the boathouse. He showed Curnow a bundle of worksheets of an unfinished poem, 'In the White

---

* Curnow later recalled the month as October (e.g. *Look Back Harder*, p. 320), but this is wrong. In a letter of 19 September he describes the trip to Betty, and appears to have recently returned. The original of this letter has not survived, but Curnow made typed extracts from it (and others) in 1954, when he was trying to write a memorial piece about Thomas for *Landfall*.

Giant's Thigh',[41] and the draft of his unfinished *Under Milk Wood*, at that stage
with the title 'The Town That Was Mad', explaining the basic situation of the play
and the derivation of the town's name, 'Llareggub', from 'bugger all'. 'He admired,
and read over aloud bits of "At Dead Low Water" & some of my old sonnets.'[42]
Thomas was also preparing for his tour of the United States the following year,
reading Oscar Williams's *Little Treasury of American Poetry*, and tried out a number
of readings on Curnow, including Thomas Hardy's 'Lisbee Brown' and poems by
W.H. Davies.

     Towards the end of his visit Thomas asked him to stay on, and 'join him on
some jaunt to the Rhondda',[43] but the option was impossible since Curnow
had arranged to begin an additional month's work at the *News Chronicle* on the
Monday after his return. Curnow often recounted the simple events of his departure from Laugharne as a sign of Thomas's unaffected generosity, the opposite
of the image of him as 'a man who exacted the utmost from others in social
or domestic tolerance, & *gave* only by his genius',[44] as if he were deficient in
ordinary human feeling. Thomas took Curnow to the pub in Laugharne an hour
before the bus was due to depart, rang the St Clears station to change Curnow's
booking on the night train to Paddington to ensure he had a third-class *sleeper*,
and as the bus pulled up called out from the pub and ran down with a bottle of
beer and the words, 'for the train'.[45] 'He was kind, and thoughtful for friends.
I always found him so.'[46]

To stay or not to stay in London?

The additional month's work at the *News Chronicle*, from later September to
later October, was hardly what Curnow wanted, but as his initial three-month
contract came to an end, in August, he realised that he did not have enough to
survive on for the rest of his planned stay in England. The British Council had
not informed him whether they could assist with the cost of his passage back
to New Zealand. There was also a possibility that he might be able to return
to New Zealand via the United States, if he were assisted by funds from the
Carnegie Corporation, but he had heard nothing as yet from that source either.
To add to his anxieties, Betty was finding it hard to manage on what he had left
for her, sending a list of unanticipated bills, which Curnow hoped to be able to
meet by the end of October.[47] He also admitted that he had underestimated the
costs of living in London, especially the expenses of meeting and socialising with
writers, and gave a number of instances. He was trying to explain – given, one
imagines, that his lively accounts of all his doings in London to Betty no doubt
gave the impression that he was spending freely while she was struggling to make

do – that he was being as careful as he could be. 'On the whole', he wrote, 'I am not extravagant here.'[48]

However, by the end of September, halfway through his additional month with the *News Chronicle*, his financial situation looked considerably more promising. Whitney Shepardson, of the Carnegie Corporation, raised the prospect of US$1,500 to support him for three months in the United States and pay for his passage from the US back to New Zealand, provided that the British Council paid his passage from London to New York (as it eventually did). 'By mid-October', Curnow wrote to Schroder, 'I shall be free, and what is more, really free of uncertainty for the first time since I arrived.'[49]

These developments were a huge relief, though he abandoned earlier plans to visit Europe and Dublin (at the invitation of Patrick Kavanagh). After he had finished up at the *News Chronicle* in mid-October he decided that he would use the three- to four-month period from then to the end of January to 'digest all I've done & seen',[50] to visit ancestral sites in Norfolk and Cornwall, and 'to get something written'.[51] He would also be able to send money back to Betty to cover the additional time (about six weeks) he would be away from New Zealand.

There was a significant complication which Curnow had to work through with Betty before he settled on these plans for the remainder of his time abroad. Betty herself, perhaps because of the interest Curnow's accounts of life in England had created for her, had become determined that she and the children should move to England and that the whole family should resettle there, at least for a few years. None of her letters to Curnow have survived, but it is clear from his to her that sometime in September or earlier she had gone as far as pencilling in bookings for the family to travel en masse to England later in the year or early the following year, and that she had come to detest the 'overcrowding & struggle'[52] of life at Leinster Road in what she described in her diary as 'this crowded difficult dirty old house'.[53]

The idea of staying on in England had *also* been in Curnow's mind for some time, until the Carnegie grant to the USA and Betty's forcing the issue compelled him to a decision, which he explained in a long, closely typed three-page letter in mid-October, 'deliberately putting aside all my own feelings about London, & this country, where I do feel the fascination of so many things'.[54] 'This Fleet experience forms a kind of crisis for me', he wrote:

> If I were prepared to turn my back on everything except success in London journalism I might (with luck & hard grind) achieve something like it. But it would mean – far more than in New Zealand – almost wholly forgetting all the work I might call my own.

I would do this, for the 'year or two' you suggest, for the sake of staying here & getting you here – because I know you want it so much. But *only* if we could make a home for ourselves that would be at least as good as the one we have; if I could be sure of the brats' future; if there were the remotest chance of saving anything here to pay our way home eventually. And the chances of those 'ifs' being satisfied just don't look possible.

I've worked here long enough to know that it's impossible even with my free time all my own – to see much & do much that matters outside the job itself. And with family cares added, I don't see that the 'overcrowding & struggle' could be any less than at home.[55]

He also provided a detailed statement about what he estimated the family's weekly living costs might be in London, and was also worried about the cost of schooling, especially for Wystan. 'What a Hell of a question it all is!' he went on, coming back to 'my own real aims in life, such as they are':

Any real effect I have made has been on N.Z. & in N.Z. And it has been made by devoting myself to the one field of poetry – other peoples' [sic] as well as my own. I think I have done what I could.

Only the necessity of earning my bread here has pushed the other possibilities – journal-istic – right under my nose. I still have to consider what is after all my real and only purpose for being here at all. That's why I have looked forward to freeing myself from the N.C., & why I have already got the subject for a new verse play sketched out in my head – something to get on with the moment I have time for it, & freedom from this hospitable but rather crowded & distracting flat.[56]

He mentioned that he would sound out the possibilities of full-time employ-ment, and the question of salary, with the *News Chronicle*, but had effectively decided against settling in London, hoping that the Carnegie grant might enable him to bring some money back with him, and that in New Zealand 'we may be able to fight our way into a better sort of house, which will be worth a great deal'.[57]

A few days later he wrote that Noel Joseph had indeed been positive about a permanent position at the *News Chronicle*, but he had nevertheless firmed up in his decision not to pursue the question of staying in England any further:

Fleet Street wld mean utterly wiping out so much that I have built my life on. . . . It's a straight out choice between carrying on with my own rather small and (in the world way) insignificant work in NZ, and giving it all up to do a job here which will claim every atom of energy & which hundreds of others cld do just as well, if not better.[58]

Death of Tremayne Curnow

In one of her letters of later September, Betty must have referred to Tremayne's uncertain health, since her comments drew an immediate reply:

> As for T. the thought of something happening to him while I am away has often occurred to me & worried me. He looks to me in ways he would never exactly express, & I have thought of him much more since I have been here.[59]

Tremayne wrote to Allen in mid-October, shortly before he moved into his Paddington bedsitter. His letter suggested nothing at all especially amiss. It asked after Tony and Ursula, was laced with literary quotations that were part of his conversational style, and referred good-humouredly to his arthritic leg. However, within days of Curnow receiving this letter a cable arrived from his mother, on 31 October, with the news that Tremayne had died that day. He was 68. Curnow was deeply shocked and wrote to her immediately, but was unable to express his feelings in a letter to Betty written a week later.

As always, Curnow's answer to events which most moved him – for which speech seemed inadequate or impossible because of the strength of the feelings involved – was a poem, or the effort at a poem. In mid-November he made his long-delayed visit to Norfolk, spending several days exploring the ancestral sites associated with his mother's Allen and Gambling family origins. The ambiences of that trip, the reminders of personal history which it provoked, the bleak late-autumn English weather in which it took place, and the particularities of the English scene and climate there and in London, fed into his fine 'November Elegy', later called simply 'Elegy on My Father', which he had completed by the end of November. It was the first serious poem he had written (leaving aside the two vignettes of Cristobal and Curaçao dashed off on the voyage to London) for more than two years.

The poem is built on seasonal and geographical oppositions and paradoxes. Spring in New Zealand, season of melting snows, of new life and growth, 'river-mouths all in bloom', is the *unseasonable* location and time of his father's death. Autumn in Paddington, London, on the other hand – season of dank, leaden, marble skies, of leafless, decaying ('mouldering') nature, of fog ('a yellowish-red glimmer of sun midday is all the daylight there is', he had written to Betty on 19 November, and in the poem, 'Day's nimbus nearer staring, colder smoulders') – is the *seasonable* location of the poet's grief and sense of bereavement, intensified by his absence on the other side of the world. Yet the poem moves towards resolving the anguish of distance and loss.

Autumn in England *is* the appropriate season in which the poet can mourn and acknowledge the fact and finality of death. The 'crutched and stunted spires' of London's Wren churches 'thumb heavenward humorously', as if seeking a ride to heaven, but the sky's marble lid, like that of a tomb, remains 'unriven'. Spring in remembered New Zealand, however, in the poet's imagination, becomes the scene of Tremayne's 'survival' – if not resurrection (though many of the images are biblically derived) – in the poet's vivid recollections of scenes from his active life as a priest. The marble ceiling of the November sky in England becomes the 'dazzling floor' inhabited by Tremayne's soul, as the poet lovingly celebrates the vitality of the man he knew:

> The ends of the earth are folded in his grave
> In sound of the Pacific and the hills he travelled singing,
> For he ferried like a feather the whelming dream, bringing
> The Word, the Wine, the Bread.
> Some bell down the obliterating gale was ringing
> To the desert the visiting glory; dust he trod
> Gathered its grains for a miracle....*

It is the double-sidedness of Curnow's sense of the antipodean that enables him to convey so convincingly and movingly the co-existence of extremities of feeling and understanding in the poem: 'The ends of the earth are folded in his grave'; 'One sheet's enough to cover / My end of the world and his.' If he is 'robed' for death in a sheet, he is also, later, 'robed' as a 'mass-priest' celebrating the Eucharist and the Resurrection. In the final stanza Curnow compares the fragile, wooden-built New Zealand church in which Tremayne preached with the seemingly permanent stone structure of Norwich Cathedral, dedicated to its founding bishop, Herbert de Losinga. But for the poet it is the fragile New Zealand 'nave' which 'loom[s] loftier' and 'lonelier', sign of the closeness and intensity of his feeling for his father, and the poem ends with a personal prayer in which feelings of grief and guilt at separateness, and closeness and warmth, are combined:

---

* In the revised version of this stanza which he published in *Poems 1949–57*, the human vitality of his father is emphasised even more, and the big Eucharistic abstractions reduced to metaphorical hints:
> The ends of the earth are folded in his grave
> In sound of the Pacific and the hills he tramped singing,
> God knows romantically or by what love bringing
> Wine from a clay creek-bed,
> Good bread; or by what glance the inane skies ringing
> Lucidly round; or by what shuffle or tread
> Warning the dirt of miracles.

and the nave

He knelt in put off its poor planks, loomed loftier
Lonelier than Losinga's that spells in stone
The Undivided Name. Oh quickening bone
Of the mass-priest under grass
Green in my absent spring, sweet relic atone
To our earth's Lord for the pride of all our voyages,
That the salt winds which scattered us blow softer.*

Curnow was extremely pleased with this poem, sending it at the end of November to Brasch, and following it up a few weeks later with some revisions and the comment: 'I do feel, at last, that some small recovery of poetry is coming to me.'[60]

Curnow achieved a great deal on his own account in the month – November – after he left his job and moved to Bayswater, and recovered something of the energy of the weeks when he first arrived in London ('When I think it's only a month since I left the grindstone of Fleet Street, I realise what I might have done if I had been free all those months', he wrote to Betty.)[61] Yet he was again under pressure from Betty, who let him know that a position in English at Auckland University College (the position based at Ardmore Teachers' Training College) was becoming available. Not only that, she had also contacted Professor Sydney Musgrove, and worked with others to prepare a CV. Curnow sent in an application, though he had mixed feelings about it, partly because it would mean abandoning his trip to the USA, but more because he was unhappy about Betty's efforts to involve others in organising a job for him, and anxious not to have another knock-back from Auckland, after his failure in 1945:

> I shall make some sort of application to A.U.C. though I see by their conditions that they 'require' an honours degree in English, which I don't have. But you must know how my heart sinks & my stomach heaves at the mere thought of another refusal.[62]

As it happened, the job was put on hold for a year, pending redefinition – it ceased to be an Ardmore-based position and became one of two additional positions in the English Department on the main city campus, with Ardmore duties rostered amongst staff. Musgrove, however, aware of Curnow's interest, approached him again the following year.

---

* In the revised version for *Poems 1949–57* Curnow changed the past tense of the verbs in the first line to the present ('puts', 'looms'), giving Tremayne's actions an ongoing life in the poet's present; and the words of the prayer itself, in the final five lines, are changed to italics.

In November, also, Curnow drafted the first act of a new play (almost certainly the beginnings of what, a decade later, became *Moon Section*), though by the end of the month he was unsure about it:

> [It] has stuck for the time being, with one act roughly copied out. It's so far a dismal tragedy of domestic loves & woes: the idea is to *begin*, instead of ending, with woe & disaster & to show how very much worth while it is to be alive in spite of all this, & perhaps even because of it. But before I go on, I must have a firm ground-plan worked out for plot – and I haven't managed that yet. I may have to be brave & scrap what I've done so far; it will have been practice.[63]

He made contact with Ngaio Marsh at this time, and saw a considerable amount of her until his departure, discussing her scheme for a National Theatre. At her suggestion he sent the script of *The Axe* to Alec Clunes, actor-director of the Arts Theatre Club, but as with the approach to the BBC earlier in the year, nothing came of it. However, he was pleased at this time to be publishing in *Poetry London*, to whose editor, Richard March, he had sent a copy of *At Dead Low Water and Sonnets*. March was full of praise for the collection, especially 'the two grandmother sonnets',[64] which he asked to publish. Curnow proofread them in November, and they appeared in the January 1950 issue of the magazine.

Visiting Norfolk

Throughout Curnow's three-day pilgrimage to Norfolk (10 to 12 November), staying at Norwich, the skies were leaden and the weather a persistent drizzle. He visited Caistor St Edmund, three miles south of Norwich, and made his way to the 'little, flintstone, Norman church'[65] where he discovered the tomb of the great-grandfather who had provided his own first two Christian names, Thomas Allen, as well as those of other ancestors of his grandmother Gambling's generation – names familiar to him from her stories during his vicarage child-hood. Oddly, what struck him about the graves was their *recentness*, partly an illusion created by the clarity of the lettering on the headstones, which the rain had washed and cleaned, and partly a fact, relative to the ancient, centuries-old history represented by the Norman church itself and the even more ancient history associated with the origins of the name Caistor, once the site of a Roman encampment: his ancestors were 'real, after all';[66] the 'ghosts' that haunted his New Zealand childhood had been replaced by 'memories'.

About a mile from the church Curnow found Markshall, the still-standing original house on Thomas Allen's farm, 'probably built in Regency times',[67] largish but not grand or stately, 'nicely proportioned of the square latter-day Georgian style'.[68] He recognised the place immediately from one of his grandmother's photographs, though much of the original internal décor had been destroyed and replaced during the current owner's tenure. He was made welcome by the owner's wife and shown around the house. But, as with the graves at the churchyard, it was the sense of the recentness of his Allen connection which struck Curnow. He looked in vain for names, on the walls of the house and its surrounding buildings, which 'might connect Markshall with my own family'.[69]

Such experiences were not so much disappointments as the laying of ghosts. On his mother's side he had grown up, fed by the stories and pictures of his grandmother, to associate his English connections – England itself – with permanence, stability, a fixed centre. What he discovered, as 'real, after all', about his ancestors, was a sense of transience, change, recentness. It was a *key* discovery at this point, in the wake of his father's death, making possible the double perspective from which his elegy was written. His father's New Zealand life was not to be seen as lived on the margins, nor his death to be lamented in a narrative of isolation and displacement from the centre of the world; he was himself the *centre* of the world in which he lived with such energy, and that world was the *same*, in its qualities of transience and recentness and mortality, *everywhere* – in rainswept Norwich and fogbound Paddington, or burgeoning spring in the South Island.

As well as exploring Norwich itself, and Buxton Lammas nearby, where the Gambling family's milling business had been based, on his way back to London Curnow spent a night with John Gambling's youngest brother, Willie Gambling, and his wife Joey, who lived near the sea in Suffolk at a village called Summer-Leyton.[70] One of his mother's cousins, Vera Gambling, whom Curnow had met when she visited New Zealand in the 1930s, dropped in while he was there. The conversation was general and no family stories were volunteered, Curnow himself not wishing to initiate them. Soon after he returned to London he wrote an account of his Norfolk trip for possible use by the BBC, which was eventually used on their Overseas Service and published in its weekly magazine, *London Calling*, with the title 'New Zealander in Ancestral Norfolk'.[71]

There were other signs that now that his time was his own Curnow was beginning to expand his literary activities. Early in December he joined Katherine Harman, a Canadian writer and editor, to record a quarter-hour interview with John Arlott for the BBC Overseas Service, which was subsequently also broadcast on 2YA in New Zealand, in its 'Critically Speaking' series.[72] He also expanded his literary acquaintances during his last two months in London. Although his efforts to contact T.S. Eliot were unsuccessful (Eliot was abroad for much of the time that Curnow was in London), he met the poets George Barker,

W.S. Graham, Roy Campbell and Stephen Spender, and (through his contact with Harman) the novelist Saul Bellow:

> At a party with young Canadians . . . I met a US novelist, Saul Bellow, once a colleague of poet Robert Penn Warren, to whom he gave me an intro. to U. of Minnesota. Also present, Harry Roskolenko, that brash little monger of letters . . . [and] Lionel Monteith.[73]

Monteith was the editor of another London-based poetry magazine, *Poetry Commonwealth*, whose policy of deliberately promoting Commonwealth poetry (unlike that of March's *Poetry London* or Lehmann's various ventures) immediately raised Curnow's hackles. He remained highly suspicious of the notion of 'Commonwealth poetry' for the rest of his life. 'What on earth or heaven does it profit us to make Commonwealth poetry into a Cause?' he wrote to Schroder:

> There lies the trap for those who make a value of Values or a cult of Culture. Your poem is good or bad, paltry or precious. 'New' Writing has a banner anyone can understand, but Poetry 'Commonwealth', like the ill-fated 'N.Z' New Writing, is one of those strange devices that defeat their own project. . . . One poem or story placed on its merits with an editor who has no Empire axe to grind is worth twenty issues of 'Poetry Commonwealth'.[74]

There could not be a clearer statement of the reasons behind Curnow's later admiration for the English literary editors Anthony Thwaite and Richard Mayne (*Encounter*), Alan Ross (*London Magazine*), Michael Schmidt (*PEN Review*), and Karl Miller and Mary-Kay Wilmers (*London Review of Books*), and of the reasons why he valued publication in these magazines.

The prospect of the trip to the USA also began to loom excitingly on Curnow's horizon by December, when he heard formally from Shepardson at the Carnegie Corporation of the $1,500 award to cover two and a half months in the USA and a passage from Vancouver to Auckland – the only ship available leaving from there on 27 April. With his passage to New York now paid for by the British Council, Curnow was hopeful of being able to send a further £100 to Betty when he left London on 8 February 1950, and also thought there might be a prospect of saving something from his Carnegie award. On one of his encounters with Dylan Thomas late in the year they swapped notes, and learnt that they were likely to be in New York about the same time in February, 'and may even be of use to each other there', he wrote to Brasch.[75] At this stage Curnow was planning 'broadly for New York, Boston-cum-Harvard, U of Louisiana, & Chicago – university poetry teachers & professors a large item on the agenda'.[76] 'Instructive for N.Z. purposes', he added.

Visiting Cornwall

Curnow spent Christmas of 1949 with Vivian Lee and her mother at Marlborough Place in London, and early in the New Year embarked on the second of his planned ancestral pilgrimages, to Cornwall. It turned out to be eventful, illuminating, and also productive of poetry. He spent three days in Cornwall, leaving London by train on 8 January to Penzance and from there taking a local train to St Ives, arriving in the dark at 5.30 p.m. and basing himself at the Western Hotel. He made notes about the trip at the time (referring to his wish 'to catch at some incident to serve as mnemonic for the scene') – including an atmospheric description of the train's departure from London in thick fog and smog through ugly industrial suburbs – and took photographs, as well as writing in detail to Betty about it, and sending postcards of places he visited.

He was unable to trace any direct connections with his grandfather John Curnow, born in St Ives (it was much later that the scholar and Cornish genealogist A.L. (Leslie) Rowse told him that the likeliest location of his branch of the family was Towednack), but was fascinated to find how common the Curnow name was in the St Ives region, and also noted that the name took different forms, including Curno and Curnoe – indeed that it had the same root as the word Cornwall itself. However, as had occurred earlier at Laugharne and at Caistor St Edmund near Norwich, it was the quite distinctive ambience of place and people which fascinated him. The Cornish habit of referring to people by nicknames (often to the point where a person's actual name might be forgotten) intrigued him. He believed the habit might have derived from Cornwall's earlier 'lawless days of smugglers and wreckers',[77] and collected examples for use in a poem, 'Sea Tryst'.

Curnow discovered the small 'art colony' at St Ives ('a very active & useful one', he thought),[78] and met several artists associated with the place. Guido Morris was a printer and typographer who ran his own Latin Press and whose aesthetic philosophy of life may have reminded Curnow of Eric Gill. But he had so pure a sense of the printer's art that he used only one typeface, the idiosyncratic Aldine Bembo, and only the finest handmade paper, and even Glover was moved to comment, when Curnow sent him a package of examples, that there might be limits to the kinds of text which could stand such a typeface. Curnow greatly enjoyed his company, at the Castle Inn and other pubs, and at his printing press.

Also living on St Ives Point, a promontory above the township known as 'The Island', was the sculptor and painter Sven Berlin, later a widely published writer. At that time he was a much-admired younger sculptor in England (wearing 'gold rings in pierced lobes, black-bearded, long black hair, as if he enjoyed playing pirates rather than any affectation')[79] who worked with Cornish granite, Sicilian marble, and alabaster. Curnow purchased one of his sketches for a piece of sculpture, in 'pencil and pinkish oil wash', for £5, and was interested in his conversation about art:

> [He] talks a good deal of primitive forms & revelations, but in fact his pieces look thoroughly in keeping with some balance of Western forms with his own slight personal intransigeance [sic]. The intransigeance [sic], I am prepared to believe, feeds itself upon primitivist inclinations & meditations. He writes (cf Cornish Review) of indwelling *forms*, i.e. in the stone itself; this is I take it a sculptor's myth, or a myth verbalised out of technical compulsions: for on these lines he explains the diff. *betw*. *sculpture* proper & modelling for bronze.[80]

He was especially interested, because of its personal relevance, in Berlin's 'retreat from London':

> [It] is a matter of faith & myth; but how much of his [wholly *adoptive*] Cornish myth-ing, as of Earth-god, sea-god, male-female, is only what he is obliged to tell himself to keep on working? – I wonder.[81]

One afternoon Curnow walked for five miles across the moors to Zennor, once a coastal fishing village, and the location of the legendary Zennor Maid, a Lilith-like changeling – part beautiful woman, part fish – who lured men to their death by drowning and whose image is engraved as a warning to the faithful in the small church dedicated to the virgin Saint Senar, after whom the village is named. It was a stormy afternoon, misty and windy, most of the walk along paths between rocky granite outcrops and broken stone walls (some of the stones as large as 6 feet long and 3 feet wide) overgrown with briar and bracken. It was 'grim, fascinating country', he wrote to Betty, 'not to be described in a few words',[82] though he made some notes soon afterwards. He arrived at the Tinners' Arms, in Zennor village, soaked through, just before dark, and dried off by an open stove in the bar.[83]

On another occasion he took a bus from St Ives to Zennor, and walked to Gurnard's Head, two miles along the coast, in order to see the grey stone house of another Curnow who farmed there. The poem he wrote shortly afterwards, originally entitled 'Zennor Moors', and published in the *Cornish Review* with the title 'A Walk', was a companion piece to 'Sea Tryst', evoking the grim desolation of the moor and the ghostly tin-mine ventilation chimneys. It is a landscape which might generate legends, though the poet's voice here is more sceptical:

> Babylon could have come to a muddy doom.
> Foundering stone in a wet wind might sink
> But never deep, and the bitten gorse bloom
> Rooted above ground in a field-wall's chink.

Desolation has its own discipline.
Those topless chimneys needing no command
Stand up and stalk me limping through the rain.
This is in order. We both understand.

They should be lungs of lifeless mines but are
Field-wise as any footless ghost
Familiar as the prickle of death. Once there
Were giants to gasp at camped upon this coast

Kneedeep in storm bowling stark uptorn crags.
I saw none. Very likely it was a tale
Told at the Tinners' Arms by one in rags
Mumbling old magics for a pint of ale.

Why Curnow never reprinted this lively poem is a mystery. In the case of 'Sea Tryst', which was also never reprinted, the answer is likely to be that he regarded 'The Changeling' as a revised version of its central idea, though in the end the revision was so substantial that they might be seen as two poems.

Curnow kept in touch with Sven Berlin for a year or so after his return to New Zealand, and in one of his letters sent him a copy of his earliest version of 'The Changeling'. Berlin and his partner Juanita had been forced out of their premises ('The Tower') at St Ives by conservative religious forces on the local council because of their unconventional lifestyle, and had moved to Nancledra in Penzance, close to Anelebra, the site of a Curnow farm named in Curnow's own 'Sea Tryst'. Berlin spoke of the 'mythic' ambience he associated with Cornwall:

> The Tower was always for us a place of creation where my ideas & my creative life could be worked out. It may be because of this, & because it was built in so lonely a spot on the edge of the sea, that the forces of destruction not only assailed it like the gales raging at its windows, but permeated like spirits into its very walls and atmosphere. I have long believed that in Cornwall one is particularly near to the primitive energies that not only exist in the roots & origins of life but also in the deepest places in our own minds – & unless they can be directed into creative channels they will destroy one: madness & death will ensue.[84]

Curnow had mentioned in his letter 'the condition of light just before sunset' – often in his own poetry a prelude to a special kind of vision or awareness – and Berlin described similar experiences, involving objects giving out darkness as well as light, interpreting them as states of 'personal illumination' related to the 'psychic condition of the beholder'. 'I grant the wind is mostly nor'west', he went on, in case Curnow might mistake his speech, as some did Hamlet's, for madness.

Curnow must also have spoken somewhat negatively about the poem 'Sea Tryst', which had appeared in the *Cornish Review* in 1950 – after sending it to Brasch for *Landfall* he had asked Betty to tell him 'that the long Cornish poem isn't good enough & that I must revise it considerably'[85] – but Berlin insisted how strong its impact remained, its only mistake a technical one: the spelling of Anelebra as 'Anlebra'. He also liked 'The Changeling' – mentioning that he was 'honoured to have my name to it. A tribute which, coming from your far off planet, moved me.' Curnow presumably removed the acknowledgement subsequently, when its earliest published versions appeared in the *New Zealand Listener*[86] and the *Cornish Review*.[87] But Berlin's comments reveal how important their conversations had been to the conception of the poem.

Certainly Berlin did not remark on its relationship to 'Sea Tryst', though its central focus – the changeling figure of the 'girl-fish' – was at the centre of 'Sea Tryst', and many other phrases and images are similar to those found in 'The Changeling', though nothing of the opening stanzas, a roll call of the Curnows he had discovered in and near St Ives:

> Curnow of Anlebra [sic] farm at Nancledra, Curnow the sweep,
> Curnow the mercer and councillor, Curnow the barber,
> Curnow of Gurnard's Head over by Wikka where deep
> In the scoop of the Western swell is your grey hulk's harbour
>
> Death, fisher of men, your nets of granite and foam:
> Surely you haul us all in, the shoal of our lives,
> Mine of a strange sea native, Pacific my home,
> And my tribesfolk, men of your tetrarchate Saint Ives.

Already, in the central stanzas of 'Sea Tryst', which evoked the Zennor Maid, Curnow had taken her on a strange undersea voyage to the other side of the world – 'Down, down, deep as the locked Antarctic streams / And the blind isles where the bread of my birth was thrown.' – a dream figure embodying sensuality, flesh, and desire who scorns the moral rectitudes of the pious. But in 'The Changeling' all traces of Cornish particularity, and the particularity of the legend of the Zennor Maid, have been removed: its focus, after Curnow arrived back in New Zealand, shifted wholly to New Zealand – in particular, Lyttelton Harbour, and the change-ling was generalised to include *any* of the legends involving such a figure.

Sketch by Rita Angus (Cook) of a 30-year-old Curnow, in a very Yeatsian, dandified pose. Rita stayed with the Curnows after Wystan was born, assisting in the house and doing sketches in exchange for meals and accommodation. This sketch was included in Glover's fifth issue of *Book*. (Book 5, *Christchurch, The Caxton Press, 1942*)

Right: Curnow at his typewriter, intensely focused on his writing. He often worked late at *The Press*, and would 'get down to' his poetry after he came home. (*Privately held*)

Below: A typical morning for Curnow and Betty, in their dressing gowns in the front garden at Leinster Road. (*Privately held*)

Family life was intensely busy during the late 1940s with three 'healthy, noisy, & ebullient children'. Above: Photographs of Curnow, Betty and their three children, Wystan, Belinda and Tim, not long before Curnow left for England in 1949 on a Literary Fund grant. In the photograph top left, Wystan is wearing an air-force cap, a present from his Uncle Tony (Curnow's younger brother). (*Privately held*)

Above: Curnow and Glover, who was to become his longest-standing literary and personal friend. Curnow would miss their often daily meetings at the Caxton Press or in pubs after Glover joined the Royal Navy in 1941 and left Christchurch on war service. *(PAColl-7404-2-23-1, Gordon Ogilvie Collection, Alexander Turnbull Library, Wellington)*

Below, from left: Curnow with his literary friends Denis Glover and Bob Lowry, and Captain Donald McWilliams, photographed in Christchurch in 1946 in front of a poster for a film. *(Betty Curnow, PAColl-2146-008, Bridget Williams Collection, Alexander Turnbull Library, Wellington)*

Opposite: On the *Empire Star* in March 1949, en route to England via the Panama Canal. The excitement at the prospect of seeing new places and people was palpable. 'Simply by sailing in a new direction / You could enlarge the world'. *(Privately held)*

Photographs of Curnow, Dylan Thomas and the Boathouse at
Laugharne, Wales, taken by Thomas's wife Caitlin on Curnow's
old box Brownie camera on his four-day visit there in September
1949. The tidal view across the estuary and the ambience of the
location made a deep impression on Curnow. (*Privately held*)

Above: The house at 13 Herbert Street on Auckland's North Shore, where the family moved in November 1951. It overlooked the tidal shell spit and mangroves of Shoal Bay, and the scene for Curnow's poem 'A Small Room with Large Windows' was observed from its south-west-facing sitting-room window. (*Privately held*)

Below left and right: Betty and Curnow in the garden at Herbert Street in the early 1950s. The house was isolated in the days before the Auckland Harbour Bridge, and Curnow would travel to work by bus and ferry across the harbour to Auckland University College. (*Privately held*)

Above: With the help of fellow poet A.R.D. (Rex) Fairburn, who also lived on Auckland's North Shore, Curnow purchased a clinker-built dinghy for fishing around the Waitemata Harbour. (*Privately held*)

Left: Curnow with freshly caught snapper. (*Privately held*)

Chapter Sixteen

United States, February–April 1950

If the psychologists have taught us anything, it is that opposites combine in a single state of mind. America is today expressing that doubleness, ambivalence of mind. Destruction on a sufficiently huge scale fascinates them: it is the obverse of their passionate admiration (and achievement) of construction on the grand scale. And they have not the heart they once had for construction.[1]

Last weeks in London

When Curnow arrived back in London from his trip to Cornwall he had less than a month left before his departure for New York. The two Cornish poems, 'Sea Tryst' and 'A Walk', were written quickly, and when Curnow sent them to Brasch a week before the end of January he mentioned that they had already been accepted for the *Cornish Review* by Denys Val Baker,[2] who edited the quarterly from Penzance. To Schroder he wrote that it was 'one of the freshest & most interesting of the more regional reviews . . . gaining much from the sense of place – place to look in upon, & place to look out from'.[3]

Soon after he got back to London he also sent off to Ronald Lewin, head of talks for the BBC Third Programme, a slightly revised version of the 30-minute script he had written at W. R. Rodgers' suggestion six months earlier, and was delighted to hear, this time very quickly, that it had been accepted. He had actually done very little to it, beyond giving it a fancier title, 'Poets of the S. Pacific: A New Zealand Cultural Study'. To Schroder he described the talk as 'almost

... a radio adaptation of my anthology Intro'. He included complete poems by Fairburn, Mason, Glover and Baxter which the BBC was hoping to get Dylan Thomas to read, though Thomas was himself frantically busy preparing for his US trip and turned out to be unavailable. Curnow described the making of the recording itself – completed less than a week before his departure, and due to be broadcast in April – to Betty, in the last of his letters to her from London:

> ... I had more compliments upon my voice & delivery than I've ever had in my life, or ever expected. The irony of it is that if this script had got into the right hands from the start, *Third P.* wld have had other jobs to offer me – using my voice, that is. Never mind. I've taught myself quite a lot about broadcasting, or the *talking* side of it. *Third P.* is of course, unlike any other service in the world; the only one, I suppose, where you can take for granted a certain level of interest & intelligence in your listeners.[4]

It was an upbeat note on which to leave London. He'd been able to add the fee of 30 guineas to the money he sent back to New Zealand. In the busy last few weeks he had also seen quite a lot of Jock [W.S.] Graham, a Scottish poet and close friend of Sven Berlin, as well as Stephen Spender and George Barker. He had visited Zwemmer's, the art bookshop, and sent off to New Zealand a carton of book purchases from his time in England. He had made a last visit to the *News Chronicle* to say farewell to Noel Joseph and Geoffrey Cox, and other colleagues there. The painful shadow over his departure, however, was leaving Vie Lee. Later in life, he commented that at the time he believed he was in love with her, and that she was 'pretty fond' of him too, and in different circumstances might have asked her to marry him. However, nothing was ever discussed, because of the tacit understanding that such a future was impossible.[5] He began working on a number of love poems, including 'When the Hulk of the World', exploring the intense sense of loss he felt.

Whether Curnow's departure was quite the painful event for Vie that it was for Curnow is not so clear. She was a good friend of Tony and Ursula (especially Ursula), and also of Pocock, belonging to a circle of friends who socialised at Peel Street, Notting Hill Gate, and later at Doughty Street, Bloomsbury, where Tony and Ursula shifted in 1951. Certainly, after Curnow's departure she did not disappear from the Peel Street scene, and the following year (1951) she went with Ursula to the Edinburgh Festival. Pocock wrote matter-of-factly to Curnow about her presence in the 'Doughty Street colony' that year. He had taken her to hear Dylan Thomas read, in London, and not been especially impressed by the reading, and she had offered to type up his Cambridge thesis for him:

> As I certainly don't mean to sacrifice twenty pounds to my offended dignity, I shall no doubt be calling there when the thing is ready for treatment. You have probably heard

of the grotesque tangle of personal relationships which developed there some months ago. I have nothing whatever to say about it.[6]

Quite what the 'grotesque tangle of personal relationships' was, is unclear. At all events it hardly suggests that Lee retreated into her shell in the wake of Curnow's departure, and a little later Curnow heard from Tony that she had remarried.

Curnow had said nothing to Betty about Vie Lee in his letters, and the fact that he felt so strongly about her during the period leading up to his departure would have produced difficult emotional conflicts within him. 'His real life', Brasch commented astutely on first seeing Curnow after his return to New Zealand, 'must go on deep inside him, carefully hidden from other people.'[7] Vie Lee's presence in London, and his feeling that he was abandoning her, clearly affected his feelings about leaving the place, though it was also the sense of doors opening, of small but significant literary achievement, which had at last made him feel a little more at home there: 'I'm sad, very sad, to leave London', he concluded his last London letter to Betty, 'a dirty, shapeless, wicked, & very loveable place. I'll write next from New York.'[8]

New York and the United States

Curnow sailed from Southampton on the *Queen Mary* on 8 February 1950 on what turned out to be a stormy transatlantic trip, arriving a day late in New York around 14 February, where he was based throughout his United States stay at Midston House, a hotel on Madison Ave at East 38th Street. Apart from the rough weather the trip was uneventful, though he received his first taste of the McCarthyite era in the USA when he was specifically interrogated by the immigration official as to whether he had any Communist Party affiliations.[9]

He had formal letters of introduction from the Carnegie Corporation, which had made a number of contacts for him, and from Professor Henry Seidel Canby of Yale University's English Department (whom he had interviewed in New Zealand during Canby's lecture tour in 1945), and planned to spend the greater part of his two-and-a-half-month stay in New York, with a scheduled visit to Boston and Harvard for a week in late February and early March, and to Washington in early April. Later, in April, he would spend the last couple of weeks travelling west through Chicago to San Francisco, thence to Vancouver by 27 April for his passage back to Auckland.

Soon after his arrival he contacted J.M. Brinnin, at the YMHA (Young Men's Hebrew Association) Poetry Center, whose address Dylan Thomas had given him. They discussed the literary furore over the award of the Bollingen Prize to

Ezra Pound for *The Pisan Cantos* – a topic of controversy throughout Curnow's stay – but Brinnin was more concerned about Thomas's impending reading tour, which he was sponsoring, and 'full of anxiety',[10] in the wake of exaggerated hearsay and gossip about Thomas's life, that he was 'buying trouble'.

Curnow tried to reassure him, but also had his own increasingly busy schedule of events and meetings, many of which he reports on in detail in a notebook covering different periods of his American stay. In addition to Canby he met Howard Moss, poetry editor of the *New Yorker*, R. Linscott, director of the publishing firm of Random House, and John Finch, 'formerly of Harvard University (a student of F.O. Matthiessen), teacher at Dartmouth, and also director of a summer school of European students at Salzburg',[11] who introduced himself to Curnow when he saw him reading *The Pisan Cantos* in the Midston House bar. He also met the poet and anthologist Oscar Williams, and William Rose Benét, 'the man', according to Canby, 'who knows all the poets'.[12]

Eliot's *Cocktail Party*, which had been much better received in New York than in London – perhaps, Curnow astutely commented, because Broadway audiences were more likely to be impressed by a central character (played by Alec Guinness) who represented 'something between a priest and a psychologist' – was a major literary topic of conversation, alongside the Bollingen Prize controversy. Curnow's reservations about the play meant that he often found himself 'one of a dissident minority when the play was being discussed – chiefly at literary cocktail parties where it was impossible to avoid discussing it'.[13] During the first fortnight he was also finding his way around wintry New York, visiting galleries and bookshops, planning later meetings, and working at poems, and did not warm to the city:

> My distaste for NY grows; it is a crude, shallow city; the good things all belong elsewhere; the indigenous are the vulgarities. The good people know this. For its size & its power one must have a special respect, but this need not inhibit other responses. It is an object lesson against a certain kind of urban planning: the effects in NY are mathematical, mechanical, characterless. There is dehumanized comfort; the apparatus of comfort is generalized, and becomes a common denominator, like money.[14]

A week after his arrival Brinnin telephoned him from the twenty-third floor of the Beekman Tower Hotel, and put him on to Thomas, who had just arrived after a rough seventeen-hour transatlantic flight and suffered badly from vertigo high up in the glass-walled hotel. Curnow went round and Brinnin took them to Greenwich Village for the evening. They dined at the Gran Ticino restaurant, not far from Washington Square (where they were joined by Howard Moss and a young poet protégé of Brinnin's, David Boland, who wished to meet Thomas), then drank at the San Remo bar before moving to Moss's Village apartment.

Thomas and Curnow left Moss and Brinnin at the apartment and went back to the San Remo until it closed at 4 a.m. (sending Boland on his way about 3 a.m.), then on to the back room of a small restaurant (where they could continue drinking) until 5 a.m., when Curnow arranged a taxi to take both of them back to their mid-city hotels.

Curnow was at pains, in the narrative he drafted for William Latham, to correct Brinnin's later sensationalised and inaccurate account of this and other occasions at which Curnow was present. In Curnow's account of this first evening, Thomas was tired but excited, went out of his way to accommodate his host, spoke kindly and encouragingly to Boland about poetry, decided to try to stay up all night in New York but eventually, not drunk but exhausted after drinking a great deal, fell asleep, when Curnow saw that he got home safely.[15] Hardly the stuff for a sensationalised account of his first night in New York, which Brinnin presents as if it was a sign of things to come.

Two days later, on 23 February, Thomas gave his first reading to an audience of a thousand at the Teresa Kaufmann Auditorium in the YMHA Poetry Center, the first of many superb, but completely exhausting, performances. As, white-faced and distressed, he was being mobbed by a hundred or more admirers after he left the stage, Curnow believed he 'read his thought plainly'. 'Don't you think he's had enough of this?' he commented to Brinnin and Moss, who then moved in to rescue him.

The next day Thomas rang Curnow in distress from the Beekman Tower ('Allen, I'm in a terrible fix'), which he needed to vacate at short notice because of a double-booking. Curnow arranged for him to be transferred to a room next to his own on the ninth floor of Midston House. He was not well, suffering from exhaustion and fatigue, and both Curnow and Oscar Williams (who arranged for his doctor to attend) regularly kept him company as he prepared for the next stage of his reading tour. Curnow was due to leave for Boston and Harvard for a week on the following day (25 February), where he had arranged to see F.O. Matthiessen and John Sweeney (in charge of the Woodberry Poetry Room at Harvard's Lamont Library). Brinnin arranged for him to stay with the poet Richard Eberhart and his wife Betty, then living at Cambridge, and also asked him to meet Thomas (who would be on his own) off the train at Boston a few days later, where Matthiessen was hosting his reading at Harvard.

Curnow had a very busy week in Cambridge and Boston, travelling there in the company of John Finch. Eberhart and Betty (Eberhart was vice-president in the Butcher Wax Company, his wife's family business) became long-standing friends, and Eberhart – from this time on – became one of the earliest poets to profit from the burgeoning university phenomenon of visiting poetry professors, spending much of the rest of his life in various such positions attached to universities. At the

Eberharts' Curnow also met Jeanne Tufts, who later married Frank Cassidy, both active in the theatre world (she as a drama teacher) in New York and elsewhere and both, also, to become long-standing friends.

Curnow greatly enjoyed his meetings with Matthiessen, 'that fine scholar and critic, and good man',[16] dining with him in his Boston apartment on his second night in Cambridge. He was familiar with Matthiessen's work on Eliot (he was also preparing an Oxford anthology of American poetry and a book on Theodore Dreiser), and he was extremely interested in Matthiessen's socialist analyses of American society, his hatred of McCarthyism and the growing anti-communist hysteria, and his uneasiness about the conservative politics of Eliot, Pound and Yeats. Matthiessen had been accused the previous year of supporting communist-front organisations, and was deeply depressed about the international situation. Curnow was shocked, little more than a month later when he was in New York, to learn that Matthiessen had committed suicide, a casualty of the McCarthy era.

Eberhart was very hospitable ('the most charmingly easy household I've ever dropped into'),[17] showing Curnow around Cambridge and Boston, including its historic literary sights, and giving him a feel for New England culture and architecture. He introduced him to numerous Library of Congress recordings of American poets reading their own works. There was also considerable discussion of W.H. Auden, whom Eberhart had known very well when Auden first immigrated to the US, and on one evening Eberhart took Curnow to a 'poets' party at the home of the poet and translator John Ciardi in Boston':

> [T]hese are all friends who now & then meet at each other's homes to read aloud any new poems they have, & criticize freely, over the usual stream of (in this case) Scotch & Bourbon & ice. . . . Eberhart, Richard Wilbur, John Holmes, May Sarton. Like all American poets except Cummings, they read their work atrociously with almost no regard for the form: two new sonnets of mine were admired, I think excessively, because in that company they sounded so much better as I read them.[18]

The sonnets, whatever they were, never survived. Curnow added a footnote to his letter to Betty: '[T]heir rule was that the work read out should be new. I took these sonnets along, R.E. [Eberhart] having determined that I should join in the game. I blush to look at them now, they are so bad.'[19]

Early in March, Curnow kept his appointment to meet Dylan Thomas at the South Station, Boston, accompanied by Jeanne Tufts and a young man officially appointed to meet him. Thomas was still recovering from his reading at Yale the evening before, and after the four-hour train trip had only two hours before his Harvard reading at 5 p.m.: he 'was in dread of formalities and fuss & wanted to sit over some beer'.[20] His schedule was to attend a faculty afternoon tea party before the reading, a post-reading party with invited guests between 6 and 7 p.m., dinner with guests at Matthiessen's apartment after that, followed by a post-dinner gathering at Richard Wilbur's apartment. First thing the following morning he had to depart on a journey of several hundred miles to Mt Holyoake for another reading. For Curnow, who was with Thomas for the whole time of his visit to Harvard, the punishing schedule epitomised the entirely unreal expectations of the tour's organisers – and the astonishing stamina and courtesy with which Thomas attempted to meet their requirements.

Matthiessen's role was exemplary. He understood perfectly Thomas's wish *not* to be caught up in a round of tea-party socialising before his reading, found a quiet bar, and cancelled the event. The reading itself was 'first-rate', with Thomas 'in entire, composed command of his audience',[21] and the cocktail party afterwards – in which Thomas mingled with a hundred guests – was entirely without incident, except for his comment to a young woman with a low-cut dress wishing to talk to him about her poetry: 'I'd like to be suckled at those breasts.' Matthiessen's dinner for Thomas was a small affair – the only others there were John Sweeney and his wife, and Curnow – and after dinner some guests arrived: Richard Wilbur (then Literary Fellow at Harvard) and his wife, the Eberharts, and Archibald Macleish. The conversation was lively, and Thomas full of amusing anecdotes, and at midnight the guests departed, with Thomas, for Wilbur's apartment in Cambridge:

> Here it was altogether more relaxed, a small party with drinks, like a hundred other small parties with drinks. There was a radiogram for music. Dyl, I remember distinctly, dancing a kind of sailor's hornpipe step up & down the room till his shirttails flapped loose. Everybody in good spirits, if tired, and nobody disagreeably 'plastered'. No roughhouse. No disorder. . . . The Eberharts & I guided Dyl to his sleeping quarters in Harvard Yard. By this time he did need a little support, & no wonder. . . . Betty Eberhart pulled down the bedclothes, & Dyl was rolled into bed.[22]

According to Brinnin, the upshot of the late night was that Thomas was late for a recording appointment the next morning, and had to be driven at breakneck pace to Mt Holyoake for his next reading – a drive, Thomas later told Curnow, which 'terrified him'.[23] Later Curnow made the simple point that Thomas 'was in the hands of his hosts, who were all having the time of their lives'.[24] 'I've barnstormed as I've never barnstormed before', he remarked to Curnow at one point.[25] Much later Curnow generalised that what Brinnin ('and, one must add, Dylan') attempted on such a scale was 'almost insanely reckless':

> It had to end as it did. It was like a murder/suicide pact. Nobody understood that genius is not indestructible by public smothering; nor is understanding helped by a book like Brinnin's where the destructible poet becomes himself the destroyer.[26]

While he was still in Boston Curnow was interviewed by Cid Corman for WQXR radio station, and Corman later asked him if he would 'act as my contact to material in yr part of the Pacific' for a new magazine, *Origin*, which he was planning.[27] (At that time, early in 1951, Curnow was too preoccupied with starting a new academic career to undertake the job.) He also spent further time at the Woodberry Poetry Room at the Lamont Library at Harvard, where Sweeney asked him to autograph its copies of *Island and Time* and *Sailing or Drowning*, and he also donated a copy of *Jack without Magic*.

On 3 March, a day or so after Thomas's Harvard reading, Curnow returned to New York with Oscar Williams, unfortunately missing his Boston train and as a result missing a meeting that afternoon with Allen Tate at the Princeton Club in New York. (It was not until 1961 that he met Tate.) For much of the rest of March he was based in New York, though he spent a week with Dr Harry Segal and his wife Evelyn at Rochester (NY). Evelyn had numerous literary contacts, including in New York, and on one evening took Curnow with Thomas to meet E.E. Cummings, one of the highlights of his American trip. Through William Rose Benét and John Hall Wheelock (an editor for Scribner) and his wife, who had been an early London friend of Ngaio Marsh – 'everyone seemed to be at their parties'[28] – he met 'Edmund Wilson, Delmore Schwarz & other Partisan Review boys',[29] and while Brinnin was accompanying Thomas on the Washington reading circuit Curnow took his class, on Gerard Manley Hopkins, at the YMHA Poetry Center.

It was through Reyenna Metz, a friend of Brinnin and Moss, that Curnow also met a youthful Allen Ginsberg, hardly recognisable, in Curnow's description of him as a nineteen-year-old in 1950, from the unconventional Beat figure he was a little later to become:

> A trim little chap, dark suit, clean white collar & tie, crisp dark curly hair, talking about poetry (mostly) to anyone who would listen. . . . Young Allen was thoroughly 'house-broke' in the American sense, meaning his company manners could be counted on. . . . Another time Allen and a male friend (later famous for all I know) enticed me to Birdland on Times Sq., to hear an impressive group of piano, string bass & sax, more to their liking than mine.[30]

Curnow saw Thomas at Midston House after his return from his reading tour to Harvard and elsewhere, and again a week or so later, after Thomas's return to New York from Washington. On this occasion Thomas left a telephone message for Curnow to call him immediately, 'whatever hour of the night it is'.[31] Curnow and Jeanne Tufts (staying overnight on the segregated women's floor of Midston House, because she'd missed a train) arrived at Thomas's Hotel Duane about 1 a.m. He could not sleep and simply wanted to talk about his Washington trip, which he had enjoyed greatly. He also insisted on providing Curnow with addresses of people to see:

> He had done me more than one good turn in Washington, knowing I meant to go there. That is, he had spoken of me, and made welcomes which I could hardly have made for myself. I think of such kindnesses ('thoughtfulness' as we say) when he must have been at full stretch in the capital, & how ill they fit Brinnin's image of him.[32]

At this point Thomas embarked on a crowded six-week tour westwards, and Curnow did not see him again, except very briefly, when he was himself in San Francisco and Thomas was about to return to New York.

Curnow was due to travel to Washington on 2 April. A few days before (30 March), he travelled to Yale to meet Cleanth Brooks, an *academic* highlight (alongside his meeting with Matthiessen) of his American stay. He made substantial notes of their discussion, which touched at length on cultural differences between the North (New York / New England) and the South, on Brooks's detestation of commercialised New York culture, on Allen Tate's view of regionalism and provincialism, on William Faulkner and Lionel Trilling. Although Curnow never accepted the politics of the Deep South 'Fugitives' (an influential literary group based at Vanderbilt University, Nashville, to which Tate and Brooks were connected), he remained deeply interested in their cultural analysis of the commercial-industrial North, in their formalist poetics (though he was sceptical of its reductive, 'scientific' tendencies), and in the poetry of John Crowe Ransom, Tate and Robert Penn Warren.

Curnow's trip to Washington was relatively brief, and his main contacts there were Elizabeth Bishop, Poetry Consultant at the Library of Congress, and Robert Richman, director of the Institute of Contemporary Arts (ICA), though he also met Katherine Biddle (the poet Katherine Garrison Chapin), then a Literary Fellow at the Library of Congress. The Richmans insisted that he stay with them, and they became close friends, meeting again when Curnow, on his first sabbatical leave from Auckland University College in 1961, was formally appointed to a fellowship at the ICA. Elizabeth Bishop, whose poetry Curnow admired, organised recording sessions at the Library of Congress, over two days, during which Curnow read his own poetry for the Congress archives. At the end of the first day, over a Chinese meal and drinks at a bar, Bishop talked at length about Ezra Pound, whom she saw regularly at St Elizabeth's psychiatric hospital in Washington. He was, she said, 'usually v. nice to her',[33] though suffering from the delusion that she was about to arrange for his release to Italy.

Curnow's movements after his return to New York from Washington – during the three weeks prior to his departure from Vancouver on the final passage home on 27 April – are a little harder to trace. He visited Karl Shapiro, editor of *Poetry* (Chicago), whom he had met in New Zealand during the war and was now at Johns Hopkins University, Baltimore; and spent time in Chicago during the long trip westwards across the continent to San Francisco, leaving Chicago on 19 April, travelling for two days and nights in a train which 'rocks like buggery',[34] and staying for three days there, until 25 April, before travelling (again, by means of a long train trip) to Vancouver.

He caught up with Thomas in San Francisco on 24 April, the day of Thomas's departure for New York, and his last memory of him was at the airport:

> Found Dylan yesterday, unhappily only a few hours before his plane left for New York; but his hostess, a Mrs (Ruth) Witt-Diamant, an English professor (at State College) here, had us both to lunch & I saw him off at the airport. . . . [I was] sad to see the last of him, & the last (it seemed) of England flying away eastward.[35]

San Francisco was also Curnow's last stopping place, and Professor Ruth Witt-Diamant became another friend and colleague whom he was to meet on most of his later trips to the United States.

'The Hulk of the World'

In addition to the notes he made about people and places, and the drafts of poems he worked at, Curnow also drafted, in the wake of his visit to Chicago, a brief analysis of the American response to the new era of the atom bomb. He had found New York (and the country) 'moody, jittery about its vast, brittle, vulnerable skylines, highly atom-bomb conscious'.[36] During the first week after his arrival there, he had read, in neon lights on Broadway, of a secret Congressional Committee inquiring into 'the state of the nation's civil defences against atomic attack'.[37] It was a primary topic of conversation wherever he went, and he had been deeply affected by the McCarthyite context of Matthiessen's suicide. His prose analysis begins with a moment when his host in Chicago, 'a Chicago surgeon, amateur musician and painter', drove him to a spot near the University of Chicago in which a plaque commemorated 'The first Self-sustaining Chain Reaction' on 2 December 1942, initiating 'The Controlled Release of Nuclear Energy'.[38] Appalled by the unintentional irony of the word 'controlled', he compared this moment to others during his trip – being driven by Eberhart past the Massachusetts Institute of Technology, 'this famous seat of atomic science', in Cambridge, and Ruth Witt-Diamant, 'from a hill in San Francisco', pointing out 'the buildings of the atom research centre across the harbour on the Berkeley side'. As Curnow read the national mood, both fascination and fear of the atomic era was contributing to a 'shift in social & national perspectives':

> Like other [shifts] which have either begun or assumed mass proportions in the USA, it may point to a worldwide shift wh. other countries have yet to experience.... If the psychologists have taught us anything, it is that opposites combine in a single state of mind. America is today expressing that doubleness, ambivalence of mind. Destruction on a sufficiently huge scale fascinates them: it is the obverse of their passionate admiration (and achievement) of construction on the grand scale. And they have not the heart they once had for construction.[39]

In Chicago he also made contact with the famous magazine *Poetry*, founded by Harriet Monroe earlier in the century, in which a number of Curnow's poems had appeared during the war. The magazine was also soon to publish a new poem by him, which he had been working on since leaving London and finished in time to give to Karl Shapiro at Johns Hopkins, who had just taken over editorship of the magazine. 'When the Hulk of the World' was accepted and published remarkably quickly, appearing in the May issue, with a contributor's note saying that Curnow 'is en route from England to his home in New Zealand [and] passing through the United States'.[40]

The poem was one of the most intense love poems Curnow ever wrote, conveying feelings of grief and guilt as the ships carrying him across 'the hulk of the world' to New Zealand reinforced his sense of unbridgeable separation from Vie Lee. It is an antipodean imagination, conscious of seasonal polarities, time polarities, weather polarities, which creates so powerful an image of the destructive effect of distance on intimate personal experience – almost certainly why the poem had the immediate appeal of originality to *Poetry*. In no other poem up to this point (except for parts of the elegy for his father) had the brute fact of physical space, the 'hulk' of the world, its separation of a *here* from a *there*, been seen as quite so absolute a condition of the personal world in which the poet lives, or to place such sheer limits on human relationships.

The poem combines private memories with some astonishingly idiosyncratic perceptions, rising to an anguished eloquence of utterance at its conclusion. The loved one is described as a 'sweet claustrophobe', remembered on a walk through the leafless trees of St John's Wood, London, in a darkness so intense (and presumably claustrophobic, for his lover) that 'we missed the middle of the road'. The occasion for the poet's upwelling sense of loss appears to be a moment on board the ship, during the transatlantic crossing, when the broken reflection of moonlight in the rough waters creates the extraordinary optical illusion of a squid's eye, staring at him accusingly from the depths:

> When the hulk of the world whirls again between
> Us for the ships shift me where your dusk is dawn
> > My skyblue side of the globe,
> Where the mooncast squid's eye of the mobied ocean
> Goggles till it gets me in the beam of its brine....
> > Can spring condone, redeem
> This treachery of departure from our life
> My four fair English seasons and my love?

Curnow later revised the somewhat obscure literary reference in his neologism 'mobied' – presumably intended to suggest the Leviathan-like whale in Melville's *Moby Dick* – to the more prosaic 'downcast'. He also changed the final two lines in later years in order to make the reference less personal, perhaps acknowledging that the love evoked in the earlier version had cooled with the passing of time, perhaps thinking that 'My four fair seasons' struck a slightly false, 'literary' note, in describing the ten months he spent in London:

> > Can spring condone, redeem
> One treachery of departure from that life,
> Shiftless to fetch this love?

There is no denying the sheer eloquence of the poem's concluding sections, and the anguished momentum they sustain. 'Seas will be seas, the same' – that is, permanently separating the lovers – and even if the earth's antipodean poles, fruitlessly chasing each other on the spinning globe's axis, were to collapse, the lovers would still be denied the pleasures of seeing and holding each other:

> Thick as our blood may flood, our opposite isles
> Chase each other round till the quiet poles
> > Crack, and the six-days top
> Totter, but catch us neither sight nor hold;

The tottering of the 'six-days top' may refer to the biblical creation story, and hence to the end of the world; but it is also a more homely image: a circus-top, with its spinning roundabouts and merry-go-rounds.

If seas will be seas, the same, 'place' also, he continues, 'will be place', simply itself, stubbornly resistant to any transcendence; even dreams offer no compensation for the intimacy of the lovers' physical embrace, their 'natural death': 'limbs may not fold / Their natural death in dreams.' In the poem's concluding lines the poet urges his lover, as spring arrives in London, to forgive him, while offering the consolation – which he knows is hardly a consolation at all – that the only togetherness they now share, and will always share, is that of being ghosts to each other:

> I pray, pray for me on some spring-wet pavement
> Where halts the heartprint of our salt bereavement,
> > Pray over many times
> Forgive him the seas forgive him the spring leaf,
> All bloom ungathered perishable as grief,
> > For the hulk of the world's between
> And I go like a ghost already gripping on the wind
> That lifts us both so lightly but so bound
> > Never to be ghost alone.

Return to New Zealand, mid-May 1950

On 27 April 1950 Curnow left Vancouver for Auckland on the *Aorangi*, which he described to Betty as an 'old hell-ship' whose third-class quarters, in which he was travelling, were 'prison-ship style'. Nineteen days later he arrived in Auckland, where Betty met him, and before returning to Christchurch they made brief further enquiries about the possibility of a job at Auckland University College the following year, and also talked to Fairburn, who had temporary employment in the English Department there, and was a close Devonport friend of Musgrove. Within a few days they were back at Leinster Road. Although he was tired, with an inevitable sense of let-down after the excitements of the previous fifteen months, he needed urgently to start earning money again at *The Press*. Meeting him in late May a day or so after his return, Brasch was disappointed. Curnow seemed tired and the conversation was mainly small talk ('we made no contact'). A fortnight later, however, Brasch noticed some of Curnow's older animation returning:

> Curnow came into the Press at tea time, & we sat down to a long talk which quite changed my feeling about him. He must have been tired, & possibly out of sorts, when I last saw him; at any rate today he was quite warm & forthcoming & ... he talked well, with a largeness of intellectual grasp at times that makes him stimulating

& lifts him above the run of NZers, even the intelligent ones. He is back working for the Press & naturally hating it....[41]

Curnow was interviewed twice immediately after his return. In *The Press* he provided detailed information about the poets he had met, but the events Curnow singled out were his Third Programme poetry script, Thomas's interest in the Caxton anthology and Mason's verse, Eliot's *Cocktail Party* at the Edinburgh Festival, and, in the United States, the growth in the recording of poets reading their work, and in criticism as a professional industry. The publishing industry, he felt, was insufficiently interested in printing new poetry, and the drift was 'all towards new volumes of criticism and interpretation'. In an address to graduate students at the State College of San Francisco, he commented, 'I could only tell them what had struck me forcibly in America, that there were dangers as well as advantages to poetry in having many teachers, many critics, and not enough readers.'[42]

Curnow made the same points in an interview in the *New Zealand Listener*, where he was described as 'a tall, lean man of 39, with dark wavy hair that is always flopping over his forehead, poet fashion, and sharp brown eyes behind his spectacles'.[43] He also registered uneasiness with 'the enormous amount of clever and brilliant, highly verbalized . . . but intellectually derivative poetry' in the United States, and responded at some length to a question asking him to compare the literary scene in the United States and Britain:

> I could put it this way. There is still a healthy relation, in the literary sense, between London and the rest of Britain, but there is an unhealthy relation between New York and the rest of the United States. They repudiate New York in other parts of America. They say it isn't America. There's a nervous insistence on this point. Cleanth Brooks, for instance, described New York as a running sore spreading corruption into the back regions of America. There is also a kind of cold war between your ordinary, commercial, small-town America on the one hand and academic literary America on the other. The English poet and artist links up into the social order wherever he happens to be, but in the States these people, many of whom seem eventually to congregate in New York, are all huddling together for warmth.[44]

New Zealand poetry, he went on in answer to a question about how New Zealand poetry compared with British and American poetry, contained no poet of the highest order with 'the essential stamp of genius', but belonged to a 'second order' whose value was related to imaginative tensions significant to the time and place in which it was written. American writers, however, although they had put into the background 'the schizophrenic problem' of their separation from England and

Europe, still felt such imaginative tensions, and in that sense provided a closer comparison with New Zealand. For that reason also, Curnow commented, Americans understood 'the problems of an outlying or germinal culture far better than the English'. Curnow's journeying around the globe had brought him back, if not to the point at which he had begun, to the unfinished business of being a poet in New Zealand.

Chapter Seventeen

Moving to Auckland,
June 1950–November 1954

*[Auckland's] cloudy & portentous idea of itself as a city is apt to float
some thousands of feet up in the air, an intermittent Fata Morgana,
& one doesn't know whether it is seeking a place to land or whether
landing is the last thing it wants to do. The striking fact is that it has
such an idea; unlike Christchurch, where they started expressing one
in stone, & later forgot what it was . . . .[1]*

Last months in Christchurch, 1950

By the end of May 1950, Curnow was back at his old job on *The Press*. The
possibility of his replacing John Schroder as literary editor on his return had
arisen while he was in England, but Curnow believed that he needed more than
one day's relief from other duties in order to edit the Literary Page properly, and
the job went instead to R.H. Launder.

From the moment of his return to Christchurch, however, Curnow was determined to get a job elsewhere. Betty was in full agreement. Professor Musgrove had
unofficially offered him a lectureship at Auckland University College, at a salary
(£750 per annum) which he thought would be difficult for the family to live on.
He also rethought the option of returning to London, after hearing that there

was a vacancy with the New Zealand Press Association there, at a salary of £950 plus expenses – more than he had imagined might be possible when he discussed with Betty the previous year the option of remaining in London as a journalist. He wrote off immediately about the job, asking Geoffrey Cox and Noel Joseph at the *News Chronicle* to be referees, but was not successful. He remained interested in London, expanding on his reasons, to Schroder, six weeks later:

> If I am a reluctant repatriate, it comes mostly of certain pangs from things begun abroad & unpursued (inevitably, I tell myself). POETRY LONDON sends me a proof of an Elegy. . . . POETRY (U.S.A.) sends its May issue with another poem. . . . Elizabeth Bishop writes from Library of Congress to say that the full set (5 albums) of their poetry recordings is on the way . . . ostensibly for reviewing.[2]

In July, after a long delay, the Caxton Press published his verse play *The Axe*, and reviews slowly appeared over the next few months. Curnow also had a backlog of his own poetry reviews to write for *The Press*, some of them held over until he returned, including reviews of the criticism and poetry of John Heath-Stubbs and the poetry of Mervyn Peake, from England, and of New Zealand volumes by J.R. Hervey (*Man on a Raft*) and Alistair Campbell. Hervey's poetry, he felt, as the review's title suggested ('Raft Becalmed'),[3] had failed to develop. Campbell's *Mine Eyes Dazzle* received high praise, although he was less success-ful when he attempted to move beyond the pure lyric mode, in Curnow's view. However, there seems little doubt that if Curnow had had access to *Mine Eyes Dazzle* at the time of making his selections for the second edition of the Caxton anthology, he would have included several of Campbell's poems. He had made these selections at the end of 1948 and the beginning of 1949, and the anthology should have come out long before he returned from abroad. Because of delays he was actually proofreading the volume at the time he wrote the review of Campbell nearly two years later – far too late to make any changes – and it did not come out until the following April, 1951. Because of these accidents of publication it seemed, then, to Baxter, Campbell, and a number of other younger poets, that Campbell was amongst those who had been ignored.

Curnow was also hopeful of producing some new poems himself, in the months after his return, writing in July to Schroder that '[w]ithin a few weeks, if I read my own symptoms rightly, I should be . . . deep in some writing or other';[4] and in August he sent his poem 'The Changeling' to Fairburn to consider for volume 7 (the last issue to appear) of the *Yearbook of the Arts in New Zealand* (1951), commenting that he had been 'chipping away at one or two poems – like trying to cut figurines out of Cornish granite'.[5] Shortly afterwards he sent Fairburn another poem, 'Logbook Found on Ararat', which also appeared in the same issue of the *Yearbook*.

Like 'The Changeling', with which it was later linked as a companion piece (under the title 'Evidences of Recent Flood'), 'Logbook' revealed Curnow's growing interest in myth as a subject for poetry, and for poetry itself as a kind of mythopoeia, a renovation or re-interpretation of myth as a means of comment on nature and human nature. Noah's imaginary journal, full of vivid, appalled and horror-struck observations of the natural and human devastation wrought by storm and maelstrom – a manifestation of the 'rage' of 'the All-Duplicity on high' – records Noah's disillusioned realisation that the Flood has changed nothing, that the world, even as new life burgeons amongst the receding flood's detritus, remains incorrigibly fallen. There is no rainbow in Curnow's poem, no sign of God's new covenant with humanity, and the doves (far from emblem-atising peace) bicker and fight with their 'mortal talons', bloodied beaks and claw-tips, 'at each other's throats'. The poem's final image is not of Noah saved and the vision of a civilisation starting again with a new chance, but of the Ark 'shipwrecked', hooked 'by the gills on Ararat'. Noah sees himself and his family as 'grounded for our pains', facing a future as earth-bound, mortal and suffering, as in the prediluvian world.

Despite his hopeful comment to Schroder, 'Logbook Found on Ararat' was the last poem Curnow was to write for nearly three years. 'Time has hardly existed since I arrived back in May', he wrote to Heenan in October, 'what with starting again at THE PRESS, Whim-Wham, & getting a new edition of the N.Z. anthology through the Caxton Press.' 'Possible poems become deferred hopes', but, he added, perhaps to reassure Heenan, 'will find their way into being somehow.'[6] The reason for this letter was to seek his assistance as a referee for the lectureship in Auckland – the position had now been formally established – which Heenan readily provided, as did Schroder. The job was offered, and Curnow accepted.

It was an inspired decision by Musgrove. Curnow's appointment inaugurated a long-lasting shift in the identity of the English Department at Auckland, not only signalling the possible development of New Zealand literature as part of the English curriculum but valuing the contribution to be made by academics who were themselves creative writers. Michael Joseph had been on the staff for a number of years, though his career as a creative writer had hardly yet begun, and Fairburn was employed there on a casual basis. During the course of the decade, W.H. (Bill) Pearson and C.K. Stead were also appointed, and the practice of such appointments was continued in succeeding decades.

But before moving to Auckland, Curnow had a smallish number of commit-ments to fulfil. In his conversations with Schroder, who was now director of the New Zealand Broadcasting Service, he had been active in promoting the use of suitable BBC Third Programme material on New Zealand radio (including the idea of a weekly radio newsletter from his 'very good friend' at the BBC, René Cutforth), and had also asked about radio work for himself. One of these commissions was for a series of thirteen half-hour poetry readings ('Poems from Four Centuries'), which began on 2YA towards the end of 1950 and was later repeated on other stations throughout the country. It was an ambitious programme, but his choices and reading style often aroused debate in the columns of the *New Zealand Listener*, and stimulated a call for much more *New Zealand* poetry to be read by its authors on radio:

> [I]f Allen Curnow reads poetry so well, or at any rate in a way to stimulate interest and perhaps argument, why not have him reading his own verse? Why not let New Zealanders hear New Zealand poets reading their own verse as often as possible. . . . I should like to hear James Baxter . . . Mason, Fairburn, Brasch, Glover and others. . . .[7]

A piece Curnow wrote for the Canterbury centennial issue of the *Listener* on 8 December, 'Painting in Canterbury' – one of the very few forays he ever made into the fraught territory of discourse about New Zealand painting – was much more controversial. He wrote positively about Leo Bensemann, Rita Angus, Eve Page, Colin McCahon and the phenomenon of the annual Group exhibitions, but attacked the earliest landscape painters for adapting a 'failing romanticism' to colonial taste, and traced 'a history of aimlessness' in their imitators and adapters, in the conservatism of the Canterbury College School of Art, and in the triumph of respectable taste whose most telling sign – Curnow reserved this for his final paragraph – was the Christchurch City Council's rejection the year before of Frances Hodgkins's *The Pleasure Garden*:

> It is to be hoped that Christchurch will at least purge, somehow, the contempt earned by its public authorities in their rejection of a fine Frances Hodgkins – and as a gift! For that is, without doubt, Canterbury's most conspicuous self-disclosure in the matter of art: a wanton attempt at policing the public taste. It is remarkable that such strength existed, and should be exerted, to fight off the peril of a single picture.[8]

The article deeply offended the Canterbury arts establishment, who attacked Curnow's credentials as an art critic, his poetry, and his theatrical ambitions, in the correspondence columns during the next couple of months. 'Do you see the profession has closed its ranks against Curnow, in *The Listener*?' James Bertram wrote to Brasch, adding, 'When did you last exhibit a painting, Charles Brasch?'[9]

By that time Curnow was about to depart for Auckland. He was in his fortieth year. Perhaps the deliberate provocation of his final paragraph was intended as a parting gesture to the city in which he had lived, worked and written for so long.

Earlier in 1950, Lilburn had given up the room in Cambridge Terrace which he had kept for use during vacations from his job at Victoria University College. By the end of 1951, Glover had ended his association with the Caxton Press. Curnow's 'Christchurch', in which these two long-standing friends and fellow artists, more than any others, had given purpose and meaning to his life as a poet, and who were intimately linked in his mind with whatever of value he had achieved there, ceased to exist.

A stressful first year at Auckland, 1951

The outward confidence Curnow often seemed to exhibit when he took on major new activities or directions in his life invariably masked deep-seated anxieties and uncertainties about his capacity to do them well enough, and these fuelled a huge, single-minded ambition to succeed, to prove himself. There had been two such crucial formative crossroads in Curnow's earlier life: his youthful decision to train for the ministry in the Church of England, and his decision four years later to abandon the career of a clergyman and enter the world of journalism. Fifteen years later, he now faced a third crossroads, having decided to abandon the world of journalism and enter the world of academia.

For Curnow, proving himself in the academic world – at an institution which still carried the aura of the place where two decades earlier he had made his own excited discovery of modern literature, of the life of the intellect, and of a lifelong commitment to being a poet – was an even greater challenge, and the stakes carried by failure even higher. He was also conscious that he lacked the formal qualifications for a university lectureship, which at that time were beginning to become the norm for academic appointments. The department he joined had only four permanent staff, apart from Musgrove. Elizabeth Sheppard, John Reid and Jim Walton (who arrived from Ireland later in 1951) all had doctorates and Joseph had a postgraduate BLitt from Oxford in addition to his New Zealand MA. Curnow had a Bachelor's degree, but not a Master's degree let alone a doctorate, and had not studied overseas for a higher qualification. Although he had written influential criticism and had outstanding editorial talent he did not have conventional research publications, nor was he a scholar in the conventional sense. Moreover, all of his strengths as a creative writer and critic were in the field of New Zealand literature, which university curricula ignored as being unworthy of academic study.

Curnow stayed with Robert (Bob) and Irene Lowry when he first arrived in February 1951. He began house-hunting and preparing lectures for the beginning of term in March, while Betty finalised the packing of their belongings in

Christchurch. His mother Jessie had lent Curnow £500 as a deposit on a house in Auckland, which entitled him to a loan of £2,000 from the government's State Advances scheme. But he quickly found that the valuations on which the loan was based were significantly lower than the asking price for houses in Auckland. His letters to Betty at the time became increasingly panicky, as housing prospects fell through (in one five-day period two deals involving houses in New Lynn collapsed). Just as Betty arrived with Wystan aged twelve, Belinda aged nine and Tim aged seven, at the beginning of March, yet another house deal 'melted away'. With the assistance of Fairburn the family eventually moved into temporary rented accommodation at 38 Leslie Avenue, Sandringham. Writing to Brasch a few months later, Betty was not impressed either by the Sandringham property or by Auckland:

> I hate this city the whole atmosphere is restless, careless, shoddy & dirty. Everything is rough & goes too quickly. Weather is quite bats. Some day when we can move nearer the sea perhaps I will like living here better but as the children (who are taken for English children here because they haven't the Auck accent yet) say, 'I am homesick'.[10]

Curnow's first two years in Auckland were a nightmare of stress and anxiety which affected his health, causing temporary alopecia. They were also years of real financial hardship. His salary was less than he had earned as a senior journalist on *The Press*, the cost of living in Auckland was higher, and he struggled to meet monthly bills. He did, however, achieve something of a coup in renegotiating the terms on which he was prepared to continue to write verses as Whim Wham, since he initially saw his shift to Auckland as an opportunity to be rid of this weekly chore. Approached by *The Press*, he asked for £10 for each piece – more than treble the 3 guineas he had been receiving since his return from overseas in 1950, when his fees had been doubled – and fully expected to be refused. *The Press*, however, came to an arrangement with the Auckland-based *New Zealand Herald* to publish them in both newspapers, and each would pay £5. Curnow could hardly refuse. His income from Whim Wham was more than half his salary as a lecturer, at a time when he was struggling to purchase a house and support his growing family. It is hardly surprising that Curnow wrote nothing on his own account – either poetry or criticism – during the next two years (except for a review at the end of 1951), since he was wholly focused (as he had been when he first became a journalist) on learning the professional ropes of his career as an academic.

On 3 October 1951 Curnow organised one university-related activity which drew directly on his work as a creative writer and critic – a highly successful poetry reading in the Great Hall of Auckland University College, involving readings by

Fairburn, Mason, Joseph, Sinclair, Smithyman (whose verse was read by Robert Chapman), Musgrove and himself, which attracted an audience of more than 400. The success of this event had a substantial influence on Auckland's poetry scene. For more than a decade such readings, at the university or other venues such as the Art Gallery, became a regular feature of the city's cultural calendar.

Earlier in the year, Curnow had attended a New Zealand Writers' Conference, held at Canterbury University College over four days, 8–11 May 1951, sponsored by the New Zealand Literary Fund and the Canterbury Centennial Association. He was involved in two events: chairing a session on 10 May at which Baxter delivered a lively paper, 'Recent Trends in New Zealand Poetry', and reading his own poems, alongside Glover, Baxter and Basil Dowling, at the final session.

A considerable mythology has developed around this conference: that it marked the crucial beginnings of a bitter generational feud, the drawing up of battle lines, lasting throughout the 1950s, between older poets led by Curnow and younger poets led by Baxter. If this was so, both the beginnings of the feud and the setting up of battle lines were entirely lost on Curnow. He was a reluctant participant, frantically busy coping with the demands of his new career, but saw the few days in Christchurch as enabling him to tidy up matters left unattended in the shift to Auckland, to catch up with Glover (who looked forward to seeing him *outside* 'the Confluence of Cacklers' in Christchurch),[11] and in particular to see his mother, now on her own at Meadow Street in Papanui. Although he did not attend the conference a great deal, he found Baxter's address extremely stimulating, and was quoted in *The Press*, two days later, as declaring it 'one of the most enthralling and richly packed hours on New Zealand verse'[12] – hardly the words of one who saw it as a manifesto or declaration of war, let alone one in which he was himself the prime target.

His absence from much of the conference may have contributed to a perception that he was standoffish, and Curnow later recalled a meal with Frank Sargeson at the time in which Sargeson warned of negative murmurings about him from some younger poets, especially in the wake of their exclusion from the delayed second edition of the Caxton anthology, which had appeared just the month before the conference. Neither Campbell (for reasons explained above) nor Louis Johnson, nor a number of other poets like W.H. Oliver and Pat Wilson whose work had appeared since Curnow made his selections in 1948 and early 1949, before his departure for England, had been represented in it. Sargeson did not mention any names, however, and Curnow did not take much notice:

> Sargeson's news made very little impression on me. I knew enough of the *genus irri-tabile vatum* – the short fuses of poets – to be unsurprised. . . . I was a little mystified by Sargeson's having taken it so seriously. . . . Besides, it simply hadn't occurred to me

that a place in my book was a thing to cut throats for, their own or mine, let alone shake the nation for the next twenty years.[13]

Perhaps he was also aware of the mischievous delight in conspiracy theories taken by Sargeson, who might also have retailed such stories simply as an oblique way of discomforting Curnow himself, whom he had never personally liked, though he acknowledged the force of his poetry. Presumably Curnow's shift to the academic life was the most immediate example in Sargeson's mind of Curnow's willingness to compromise with society and an obvious sign of his detested intellectualism, though he would have held the same view of Curnow's career in journalism. Curnow reciprocated Sargeson's dislike, though after he shifted to Auckland they often found themselves at the same parties, and on occasion visited each other's homes.

Curnow's close friendship with Fairburn may also have fuelled Sargeson's antipathy. At the time Curnow arrived in Auckland, Sargeson and Fairburn were not on speaking terms, partly because of Fairburn's outspoken attacks on state patronage (of which Sargeson was a recipient, in the form of an annual pension), and his homophobia. Curnow did not share Fairburn's homophobia, but (despite his own Literary Fund travel grant in 1949) understood Fairburn's hostility to state patronage.

Restatement of poetic credo, 1952–53

In a letter to Dan Davin, Curnow had mentioned his desire to 'get a house by the water & play boats with Fairburn',[14] and throughout their time at Sandringham, Fairburn had been assisting the Curnows to find such a place. The small house they found, and shifted into in mid-November 1951, was at 13 Herbert Street, Takapuna. Its large south-west-facing sitting-room windows overlooked the harbour, with mangroves and the shell spit of Shoal Bay in the foreground, and what Brasch called (after his first visit to it at the end of 1952) 'that lovely nest of pines on your promontory'.[15] At that time (well before the Harbour Bridge had been built) the house was isolated, and the Curnows still could not afford a car. Curnow travelled to work across the harbour by bus and ferry. Fairburn also assisted Curnow to purchase a small, clinker-built boat from Brian Donovan, a boatbuilder who lived next door, which was suitable for fishing and pottering around the harbour, and which he kept moored below the house.

One of the great pleasures, if not consequences, of Curnow's shift to Auckland was the reopening on a quite regular basis of correspondence with Lilburn and with

Glover.* Renewed correspondence with Lilburn, in particular, in 1952, provided a stimulus for Curnow's creative thinking at a time when the demands of his academic career still occupied almost all of his attention. He said little to anyone about this work, except on one occasion (to Lilburn) when he expressed evident pleasure at giving a whole Stage I lecture on a single sonnet, Gerard Manley Hopkins's 'The Windhover'.[16] In March 1952, Lilburn wrote on David Farquhar's behalf seeking permission for 'Wild Iron', which Curnow had written in 1941, to be set to music. It prompted Curnow's typically mystified reaction to the poem's popularity: '"Wild Iron" as a poem has always looked strange to me: I seem to have been absent from the place where it was written, or at least not especially aware of what was going on.'[17] In return he asked Lilburn if he would compose some music to accompany the poetry reading he was organising again for August of that year, and invited Lilburn to come and stay.

Lilburn was interested in the request for incidental music, and wanted more detail about what was planned. Because of the costs involved, most of the poets had to be from Auckland, but the key new participant for 1952, whom Curnow was anxious to introduce to an Auckland audience, was Baxter. The extraordinarily detailed response he sent to Lilburn about his plans for the reading revealed how professional his approach to the event was: including the order of poets (Fairburn, Sinclair, Curnow, Joseph, Baxter, Smithyman and Mason), the nature of the space, the timing of readings and intervals between them, and diagrams which amounted to a kind of choreography of the event.[18] The incidental music for violin and piano which Lilburn wrote (later entitled 'Seven Salutes to Seven Poets') was very warmly received, though he was unhappy that on the night itself a decision was made to play each piece after the poet had read rather than before.[19]

Like Curnow, Lilburn also found himself at this time resisting the terms 'national myth' and 'South Island myth' which younger poets and critics (in Wellington and Auckland) were bandying about as a way of qualifying or belittling the achievement of earlier poets, no doubt feeling that his own music came within the ambit of such attacks. In a review of the first issue of a new annual *New Zealand Poetry Yearbook*, edited by Louis Johnson, Curnow had already challenged the use of the term 'national myth' in a commentary by Erik Schwimmer and queried what he called 'the baited trap of a spurious "internationalization of culture"'.[20] The review welcomed the new journal and praised Johnson's work as editor, but saw little

---

* Unfortunately, none of the regular correspondence between Curnow and Glover during Curnow's 1949–50 trip abroad has survived (though while he was away Curnow occasionally suggested to Brasch and others that they read his letters to Glover for a full account of his literary activities). However, for the next 30 years, in the case of Glover, and the next 50 years, in the case of Lilburn, much in the rich correspondence record has survived.

that was new or exciting amongst either the older or younger poets (including his own contribution in that generalisation), noting that Baxter, Smithyman and Sinclair all seemed 'in need of a change'.[21] But he exempted Ruth Dallas, Hubert Witheford and Mary Stanley from the general thrust of his comments.

The discussion prompted Curnow, in a letter to Lilburn, into a much more passionate restatement of his poetic credo, which is worth quoting at length because it seems to mark, after a longish time, the resurgence of his old combative intensity:

> To call it a 'myth' (none of *us* did) is cheating on their part; they thus acknowledge the force of it, & at the same time hint 'myth' in the pejorative sense. 'Myth', I suppose fairly enough, in the sense of some dramatic *idea* by which a community sustains itself: & I imagine that nothing ever written by Fairburn or Glover or Holcroft or Brasch or me (or you as far as you acknowledge us in music) went unrecognizably beyond such ideas as had already exhibited some embryonic shape in the country's mind.

> If we are to talk of 'myth', let's be clear that we don't mean some private fabrication, foisted upon the country by a group of (but why South Island? – Mason, Fairburn, E. Duggan? – I suppose they think I *wrote* everything in that anthology!) poets. Let them look *back* a bit, & *round* them a bit, let them even learn to read & *then* read my Introduction, & they'll see that whatever they call 'S. Island myth' was part of our common consciousness, & even struggling to be articulate 50 years before. In the *crudest* of interpretations, there was no more to do than to set in order certain facts of history & geography: facts to which a younger lot seems blinder than it need: no tuppeny [sic] buses run from Lambton Quay to Notting Hill, or Greenwich Village or the Left Bank. That kind of 'internationalism' shld be spelt Provincialism with a cap. P.

> It seems they believe we want all poems to be about islands & unknown lands & encircling seas, etc; there was never any such manifesto, & they are not being straight with themselves if they imagine themselves heroes of any such teacup revolution. I believe it amounts to this: that a timid or tired or half-baked talent wants to live in some dream or reverie of aesthetic consummation, & this it creates out of the fragments of its current reading – not reflecting, maybe, that men & poems are not to be equated with the colour schemes you can make on a bookshelf with a few favourite translations, poets, Penguins & Partisan Reviews.

> It's a dream which has tempted us all: in earlier years, maybe we were naive to hope so much from history & geography; yet we felt some pulse of reality there. If I reject – critically, too, not personally – Wilson, Oliver, & Johnson (except that the last now & then speaks truth in innocence) – it's by no means because they don't treat the

subjects (or *objects*) we used to favour; but because they seem to me to have *no* subject except themselves-as-poets, & if they can do no better, let them consider if there wasn't a direction shown them, which they might profit by.

You & I (if I may preach on) may receive this lesson: that we must grapple to our own subject, or what we can perceive of it; & that we long ago passed beyond the stage at which these quarrels can profitably trouble our minds. I feel, myself, that I do not want to criticize much of what is being done, let alone set up as a pundit. I want Baxter to write better, & bigger, with less self-involvement: somebody (it might be me, even) to write another verse play. It is so *wrong* (I had this out with Johnson) to imagine an 'older generation' *resisting* the advance of a newer – if only somebody *would* advance! What a blessed consolation that wld be for our own fallings short & failures! – I know, I know what they mean: the Anthology is in the schools & colleges: an ignorant approbation has put its rubber stamp all over me & others. That must be galling, I suppose, to the young men – but dear Heaven! if *that* is all they want!!

It was not until the following year that he pursued in print the issues around the term 'myth' to which he reacted so strongly in this letter, written more than a year after his shift to Auckland, which concluded with an acerbic comment on the place – a clear sign of the difficulties he was having in settling in:

I can tell you nothing about Auckland. It is, I think, the most parochial, provincial town in N.Z. That it's the largest doesn't alter that: for it inclines to participate in nothing but itself, & the little that the other 2/3rds of N.Z. has gained by some sense of sharing place & time, is hardly grasped here: it is a third island, & sometimes I think might as well be in mid-Pacific.[22]

In the summer vacation of 1952–53, after a visit from Brasch, Curnow began his first piece of serious critical writing in Auckland, a review of Holcroft's *Dance of the Seasons*. 'It's time someone of our generation redressed the balance and gave Monte his due', Brasch wrote. '[T]o the young now he seems to be almost non-existent.'[23] Curnow sweated over the piece, more an article than a review, over the next five months, apologising to Brasch in March 1953 that he needed to give attention to Holcroft's other books, and wondering if he was the right person to do the job: '[Y]ou will see when you get the copy. It's apt to turn into a critique of M.H. and may run to length.'[24] He eventually sent the review to Brasch at the end of May, still unsure about it, although 'some parts I feel are well said', and explaining:

There's a point I am trying to fix, where his practical thinking, i.e. about N.Z., stops & the less distinctive & altogether less original thinking begins; & the trickiness is, that MH doesn't help us, rather the contrary, to draw the line which seems to me so important. . . .[25]

Brasch praised the review tactfully, and it appeared in the September 1953 issue of *Landfall*: 'I welcome your Holcroft; with all its length. . . . [I]t was worth doing, and much of it needed saying.'[26] Much of the review worked closely on passages of Holcroft's prose in *Dance of the Seasons*, and on the distractions of his adoption of a fictive persona in the book. He attempted to differentiate Holcroft's specific critiques of New Zealand ('the valuable part of his work',[27] especially in his earlier essays of the 1940s) from the 'quasi-philosophical language' in which he tries to express a Platonist 'nature creed', 'some all-resolving assertion of a mystically apprehended Whole, God-nature-man'. In his concluding paragraphs he turned to the pejorative use of the term 'South Island myth', as a 'local and vulgar error'[28] by a younger generation, held to be in large part Holcroft's and his own invention. Perhaps it was *because* he was so aware that the term 'myth' was capable of much more complex meanings (indeed many of his own poems had begun to explore them) that he reacted so strongly to the implications of falsity and 'bad faith' directed at his own 'myth-making' generation:

> '[M]yth' is a curious term to use for what is simply a way of looking at history, to be judged as such, and upon the effectiveness of its expression. . . . The word means either too little or too much, and is inapt on whichever side you load it. The proposition itself, that some special modification of the-world-as-seen-and-known takes place when slips of an old culture are planted in a new land, and that poets many be *conscious* agents in this process, is one (I feel sure) that Mr Holcroft and others took to be self-evident. Or, pursuing it practically, that the Nature around us, present and actual, sooner or later calls the bluff of a copyist art which has taken leave of its five and country senses.[29]

At the same time as he was writing the Holcroft piece Curnow also reviewed the second *Poetry Yearbook* (for 1952) in the May issue of *Here & Now*, in the form of a letter to its editor, Louis Johnson. The device was intended to introduce a lightness of tone into what were a series of deeply critical observations about the country's socially conformist culture in the 1950s and of a parallel tendency amongst many of the poets in the *Yearbook* to produce what he felt to be a standardised commodity – superficially exhibiting 'the external criteria of good verse' but basically motivated by a desire to conform to an idea of 'the poet' suitable for consumption by an enthusiastic but undiscriminating readership. 'A poem', he wrote, – by which he meant a *good* poem – is 'what a poet makes when he is passionately interested in something else', not simply in conforming to a preconceived idea of what it is to be a poet. He went on to suggest that there were *structural* similarities between the 1950s and the 'flimsy [but ruling] coalition' of '"poet"–editor–reader'[30] in the 1930s which younger poets rebelled against.

The argument was bold, challenging, and tendentious – typically, an effort to construct a local historical and social context for the practice of poetry in the 1950s – but Curnow misjudged the tone of the device (the letter) in which he framed his comments, so that when he tried to illustrate it by reference to particular poems and poets, he often appeared unintentionally patronising and preachy, and it was this that irritated the readers (and poets) who disagreed with him. The message he preached was, essentially, 'Don't waste or squander your talents by writing to conform to some *idea* of what it is to be a poet, derived from the latest fashion in New York or London, or from a local public interested in poetry as some kind of social accomplishment or piece of cultural décor. Attend passionately to the transaction between yourself and your *subject*. A good poem *might*, or *might not*, result from such attention, but without it a good poem is impossible.'

It was the kind of advice that Curnow applied to himself at every stage of his poetic career, far more severely than to any of the poets he mentioned in his review, though the review's readers might hardly be expected to know that. It was later seen as a full-scale 'attack' on Baxter and others, though he praised a number of poems and poets and began with the comment: 'Your second Poetry Yearbook is better than the first one. It has more good or at least interesting verse in it.'[31] His criticisms of two of Baxter's poems – which were often seen as personal, though that was not the case, and Baxter did not take them that way – were detailed, considered, and framed within a judgement that 'he is far and away the most gifted of our younger generation of poets; even at his worst, you might say it was a poet writing badly, not a bad poet'.[32] They were written at the same time as he was citing 'a fine poem ["The Fallen House"] in James Baxter's newest book, in which "the meaning of solitude" moves towards realization' in his review of Holcroft's *Dance of the Seasons*.* [33]

Tentative new beginnings in poetry and drama, 1953–54

Perhaps the strength of feeling that underpinned Curnow's argument in the *Yearbook* review was reinforced by the continuing difficulty he himself had in writing poems which satisfied him – and his awareness that he could readily churn out publishable stuff if he wished to. He published one poem in 1953, which appeared in the *New Zealand Listener* in April of that year, the first since

---

* *The Fallen House* was Baxter's third volume, published in 1953.

'Logbook on Ararat' written nearly three years earlier. 'Jack-in-the-Boat', based on the box of a toy purchased for Tim, was a delightful *jeu d'esprit* tinged with sadness. The damaged clockwork toy suggests a metaphor for human life, but it is the ambivalence of metaphor itself, as a means of access to truth, which at the end of each stanza hints at the poem's real subject:

> Children, children, come and look
> Through the crack in the corner of the middle of the world
> At the clockwork man in a cardboard house.
> He's crying, children, crying.
> *He's not true, really.*
>
> Once he was new, like you, you see
> Through the crack in the corner of the middle of the night,
> The bright blue man on the wind-up sea,
> Oh, he went so beautifully.
> *He's not true, really.*[34]

The decelerating rhythm of each stanza, which enacts the gradual slowing down of the clockwork mechanism, made it a favourite for children's anthologies, as well as for musical settings.*[35] (One literal-minded reader, 'Satisfied Customer', thanked Curnow for bringing the toy to his notice: he had purchased a Jack-in-the-Boat for his four-year-old son, who was 'well pleased' with it.)[36]

Despite Curnow's efforts, however, other poems remained unfinished, as he wrote to Brasch, who regularly let him know that new poems by him would be welcome for *Landfall*:

> I have a number of poems or drafts of poems skewered on nails in my basement here [at university], which I use for work. I don't feel very sure about any of them; it is almost like beginning again, & I don't want false starts, even the kind that are interesting in themselves.[37]

At this time plans were well advanced for a new production of *The Axe*, to be produced by Musgrove and the Auckland University College Dramatic Club in the Elam School of Fine Arts Little Theatre from 27 August to 2 September 1953,

---

* Nigel Williams, of St Paul's Collegiate School in Hamilton, composed music for a choral performance of the poem, with piano, flute and snare drum, on 26 August 1993, at the Keyboard Festival, Newcastle University Conservatorium of Music, 23–28 August 1993. In 1994, Graham Parsons, of the Music Department of Palmerston North College of Education, set the poem for a four-part choir unaccompanied and for a vocal solo with piano accompaniment.

and Curnow was anxiously tinkering with the text yet again, rewriting the opening of the second act and adding a new chorus. There was some excellent advance publicity, in the form of interviews with Curnow and Musgrove in *Craccum*,[38] and an article by John Pocock in the *Auckland Star*,[39] and the newspaper reviews were welcoming. However, for a number of reviewers in the local magazines (including Bob Lowry in *Here & Now* and 'P.M.' in *Parson's Packet*),[40] the play failed dramatically, despite its promise, because it did not define its central questions clearly enough or provide clear-cut answers. The issue was a difficult one for Curnow, since he had never conceived the play as providing 'answers' to the issues it raised, but as deliberately avoiding a black-and-white statement, challenging audiences to question their own attitudes and come to their own judgements. In the meantime, he set his mind to the new play which he had been determined to write for a number of years.

In January 1954, however, before he settled in to this work, he wrote his first substantial poem for more than three years, 'In Memory of Dylan Thomas', an elegy on the poet who had died in New York in November the previous year. Soon after Thomas's death, Brasch had asked Curnow for a note about Thomas for *Landfall*,[41] and Curnow had immediately agreed, adding that 'some unsatisfactory expression like "burning himself out" explains his death. "Virtue went out of him" continually, & he had little or no knowledge or control of that expenditure.'[42] Curnow worked hard over Christmas and the New Year on this reminiscence, but wrote to Brasch that he found the 'dilemma between the critical & the personal "note"'[43] difficult to resolve. The elegy seems to have been (at least partly) sparked by this dilemma. In the same letter he wrote:

> Some days ago I began to be busy on a poem, of some length, about Thomas, his land-scape, et al. And couldn't combine this with any prose about him. The poem, which isn't (of course) personal reminiscence, unless by inference, should run to 60–70 lines when complete. I wonder – would you care to have the poem, supposing you like it? I can't really offer you a poem 'blind'; but this looks a success to me, so far. I've been so dry, of verse, in late years, that I'm inclined to drop everything else in favour of this.[44]

'Of course you are right to drop everything for a poem when one comes', Brasch wrote, and was 'most delighted' when he saw it. 'What a happy visitation!' he added – praise indeed from Brasch, who rarely reached for superlatives.[45] When some years later he came to publish a selection of *Landfall* contributions, *Landfall Country* (1962), it was the Thomas elegy he chose to represent Curnow.

The finished poem was considerably longer than the '60–70 lines' Curnow had first mentioned, when it appeared in the March 1954 issue of *Landfall*, together with three of the photographs taken by Curnow at Laugharne: one of

Thomas, and the others of the house and of the boatshed which Thomas used as a work space. In five sections, each prefaced by a quotation from the poet's favourite book of Genesis, within which different aspects of Thomas's life and art are framed, and each with its own different rhythmical and rhyming scheme, the poem richly evokes Thomas's delight in the life of the senses, his vivid and specific sense of Welsh place (especially the landscape, tidescape and natural life at Laugharne), his unsentimental identification with and celebration of human life and energy in a fallen world, time- and death- and violence-ridden – above all his remarkable transmutation of this world into art.

The elegy never directly refers to Thomas's poems by way of quotation or allusion, but constantly *suggests* many of them: the childhood pleasures recollected in 'Fern Hill'; the moving poem about the death of a child in wartime, 'Ceremony After a Fire Raid'; the defiant energy of 'Do Not Go Gentle into that Good Night'; the remarkable elegy for the birds slain by a hawk in 'Sir John's Hill' near Laugharne. The poem's moving conclusion evokes the death-dealing hawk of this last poem by way of contrast with a biblical image of Thomas's death amongst New York's millions, the poet imagined as choosing the role of one of the homeliest of Christ's fallen sparrows:

> 'Ware the hawk, 'ware the hill,
> Claw clenched for the trilling throat,
> The shadow, the shudder, the kill,
> Feathers afloat –
>
> But in the map of mercy among a city's
> Dying millions he fell,
> Who chose of heaven's thousand thousand pities
> The sparrow's one, and all.

Glover, like Brasch, was immediately impressed by the elegy, comparing it in his own inimitable way with the earlier elegies, 'Crash at Leithfield' and the wartime sonnet to T.C.F. Ronalds:

> Your lucubrations have been, sometimes, so involved that I have had to defend you against all comers.... The really hard thing to do was on TCF or was he TFC? Curious that I should be so moved by your tributes to the dead. (You old bastard, I intend to outlive you!)[46]

On 26 March, Curnow read the poem in a programme by the Poetry Reading Society in the Central Library Hall, Wellington, alongside contributions by

Baxter, Johnson, Anton Vogt and Brasch, and the following day read 'Landfall in Unknown Seas' in the Wellington Town Hall concert given by the Alex Lindsay String Orchestra as part of a cultural exchange of music programmes between the cities of Wellington and Birmingham, Alabama.[47] It was one of two readings of 'Landfall' which Curnow gave in 1954, the second one in Auckland on 21 August (the first Auckland performance) with the Auckland String Players conducted by Maurice Clare and Barrie Trussell.

When he got back to Auckland from the Wellington performance, he had written apologetically to Lilburn about a public comment he had made about their 'Landfall' collaboration – perhaps during the concert itself – fearing that he might have caused offence:

> Something did come out, under strain, which I ought to hope you will forgive – about your putting some burden of explanation on me. The burden is really myself, trying to pass some counterfeit wisdom or precept, when that is not called for at all; & this happening when affection is so deep & is tormented by having nothing better to offer, even if the precept happened to be sensible.[48]

He went on to speak with some enthusiasm of possible plans for the rest of the year, in the wake of a discussion with Eric Westbrook, director of the Auckland City Art Gallery. These possibilities included a reading (with William Walton's music) of Edith Sitwell's 'Façade', organising a Dylan Thomas programme and a programme of Lilburn's settings of New Zealand poems, and 'if there is enough of the new play by this winter, the Wertheim room [in the Art Gallery] is open to me for a reading or part-production if it can be arranged'.[49] His letter was also laced with comments about Auckland, only slightly less acerbic about 'this sprawling, incoherent place' than during the first years after his arrival there, but aware of its 'crude energy':

> [Auckland's] cloudy & portentous idea of itself as a city is apt to float some thousands of feet up in the air, an intermittent Fata Morgana, & one doesn't know whether it is seeking a place to land or whether landing is the last thing it wants to do. The striking fact is that it *has* such an idea; unlike Christchurch, where they started expressing one in stone, & later forgot what it was . . . .

> [I]t's so important for the northern *third* of the country to be conscious of the rest – so much idle bragging about its own size & importance, & 'cultural centre' (which is worse), & so little effort to make this real by calling upon the best the country has.[50]

Curnow worked hard at the new play over the next few months, but said little about its subject or theme to others at this time, and it was not advanced enough for the reading from it that he had hinted to Lilburn might occur at the Art Gallery during winter. In August, Glover was in Auckland for a poetry reading, at which Baxter had disgraced himself. 'Jim, I feel is in a fair way to debasing his poet-ego to the role of bawd, pimp or pandar to his thoroughly vulgar little libido', Curnow wrote to Glover afterwards, before reporting on the efforts he was putting into his 'projected play', and on his current reading of 'Hitchings's psychiatry textbooks' in order 'to fix the limits of the plausible & the possible in an important female character'.[51] However, by December he was less confident, referring only to 'fragments of [my] half-attempted play'.[52] It was not until 1957 that a first draft of the play, called at that time 'Bright Sky', was completed.

By 1954, in his fourth year in the Department of English, Curnow was more comfortable and confident in his role as a lecturer, and the arrival of Bill Pearson (whom he had previously met in Christchurch in the company of Baxter, and entertained at Leinster Road, during the year before his trip overseas) began a long-standing friendship. At the end of 1955 he was promoted to senior lecturer.[53]

Unlike Joseph and Reid, whose lectures were models of lucidity and orderliness, mixing scholarly and critical and biographical information, delivered with appropriate pauses for student note-taking, and repetitions of key points, Curnow did not deliver his lectures from a formally written script. Nevertheless, Curnow's preparation was equally rigorous and time-consuming, and consisted of reading and re-reading the poems he was to lecture on, annotating their margins copiously, rehearsing the reading of them aloud, and selecting from amongst current criticism and scholarship a few salient points to be argued with or agreed with during the course of the lecture.

The lectures themselves were text-focused and exploratory – giving the appearance of an impromptu monologue in the form of a conversation with himself – and more often than not he would arrive to give his lecture carrying only the text on which he was to lecture, inside which was a card with brief notes of key points to be covered. There was a considerable degree of risk in such a lecturing style, a waiting upon insights to emerge from the exploratory process, and they required an appropriate kind of involved attentiveness on the part of students.

Curnow may have felt somewhat dispirited about the fragments of his half-attempted play when he wrote to Glover in December 1954, but he also enclosed a recently completed poem, entitled 'Spectacular Blossom'. His comments on it were somewhat offhand ('You might tell me what you think of the lyric I enclose, regarding it strictly as a piece which needs working over some more'). The letter had a postscript, added two days later:

The poem is much worked over *since*, & now looks about finished to me. Something *obstinate* about its external shape that bothers me, but eventually I let it have its way

& concentrated on inside things. A *poem*, anyway, God be thanked. I want to know how it strikes you.[54]

Although he said nothing to Glover at this point, the poem had been the immediate result of an event which transformed the rest of his life. On 20 November he attended a party in Bayswater where he met Jenifer Tole. The rapport was instantaneous. For the rest of his life, Jeny was at its centre.

Chapter Eighteen

A New Life and New Poems, 1955–57

I was willing to risk going off together but not at the price of Allen losing his children or they him. As he put it, 'There are four corners to my world.' We knew then and always after, that some time we would be together all the time.

Jeny Curnow[1]

Meeting Jenifer Tole

Jenifer Mary Tole was 23 years old, and Curnow 43, when they first met. Born in Auckland in 1931, she was the only child of George Edmund Tole and Janet Mary Tole (née Clarkson). Her parents separated when she was two and her mother later married again (to David Osborne) and moved to the United States, where she lived for many years in upstate New York. Jeny was brought up by her father and aunts, first at 536 Remuera Road and later at 60 Ascot Avenue, Remuera, and she was educated close by at Baradene Convent of the Sacred Heart. George Tole was a distinguished architect, whose designs included St Michael's Catholic Church in Remuera and other church buildings, numerous provincial cinemas, and the Mission Bay fountain. Two of his brothers, John and Charles Tole, were accomplished painters, becoming members of the Thornhill group of artists which included John Weeks and Louise Henderson, and Charles in particular became well known as a painter of semi-abstract landscapes and industrial scenes.

Jeny graduated from Auckland University College in 1951, and the following year became engaged to Bill Hoare, a gifted young reporter on the *Auckland Star*. The engagement was broken when it was revealed that Bill was homosexual. Jeny then visited her mother and stepfather in the United States before travelling to London where, aged 22, she taught at Chingford Secondary Modern School for Girls in 1953 and 1954. Returning to Auckland to the family house in Seaview Road, Remuera, she began teaching in 1955 at her old school, the first of a number of teaching and counselling positions she held during the next 20 years, at Tamaki College, Westlake Girls' High School and Selwyn College.

When Curnow and Jeny met in November 1954, the personal lives of both were in a state of drift. The previous year Bill Hoare had committed suicide in London, where he had hoped to find an environment more accepting of his homosexuality,[2] and Curnow's marriage was by this time held together only by the commitment of both parents to their children. Within a few days, however, they had decided to meet regularly, and the relationship quickly developed into a long-term commitment, though they did not marry until 1965.

The tumult of Curnow's feelings is vividly realised in what was to become one of his best-known poems, 'Spectacular Blossom', written within a few weeks of their first meeting. Its immediate occasion is the beauty of the scarlet-blossoming pohutukawa tree in December. The poem is suffused with a sense of transience and brevity, but age and death and loss are seen as a necessary part of the scheme in which such transformative moments can recur, in the seasonal recurrences of nature and the rhythms and cycles of human relationships (male/female, age/youth) – a scheme and a rhythm, the poem suggests, which enact a universal drama of ritual sacrifice and renewal. The poem is not a personal love poem, but caught up into it are his astonished reaction to Jeny's youth, grace and Botticellian beauty, his sense of the age difference between them and of ageing as a fact of the world which they both inhabited and would continue to inhabit – perhaps also a feeling for what had irretrievably died in his relationship with Betty.

For nearly seven years, however, the relationship with Jeny had to be tested and forged in secrecy. It was several decades before marital breakdown began to be treated in a more civilised fashion by the law and social attitudes changed, and it is hard to imagine now the extent of the opprobrium directed at those deemed to be at fault in the 1950s, or the salaciousness with which newspapers, and weeklies like *New Zealand Truth*, reported court stories of errant behaviour, or the threat to employment in jobs which required unblemished marital records. Those in the teaching profession, particularly, were expected to be moral guardians of their students, and role models in their personal lives.

Both Curnow and Jeny had family obligations and commitments. For Curnow there was no question of leaving the marriage while the children were still growing up; and although he had long since abandoned the Church, the force of his own parents' expectations about marriage obligations remained strong. Jeny had grown up in a loving family of father, uncles and aunts, which was nevertheless strictly Catholic in its expectations. For neither was the option of living openly together a possibility, when both their jobs would be potentially at risk.

Until 1961, when Curnow finally left the Herbert Street family home, and Betty initiated divorce proceedings, he and Jeny continued to meet in secret, making their relationship known only to a few of their most trusted friends. For Curnow, that meant Denis and Khura Glover and Lilburn, and amongst his colleagues at university Bill Pearson and Jim Walton. Jeny's closest confidantes, both becoming long-standing friends, were Joan Hoare – Bill Hoare's sister, who had accompanied Jeny to the party where she met Curnow – and Ruth Hirsch, who later moved to New York where she practised as a social worker.

Early in 1955 during Curnow's annual visit to his mother in Christchurch, Jeny travelled down separately and spent the week with him at a hotel. Hardly surprisingly, he did not see a great deal of his mother on this trip, and Jeny did not meet her at this time, but it was a sure sign of the seriousness of their relationship, within six weeks of their first meeting, that he introduced her on this visit to Christchurch to his closest cousin, Patricia, her daughter Angela, and Patricia's mother, Irene Ronalds, who became from this time on close friends of Jeny as well. 'Going back separately and to partially separate lives was hard', Jeny later wrote, since in Auckland they were never able to meet during weekends, or on public holidays like Christmas.

The most precious times they had together during these years were when Curnow was away from Auckland, either in Christchurch each January when he visited his mother, or when his research commitments took him to Wellington during the May and/or August university vacations, or occasionally when he undertook a programme of lectures in adult education courses held outside Auckland. The first such trip, a milestone in their relationship, occurred in the May vacation of 1955, when Curnow travelled to Wellington to read New Zealand poetry in the Alexander Turnbull Library and the General Assembly Library for the Penguin anthology he had embarked on a few months earlier. Jeny arrived by the early train the day after Allen, who took her immediately to meet Denis and Khura Glover (then flatting in Hill Street near the General Assembly Library). Glover had arranged for Curnow and Jeny to house-sit for a friend who lived in Wadestown.

Curnow worked hard every day in the libraries as he was determined to read *all* earlier New Zealand poetry in making his selection, but the week provided a first inkling of what life together, shorn of subterfuges, might be like. 'It was here on one of our last nights', Jeny later wrote, 'that we talked of our future':

I was willing to risk going off together but not at the price of Allen losing his children or they him. As he put it, 'There are four corners to my world.' We knew then and always after, that some time we would be together all the time. I did not have any guilt feeling about Betty. It was plain that the marriage was not good and that eventually Allen would have left her, if not for me for someone else, probably not making such a special relationship as ours.[3]

There was a further visit to Wellington in August that year, and in January 1956 they stayed with the Glovers at a flat in Vivian Street, where Jeny met Allen's brother Tony, recently returned from London with Ursula and their young son Simon, and about to take up a post with the Government Tourist and Publicity Department. The pattern of vacation research trips continued in 1956 and 1957. In January 1957, before travelling to Christchurch, they stayed with the Glovers at 'The Ranch', a small two-bedroomed bach they had recently moved into in Raumati South on Wellington's west coast, and again in January 1958:

> Each summer went like this until 1961, and for the last couple of years we rented a small sleep-out in Raumati South. . . . We loved that Kapiti coast, swam, collected pipis, took a dinghy to Kapiti (at some risk as the sea could and did come up very suddenly), fished for kahawai.[4]

The story of those seven years in which – apart from the three week-long oases each year out of Auckland in which they could freely pursue their lives together – they had to engage in elaborate subterfuges to preserve the secrecy of their relationship, is a remarkable love story; a story also of tenacious loyalty and devotion in a situation where it was unclear to both when they would be permanently together.

In retrospect it might be said that Curnow made the wrong decision in not separating earlier from Betty, and Jeny in agreeing to that course of action, but in affairs of the heart there are never clear-cut answers, and there were as many risks in not separating as in making the break earlier than he did, in 1961. For Betty the stresses were acute, in a situation which was not directly of her own making, though the causes of the decline of the marriage went back much further and blame could hardly be apportioned to one side only, as those who had known Curnow longest knew. Betty was aware that there was an ongoing affair, and fought hard to break it up.

Jeny, in turn, knew she would have to deal with her own deeply disapproving family, as well as the anxieties of never knowing when the separation would occur. The divorce, according to the rules of the time, was not finalised until 1965, and several months before their marriage that year, her father wrote sternly to Curnow telling him that he was responsible for his daughter losing her soul, and that what should have been the happiest day for all the family was to be a tragedy.[5] He declined to attend the civil wedding ceremony, but relented a little a few days before it, meeting Curnow and describing him as 'a scholar and a gentleman', and providing a lavish reception for them after the wedding at the Seaview Road home.

In September 2000, Curnow remembered George Tole, who died in 1972, in the second-to-last poem he ever wrote – the last of his poems to be set at Karekare Beach – a sonnet written in an unusual syllabic measure, entitled 'The Pocket Compass'. His father-in-law is remembered as providing 'bearings', meticulously tracing the design of the compass rose from his pocket compass onto the timbered deck railing of the Karekare bach, from which the poet later chiselled in the cardinal points:

> for me to get my bearings
> by, for you to see our world the right
> way round. The blaze of a late sun half
> blinds us. Later, my chisel will have incised
>
> the upper case cardinal points, years after that
> the rotted rail will have been replaced,
> pencil or chisel can't replicate
> the rose in the mind's eye, indelibly true
>
> north by needle. I paint it over again
> in sight of the sea with one more sun to drown.

On Curnow's mother's side the friendship was immediate when she and Jeny eventually met, after the separation, and Jeny enjoyed visiting her when she and Curnow were in Christchurch, and corresponding with her.

Creative spring: *annus mirabilis*, 1955

'Spectacular Blossom', and the relationship with Jeny in which it had its origins, released a remarkable spring of creativity. Curnow was pleased and confident about the quality of the poem and showed it to Glover, as well as to Stead, the first of many poems which he later tested for Stead's response. Glover liked it, but queried the title, as did Holcroft, who published it in the *New Zealand Listener* on 4 February 1955. Neither seems to have picked up the multiple connotations of 'spectacular' in the title, which, in addition to its popular sense hinted at the theatrical idea of 'spectacle' as well as the primacy of the eye, of vivid visual imagery, throughout the poem. Glover also found the relationship between each stanza and the refrains which followed them (with seemingly slight variants in each instance) unclear, a criticism with more substance to it, and one which later commentators also found difficult and challenging. However, Curnow firmly resisted making any changes.

Within eighteen months Curnow had completed ten more poems. Four of the poems from this intense period of creativity – 'Spectacular Blossom', 'To Forget Self and All', 'A Small Room with Large Windows' and 'The Eye Is More or Less Satisfied with Seeing' – were a remarkable statement of a new direction in his poetry. Mature and memorable in their own right, they would form the core of a new collection, *Poems 1949–57*, and would be often quoted, much discussed and frequently anthologised.

'To Forget Self and All' was written immediately after 'Spectacular Blossom', and also experimented with a refrain, the final three lines in each of its three stanzas containing variants on Caliban's absurd, self-deluded cry of 'Freedom, heyday' on Prospero's island in Shakespeare's *The Tempest*. Curnow sent it to Glover in January 1955, commenting that he thought it 'much better – livelier anyway – than the Spectacular Blossom' (though that may have been his way of acknowledging Glover's reservations about the earlier poem), and felt 'ridiculously pleased with it'.[6] He did not think Holcroft would care for the poem for the *New Zealand Listener*, but added:

> If you see him, you might care to show him this new one, which looks so non-Listener to me that I didn't bother him with it: I might be quite wrong about that, so you could let him know that it's his if he cares to have it.[7]

He was quite wrong about Holcroft's response, and the poem appeared in the *Listener* on 7 April 1955. It was also accepted for the September issue of *Poetry* (Chicago) that year, together with another poem written shortly afterwards, 'He Cracked a Word', a witty, conundrum-type poem about the mood, mental processes and linguistic habits out of which poetry might emerge, 'the beginnings of his joy'.

Curnow later chose to open *Poems 1949–57* with 'To Forget Self and All', where it functioned as a kind of epigraph to the volume as a whole. Its subtitle might have been 'Attitudes for a New Zealand Poet', its three intricately rhymed stanzas reopening, and updating, the questions explored in his three-part sequence of the earlier 1940s. Lurking behind its sceptical questionings of the relationship between self-as-poet and the world were the issues about internationalism versus local and national identity – at base issues about poetic aims and motivations – which increasingly preoccupied critical discourse in the country in the 1950s.

Its first two stanzas wittily demolish, as illusory dreams, the 'attitudes' which represented the terms *local / universal, national / international, provincial / cosmo-politan* as mutually exclusive, self-contained totalities, as if one were right, the other wrong, one a true aim and perspective, the other false. The third stanza, sceptical and self-mocking like the others, densely textured with puns and cleverly worked allusions to Milton's account of the expulsion of Lucifer from Paradise and Yeats's golden bird of Byzantium, contained the core proposition of the poem, that the greatest delusion of all, the greatest betrayal of self, for a poet, would be to abandon 'the phenomenal enterprise' entirely:

> To sink both self and all why sink the whole
> Phenomenal enterprise, colours, shapes and sizes
> Low like Lucifer's bolt from the cockshied roost
> Of groundless paradise: peeled gold gull
> Whom the cracked verb of his thoughts
> Blew down blew up mid-air, where the sea's gorge rises,
> The burning brain's nine feathering fathom doused
> And prints with bubbles one grand row of noughts?
> Why that'd be freedom heyday, hey
> For freedom, that'd be the day
> And as good a dream as any to be damned by.

The 'phenomenal enterprise' to be embraced is the kind which Curnow cele-brated as at the core of Dylan Thomas's art in the elegy he had written a year earlier. It implies not simply an engagement with the life of the senses and of perceptions, though it includes these, but with the *conceptions*, feelings and inner psychic compulsions – as he later wrote – which disturb, interrupt and accompany perceptions: 'aberrations, nightmares, daydreams, fantasies; even the phenomena, the perceptions – so far as we can fix and focus them – keep on joining, disjoining, connecting, conflicting, relating, failing to relate'.[8] Perhaps Yeats's thinking about the imagination is the main inspiration for the poem, with its sense that the 'self' has constantly to be remade, that there are no short cuts on the road to Byzantium's golden bird (Yeats's sculptured image of the timeless, universal work of art), that all true poetic enterprise has its sources in 'the foul rag-and-bone shop of the heart'.[9]

Curnow sent 'He Cracked a Word' to Glover in March 1955, together with two other poems. 'Times without Number', dated March 1955, was a first version of 'Keep in a Cool Place' (revised for *Poems 1949–57*), a poem sparked by the floral clock in Albert Park, Auckland, which attempts to 'arrest' a midsummer Auckland urban and harbour vista full of sensuous intimations of movement in time and space. The second poem, 'Turn, Summer', was never published. Glover thought it 'of lesser calibre' though 'beautifully "turned"'.[10] Perhaps more directly alluding to his new personal situation, it is a pity Curnow did not include it in *Poems 1949–57*:

> Turn, summer, torpid summer.
> There is a life that lovers lead,
> The earliest and the latest comer.
> Earth will bury what earth must breed.
>
> Days crowd stooping to the quayside
> Where the loose tides lap the town.
> Evening lolls along the glazed
> Street that follows the whole day down.
>
> Earth will breed what earth must bury.
> Out of the city two and two
> Face to the guttered sunset hurrying,
> Pardoned, knowing not what they do,
>
> Two and two and alone forever
> Count their losses and cut their gains.
> O summer so light, so flushed, so clever,
> Turn, summer, the night remains.

In August 1955, shortly before he travelled to Wellington with Jeny to work again on his Penguin anthology, Curnow wrote to Glover that he had two new poems, 'very spare & metaphysical', for him to see.[11] The poems were likely to have been 'To Introduce the Landscape' and 'A Small Room with Large Windows', which appeared in the *New Zealand Listener* later that year (on 11 November and 9 December), though it is possible that 'The Eye Is More or Less Satisfied with Seeing' – which was certainly completed by the early months of 1956 – was one of them.

'To Introduce the Landscape' was the slightest of these, a sonnet which sceptically undermines the notion that *representation* or *mimesis* – of the world by language, of things by words – is a simple, unproblematic, one-for-one mirroring transaction. There is an unbridgeable *gap*, the poem suggests, between the landscape and the language. What is 'out there' remains stubbornly resistant to efforts to describe or reveal it, let alone embody it in poetry, which is always reductive of the sheer, energised otherness of the world: 'No self-staled poet can hold a candle to / The light he stares by.'* [12] The anxieties evoked in 'To Introduce the Landscape' about self and other, about the relationship of words to things, and about the nature of poetry recurred in the second section of 'A Small Room with Large Windows'.

Appearing in the *New Zealand Listener* on 9 December 1955, 'A Small Room with Large Windows' was one of the major poems of Curnow's career. It was a scene with an actual location, observed through the sitting-room windows of the house at Herbert Street, and it took some time for its possibilities, as an occasion for poetry, to emerge. The poem was chosen by Geoffrey Moore, editor of the Penguin anthology *Modern American Poetry*, who described it as by far the best of any of the New Zealand and Australian poems he had read for that year, for inclusion in the tenth annual edition of the New York-based journal *New World Writing* (1956).[13]

In its final version it consisted of four parts – a sequence whose order emerged not from any overt logical or narrative progression, but from the tensions between each part, with their vividly dramatic oppositions of form, image and motif, and poetic mode. The structure of the poem in effect *mimed* the irreducible particularity of the world, and the singularities of perception of it, which it celebrated.

Driven by epistemological scepticism, the first three sections undermine idealist claims to absolute truth in a variety of different fields of discourse: monolithic and abstract philosophical and poetic thinking in the first part; the anxiety-ridden, self-serving religious-moral fictions which consciousness imposes on a world whose otherness is deeply threatening in the second; and social conformism, the rule of the norm applied to human behaviour, in the third. In its brief fourth section the poem offers a series of striking, self-contained, disparate images of objects and events observed through the windows of the poet's small room.

The ironies, throughout, are not those of anxiety and defensiveness, but of energetic, delighted pleasure in the removal of what Blake called 'mind-forged manacles' and the discovery of the inexhaustible possibilities of a world seen afresh in every perception of it, and this sense of discovery is conveyed by the vitality of the poem's imagery and language. Although much of the poem engages in ironic demolitions of the philosophical and religious fictions by which the illusion of absolute truth is sustained, and of the socio-moral cant by which a

---

* There was an unfortunate misprint in the *Listener* version, which printed 'steers' instead of 'stares', conveying the opposite to what Curnow intended: all the poet actually has to 'steer' by is a candle, an absurdly inadequate substitute for the light of the sun, the very ground of his awareness of the irreducibility of the phenomenal world.

deeply conformist nanny state attempts to preserve the illusion of the normative through legal and educational control of its citizens' behaviour, few of Curnow's poems ever offered quite so delighted a celebration of the vitality of what is fresh, strange, irreducibly other, infinitely diverse, in the world as perceived through large windows in the poem's final part:

> A kingfisher's naked arc alight
> Upon a dead stick in the mud
> A scarlet geranium wild on a wet bank
> A man stepping it out in the near distance
> With a dog and a bag
>   on a spit of shell
> On a wire in a mist
>   a gannet impacting
> Explode a dozen diverse dullnesses
> Like a burst of accurate fire.

As critics later astutely pointed out, there is no transparent, pure representation of 'otherness' in this final section. The 'fixing' of the particular scene – which would have been different one second before the poet perceived it, and changed continually throughout the duration of the process of perception, let alone in the time it might take for the poet to put pen to paper – is itself an illusion mediated by language, and in this case by a particular poetic theory of the kind of language most suited to capturing such moments, the theory of imagism. Imagism could hardly be exempt from the kinds of scepticism to which other conceptions of the real are subjected in the earlier part of the poem.

Curnow was hardly an innocent in such matters, but the aim and effect of the illusion he creates in the final section was not so much to assert a superior kind of truth, a superior way of looking at and talking about the world, as to *release* the worlds of the previous sections from their deflating ironies. The philosopher-cum-mathematician who absurdly imagines a compass in which only one point (perhaps north) is *true*; the gravitationally minded physicist who conceives life simply as the parabola followed by an exploding fireworks rocket; the poet whose only role is 'a word on arrival, a word on departure', since the intervening space of his life is an undifferentiated sameness; the lugubrious, consciousness-wracked pine trees who read in the spectacle of gathering storm clouds the end of the world and a final judgement, and damn as inferior the slime-suckled mangroves, blindly and unconsciously participating in the flux of the tides, unaware of past, present or future; even the posturing bureaucrats of the third section with their utopian dream of a socially engineered society in which personality is normalised, protected from 'all hazards of climate, parentage, diet, / Whatever it is exists' – in the end *all* of these weird and absurd utopian imaginings of a world in which final truth, morality and social order have been achieved become *part* of the strangeness and irreducibility of the world the poem celebrates.

Creative spring: more new poems, 1956

Sometime in the second half of 1955 or the early months of 1956 Curnow completed the fourth of the remarkable quartet of poems he wrote in the productive eighteen months from the end of 1954 to mid-1956. 'The Eye Is More or Less Satisfied with Seeing', which he described enigmatically to Glover as 'about a two-faced persona',[14] was perhaps the knottiest and most paradoxical of all the 'metaphysical' poems he wrote at this time. Written in terse three- and four-stressed lines, and shaped into rhymed or half-rhymed distichs, many of which carry an epigrammatic force, the poem's central image of human consciousness and perception is that of the 'janus-face' – the two-faced Roman deity, one face looking forwards, the other backwards, who presided over the ending of the old year and the beginning of the new:

> Wholehearted he can't move
> > From where he is, nor love
>
> Wholehearted that place,
> Indigene janus-face,
>
> Half mocking half,
> > Neither caring to laugh.
>
> Does true or false sun rise?
> > Do both half-eyes tell lies?
>
> Cradle or grave, which view's
> > The actual of the two?
>
> Half eyes foretell, forget
> > Sunrise, sunset,

The phrase 'indigene janus-face' – its erudite formality reminiscent of Wallace Stevens – might suggest the New Zealander's particular situation (as John Pocock suggested, linking the poem to earlier poems of the 1940s), but the 'indigene' is not simply 'native' in this national sense. Human consciousness is 'native' to a spatio-temporal world, anywhere and at any time, which is irretrievably contradictory in our perceptions of it, our feelings about it, our efforts at understanding it: there is always a conflict, a distancing, between *here* and *there*, between this place (where we are) and that place (where we once were or might be), and our efforts to bridge such distances, in time and space, will invariably be provisional, uncertain, unresolved.

In the second half of the poem the persona links the possibility of such a resolving, of tensions and belief, by imagining a brief moment in which the closed eye 'snares', whole and undivided, the fullness of what it has perceived, a moment of 'immobile plenitude' in which the eyeball is likened to a moon 'brimming astride' the full tide of the light momentarily trapped beneath the eyelid. The suggestion behind this extraordinary image is that imagination – art – contains this unifying, resolving possibility. But it is a possibility only, and the poem ends with a sceptical questioning of what one might read into such fleeting moments:

> Snap open! He's all eyes, wary,
>   Darting both ways one query,
>
> Whether the moonbeam glanced
>   Upon half to hole enhanced,
>
> Or wholly the soul's error
>   And confederate mirror.

By mid-year 1956 Curnow had also completed a memorial poem to Wallace Stevens, who had died in August 1955, as well as a shorter poem, 'A Leaf', both of which he sent to Glover, along with passages from half a dozen translations of Maori poems he was working on with a colleague at the university, the anthropologist and linguist Roger Oppenheim, to open his Penguin anthology – a bold, innovative move, intended to remind or inform readers of the richness of a tradition which long pre-dated the arrival of Europeans in the country, and also to provide a glimpse of the kind of access to the poems which might be possible for contemporary English-speaking readers, if plain, undecorative versions were aimed at, different from the romantic, poeticising habits of the hordes of enthusiastic colonial versifiers of Maori poems and legends. The Stevens poem he sent to Glover, 'Mementos of an Occasion', was close to its final version, though at this stage the final three shortish sections were a single block, and Curnow added to Glover, 'I hardly dare publish [it] with all that list of memorial poems behind me'.[15] The Maori poems he described as now in their third draft, a matter of painstaking work with his collaborator.[16]

'Mementos of an Occasion' had nothing of the personal character which marked the elegies to his father and to Dylan Thomas. It was in fact less an elegy than an elegant, witty tribute to the poetry and to Stevens's complex conception of the relationship between imagination and reality, imitating Stevens's fastidious concern with the precision of words, syntax, images and symbols, his interest in the meanings carried by the etymologies of unusual words, and his fascination with poetry as a subject for poems. In his brief concluding section Curnow paid tribute to the unsentimental scepticism underlying Stevens's approach to poetry and the world, seeing in his work, perhaps, an attitude similar to that expressed in his own poetry: 'Capable to detect where reality was not / And scrupulous what to put in place of it.' His characterisation of Stevens's poetic method (very different from his own), and of the reasons for it (the never-ending pressures of reality – the 'ranting sun' – and the chaos of one's perceptions of it – the 'rabble retina'), is brilliantly conveyed in the opening to the poem's second section:

> A well-set-up shade passed
> Forth between ranting sun and rabble retina,
> Announcing a prim masque, a conducted illusion
> Out of worse nothing.

Curnow had purchased as much of Stevens's poetry as he could during his trip to the United States in 1950, including a first edition of *Harmonium*, and the poem marked the emergence of Stevens as a significant influence on Curnow's thinking about poetry, alongside Yeats.

'A Leaf', much slighter than either 'A Small Room with Large Windows' or 'Mementos of an Occasion', continued the mode of epistemological questioning found in those and other poems at this time:

> The puzzle presented by any kind of a leaf,
> One among millions to smudge your airy sceneries
> Or among millions one your window tickler
> Gust upon gust agitates, a trifle sharp
> Enough to murder sleep:

The puzzle – to define any particular leaf, as well as the word itself (which carries multiple meanings) and its relationship to the natural leaf – remains unsolved, despite the efforts to describe its shape, size, colour, the stage of its growth, as well as its precise location in relation to the poet's world. Driving the poem is a fascination for, and an anxiety about, the issue of representation, and behind this the question of the epistemological status of objects whose 'reality' eludes us. Like all the other poems that Curnow wrote in this eighteen-month period, they introduced concerns which were to become central in the poetry of his later career.

'The Eye Is More or Less Satisfied with Seeing' was published by Brasch in the December 1956 issue of *Landfall*, but 'Mementos of an Occasion' and 'A Leaf' remained unpublished until *Poems 1949–57* appeared, as did 'Keep in a Cool Place', written the year before. A remarkable period of creativity had come to a close. It was to be another fourteen years before anything like the efflorescence of those eighteen months was to recur.

Preparing a new anthology for Penguin Books, 1955–56

In March 1953 when Curnow sent 'Jack-in-the-Boat' to the *Listener*, he thanked Holcroft for putting him in touch with Allen Lane, the director of Penguin Books in England, who was then visiting New Zealand. Lane visited Curnow at the university. He was interested in the possibility of publishing an anthology of New Zealand verse, alongside planned Penguin anthologies of modern American, Canadian and Australian verse, and also in sounding out Curnow as a possible editor. Curnow wrote to Holcroft in some excitement:

> [Lane] was interested enough to spend money on a call to Christchurch, so that we could find out the state of the present anthology [the 1951 edition of the Caxton *Book of New Zealand Verse*]; it should be sold out by 1955, which is about the time Penguins [sic] cld get one out. I am to hear from Lane.[17]

It was in August 1954 that Eunice Frost, a senior editor (later, director) at Penguin Books in England, finally contacted Curnow to say that the firm was interested in pursuing a New Zealand anthology and asking to see a contents list; and in March 1955, after seeing a rough outline of the field to be covered, Allen Lane agreed that Penguin would like to go ahead. The book was scheduled for production in 1957, and Frost initially proposed a manuscript deadline of June 1956, an impossibly tight schedule for Curnow. The contract eventually contained an agreed delivery date of the end of February 1957, for publication later that year. Curnow immediately set to work on the large task of reading New Zealand poetry from its beginnings to the present – a much more substantial task than for the first Caxton anthology, which was confined to the years 1923 to 1945. This occupied the first year of his work on the project, in whatever time he could devote to it, during trips to Wellington in May and August of 1955 and January 1956, and during the summer vacation of 1955–56. In May 1956 he began the work of assembling permissions and biographical information from the poets themselves.

At this stage, the assembling of permissions went smoothly enough, except in two instances. One of them must have amused Curnow at the time. On the day Louis Johnson received Curnow's letter requesting permissions, he had himself posted what he later apologetically called 'a strange missive' to Curnow after being told by Baxter, for some unfathomable reason ('Jim seemed to think the worst'), that he had been excluded.[18] His reply to Curnow, perhaps expressing his relief that Baxter was wrong and that he *was* to be included, was fulsome in its praise of the poems Curnow had selected:

> Oddly enough, the three you've chosen pleases [sic] me as a representation more than Chapman & Bennett's ten. The C & B [*Anthology of New Zealand Verse**] simply shows that we have only one anthologist – yourself. . . . As I say, I'm happy about your choice – so do as you wish – if you prefer something else I've sent, over to you.[19]

The other hiccup was probably more predictable. Eileen Duggan did not agree with Curnow's choice of the six poems for which he sought permission, believing that it was too narrowly focused on her earlier work. Curnow was extremely keen to include her, and anxious to avoid the impasse which had occurred with the Caxton anthologies. He was delighted when John Reid, a trusted friend of both, offered to act as an intermediary and negotiate a selection, and by August, Curnow and Duggan had largely agreed on a list of six poems, with expressions of goodwill on both sides. At this point, when he was fully engaged with the writing of the introduction, he must have felt confident and pleased that all would be plain sailing.

By early September 1956 Curnow had completed a 12,000-word draft of the preface ('& about twice that in wastage', he wrote to Glover),[20] and over the next three months continued to revise and refine it. 'I go over each page in fear & trembling', he wrote to Brasch in October,[21] and was a little anxious that Penguin might object to its length, not realising, he wrote to Glover, that it is 'mainly a consolidation of all the scattered critical matter they have had in other anthologies'.[22] Eunice Frost reassured him, however, after he had given his reasons, that she would be 'quite content to leave it as it is'.[23] Towards the end of November he sent his only copy of the preface to Brasch, 'the final job, after months of drafting, redrafting & revision',[24] and waited anxiously on Brasch's response, before sending the complete manuscript off to Penguin before Christmas – two months earlier

---

* Robert Chapman and Jonathan Bennett, *An Anthology of New Zealand Verse*, Oxford University Press, London, 1956.

than the deadline of the end of February. 'This is plainly a preface written to stand', Brasch wrote, adding presciently, 'to be read and re-read and quarrelled with and returned to; the most substantial statement yet about poetry in N.Z.'[25]

The completion of the Penguin manuscript in a little more than eighteen months, in advance of the deadline and during a period when he also wrote some of his most important poems, was lecturing full-time at the university, and producing weekly Whim Whams, showed astonishing energy, determination and sense of purpose. He was not to know, at this time (the end of 1956), that a substantial set of obstacles would have to be negotiated over the next few years before the book was actually published.

The first of these obstacles was the hostility with which D.L. Donovan at the Caxton Press pursued what he felt was a breach of contract for failing to produce a third edition of the Caxton anthology. The Caxton agreement also included the sentence 'nor shall the Author prepare otherwise than for the Publisher any work which shall be an expansion or abridgement of the said book or of a nature likely to compete with it'. Perhaps naively, Curnow had not taken his obligations under the contract too seriously. However, the letter which A.C. Brassington (Donovan's lawyer) sent to Frank Haigh (Curnow's lawyer) some three months after the Penguin manuscript had been sent off left no doubt as to the threatening nature of Donovan's intentions: 'Our client company is not unwilling to place the full facts before a Court....'[26]

For several months there was a stand-off between the parties, which was only resolved when Caxton failed to notice that a three-year limit on the terms of a third edition had passed, releasing Curnow from his obligation. It was probably not a coincidence that in August Penguin informed him that they were not able to include the anthology in their 1957 publishing schedule, that 1958 was already full, and that the anthology would be published in 1959. Almost certainly Donovan had informed Penguin of his legal dispute with Curnow. Curnow wrote forcefully to Penguin and persuaded the firm to include the book in their 1958 schedule, a delay of one year instead of two. He had learnt a hard lesson in the matter of contracts which he was never to forget. Henceforth, assisted by his son Tim after he became a literary agent in 1971, he gave the most minute attention to the wording of every contract he put his signature to, on occasion testing the patience of his publishers.

Preparing Poems 1949–57

The completion of the Penguin manuscript left Curnow free for other projects. 'I feel happier on these jobs than on anything for a long time', he wrote to Glover in February 1957. One such job was the preparation of a long-overdue collection of R.A.K. Mason's poems, to be published by Glover under his new imprint of the Mermaid Press; the other, also for Glover, was a new collection of his own poems.

Work proceeded apace during the next three months on the Mason collection. Glover and Curnow exchanged ideas regularly on editorial and selection questions. Curnow was anxious to include all of Mason's earlier collections, and worked with Mason with suggestions to revise those which he had not already revised for his publications in the 1930s. By May, Curnow had sent Glover a list of the contents, and was promising the introduction by the end of the year. However, its completion was to be delayed for several years, a casualty both of Glover's difficulties with the Mermaid Press and Curnow's difficulties with the Penguin anthology.

By this time, Curnow had finalised the manuscript of his own new collection of poems. Glover had first approached him about it in October the previous year, and he had agreed to what he thought would be a 'small assortment of new work'. By February 1957, Curnow was spending some hours a day on the collection, writing to Glover, 'Am horrified by some of the slipshod places in poems I have let into print, & revising where I can.'[27] Sending them off in May, with the provisional title *A Small Room with Large Windows*, he apologised for the delay:

> I've not really been dilatory about this, though I'd forgive you for thinking me so. Nothing is ever quite so ready as one thinks, when it comes to typing out fair & forever. There were things wrong, which I've always known to be wrong, with several pieces; but now put right or as near as can be. In fact the 20 poems have as much work behind them as anything I've done....
>
> The order of poems has been thought over; any suggestion from yourself, of course, as welcome as ever. The title? I can't think of a better, so far. 'The Eye is More or Less, etc', too long: any of the other poem-titles seem, to me, likely to put a slant on the whole collection which I don't intend. But again, if you think 'A Small Room with Large Windows' is too flat or otherwise faulty, I'm not all that wedded to it.[28]

During the winter months there were many exchanges between Curnow and Glover as the design of the volume gradually took shape. Glover thought the title 'A Small Room with Large Windows' was 'open to parody' and suggested, simply, *Poems*. Curnow agreed with this criticism, accepting Glover's title but adding the dates *1949–57*. He also accepted a suggestion from Glover that involved a 'slight' transposition of the order of one or two poems,[29] commenting that 'the order was in part what seemed to make tolerable sense, or rather decorum; in part, just mechanical, to avoid a clot of elegies'.[30] Apart from the opening three poems, all of which might be seen as exploring aspects of the poetic imagination, and the concluding poem, 'A Small Room with Large Windows', which could be seen as a kind of summation of the whole, it is difficult to discern quite what principles governed their ordering. Certainly, the order bears no relation to the date of composition, or date of first publication, of the poems.

Glover decided, late in production, that the volume 'demands case-hardening',[31] and the result of all his design and typographical attentions was a superbly produced book – Curnow was delighted when he received advance copies early in December. Yet he was also extremely anxious about how it would be received. It was a slim volume. In nine years he had produced eighteen poems, a period in which some of the younger poets (with, as he saw it, access to easy publication) had published hundreds. In effect, he saw the volume as putting his critical position in relation to the poetry scene in the 1950s on the line, subjecting it to the test of his own poetry.

Death of Fairburn

At this time, and in the months prior, Glover's correspondence contained anxious enquiries about A.R.D. Fairburn's health. Fairburn was still only 53 years old. Like others, Curnow knew that he was very ill, and battling against cancer, but felt diffident about asking too many questions or intruding on the privacy of the family and of Fairburn himself, a man who had always prided himself on his robust physical energy. 'I think I did know how ill he was', he said in an interview with James McNeish. 'Perhaps I had a kind of compact with him. . . . This was not the kind of thing, this illness, I was prepared to contemplate.'[32] On one occasion Curnow asked Fairburn's doctor and friend, the eminent surgeon Sir Douglas Robb, what the illness was. His brief reply, 'Oh well, when lightning strikes',[33] was not unexpressive, at that time, of both the nature of the disease or the shock felt at the fact that nothing could be done, though Curnow and others always hoped that 'in some way one of these remissions might happen and Rex might survive'.[34]

In one of his last letters to Curnow, Fairburn had written, 'I'm unable to get to the phone much, except for short sharp calls.'[35] On 11 March, Curnow wrote what was to be his last letter to Fairburn, beginning: 'I can't ring and must address this to your bed.' He confined himself mainly to literary gossip – to his pleasure in Fairburn's recently published parody of Thomas Bracken, 'Not Understood', to 'Jim Baxter's full-length plagiarism from *Under Milk Wood* – called *Jack Winter's Dream*', and to a story about Yeats in the back stalls of a theatre with his head in his hands, 'moaning over & over, "Oh, the horrible clarity of the words"' – but concluded that he hoped Fairburn would have a time when he could visit.[36] A few days later he did visit him, and came away deeply shocked by the physical change:

> My memory of him? Wasted. But he was sleeping a lot . . . heavily sedated. But the sedation wasn't so heavy, even some weeks before. He called it in, as it were. He called it in when desperate. Against pain.[37]

Perhaps Curnow was remembering Fairburn's courage in the moving sixth section of his late poem, 'Ten Steps to the Sea':

> Telling us about
> his cancer, he said: 'They can control
> the pain till there's well really
> no pain, but then there's no reality.'
> He said: 'I try to balance
> the two, as little pain
> as possible, as much reality
> as possible.'

When McNeish asked Curnow what he most missed about Fairburn, his answer was immediate, 'Oh. His presence.' He also missed 'obvious things': 'He wldn't be on the telephone again. He was a telephone talker. If he'd knocked off a comic trifle he'd ring up and recite it to you.'[38] Perhaps also he missed their robust conversations at North Shore parties, described – according to Fairburn's biographer, Denys Trussell – as 'a meeting of the unstoppable force and immovable object'.[39]

There had been one source of tension in 1955 – Curnow's disagreement with a City Council proposal supported by Fairburn and others to place the Auckland City Art Gallery and its director under the oversight of an advisory panel of qualified experts, which he saw as compromising the independence of the director and exposing the management of the gallery to 'local art factions and their devious, muddleheaded politics', as had occurred in Christchurch at the time of the Hodgkins controversy in 1949. Fairburn, in turn, accused Curnow of being 'commissioned' by the *New Zealand Herald* to attack the proposal, in an article Curnow published there entitled 'The Art Gallery Controversy: A Precedent to be Avoided'.[40] But the disagreement was not such as to affect their underlying respect for each other, nor – after Fairburn's death – Curnow's continuing loyalty to the man and his work, which was tested on a number of occasions, including (in the later 1960s) when Stead wrote what Curnow thought was an unbalanced and ill-considered attack on Fairburn's life and poetry.

After Curnow's account of his visit to Fairburn, Glover agreed to his suggestion that he should come up to Auckland as soon as possible and stay at Herbert Street. However, before he could finalise his arrangements Curnow cabled him, on 26 March, with news of Fairburn's death. Glover was devastated. His friendship with Fairburn was as close as with Curnow and their temperaments much more alike. He came up for the funeral, at which Curnow delivered the eulogy, and in the months following he and Curnow conferred regularly, as did others, about what might be done to assist with Fairburn's literary affairs and ensure that literary executors were arranged.

For the rest of his life, Glover, in particular, remained actively involved in Fairburn publishing projects: his collected poems, a selection of his prose writings, a selection of his letters. More immediately, Curnow assisted W.H. Oliver – who was acting editor of *Landfall* at the time while Brasch was overseas for a year – with advice about contributors to a special *Landfall* commemoration issue, and he was strongly involved in the organisation of a poetry reading, 'Homage to A.R.D. Fairburn', held in the Auckland University College Hall on 20 July 1957, at which he was one of the readers, alongside Baxter, Glover, Smithyman, and Musgrove, who also chaired the event.

Satirical broadsheets, 1957 and 1958

On 24 May 1957, a few days after Curnow sent the manuscript of *Poems 1949–57* to Glover, he gave a reading of a biting satirical poem, in the manner of eighteenth-century broadsheets, at the Auckland City Art Gallery, entitled *The Hucksters & the University or Out of Site, Out of Mind or Up Queen Street Without a Paddle!* Its subject was a proposal to move the university from its commercially valuable 9-acre central city site, and its targets, ferociously attacked and ridiculed, were the Auckland businessmen and developers behind the proposal and their supporters on the Auckland City Council and on the University College Council. It pulled no punches, in any of its nine stanzas, including the following, describing the City Council's infiltration of the College Council in order to advance its pro-development agenda:

> For a greasy ha'pennyworth of Rates,
>   They mixed their Poison black.
> They smuggled it up to Princes Street
>   And sneaked it in at the Back.
> Cumberland carried the mixture in –
>   'Twas to save sick Learning's Life!

Robinson stood with a Bowl for the Blood,
  And Surgeon Robb with a Knife.

And round the Bed and behind the Door,
  Lurking to snatch the Loot,
Were your City Fathers as cool as Judas
  And a good deal more astute,
With one Fish-eye on the Invoice Sheet
  And the other One on the Rent –
So long as the Truth stood out of their Way,
  They didn't care where it went.

 . . . .

And the Queen Street Business Mongrels yelped
  To be in at the Death at last,
There was ringing of Tills and thumbing of Bills
  When the Council's Vote was cast:
While the rent-roll Rats laid Plans for Flats
  To fatten a Queen Street Shop,
And Fletcher figured his Contract price
  As a Hangman tests his Drop.*

A few days later, Bob Lowry of Pilgrim Press published the poem anonymously (because of the dangers of a lawsuit for libel) as a broadsheet for one shilling. Curnow was happy (if somewhat foolhardy) to put his name to it, and largely managed the distribution himself. As word spread, there was a heavy demand, and within a few weeks the first printing of a thousand copies had sold out. By the end of June it was into its third impression and by the end of August it had become a collector's item.

 The poem attracted many admirers, but it hardly endeared Curnow to those he pilloried by name, nor the city business and cultural establishment who supported them. Curnow was not sued for libel, though he sailed close to the wind. Members of the National Government, struggling then to deal with the chaotic dysfunction of governance in Auckland, enjoyed the satire. 'A fine piece of caustic humour', wrote R.M. Algie, then Minister of Education and a former professor of law at

---

*   Kenneth Brailey Cumberland was professor of geography; Dove Myer Robinson (later Sir) became Auckland's longest-standing mayor; surgeon, 'medical statesman', and writer, George Douglas Robb (later Sir) was vice-president of the College Council, and became chancellor in 1961; businessman James Fletcher was chairman of Fletcher Holdings.

Auckland, adding, 'I offer no comments on its relation to the law of defamation.'[41] Curnow received many congratulatory letters, but it was the praise of his
close friends which most pleased him. 'Oh swingeing balladeer, / A lovely effort',
wrote Glover,[42] who assisted in the distribution of the broadsheet in Wellington.
Jim Walton, writing from Dublin, described it as 'grand stuff which made me
feel ten years younger. It is one of the best hate poems in the language.'[43] Lilburn
and Richard Campion (artistic director of the New Zealand Players Theatre
Trust) were waiting for a performance to begin at a theatre in Wellington when
Maria Dronke, recently returned from Auckland, 'passed a folded sheet of paper'
to the latter: 'Douglas Lilburn and I read it side by side & the room became hot.
Your broadsheet. Wonderful stuff. These are the trumpets that will bring down
the walls of Jericho.'[44]

In July the following year, Curnow published a follow-up broadsheet at the
Pilgrim Press, *Mr Huckster of 1958*, 'aimed', he wrote to Glover, 'chiefly at City Cr
John Carpenter, who said a new University would be "a cancer at the heart of the
town"'.[45] The poem did not have the impact and shock value of its predecessor,
and was more narrowly focused on an individual, but it was nevertheless highly
effective satire.* [46]

Last newspaper reviews and the new play

Curnow also wrote two poetry reviews for *The Press* in August and September of 1957,
the last newspaper reviews he ever wrote. One was of Brasch's *The Estate* and the
other of Oliver's *Fire Without Phoenix*. Both were lengthy and considered: in
the case of Oliver an attempt to be fair to a poetry he thought very uneven;[47] in the
case of Brasch an attempt to grapple with a poetry which he deeply respected and
valued, but which was so different from his own.[48] James Bertram thought the
Brasch review unforgivably 'condescending',[49] but Brasch himself did not read
Curnow's review in that way at all:

> Allen Curnow in the Press, generous admiring & critical, taking the book seriously, &
> unerringly pointing to some of its worst weaknesses; this is all I could wish, although
> I don't agree with everything he says & feel that he hasn't covered all the ground –
> but then he couldn't in one review. – When I read it again, I began to learn from it,
> & to see how well produced, how well founded on general ideas it is, a product of

---

* Algie (now in Opposition in Parliament) was even more impressed, and fascinated by Curnow's flirting
  with the possibility of a writ for defamation, wrote: 'Very best wishes, but – if you'll accept gratuitous legal
  advice (never any good) do what the Jew did and put all your property in your wife's name.'

perceptiveness & intelligence working finely together. No one else in this country could have written so able a review.[50]

The loss of Curnow to newspaper reviewing – though it was not at all a conscious decision on his part – was significant, and Brasch's response encapsulates the reasons why, during the previous 20 years, Curnow had established such pre-eminence. A review, for Curnow, was never something to be written off the top of his head, aided by a book's blurb, and never something written to please the author's constituency, or to praise a friend. He agonised over the reviews he wrote, engaged with particular texts, and related them to general ideas. Few poets, reading his reviews, would not, as Brasch recognised, learn something about the practice of the art or be challenged to think about their own practice as poets. In addition to seriousness, Curnow's reviewing had unusual integrity. Those who thought of him as condescending, as magisterially and patronisingly dispensing judgements, completely misunderstood him. He never asked a question, of the practice of other poets, which he did not ask – far more agonisingly – of his own poetic practice, though it may be that there was a certain naivety in his belief that by improving the quality of newspaper reviewing of books he could change the culture, persuading general readers to think more seriously about poetry and the life of the arts than they were accustomed to.

In November 1957, Curnow suddenly announced to Glover the resumption of interest in his play:

> Have written 3 weeks non-stop, since end of lectures, finishing the long-deferred new play. Better than the *Axe*, & I hope, also than a *Forest* of *Pohutukawa Trees.** Called, just now, *Out of the Bright Sky*. Can't help it if it sounds like Witheford's next book of verse . . . . But it could be called any of several alternatives, of which *Fine for the Weekend* or *Big House, Little House*, or *Decent Burial* could be preferred.
>
> Don't ask me what it's about. If it ever goes on, I may find out. The hardest bit of *hard writing* I've done in years, counting in the sleepless hours unpicking each day's work.
>
> Final curtain line may be all too significant: spoken by a woman doctor to a builder – '– I expect you think that's not a very good answer.'[51]

He added a little more background, to Glover, a month later:

---

*   A joking reference to Bruce Mason's play, *The Pohutukawa Tree*, first performed in 1957, and D'Arcy Cresswell's verse comedy, *The Forest*, published in 1952. [Editor's note: Emeritus Professor of English at the University of Auckland Macdonald P. Jackson and former director of Auckland University Press, Elizabeth Caffin, are acknowledged for providing this information.]

The new play has caused much pain & stress, not (I believe) all out of proportion to its worth; its immediate fortunes . . . Festival choice or not, to be decided in a day or two, are causing me anxiety. In the fevered 3 weeks of its main composition, it fed pretty well on everything I've ever imagined, going right back to Leithfield & *House & Land*. . . . No more plays, I think. This one oughtn't to be offered for print until it's been through the production mill at least twice.[52]

Like the Penguin anthology, which he informed Glover at this time[53] was at last going into production for publication in 1958, the play faced numerous obstacles before its performance, with the title *Moon Section*, in mid-1959. And it was not the last play Curnow was to write. For the next three years the anthology, and drama, were to occupy most of his attention.

Chapter Nineteen

Penguin Anthology Delays, 1958–60

*The last three months have been fuller of stress than any I remember
across the minefield Baxter, Johnson & Campbell laid for it; & lastly,
a costly and abortive struggle with Miss Duggan & her solicitors.[1]*

Background to the delays

In March 1958 Curnow received the galley proofs of the Penguin anthology, and
wrote back promptly to say that the corrections would not take too long. Penguin
also sent a copy of the galley proofs to Richard Hollyer, their Wellington representative who had recently arrived in the country, to show at his discretion to potential
purchasers – especially the universities and training colleges. In early June, Hollyer
confirmed to Curnow that the book was on schedule for publication in November.
However, Curnow was taken entirely by surprise later in June when a number
of poets in Wellington – Alistair Campbell, James K. Baxter and Louis Johnson,
acting together, and Eileen Duggan, acting independently – attempted to have
their poems withdrawn from the anthology. Penguin put production on hold until
the matters were resolved. By September, when Campbell, Baxter and Johnson
agreed to appear (a course of action Penguin preferred, rather than simply publishing on the basis of the permissions they had given two years earlier), the book had
had to be removed from the 1958 publishing schedule.

Curnow's method of seeking permission for the Penguin anthology – the same
that he had used, without any problems, for the Caxton anthology – was to send
to contributors a list of their poems which he would like to include. His intention

was not that *all* the poems he named would be included, but that the permissions would cover all that he finally selected – leaving him necessary space for fine-tuning and adjustment as the book gradually came together. In almost every instance he sought permission for a greater number of poems than he finally included – in Brasch's case, for example, he named fifteen poems and eventually included twelve, and in the case of a number of poets, like Glover and Fairburn, the authors immediately gave him carte blanche to include whatever he liked. There were many poets who did not necessarily agree with the choices he had made from their work, but none, apart from the four dissenters, questioned his right as editor to make his own decisions.

Curnow was aware, of course, that his review of the second *Poetry Yearbook*, six years earlier, had triggered debate and dissent. No doubt he was pleased about this, since that in fact, as always, had been his aim. Furthermore, numerous literary episodes had occurred during those six years, in small magazines and in the *New Zealand Listener*, in which sides were taken and disagreements aired, about the issues Curnow had raised in that review. Curnow himself took no public part in these debates and disagreements. The crucial test, for him, his 'public contribution' as it were, was not what he *said* in public but what he might *demonstrate* in the poems he was writing. However, he seems to have been entirely unaware of the personal animus which some poets felt towards him, and it was at this time that the myth of Curnow as an *éminence grise*, a malign behind-the-scenes controller of poetic reputations, had its origins.

Curnow had every reason to believe that whatever particular judgements he had made, he had been generous to the 'younger generation' of poets. His anthology, covering the whole of New Zealand verse, contained 39 poets. Of these, no fewer than seventeen (more than 40 per cent) belonged to the post-Second World War period – in effect had emerged during the last decade (1945–1956) covered by the anthology. In addition to Baxter, Campbell and Johnson, these were William Hart-Smith, Charles Spear, Paul Henderson, M.K. Joseph, Gloria Rawlinson, Ruth Dallas, Hubert Witheford, R.M. Chapman, Keith Sinclair, Kendrick Smithyman, W.H. Oliver, Pat Wilson, C.K. Stead and David Elworthy. These poets contributed 67, or one third, of the total number of poems in the anthology. If one were to add to these the post-war poems of older poets whom Curnow included – Brasch, Fairburn, Glover, and Curnow himself – nearly *half* the poems selected had been taken from the post-war period. Far from exhibiting a bias *against* the most recent poetry, as Baxter and others claimed, the selection might more accurately have been accused of exhibiting a bias in *favour* of the most recent poetry.

It needs to be emphasised that only three poets were involved in the attempt to derail the book, although it was Baxter's involvement which most distressed

Curnow, and which most threatened its viability. The absence of Johnson and Campbell would have significantly weakened the anthology. However, Baxter's absence would have all but destroyed its credibility, and it is a moot point whether Penguin would have gone ahead with the anthology without Baxter. Curnow regarded Baxter as a friend, felt deeply betrayed by behaviour which he regarded as devious, and simply could not understand Baxter's motivation other than as a personal desire for notoriety amongst mainly Wellington-based acolytes who gravitated towards him as a leader in what they saw as an intergenerational battle for supremacy. He knew, of course, that Baxter dissented from some of his own critical positions and valuations of poets and poems, and urged Baxter (as well as Johnson and Campbell) to have this debate *after* the book appeared rather than try to delay or obstruct its appearance altogether. What Curnow missed, in his efforts to understand Baxter's personal motivation, was the element of protectiveness that Baxter felt towards friends whose poetry he believed Curnow undervalued.

The experience of those years, especially 1958, left permanent scars, though Curnow later tried to downplay its significance. At the time, however, in letters to the only two people he kept regularly informed about what was happening, Glover and Brasch, he described the experience, repeatedly, as a nightmare. His realisation of the extent of the hostility directed at him, when it emerged that a calculated attempt was under way to weaken his credibility with Penguin, with a view either to blocking the anthology's publication or rendering it a laughing stock, came as a total shock.

'A calculated attempt to mutilate or destroy my book': the dispute with Baxter, Campbell and Johnson

Curnow was confident that he had produced a first-rate anthology, and believed that he had been entirely open in his dealings with all the poets he wished to include in it. However, in the course of the voluminous correspondence he had had with poets during the preparation of the manuscript, he had omitted to get Campbell's permission for a poem he had included, 'The Coming of Spring'. He also made a late change, at galley proof stage, to his selection from Duggan, including two poems, 'Augury' and 'Service', which were not in the original agreed list of six poems, and only at this late stage sought permissions from her. In both cases (though this was true for almost *all* the poets in the anthology), he had not included all the poems for which he had originally gained permissions. He had permissions from Campbell for four poems, and included two; he had permissions for six from Duggan and included four.

His nightmare began in the last weeks of June when Campbell wrote to him asking for an apology and an explanation as to why he had not included all four poems for which he had given permission and included one for which he had not given permission, adding that 'if possible, I would like to withdraw altogether'.[2] Curnow immediately replied apologising for the oversight, and begging him to think better of it and cover the lapse with his present permission. He also tried to explain that his original permissions letter did not mean that *all* poems would necessarily be included.[3] 'I'm afraid I can't let you get away with that one', Campbell wrote back, adding, 'I think any court of law would uphold me on this point.' He went on to quote back to Curnow his earlier praise of the four poems for which he had sought permission, ridiculed his editorial judgement for being 'as changeable as a Wellington summer', and vaguely threatened that although Penguin might be free from 'damages' the firm might not wish to attract 'unsavoury publicity'.[4] Curnow replied stating firmly that he did wish to withdraw 'The Return' from the anthology, for which he had permission, and that he simply did not have room to include all the poems he liked.[5] Campbell remained adamant, however, adding, 'I will say this much for you, you're a worthy adversary.'[6] 'I have never thought of myself as anyone's adversary or not', Curnow replied, 'so must shyly refuse the compliment', adding that he would let him know his decision in due course.[7]

Campbell had at least confronted Curnow directly about his concerns, and informed him that he was writing to Penguin. Like Campbell, Duggan also communicated directly with Curnow at this time, sending a blunt cable on 26 June: 'I refuse my consent and withdraw altogether from your anthology.' Two days later he received a cable from Eunice Frost at Penguin: 'SENDING LETTER COMPLAINT BEHALF SEVERAL CONTRIBUTORS ANXIOUS WITHDRAW POEMS DO YOU KNOW OF THIS STOP MATTER URGENT HOLDING PROOFS FROST'.[8] Curnow immediately cabled back seeking the names of the complainants, and wrote that he was only aware of two, Campbell and Duggan.[9] Penguin cabled back: 'BAXTER CAMPBELL JOHNSON' and Eunice Frost wrote, 'Naturally, I have held up all work on the anthology'.[10]

By this time Curnow had become thoroughly alarmed, 'haunted by the fear', he wrote to Brasch,[11] that even a short delay might mean that the book would be dropped off the publishing schedule for later in the year, after his strenuous earlier efforts to advance it from 1959 to 1958. He had since learnt from Hollyer, Penguin's rep, how the proofs came into the possession of Campbell, and thence to Baxter and Johnson, and felt that they had not dealt straightly with him. Hollyer had sent the page proofs to Campbell at his request at the Department of Education's School Publications Branch, where he and Baxter were working, leading Hollyer to believe ('intentionally or otherwise?' he later wrote) that he was asking to see the proofs on behalf of School Publications. 'On reflection', Hollyer wrote to Frost later, 'I think I should have been more acute than I was, but I did not then know that [Campbell] was one of the contributors to the anthology.'[12] Curnow later saw the situation at the end of June as follows:

> Having got possession of the proofs, on pretext of official employment, they immediately called in their friend Louis Johnson – who had nothing to do with School Publications – and embarked, all three, on what can only be regarded as an attempt to ruin the book, to damage or destroy the publishers' confidence in me, as editor, and to discredit me on the grounds of critical incompetence, partiality towards 'my own generation', and the pursuit of 'a thesis, personal and highly debatable'. All this is expressed in Baxter's long, carefully designed letter to Penguins [sic] of 21 June.[13]

His strategy at the time was to preserve the integrity of the book and keep it on schedule. He believed that if Penguin were to state firmly and politely to Campbell, Baxter and Johnson that it was impossible for them to withdraw from the book at this stage, and that their permissions were legally binding, they would withdraw their opposition. He also believed that Duggan could be persuaded, quite quickly, to withdraw her objections. On almost every count he misread the situation. Penguin was quite unwilling to proceed to publication without exhausting every possible means of gaining the consent of the disaffected poets, and Campbell, Baxter and Johnson remained firm in their opposition for two months. By August that had ensured the removal of the book from the 1958 publishing schedule, and Curnow was deeply mortified to learn of this in a copy of a letter sent by Penguin to Baxter, after repeatedly himself asking for information from Penguin and receiving no direct answer.

In the meantime Curnow waited anxiously to see the letters from Campbell, Baxter and Johnson, which Penguin had said they would send him for comment before they did anything else. They did not send Johnson's, which was likely to have been colourful, if not inflammatory. Campbell's letter was brief, reiterating the points he had already made to Curnow. Baxter's letter was much longer. He insisted that there was no 'personal acrimony' in his decision, 'with genuine regret', to withdraw from the anthology, and that he did not feel that Curnow's selection of his own verse was inadequate, nor that his treatment of his verse in the introduction was unfair. He listed four reasons for his decision, although the fourth was of a largely summary nature. First, although the introduction was 'brilliant . . . in parts' it was excessively biased towards landscape poetry, which had been 'selected to illustrate a thesis, personal and highly debatable'. Second, he was uncertain of the accuracy of the Maori translations, questioned their relevance to 'the main body of New Zealand verse', and argued that their inclusion meant that Curnow had himself written 'a third' of the anthology, a procedure whose 'literary ethics' should be questioned. Third, 'the most important factor' was the injustice of the anthologist's selection from individual poets. Because of his bias towards a 'poetry of place' he had selected very few poems of Hubert Witheford, Campbell, Pat Wilson and Johnson, who had each produced work of 'nearly comparable quality' to that of Mason, Fairburn and Glover, and he had omitted Mary Stanley, 'a most forcible and mature poet'. Fourth, Curnow's judgement appeared to be sound only when he selected from poets 'of his own generation'.

In a concluding paragraph he repeated that his motive was not a personal one, but an expression of 'deep misgivings' about the false impression the book would give to readers who lacked personal acquaintance with New Zealand letters. His final sentence, which Curnow read, correctly, as an effort to discredit the enterprise as a whole, and to persuade Penguin that if they were to go ahead with publication they would be lending their name to an unjust selection, was, 'An entirely new selection, more justly handled, would be necessary before I could permit publication of any of my own poems in this anthology.'[14]

Curnow sent a copy of his reply to Baxter's accusations, and of other correspondence, to Brasch and to Glover, commenting to Brasch about his 'nightmarish' experience:

> Baxter's letter raised questions cutting at my competence, my integrity, in such a form and from such a distance, that I judged only a full answer would serve. In the interests of the book, I had to use a harsh and unmistakeable [sic] outline. It cost me five hours, late into the night.[15]

Curnow's six-page reply to Frost indeed had a harsh and unmistakable outline, and is clearly designed to protect his literary reputation in case Baxter's letter had raised doubts in Frost's mind, and to demonstrate his bona fides and competence as an editor. He asserted that Baxter's letter lacked candour in not explaining how he came to see the galleys, and believed that he had not acted 'independently', as he claimed. He then took up each of Baxter's points. He quoted Brasch's opinion of the introduction, and attacked Baxter's view of it as itself a 'personal and highly debatable opinion'. He pointed out that Baxter's assertion that he as editor had written one third of the book was quite incorrect, and cited Dr Bruce Biggs, Mr Te Hau, Pei te Hurunui Jones, Eric Ramsden and Erik Schwimmer (editor of *Te Ao Hou*) on the quality of his and Roger Oppenheim's Maori translations. He defended the book's disposition of space, including that devoted to his own poems. He attacked Baxter's selective singling out of 'the great deal of space' allowed to Mason, Fairburn and Glover, ignoring the 'more or less equivalent' space allowed to numerous other poets, including Baxter. He then dealt seriatim with his reasons for the selections he had made from Witheford, Campbell, Wilson and Johnson, and for not including Mary Stanley, and quoted at length from two highly critical recent reviews of Baxter's poetry by E.A. Horsman and M.K. Joseph. On his concluding page he apologised that he had 'had to answer personalities with personalities, which is nasty and I don't like it; but in the interests of the book as well as justice to myself, it had to be done', and asked to be forgiven 'if personal feeling has overflowed into these comments in parts'.[16]

After further correspondence with Frost, who tried to reassure Curnow that Penguin had full confidence in him as editor, Curnow embarked in mid-July on a round of letters to Johnson, Baxter and Campbell. These were his first communications with Johnson and Baxter, and they had not to this point been in touch with him. The letters were courteous and polite, and aimed at friendliness ('Dear Lou', 'Dear Jim'), emphasising that he was writing with Frost's authority and agreement to their contents, stating that he could not agree to the withdrawal of their poems from the book and hoped that disagreements with it would be pursued *after* it had appeared, and concluding with a statement of the value of their poetry to the book:

> Any deference to the complaints of any poet – based on an accidental opportunity of seeing the proofs – would (you will agree) be improper, and hardly fair to other poets who have not had that kind of opportunity to form opinions of the book as a whole. These general disagreements are surely matters to be sorted out after the book has appeared.[17]

Johnson's reply was colourful, and personally aggressive:

> It is a matter of complete indifference to me that your publisher has confidence in you – that is his misfortune – my purpose is simply to get as far away from your vanity bag anthology as possible.[18]

His reason for withdrawing, he stated, was not because of disagreement with his editing ('and God knows it's bad enough'), but because of Curnow's 'breach of contract' in not including the four poems for which he had originally received permissions, and for substituting a different one from those four in the three poems he *had* selected. Curnow's belief, surely reasonable, that Johnson's permissions letter ('do as you wish – if you prefer something else I've sent, over to you') gave him freedom to consider other poems was simply an 'arrogant interpretation of [his] editorial rights' which no reputable publisher would accept. Even if Curnow were prepared to give him 50 pages in the book he wanted no further personal dealings with him. He concluded that unless his poems were withdrawn within a week he would seek whatever publicity he could, and 'make claims upon the publisher'. His final words were, 'in the event of the book's appearance, I will take the greatest delight in punching your bloody nose'.[19] Curnow replied briefly, 'Dear Johnson, I have received your letter of 19 July and have noted its contents carefully. Yours faithfully . . .'[20]

Baxter's reply attempted a greater equanimity of tone, but nevertheless firmly restated his position, and he probably guessed that Curnow had seen the letter he had written to Penguin. He reiterated that he had no personal animus towards Curnow, and claimed that the reason he had written directly to Penguin was that if he had made personal contact he feared that their 'long acquaintanceship etc.' would make it difficult to insist on the withdrawal of his poems. In the main paragraph of his letter he attempted to argue that it was not appropriate to wait until the book came out to engage with its limitations because it was not a case, with Curnow's anthology, of 'ordinary editorial bias' but of a book 'grossly overweighted in favour of the 'thirties', which 'does not begin to give a representative selection of the poetry of the past twelve years', and exhibits 'gross unfairness to five or six poets'.* 'If you are not culpable in the matter', he went on, '(and I would not try to judge that) at least you have been carried off your course by excessive prejudice.' It is difficult to know quite what Baxter intended by that sentence, but it seems to advance the innuendo, again, that as an editor Curnow lacked integrity or ethics. He allowed himself one colourful phrase at the end of his letter, before repeating his threat of withdrawal:

> The pig must have the right to squeal if its throat is being cut – the pig in this case is N.Z. poetry. Unless you decide to make the anthology more representative, I intend to insist on the withdrawal of my poems from it.[21]

Curnow's reply to Baxter ('My dear Jim') was also brief, saying that he seemed to have missed the point of his own letter, that Baxter's poems were in the book, as selected, 'beyond recall', adding, 'The decision is with Penguins [sic] and myself, and it has been made.' His last sentence alluded to Baxter's references to himself as lacking 'personal animus': 'I'm glad you say there was no "personal animus". Whoever suggested there was?'[22]

Curnow wrote to Frost at this point urging her to proceed with the book with the poems included, insisting that he did not believe the negative responses to his letters 'should be taken at face value',[23] insisting also that if Penguin were simply to inform the poets, politely but firmly, that it was too late to withdraw their poems, they would drop their objections. The truth was that he was becoming

---

* Presumably a distinction was being made here between acceptable 'ordinary' bias and unfairness and unacceptable 'gross' bias and unfairness!

desperate, and was far less confident than he expressed himself to be. His own letters had failed to produce the results he had expected, and he was unsure how Penguin would react. At the end of the month he received a cable from Frost, informing him that she had 'today received further letters confirming their decision to withdraw', and asking him to send her copies of the letters he had sent to the poets. The ball was now firmly in Penguin's court.

In mid-August, Frost decided that she would herself write a letter to each of the poets, 'appeal[ing] to them not only firmly but in a most friendly and co-operative way while fully supporting you'.[24] Curnow was deeply worried that any suggestion from Penguin admitting the poets' right to withdraw would 'flatter them into persisting'[25] and 'give them a platform (however insecure) on which to base some attempt to discredit the book',[26] but he had little option but to agree, reiterating that their opposition was 'bluff'[27] and that if a firm undertaking to include their work was made it would collapse.

At this time, he received one piece of good news. He had tried writing to Campbell again, despite Campbell's constant ridicule, saying that he had reconsidered his inclusions and proposed to restore 'Hut Near Desolated Pines' (for which Campbell *had* given permission) instead of 'The Coming of Spring'.[28] Campbell at last agreed to withdraw his objections. 'I am not overjoyed, although it is a move in the right direction', he wrote. Perhaps he felt that what he called his 'wounded vanity', in his very first letter to Curnow, had been sufficiently appeased. He concluded with 'a parting shot':

> I'd like you to know that I think, quite objectively, that your anthology stinks. It is what an anthology cannot be if it wishes to impress or to survive: it is dull. But then, perhaps, taken all in all, New Zealand verse *is* dull.[29]

Curnow thanked Campbell politely, and allowed himself only a brief allusion to Yeats in response: 'Don't let's get too downhearted about the dullness. There's nobody but ourselves to brighten it – if that's not simply the complacency of one who died in 1939.'[30]

Whatever relief Curnow felt was short-lived. He was able to cable Frost that he had secured Campbell's consent, saving her one of the letters she was about to write. However, when he saw the copies of her letters to Johnson and Baxter, which she sent to him, he was deeply upset that they did not unequivocally support his position that they should be held to their permissions, thus opening the door for further delays and perhaps inviting the possibility of changes to the selections. In fact, Frost's letters were small masterpieces of tact and diplomacy. She was a very experienced senior editor at Penguin, and she later admitted to Curnow that she knew she was running the risk of disappointing him by appearing less than wholehearted in her support of him, but that to do so, in an approach to the poets which was in the nature of a friendly and personal appeal for the sake of the book, ran the risk of inflaming the situation even further. In her letter to Johnson, Frost detailed the 'inconvenience, loss of time, and expense' that the delay was causing, and then got to the main points:

> While I am most reluctant to do anything which would seem to ignore your wishes and point of view I do believe that we too, as publishers, have a case.

> I should be very sorry, from every point of view, were you to insist on being excluded, and with this I am sure Mr Curnow would agree, and while in no sense do I wish to hold you – against your wishes – to inclusion surely it is not impossible for all of us to settle this in an amicable and mutually helpful spirit? . . .

> May I hear from you if you are willing to make some further attempt to meet my very personal wish that you be represented in the anthology?[31]

The gist of her letter to Baxter was similar, though (perhaps significantly) it did not include the sentence about not wishing to hold the poet to inclusion against his wishes, offering a different form of words: 'While I do not want to seem to go against your wishes, I should like to be able to ask you to reconsider your decision. Is there no way in which you feel you can meet my very personal wish that you be included in the anthology?'[32] The differences between the two letters suggest that Penguin's plan, if both continued to hold out, was to let Johnson go (perhaps because he had threatened legal action) and retain Baxter (not only because of his value to the book, but because he had already stated to them that he had no objections to Curnow's selection of his poems or commentary on them). If Baxter and Johnson compared letters, this difference might not have escaped Baxter, in particular.

Curnow was, however, by this time exhausted and deeply dispirited, and he read Frost's invitation to Johnson 'to make some further attempt' to be represented, and to Baxter to find some 'way' of being included, as opening the door for the selections to be changed. (Indeed, Johnson *did* read it this way, commenting to Curnow later that he planned to seek the restoration of all four of the poems for which he had given explicit permissions.)[33] When nothing had been heard for nearly a fortnight Curnow feared the worst, and began to contemplate his own options, as editor. He was clearly ready to throw in his hand. To Brasch he wrote that he could not acquit Baxter and Johnson of 'a calculated attempt to mutilate or destroy my book', adding, 'One thing you may be sure of. My name will come off the title page if there is any move by Penguins [sic] to make the slightest change to suit Baxter or Johnson.'[34]

Nevertheless, he decided on one last personal appeal to Baxter and Johnson, in the wake of their receipt of Frost's letters. His letters were brief, friendly ('Dear Lou', 'Dear Jim'), and their restraint, given the strength of his feelings of anger and humiliation, must have taken a huge effort of self-control. To Johnson, he concluded:

> I realise that you acted as soon as you could, when it seemed necessary to you. But now it has all (I hope) been explained, I am sure you will welcome an opportunity to help us out of a situation which can only be considered the result of a misunderstanding.[35]

To Baxter, who was soon to depart on a trip to India, he wrote:

> I know you will be glad to have misunderstandings cleared up. I think you will agree that the publishers have been most helpful and forbearing. Shall I hear from you before you go? Good travelling.[36]

By sheer coincidence his letter to Baxter crossed with a letter from Baxter, written the same day. Baxter had changed his mind. He informed Curnow that he was authorising the inclusion of his poems in the anthology because he did 'not see any point in stonewalling when no useful object is to be gained by it'. Perhaps he had taken the hint that Penguin would proceed anyway, in his case. He did not think Curnow had been 'wholly frank or wholly fair' in his handling of the situation, but realised that he had been obliged to defend 'a nearly-completed project'. He repeated his criticisms of the anthology, and concluded:

> Are we too close to these issues to see them straight? I sincerely hope not. I have tried to avoid acting in a partisan spirit; and I regret having caused you personal anxiety or inconvenience by this clash, though I cannot apologise for protesting or for the manner in which the protest was made.[37]

Curnow's reply was brief and polite. Perhaps he did not trust himself to write at length. He thanked Baxter, assured him that Frost would be glad, and concluded: 'I hope you will excuse this brief acknowledgement now. Perhaps there will be an opportunity for discussion after your return from abroad.'[38] A reply by Baxter to Curnow's own letter then arrived, confirming the withdrawal of his 'go-on-strike decision' and attempting to smooth relations. It was well-meaning, but utterly misread the depth of Curnow's sense of betrayal, which made him read almost every phrase in it as false or hypocritical. 'Well, there's no need for any more bitching between us', Baxter wrote:

> Probably this lot was not entirely necessary. I don't know how much of my own
> tendency to haul out the sabre is straight aggressive criticism and how much comes
> from the gnawing of a private devil; but I suspect that the second category covers
> more than I once thought. Not contrite, but prepared to call it a day. Good luck.
> I hope all goes smoothly now that you have got through the Clashing Pillars. I do not
> like this *Argo* yet I respect her captain.[39]

Curnow did not reply. But he wrote the angriest letter he ever wrote about
anyone, to Glover, about what he saw as 'the labyrinths of dishonesty' in it: 'You've
seen *all* my letters. When was there any "bitching"? . . . His "sabre"! His "private
devil"! Jesus!'[40]

At this stage there was still the question of Johnson's response to Frost's letter.
Curnow did not have to wait long, and received a jaunty letter from Glover (then
working at Whitcombe & Tombs) a couple of days later:

> The laddie called Lou has just been in, & I think I have persuaded him to hide his
> rare pride with an acquiescent shrug. . . . He says the others have 'ratted' (yes, ratted)
> on him! Scabs, he says they are. I learn you have done me a disservice by putting so
> much of mine in. . . .[41]

It remained for Curnow to apologise to Miss Frost at Penguin, which he
did, handsomely, 'for every tone of reproach & foreboding in those last letters of
mine', and to acknowledge that her course of action had been the key to resolving the issues.[42] Frost, in turn, replied graciously, saying how relieved she was,
'especially for you, at this happy outcome of what had become, or looked like
becoming, something of an out of proportion problem all round'.[43]

In retrospect, Curnow's selection of three poems by Johnson and two by
Campbell, despite the generous space he allowed to poetry written in the decade
after the war, *was* harsh (though Johnson's best work was written much later, in
the mid-1960s and after), and if he had thought more highly of it he might have
made space for two or three more poems from each (and perhaps introduced one
or two by Mary Stanley) by reducing the representation of D'Arcy Cresswell,
whom most commentators later believed he overvalued. It may be that, as had
happened with the second edition of the Caxton anthology, if delays in publication
had not occurred (it was published four years after he sent the manuscript off at
the end of 1956), the weightings and selections might have been slightly different,
though Curnow denied this when the book was published. His most intensive
reading for the book was done in 1955 and the first half of 1956. If he had begun
this intensive reading two or even three years later, Johnson's significant volume
New Worlds for Old (1957) would have been available, and poets like Peter Bland,

Fleur Adcock and Hone Tuwhare might have come within the frame. From early 1957, when Curnow had sent the completed selection to Penguin, his capacity to make changes, even if he had wished to, was very restricted.

During the two-and-a-half-months in which he was dealing with the nightmare of Baxter's, Campbell's and Johnson's threatened withdrawals, Curnow had confidently reassured Frost that negotiations with Eileen Duggan were being resolved. They were not, and almost immediately after the participation of the other poets had been secured, negotiations with Duggan broke down. The hapless book was plunged into a new crisis which proved far more difficult to resolve.

A 'passion for completeness': the effort to include Eileen Duggan

There is a polite but curt letter from Eunice Frost to Curnow, which he received in May 1959, nine months after the permissions of Baxter, Campbell and Johnson had been confirmed, in which she informed him that before the book could be published Penguin required a statement in writing from Eileen Duggan's lawyer, C.I. Patterson (of Barnett, Corry, Watts & Patterson in Wellington), confirming that he accepted Curnow's form and wording of a two-sentence statement that Duggan's poems were not in the book, a statement which had already been approved by Curnow's Wellington lawyer, George Swan (of Swan, Davies & McKay). Perhaps while on the telephone to Swan about this letter, Curnow doodled in the margins. The doodle has the unmistakable shape of a spider's web.[44] Perhaps, even at this point, he did not consciously realise how completely he had been ensnared in his dealings with Duggan and her lawyer over Duggan's representation in the Penguin anthology. Perhaps he never did.

It was not for another fifteen months, in July 1960, only four months before the book appeared, that Patterson – having examined the page proofs – gave Penguin the final assurance they needed to go ahead. His letter has the supreme confidence of one who knows he has total control over the fate of the book. If he had expressed the slightest demurral, the book would not have been published. 'I have studied the proofs', he wrote to Frost, adding, '. . . I had to spend some time arranging these in sequence, which did not please me'. He went on, 'I do not regard the passage at pp 41–42 as a "satisfactory" (to use your own word) reference to Miss Duggan, but I recognize that Mr Curnow may express his opinion within legal limits.' In actual fact there were no references to Duggan in the passage in question. All references to her had been removed, as required by Patterson and Duggan under an earlier agreement. He concluded, 'Miss Duggan instructs me to say that she has accepted my opinion and that accordingly she will not take any legal proceedings if the book appears in the form of the proofs.'[45]

The whole dispute had its origins in Curnow's failure to understand the depth of Duggan's continuing distrust of him, as an editor and critic of her own writing, after his *Press* review of her work in 1940 and his comments about her poetry in the Caxton anthology in 1945, and his misplaced confidence in his own capacity to persuade her of the genuineness of his motives. He also underestimated Duggan's toughness and determination to look after her own interests. But it was (or became) a dispute only in the sense that Curnow did not wish to accede to her withdrawal from the anthology and for more than a year tried, stubbornly, various means of persuasion to achieve this. The publication delay that this entailed – a further eighteen months, until the end of 1960 – was in this sense entirely of his *own* making. It also achieved nothing. Not only did Duggan succeed in having her poems removed from the book, but all references to her in the introduction were removed and, as outlined above, the book was not published until her lawyer had vetted the page proofs to ensure that such was indeed the case. Duggan's victory was comprehensive.

Curnow had spoken to Hollyer about the 'passion for completeness' which had impelled him to persist in trying to negotiate Duggan's presence,[46] and was later at pains to deny that *Duggan* had delayed the book. True, it was never her wish to obstruct the *book*'s publication, as it was with Campbell, Baxter and Johnson, but she was only prepared to appear in it if she controlled the selection of her poems and what was said about her. If Curnow had simply been prepared to accept her initial wish to withdraw, or at any point afterwards to accept the terms she (or her lawyer) required, there would have been no further delay at all.

He did have one minor victory though. During January and February 1960, Curnow worked busily on updating the galley proofs. There was a considerable amount of work to do on them, since he found that Penguin had taken in no changes whatever since June 1958, when his problems with Campbell and Duggan first began. The space made available by Duggan's non-appearance was filled by additional poems by Mason, Smithyman and Stead. When he returned the galleys to Penguin he commented that the passage with Duggan's name removed was *not* the same as the one which Patterson had approved. He had written the passage Patterson approved 'in haste', and felt that 'some re-writing was necessary, in order to preserve the continuity of the Intro', though he added that Penguin might use the Patterson-approved passage if they wished.[47] Fortunately, Penguin used Curnow's revised passage. It contained some of his most elegant, often-quoted sentences, including: 'The shocks of colonial translation had imparted their own subtle twist to the ever-twisting and shifting accommodations between literature and living. . . . Some working relationship had to be recovered, between the sense of actualities and the sense of poetic values. . . . But in the small island frontier society, which rashly chose to be born in the mid nineteenth century, life and art were sundered with a peculiarly brutal absoluteness . . . .'[48]

Patterson could do little about it when he saw the proofs in July (though no doubt if he and Duggan had been able to find even the remotest suggestion that she might be included in such generalisations they would have regarded them as defamatory), and finally gave the clearance which Penguin sought: 'Although the passages in the Introduction do not follow the agreement with Mr Curnow . . . in my opinion [they] are not defamatory of her.'[49] Curnow may have had the small satisfaction of feeling that his text had not been entirely dictated by Patterson and Duggan.

Six months after the book appeared Patterson reported finally to Duggan that he had looked 'for any references to you in reviews of the kind we feared', but had not noticed any. 'I think the whole episode may now be forgotten', he said, but added, 'I will retain the file of papers in this matter which I will keep in a safe place in case it becomes necessary later on to refer to the correspondence.'[50] He need not have feared. Curnow later described Duggan as having 'no weak-minded illusions about the power of an editor's choices . . . to make or break a poet'. About the Penguin 'episode' he wrote:

> [I]t was plain to me that she would have consented, if she were given control of the selection of her poems, and of my commentary printed in the book; her Wellington solicitor wrote to the publishers warning them to be careful about any 'reference to our client': terms no honest editor could think of accepting.[51]

The comment is true, but leaves out a little. Curnow was willing to concede a great deal to her control, in the selection of the poems, provided his commentary on her remained, and although he refused to accept Duggan's control over the commentary he had written specifically about her, in the end Duggan wholly controlled his right to say anything about her at all.

Chapter Twenty

More Plays, 1958–61

*Auckland in particular, N.Z. in general, have been too much with me
these last few years. We haven't got on very well together. My poems are
too dry & stringy for them . . . . My plays bewilder or disgust them . . . .[1]*

Reception of *Poems 1949–57*

The year 1958 promised to be Curnow's most active year of publication since
arriving in Auckland in 1951. *Poems 1949–57* was about to appear in the bookshops,
the Penguin anthology was on track to come out around midyear or soon afterwards, the manuscript of Mason's collected poems was close to completion, and
Curnow was actively investigating the performance possibilities of his recently
completed play, *Out of the Bright Sky* (later changed to *Moon Section*). Blackwood
Paul was also keen to publish a new selection of Whim Wham's verses. However,
only the first of these projects actually came to fruition in 1958, largely because of
the disruption associated with the Penguin anthology in the second half of the year.

Poems 1949–57 was published in 1958 and although Curnow was disappointed
by its reception there were perceptive reviews by A.W. Stockwell in *Landfall*[2] and
Alexander Craig in *Poetry* (Chicago),[3] and the volume was awarded the Jessie
Mackay Memorial Prize for poetry for 1957. Newspapers in Auckland hardly
noticed it. Bertram reviewed it in the *New Zealand Listener*, on the whole positively, but with an edge, throughout, suggesting that Curnow's 'involved, elliptic,
gnomic style', his 'technical accomplishment' and 'polish', more often than not
did not justify the 'severe demands' they made on 'the most agile intelligence'.[4]

Oliver published a long review in *The Press* which mounted a full-scale attack on the book as a whole, whose 'moments of joy' were 'hedged in by annoyances', revealing a poet who had taken a new road from that of his earlier verse but had largely failed, resulting in a loss of direction. The defect that haunted the book was 'clearly psychological rather than technical', an obliqueness of approach where the poet 'seems to be deliberately fending the reader away from his meaning', and his major instance of the failure of Curnow's 'oblique, sideways entry into his material' was 'Spectacular Blossom'.[5]

If Curnow was disappointed by such responses he should hardly have been surprised by them. Every volume he ever published had aimed to challenge readers, to destabilise assumptions about how poems should be read and valued, and had attracted reviews complaining about the poet's incomprehensibility. There is some irony in Oliver's listing of Curnow's admired earlier achievements – by way of contrasting their 'true voice' with what he saw as Curnow's current loss of direction – when those earlier achievements had invariably been met by some with the same criticisms he now applied to the latest.

To a certain extent Curnow *needed* the stimulus of such misreadings, or negative readings, though he also needed the approbation of at least a small number of people whose judgement he trusted. If Oliver considered 'Evidences of Recent Flood' an abject failure, Curnow knew that Glover and Bertram thought very highly of it. If the reviews generally attacked 'In Memory of Dylan Thomas' as merely derivative of the style of his subject, Curnow knew that Brasch thought it the best of all Curnow's poems which he had published in *Landfall*; if Oliver found 'Spectacular Blossom' incomprehensible, and Bertram deemed it a mere 'bittersweet marine flower-piece, oddly named', Curnow knew that Stead thought it one of his richest later poems.

Brasch was as exercised, uncertainly, over Curnow's 1950s poems, writing in his journal:

> Allen Curnow's new book of poems: very accomplished, skilful work, that of an old hand, a virtuoso: it *is*, but it hardly *says*, or what it says is so darkly wrapped up that I can only get flashes of it here & there, through chinks in its own armour. A.C. has been wrapping up his meanings ever more obscurely in successive books as if he were moving further & further away from us & wanted less & less to communicate, or had less to communicate – which is always my suspicion. His poems are now like non-figurative paintings, full of suggestiveness, rich in sound, with a life of their own only remotely related to our life.[6]

Two months later he pondered the relationship between poetry and journalism in Curnow's work:

I used to admire Allen Curnow for his ability, when he worked for so long on the *Press*, to keep journalism & literature distinct & allow no trace of the former to infect his poetry or his critical prose. Now I wonder if the increasing difficulty of his poetry is not due in part to the effort to keep all journalism out of it, so that he has made it as different & as pure as possible, to the extent of banishing prose from it entirely.[7]

To Curnow himself he was characteristically direct and open, again invoking MacLeish's dictum that 'a poem should not mean – but be':[8]

I am absorbing your poems piecemeal. 'A Small Room' is delightful; 'Evidences' I find hard reading; when I know it by heart it will tell me more. You not only warn off the casual running reader, but look frowningly at all who approach; don't put too much obliquity in our way. I should like you to say more openly what you have to say: more saying, a little less being: poetry is impure of necessity.[9]

Brasch's suggestion of an analogy between Curnow's poetry and non-figurative painting, and his proposition that poetry is impure by necessity, would have interested and troubled Curnow (both Glover and Lilburn would have agreed with Brasch's proposition), as he wrote to Schroder, delighted with his positive comments on *Poems 1949–57*, as judge of the Jessie Mackay Award:

These last six months have been troubled by thoughts that I had, perhaps culpably, written myself out of reach of any deserving audience – I mean, deserving the best I can do – thoughts now banished completely.[10]

Schroder had written to Curnow that he 'had read no verse so genuine in its springs & texture for a long time, & there's very little in N.Z. poetry that I know, to come near it',[11] and in his report commented that the volume 'excels . . . in grasp of subject and of significant form' and that although the difficulty of the poems was 'in part due to something rather wilful and arbitrary in his control . . . [it] never hides emptiness'.[12] Curnow also expressed his frustration at the grosser kinds of opposition between form or technique and meaning that had recurred in the reviews:

I've had (in both senses) this 'technique' thing; not only J.M. Bertram . . . in the *Listener*, but from young Bill Oliver, who took a column in *The Press* to tell us what he didn't find, & nothing about what he did. I wld have thought – we would have thought – that 'technique' which displayed itself to the detriment of the poetry was *bad* technique; what nonsense it makes, to profess admiration of the 'technique', & by so much to diminish the value of the result! Me, so far from idolatry of technique-an-sich, I've always felt myself trying – the analogy's from experience – to take down an outboard motor with the wrong spanners, little knowledge of engines, & numb fingers. I *knew* there was nothing in the book that wasn't mine, for better or worse, & I'd used what means I had to make the best poems I could. . . . *You* haven't suggested that I have been clever just for the hell of it – or blamed 'technique' when the real trouble is the lack of it! *Nor* have you professed (like J.M.B.) to discern the 'influences' of Stevens & Thomas, because I happen to have made poems about both of them![13]

Ronald Barker and the CAS Theatre

During the first half of 1958 Curnow spent all of his available time substantially revising his stage play *Out of the Bright Sky*, whose first full draft he had completed during a concentrated burst of activity in November and December of the previous year. It had not been selected as an Auckland Festival play for 1958, and he was unsure about it, feeling, he wrote to Glover early in the New Year, that he was 'tampering with a *kind* that's not mine, probing forbidden mysteries'.[14] Glover did not especially like it when Curnow showed it to him during his visit to Wellington later that month, but the newly arrived Auckland theatre director Ronald Barker was deeply impressed by its possibilities, and in February spent a number of days working with Curnow to suggest the lines along which revisions might be made, with a view to production the following year.[15]

Barker, an Englishman who had been involved with the Cambridge Arts Theatre and was founder-editor in 1953 of the London theatre journal *Plays and Players*, came to Auckland in 1958 to take up the post of director of the Community Arts Service (CAS) Theatre, a small professional company run (and funded) by the Adult Education Centre of Auckland University College, whose aim was to serve the city of Auckland and the rural centres of Auckland province. Barker brought astonishing vigour and resourcefulness to rejuvenating this moribund organisation, and over the next five years directed and toured ten major productions (including works by Shakespeare, Chekhov, Shaw, Synge and Beckett, and in 1959 Curnow's new play, renamed *Moon Section*) as well as conducting theatre workshops and involving himself in many other one-off productions and performances. He was a controversial figure, subject to suspicion and obstruction from entrenched local amateurism, hampered by the committees in Auckland and in the provinces with which he had to negotiate, but an energetic and valuable member of the planning committees of the annual midwinter Auckland Festival of the Arts. In 1963 he left CAS and with his wife, Lilian, set up a small company (Ronald and Lilian Barker Ltd), which continued to sponsor lively contemporary plays, unsubsidised, until Barker's early death in 1968. 'His was not the spirit of a visitor, or of those I think of as "campers" no matter how long they stay', Curnow wrote in appreciation after his death. 'He released us from the provincialism which confined us to the safe modernities of the past 20 years.'[16]

The presence of Barker, who became a close friend and whose work Curnow greatly admired ('I can think of only two others [Miss Ngaio Marsh and Mr Richard Campion] whose contributions to theatre in this country could be said to match his', he wrote in 1963),[17] provided a key motivation for Curnow to write for the stage during the next few years:

> I myself . . . had the experience (to me greatly enriching and instructive) of working closely through with him, successive drafts of two full-length plays of my own. One of these [*Moon Section*] he produced and toured with the CAS company; if it is still debated (if not generally liked) in this country, that is wholly on account of Mr Barker's perception of its possibilities, and the guidance he gave me to fit it for the stage. Attendance at all his rehearsals was the best education I have had in writing for the stage. The second of these two plays [*The Overseas Expert*], since presented nationally by the NZ Broadcasting Corporation, also owed much to Mr Barker's guidance.*[18]

By late May 1958 Curnow had made steady progress on his revisions and was able to inform Brasch that Barker had accepted the play for CAS. He also hoped to send Brasch a fair copy when it was complete: 'It is, really, a *terrible* play; I can't help it if some think it was written out of hatred, not love. Both, I think. (But perhaps I daren't guess which!)'[19] For the rest of the year progress was fitful and difficult. In early September, however, he wrote to Brasch that he had finished his revisions of the first two acts:

> Barker seems well satisfied with the revised Acts I and II; and I shall be full time on Acts III and IV a few weeks from now. In addition to a CAS tour, Barker has (while in Australia lately) interested Hugh Hunt of Elizabethan Theatre Trust in the play, & has plans to take it on tour there.[20]

The full-time work on it which he anticipated never eventuated, since he was plunged almost immediately and for the rest of the year into the escalating Penguin anthology crisis. However, he did manage to meet Barker's deadline of November, and Barker was excited at the prospect of staging it the following year,

---

* Robertson was registrar at the University of Southampton, where Barker at this time applied for the position of director of drama at the Nuffield Theatre.

now accepted as an 'official' play of the Auckland Festival. But when Curnow sent Glover a copy early in the following year to consider for publication, Glover remained unconvinced and simply refused: 'Nothing will alter my conviction that plays are unpublishable. . . . But I still think you are nuts in thinking of a printed version before it has been hammered out in a producer's bellows.'[21] Disagreement about the play (and Curnow's delay in completing the Mason manuscript, which Glover was keen to publish) caused a significant estrangement between them, and they were not in touch with each other for another five months.

In Auckland, Barker was strongly supported in his CAS arrangements for the play by Stuart Morrison (Auckland director of Adult Education) and by Musgrove, who was also on the Auckland Festival committee – all of them interested in developing the CAS as a second *national* professional theatre company alongside the Wellington-based New Zealand Players. Two perform-ances were arranged for Wellington, in addition to the Auckland provincial tour, and Curnow had shown Ngaio Marsh his earliest draft of the play, and sent her a copy of the revised version, commenting: 'You will find the play very much revised & rebuilt since you saw it a year ago. It's already in debt for your kindness then.'[22] She still had quite serious doubts about it, though none about the importance of its being staged:

> Of course your play should be heard & seen all over New Zealand. Even if it turns out to be not, in its essence, the stuff of the theatre, it is the work of a distinguished, serious & important poet & dramatist & must be subjected to the ordeal by fire that awaits all dramatists. . . .
>
> My doubt – & please don't make too much of this – is whether the fundamental element of the play: the One Thing that every play must be about – is sufficiently established for presentation to an audience. I wonder perhaps if there is an uneasy ambivalence between the theme itself & its application in specific New Zealand terms. . . .[23]

Curnow's comments to others about the play up to this point had been brief and enigmatic, inexplicit about its subject matter or theme or style, but constantly implying that it drew deeply on buried psychic materials in himself that he did not fully understand. The play had caused 'much pain & stress', he had written to Glover, 'feeding on pretty well everything I've ever imagined, going right back to Leithfield and *House and Land*'. To Lilburn, shortly before it went into rehearsal, he repeated a comment that he had made to Brasch, that it was 'a sad & terrible piece': 'But if people don't (as many well may) misconstrue the feelings they get, it shld not seem destructive; or perhaps a kind of slum clearance.'[24]

Reception of *Moon Section*

Never published, *Moon Section* is basically a family tragedy. Set in the 1950s on the shrunken 17-acre remnant of what was once a 2000-acre landed estate established in colonial times, it tells the story of the deaths of the three surviving descendants – a father, and his son and daughter – who had inherited what was left of the estate. Their deaths signify the final collapse of the original settlers' 'new world' colonial dream of a fresh start. The two main characters, both richly and complexly drawn, are the father, Thomas Judd, and his daughter, Nance. Judd is the sole survivor (and youngest) of five sons in whom the original emigrant dream was to be realised, but is now aged, ill, deeply embittered and disillusioned. His daughter is a nurse who at the beginning of the play still lives the dream of a fresh start, hoping to rejuvenate the farm, and fulfil a domestic ideal of marrying and raising a family. The third member of the family, the son Jack, has died a year prior to the action of the play – accidentally shooting himself with his own rifle, according to the inquest, but the mystery and intrigue surrounding the real cause of his death provide much of the plot momentum.

The fortunes of the Judd family, as they unfold inexorably towards their tragic ending, are intertwined with the lives of three other characters. Two of these belong to the newly emergent professional elites of New Zealand's post-war welfare state: Stephen Bailey, a young, manipulative, entirely self-centred, philandering schoolteacher-poet whose professed Christianity is as much an affectation as his poetry, and Janet Colebatch, a self-assured but equally self-centred and status-conscious young woman doctor. The third of these characters is Margaret Watson, a woman whom Bailey has recently become engaged to after abandoning relationships first with Nance Judd and then with Janet Colebatch. She is a young, city-bred woman, sensuous, independent, sophisticated but – unlike either Bailey or Colebatch – possesses qualities of empathy and imagination which give her an insight into the tragic events in which she becomes unwittingly involved. The cast includes two other characters – a builder, Hal Singleton, and a carrier, Mac Derbidge – who function throughout as stereotypes of decent, average New Zealanders going about the material business of building a comfortable society, making a living, bringing up a family, and whose words and actions often provide an ironic, down-to-earth 'choric' comment on the intense passions unfolding around them. The action takes place during two acts, each consisting of two long scenes (the four scenes covering four consecutive days), on a single set. Seen under the revealing light of the moon in the final scene, 'moon section' – the section (Judd's property, New Zealand, human life as a whole) – is revealed as a place of death, dust, the destruction of dreams.

The play was hugely ambitious, and utterly unlike anything by a New Zealand playwright which had ever appeared on the New Zealand stage – a deliberate challenge, as Curnow put it, to 'the popular dream of N.Z. as epitomizing all the social virtues and "normalities"'.[25] Tragedy was the mode in which he chose to confront the myth of God's Own Country (the myth, that is, of a country specially favoured by providence), offering a means of probing beneath the comfortable platitudes of welfarism and prosperity in post-war New Zealand by construct-ing a counter-narrative of defeat, loss, disillusion, the maiming of hopes and dreams. Judd's family history offers a story of those 'many', as Curnow had put it in a biblical metaphor in an earlier poem, 'The Unhistoric Story', who were not 'called' – to participate, like the lucky others, in the achievement of the vision of a new society – but 'left at the start', casualties and victims of that vision. To Ngaio Marsh's acute query as to whether the play convincingly *established* 'the theme itself & its application' to New Zealanders,[26] Curnow might no doubt have replied that he believed there was a 'Judd story' – a tragic story of failure and waste – in the lives and histories of most New Zealand families, even if the precise terms were different, the tragedies of varying intensity, and memory of the personalities and events largely repressed:

> Tragedy gets its impact and its music by playing on the concealed tensions in the heart of a people. It is the most ancient and the most universal dramatic form. . . . [O]ur madness is simply an acute form of what mankind has suffered from for centuries. I think it's a commonplace that New Zealand has set the pace for the modern world, in its effort to develop a way of life which is supposed to be painless for everybody.

> Right back to the early colonists, New Zealand can be seen as a product of modern man's vain struggle to get away from himself by going to live somewhere else – the illusion of the clean break and fresh start.[27]

Whether Curnow succeeded, theatrically, in tapping into the buried psyches, the memories, of his audiences depended, of course, on how effectively the play worked on the stage. The particular tragic mode which seems strongest as an influence on the play is the mode of social tragedy of Ibsen's later plays, like *The Master Builder* and *Hedda Gabler* – plays in which naturalism of action is absorbed into a highly symbolic drama, and the tragedy of the main character's life carries with it a broad social and political significance. Ibsen's interest in family histories, and in family history as a kind of tragic fate inherited through successive generations (of which *Ghosts* is his most powerful example), is also highly relevant to Curnow's representation of the Judds in *Moon Section*. But there are other influences as well. Nothing like the intensity of Judd's half-crazed ferocity towards others and himself can be found in Ibsen, but it can be found in Strindberg's theatre of lacerating and self-lacerating domestic relationships.

Strindberg's late plays were also much more closely attuned to the expressionist impulses that underpinned the bold experiment of Curnow's final act, in which lighting is deployed to generate a double perspective on people and events, as if people exist in two dimensions: their ordinary daytime selves, and their selves as part of a larger, universal pattern in human behaviour.

The set deployed by Curnow, with its simple properties – a hole in the ground with a pile of earth and a spade, a trunk filled with bric-à-brac, a bucket with night soil – also suggests the new existential impulses in European theatre in the 1950s, with the reduction of the stage to simple symbolic objects, as in Beckett's plays, and Judd himself, raging futilely against the world and himself, as a kind of existential anti-hero. It is possible also to read in Curnow's play the traces of Greek (Sophoclean) tragedy: the fated downfall of the Judd dynasty, as if predetermined and dealt by some malign force out of the characters' control, the metaphorical emphasis on the 'house' (in the play's physical setting) as a metaphor for family dynasties, perhaps also the association of the three women (Nance, Janet and Margaret) with the three Graces or Fates.

Moon Section was well publicised, as the official play of the Auckland Festival, and received ten performances at the Concert Chamber from 9 June to 14 June 1959, following a similar-length season of Ray Lawler's Australian play, *Summer of the Seventeenth Doll*. However, its immediate fate was heavily dependent on the reviews it received in the two Auckland newspapers, the *New Zealand Herald* and the *Auckland Star*, both of which were hostile, offering only the faintest of praise, and 'did damage out of all proportion to their significance *as* crits',[28] 'seemingly designed', Curnow felt afterwards, 'to knock the piece cold & leave it for dead'.[29] The *Star*'s review, headlined 'Gloom-steeped "Moon Section" fails to match bright expectations', attacked the content of the play.[30] The *Herald* review had an equally off-putting title, 'Puzzling Festival Play', describing it as winding through 'such a Hampton Court-like maze that it is sometimes difficult to say in what direction it might be going. And so many of the paths appear to be deadends that the true one is extremely hard to trace.'[31]

The size of the audiences was affected by the reviews, although not as badly as might have been the case, and during the ten performances approximately half the available 5000 seats were sold. Some members of the festival committee reacted badly, and there was an effort after the first night to force Barker to remove a bucket of night soil from the stage. Curnow was almost certainly correct in believing that, whatever theatrical weaknesses the play had, those who were most outspoken in objecting to it were much more bothered by its socially unacceptable 'realism' than by its supposed obscurity and intellectualism.

During its North Island tour – to 21 provincial centres – the play was often quite well received, and there were a number of excellent reviews, with regular praise for Peter Varley's performance as Judd, and for the 'poignant tragedy' of Olwen Barr's performance as Nance. The play's two performances in Wellington at the end of June received mixed reviews, one (by Bruce Mason in *The Dominion*) singling out Judd as 'the most memorable character in New Zealand stage literature'.[32] The other (by EHB in the *Evening Standard*) described the play as painting 'a disjointed, left-handed sort of picture': '[it] moves in stops and starts, strands characters then rescues them, makes sense then nonsense, switches from poetry to prose, from symbolism to reality, and develops clumsily'.[33] However, the publicity in Auckland effectively stopped the play in its tracks, as far as the further plans – for a tour of the South Island and, under the auspices of the Elizabethan Theatre Trust, of Australia – were concerned.

Barker, disappointed that the Auckland reviewers recognised neither the quality of the writing nor of at least some of the play's dramatic moments, maintained strong faith in it and urged Curnow to revise it both for print and for further productions. Sarah Campion, critiquing the play (but not the production) favourably in *Landfall*, also strongly advocated publication, given its complexity and the richness of its language, much of it difficult to take in on a single viewing.[34] Curnow approached both Blackwood Paul and the Pegasus Press, unsuccessfully,[35] about publishing a tidied-up version of the acting text, and the possibility of a substantial revision was on his mind for the next 20 years. He did not include it in his 'collected' edition of *Four Plays* in 1972, but mentioned in his preface that he might yet go back to it, 'to justify [Barker's] faith in the play and in the possibility of a *New Zealand* theatre',[36] and in 1977 when he sent John Coulson's model of the set design to Peter Harcourt for his theatre archives he commented: 'I still haven't given up the thought of revising the play.'[37] It was not until 1982, when he deposited an actor's copy of the script in the Alexander Turnbull Library, with revisions made during the course of production, that he seems finally to have abandoned the idea of ever taking the play further.

The Overseas Expert and a new Whim Wham selection

In the meantime, even before *Moon Section* had finished its North Island tour, Curnow had begun another play, 'to vindicate (or make amends for) *Moon Section*'.[38] Barker, again, was the begetter, and the new play was an altogether much lighter affair. Curnow gave his fullest account of its background to Brasch in October 1959, when it was close to completion:

> The title of the play is *Fool's Gold*; it's a 'satiric comedy of NZ city & family life', all
> at the expense, & I hope for the instruction, of the more pretentious & prosperous

commercial section: in *part*, my riposte to that Auckland element which (through *Herald* & *Star*) attempted to dodge the meaning of *Moon Section* by calling it 'symbolic', 'intellectual', 'puzzling' etc. *And* a few people who also said they couldn't understand it, but were quite sure it was 'dirty, sexy' or 'disgusting'. (I might have told you that at least 10 of the 20 *country* audiences on the subsequent tour had no difficulty at all about the meaning, only the half-baked city sophisticates, of whom the two press reporters happened to be prize examples.) So I am giving them now, if we get it on to the stage, something so open, of so indisputably recognizable a comedy genre, that they'll have to think of a new evasive manoeuvre, & that won't be easy for them.* [39]

The play was finished in February 1960, but never had a stage production, though it was performed twice on radio, in 1961 and 1963. Ngaio Marsh thought it 'would act well and rings distressingly true', but (as might be predicted given her own very different, somewhat idealised English 'overseas expert', the detective Roderick Alleyn, in her New Zealand detective fiction) took exception to the portrayal of Mandragora, the villain who passes himself off as a titled, wealthy English gentleman of impeccable manners and pedigree and is as utterly improbable as his name.[40] Curnow published it in *Four Plays* (1972), with a small number of updatings of topical references (including allusions to the Vietnam War), and spent some time in his preface drawing connections, somewhat improbably, between its themes and those of *The Axe*. Its closest connections are with the kinds of social satire at which Curnow excelled as Whim Wham, not only targeting the dogmatic conservatism and anti-intellectualism, desire for wealth and status, and obsequious reverence for English privilege of Auckland's self-styled social elite, but the more intimate details of language, cuisine, décor and dress fashion through which their pretentiousness is expressed.

In July and August 1959, while he was working on the first draft of *The Overseas Expert*, Curnow also completed a new selection of verses by Whim Wham, *The Best of Whim Wham*, for publication by Paul's Book Arcade for the Christmas market that year. Blackwood Paul had approached him two years earlier, and he eventually agreed to make the selection early in 1959. It was his first published selection since 1943, and he decided to confine his coverage to the 1950s, choosing roughly seventy pieces from more than 400 (the most recent written in July 1959) which he had contributed to both *The Press* and the *New Zealand Herald* since returning from his trip to England and the United States.

At the centre of the volume, as Robert Chapman astutely noted, is 'the world that welfare built',[41] the subject of many of Whim Wham's most pointed satirical

---

* The play was initially entitled *Fool's Gold* but later changed to *The Overseas Expert*, because *Fool's Gold* had already been used by someone else for a novel.

jibes. His target is not welfare itself, as a means of addressing poverty and material inequities in society, but the widespread assumption that the *only* human needs are material needs. Welfarism seemed to carry with it an increasing reliance on state control and bureaucratic interference as a means of 'normalising' all aspects of human behaviour (through the education system, censorship, control of drinking hours, and the like), and the emergence of a deeply conformist, deeply complacent society, hostile to any signs of difference and to foreigners, suspicious of the life of the mind and spirit, smugly believing itself to be God's Own Country specially favoured by providence. Beneath such platitudes – and the often angry insistence with which they were voiced, whenever challenged – Whim Wham detected a deep unease and uncertainty in New Zealand society. Both *Moon Section* and *The Overseas Expert*, with their very different styles and subject matter, were profoundly motivated by the kind of reading of New Zealand society in the 1950s which is to be found in these light verses, some of the best Whim Wham ever wrote.

Curnow's selection was weighted towards pieces of local interest, and unlike his earlier collections did not organise them under thematic or other headings, so that similar topics (drinking and eating habits, the punditry of educationists and politicians, the self-inflating rhetoric of the tourist industry, censorship) recur randomly throughout. Amongst the local topics he distributed a smallish number of the many globally focused pieces he wrote throughout the 1950s, whose main topics were the Cold War, nuclear testing and the armaments industry (especially the complicity of science in the arms race), and space exploration. Shortly before the collection appeared, Brasch by coincidence asked Curnow if he was planning one:

> I'd hoped to say a word to you too about your Whim Whams, which I read every week, and often with delighted admiration; that's an astonishing performance you're putting up, and, if I may say so, quite a contribution to social and political history. I've long been wanting to get someone to write about them, and hope I shall find the person in time; have you plans for another collection? It is such ages since the last. . . .[42]

'Do you know, I'd never supposed you thought much of *Whim Wham*', Curnow replied, '& for obvious reasons (the conditions of composition, etc)', adding, 'I've fallen into an oddly confused attitude to them – acquiescence, self-reproach, disgust & vanity all mixed up.'[43] The reviewer Brasch eventually found, Robert Chapman, gave Whim Wham the most intelligent discussion he ever received, and R.A. Copland in *Comment* captured the lively entertainment values essential to Whim Wham's effectiveness, which made 'his latest verse . . . almost as essential an item to be carried in the head on Saturday evenings as a handkerchief or cigarettes in the pocket'.[44] Curnow was to find that many of the pieces in the collection were reprinted again and again over succeeding years in anthologies, especially in the schools, and in books of social history.

In the second half of 1959, too late for inclusion in *The Best of Whim Wham*, the first three examples of what was to be a major, continuing topic for more than two decades appeared. They were devoted to a decision by the New Zealand Rugby Football Union that year to send to South Africa in 1960 an All Blacks team in which no Maori would be included. The Rugby Union had remained intransigent in the face of oppositional voices, as had Walter Nash's Labour Government, insisting that it would not interfere in sporting matters. For Whim Wham the issue became a key test of race relations *within* New Zealand, and a test of the country's willingness to *act* in a principled way against apartheid, in one of the few areas in which it could be effective on the international stage. Shortly before the All Blacks departed in May 1960, Curnow produced under his own name another satirical broadsheet, *On the Tour* (to be sung to the tune of 'On the Ball'*), published, like the *Huckster* broadsheets previously, by Bob Lowry at the Pilgrim Press.

Curnow's full title was *On the Tour: Verwoerd be our Vatchwoerd!, or, God Amend New Zealand*, and it was dedicated to T.H. (Tom) Pearce, 'Manager of the 1960 All White Rugby Team', 'in sincere if astonished Admiration of his exemplary Devotion to the Rugby Broederbond, unswayed by popular Clamour, undaunted by seditious Conspiracy among the nation's Religious Leaders, Catholic and Protestant, and unswerving before the Racial Intolerance of the Maori People'. Curnow hoped it would sell 2500 copies,[45] describing the poem to Glover as containing 'some pretty rough balladry, & some few prosodic atrocities',[46] and to Musgrove as 'a bit of abstract hatred, but heartfelt, in pretty rough-and-tumble verse'.[47] However, despite such desperate rhymes as Stellenbosch and brainwash, the stanza-plus-refrain structure worked effectively as satire in passages like the following – certainly, effectively enough for Curnow's daughter Belinda and Pearce's daughter Helen to both later enjoy remembering their fathers 'raving at each other over the telephone' and Pearce threatening to sue Curnow, in the wake of the satire's publication:[48]

> Let political Thought never sully our Sport,
> > Let us play on that purified Plane –
> Where Verwoerd's Police and their Guns keep the Peace,
> > While they join in our Rugby Refrain:

---

* Editor's note: 'On the Ball' was composed by Manawatu rugby forward Edward Secker in 1887. See the discussion of rugby and music in Ron Palenski, *Rugby: A New Zealand History*, Auckland University Press, Auckland, 2015, pp. 87–90. The cover of Curnow's *On the Tour* is reproduced in the third photographic insert of this book.

On the Tour, on the Tour, on the Tour,
For God's sake, let's keep the Game pure!
We can't win a Test if we're under Arrest,
So our Policy's plain for the Tour!

If there's Blood on the Hand we shall shake as we land,
     Soft Speeches will soap it away.
We'll be deaf to the Wails of the Nameless in Gaols,
     Where the White Fury battens its Prey:

On the Tour, on the Tour, on the Tour,
We're on Side with the 'Bok and the Boer.
While each poor censored Rag dribbles Lies through its Gag,
Their Press won't lack Space for the Tour!

Another collaboration with Lilburn: *The Axe* on radio

With the completion of *The Overseas Expert* early in 1960, Curnow had by no means exhausted his interest in drama at this time. Towards the end of 1959 he had arranged with the New Zealand Broadcasting Service (NZBS) to do a radio adaptation of *The Axe* and spent much of the 1959–60 summer vacation annotating, cutting and revising the text, as well as making an elaborate plan for musical themes and sound effects. Writing to Musgrove, he explained that all the changes made for the 1953 production had been retained, but he had 'trimmed away' 'redundant or superfluous words and phrases', and much of the 'excrescent writing, anxious over-writing'.[49] At the end of February 1960, when he sent the adapted text to the NZBS, he also wrote to Lilburn, asking him if he would consider composing the music for the production: 'I would be tremendously proud & delighted if you cared to do it. No-one else is within years of understanding the play as you do. . . .'[50] Lilburn assured him that he would be 'honoured to try my hand at some music for it'[51] once the final script had been settled on. The chief producer of the NZBS, William Austin, had assigned the task of production, and assistance with the adaptation, to Bernard Kearns in the Christchurch studio, a choice which delighted Curnow because Kearns had acted (as one of the chorus duo) in the original 1948 production in Christchurch.

Kearns got back to Curnow towards the end of August, in some trepidation, with detailed proposals for the adaptation, which were of two kinds: cuts to the script of less relevant material in order to get the play to a suitable length for radio, and many small adjustments throughout, where the stage text assumed *visual* knowledge, to ensure that information was clear (about *who* was speaking and to whom, for example) and to avoid any aside lasting longer than two lines, in the sound medium of radio. He also cut Curnow's scheme of 38 musical cues to 20.[52] Curnow was extremely impressed, regarding Kearns's major rearrangements as 'brilliant and, once seen, inevitable'. He was happy to rewrite occasional passages in instances where cuts had had to be made, making a few further small suggestions of his own, which he hoped confirmed what Kearns was aiming for in production, and adding, 'I rely absolutely on your final decision on all these points.'[53]

By November the script was ready for Lilburn, who wrote to Curnow asking him which version of the hymn 'Jesus Shall Reign' he had in mind to accompany Davida and the Christian missionary presence in the play. Curnow wrote back that it was not the Truro version but the alternative, 'the one with the congregational, evangelical rock 'n roll'.[54] But he was anxious (much as he liked his suggestion of 'Jesus Shall Reign') that Lilburn should simply make his own decisions about music for the play.

In fact, as Lilburn wrote later, the two-page list of musical instructions (Curnow's original 38 reduced to 20) which he first saw in November 'alarmed' him, and was far too demanding of resources, in any case, for the music division of the NZBS to cope with. However, as he worked on the play over the next two months, experimenting with different sounds and with makeshift facilities, he became increasingly excited at the possibilities:

> My intuitive reaction was to leave the play as uncluttered as possible, to use natural sounds, island sounds, and perhaps some authentic Cook Island drumming. So I go looking for these, Dominion Museum, Film Unit, NZBS archives, Polynesian Society, and draw almost complete blank....
>
> . . .
>
> Perhaps what I'm really after is electronic sounds, sinc-tones being put through their paces. I go back for more thorough listening to Stockhausen, Eimert and the boys. But this would be impossible because electronic studios with their specialized equipment don't exist outside Cologne, Milan and Tokyo. What strikes me forcibly though, is that this sound would again be wrong – European, machine-minded, hard-surfaced, sophisticated. My raw material must be natural sound, or something with the same quality.
>
> Then one evening I hear Fred Page giving a talk on the air on aspects of contemporary music, and in the course of it he reaches into the Steinway and plucks a string, and rolls a drumstick across some more, to illustrate John Cage. I draw my breath

and think, this is what I've been waiting for, and I can do it better! Here at least is a starting point – sound as unpremeditated as an oriental stringed instrument playing its ravishing single notes, and with the right lack of associations, timeless and not bound to place. That deep note might have come from some 'gong-tormented sea'.*

So I get Fred down to the studio again, with Ivan Sutherland who knows something of this world, to record, and together we stir up the resonant bowels of the piano, a free improvisation with bare hands, drumsticks, and toothbrush on the high strings. The tape, played back, was vivid in colour, and half a dozen technicians gathered around in excitement. I went off with it feeling elated.[55]

The result was a remarkable production in late September 1961, which Curnow was able to hear soon after his return from the United States. For Lilburn, 1961 was, as his biographer has written, 'a watershed year'.[56] *The Axe* had stimulated Lilburn to produce his first work in the new medium of what was then called *musique concrète*, music based on artificially manipulated natural sounds (as distinct from electronic music, based on electronically generated sounds), and it was closely followed, in the same year, by the last and greatest of his works for traditional instruments, his *Symphony No. 3*. Writing to Lilburn immediately after he listened to the performance Curnow was deeply moved:

> I had never heard *The Axe* till Friday night, & I mean *never*, & your music fulfilled all my best hopes; a most subtle & marvellous enhancement of the play – lucky play & lucky author, to deserve the work! So proud to have your *company* & confidence again – & can't describe the experience without vain words – your thrilling *sounds* & the familiar words of the play – had not expected to be so moved. The music *acted* – & so did the actors themselves.[57]

There were a number of other performances of Lilburn's musical settings of Curnow's work during the late 1950s and early 1960s. His setting of 'The Changeling' in a three-part series – *Three Poems of the Sea* – suggested by Maria Dronke and composed for her in 1958 (the other poems were the ballad 'Sir Patrick Spens' and 'Ariel's Song' from *The Tempest*) received performances from the Alex Lindsay String Orchestra in 1959, and again in 1960. Listening to a disc of Dronke's reading, Curnow commented to Lilburn:

> Your music, lovely in itself (I never have words to describe music), seems wholly right as a reading of the poem – a poem I'm never sure of how I read (I mean understand)

---

* W.B. Yeats, 'Byzantium' (1930).

myself. M's speaking of the poem – first time I wondered, then it took me, as much by its skill at first as by anything else; then some sensitively felt & pictured qualities, then one or two touches of the more *conscious* thing – on the edge of stagi-ness, but so are parts of the poem! Virtuoso work by Maria, all round, & who else, even liking the poem as much, could have brought it off, as she *has*.[58]

At this time, also, 'Landfall in Unknown Seas' was recorded on disc for the first time, the featured work on the first LP of New Zealand music made by A.H. & A.W. Reed on their new Kiwi label. Curnow read the poem especially for the recording, and the music was again by the Alex Lindsay String Orchestra. 'I felt the pressure of the studio, & the *finality* of that disc-making', he wrote to Lilburn, 'had 2–3 shots at parts one & two, but part three is just as it came the first time.'[59] Lilburn was impressed by the result:

> Ugly ducklings into swans, rare trees which bloom after 20 years. I found it strange & exciting today to listen to the *Landfall* recording, moving to hear you speak the poem so firmly as you do, to have something put so well into permanent form & reach out to those many for whom it was intended.[60]

And Curnow himself was pleased, after receiving a copy of the finished disc in mid-June:

> I hardly know what to say about it, except echo your letter; that there it is, now, for so many people to hear; that I can't remember, ever, hearing so much that is in the music, or being so moved; & if I shall never speak the poem well enough, I think this reading isn't less than the best I can do. I wish you could have seen the excitement of a few – Carl Stead [sic] in particular – who have heard the work for the first time from this recording. It is all so familiar (if never *all* familiar) to us, that I expect you have been delighted, as I have, by the response of people to whom it is quite new.[61]

Preparing for leave, 1961

In the first term of 1960 Curnow heard that he had at last been successful in his application for sabbatical leave, and was granted leave for the year 1961, with a travel grant of £300. He had been lecturing full-time in an understaffed depart-ment for ten years, and was exhausted. '[T]he last ten years' unremitting labour in this learnery have brought me, this year, almost to a dead halt', he wrote to Jim Walton. 'I crawl to my lectures like a whipped cur & hate books.'[62] During the previous two years the efforts he had expended on negotiating the impasse with authors and Penguin over his anthology, and his unevenly received forays into the fraught territory of local theatre, had also taken their toll. He was drinking heavily, and his marriage had reached breaking point. To Walton he explained how desperately he needed to get a break from the insularity of the local scene in which he felt bogged down:

> Auckland in particular, N.Z. in general, have been too much with me these last few years. We haven't got on very well together. My poems are too dry & stringy for them (both Auckland papers, anyway, completely ignored my last book – 1958 – though TLS [*Times Literary Supplement*] & one or two others were kind). My plays bewilder or disgust them: both papers panned *Moon Section*, ignorantly & malevolently, when it went on as last year's Auckland Festival play. . . . And I've had to fight four years to ensure the integrity of the *Penguin Book of N. Z. Verse* – against every sort of under-hand sabotage. . . . I enjoy fights: but this one has been too long, too sordid, too exhausting, like trench warfare.[63]

Financial circumstances, as in 1949, dictated the arrangements Curnow made for his leave. All of his salary was required to support his family at home, and the £300 grant to support his leave expenses meant that travel to England (his preferred option) was impossible, as was the possibility of spending the full year away. He decided to try to arrange a trip of six months to the United States, where the possibility of finding additional funding to meet his living costs was better. The Carnegie Corporation (which had assisted him in 1950) informed him that it was not possible to have a second grant, but with support from Brasch, Joseph (acting head of the English Department while Musgrove was on leave), and his old friend Richard Eberhart in the United States, he was awarded a Fulbright travel grant. Eberhart also spoke to Robert Richman, director of the Institute of Contemporary Arts in Washington, whom Curnow had met in 1950. Richman immediately offered Curnow a six-week fellowship at the ICA, worth US$1,000, and promised to arrange several 'one-week visiting professorships' to American universities.

With these arrangements in hand Curnow could at last look to make travel arrangements, sailing from Auckland to Vancouver via Fiji at the beginning of March 1961 and returning later in September that year. He hoped to complete most of his money-earning assignments during the first half of his leave, and to spend the rest of it based in New York. New York was central to the main research task he had mentioned in his application for leave, which was to reconstruct Dylan Thomas's first visit to the United States in 1950, in order to set the record (of Brinnin and others) straight. But New York was also central to his creative interests, and of these, drama remained exceptionally strong: he especially wanted to discover everything he could about new theatrical impulses, to see as much contemporary theatre as he could.

In the six months before his departure Curnow had two unfinished projects that he wished to complete, the manuscript of Mason's collected poems and a selected poems of his own which he had been invited by Dan Davin to submit to Oxford University Press. Curnow had raised the possibility of a selected poems when Davin visited New Zealand in 1959, imagining a slim volume with perhaps 30 poems chosen from the 1940s (nothing from the 1930s) and a dozen or so from his most recent volume, *Poems 1949–57*, and promising a manuscript by October 1959. However, he seems to have felt a lack of confidence in making the selection, which was not at all relieved by the recent reception of *Moon Section*. '[S]o much seems horribly jejune & infantile to me now', he wrote of his earlier work.[64] He also recalled Mason's attitude to his own earlier work:

> I remember how some years ago it was *impossible* to interest Ronald Mason much in any plans for publishing his [poetry]; & I have been a little surprised & alarmed to find myself showing symptoms of the same complaint. . . . I have shaken it off. . . . I am indeed very, very much interested, & more grateful than I can say that you are willing to channel them.[65]

It was to be another sixteen months before he finally sent the manuscript off to Oxford, just days before his departure for the United States, and more than a year after that, in 1962, before *A Small Room with Large Windows* appeared. For the next dozen years this slim volume of 50 poems, heavily selective from his earlier work, provided the only immediate access to any of his poetry, all ten volumes of which were out of print.

Shortly before his departure Curnow also sent the completed manuscript of Mason's collected poems to Glover, with a newly written introduction which he had taken many pains over, including, he wrote to Glover, 'five prolonged telephone talks with Ron to get all the facts as straight as they need be'. The 'facts' related especially to the datings of poems, which required a more complex account of Mason's poetic development, he felt, than had been advanced by critics like Eric McCormick. He added that he had read the whole introduction to Mason, 'who is delighted with it: especially in the matter of the 'thirties & politics, the revolution, etc., on which McC[ormick] has jumped to quite wrong conclusions insufficiently based on the facts & the dates'.[66] Glover was also delighted with the introduction:

> I think it's all pretty top line & must go in . . . [despite] that touch of the funeral oration [which] will be completely removed by a separate publisher's note. . . . It puts

Ron so much more authoritatively on the map than a barer presentation would . . . .
The detective work is fascinating.[67]

However, there were to be further delays in the production of the book, and
Curnow returned to it again before it finally appeared later in 1962. 'I only hope',
Mason wrote to Curnow then, as further details were being resolved, that 'the
miracle has happened and we are ending up with the immaculate conception.'[68]

The late 1950s and 1960s had seen numerous changes as Curnow's family grew
up. Wystan had left home in 1958 and was attending university at Auckland,
hoping to complete his Master's degree in English in 1962 and go overseas to
the United States. 'He has turned out', Curnow wrote proudly to Jim Walton,
'to have an excellent critical head (for pictures, I'd say, the best in the place),
writes well & should paint well too.'[69] Belinda had also left school, and in 1960
was studying at Elam School of Fine Arts, where she met Bruce Morley and
became pregnant, marrying him in December that year. Betty's plans for the
wedding 'were well advanced before Allen was even told of the pregnancy',[70] and
he was deeply upset about what had happened. Tim in 1960 was in fifth form at
Westlake High School, and was to leave at the end of the following year.

In 1960 Tony's marriage to Ursula broke down, and both Tony and Curnow
were concerned about how their mother was likely to react to a situation which
(as Curnow put it) 'she is going to find pretty intolerable'.[71] No doubt Curnow
was concerned, also, with the second blow she would receive, when (as was inevitable) she heard of his own marriage breakdown. He thought Tony had informed
his mother far too directly and 'abruptly' about the breakdown, and too readily
allowed himself to accept the blame for it. Curnow's attitude towards his mother
was more protective; Tony thought her more resilient, and seems to have felt less
need to specially justify himself.

In 1960 Curnow also arranged for a number of alterations to the house at
Herbert Street (begun much earlier but unfinished) to be completed. To Jeny,
who this year had herself left her family home and taken a flatette in Radnor,
Waterloo Quadrant, then moved to a better flat at Courtville, Parliament Street,
this development seemed to be delaying their permanently living together.
Perhaps the hardest parting Curnow and Jeny ever had to make from each other
was when he left for the United States in early March 1961. Curnow's life had
changed radically after his first trip overseas in 1949–1950. After this second trip,
it was to change even more radically, and permanently.

Chapter Twenty-one

United States,
March–September 1961

*[S]ince no man is himself alone, but a member of mankind, the poem,
if it is new and good, finds and transmits some news about us all.[1]*

Washington spring, April 1961

Curnow left New Zealand in early March 1961, sailing on the *Orsova* to
Vancouver, with stops at Suva and Honolulu. It was an uneventful voyage, except
for the arrival in Honolulu of a letter from his colleague Bill Pearson enclosing a
letter drafted by Stead on Curnow's behalf in response to a long, hostile review
by Baxter of the Penguin anthology which had appeared in *Education*[2] soon after
Curnow's departure.

Since its appearance at the end of 1960 the book had attracted many reviews, all
of them recognising its significance in the country's cultural history, and most of
them acknowledging the force and interest of the selection and the introduction, as
well as the calibre of its scholarship. Curnow had already decided not to enter into
any public debate about the book except on matters of fact, trusting that in the end
it would stand or fall on its own merits. He made no exception for Baxter's review,
despite (as he wrote to Jeny) 'its half-baked & partisan views', and declined Stead's
invitation to respond, adding, 'I can't have the least suspicion of collusion with
friends to defend my *book*'.[3] On one matter of fact, he responded to a letter from
Charles Doyle in *Education* the following month,[4] to correct a misapprehension by

Doyle that his work had been withdrawn at his own request, informing readers that he had decided not to include any poem by Doyle long before receiving the request.[5]

In Vancouver, Curnow visited the University of British Columbia for lunch and dinner with Professor Roy Daniels, and then took a train to San Francisco, where he met up again with Ruth Witt-Diamant, who was still, as in 1950, at State College and head of the San Francisco Poetry Center. While there, he discussed New Zealand poetry with members of the English Department, gave a lecture and reading to Witt-Diamant's students, and recorded poems for the department's sound archives. San Francisco was a city which Curnow found immensely attractive, not only for its famous City Lights bookshop and other bookstores, but for its jazz and café ambience. He left there on 22 March, travelling via New Orleans, where he stopped for a night and a day, enjoyed the jazz scene, and observed student protest pickets against segregation as the civil rights movement gained momentum. He arrived at his main destination, Washington, early on a spring morning on 27 March 1961.

Curnow spent two months based in Washington as a Visiting Fellow attached to the Institute of Contemporary Arts, whose director was still Robert Richman. He was excited and stimulated by the people he met, among them fellow writers and artists, academics and members of the political and diplomatic world of the recently inaugurated Kennedy administration. His confidence received a much-needed boost from the courtesies extended to him. His poetry and opinions were respected by others, and his interest in the intellectual life simply accepted as part of normal, civilised discourse. Although he found the round of engagements during this two-month period exhausting, it was quite different from the feeling of being ground down by petty hostilities and jealousies, by personal attacks on his integrity as an editor and critic, and by the pressure of overwork in an understaffed department, which he had experienced during the previous three years in Auckland.

From the moment of his arrival, Curnow was treated as a distinguished guest at the ICA. On his first day he attended a lunch at the Library of Congress for the Mexican poet and diplomat Octavio Paz, and that evening dined at the Cosmos Club with Richman, who then took him to a lecture and reading by one of America's most admired poets and novelists, Robert Penn Warren. Afterwards they went to a small party for Warren at the home of Milton and Zaro Starr, from which he finally arrived home at 1 a.m. Some welcome news on his first day in Washington was a letter from Davin to say that John Bell, poetry editor of OUP, liked Curnow's selected poems very much and looked forward to publishing them.[6] The next day he visited his old friend Richard Eberhart and his wife Betty. Much sought after on the burgeoning and well-paid poet-in-residence university circuits, Eberhart was coming to the end of a two-year stint as Poetry Fellow at the Library of Congress.

Curnow spent a week over Easter staying with the Starrs, 'two of the best Americans alive'.[7] Milton had been at Vanderbilt University with Robert Penn Warren, John Crowe Ransom, Allen Tate and Merrill Moore, members of the Nashville Fugitive movement, and was now managing a chain of theatres in the South which he had inherited. On Easter Sunday the Eberharts took Curnow to Georgetown to meet the 'really great critic & poet'[8] Allen Tate, whom he had missed seeing on his earlier trip. They 'clicked at once over the evening high-balls'.[9] Tate was a close friend of Dan Davin, and interested in the possibility of Wystan's becoming a postgraduate student in his own English Department at the University of Minnesota. He took Curnow to visit the novelist Katherine Anne Porter, 'a delightful old lady'.[10] 'What a fine real man', Curnow described Tate to Stead, 'with an equally real touch (just a touch) of Old South *politesse*.'[11]

Curnow's first formal engagement was a public reading at the ICA's Meridian House on the Friday after Easter (7 April), which he approached with his usual trepidation. The afternoon before, he went for a long walk to the zoo, where he 'gazed at some enormous *owls*, looking absurdly like *owls*', storing up a memory that was to be used later in a poem entitled 'Friendship Heights'. The reading itself, to a full house of about 150, went extremely well, especially of 'Spectacular Blossom'. Immediately after the reading Curnow began preparing the paper he had to give later in the month to the Third International Congress of Artists and Writers. He was scheduled to visit the University of Pennsylvania in Philadelphia from 17–22 April, so the bulk of the paper needed to be written in the week or so beforehand. The assignment was 'terrifying & unexpected', he wrote to Wystan.[12]

The general theme of the International Congress was provided by C.P. Snow's influential Rede Lecture 'The Two Cultures' given in 1959, which had argued that there was a widening and disabling gap between the humanities and the sciences. A variety of renowned speakers had been assembled to deliver six papers over four days: Professor Milton Babbitt, a musicologist at Princeton, and British historian Arnold Toynbee on the first day; Curnow and Dr Harold Urey, a Nobel Prize physicist, on the second day; architect and designer Charles Eames and C.P. Snow himself on the third day. Other distinguished guests included Aaron Copland, Nadine Gordimer, Octavio Paz, Richard Eberhart, the magazine editors Robie Macauley (*Kenyon Review*) and Robert Mueller (*Poetry* (Chicago)), and the Yale philosopher Paul Weiss, who were invited to discuss and debate the papers given the previous evening on each following morning.

Each speaker addressed the relationship of their own specialist interest to the general theme, and Curnow's topic was 'Poetry and Other Cultures'. Given the company in which he was expected to perform, and the importance of the event in Washington's cultural calendar, Curnow's trepidation is understandable. Being selected to give the paper, from amongst the distinguished writers attending the

Congress, let alone from others in the United States who might have been invited, was a remarkable tribute to the esteem in which he was held by Richman and those (like Eberhart, Tate, Cleanth Brooks and others) whom Richman had consulted.

Curnow had completed a draft of the paper by the time he left Washington by bus, on Monday 17 April, for Philadelphia, where his host was Dr Tom Haviland of the English Department. At a faculty function the following day he met Eric and Birgitta Sellin, who became long-standing friends. The next three days were frantically busy, with two-hour classes for creative writing students followed up by individual consultations, a public lecture and reading, and a dinner with English professors. Curnow also made time for an interview with the student newspaper (an enthusiastic item, with some grotesque misreportings, including the spelling of A.R.D. Fairburn's name – to Glover's huge merriment later – as Art Furbend). He was greatly impressed by the university itself, as well as its location. His visit was highly successful and Sellin wrote to him shortly afterwards:

> Here all has subsided back into routine since your wonderful whirlwind passage through provincial Philadelphia. We both grew very fond of you and when you left there was a sense of emptiness in the various classrooms, lecture halls, and automobiles you occupied . . . . The students you met here during your stay were all very impressed and thought you were magnificent . . . as did I.[13]

He had not known that his visit was of the nature of a pilot project for the university, which did not at that stage have a full-scale artists-in-residence programme, and its success did lead to the establishment of a permanent programme.

Curnow arrived back in Washington late on Saturday 22 April, to face the busiest and most testing week of his overseas trip. He spent all Sunday and most of Sunday night finalising his paper for the International Congress, a nineteen-hour stretch. On Monday the Congress participants met each other and the press and then attended a formal luncheon, where he particularly enjoyed the company of Milton Babbitt, Paul Weiss and Robie Macauley. In the evening the first two papers were given by Babbitt on 'Music and Science' and Toynbee on 'Civilisation and Quantity', Curnow commenting on Toynbee, 'that windbag', 'freewheeling & talking a lot of utter commonplaces & truisms'.[14] He left early, to catch up on some sleep.

The next morning he worked on his paper again for several hours, then joined the late-morning discussion session on the previous evening's papers, where he found a ready ally, against Toynbee, in Weiss. After the formal lunch he walked into the city, found a bar, and wrote a concluding paragraph to his paper, before meeting up with Mueller and making his way to the Lisner Auditorium at George Washington University at 5.15 a.m. to address an audience of 500 to 600 people.

Harold Urey spoke first, and irrelevantly, on the use of science to win the Cold War, then Curnow:

> [T]hey all listened like mice; & the best part, afterwards, was both Weiss & Babbitt, & a French architect, Beer, & Eliot Coleman (poetry teacher at Johns Hopkins) & several complete strangers, all pressing round & thanking & congratulating really enthusiastically. Seeing that I'd contradicted Snow, dissented from Toynbee, & ignored Urey, I was pretty glad of all this support. – Oh what a *brag* this all sounds, but it was, it *was* one of my most successful appearances ever & if one *is* faced with an occasion like that, one *must* bring it off; I was glad I'd put the work into it.[15]

The papers were followed by an 'InterAmerican' Music concert including new, commissioned works by Aaron Copland and by a young composer, Robert Evett, which particularly appealed to Curnow, followed by a reception for both composers. Curnow arrived home at 1.30 a.m., to prepare himself for the debate and discussion of his own and Urey's papers at Meridian House later that morning. 'I hardly know if the chap doing all this is me', he wrote later in the day to Jeny, 'or some other man of the same name.'[16]

During the discussion he had to deflect an effort at a put-down by Lady Snow (Pamela Hansford-Johnson), who wondered if Snow's position had been fully understood, and responded that his paper was not concerned with literary crusades, 'but with poetry & how the proliferation of knowledge, science, etc., concerned the poets'. But both Toynbee and Snow himself drew attention to points he had made, Weiss was 'formidable', and he felt at the end that he had 'weathered the storm'. His paper was also publicised in the *Washington Star*, and prompted the French architect Abraham Beer to say that he'd never known any ICA fellow to have such a publicity success in Washington.[17]

Curnow's address: 'Poetry and Knowledge'

Like a number of his unpublished writings, Curnow's address to the Third International Congress of Artists and Writers deserved a much wider audience than those who heard it at the Lisner Auditorium. He offered a set of reflections on two related questions: How much knowledge does a poet need? Is poetry of itself a way of knowing – a different way of saying what we know already, but something we wouldn't otherwise think of saying?

> I think the two questions belong together; the way we answer one will affect the way we answer the other. If poetry is regarded as being itself a means of getting at

truth, of finding out and passing on knowledge, then it would seem that the poet's curiosity, if any, about other kinds of knowledge and of their appropriate disciplines – of the sciences, say, or even the special disciplines of literary scholarship itself – need be no more nor less than the curiosity of the interested layman or private person: he will be chiefly occupied with his own kind of inquiry and his own mode of knowing and reporting.

But if poetry *cannot* be thought of as being itself a way of extending our knowledge – why, then, obviously, the poet's privilege is of a more limited kind; his licence is endorsed by a higher authority; and in a world where the prestige of science is enhanced every day by results which a child can appreciate, it will then seem that poetry – having no discoveries of its own, no part to play in any technological revolution – can have no future except as the solace or amusement of the few who have the time or the taste for it. And it will not amuse many for long, or any minds of the better sort, unless the poet can make some effort to appear multi-competent in various branches of modern learning, including the sciences. His anxiety about knowing *enough* will become acute. The question, 'How much knowledge does a poet need?' then could very well reduce him to the desperate answer, 'very nearly everything' – if he is to be sure of not writing nonsense in a world where inspirational guesswork or cranky whims won't wash any longer, and if his utterances are to be respected, as indeed many people today still do respect them, without any clear idea why they do so.

After brief references to Yeats and the linguist and critic I.A. Richards, he then spent some time discussing Eliot's 'almost comically astonishing' use of a scientific analogy in his famous essay 'Tradition and the Individual Talent' (1919) – the introduction of 'a bit of finely filiated platinum' into a chamber containing oxygen and sulphur dioxide in order to produce sulphurous acid – to describe the poetic process. The platinum – inert, neutral and unchanged during the process – is figured as 'the mind of the poet', depersonalised, and the resulting fusion of elements, the poem, generates a new 'art emotion', in readers, 'which has its life in the poem and not in the history of the poet'. Eliot thus invoked science not only in order to 'cut the individual poet down to size', but to bolster 'a calculated strategic surrender of all the time-honoured claims made for poets and poetry' – 'the claims to inspiration, to revelatory or prophetic powers, to the custodianship of ideals or morality, to the championship of truth, and to any and every kind of specially privileged status for poetic utterance as such'.

Curnow thus read Eliot's essay as offering an emphatic 'No' to his second question. The poet does not in any way 'extend knowledge', and Eliot's use of a scientific analogy to make this point is symptomatic of the anxieties poets felt about its power and prestige, its domination of the domain of 'knowledge'. He also read the essay as answering the first question ('How much knowledge does a poet need?') in ways that illustrated his contention that those who could *not* see poetry as itself an act of knowledge were likely to face the occupational anxiety of feeling they needed to know 'very nearly everything' about the knowledge other disciplines have discovered. Eliot's poet may be entirely depersonalised, even eliminated, from the poetic process, but nevertheless has to have absorbed 'into his bones' the whole history of literature from Homer to the present, a task requiring 'great labour' and bringing with it 'great difficulties and responsibilities'.

Furthermore, Eliot's essay, seen this way, was but one example – if 'strange, extreme, almost panic-stricken' – of dominant thinking about poetic theory since the mid-nineteenth century, which amounted to 'a kind of dismayed or defiant surrender of poetic pretensions' felt to be 'hopeless or absurd, in the face of scientific advance'. 'With this', he went on, in an extremely interesting elaboration, 'went a kind of retrenchment programme in poetic theory': 'this is one way of regarding all the varieties of symbolism, imagism, the poetry of social revolt, the nationalist poetry, poetry of faith, and the poets' poetry'.

At this point Curnow was ready to challenge at least one or two of Snow's propositions about the two cultures, though he chose to work not with Snow's famous essay on the subject, 'The Two Cultures and the Scientific Revolution', but with Snow's definition of the 'distorted stereotype' of scientists held by 'the literary culture' in a note to his novel *The Search* (1934): 'brash, shallowly optimistic, indifferent to the individual condition, lacking all sense of tragedy, unemotional, naïve, asexual'. Curnow responded that nothing in his reading of the best of the poets (not only his own 'eminent examples', Eliot and Yeats) had suggested to Curnow such 'unreflective dislike and contempt' for the scientist; quite the reverse, in fact: Eliot's essay 'errs, rather, on the side of a wholly misplaced reverence for science'.

Curnow shifted tack subtly at this point and argued that contrary to the 'No' of his early theory, Eliot, like all excellent modern poets, wrote poems *as if* poetry extends our knowledge, '*as if* ', Curnow went on, 'there were not two cultures but one, and one in which it is perhaps a little better recognized than it was a century ago, that knowledge is of more than one order, and that a unity of man's intellectual life – if it is a possible or desirable aspiration – can perhaps be sought only in religion if anywhere at all, and in these days without much hope in *that* quarter'.

The remainder of Curnow's paper offered a series of suggestive ways in which science and poetry might be seen as aspects of *one* culture. He gave two anonymous examples of scientists he knew at Auckland University College (in the fields of medicine and nuclear science), and could only remember two instances of a 'cultural gap'. The first was when he could not grasp a simplified explanation of the half-life of an atomic particle, which deeply distressed his friend, who prided himself on his simplifications, and didn't allow for Curnow's defective math-ematical sense. The second related to institutional fights between the arts and the sciences for priority at the university, and he wondered whether the *perception* of two cultures had more to do with anxieties and tensions over financial and other resources than with any 'actual' split. On one particular issue – Snow's belief in *educational* remedies – he was deeply sceptical: 'I close my eyes with holy dread, at the thought of the educational busybodies and witch-doctors brandishing their lecture notes & closing in for the kill.' Such a pedagogy would itself become a 'monster' devouring and displacing the real work in the disciplines of the arts and sciences, for which there was never enough time, though he added that his scepticism might well be a result of his New Zealand experience:

> Are these suspicions of mine unworthy, or absurd? Perhaps they can be partly traced to my being a New Zealander, and therefore possibly more conscious than most of the defects of a highly centralized, highly idealistic and somewhat doctrinaire edu-cation system. I believe in a great deal that educationists promise us, but I don't think they can save the world.

Curnow concluded his paper by returning again to the ways in which poetry could be said to 'extend our knowledge', though its knowledge is not of the same order as physical science:

> If it actually did no more than observe and represent for us some part of the sen-sations and perceptions of a single person, the poet himself, in some aspect of his uniqueness, it could be said to contribute to knowledge of man and his world. But since no man is himself alone, but a member of mankind, the poem, if it is new and good, finds and transmits some news about us all.

If poets' discoveries come 'capriciously, haphazardly', and if some poetry 'seems to indulge the sheer delight in design, rather than the passion for knowing and realising', he believed that at least some scientists (perhaps especially mathema-ticians) would recognise in such impulses something akin to their own processes of discovery:

> I'm not trying to make out that poetry is a kind of science, or science a kind of poetry. There is the obvious difference that in poetry new discoveries never supersede old ones. But poetry does name things, identify them and set them in an order that the mind can apprehend and employ in its dealings with reality; perhaps it can name more things than science can, and plenty of things no science has any thought of naming; and in doing all this it takes infinite pains to be accurate.

It remained for him to answer, for himself, his first question, 'How much knowledge does a poet need?' His answer was vintage Curnow, again suggesting the likelihood of a similarity in the experiences of poets and scientists:

> We can only observe that some [poets] can do with a great deal of it, others with astonishingly little. The good poet always knows exactly enough when he composes a good poem. It is part of his art, to learn to free his mind from every sort of unwanted fact or preconception or preoccupation, in order to give exclusive and total attention to the area of experience or the disturbance in his own being which has provided him with the occasion for a poem. I wonder if scientists, some of them, don't have to perform some similar act of concentration and elimination.

In conclusion he offered as an example of such 'freeing of the mind' Yeats's 'superb lyric', 'The Dawn', from *The Wild Swans at Coole*. The 'ignorance' the poem espouses ('I would be ignorant as the dawn') involves precisely that act of concentration and elimination which frees the poet's mind 'for that pure act of apprehension: when nothing is known and all is pure potency and energy of apprehension'. Even the pedantic Babylonian astronomers of that poem, Curnow suggested, if new knowledge were to be discovered, 'had also in some sense to dismiss knowledge – that is, all past knowledge – and strive to become as ignorant and wanton as the poet would wish to be'.[18]

Washington: poetry and politics, May 1961

The paper was eloquent and elegant, its polemic against Snow subtly argued, and its re-reading of Eliot's famous essay lively and provocative. Curnow had every reason to feel a huge morale boost from its reception, 'to discover one's mind at ease & respected', he commented to Betty.[19] The day after the Congress finished he gave a joint seminar at George Washington University, with Nadine Gordimer and Octavio Paz, on the theme of 'the two cultures', and was delighted when Paz picked out 'Spectacular Blossom' from the Penguin anthology: 'He pointed to the line, "The victims are always beautiful" & said, *twice*, "that is beautiful!" How much I want that poem to be praised!'[20]

After the Congress, Curnow had only a week's respite before travelling to Wilmington, Ohio, for the second of his poet-in-residence assignments. During that time he worked on a poem, 'the first serious one', he wrote to Jeny, 'since "A Small Room" . . . really not at all personal except that it expresses a good deal of Washington, Congress, etc'.[21] He was fascinated by Washington and the question of how far it had grown, or could grow, 'to live culturally as a *metropolis*'.[22] As a

capital, an abstraction, a seat of power, it was a location of 'functions & func-
tionaries, processes & projects, powers & principalities, a control top with its
lights, levers, dials & buttons, which may charm the naïf spectator or citizen in
inverse proportion to his understanding of what goes on'.[23] He was particularly
fascinated by the abstract symbolism of the Lincoln Memorial, the Washington
Obelisk and the Capitol:

> Can that grandiosely conceived triad … – so superbly raised & distanced, yet somehow
> embarrassing to the imagination – be felt to express the city *itself*, not merely to be
> located there, as if the American spirit had needed such massive symbols, as it needed
> a seat of Govt; and as if the city had been, as it were, co-opted to serve for a site?[24]

The poem Curnow worked on, which he called 'Capitoline Spring', was
longish and in four sections, like 'A Small Room', 'all impressionistic about
Washington', he wrote to Jeny, though the impressions were 'all compressed &
synthetic', including a spring thunderstorm bursting over Friendship Heights
and the Lincoln Memorial, its energies reflecting pulses in the blood of young
lovers and in the spring flowering of trees, in the face of which the stone
monument remains impassive, stillborn. By 'synthetic' Curnow meant that many
of the impressions belonged to different occasions but were brought together for
the purposes of the poem. Curnow was less sure about the poem after he had
given it to Mueller for consideration for *Poetry* (Chicago), Mueller eventually
returning it with the comment that readers thought it needed more work.
Although Mueller was interested to see the poem again, Curnow put it aside. It
would be a decade before he returned to it, raiding it for other poems (especially
'Bourdon' and 'Do It Yourself') in *Trees, Effigies, Moving Objects* (1972).

On 7 May, Curnow set off for the tiny township of Wilmington, travelling
to Ohio by car with Mueller who was returning to Chicago after the Congress.
It was an exhausting eighteen-hour trip overnight, westwards across West
Virginia. Arriving at 9.30 a.m. on a Sunday, he slept most of the day and
later met his host, Joel Climenhaga, a creative writing teacher at the small,
650-student, mainly residential Wilmington College. His work there included
one-to-one interviews with students, a formal lecture ('my usual, an account of
NZ through readings of the poems, the Maori first, then Mason, Fairburn &
Denis: – magpies, as always, a big success'),[25] a creative writing seminar, and a
formal reading of his own poems. Like his visit to the University of Pennsylvania
the previous month, it was an unusual success, and on 14 May he returned by
train to Washington for his last three weeks at the ICA. After two months of
demanding work and travel he could now look forward to an interval when he
would have more time to himself.

The period Curnow spent in Washington was marked by difficult crises for the Kennedy administration, with a communist insurgency in Laos and a crisis in relations with Cuba under Castro, whose socialisation programme led to retaliatory measures by the US government and an abortive invasion by Florida-based, CIA-trained Cuban exiles at the Bay of Pigs in April. Curnow found that he had 'to walk a bit warily' with many of his American friends like Richman and Eberhart, established liberals and strong supporters of the Kennedy administration, about which he felt considerable disillusion. With Richman he found it easier to negotiate their differences, but relations became somewhat strained with Eberhart, and were exacerbated by his wife, who Curnow believed strongly influenced her husband's blatant self-promotion amongst Washington's cultural and social elites.

However, if Curnow imagined that he would have more time to himself for the rest of his stay in Washington he was quite wrong. He had a memorable evening with Robert Graves, accompanying Maida Richman to dinner with him at the home of Francis and Katherine Biddle (Katherine Biddle was the poet Katherine Garrison Chapin he had met on his previous US visit, and Biddle himself, 'a fine man and mind' according to Curnow,[26] had been a member of the Roosevelt administration). He then accompanied Graves to a poetry reading, and after that to a small party, including the composer Robert Evett, at Marcella du Pont's place. He enjoyed Graves's company, though he had not expected to (remembering Graves's 'sneers at Yeats in his essay, "These be thy Gods"'), and was extremely impressed by Graves's reading of his own poems, especially his short love poems – 'about the most civilized [reading] I can remember hearing'.[27] To Glover he wrote that Graves was 'a fine man & worth 10 Toynbees & all the Snows of yesteryear'.[28]

Before leaving Washington, Curnow had a half-hour television interview and reading on NETV (National Education TV), which went out to 50 stations in the US. He had asked Joel Climenhaga to come from Wilmington to conduct the interview. It was Curnow's first television appearance ever, and he was understandably nervous:

> I did the best I could; Joel draws me out with a few questions, & I reply & illustrate by reading a few poems, mostly gazing steadily (as directed) into the big square eye of the camera, & feeling the heat of the lights. It was all done sitting; in two fancy blue-padded modern chairs, with a coffee table in front of us. I read Unhistoric Story, Tomb of an Ancestor, Spectacular Blossom, Jack-in-the-Boat, & A Small Room. It prolonged the ordeal rather, that they have to cut & stop to reload the cameras twice during the 30 min; & you have to remember when they start again if you had your legs crossed or a book in hand, etc.[29]

He also had a long-delayed meeting over lunch at the Cosmos Club with New Zealander Sir Leslie Munro (invited as a guest by Richman), about whose time as president of the United Nations General Assembly Curnow had heard the most positive comments throughout his stay in Washington. Several days later Curnow attended a dinner in his honour put on at the New Zealand Embassy by the ambassador George Laking and his wife Patricia:

> The Embassy dinner party was very informal, & would have been pretty dull but for one young (well, late thirties) couple, Bill & Mary Bundy (she a daughter of Dean Acheson [former Secretary of State in the Truman administration], & made a fuss of me, which I suppose is why I liked them best....)[30]

Curnow saw a great deal of the Bundys during his last ten days in Washington. The relationship gave him an insight into the inner workings of the political circles close to the Kennedy administration. Bill Bundy was a deputy assistant secretary of defence for international affairs and worked at the Pentagon, a 'political appointee' (as Curnow describes him in his evocation of the Kennedy era, 'A Framed Photograph', in *Trees, Effigies, Moving Objects*). The Bundys invited him to join a drinks and dinner party with them in Washington where he met a number of White House economists and advisors, then to dinner at their own Washington house, furnished in 'excellent taste of the quiet sort', its atmosphere putting him in mind of 'so much of the old, real New Deal Roosevelt era: on her side mostly, with the Acheson background, & family friends with Archibald MacLeish (poet) when he was Librarian of Congress back in the 'forties'.[31]

He made three visits to the Bundys' small 50-acre farm in Maryland with 'an old 2-storey stone house built in 1790 & restored', some 30 miles from Washington, being driven there either by the Bundys themselves or the Richmans. On the first occasion (Sunday, 28 May) the Lakings were also invited, and Dean Acheson arrived with his wife after lunch. Curnow was fascinated by his appearance, his manner, his conversation:

> Tall, well-nourished, grey-to-white haired; a trace of the dandy, in a dark check summer jacket with dull metal buttons, & a pale blue silk choker which I could have stolen from him; small, white moustache combed up at the ends in a waggish sort of way. Odd to sit there hearing him tell us that Harry Truman had shown him the speech he meant to make at the Democrat dinner the other day (6000 guests, $100 dollars [sic] a plate to the party funds); Truman was going to make a real old rousing Mid. West harangue against Nixon & the old Admin. Acheson said he just couldn't do that, & told him JFK had to be given a chance to live down his mistakes, & now was not the time 'to start throwing rocks around in the greenhouse'. Truman of course did as he was told.[32]

Writing to Wystan in the wake of these encounters with the Bundys and Acheson, 'a man of uncommon poise, & sense of humour & strength of mind',[33] Curnow took a somewhat more positive view of Kennedy than he had earlier, emphasising the 'whirlwind sowed by his predecessor [President Eisenhower]' and the dangers of 'a really crashing failure by JFK'. He also recounted the Washington story (later used in 'A Framed Photograph'), told very much in Kennedy's favour, of a press conference in which he justified the appointment of his 34-year-old brother, Robert, to be US Attorney General by saying, 'I thought I owed him the chance of a little experience before he goes into practice.'[34]

Curnow had one last formal engagement before he left Washington, record-ing on tape a reading of his poems and an interview with Eberhart at the Library of Congress on 2 June. He was pleased, afterwards, when Eberhart spoke openly and frankly to him for the first time about his life as a poet – his naive enjoy-ment of the Washington scene, and his intense unhappiness at the prospect of returning to Dartmouth College after two years. Curnow also had numerous others besides the Eberharts to see and thank in his busy last days, especially the Richmans, the Starrs, the Lakings and the Biddles.

On 5 June he travelled to New York for the next, two-month stage of his leave. He had been uncertain where to stay, seeking the advice of Jeny's friend Ruth Hirsch who was now living there, but during his last fortnight in Washington had been invited by Jeanne Tufts Cassidy and her husband Frank to use their East 85th Street apartment, since they would be away for most of the summer on various theatrical assignments in which they were both involved. It was a lucky chance, and Curnow leapt at the offer.

New York heat wave: theatre, a poem

When Curnow arrived in New York in early June, for what he later described to Stead as '5 weeks ... of a minor adventure in solitude', the city was in the grip of a heat wave which lasted for most of his stay there. In the absence of air condi-tioning in the Cassidy apartment at 526 East 85th Street he found the heat close to unbearable. 'Don't try to imagine what the full blast of NY summer heat & humidity is like', he wrote to Wystan:

> [I]t has to be experienced to be believed; life under a mushroom cloud of dirty whitey haze; one feels quite literally *ill*; there's neither fan nor air-conditioner in this little apartment, & I go soon to seek relief in Met. Mus. of Art, so very close here on 82nd. East River in the heat haze looks a grotesque (& unappealing) mix of Turner & Whistler, a mock nocturneresque horror, an opinion which is of course ¾ *mood*.[35]

Curnow's main activity in New York was to inform himself about new work in the theatre, then heavily influenced by the absurdist movement. He was interested in Albee, whose double bill of one-acters, *An American Dream* and *The Death of Bessie Smith*, he saw twice while there. He described Ionesco's *Rhinoceros* as 'a wonderful farcical-satirical comedy *for B'way*' even though 'as satire, it wouldn't hurt a baby'.[36] However, the playwright who most interested him was Genet. The production of *The Balcony* – 'what a superbly savage play, as mad & as fierce & brilliant as Swift, & on the whole magnificently done'[37] – taught him 'more about modern theatre & presentation than I could have dreamed of',[38] but *The Blacks*, which he managed to catch shortly before leaving New York, left him speechless:

> I can hardly speak about it; it was theatre such as I couldn't have dreamt about . . . the all-negro cast giving a performance both dramatically brilliant & disciplined & inspired. It made all other plays seem insipid & dull.[39]

Curnow did not see a great many people during his five-week stay in New York. He made immediate contact with Jeny's friend Ruth Hirsch, with whom he went to the theatre several times. Jeanne Cassidy visited briefly, on her way to join her husband running a summer theatre programme in Philadelphia. Eric and Birgitta Sellin visited from Philadelphia, and later in the month he met up with acquaintances of 1950, Evelyn and Harry Segal (Evelyn a painter and Harry a medical teacher), both based at the University of Rochester in upstate New York, who wished to arrange for him to read and lecture there in late July.

Although Curnow had no formal literary engagements during this period, in late June he recorded a radio interview with Sidney Paul for Voice of America (Paul offered straight questions and wanted 'short sharp answers', 'which I gave, to his great satisfaction'),[40] and he also read 'Spectacular Blossom' and 'He Cracked a Word'. He was also in touch with John Bell at Oxford University Press to finalise the text of *A Small Room with Large Windows*, as his selected poems was now entitled, removing 'Crash at Leithfield' and later adding two new poems written towards the end of his stay in New York. These were in fact self-contained parts of a single poem about New York which he worked on during the first week of July. In his first completed version they were given subtitles: '1. The Dog' and '2. The People', under the general title 'Temperatures in the Lower Nineties'. In the final version they were given the general title 'An Oppressive Climate, a Populous Neighbourhood'.

Last weeks in the US: Montauk Point, Maine, Rochester and San Francisco

On 6 July, Curnow was to be picked up in Hyman J. Sobiloff's private plane and flown to his mansion at Montauk Point, at the far eastern end of Long Island, for a week. His meeting with Hy Sobiloff was a remarkable piece of good fortune (in both senses) and occurred through the good offices of Curnow's old New York friend Oscar Williams. Sobiloff was an eccentric millionaire business-man and philanthropist interested in writing poetry, a friend of Tate, Conrad Aiken, Eberhart, Williams and others, whose advice he sought about his poems. Williams had proposed Allen Curnow as well, and then organised the week-long stay for him at Montauk Point, for which he would receive US$500. Curnow thought it 'the most astonishing American thing' he had ever encountered: 'I told Oscar, "you've made it all up," and he said, "It's all arranged. Your air tickets for the plane will be posted to you."'[41] Before he visited Sobiloff, Curnow arranged for Glover to send him a copy of his *Poems 1949–57*.[42]

The week Curnow spent at Montauk Point lived up to his imaginings, though it ended somewhat farcically when Sobiloff was taken to hospital after a fall in the swimming pool which produced a nasty head wound. Sobiloff held numerous board memberships and bought and sold retail businesses in New York, Los Angeles and Pittsburgh as well as owning property in Nassau in the Bahamas. During Curnow's stay he conducted most of his business by telephone. His house, looking out over Long Island Sound, had two two-storey wings, a lawn and gardens with a swimming pool, and there were gardeners, servants and business advisors who came and went, mixing formality with informality. On his first day Curnow took an instant liking to Sobiloff:

> How on earth to describe Hy Sobiloff? To begin with, a burly, excitable, highly intel-ligent man of about my own age: the poetry is serious, I mean, to be taken seriously; he has two books in print, & one with a Foreword by Allen Tate, the other introduced by Conrad Aiken. Making poems & making money & living with Jo [Jo Huntly-Wright, his partner of fifteen years, interested in acting] are the 3 components of his life. We all got on well; no, *very* well, that's an understatement.[43]

The next day he settled into the 'work' arrangement: each day after breakfast he would spend an hour or two on his own reading a few of Sobiloff's poems and making notes. From mid-morning until lunchtime he would spend time with Sobiloff discussing them and making suggestions. In one session they discussed three short poems. In another, he assisted Sobiloff to 'straighten out a few things in the longest & newest of the poems for his new book':

[T]here were three drafts & I'd read them all over b'fast . . . & typed it out for him – he can't type, & Jo can't read his writing (neither can I). Quite an extraordinary experience . . . because the man as it happens isn't a joke but in his half-primitive half-sophisticated way a perfectly genuine poet; if he has nothing specially new or profound to say, he hits off some original & subtle ways of saying it, & has a fine intuitive grasp of small natural things & occurrences. . . . All in all, Hy is a loveable person, & in this kind of relation he's as candid as a child & has no vanity at all; his worst poems are never pretentious, but genuine failures.[44]

Curnow's friendship with Sobiloff continued through the 1960s, and he visited him again in 1967 with Jeny. Sobiloff died, suddenly, of a heart attack in 1970. In 1971, by way of memorial, Curnow wrote an unusual serious piece as Whim Wham ('Portrait of an Artist: H.J.S. 1913–1970'),[45] a piece admired by Tate, Aiken and others of Sobiloff's friends, which presented his life as the epitome of 'real' culture in action, as distinct from the factitious culture fostered by state subsidy.

Immediately after his return to New York, Curnow flew to Bangor, Maine, and thence to Undercliff at Cape Rosier on the Atlantic coast where he was to join the Eberharts for ten days at their summer residence and on their 36-foot launch *The Rêve*. There were tensions in his relationships with the Eberharts, especially with Betty. It was her family money, from the Butcher Polish Company, which financed their houses and launch, and Curnow felt that she patronised her husband, regarding his reputation as a poet primarily as a social asset which might assist in advancing her in the circles to which she aspired. She had been jealous of Curnow's friendship with the Bundys in Washington, attacking them – to Eberhart's embarrassment – in front of Curnow. At Undercliff matters reached something of a climax one evening when, after a harangue about a neighbour's divorce (which may, or may not, have been meant to embarrass Curnow), her conversation turned to international politics:

> Betty talks at you, that kind of demanding support for her opinions, & gets cross if you don't quite agree: then it went to politics & Russia – the crisis came when I said quite coolly that *if* people felt that way about Communism they ought to stop *talking* about it & set about destroying it; it was evidently a Christian duty to wipe out Russia with nuclear weapons, at whatever cost, *if* Americans had the courage to act on the logic of their words. At this point, Betty lost her temper & said I did nothing but criticise America (which is nonsense); next morning she apologized . . . .[46]

The weather at Maine for much of the time Curnow was there was extremely foggy, so that the opportunity for launch trips was limited, and the family and guests were forced to stay inside. On occasions when the fog lifted, however, there were several trips, one to Penobscot Bay, which Curnow greatly enjoyed, and he also enjoyed the company of Roy Basler (of the Library of Congress) and his wife Virginia who arrived a few days after Curnow. For the last three days he escaped from the 'relentless vacation-planned society of Undercliff'[47] and relaxed with Robert and Maida Richman at their beautifully restored 1770s house on Cranberry Island, one of the furthest islands to the north-east, to which he travelled by launch with the Eberharts.

At Cranberry Island Curnow took 'a fine cruise out into the Atlantic swells' with Richman on a 20-foot launch, feeling 'that great up and down of the sea like the Tasman off Raumati', and also had leisure to take in the landscape:

> There are big hills of Mount Desert Island (2000ft) to the east, across some miles of water; a few other small islets in the same quarter; the [Atlantic] ocean on the east. Big vegetation is all stiff spruces & brushy larches; little vegetation, anything from wild roses & raspberries to alders & sycamores & silver birches, though the birches are as tall as anything in sight.[48]

Curnow returned from Maine to New York for one night and on 27 July flew to Rochester in upstate New York to stay with Evelyn and Harry Segal for four days ('no two people could have done more, or have been so mindful & kind'),[49] giving an interview to the local newspaper and reading his poetry to summer school students at the University of Rochester.

By 31 July, Curnow was back at the Cassidys' apartment in New York for the last two days of his stay there. He had packing and tidying to do, made farewell visits to Ruth Hirsch and Oscar Williams, and on 3 August flew to San Francisco, travelling the following day to Carmel Valley where he stayed for ten days with Ruth Witt-Diamant and her family (a son and daughter-in-law and grandchild). He relaxed, visited Big Sur country and Steinbeck country, read much of the poetry he had purchased at the City Lights bookshop in San Francisco (including the newest Ginsberg volumes, and others 'around the so-called "beat" (but the best of it is not "beat") poetry',[50] and also began to think about possible writing projects:

> I need a day or two alone with a typewriter, to tidy up the Dog poem & its companion-piece, & see if I can reorganise the *Capitol* poem (something wrong with it, I know – but I suspect that it may have to wait for some editor to catch on to the pattern the poem has). I'm at war with something that persists in telling me my poems won't do & aren't worth the bother; the confusion of poetic voices here may have something to do with this loss of nerve; besides, the coarse woodenness of the NZ reception of the *Expert*. A new play is probably the thing I want, to get rid

of the feeling that everything I write is half-baked. [P]erhaps I have to have anxieties if I'm to write at all; but if they're too pressing, they stop the writing.[51]

Back in San Francisco for his last few days in the United States he worked hard, but unsuccessfully, on a homecoming poem for Jeny:

[O]f course I had to pick the Odyssey for a comparison, I suppose expecting the impossible, that I could give the idea some original turn & something personal to us. The only lines that get at all near it are three which try to mix flying by jet with Homer's ships, with 'wine-bright sky' in place of Homeric 'wine-dark sea', & speaking to Odysseus as a fellow-passenger:

> This wine-bright sky is a track, no matter how beaten,
> You follow & I follow, first fellow-passenger
> Dashing your oars into the dawn.

But I don't care for that fuff-fuffing alliteration of f's; in fact it won't do at all....[52]

When Curnow left San Francisco for Sydney, he could reflect on numerous positive achievements during his second visit to the United States. However, the very success of his trip left him unsure quite where his own writing – especially his poetry – would go, from this point. For Curnow, it could never be a case of simply repeating what had been done, and done well. The fate of his 'Capitol' poem, about his experiences in, and of, Washington, epitomised the issues he faced. He had thought of it as one of his best – as indeed it was – and compared its method and approach with another of his best, 'A Small Room with Large Windows'. But it had not been accepted by *Poetry* (Chicago). His comments about the poem to Jeny from San Francisco show that he was torn about what to do: whether to persist with it with other editors who might 'catch on' to its pattern, or try to discover the 'something wrong' with it which he reluctantly acknowledged might be the case. He did not send it to other editors, though there is not the slightest doubt that as it stood it could easily have found publication elsewhere. However, the problem was not, exactly, that there was 'something wrong' with the poem. What Curnow eventually did was dismantle the poem entirely, and reshape its materials into a quite new way of writing. Bits of the poem appear in all four of the 'American' poems in his next volume, the sequence *Trees, Effigies, Moving Objects*. It took almost a decade for this to happen, but the result was the beginning of what (given the ten-year gestation of the new style) became a second career, in which much of his finest poetry was written.

Deciding to leave his marriage

For Curnow at the time, the many public achievements of his American trip are likely to have paled into insignificance beside the personal decision to leave his marriage to Betty. Curnow and Jeny wrote to each other almost every day during the five and a half months that they were apart. The letters were deeply personal and intimate, and Curnow's also provided a remarkably detailed 'diary' of everything he did and saw – the people he met, the events he was involved in, the landscapes he travelled through, the social and political life he observed, the meals he ate – as well as commenting on the information Jeny sent him about her own daily routines and the people she met.

In Washington he got into the regular habit, often later in the afternoon or evening, of walking along the six-laned Wisconsin Avenue of Friendship Heights, with its noisy fugue of traffic and green canopy of leaf-covered trees, to post his daily letter to Jeny in the iron receptacle marked 'For U.S. Mail'. He also timed his movements so that at 11 p.m. New Zealand time on 20 May he and Jeny drank their six-monthly toast to each other, celebrating the precise moment of their first meeting on 20 November 1954, a ritual which they observed throughout their lives together; and on the same day they sent cables to each other. On one special occasion shortly before he left Washington, when his thinking about Betty and his marriage reached a new point of resolution, he stopped to gather a leaf from one of Wisconsin Avenue's trees for the letter he was posting:

> Picked this leaf off a tree on my way to the street letter-box (an elm, I think) – 'made flesh before the word' like the leaf in my poem, & send it because I can trust it better than the words. I wanted a flower, but the shops are shut.[53]

The separation was harder for Jeny, since Curnow had at least the constant stimulation of meeting new people, catching up with old friends, and under-taking new activities. Her closest confidant was Bill Pearson, who visited her regularly at Courtville in Parliament Street to see how she was and share a drink, keeping her informed about the English Department and other literary gossip, and catching up from her with news of Allen's activities overseas. She also saw Lilian and Ronald Barker occasionally, and in the May vacation spent almost a week with the Glovers at Paekakariki. Jeny's visit was 'a joy, a positive delight', Glover wrote to Curnow,[54] and Jeny herself felt thoroughly spoilt, swapping news about Curnow and bringing them up to date with his current activities and plans. Her friendship with Khura flourished, and she was surprised when Khura mentioned that three or four years earlier, when Betty visited the Glovers at

Raumati, she had told Khura that she had asked a lawyer about getting a divorce but had been advised against it.

For Curnow the information was important: 'it clears my mind on quite a few things, & relieves me of a big anxiety. You see, I've still had the burden of believing there's some kind of desperate devotion there, the *dependence* which I've had to assume in the absence of anything really known to the contrary.'[55] Curnow and Jeny had arranged to spend the last three weeks of Curnow's time away, from 19 August to 10 September, together in Sydney. Throughout June, as they exchanged letters and Jeny offered clear-sighted, sympathetic comments on Curnow's lingering uncertainties and doubts (not about the relationship itself, Curnow emphasised to Jeny, but about *himself* and his worries about the effects on others of his walking away from his marriage to Betty), Curnow's resolution firmed to make the break from Betty at the time of their return from Sydney, and he asked Jeny to find a small central flat. Reaching this decision was a huge relief to Curnow (as well as to Jeny), and throughout July and the first two weeks of August (the last six weeks of his stay in the United States) the enthusiasm and energy he had felt throughout his time in Washington returned.

There were two other family matters which affected Curnow while he was away. One was the sadness of learning in early May from his mother that cousin Irene Ronalds, Patricia's mother, had died. Irene had been 'such a very dear part of my life', he wrote to Jeny, '& was of old T's too, & can't help but remind me of his dying when I was away ten years ago'.[56] The other was the pleasure of learning of the birth of Belinda's first son, Matthew, his first grandchild, on 23 June. 'What exhilarating news . . .!' he immediately wrote to Belinda, '*L'art d'être grandpère* I shall take time over':

> Take care of yourselves. Nothing worse for everyone than anxious parents. He won't stop breathing if you take your eyes off him. Babies are almost indestructible. Very jejune advice, but I can think of no other.[57]

On 19 August, Jeny travelled to Sydney to meet Curnow, who had arrived shortly before from the United States. For three weeks they had the use of Angela Harman's flat at Potts Point, while Angela (Patricia's daughter), who was touring New Zealand as a publicist for the touring opera singer Luigi Infantino, had the use of Jeny's flat at Auckland. Curnow had only one engagement in Sydney, an interview and reading on ABC radio. Apart from this it was to be a holiday together for both, and also a time, after so long apart, to talk and plan for the future. Curnow had written half a dozen times to Betty during his time in the United States, with information about his activities and movements. Shortly before their return from Sydney he wrote again, briefly and clearly, saying that he would not be coming back to Herbert Street and assuring her that he was concerned to make proper provision for herself and Tim, through their respective legal advisors:

> I came to this decision finally some months ago; but you know that it has been my wish for years to re-marry, as soon as it seemed to me not unjust to anyone dependent on me.

> Please believe that there is no bitter feeling on my part. Simply that I don't mean to resume a situation where I have nothing for either except strain and distress.[58]

Chapter Twenty-two

Separation and Remarriage, September 1961–August 1965

Perhaps it is possible for two people, each in their own way holding
hard to an idea (ideal?) of a right relationship, to hold on, & on, &
on – till something, someone, has to break? Nobody knows, quite, how
every effort only tightens the knot to breaking-point? I don't, seriously,
rationalise like this; it runs too easily into self-flattery or unjust blame
– doesn't it?....Jeny Tole has made my half-world round, & rounded
for the years that remain.[1]

Leaving Herbert Street

After his return from Sydney, Curnow moved into a temporary bedsitter in Balfour
Road, Parnell, and after a few weeks into a small basement flat in Ferncroft Street,
Grafton, where he remained until May 1962 when a university flat at Sonoma in
Alfred Street became available. He was on leave from the university for the rest
of 1961 and remained largely out of contact for some weeks, anxious to avoid any
situation which might lead Betty to believe that his mind could be changed. He
contacted his lawyer (David Beattie) immediately after he returned, and had
advised Betty to contact Martyn Finlay. Curnow never discussed the breakdown of
his first marriage publicly. He did not invite sympathy. He regarded it as a private
matter, and refused any comment of any kind – whether of blame, recrimination,
or self-justification – which might feed the speculations of others.

Betty was distressed, and uncertain about the future. Perhaps she did believe, for the first few weeks, that he would see the error of his ways and return, and although she was angry that he was unable to be contacted she said little to anyone except close friends. However, she soon realised that no rapprochement was possible. To Lilburn, who wrote sympathetically to her a month after Curnow had left, she confided that she had hoped his recent trip to America 'would mend things rather than completely break them', though she laid much of the blame for the break-up on the 'ambition' which his first trip overseas in 1949–50 had aroused in him ('I think I was aware even when he came back then that this might happen in the end').[2]

Curnow was also concerned about the effects of the separation on Wystan, Belinda and Tim. All three were angered by their father's behaviour – especially the manner of his departure – and Wystan and Tim carried a great deal of the responsibility for helping their mother to cope with her new circumstances. Perhaps unwisely, Curnow decided not to initiate contact with any of his children until arrangements with Betty had been sorted, hoping that this might happen reasonably quickly, and that whatever strains he placed on the children's relationship with him would gradually dissipate.

Eventually Betty decided to petition for divorce, but negotiations over the settlement agreement were difficult. For Curnow there was absolutely no question of the need to make fair financial provision for Betty's future, and he did his best to meet her wishes: so much so that it was against his lawyer's advice that he eventually agreed to a settlement that was very favourable to her.

Despite the turmoil of the separation, by the end of 1961 Curnow was able to express the relief he now felt to Glover: 'J & I can at last lead our own life now; and at least for the time being, the drawback of separate flats seems little enough, after the contrivances of the past 7 years and the separation during my travels.'[3] His relationships with Wystan, Belinda and Tim had also resumed, although some constraints remained. These were least with Belinda, who took matters into her own hands, anxious to show her baby to her father, and visited him at his flat in Ferncroft Street, where she met Jeny for the first time. In October, at the suggestion of Pearson, Curnow visited Wystan in his Beresford Street flat, and Wystan and Sue [Susan Matthews], who were soon to be married, then visited Jeny and Curnow at Jeny's flat at Courtville. Tim, in his University Entrance year at Westlake High School at the time of the separation, was the most immediately affected by it, resenting his father, as he later put it, for not meeting his mother face to face.[4] After he was accredited with University Entrance aged seventeen and having heard nothing from his father about his future, he decided to look after himself. He applied for and was offered a job as a technician in the Geography Department at the University of Auckland. He was determined to preserve his own independence, refusing an offer from his father of a weekly allowance to enable him to enrol full-time for a degree. The allowance was the same amount as had been offered to his older brother Wystan, who had already started his university studies at this time, and who advised Tim that it was not enough to live on and had to be supplemented by taking out a teacher's scholarship. The following year after a period as a warehouse assistant for Hick Smith, a firm of book distributors, he joined the staff of Paul's Book Arcade in Auckland's High Street as a bookseller, becoming shop manager before joining the publishing firm of A.H. & A.W. Reed in Wellington in 1966 as educational editor.

Glover, who had now left his job with Harry Tombs at the Wingfield Press, was pleased to see Curnow and Jeny early in 1962, though Curnow was unsure of how his mother might react to the separation, when he and Jeny visited Christchurch during the same trip south. In the event, Jessie liked Jeny and they got on very well. One of Jessie's main worries was that because Jeny would be married outside the Church, and the Toles were such a long-established Catholic family, there would be Catholic Church reprisals against her son.[5] For the first two years after the separation agreement was signed in May 1962, Curnow and Jeny maintained their separate flats, but a makeshift and primitive bach at Karekare provided a welcome escape from the city, where they could be alone together.[6]

Curnow had given the US$500 he had received from Hy Sobiloff during his trip to the United States to Jeny and on Labour Weekend later in October 1961 they had set out for Whatipu on Auckland's west coast to begin searching for a modest section. By accident they met Pat Odlin at Karekare, whose family were about to sell their farmland, and quickly settled on a small bush site which had a sea view, about a kilometre from the beach on the winding access road, Lone Kauri Road, which looped from the main Piha Road to the north. They then found a cheap knock-down bach (16 x 10 ft) at Browns Bay, and after Curnow and Jeny had got the levels fixed, Ronald Barker helped Curnow re-erect it on site. It remained for both 'a most special place' until Curnow's death:

> We spent all our summers there and long weekends and winter vacations when we were both teaching. It was a place where we could be alone, where we both worked and where we swam, fished and walked.[7]

There were visits there, early on, from Wystan and Sue, from Belinda and her family, and from Tim. In September 1962, Tony (visiting New Zealand for a month with his second wife, Cheong Soo Lan, a Chinese teacher and painter) had the use of the flat at Sonoma, and towards the end of 1962, Jeny's mother, Janet Osborne, who returned to New Zealand for a visit of nine months after her second husband died in the United States, also stayed for much of the time at Sonoma while Curnow moved in with Jeny at Courtville.

Jeny had inherited much of her independence of spirit and determination from her mother, who was lively and fun-loving. Janet enjoyed meeting the Glovers when she travelled to Wellington with Curnow and Jeny in January 1963. In May that year she entertained Glover in the Grand Hotel, where she shifted briefly while Glover – in Auckland to give a poetry reading with Curnow, organised by Barker* – stayed at Sonoma with Khura. Later in 1963, Janet moved into a small two-storeyed house at 1 Maunsell Road, Parnell, near the Auckland Domain, with Jeny and Curnow. Karl and Kay Stead had been previous tenants and it provided the location of Stead's well-known story 'A Fitting Tribute' (1965). Maunsell Road was Curnow's fourth shift of residence in two years. He and Jeny lived there for two years, until later in 1965 they purchased the house in Tohunga Crescent (opposite the Steads) which became their permanent home.

In October 1963 they also made a small number of modest additions to the bach at Karekare, adding a small bedroom, a washroom and a sundeck – almost doubling its space, though it was still quite small. The original bach had been assembled without a building permit and had lost its roof during a storm in the winter of 1962. They were now required to install new foundations, which Curnow paid for with his half-share (£50) of the Jessie Mackay Award for *A Small Room with Large Windows*, shared with R.A.K. Mason's *Collected Poems*.[8] 'Karekare you'd hardly know', Curnow wrote to Wystan, who had recently arrived with his family at the University of Pennsylvania to begin study for a doctorate in American literature.[9]

A miscellany of writings, 1962–64

Despite the pressures on his personal life and his makeshift living arrangements during the years immediately following the separation, Curnow worked at a range of small projects. There were few poems, however, apart from 'one or two odd sort of dry poems which I'd like you to see', he wrote to Glover soon after returning from the United States. He was still more interested in writing plays – perhaps encouraged by the success of the radio production of *The Axe* soon after his return to Auckland and the prospect of a stage production of *The Overseas Expert*, and stimulated by the new theatrical impulses he had encountered in the United States.

Brasch decided to publish the two New York poems in *Landfall* – they were 'very enjoyable cunning poems', he wrote to Curnow[10] – but withdrew both, testily, after

---

* Auckland Art Gallery, 18 May 1963.

one of them* was also accepted by the *Times Literary Supplement*. Curnow could hardly refuse the *TLS* acceptance. 'First time I've ever tried anything with TLS', he wrote to Schroder, '& was delighted when they took it; it circulates so much further than the monthlies & quarterlies, esp. the very literary ones, & will reach, for instance, friends at the Library of Congress & elsewhere on that continent.'[11] Brasch did, however, publish three further 'Songs from the Maori', co-translated with Roger Oppenheim, in the first issue of *Landfall* in 1962. But there was to be no further new poem until 1965, when 'A Year and a Day' – a fiftieth-birthday tribute to Douglas Lilburn – appeared in the *New Zealand Listener*.[12]

In November 1962 *A Small Room With Large Windows* appeared under the Oxford University Press imprint. It was the first time Curnow had ever put together a selection of his work, covering two decades, and ought to have been the occasion for widespread appraisal of his achievement. The newspapers, however, made no special occasion of the event, and the *New Zealand Listener* 'buried' what Curnow called 'an ignorant & inadequate scrap'.†[13] According to OUP,[14] overseas reviews were 'rather sparse', but there were 'some good ones among them', most notably in the *Times Literary Supplement* which, though wishing for more 'lucidity' in the later poems, concluded that 'there are few poets writing in English today who surpass him as an artist'.[15]

Publicity for the book should have been helped by a radio reading Curnow gave on the YC Poetry programme on 21 November 1962 (in a series organised by James Bertram) which included 'To Forget Self and All', 'An Oppressive Climate, a Populous Neighbourhood', and, unusually, the first part of 'Evidences of Recent Flood', 'Logbook Found on Ararat', as well as the much better known second part, 'The Changeling', of 'Evidences of Recent Flood'. Bertram was especially excited by Curnow's reading of 'Evidences' and remained impressed after the programme went to air:

> I thought Evidences was the most effective of all; and really, this was quite a terrific reading. It's nice to have some of the externals noted: I'd forgotten about New Brighton, and had been transposing to the Waitemata. But it's your mangroves I particularly like, and they are very local.[16]

Amongst the dearth of substantial critical notices in New Zealand, however, there was one – a full-length article by Stead, 'Allen Curnow's Poetry', in

---

* 'An Oppressive Climate, a Populous Neighbourhood', published in the *Times Literary Supplement*, 2 August 1963. Note, only part I was published in the *TLS*, and parts I and II of the poem appear in *A Small Room with Large Windows* (Oxford University Press, 1962). The poem would have been accepted for publication by the *TLS* in 1961, but not published by them until 1963.
† The review was by Martyn Sanderson, 7 Dec. 1962.

Landfall[17] – which more than made up for the deficiencies of the rest. It was not only a brilliant critical reading of Curnow's poetry, deeply influential on subsequent understandings of it, but a seminal piece of criticism in its own right, demonstrating how New Zealand poetry might be read in the light of sophisticated critical practice elsewhere. The article contextualised its approach to Curnow with discussions of his critical method in his anthology introductions, and by reference to some of the central imaginative preoccupations of modernist poetry elsewhere (citing Yeats, Eliot, Allen Tate, and ideas of tradition and the individual talent, regionalism and provincialism), but its main force lay in the persuasive depth and detail of its discussion of particular poems – including 'Discovery', 'House and Land', 'In Memoriam, R.M.L.G.', 'Spectacular Blossom' and 'A Small Room with Large Windows'. The article was an implicit engagement with critical detractors (none were named though they had existed from the time of Curnow's very first volume) who complained that the poetry was 'too difficult', or too exclusively concerned with technique at the expense of substance. Stead's particular readings and his critical framework would later be disputed, but again and again his approach revealed the connection between complexity of form and depth of historical, social, philosophical and aesthetic meaning in the poetry. Stead and the anonymous *TLS* reviewer were the first critics to acknowledge that Curnow was one of the most significant poets writing in English.

Brasch had asked Curnow if he would write a piece for *Landfall* about William Carlos Williams, who died in March 1963, but Curnow remained undecided about Williams's poetry, and cited the pressure of other commitments as an excuse, one of which was the preparation of a lecture for the 1963 Winter Lecture Series at the University of Auckland, whose general title was 'The Future of New Zealand'.

He spent a great deal of time on his lecture, 'New Zealand Literature: the Case for a Working Definition', which revisited some of the arguments advanced in the Penguin introduction, but was not simply a restatement of them. He was concerned to *problematise* the term 'New Zealand Literature', devoting some time to the ideas of 'nationality' and 'universality'. He had touched on these ideas in his Penguin introduction but had not anticipated how loosely the term 'universal', and its cognates, would be used in attacking his own approach. He also discussed the limitations of organic metaphors of national development: New Zealand literature as a 'sprout' or 'offshoot' of a main trunk, or as the 'tributary' of a mainstream. He was concerned primarily, that is, with 'the *possibility* of discussing New Zealand literature at all; and [with] the possibility that this expression in general use is not nonsensical':[18]

Is it supposed that any work of original merit, whether poem or story or play, can be composed without distinct references to sensible objects, actual memories, images of a home, a climate, a city or a mountain? Or that these references can occur without accompanying tones of acceptance or denial, responding to the pressures of a society, a tradition, a people? – why not say 'a nation', if by that we mean to dignify the idea of nationality, not to degrade the idea of art? Can a poet, for instance, write poems of love, hate, death, without imaging the physical tensions and resistances of objects known and experienced?[19]

He also drew broadly on other cultures for the purposes of comparison, and two of his examples came directly from his recent trip to the United States. One recalled his meetings with Octavio Paz:

Less precisely, our case could be compared with literature like some of the Latin-American, or the Spanish literature of Mexico. I am thinking of the Mexican poetry in Spanish of Octavio Paz: so filled with native Mexican tradition and scene and climate, that when he reads it aloud in his imperfect English or talks about it (I have heard him do both) it is the non-European vision that strikes you first. This is poetry in Spanish, certainly, but such as only a Mexican could have conceived and written, and so properly to be called Mexican poetry. Paz called it so. He is no primitive, but an 'intellectual' besides a lover of his country.[20]

The other recalled his summer visit to the Eberharts and the Richmans on the Maine coast:

A couple of years ago, during a fortnight among the Atlantic bays and islands of New England, I think I understood for the first time why T.S. Eliot's 'The Dry Salvages' [part of the *Four Quartets*] is the most beautiful and profound of his longer poems. The colours, the smells, the weather of that coast supplied the physical experience, the physical aspects and details of the area of reality to which the poem refers. It was one of those accidental corroborations . . . which serve to remind us of how much that is called 'imaginative' or 'creative' or poetic in some confused sense of those words, consists really in an exceptional gift for matching accurate and commodious memory with precise and (in the first place) denotative language. There is always less 'poet's make-believe' in good poems than we are apt to suppose.[21]

Curnow spent some time revising this lecture for publication, expanding it to include examples from New Zealand fiction. He proposed to submit his main published work to be examined for a DLitt in 1964, and the lecture would make 'a useful P.S. to my anthologies'.[22] In addition to the anthologies and the Winter Lecture, he submitted four *Landfall* articles (including the piece on Holcroft's *Dance of the Seasons*[23] and his lengthy review of Eric McCormick's study of Frances

Hodgkins, *The Expatriate*[24]) and a recently published review of Bill Pearson's *Coal Flat* (in *Comment*) which Stead thought 'one of your very best pieces of criticism'.[25] The moderator of the examining panel, Professor John Garrett of the University of Canterbury, later asked Curnow to add his Oxford selected poems to the submitted works. 'I fancy they will give me the degree', he wrote to Wystan, '& having done so, won't be likely to turn me down *this* year [1964] (as they did last) for an Ass. Prof.'[26]

Curnow had applied for promotion to associate professor in 1962 and 1963, and on both occasions had been turned down. Although he was awarded a DLitt in 1964 (the first such degree awarded by the University of Auckland), he would not receive promotion to associate professor until his sixth attempt, in 1967. He felt 'slighted' at this time at being turned down, especially as Stead had been promoted ahead of him. 'I find it hard to rid my mind of the thought', he wrote to Pearson, 'that at this point the race is really a rat-race: one for which Karl has been in rigorous training, both tactically and intellectually, & in which I rate as an outsider.'[27] For the remainder of his time at the university, Curnow maintained a certain reserve in his personal relations with Stead.

Aside from the Winter Lecture, Curnow was active on other literary matters in 1963. On 17 October he gave a fine memorial address about Louis MacNeice on radio, which Brasch immediately sought for publication in *Landfall*.[28] In that year he was also approached by Blackwood Paul and agreed to a proposal to edit an expanded, updated, hardback edition of the Penguin anthology. However, in November, when it emerged 'suddenly and unexpectedly' that the first edition of 25,000 copies had almost sold out, Penguin considered reprinting themselves rather than coming to an arrangement with Paul's. There was a delay at this point, and it was not until the end of 1964 that Penguin decided not to proceed themselves but to give Paul's a five-year right to reprint the paperback, and not until 1966, after a blundering effort by Paul's to persuade Curnow to change the title to *The Curnow Anthology of New Zealand Verse*, that the Paul's reprint (of 10,000 copies) finally appeared.* [29]

In 1963 the National Government introduced an Indecent Publications Bill – 'a monstrous document', as Curnow described it to Wystan[30] – which proposed a specialist tribunal, with very considerable powers of secrecy, to vet all books (including literary manuscripts) and sound-recorded materials submitted to it. Curnow wrote an article on the issues for the *New Zealand Herald* (which was quoted at length in a piece entitled 'Shadow of Secret Censorship' in the British *Manchester Guardian*), made a strong submission to the government, and worked

---

* As part of a series of country anthologies produced at that time, 25,000 copies of the New Zealand anthology would have been a standard run for sale worldwide (the old British Commonwealth market and the US), making the Paul's reprint optimistic as their only market was New Zealand but with potential educational sales.

on a university staff committee which drafted a 3000-word article published by the *Auckland Star*.[31] He also resigned from PEN, the New Zealand writers' organisation chaired by John Reece Cole, in protest at PEN's view that the bill was a liberalisation of existing law. Other writers – notably Maurice Duggan and Eric McCormick – shared Curnow's dissatisfaction with PEN. In his letter of resignation Curnow wrote that he could not regard a bill which envisaged 'a special class of books' which would be made more readily available to 'a special class of reader' as a liberalisation at all:

> 'Liberalisation' which refers to some implied privilege for the few, and which is to be bought at the price of a violation of rights which concern the whole adult community, is surely a miserable purchase. And this is a miserable defence of the Bill.[32]

This was also a key point Curnow made in a lively piece by Whim Wham ('A Little Common Sensorship') at the time the prospect of legislation was first raised:

> The Qualifications have to be special,
>   Oh very special indeed,
> Of those who decide for Us what is decent
>   And what is NOT, to read.
>
> Persons of Probity, Persons of Taste,
>   Of incorruptible Soul –
> Who can scan all Manner of poisonous Print
>   And keep their Conscience whole.
>
> If a Book's not fit for You, Sir,
>   Or Me, it isn't the Stuff
> For common Readers whose Qualifications
>   Just aren't Special enough.
>
> For the Likes of Us need Specialists –
>   Not One, but three or four –
> To judge for Us whether the Author's an Artist
>   Or a nasty-minded Bore.
>
> Of course the most highly qualified Team
>   Are a fallible Bunch, at best –
> Parsons, Professors, whoever you like,
>   Can make Mistakes like the Rest.

> The Minister in his Wisdom, Sir,
> > Has thought of that One, too.
> Why, COMMON SENSE, he happily adds,
> > Plain Common Sense will do!
>
> IF THAT's the Case – and with all Respect
> > To our specially qualified Leaders –
> Can't Common Sense decide for Itself,
> > i.e. the Common Reader's? *33

In February the following year the 'unhealthily miasmic' climate created by the censorship act was in the headlines again, when the New Zealand Literary Fund made a grant to Louis Johnson's *Poetry Yearbook* conditional on the removal of six poems (which the chairman, Ian Gordon, said 'might have given offence to the taxpayer'), and the Indecent Publications Tribunal (of which Gordon was also a member) was asked to make a precedent-setting adjudication on James Baldwin's novel *Another Country*. Paul's bookshop was asked by the Customs Department (a major conduit of materials to the Tribunal) to supply a copy of Joyce's *Ulysses*,† and the vice-chancellor of the University of Auckland required an issue of the student magazine *Craccum* to be withdrawn, because of a parental complaint about an item by Baxter and a review of the novel *The Group* by Mary McCarthy.

Curnow regarded himself as 'too well marked as a censorship publicist'34 to appear before the Tribunal as a witness in its investigation of *Another Country*, but voiced his disquiet in a lively piece written for the *New Zealand Herald* entitled 'Signs Point to Growing Pressures on Liberty of N.Z. Writers'. Curnow's initial target was the Literary Fund which in its decision about the *Poetry Yearbook* had implicitly introduced a new criterion into its decisions, 'that the book has been passed and certified as free from morally offensive matter':

> State pressure on the grant-hungry author or publisher, the benevolent nudge in the direction of 'safe' or 'inoffensive' writing, must affect the climate in which the writing is done. . . . This pressure is intangible, for most; the wind blows from a familiar quarter [the government], and the Literary Fund committee room has turned out less weatherproof than might have been hoped.35

---

*   There were several other pieces by Whim Wham on the issue. 'Comfortable Up There?' (14 Sept. 1963) attacked the views of John Reece Cole, president of PEN; 'It's Dark Outside' (5 Oct. 1963) pilloried the Minister concerned, J.R. Hanan; and 'A Decent Bunch' (28 Dec. 1963) poked gentle fun at the membership of the Tribunal ('Here's the mysteriously potent FIVE / That guards the DECENCY for which we strive'), amongst whom was his long-standing friend and mentor, John Schroder.
†   Joyce's *Ulysses* and Baldwin's *Another Country* were both cleared by the Indecent Publications Tribunal.

Curnow then turned to the personnel on the Tribunal, and in particular to the fact that Gordon was 'the leading literary personage' on the Tribunal as well as chair of the Literary Fund. His elegant understatements intensified the barbed nature of the comment:

> If a book before the tribunal has already been before the [Literary Fund] committee
> – and accepted or rejected for a grant – Professor Gordon will be specially well placed
> to evaluate it. He may, in fact, be already committed to an opinion on its freedom or
> otherwise from offence. . . . The benevolent nudge – 'play it safe, and get your grant'
> – and the prohibitory check may in fact be administered by the same pair of hands.[36]

He concluded by drawing attention especially to the narrowly Wellington-based, English Department-concentrated membership of the Tribunal:

> It cannot have been Government policy to link State patronage and censorship so
> closely, or either of them with the personnel of a single university department. If we
> are to benefit from patronage, or tolerate censorship, this situation calls for examin-
> ation and correction. Gratitude for the zealous, unremunerated service of persons
> who have happily shouldered the burdens of their Wellington citizenship should not,
> one feels, stand in the way.[37]

Curnow put a great deal of effort into this article, initially drafting 5000 words which he reduced to 1500, and hoped that it might 'draw fire'.[38] After it appeared he was less certain of its impact:

> Now I see it, I think it is too *tempered*, & dully written. Yet, how to *force* the topic into
> prominence, when the public lead is lacking?? I fear that anyone who will take the
> right conclusions from it will have drawn them in any case.[39]

Censorship remained an issue for much of the decade, and at various times in the 1960s Curnow himself was not immune from attempts to censor his own writing. In September 1962 he had been extremely angry at one of the rare instances in which Whim Wham was subject to censorship, when *The Press* 'warn[ed]' him to cease writing verses about New Zealand's response to the prospect of Great Britain's joining the European Economic Community, commenting that although Curnow's attitude coincided with the editorial policy of the *New Zealand Herald* it was different from *The Press*'s: 'Could we agree that you have now had your fair share of our space for the purpose?'[40] Britain's possible entry into the EEC was a highly significant event for New Zealand, in Whim Wham's view, and he took issue with the government (and others) whose policy was to present New Zealand as 'a special case', deserving 'special privileges'. Whatever the cost and whatever the difficulties for the future, New Zealand could and should no longer either expect special treatment, or appeal to colonial ties that had long ceased to be relevant. Curnow replied to the editor Arthur Rolleston (Rolle) Cant that he had no idea what *The Press's* policy was, that he worked professionally and managed the best verse he could each week, had 'never argued with a rejection slip', and deserved an apology.[41] Cant regretted if his letter had caused offence, but did not back down on his main point: 'If your professional working methods forbid your accepting the courtesy of prior notice of what is unacceptable, I, for one, have no objection to indulging your preference for rejections slips.'[42] There the matter rested.

A second instance occurred in August 1964 when Curnow was asked by the New Zealand Broadcasting Corporation (NZBC) to contribute two opinion pieces to a weekly current affairs radio programme, 'Looking at Ourselves'. For the first he addressed the belief that there should be no 'political interference' in rugby tours between New Zealand and South Africa, and found that without consulting him his talk had been edited to remove comments that the rugby administrator T.H. (Tom) Pearce was politically sympathetic to the apartheid system. Despite his anger he went ahead with his second contribution, a lively expression of his approval of Sir Basil Spence's 'beehive' design for a new parliament building, arguing against the proposal that another design be sought from specifically New Zealand architects.

In February 1964, at the request of his brother Tony, Curnow recorded a programme on New Zealand poetry for SEATO (one of a series of cultural programmes by member countries), basing it on the talks he had given at universities and colleges in the United States. He was then asked if he would do a similar programme on British poetry, but declined. He was beginning to get anxious about the play he had promised to Ronald Barker. By the end of summer, after three weeks at Karekare during which he read a great deal of Henry James, Diderot and Gide, and caught 'a few good fat rock cod off south rocks' as well as finding the mussels 'big & excellent', he had only 50 lines on paper and a 'shadowy scenario in mind'.[43] He had also promised Pearson, on leave overseas in 1964, to proofread his edition of Sargeson's *Collected Stories* for Paul's – a task which made him 'realise as never before how big Frank's performance is'.* [44]

Dr Pom, 1964

Earlier in 1963, Barker had asked Curnow if he could write 'a one act play of a man and a woman' for his new shoestring theatrical company, Ronald and Lilian

---

* He also recast the jacket blurb at Pearson's request, having earlier done the jacket blurb for *Coal Flat*.

Barker Ltd.[45] He was still interested in staging *The Overseas Expert*, but the play would now have to wait until he had assembled an adequate cast. Later in 1963 Barker toured New Zealand with Marguerite Duras' *The Square*, which Curnow found very moving, despite the mixed reception it received. 'If it's the last thing I write', he commented to Wystan, 'I shall do them the play they have asked for, for next year – but what shall I write about?'[46]

By mid-1964 Curnow at last began to get a good deal of the new play on to paper. He had 'not much time to spare, just now', he wrote to Schroder in September, for anything but *Dr Pom*:

> I've written for eleven players (*The Axe*); for seven (*Moon Section*); for five (*The Overseas Expert*); & now for two, with one walk-on part. During the year I've thrown away two false starts: both tragic-satiric, & neither very promising. *Dr Pom* is comic-satiric: utterly unlike Jarry's *Ubu Roi*, which I thought was going to be a model; & if it has any scenario, it comes from the Grimms' wonderful story of the Fisherman & his wife; all the rest is my own invention, like the White Knight's, & really (if anyone ever cares enough to work it out) so much the same old subject of all my scribbles, serious or funny, that I hardly know whether I saw it or dreamt it.[47]

Dr Pom was intended for a season of plays (for two actors only) which Barker was putting on from mid-October to early December, beginning with Strindberg's *Miss Julie*, followed by Beckett's *Happy Days*, and concluding with a double bill of one-acters – Pinter's *A Slight Ache* and Curnow's *Dr Pom*. Curnow never published the play, and the production later in the year was so disastrous, so remote from anything he had intended, that he never regarded the play as having been performed at all. Like *Moon Section*, it deserved a better fate.

A lively, fast-moving, often hilariously funny farce in the style of Ionesco, drawing on some of the absurdist theatrical techniques Curnow had encountered in New York in 1961, as well as on the Grimms' tale *The Fisherman and his Wife* for the general idea and structure, *Dr Pom* can be seen as a boisterous satirical parable with a number of targets. It mocks reverence for things British in New Zealand, attacks the old British colonial assumption of smug superiority, and sends up the country's mindless bureaucracy, its paranoid fear of communism and of Asians, and its willingness to accept the curtailment of liberties by those in authority. The play's provocative concluding fantasy, which can be read either as a successful Asian invasion and the establishment of a new democratic order, or as a successful democratic revolution from within, emphasises that it is not possible to turn the clock back, to expel Britishness from 'Zelania' as if it had never existed, even if the ways in which it might survive, adapt, or fail to adapt in such a world are left unexplored. The English-born Poms clearly regard living the rest of their lives in a democratic republic from which the British apron strings have been cut as tantamount to a sentence of death.

By the end of October, with the play all but complete, he described it to Wystan as 'a snarling little satire (less than an hour), but shld not make me any enemies among my friends'. The play was '[f]ull of laugh-lines which should (I hope) take effect the moment before it dawns on them, *what* they are laughing at'.[48]

By the time the play was finished, Barker's season was under way at the small Rembrandt Art Theatre (originally the Lewis Eady Hall, and by day functioning as the Paris Boulevard coffee shop, with an entry from High Street). Each play had eight performances during weeknights over the period of a fortnight, *Miss Julie* first, then *Happy Days*, with *A Slight Ache* and *Dr Pom* scheduled to begin on 23 November, only ten days after the completion of the season of *Happy Days*. Barker's two actors in all the plays were the wife-and-husband team of Sybil Westland and Des Lock. Curnow thought them highly talented, and had been much moved by their performances in *The Square* the previous year. Unfortunately the pressures placed on them by such a schedule – especially given that plays with only two actors were much more demanding than plays with larger casts – were impossible. By the time *A Slight Ache* and *Dr Pom* began the actors were exhausted. Curnow believed that Barker himself should have foreseen the difficulties of trying to sustain the programme and dropped *A Slight Ache*, so that the actors could focus wholly on *Dr Pom*, which had been billed as the main play. He provided a graphic description of the disaster of the production to Wystan:

> Alas, poor Pom. He deserved better, & Barker should have known better. On the first night, the two actors . . . did not know their lines. I don't mean the occasional prompt, common enough on first nights. I mean that after the first two short scenes, the remaining four were taken over by prompt almost entirely, both actors ad libbing frantically – pace, punch, timing, sequence, dramatic sense of any description completely lost – privately I wholly disclaim authorship of what occurred, & would do so publicly if that were possible.[49]

He did not blame the actors at all, both of whom had day-time jobs, and had 'an inhuman burden of line-study':

> Ronnie knew damned well he was driving both plays straight for the rocks, but held on like a mad sea-captain – & I must say that until the night, I stifled my appre-hensions & counted on the miracle that wasn't going to take place. After an hour of Pinter . . . the audience may have been too numb with boredom to suffer the worst effects of the wreck of Pom. You will imagine that I was far from numb. One of the

worst evenings of my life. . . . R.B. called the next day, hoping to discuss cuts. Cuts! Not dramatic cuts, mind you, but cuts to relieve the actors of vital lines & whole passages they didn't know. I told him to cut what he b--- well liked & that I took no further responsibility. . . . Well, he did cut, or gut, as best he might. . . . I'd mind all this less if R.B. were willing to admit that he had gambled outrageously with my name & work, & (with whatever desperate intentions) let us all down. As for the play, as written, I make no claims & admit no faults, since it has yet to be performed. . . .[50]

Wystan wrote sympathetically, but also ventured a direct comment on Curnow's own propensity for getting himself into foolish situations:

That is very sad about *Dr Pom*. I hope you won't fall out with Ronny over it and that the play can have a decent birth in spite of the premature burial. Ronny is the victim of some of his own virtues – he pushes too hard, fights too hard and maybe the pushing becomes the end rather than the means to something. In New Zealand this would seem a likely malady. But without Ronny your playwriting efforts would be even less rewarding than they are now. All this makes me realise what a hellava thing it is you are trying to do, that none but a fool would try to write plays in New Zealand. But you have a weakness for manoeuvring yourself into such 'foolish' positions. This surely is the most foolish of them.[51]

Curnow did not fall out with Barker, despite the strain on their relations at this time, and '*noted* ruefully' his son's remarks on the folly of writing plays in New Zealand.[52] As for his aptitude for getting himself into foolish situations – 'I'm still wincing a little from that', he wrote, 'but indeed it's true.'[53] When Curnow came to collect four of his plays together for publication in 1972, his preface makes no mention of *Dr Pom* whatever, as if it never existed. It is a pity he did not revise and publish the play then, since it did indeed deserve 'a decent birth' rather than 'premature burial'.

Marriage, 31 August 1965

Early in the New Year of 1965, Curnow and Jeny made a shorter than usual trip south, staying only one day with the Glovers before visiting Curnow's mother in Christchurch, and they spent much longer at Karekare, which was 'full of surfing & fresh fish'.[54] The divorce petition was now under way, and although they were a little unsure when the divorce would be finalised in the courts, they began to make plans for their wedding. 'I think you know better than anyone else can, how we are looking forward to this', Curnow wrote to Pearson, adding: 'You *are* going to be Best Man, as we've always hoped? (Not just ritually BM, but literally so, to us both.)'[55] At the last moment Betty decided that she would not file or serve the petition until she had seen signed contracts for repairing the house and Curnow had lodged the money to pay for it with her lawyer.[56] Although they had hoped to marry in May, by that time only the *decree nisi* had been announced; they settled on a date at the end of August, only a few days after the *decree absolute* came through.

In the meantime, in February, Curnow had accepted a commission from the Poetry Book Society (PBS) in London to write a 200-line poem, possibly with music by Lilburn, for performance in a poetry-reading programme at the Royal Court Theatre as part of a Commonwealth Arts Festival in the week 26 September to 2 October. It was another of his 'foolish' decisions, made on the spur of the moment, he wrote to Wystan,[57] and he regretted making it almost immediately.

Despite increasingly anxious efforts over the next few months the poem quite simply would not materialise. His description to Wystan of what he was aiming to do might almost be an account of what he eventually *did* do five years later in the poems of *Trees, Effigies, Moving Objects*:

> [The poem] is immensely important, & all must take second place to it. It means rediscovering myself, the place, and the first focus, hearthstone or omphalos, which must be the West Coast, but *from* there, not *to*. It also means putting out of mind everything anyone else has written – not *else* – anything I've written myself as well.[58]

In 1965 the time was simply not yet right. In August, he had, finally, to admit defeat to the PBS, apologising for being so 'troublesome' and adding, 'Circumstances have not been at all helpful, but I would be ashamed to blame *them*.'[59] The experience quite simply confirmed to him that (despite the lucky chance of 'Landfall in Unknown Seas' more than two decades earlier) he could not write poems 'to order'. Stead, who had managed to produce a fine poem of his own for the festival ('You Have a Lot to Lose'), read several of Curnow's in his absence.

On 31 August 1965, Curnow and Jeny were married at the Auckland registry office. The wedding ceremony itself was a small, private occasion. Pearson was best man, and Curnow's brother John was also present; Jeny was accompanied by Shirley Andrews as matron of honour and her godmother, Audrie Jacobs. None of Jeny's family and relations attended, but her father arranged a lavish reception at his Seaview Road home, with fine catering and French champagne, and invitations for 60 guests. '[I]t was heroism on their part (and, of course, sheer affection for Jeny) to lay aside Catholic scruples', Curnow later wrote to Wystan.[60] It was a lively affair, with numerous speeches – accompanied by interjections from Khura Glover, who travelled to Auckland especially for the event. They received warm messages from their close friends – from Patricia Harman, Ted Wall, John Schroder – as well as from Jeny's mother, and from Tony in Geneva, and Belinda, who had now moved with her growing family to Sydney. Wystan was more circumspect, but generous despite his conflicted loyalties: 'I am glad to hear that the marriage business went off smoothly and pleasantly. I do wish you both well.'[61]

The day after the wedding they travelled to Northland for four days. It was Curnow's first trip north of Auckland, and they visited the Hokianga where his Monro ancestors had first settled in the 1830s, as well as the Bay of Islands:

> What a spectacular *region* it all is! Those tree-high mangroves on the Hokianga – which is surely *not* just another lovely NZ inlet; it exceeded all my expectations. At Horeke we called at the old pub, which has that rare character, a local historian as licensee. He directed us to the Mangungu cemetery, & there was the grave of William Frederick Mosely Monro, evidently the eldest son of Peter (who arrived there in 1835). W.F.M. Monro, b. 1819, d. 1862. I conjecture that Peter, who served as a youth at Waterloo,* christened his eldest only 4 years later, after Frederick William of Prussia! Then to Kaitaia, *Mangonui*, a remote inlet; then Whangaroa; then Russell, & back to Auckland. At Russell, on a glassy calm, I hired a dinghy & rowed to Kororareka Point: five fine snapper between the two of us in an hour.[62]

To Schroder, he added more about the Bay of Islands part of this 'long-dreamt-of journey':

> The Waitangi treaty house, charming enough, almost too well kept, an invisible glass case encloses the whole spot. The tourist dept. hotel a sheer horror. As if the first-class decks of the Oriana had run aground there & been abandoned by the crew. Russell's the place. The old Duke of Marlborough, reasonable & comfortable. History here, all the more for not striving to be historic.[63]

Already, as he returned from this first trip to Northland, Curnow was storing up memories for future poems, and a play.

---

*   See footnote to page 16.

Chapter Twenty-three

Transitions, 1965–71

When am I going to make finished poems out of a small pile of notes for
lyrics, begun & put aside over some years now?[1]

'Here be "all manner alchemical electronic tinctures"':
another poem for Lilburn

Finished poems remained elusive throughout the second half of the 1960s,
though drafts of poems (mainly worked on during visits to Karekare) began to
accumulate during these years. Driven by Ezra Pound's poetic dictum, 'Make it
new!',[2] Curnow needed time to assimilate the many changes that had occurred in
his personal life, his experiences in the United States, and his encounter with the
rich coastal landscape at Karekare – to find some central imaginative idea around
which such disparate experience might cohere, and a way of writing which might
be adequate to it.

   It was Glover, two decades earlier, who had identified Curnow's distinctive
gift as the 'collective impressiveness' he achieved with 'a number of poems on
some central idea'.[3] He might have been describing *Trees, Effigies, Moving Objects*
– the breakthrough volume which eventually emerged in 1971–72 – as much as
the poems of *Sailing or Drowning* in 1943. In the meantime Curnow could only
keep working intermittently at drafts of poems, read deeply, especially in the
poetry of Wallace Stevens and the philosophy of Nietzsche, and wait patiently,
or impatiently and anxiously, in the hope that poems satisfying Pound's dictum
might emerge.

He remained active in many other respects during the second half of the decade. A new Whim Wham collection was published, and a much darker Whim Wham emerged – anticipating a shift in his serious poetry – as international events (the Cold War, the Vietnam War, war in the Middle East, escalating racial and religious conflicts, the intensification of the nuclear armaments race) seemed to spiral grimly out of control. He wrote two new radio plays, one of them (*The Duke's Miracle*) as good as anything he had written, making a total of five new plays written in the decade 1958–68, and he spent considerable time in 1970–71 revising four of them for publication in 1972. He also worked hard preparing a collection of his critical writings for publication, entitled 'Origins', including in it a substantial new essay based on a paper he gave at the Commonwealth Literature Conference in Brisbane in 1968. The volume in the end did not appear – at this time the market for such writings in New Zealand was too small for publishers to take the risk – but alongside his other literary activities, it suggests that the period covered by this chapter was one of transition for Curnow: his playwriting career was coming to an end, as was his career as an active critic of New Zealand literature; a new, international poetic career was about to start, which would henceforth become the single focus of his writing.

After their brief trip to Northland in September 1965, Curnow and Jeny began looking for a house, and before Christmas shifted to 62 Tohunga Crescent, Parnell, a narrow street off Brighton Road which wound its way for about a kilometre to the western edge of Hobson Bay. The house was a modest two-bedroom bungalow – the mortgage deposit assisted by a wedding gift of £500 from Jeny's father – and overlooked the bay with its tidal mangroves to the south-east, and beyond these, Shore Road, which skirted the bay towards the Orakei Basin and the eastern suburbs. This place, too, once assimilated like Karekare into the imagination, became a rich location for later poems.

In October 1965 the *New Zealand Listener* published a number of tributes to Douglas Lilburn on his fiftieth birthday, by fellow musicians (Owen Jensen, Alex Lindsay, Jenny McLeod, Frederick Page, Larry Pruden) as well as by the poets Glover, Campbell and Curnow.[4] Curnow's contribution was a poem, the first he had published for four years, entitled 'A Year and a Day'. Lilburn was delighted that in Curnow's elegant poem he included his new work in the allusions to his musical career and achievements, evoking Faustus's delight in alchemical magic (in Marlowe's *Dr Faustus*) to convey the magic of Lilburn's own experimental insights into the new world of sound opened up by electronic composition. Lilburn was Curnow's most immediate example of an artist whose credo might be 'Make it new!':

The days and the midnights between the days,
Shades, alterations, novelties,
The written score affirms.

In part, you will be persuaded to allow,
The music affirms, makes room at least
For silence to loom in,

Larger than in the hills where it first harboured:
Spied upon, eavesdropped upon.
The idea was never to break it!

Is it fiddler's armpit sweat or the punished
Underskin of drums, spittle of brass,
Cock-pitted against silence?

Or bloodbeat, waterdrop, all manner alchemical
Electronic tinctures? *'Tis magic,*
Magic that hath ravish'd me!

Curnow's poem sparked an unusual mood of reflectiveness in Lilburn, about
the directions both had taken since the 1940s:

[W]hen we both began I don't think we had anything of this kind in mind. [That
is, public accolades.] Rather it was some personal attempt to come to terms with
some vast, new, exhilarating human context, that feeling of discovery which ran
through our myth-making then. And all begun a quarter-century ago under those
apocalyptic Canterbury skies, on those timeless hills, in that human-size town with
its river, in that youthful human web. And how scattered & disenchanted we all are
since then.

I think I've never quite been whole since then, or never taken wholeness for granted
& reasonable to expect as I did then. Necessary? Of course, & you know it too. It was
valid but cosy. And we become larger since then, but in a bitter, or ironic, or more
fragmented way.

But necessary. And your poem suits my mood. I'm raw to it still, conscious of your
own half-century of experience, of its marvellous asides & half-lights, its quizzical
reflecting & irony, its deftness – allusions & ambiguities, its injunctions. How lightly
you touch the old loyalties, the painters & poets, the hills & silences. But all there,

& full measure for the new, too! I may hang on the new studio wall – Here be 'all manner alchemical electronic tinctures'.[5]

Immediately after Curnow's return from Northland there was also a small avalanche of correspondence with Glover about Fairburn, whose collected poems Glover was in the final stages of editing for the Pegasus Press. In September 1965, Curnow also accepted a commission from chief producer William Austin to write a 60-minute radio sound play for the NZBC on any topic, and towards the end of the year agreed to prepare a new selection of Whim Wham pieces for Blackwood and Janet Paul. At the time he was beginning to plan for a sabbatical leave of six months in the United States the following year, and these two projects were essential to complete before his departure at the end of August 1966.

The author loves it notwithstanding: *Whim Wham Land*

Whim Wham Land (1967) was the last of the selections Curnow himself made from his weekly verses, and the most carefully selected and presented, with a lively, tongue-in-cheek introductory 'Note in Collusion' offering the fullest account (brief as it is) he ever put into print about the aims of Whim Wham. Glover devised a clever jacket design with some *trompe l'oeil* effects: the northern half of the North Island, upside down, appears above the southern half of the South Island, also upside down, with Foveaux Strait in the middle. The grey of these inverted pieces of the country is surrounded by an orange sea, but the optical effect makes this sea appear as a large landmass and the islands of New Zealand as oceanic inlets. There is no place for the country's political and administrative capital, Wellington, in Glover's upside-down rendition of New Zealand, but a compass map shows all points W – as if, perhaps, Wellington loomed on the horizon from anywhere in the country.

The volume's coverage, of fifteen years from 1950 until 1965, overlapped with that of his previous selection, *The Best of Whim Wham* (1959), from which some 30 pieces were reprinted, alongside a further 100 pieces chosen from the seven years 1959 to 1965. Curnow took some care, in his selection, to group pieces thematically, according to his mock-ethnographical note about the nature of Whim Wham's interest in the place. Whim Wham Land, he wrote, 'may be thought to resemble New Zealand, quite strikingly in some respects':

Whim Wham Land is an odd country. The Author loves it notwithstanding. He has devoted (if that is the word) half a lifetime to the study of its history, its language and literature, its arts, its flora and fauna, its social traditions, and its national institutions.

He has lived among the People and observed their quaint customs. He is an acknowledged authority on their folklore.[6]

The 130 pieces were organised into ten roughly equal sections, whose headings
each defined the range of satirical fields with which his hundreds of thousands
of readers were familiar. Whim Wham also suggested, not entirely tongue-in-
cheek, that underlying the specific topics he dealt with were the perennial objects
of satire: self-interest, power-seeking, greed and hypocrisy:

> [I]n Whim Wham Land the same old crops, weeds and blights flourish perennially,
> whoever it is that comforts his chuff in a particular Chair, whoever sits on this Fence or
> leans on that Shovel. The Author (earnestly, but somewhat obscurely, we feel) claims
> that his 'concern is with permanent values, not the trivial accidents of public life'.

In a delightfully witty concluding passage he raised the issue of bias, pleading
innocence and teasing his readers to judge for themselves:

> Like all pioneer investigators, he has his moments of panicky doubt. Has he made
> it all up out of his own head? Is it the product of cool, objective observation? Or an
> unstable mixture of fact and fancy, like the Official Year Book or the Annual Report
> of the Justice Department? The reader must judge.

Like *The Best of Whim Wham*, the new selection focused primarily on the New
Zealand social scene, introducing the international scene (with the exception
of a number of pieces on the space race between the Big Powers) mainly as it
directly affected New Zealand. 'Take your Time, History!', for instance, is deeply
evocative of the mood of those who felt, like Curnow, that Great Britain's move
to enter the European Economic Community was inevitable, and the future,
for New Zealand, unpredictable. In such a witty and moving piece, which harks
back to Feste's closing song in *Twelfth Night*, the distinction between the serious
poet and the light-verse satirist has almost ceased to exist. In its association of
profound historic change with the refrain's oceanic imagery ('*Heigh Ho, the Winds
and the Waves!*'), as if the country is cast adrift and facing a quite unpredictable future, the verse seems to reach back naturally to the deepest impulses of
Curnow's historical poems, and his play *The Axe*, in the 1940s.

The best new pieces in *Whim Wham Land* were as fresh, witty and pointed as
they always were, and particular local events of those years – mounting opposition to Springbok rugby tours, censorship issues raised by the passing of the
Indecent Publications Act, increasingly absurd efforts to deal with the country's
antiquated liquor laws, as well as the advent of television in 1960 and the setting

up of an Arts Council in 1964 – claimed regular satirical attention. However, the cut-off date for Curnow's selection, towards the end of 1965, meant that the key international event of the Vietnam War was largely outside the volume's ambit.

In July 1965, when the Holyoake Government sent an artillery battery to Vietnam, Whim Wham produced the first of many pieces about Vietnam during the next decade – typifying the much darker strain noticeable in the verses in the later 1960s and afterwards, hinting at a growing sense of global crisis which loomed large in the serious poems he was to write. Two issues – the Vietnam War and Springbok tours – featured strongly at this time, and he had to manage carefully the ways in which he engaged with his popular readership on these contentious issues.

Robert Kennedy's assassination in the United States in June 1968, two months after the assassination of the black civil rights leader Martin Luther King, prompted one of his most sombre pieces, 'Dark Week',[7] which he sent to Wystan with a comment that might serve as a motto to many of his later poems about the rituals of political violence: 'The rituals are being re-enacted; & maybe it is always the same victim &, one suspects, the same executioners.'[8] In May 1970 he wrote one of his most powerful satires on apathy, in response to the Holyoake Government's attacks on anti-Vietnam War protesters as longhairs, pinkos and beatniks:

> I was the Silent Majority,
> > I never said a Word.
> I listened to those in Authority.
> > Silently I concurred.
> I followed my Leaders loyally,
> > My Silence let Them know,
> Whatever They said, wherever They led,
> > Was the Way I meant to go.
>
> I was the Silent Majority.
> > Hitler had my Vote, –
> Never a careless Word, Sir,
> > Never a jarring Note.
> Safer to keep my Mouth shut,
> > And let the Nazis yell, –
> Only a Fool would keep a Dog
> > And bark Himself as well.
>
> I was the Silent Majority,
> > I never howled with the Mob,

I never cried, 'Crucify Him!'
    The Soldiers knew their Job.
I never provoked the Authorities,
    Like HIM, the self-styled KING.
I never doubted that Pontius Pilate
    Would do the Proper Thing.

I was the Silent Majority.
    What else did I have to be?
I never spoke for Myself, Sir,
    I let Them speak for Me.
Silent, I gave consent, Sir,
    Knowing not What I gave, –
To the last Violence, the deepest Silence,
    Of a War's common Grave.

I was the Silent Majority,
    Neither a Voice nor a Face,
I was Nobody multiplied by X,
    As Dumb as the Dust in Space.
I died in the last Atomic War, –
    Following, following fast
Wherever They led, whatever They said,
    And Silent, to the Last.[9]

Walter Pollard, on the staff of Romance Languages at Auckland and active in the anti-war movement, wrote immediately to Curnow, addressing his letter 'Cher Mâitre!':

I have just read 'The Silent Majority' & everything I have ever felt has been expressed in that poem. Five years have we laboured and only now do we know for what we laboured. Never have I seen the unformulated dreams & inexpressible hopes put onto paper & incarnated so splendidly.[10]

There was also a lively correspondence in the *New Zealand Herald*: 'This gem should be pasted up in every church, school and workplace in the nation', wrote one contributor. Others were less convinced. 'What should the silent majority really do, if its will, as expressed through a general election, is not respected by a dissenting minority?' The last word was given to a correspondent who described the poem as 'a masterpiece of word expression', but as 'based on an illusion', since 'it is the balanced person who is neither silent nor extreme who enlightens us'. Such verses reveal Whim Wham at his polemical best, engaging readers in public debate and controversy.

An obsession with death: *The Duke's Miracle*

By March 1966 Curnow had decided on the subject matter of his radio play and begun serious work on it, though he wrote to Glover, 'My own piece has started stumblingly, highly serious. Tell no-one that the scenario is Browning's "My Last Duchess".'[11] By the end of April he was close to the end of a first draft, and by mid-May it was at last taking a shape that satisfied him. He sent the completed play to the NZBC at the end of May, and received a prompt reply from Roy Leywood, then acting chief producer – 'a most effective piece of radio writing'[12] – with a cheque for £150, a welcome boost to the financial resources needed for his upcoming trip to the United States.

The Duke's Miracle, which went into production in the Wellington studios (directed by Roy Leywood) the following May (1967) and was first broadcast on 28 July that year, became Curnow's most widely performed play. He took great care to explain that it was not a dramatisation of Browning's famous poem. To Wystan, he described it as 'an "exploded" dramatic version of "My Last Duchess"',[13] and in his introduction to the published text, in *Four Plays* (1972), he also, oddly, even avoided the term 'scenario' to describe the relationship between poem and script, which he had earlier used to both Glover and Wystan:

> *The Duke's Miracle* is not a dramatisation of Browning's 'My Last Duchess', which in fifty-six lines perfectly satisfies the requirements of its own form, so far as these are dramatic. . . . The play is, rather, superimposed on the poem; the poem is treated neither as a scenario nor synopsis for the play, but as a sketch which might be developed. The play adds nothing to the poem; it does not pretend to 'interpret' it. It goes its own way and finds its own solution. If this seems an impertinence, I can only plead that no damage has been done: the poem remains intact, and the play stands or falls, without the slightest help from Browning's fame.[14]

'My Last Duchess' provides a chilling insight into the sexual politics of husband–wife relationships, and triggered some of Curnow's deepest, most abiding concerns with death and mutability. In the poem, one of Browning's most famous dramatic monologues, a wealthy Renaissance duke (of Ferrara) is so driven by an ego which can brook no opposition to or diminishment of its authority, that he 'reads' even the ordinary civilities and courtesies of his beautiful young wife towards others as a sign of less-than-complete devotion to himself. The only way in which he can secure the absolute submission to his will which he requires is to substitute for the real person (whose death, it is implied, he arranges) a lifelike painting of her which he keeps behind a curtain, controlling the display of her to others, at times of his own choice. Browning's lines 'probe, while they represent, the character of a kind of husband', Curnow wrote in his introduction, adding: 'The Duke's sickness is jealousy, to the pitch of paranoia.'[15]

Curnow retains the central characters of Browning's poem (the Duke himself, the Duchess, and her painter, Fra Pandolph), but he also introduces others – most notably, an Envoy who has come to Ferrara to arrange a new, politically strategic marriage 40 years after the death of 'the last duchess'. The Envoy is 30 years old and thus the same age as the Duke was at the time of his earlier marriage to the eighteen-year-old Duchess 'immortalised' in the painting. The complex interaction between the Duke and the Envoy is thus to an extent an encounter between older and younger selves of the Duke, and this provides the main difference between the play and Browning's poem. The play enacts a kind of self-analysis by the ageing Duke, deeply informed by the intellectual and philosophical interests to which he has become attracted in later life.

None of this knowledge and self-knowledge, however, brings the Duke to any understanding or acceptance of life (let alone awareness of the heinousness of his behaviour towards his wife) except as an arena of unresolvable tensions and paradoxes. The Duchess survives, in the preserved image of art, only at the cost of her death, possessing 'Life-in-Death'; the Duke survives, in life, only at the cost of the death of everything in that life which his 'perfect' love for the Duchess had or might have meant to him, living an ongoing 'Death-in-Life'. As in Browning's poem, the Duke in Curnow's play fascinates because he does not seek to justify morally or excuse his destructive actions. Every time he draws the curtain to display the image of his last Duchess, as he does to the Envoy, he re-enacts the destructive and self-destructive desires that motivated the original act. The play delicately balances whatever sympathy-compelling impulses the Duke/Envoy encounter has in the present with a series of flashbacks to the events themselves, 40 years earlier. In all of these scenes the Duke's paranoid jealousy, his callousness, his brutality, are variously on display.

No other play of Curnow's, except perhaps *The Axe*, has quite the same concentration of focus, dramatic skill (especially as it moves between present and past), or intellectual and imaginative depth, as *The Duke's Miracle*. It has suggestive connections to many of Curnow's poems, from the 1950s onwards, and might be seen, for example, as an excursus on the line 'The victims are always beautiful' in 'Spectacular Blossom', a poem which also contrasts youth and age, maleness and femaleness, in a context in which 'perfect beauty' is inevitably fleeting in a world of change, ageing and mortality. The mythic references in *The Duke's Miracle*, sparked by Curnow's reading of Edgar Wind's *Pagan Mysteries in the Renaissance*[16] – a book which explored the many connections between classical (neo-Platonic and mythic) and Christian thought which fascinated Renaissance philosophers and artists – became especially important in his later poetry, as he began to rearticulate the meaning of myth, emphasising its social and political importance as 'explanatory' narrative rather than as a means of access to absolute truth. The writing of *The Duke's Miracle* almost certainly assisted him in establishing the ground on which his new poetry was to be written.

United States, September 1966–February 1967

By the end of 1965, arrangements for a six-month period of sabbatical leave in the United States were beginning to take shape. Curnow had begun in May to think about such a leave, but the problem was financial and would be dependent on grants. As in 1961, his first preference was to go to England or perhaps Europe. He enquired about possible residencies at American universities, but by the end of the year he was still uncertain about finances, though he had a firm invitation from Roy Basler at the Library of Congress in Washington to give a formal poetry reading there the following year.

It was not until July that most of the arrangements were finalised. In his leave application he had identified three aims: to research the life and regional subject matter of Wallace Stevens; to reacquaint himself with developments in poetry, criticism, the theatre and painting; and to read his poems and other New Zealand work at major universities and elsewhere in the United States.[17] He was to leave at the end of August 1966, and after an initial fortnight on the trail of Wallace Stevens in Key West and Jacksonville, Florida, he planned to move to New York, and for the best part of a month undertake a demanding round of poetry readings and lectures including visits to the University of Cincinnati and then to Washington. From mid-November to mid-January he would be based again in New York, returning to New Zealand by air, via San Francisco and Hawai'i, in early February 1967.

Jeny resigned from her job as school counsellor at Tamaki College at this time after ten years, in order to accompany Curnow. Curnow's literary engagements were well paid – $1,000 for the upstate New York Poetry Circuit, $700 for his reading at the Library of Congress in Washington, and $450 for his lecture/reading at Cincinnati – enough for Jeny and himself to survive on until their return to New Zealand. The poetry readings and lectures were essential to provide living expenses for the trip, since his university travel grant of £700 did not quite cover the travel costs for both, most of his salary was required for alimony and mortgage payments, and during his absence there was no income from Whim Wham. They left from Wellington on 31 August and arrived at Fort Lauderdale, Florida, on 22 September.

In pure 'research' terms the trip to Florida was disappointing. They spent four days south-west of Miami at Key West, 'in a blaze of tropical heat',[18] where Curnow visited the local historical association and museum and advertised for information in the local newspaper, but had 'peu de joie', he wrote to Wystan, adding that such a result was not unexpected, since at the time of Stevens's visits he had 'no fame' and was 'the last man to draw attention even if he'd had it'.[19] However, the location itself did not disappoint his expectations. The 'climate, scene, architecture, all that adds up to the nebulous thing "atmosphere", are exactly the "veritable ding an sich" of a few poems'.[20] The 'porched houses, palms, & fantastic tropical thunderclouds, & all the light & colour of the place, made up the true backdrop to his Florida poems', he wrote to Tim.[21]

At Key West the Curnows met Marshall Stearns and his wife.* [22] Then, on 27 September, they flew 400 miles to Jacksonville in north Florida, where they were met by Frank Doggett, the head of a local high school and author of an excellent book, *Stevens' Poetry of Thought*, just published by the Johns Hopkins University Press. Here, too, Curnow found no traces of Stevens, though he was able to talk to one of Stevens's very few surviving friends of the earlier years, the Florida attorney Philip May.

Curnow and Jeny flew from Jacksonville to New York on 2 October, where they stayed at the Hotel Paris on West End Avenue at 97th Street for a fortnight. For the first two days they were entertained by Jeny's mother, Janet Osborne, who travelled to New York from upstate Cazenovia (near Syracuse) where she had a job as resident counsellor at Cazenovia College. Wystan visited for a day from Philadelphia – their first meeting since 1963 – and they took in the Solomon R. Guggenheim Museum, then visited Greenwich Village to listen to Miles Davis's jazz at the Village Vanguard. In New York the Curnows also met for the first time the Oxford scholar A.L. Rowse, among whose many interests were Cornish history and genealogy and who took them to his favourite Breton restaurant.

During his first fortnight in New York Curnow also worked on the month-long programme of lecture/readings he was about to embark on, and finalised their travel and accommodation arrangements for the rest of the trip. Milton and Zaro Starr invited them to stay for the week 3 to 9 November, when they were

---

* Stearns was an author on jazz and teacher of Chaucer at Columbia University, and commented on Curnow's voice that he 'would only have to read the telephone book and American audiences would be enchanted'.

due to visit Washington. Hy Sobiloff was delighted to see them in New York (where he and Curnow reminisced about his stay at Montauk five years earlier, and 'grieved together over Oscar Williams's death' the previous year). Hy invited them to stay with him in New York for a week after their return from Washington. For their last two months in New York, mid-November to mid-January, they also decided to change their accommodation from their hotel room to an apartment at Hotel Albert, 23 East 10th Street, near Washington Square. Despite primitive cooking facilities (no oven), being able to shop for food and prepare meals made for cheaper living costs.

During the fortnight 17 to 30 October, Curnow read at ten universities and liberal arts colleges on the upstate New York Poetry Circuit. The Circuit was administered by the University of Syracuse, with a visiting poet of repute each spring and fall (Curnow was the 'fall guy', he wrote to Schroder),[23] and the invitations were confirmed by the Academy of American Poets, chaired at that time by Professor Norman Holmes Pearson of Yale University. The Circuit included the universities of Syracuse and Rochester (where they stayed with Curnow's old friends of 1950 and 1961, Evelyn and Harry Segal), and campuses of the New York State University at Oswego and Oneonta, as well as Colgate, Wells, Utica, Corning and Cazenovia community colleges, and involved travel almost every day with about 1000 miles covered in all.

He began each reading with two or three of the Maori waiata from the Penguin selection ('Ritual Chant of Fire and Water', 'An Ancient Flute Song' and 'Tipare o Nui')[24] before moving on to his own work. Each reading was accompanied by a schedule of receptions, dinners and parties. The hospitality throughout was excellent, but the pace exhausting. 'Luckily, I found the performance improved as I went on', he wrote to Pearson, 'though I began to feel like an actor in a long-run musical, hamming his way through his 1000th performance. I know better than I did why this kind of thing killed [Dylan] Thomas.'[25]

On 1 November the Curnows flew from Syracuse to Cincinnati, where it snowed unseasonably for the two days they spent there. The university there had one of the bigger poetry endowments, and his engagements included 'an unnerving lunch' with some forty staff after which he was expected to lead a round-table discussion. For his lecture/reading, which focused more broadly on New Zealand poetry, he included Hone Tuwhare's work for the first time, choosing 'Lament', which he also read a little later at his Library of Congress reading:

> The Tuwhare made a magnificent reading piece; certainly nothing could have held this kind of audience better, & nothing did. It had the singleness of impact, 'dramatic' if you like, that elsewhere I can bring off only with Ron Mason's.[26]

From Cincinnati the Curnows flew directly to Washington, where Curnow's most important engagement of his stay in the United States, a reading at the Coolidge Auditorium of the Library of Congress in its prestigious Whittall series, took place on the evening of 7 November, preceded by a formal lunch hosted by Quincy Mumford, the head librarian, and Roy Basler (director of reference), at which there were many speeches to which, as guest of honour, Curnow had to reply. Robert Richman, suffering from spinal problems, was unable to come, but the support of George and Patricia Laking from the New Zealand Embassy, then and throughout their stay, was helpful in easing some of the extreme nervous strain Curnow felt.

One of the pleasures of Curnow's Washington trip was his meeting with the American poet James Dickey, 'a big, warm, loveable man',[27] who was then Poetry Consultant at the Library of Congress and a great admirer of Curnow's poetry, first encountering it when he reviewed *A Small Room with Large Windows* for the *New York Times*. Curnow was able to reciprocate his hospitality briefly in March 1968, when Dickey had a few hours in Auckland on a flight from Wellington to the Adelaide Arts Festival, long enough for a lunch at Tohunga Crescent with Kendrick and Mary Smithyman but unfortunately not long enough for him to be taken to see 'the valley of original rain forest at Karekare': 'I know this wld surprise & delight your woodman's eye; & to leave NZ without seeing it wld be like visiting Florence without the Uffizi.'[28]

Immediately after their return to New York from Washington on 9 November the Curnows moved for a week to Hy Sobiloff's New York townhouse on East 77th Street near Central Park. He and Jeny were both in need of a rest, after the strains of the month-long 'tour of duty',[29] and the stay provided 'more luxury than we're used to'.[30] Jeny had helped 'as no *ten* secretaries could have done', Curnow wrote to Pearson, and without her, 'to pack, & timetable, & share the social pressures, I couldn't have seen it through'.[31]

After the move on 15 November to their apartment at the Hotel Albert on East 10th Street, Curnow was free of commitments except for one – at Wystan's university, the University of Pennsylvania – where he gave a reading under its Leon endowment on 30 November. He and Jeny spent four days in Philadelphia, their first visit there to see Wystan, Sue and the two grandsons: Nathaniel, now four, and Benjamin, whom they had not seen before. There was a great deal of socialising during their stay, with faculty parties and meetings with Curnow's old friends the Havilands and the Sellins (Eric Sellin was now teaching nearby at Temple University), as well as with Wystan's doctoral supervisor, Morse Peckham.

Following the shift to the East 10th Street apartment Curnow also resumed work on a poem, entitled 'Veterans Day in the Metropolitan Museum of Art', which he had begun soon after arriving in New York in early October. He mentioned the poem in confidence to Pearson, as well as to Wystan:

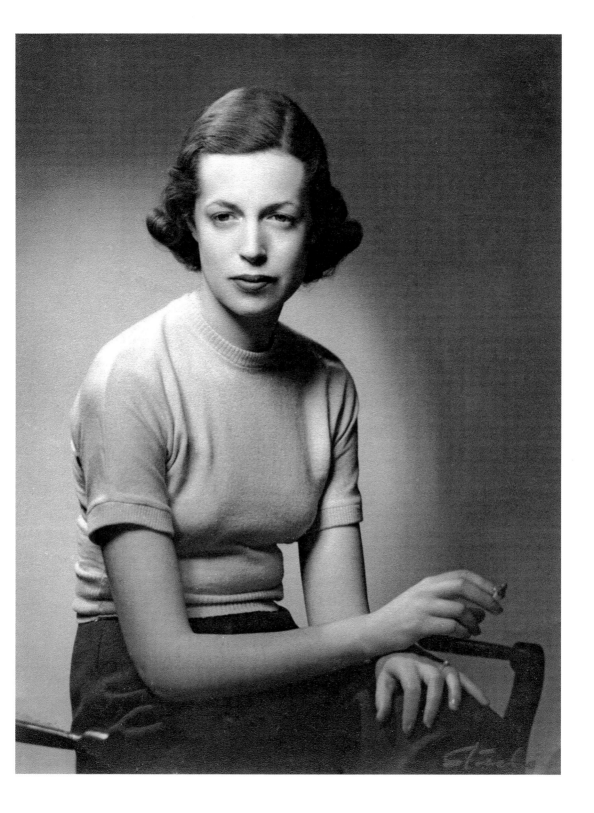

Jenifer Mary Tole (1931–2013), photographed here in 1952, was 23 years old and Curnow 43 when they first met. For many years their relationship was tested and forged in secrecy, and they did not marry until 1965. The famous poem 'Spectacular Blossom' was written within a few weeks of their first meeting. (*Privately held*)

Right: Curnow first met A.R.D. (Rex) Fairburn (right) in 1932 while a student in Auckland and they maintained a regular literary correspondence until Curnow moved to Auckland. Fairburn was godfather to Curnow's youngest son Tim, and Curnow delivered the eulogy at Fairburn's funeral service in 1957. (*Privately held*)

Below: Curnow's teaching at the University of Auckland exerted an influence on a new generation of students with a critical interest in New Zealand literature. Photographed here in 1962 after lectures, with son Wystan (centre left) and friends Tony Hammond (left) and William (Bill) Broughton (right) in the Grand Hotel in Princes Street. (*Privately held*)

Above: Curnow and Jeny on their wedding day, 31 August 1965, with best man W.H. (Bill) Pearson. (*Privately held*)

Left: Bill Pearson, photographed here in the Senior Common Room at the University of Auckland in 1988, joined the English Department in 1954 and became a close colleague of Curnow. He was one of a very small number of trusted friends in whom both Curnow and Jeny could confide. Their loyalty to him was absolute. (*Robert Cross*)

Curnow delivering a talk on poetry in the Bennett Hall Lounge, University of Pennsylvania, in April 1961 during his six-month visit to the United States. Looking on is Shakespeare and Renaissance scholar Professor Matthias Adam Shaaber, then chair of the English Department. (*Privately held*)

Left: Curnow in northern Florida on the trail of Wallace Stevens, after a day fishing on the inland waterway near Jacksonville. It was at the start of his six-month sabbatical leave to the United States in 1966, before heading to New York. 'Everything you see I caught', he writes on the back of the photograph. 'The spots on the bass are part of the fish & very beautiful.' (*Privately held*)

Below: In 1968 in Auckland with poet and novelist James Dickey, who was en route to the Adelaide Arts Festival. They first met in Washington in 1966 when Dickey was Poetry Consultant at the Library of Congress. (Dickey wrote the 1970 novel *Deliverance* on which the famous film is based.) (*Privately held*)

Not in Narrow Seas

Poems with Prose *by* Allen Curnow

Christchurch:
THE CAXTON PRESS
1939

Above: Title page of *Not in Narrow Seas* with a frontispiece by artist and printer Leo Bensemann, published by the Caxton Press, 1939.

Below: *Trees, Effigies, Moving Objects* was published by Denis Glover under the Catspaw Press in 1972. The German edition, *Bäume, Bildnisse, bewegliche Dinge*, translated by Karin Graf and Joachim Sartorius, had a preface by literary critic and poet Michael Hulse, who first met Curnow at the Toronto Festival in 1985 and was instrumental in securing the German publication in 1994.

ON THE TOUR

Verwoerd be our Vatchwoerd!

OR

GOD AMEND NEW ZEALAND

*A timely little Poem for all Ages and Races, suitable for
Recitation or Singing at Rugby Reunions, Church Socials
(leading Denominations), R.S.A. Smoke-concerts,
Hangis, Tangis, etc. etc. etc.*

By ALLEN CURNOW

DEDICATED

in sincere if astonished Admiration of his exemplary Devotion
to the Rugby Broederbond, unswayed by popular Clamour,
undaunted by seditious Conspiracy among the nation's
Religious Leaders, Catholic and Protestant, and unswerving
before the Racial Intolerance of the Maori People

to T. H. Pearce Esq.

Manager of the 1960 All White Rugby Team

This satirical broadsheet, produced by Bob Lowry of the Pilgrim Press, appeared shortly before the
All Blacks departed in May 1960 for a tour of South Africa with a team in which no Maori were
included. The topic was to become a major one over the next two decades for Curnow's popular persona
Whim Wham.

Right: The Curnow bach at Karekare provided a welcome escape from the city where Curnow and Jeny could be alone. Poems such as 'A Pocket Compass' (prompted by a memory of his father-in-law George Tole at Karekare) and the widely anthologised poem 'A Dead Lamb' drew on this much-loved location. (*Privately held*)

Below: Curnow in 1972 with Jeny on the south rocks at Karekare, a favourite spot for fishing and collecting mussels at low tide. (*Privately held*)

Have in draft a new poem of my own, too soon to say whether good or not. About the smiles on the faces of the primitive Greek sculptures in the Met. Museum, & other matters. How do you like 'a rumpus of nymphets' – not for the sculpture, but for some noisy kids round the lunch pool?[32]

Despite the work he put into it, he remained uncertain about its quality. 'Many anxious hours have gone into it', he wrote later to Pearson, '& I still don't *know*.'[33] To Wystan he expressed similar reservations:

The one I have written might strike you at once as prosy & self-deprecating. Or the pose of walking on the broad pavement as if it were a tight wire: maybe the pavement is broad, & the tight wire all in my own head; but it isn't a pose, any more than 'An Oppressive Climate' was. If it were printed anywhere respectable, I wld think well of it; at the moment, I don't so much think ill of it as nothing at all.[34]

The longish poem (some 68 lines) was never published, and it may be that Curnow decided against submitting it to magazines in the United States or elsewhere. It certainly deserved publication, as had 'Capitoline Spring' written on his previous trip. The title refers to the annual Veterans Day (11 November) in the United States, which honours those who served in the American armed forces. However, the particular veterans in Curnow's poem are numerous ancient Greek and Roman statues, in various states of preservation, on display in the Metropolitan Museum. It is a complex poem, gesturing to the present as well as the past, by implication dignifying the 'veterans' / 'votaries' whose parades he has been aware of in the streets outside, while drawing an edged connection between Roman emperors engaging in militaristic adventures (Constantine's 'legions lost in Asia') and contemporary American military adventures with new legions in Vietnam.

Curnow and Jeny left New York on 16 January 1967, flying to San Francisco, then on to Honolulu where they stayed with Jeny's stepsister Olivia and her husband Moki Kahalewai, before arriving in Auckland on 6 February. Curnow was never, again, to base himself in New York in the way he had on his first three overseas trips, 1950, 1961 and 1966–67, but it was now a city, like Washington, which he felt he knew more than superficially – not simply the place, but something of its many ambiences and contradictions. Not least of the pleasures of this short leave in the United States was introducing Jeny to people and places he knew there, and elsewhere, as well as meeting her friends and relatives there and doing new things with her. As in 1961, little resulted from his leave, in terms of conventional scholarly research: he did not publish on Stevens, though a year after his return to New Zealand he decided to substitute Stevens for Yeats in the specialised single-author Master's course he offered, a significant decision not unconnected with his own creative aims:

I have taught Yeats too long; & in trying to keep the teaching *personally* alive, have found too big a gap between my Yeats & the Yeats the students ought to learn about. Besides, WS (I find) leaves me freer to compose my own verse my own way: for reasons maybe of more personal than general validity, Yeats inhibits me. He is a mountain I tire myself climbing: WS more a region where I can visit – at least, while I'm some way from the mountains at the heart of it.[35]

More important, perhaps, were the confirmations of his status as a poet (an acceptance he never felt entirely sure about in New Zealand), and his accumulating experience of an *actual* 'elsewhere', whose value for his poetry would be hard to underestimate though it still needed time to become part of the texture of the way he looked at the world.

The big new subject he felt anxiously, throughout the 1960s, that he needed to discover, and which seemed so often to elude him, involved, precisely, a rethinking of the relationship between *here* and *elsewhere* once *elsewhere* had ceased to be a purely literary or fantasised or imaginary location, and once *here* had been freed from the dominance of the 'national' and become as particularised as the small stretch of surf-beaten coast at Karekare or the immediate environs of Tohunga Crescent and Hobson Bay. Living in the United States released Curnow from (as Whim Wham had put it) 'the America in his head',[36] just as in 1949 the sight of his ancestors' graves in the Caistor St Edmund churchyard had enabled him to say, 'They're real after all', not figures of his grandmother's colonial fantasising.

Seen in this way, the relationship between *here* and *elsewhere* becomes one of *equivalence*. It might be said that a *dynamic of equivalence*, evident also in new approaches to form and language, informs all of Curnow's later poetry. One can never be freed from the dynamic – there is always an 'elsewhere', wherever it might be in place or time, relative to a 'here' where one happens to be, and wherever *that* also might be in place or time – but understanding this introduced a huge new freedom and range into the *occasions* for poetry, and into the nature of the self-reflective processes Curnow brought to them. Misunderstanding it, one might add, also led to continuing misreadings of his poetry, as if he never outgrew a loaded nationalistic privileging of the *here*, a position which he had never espoused in any case.

Return to Auckland

While he was overseas Curnow had learnt from Pearson that his application for promotion to associate professor in 1966 had failed again. Before applying once more in 1967 he consulted Stead, who was now lecturers' representative on the university's Promotions Committee, for advice. Curnow consequently reconsidered his referees, substituting Jim Walton (now a professor at Trinity College, Dublin) for James Bertram, and was pleased and relieved when on this occasion, at last, his promotion to associate professor was approved. In the meantime, Jeny accepted a relieving teaching post at Westlake Girls' High School for the second half of 1967, and in 1968 became a part-time counsellor at Selwyn College in Kohimarama, a job she kept until the end of 1975.

On 28 July 1967 Curnow's radio play, *The Duke's Miracle*, was broadcast for the first time on the YC network, and he was delighted by the immediate response of those whose opinion he valued. The play 'has had the best "press" privately of anything I've done of the kind', he reported to Wystan.[37] Eric McCormick, praising the subtlety of the play, wished he could hear it again, adding, 'It's high time you set about collecting your dramatic pieces. How amazingly varied they are.'[38] Tim had already suggested that Reed might be interested in a book of three plays, and Curnow was interested, but daunted by the task of fitting out scripts drafted for the theatre into a form suitable for publication. McCormick's comment, however, confirmed the idea of publication:

> I am taking to heart your encouragement to print the plays. I shall try to get over a fear of exposing their nakedness, *offstage*, so to speak; & face the job of revising & finding a publisher. *The Axe*, & *Expert*, & this last one, wouldn't be so hard; *Moon Section* & *Dr Pom* both need radical rewriting.[39]

By later in August he had confirmed to Tim that he planned to work on a collection of three plays for Reed to consider, adding that he would try Pegasus Press if Reed decided against.[40]

At this time Curnow was also heavily involved in the long, 12,000-word draft of his reminiscences about Dylan Thomas in 1949 and 1950, which occupied him to the end of the year, when he sent it off to William Latham, who was planning a new biography of Thomas. In fact, more than two years were to pass before Curnow (in 1970) finally gave serious attention to the preparation of his plays for Reed, and in the meantime the performance history of *The Duke's Miracle* had taken an unusual turn, and there had been a further radio play, *Resident of Nowhere*, written later the following year, 1968. Almost certainly it was the *fluid* nature of his dramatic career at this point in the later 1960s, the fact that further new work might continue to appear and perhaps take new directions, that was responsible for the delay in attending to the 'historical' task of getting his earlier plays into print.

The Duke's Miracle was re-broadcast by the NZBC on 31 December 1967, as its 'Play of the Year', and in February the following year Curnow heard out of the blue from the NZBC that the play had been selected by DILIA, the Czechoslovak

Theatrical and Literary Agency, for broadcast on Radio Prague in its biennial National Radio Drama Festival of foreign plays. The selection of the play was an impressive comment on its quality. Altogether there were 103 entries from 33 radio centres in 21 countries, including Japan, Italy, Switzerland, Germany, Denmark, Belgium and the BBC. The translator was the distinguished Czech poet Josef Hirsal, and the contract was for four to five 'emissions' during 1968–69.

Throughout the first part of 1968 Curnow returned to a project he had begun in 1965, of preparing a selection of his critical writings. Whitcombe & Tombs had expressed interest in publishing them, but decided that the market was too small. Tim now suggested that he offer the book to Reed instead, and advised him to exclude any non-New Zealand material.[41] By early May his typescript was complete. 'I've called the book ORIGINS', he wrote to Pearson. 'Now it is all put together, I've got cold feet (chilly, at least) myself. But if they *do* print it, at least it will be what I *have* said, & not what Ian Cross or Louis Johnson *say* I said!'[42]

In an introduction, he commented that all the books he discussed:

> . . . in different ways at different times, put me to the question about the literature of this country, and its character as scene and climate for new writing. All are books which, whatever else might or should be said about them, possess at least the original- ity, and the novelty, of belonging by subject and conception to New Zealand. . . . Whatever we are, or are about to become, these are part of its origins.[43]

On the question of indigenous or 'national' emphasis in criticism, he went on, 'I shall add here only, that there has never been (as I reassure myself, reading these pieces again) anything restrictive or exclusive in the way I have taken account of the New Zealand reference':

> We speak of 'New Zealand literature'. In that phrase we marry an idea of New Zealand and the idea of literature. You can call it a *de facto* arrangement, or say that there ought to be a law. I am afraid that I must tell my younger friends that if they did succeed in breaking it up, it would only set up house again, and perhaps in a style they would dislike even more than the one I have provided. Perhaps if they had their way it would be promiscuous at best, and very likely sterile; happily, their way is illusory.[44]

However, although as late as April 1969 the book was listed by Reed for publi- cation later in the year, it never in fact appeared. By the early 1970s, Curnow's enthusiasm had also waned, as his interests turned strongly, again, to poetry. These and others of Curnow's critical writings were to remain unreprinted until Peter Simpson edited a much fuller selection for Auckland University Press in 1987 called *Look Back Harder*.

Curnow had been approached early in 1968 by A. Norman Jeffares to attend the Commonwealth Literature Conference in Brisbane, 9 to 15 August 1968, as one of its keynote speakers, and immediately after he sent the typescript of 'Origins' to Reed, began to draft the paper he planned to give at the conference. Jeffares was professor of English at Leeds University, and a key figure in establishing ACLALS (the Association for Commonwealth Literature and Language Studies) under whose auspices the conference was organised.*

Curnow enjoyed the conference. He was particularly pleased to catch up with Pearson (in the middle of a three-year research appointment at the School of Pacific Studies in the Institute of Humanities at Canberra), as well as with the Canadian poet Earle Birney, and he was intrigued by his meeting with Jeffares:

> I knew he was an old T.C.D. [Trinity College, Dublin] contemporary of Jim Walton's: that same unmistakable Dublin style, & the insouciant mistrust (at heart) of the Limeys & all their works. Jeffares is fantastically efficient. Told me he has a new Yeats book in the press (US & UK), the poems in the light of the prose, I gathered; the very thing I have been fumbling with all these years. He arrived with the Leeds contingent, including Africans, in a chartered jet.[45]

He described his own contribution, entitled 'Distraction and Definition: Centripetal Directions in New Zealand Poetry', as 'really my old sermon, with different emphases & illustrations'. He devoted considerable space to anthologisers Alexander and Currie[†] and to the poetic treatment of Maori traditions, and then offered a series of elegant critical discussions of Mason, Brasch and Fairburn, before finishing with comments on the promising quality of new work by Smithyman, Baxter and Stead. Partly, the coverage Curnow provided was conditioned by the nature of the conference itself:

> A hundred or so of us, of all countries & colours; hardly anyone had heard of anyone else's literary heroes, so we were all in much the same spot. *Papers* got rattled off somehow, two to a session of 90 minutes or less; one had to cut & extemporize in delivery, but everyone had copies cyclostyled in full.[46]

He was also very pleased to be able to spend a day with Belinda's family at Newport, Sydney, on his way back to Auckland – Belinda and Bruce, now with

---

* Towards the end of 1966, Curnow had been invited by the University of Leeds to spend six months there in the second half of 1967 as its annual Commonwealth Literary Fellow, but the £1,000 stipend was insufficient for him to live on and he had no option but to refuse the fellowship after the University of Auckland declined his requests to retain his salary, or a significant proportion of it, during the time he and Jeny would be away.

† *New Zealand Verse* (1906); revised as *A Treasury of New Zealand Verse* (1926).

four boys, had moved there in 1964 – and soon after his return prepared his paper for publication, together with other conference papers, in *National Identity* (1970), edited by the conference convenor, Ken Goodwin.

Resident of Nowhere

Although no completed poems emerged during the summer of 1967–68, Curnow persisted throughout, he wrote to Wystan, in 'trying new verse of my own – though it feels like an entirely fresh start, stumbling & groping between the wants of subject & style: given the former, of course one invents the latter'.[47] The drafts and fragments were accumulating, as were his observations of the scene at Karekare, providing a store of memories for later poems. As the summer of 1968–69 approached he again anticipated working on these accumulated notes and fragments:

> [W]ish my *appetite* for new poetry was a bit keener. . . . *When* am I going to make finished poems out of a small pile of notes for lyrics, begun & put aside over some years now? Something fell out of my Stevens volume this morning – a few lines on ship's notepaper, about Tahiti. 'Keep your imagination to cool your poems with' – now isn't that a good line? But the poem it ought to belong to is a string of bits that I can't really connect.[48]

In fact, at this time Curnow already had another project which was to engage him fully until the end of 1968, the writing of another radio play, *Resident of Nowhere*. William Austin had approached him in June to write one of six one-hour plays which the NZBC wished to commission to mark the Cook bicentenary in the following year, 1969. 'It is planned', Austin wrote, 'that each should deal with a figure that strongly influenced New Zealand's history. While the basis will naturally be factual, it is intended that the impact should be "drama" rather than ungarnished "documentary". There are many ways of tackling these subjects: epic, poetic, domestic, etc.'[49] Curnow was interested, but needed time to think about the figure he would choose. The question of finding a suitable subject was always a major problem for him:

> Before I write the first thing I feel is a craving for a subject. There is this gap and the subject for a play is what will fill it. For me this is a major problem. After sometimes months of searching somewhere, perhaps in one's subconscious or subliminal mind or whatever probings of oneself, there appears something that looks like a subject. After a bit of experimenting and some time has elapsed it may turn out that it is not the right subject after all.[50]

In August, prompting him again, Austin mentioned that the other figures in the series were Hongi Hika, Sir Donald McLean, Tamati Waka Nene, Wiremu Tamehana and Joseph Banks. Curnow wanted someone who did not cut a heroic or noble figure in New Zealand's history, and he also wanted a relatively minor figure whose role was sufficiently clear not to require him to engage in historical debates for which he felt unqualified. He chose the unlikely figure of British Resident James Busby. To Wystan he expanded on the elements that attracted him in his subject:

> I have chosen Busby: ambiguous, tragic in his way. After all, he was the first to think of assembling the Chiefs, & drafted Waitangi for sick Hobson. Where is the NZ Flag that he designed & hoisted? Every Shaw Savill ship flies it, – the company's house-flag. Then his 30 years in NZ after Waitangi, obsessively fighting his land claims; at 70, deaf & nearly blind with cataract, he went to Sydney, then London for an eye operation; the latter was successful, & part of his claim settled in his favour; he died of a chill a few weeks after. NZBC asked for some historical worthy, & I've chosen B because popular history reputes him a failure & a fool, – no part of the local hagiography.[51]

Curnow spent September, October and much of November 1968 reading for the play, in the midst of end-of-year student examination marking. 'I began by reading all I could on him', he commented, 'and I actually spent more time reading than on the actual writing of the play. This got the history out of my system before I began writing.'[52] He also drew on his familiarity with Busby's Bay of Islands location, in the wake of the visits he and Jeny had made to Russell since their marriage in 1965. In 'inventing a Busby', he wrote to Pearson, 'I don't want to make any silly historical mistakes, & must hope that my reading will be enough to save me from those'.[53]

Curnow did not start writing the play until later in November, and wrote it at speed, over little more than three weeks, utilising the same structure as *The Duke's Miracle* – a series of flashbacks, as the aged Busby, tended by his wife Agnes, obsessively returns in fevered reveries to events during the period (1833–40) of his Residency, reading, as he puts it, 'the Book of Injustice' in 'the tablets of my memory':[54] the scene of his arrival in the Bay of Islands; a scene with Henry Williams in which he learns of the moral squalor of the time; the scene – contemptuously observed by Pakeha riff-raff – of the flag-raising and signing of the Declaration of Independence; a final flashback (after Busby has been shot at in his house at Waitangi) which reveals the powerlessness of his position. Curnow was 'flat out writing it till Xmas Day itself' – 'it woke me daily at 5am. for three weeks'[55] – and it went quickly into production with Roy Leywood in

February 1969, having its first broadcast on 14 March as part of the 1969 Auckland Festival, and a repeat performance later in the year as part of the national NZBC Cook bicentenary series of plays. Its first performance attracted positive reviews from the Auckland newspapers. Robin Dudding, Brasch's successor as editor of *Landfall* in 1967, published the play in the magazine's June issue, and it was subsequently included in Curnow's *Four Plays*, in 1972.

Turning 60: the death of friends, and changing family dynamics

During the two years from mid-1969 to mid-1971 Curnow did not attempt any substantial new writing, apart from an effort in September 1970 to work on a collaborative 'words and music' project with Lilburn to mark the Auckland City Council centenary, which came to nothing. His academic work kept him busy, especially his new full-year Master's paper on Wallace Stevens, which he gave for the first time in 1969, and later that year he wrote to Wystan about his own teaching preparation habits, and the pressures of his workload:

> It is possible that my feelings about some of these things are coloured by my own work habits & the kind of work I do: e.g., I make heavy weather of annually freshing up at least some part of Spenser – such bulk here! I can't manage Hons. Stevens (any more than I could Yeats) without much brooding through the week & at least one day's full attention before the lecture; much the same for Sonnets in Hons. Shakespeare. And (as I said in my last) a profession is never *quite* so much one's own, however nearly that happens, when adopted as late in life as I did this one. It does not follow that everyone's experience is the same as mine.[56]

In 1970 he worked intensively on the preparation of his plays for publication during breaks between each term, and completed his introduction to them during the summer of 1970–71.

In 1971 Curnow turned 60, and the deaths of friends during this and earlier years were a reminder of his own mortality. He was distressed when Ronald Barker died suddenly at a relatively young age in September 1968, and wrote a warm and deeply appreciative obituary notice about his contribution to New Zealand theatre for the *Auckland Star*, as well as (with Jeny) offering emotional support for his wife Lilian and young children. A year later, Khura Glover died, also suddenly, a particular sadness for both Curnow and Jeny since she had been so much a part of the landscape of their lives, on their annual trips through Wellington to Christchurch, since they first met in 1955. 'She loved you two more than anyone', Glover wrote to Curnow and Jeny, 'and when I grumbled about Allen, as has been my wont, would fly to your defence like a fighting bantam.'[57] Quite how Glover would cope without Khura was also an anxiety, though after a second visit from Glover the following April, Curnow was much relieved to feel that he seemed well on the way to recovering from 'the near-collapse of the past 6 months'.[58] In 1971 Ron Mason died, and Curnow gave the memorial address at the university's Maclaurin Chapel to more than 250 people, speaking eloquently of the significance of Mason's life and art: 'We would be no nation at all, if we did not honour him and mourn him, as our common friend and our common pride.'[59]

In 1971, too, Curnow published one of the rare personal pieces by Whim Wham, after he learnt of the death of his old American friend Hy Sobiloff the previous year, from a heart attack. 'Portrait of an Artist (H.J.S. 1913–1970)' was the only Whim Wham piece Curnow ever contemplated reprinting under his own name, though he decided against doing so. He sent copies to Roy Basler at the Library of Congress, who in turn sent them on to Sobiloff's other poet-friends, Eberhart, Allen Tate and Conrad Aiken. Tate thought it was 'a very moving work',[60] and Aiken thought it 'beautiful' and sought a copy for the Georgia Poetry Society and for its annual report. Eberhart liked best 'Allen's addressing the (newly) dead as if they were alive', but could not understand the reason for the pen name and the capitalisations.[61] 'Dick is right about the capricious capitals', Curnow wrote to Basler. 'He was not to know that these are an eccentricity I adopted for this weekly press feature more than 20 years ago. I fancy that most of its devoted readers would hardly recognize it without them....'[62]

There were also more personal events, during the later 1960s, which made Curnow aware that he belonged to an older generation, and that the dynamics of his family relationships had rapidly changed. In 1970 his mother turned 90. She was still determined to live on her own, at her home in Meadow Street, where she received regular visits most days from a district nurse and home aid, and enjoyed reasonably good health, though her frailty was a matter of concern to all of her sons, who arranged their visits for different times of the year. Some, amongst those who knew Jessie in Christchurch (most notably and vociferously, Audrey Cotterill, Curnow's cousin, as well as some of her church friends), felt that she should be in a rest home, but Curnow – who kept in regular touch for advice from her doctor and visiting social worker – felt strongly that her own wishes should be paramount, as he explained in regular letters about her health to his brother Tony:

> [The doctor's] view was substantially unchanged: briefly, that whatever the hazards & difficulties of leaving her alone, a 'home' might well be the end of her, even if she could be persuaded against her will. Her will, as you will imagine, is as strong as ever; & although the old machine moves slowly, it has not broken down.[63]

Curnow's three children were well established in independent lives and careers, and there were eight grandsons, now all living in Auckland. Wystan and Sue returned to Auckland in 1970, with their three sons, Nathaniel, Benjamin and Barnaby (their fourth, Tobias, was born in 1972), and Wystan took up a lecture-ship in English at the University of Auckland, after two years at the University of Rochester and a further six months at York University, Ontario. His doctorate, on the American novelist and poet Melville, was awarded the following year. For a number of years he had been actively publishing his own work, short fiction as well as critical articles, and pursuing his interest in the relationship between the visual arts and literature. In 1971 Belinda returned to Auckland with her four sons – Matthew, Samuel, Joseph and Daniel – after six years in Sydney, and in that year the fifth of her sons, Jesse, was born. Tim, after successfully developing the edu-cational list at Reed (he expanded the Primary programme, introduced Secondary and Tertiary programmes, and established the Reed Education imprint along with numerous innovative New Zealand-focused approaches to texts and their design), moved to Sydney later in 1970 in order to become managing editor of the firm's office there. He was now separated from his wife Heather, and within a year of settling in Sydney struck out on his own into a new career as a literary agent, becoming managing director of the Australian company of the London literary agency of Curtis Brown. Curnow was fascinated and impressed by Tim's 'entrepreneurial' energies, his willingness to seize new career opportunities, which he thought showed character traits quite unlike his own but very similar to those of his younger brother, Tony. Belinda's situation was the hardest at this time, when she was in the process of separating from Bruce, though she was supported by both of her parents as she struggled to bring up her young family of five as a solo parent.

Curnow related to his children in quite different – much more relaxed – ways as they developed their own independent lives, and enjoyed seeing his grandchildren. Jeny, who also enjoyed her own developing relationship with the children and the grandchildren, played a key role in arranging the regular occasions on which they saw each other at Tohunga Crescent, and occasionally at Karekare. As their means allowed, Curnow and Jeny were able to make small renovations to the house at Tohunga Crescent and the bach at Karekare, making both places more hospitable for visitors. In 1969 they had power connected to Karekare, and were able to install a small second-hand refrigerator, as well as electric light; and between 1971 and 1973 a small basement space at Tohunga Crescent was turned into a guest room with its own facilities. In 1969 Jeny wrote to Tony that they had purchased a beagle pup, named Flash, 'most beautiful, & I'm afraid very spoilt. Allen dotes on him even more than I.'[64] Flash became an inseparable companion on Curnow's daily walks along Brighton Road or to Hobson Bay, as well as at Karekare, and made his first appearances in three poems of the sequence *Trees, Effigies, Moving Objects* two years later.

Wystan, Belinda and Tim, over the years, had made their own accommodations with their parents' separation, and remained close to their mother, as well as enjoying their father's evident sense of new-found contentment and security in his relationship with Jeny. Betty provided crucial emotional and practical support to Belinda during the years in which she was bringing up her family on her own, and Curnow also provided financial assistance to enable her to purchase a house in Beach Haven in 1974. Wystan, as the oldest, had the more difficult task of negotiating issues on his mother's behalf (house repairs that needed attending to, and the like) with his father, when they arose.

The complex feelings associated with death, ageing and generational change seem to have provided the personal catalyst Curnow needed to turn the drafts and fragments which had been accumulating over ten years into completed poems, during the second half of 1971. By November of that year, he had a number of poems in draft form, writing to Tony that 'Wystan's energy also sends me back to sweat over a dozen poems in draft which must be made fit to print'.[65] He had made such a comment on numerous occasions over the previous years. This time, however, the outcome was different, and a month later (as he wrote to Glover, praising the poems in Glover's recently published *Diary to a Woman*) he was contemplating sending the poems to Robin Dudding at *Landfall*:

> Only one line of my own recent hard-ground pieces seems to compare: it runs (never mind the context) –
>
> > Pray for this tissue not to be rejected
>
> But why I flatter myself so will not be apparent, unless (until) it is all in print: Lfall maybe, if Dudding will oblige to the tunes of c.400 ll.[66]

The line he quoted was from 'A Four Letter Word', one of his major poems, about the origins and nature of the mythic impulse in human behaviour. Throughout the summer of 1971–72 he continued to work on the poems, and they became a sequence of eighteen, to the 'tunes' of 571 lines. They were to inaugurate an astonishing second flourishing of Curnow's poetry – a second career – during the next 30 years.

PART III

Chapter Twenty-four

The Making of a Sequence:
Trees, Effigies, Moving Objects, 1972

When I was working on Trees, Effigies, Moving Objects, I know I was trying harder than ever to reconcile the formal pressures I feel, with some personal pressures that – in my case anyway – could only be contained by poems. . . . [I]sn't it a personal pressure, simply being the age I am? . . . . But there are other pressures – they may go back to the childhood I was trying to describe – which have more to do with being a New Zealander than being sixty. I mean the pressure of here where one is, and the there which is all the world.[1]

A new period of intense creativity – and anxiety

All except one of the eighteen poems of Curnow's *Trees, Effigies, Moving Objects* found their final shape and order during an intensive burst of activity in the spring and summer of 1971–72, and the sequence was published by Glover under his new imprint, The Catspaw Press, at the end of 1972.* A decade had elapsed since his previous volume (the selection *A Small Room with Large Windows*, 1962), and it was even longer since his previous collection of wholly new work, *Poems 1949–57*.

Although this was a long gap (and some, it seemed, had been prepared during this time to write Curnow off as finished) his poetic career had always been

---

* The exception was 'Any Time Now,' which was completed in June 1972 and placed at the end of the sequence.

marked by sudden bursts of activity followed by longish periods in which little
or nothing was published. His publication history tended to disguise this fact.
Almost all of the poems in his two main volumes of the 1930s, *Enemies* and *Not
in Narrow Seas*, were written during just fifteen months in 1936–37. Most of the
poems of *Island and Time* (1941) and *Sailing or Drowning* (1944) were written
during little more than two years between late 1940 and early 1943, and most
of the new poems in *At Dead Low Water* (1949) were written during eighteen
months between 1945 and 1946. Almost a decade then elapsed before his next
creative burst, in the eighteen months between the end of 1954 and mid-1956,
when his major poems of the 1950s were written.

Curnow did not of course stop writing in the gaps between each of these
periods of intense creativity – often he wrote a great deal in draft and occasionally published excellent new poems in magazines – but each of the intensive
periods was marked by an excited personal discovery of a new direction in his
poetry. Curnow was possessed to an extraordinary degree throughout his career
of the need to 'make it new', to avoid simply repeating what he had already done.
His anxiety in the 1960s about the absence of new poems was nothing new. He
had felt the same in the late 1930s, wondering if he had written himself out, and
again in the later 1940s, and again in the earlier 1950s. And because each new
direction felt like a new beginning it was marked by intense anxiety about how
the new work might be received by readers whose expectations had been shaped
by familiarity with his earlier work.

With *Trees, Effigies, Moving Objects* – perhaps because of the intensity of
Curnow's personal investment in the poems, perhaps, as he wrote to Robin
Dudding, because of the lapse of so many years of apparent 'truan[cy] from
poetry'[2] – he was more nervous than he had ever been about their reception.
Curnow wrote in some detail about the provenance of the poems to Dudding
(who selected seven of them for publication in the first issue of his new magazine,
Islands, shortly before the volume itself appeared), by way of providing infor-
mation and context for Dudding to use in a note to accompany the selection:

> The *facts* are that I had three folders of notes for poems, fragments, half-revised
> passages, cancelled drafts, some dating back to Washington in 1961 (not much of this),
> others done at Kare Kare or Parnell. What was wanting was one poem, at least, that
> looked ready. . . . It didn't occur till some time last year, & the poem was 'Lone Kauri
> Road'. It was good enough to bring back the confidence to work on others: then a
> few entirely new ones, e.g. Magnificat, A Dead Lamb, A Hot Time, Any Time Now.
> I began to want a kind of perspective, where one could stand on a beach, or walk
> in the street, or look out the window, or be perhaps in two places at once, & in that
> one perspective arrange (it begins to look surrealistic) a bit of Nature (the Trees stand

for that), a bit of supernature or artifice (the Effigies, anything from an advertising sign to an image of the Virgin or Lincoln), and all the agitation and variableness and flux of everything (Moving Objects, anything from a carton or a truck or a car, or a jet aircraft, to one's dog or oneself walking, to the sun going down or the tide going out). Now, the general title wasn't thought of first, as a 'scheme'. It was thought of afterwards, & took a long while to find, as the best way of describing what was in the poems.[3]

At least some of those earlier 'fragments, half-revised passages, cancelled drafts' from the 1960s have survived, as well as later working drafts of poems as they emerged during the spring and summer of 1971 and 1972. The earliest related to the United States, especially the long 'cancelled draft', entitled 'Capitoline Spring', which he had completed during the months of his stay in Washington DC (April and May 1961) and submitted unsuccessfully at the time to *Poetry* (Chicago). Ideas, images and phrases from this draft later found their way into three of the four 'American' poems dispersed through the sequence – 'Friendship Heights', 'Do It Yourself' and 'Bourdon' – especially 'Bourdon'. The other 'American' poem, 'A Framed Photograph', evoking the Kennedy era and its aftermath, was based on notes (also made at this time) of a visit to the Friendship Heights home of William and Mary Bundy during the final fortnight of his stay in Washington, where he observed a Jamaican servant dusting a framed photograph of President Harry Truman with his Foreign Secretary Dean Acheson (Mary Bundy's father) on the Bundys' drawing-room piano.

The key to finding a poetic use for the rich material Curnow had garnered during his 1961 visit to Washington lay in the discovery of a local perspective and frame for it, a frame which would not only include the particularities of the poet's physical location in New Zealand but his personal life (including the fact of ageing and the ongoing challenge of personal belief), his political understanding of the relationship between New Zealand and America during the crisis-ridden 1960s, and the articulation of an intellectual frame which might be adequate to the tensions and polarities he wished to address. Curnow gave a number of the poems a first reading to a lunch-hour audience at the Auckland Central Library in July 1972 – before any of them had been published – and introduced his reading with comments which also suggested that at the core of their varied concerns was an effort to discover (or construct) a self which might be in some way or to some extent representative of its time:

The subject is one man alone here – in the bush, by the sea, in this city where we all live – and in another city which contains the greatest and most terrible power in this world, where we all live too. The poems do the best they can, to make sense out of the cry of this human consciousness – if they are any good at all, it isn't just *my* cry – of course it *is* mine, but if it were only that, it wouldn't be a subject for poetry.[4]

During his 1966–67 visit to the United States Curnow completed a New York poem ('Veterans Day in the Metropolitan Museum'), but found no direct use for it in *Trees, Effigies, Moving Objects* as he did for 'Capitoline Spring'. Instead, in the later 1960s the drafts and fragments he wrote were mainly focused on aspects of the local scene, in particular on bush settings: the huge, decaying kauri tree, Tane Mahuta, in the Waipoua Forest which he first saw on his trip to the Hokianga in September 1965, and (as he wrote in some excitement to Pearson, surprised that he had not noticed it earlier) the 'great Northern Rata (Metrosideros robusta!)' which he first discovered at Karekare, blooming in 'the gully above the Taraires and the Nikaus', in the summer of 1968.[5] In these 'tree-poem' drafts Curnow responded to a sense of nature as threatening, violent and alien.

By the late 1960s, then, Curnow's drafts, fragments and notes seem to have consisted largely of his American 'effigy' materials and drafts of tree and bush poems – the materials, that is, for about half of the poems of *Trees, Effigies, Moving Objects*. The poetic catalyst for the sequence occurred during the second half of 1971, with the writing of 'Lone Kauri Road', a brilliantly rich if seemingly defeated attempt to 'capture' or 'frame' in language a constantly shifting, cloud-swept coastal scene at Karekare – a poem replete with moving objects, including the poet's own thoughts and feelings and sensations.

Alongside 'Lone Kauri Road' Curnow composed a number of other poems with an intensive focus on movement in time and space, extending the locations to include his Auckland urban environment. These included 'Two Pedestrians with One Thought' (a wind-buffeted walk in Brighton Road, Parnell), 'The Kitchen Cupboard' (a Hobson Bay tidal scene observed from the house at Tohunga Crescent), and the brief 'Agenda' (its location Beach Road in the central city, according to Curnow, and its mock-aphorisms presumably sparked by images on inner-city billboards). In 'An Upper Room' (on the theme of generational change, felt during a class on Milton in the poet's university office overlooking Auckland harbour) the poet identifies himself as in his 'sixty-first year', after, that is, turning sixty in June 1971. In the wake of these Auckland urban poems, he went on, over the summer of 1971–72, to write 'Magnificat', 'A Dead Lamb' and 'A Hot Time'. By the end of summer 1972 the sequence was complete, with the exception of 'Any Time Now', another Brighton Road walking poem which became the final poem.

'Lone Kauri Road' was a catalyst for the sequence not only in suggest-ing the third term, 'moving objects', alongside 'trees' and 'effigies', as a means of identifying the subject matter of the sequence, but also because it sparked the idea that the problem of representation – the teasing gap between words and the things (objects, events, abstract ideas, systems of belief) to which they refer – might provide, paradoxically, an organising principle for otherwise highly disparate poems. Almost certainly the idea of the poems as forming a sequence first occurred in its wake. Furthermore, 'Lone Kauri Road' introduced a directly *personal* perspective. The poet in his Karekare bach casually reading, observing, writing, is suddenly caught up increasingly, as the observed scene of cloud and sun continually changes and keeps 'backing away', in feelings of anxiety and threat which he struggles to articulate – feelings about ageing, death, the prospect perhaps (deeply ingrained from his childhood) of a last judgement. From such a perspective he could now think of all such commonplace acts of observing, reflecting, remembering, speaking, as carrying an imagining of a self – whose perspectives, beliefs, anxieties, pleasures, uncertainties might provide a unifying dimension in the sequence. Curnow stressed the importance of this dimension in his explanatory note to Dudding when, after listing many of the disparate objects, events and locations in the poems, he commented:

> All this has to end in paradox: that in locating or identifying such things, & arranging the 'perspective', there's an ulterior object which is to locate and identify not *them*, but the *self*. All poetry has that object. If I have invented a kind of triangulation in Trees, Effigies, Moving Objects, it isn't one I would think of justifying philosophically, literally in those precise terms. It is simply an appropriate title for these poems. . . .[6]

In fact Curnow had various thoughts about an 'appropriate title' before arriving at *Trees, Effigies, Moving Objects*. Until quite late in the process he had settled on 'Cloud Effects, Effigies, Moving Objects', but he also considered 'Continuum' (the title he gave to a much later selection), 'Omens/Exits, Effigies, Moving Objects', and – oddly – 'In a Sieve I'll Thither Sail' (a quotation from one of the witches' speeches in *Macbeth*). Perhaps the latter was intended to allude ironically to the poems' seemingly magical capacity to traverse the oceanic distances between New Zealand and Washington.

Intellectual and literary contexts – Wallace Stevens

Personal and political events provided catalysts in the emergence of *Trees, Effigies, Moving Objects*, but the poems were also deeply informed by new intellectual and literary interests. In the late 1930s and early 1940s Curnow's poetry had taken a quite new direction in the wake of his rethinking of the importance of Yeats (who supplanted the English thirties poets in his thinking) and his excited discovery of the work of the philosopher Henri Bergson. A parallel shift in his literary and intellectual interests occurred in the 1960s, especially after the mid-1960s, when his reading took him in a number of new poetic, critical and philosophical directions. In his thinking about poetry, Wallace Stevens assumed an importance. He had been familiar with Stevens's poetry since the 1950s and written an elegy on him after his death in 1955, but from the mid-1960s, when he embarked for the first time on really intensive reading of his work – not only his poetry, but his essays and, especially, the remarkable letters which his daughter published in 1966 – Stevens began to supplant Yeats as (in his view) the most pressingly and immediately relevant poet to the crises of belief and politics Curnow identified in the post-war world.

Stevens's poetry was not especially influential on Curnow – there is hardly anything in the styles and forms of the poems of *Trees, Effigies, Moving Objects* that is derivative of Stevens, except perhaps his adaptation of Stevens's trademark distichs (unrhymed two-line stanzas) in several of the eighteen poems, including 'A Four Letter Word' and 'A Dead Lamb'. Stevens's *thinking* about poetry was, however, quite a different matter. The philosophy in Stevens's writing, Curnow commented to MacDonald P. Jackson, 'may have affected me in recent work, without fear of being what I call contaminated by his style':

> One sees in Stevens an essentially modern and sceptical mind finding a ground in thinking of modern man which somehow dispenses with mythology, dispenses with theology, and attempts to face it naked, an attempt to go to reality with one's bare hands, which is possibly what we all have to do.[7]

In the later 1960s Curnow was especially interested in the burgeoning critical discourse about Stevens's later work, which emphasised his importance as a poet of intellectual preoccupations, rather than – as Edmund Wilson and Yvor Winters had provocatively argued – primarily a poet of sensations. During Curnow's visit to Florida and Key West in 1966, Frank Doggett had given him a copy of his own just-published study, *Stevens' Poetry of Thought*,[8] one of the first books to approach Stevens as a poet interested in the *poetic* possibilities of ideas. On the same visit to the United States, Curnow also purchased a copy of *The Act of the Mind*,[9] a seminal collection of essays on Stevens's poetry edited by Roy Harvey Pearce and J. Hillis Miller. Although he annotated various of the book's essays, in ways that reveal a great deal about the direction of his own intellectual interests at the time, the one which most interested him was Miller's on 'Wallace Stevens's Poetry of Being'. The disappearance of the gods in Stevens's earlier work ('they reveal themselves to be fictions, aesthetic projections of man's gratuitous values'),[10] according to Miller, drove Stevens into a seemingly endless seeking to escape from the internal conflict of a human self divided against itself:

One part is committed to the brute substance of the earth, things as they are, and the other just as tenaciously holds to its need for imaginative grandeur. Self-division, contradiction, perpetual oscillation of thought – these are the constants in Stevens's work.[11]

However, as Stevens's work progressed, Miller argued, he came more and more to discover that 'there is after all only one realm, always and everywhere the realm of some new conjunction of imagination and reality': 'Imagination is still present in the most absolute commitment of the mind to reality, and reality is still there in the wildest imaginary fiction.' The later poetry, he went on, moves 'beyond meta-physical dualism, and beyond representational thinking'.[12] Curnow commented marginally of this formulation, 'This improves immensely on RHP's [Pearce's]', and marked a number of passages in which Miller described the development of a mode of poetry of 'flickering mobility', of 'flittering metamorphosis', whose aim was to sustain the idea of the identity of poetry and life, glimpsed only in the most fleeting of moments:

> Stevens gradually develops, as his poetry progresses, a way of matching the fluidity of time. He comes to write a poetry of flickering mobility, a poetry in which each phrase moves so rapidly it has beginning and ending at once. Instead of being fixed and unyielding, a solid piece of language interacting with other words, each image recapitulates within itself the coming into being of the moment and its disappearance.[13]

At the heart of such poetry, Miller concluded, was the adumbration of an idea of 'being' different from the metaphysics of dualism. Curnow noted and ticked Miller's key phrases describing this idea of being:

> Being . . . is within things as they are, here and now, revealed in the glistening of the steeple at Farmington, in the flowing of time, in the presentness of things present, in the interior fons of man.[14]

> The mobile, flickering poetry of Stevens's later style, poetry which fears stillness beyond anything, is more than a revelation of the impossibility of escaping the war of the mind and the sky. It is a revelation of being.[15]

> Perhaps it is Stevens's way, the movement from the dissolution of the gods to the difficult apperception of being, which represents the next step forward in the spiritual history of man. . . . Central in this movement is the idea that all our spiritual height and depth is available here and now or nowhere.[16]

Rethinking myth – 1950s, 1960s and 1970s

Curnow was attracted to Stevens's deeply sceptical, humanist intelligence, his lifelong poetic effort to discover a ground for affirming 'being' in the spatio-temporal world which did not depend on metaphysical idealism or on belief in some sponsoring mythic, theological or religious absolute. Myth was a central preoccupation in *Trees, Effigies, Moving Objects*. Curnow's interest in its nature, in mythic thinking as a general human phenomenon, and in the variety of mythic systems in human history, had begun to take new directions during the later 1940s and 1950s. When he visited ancestral Cornwall during his trip to England in 1949 he had been fascinated not simply by its distinctive landscape and seascape but by the relationship between the place (and its human history) and the character of the myths and legends these had engendered. On his return to London from Cornwall, Curnow purchased Robert Graves's recently published *The White Goddess* (1948). It was a strange and eccentric work, but attracted a great deal of literary interest at the time because of its strong assertion of a connection between poetry and myth. Subtitled 'A Historical Grammar of Poetic Myth', it offered what Graves called an 'iconotropic' or etymological reading of a wide range of Celtic, European and ancient Middle Eastern myths, claiming to discern behind them an original female deity, the 'White Goddess of Birth, Love and Death', the inspiration of all poetry.

There were also local reasons behind Curnow's beginning to rethink the notion of myth in the 1950s. Early in that decade he found himself under attack as a 'mythmaker' by critics (younger, primarily Wellington-based poets, and historians like Keith Sinclair and Bob Chapman) who used the term 'myth' in a largely negative sense. He (and others like Holcroft and Brasch) was accused of inventing a 'South Island myth' (in their poetry, but more damagingly in their criticism) and foisting it as 'truth' on the country as a whole. Curnow's initial reaction to such criticism was, in effect, to *accept* the implied popular definition of myth – as a false, invented narrative, lacking credibility – and to defend his own and others' work on *realist* grounds. Far from being 'mythical' in this sense, he responded, such work at its best embodied a *true* response to historical and geographical conditions which was New Zealand-wide in its application. If the South Island mountainscapes of poets were formidably remote and icy and the northern Auckland beachscapes of Fairburn and others invitingly warm and sunny, such differences were *of the surface*, and to emphasise them was to fall into the trap of valuing mere pictorialism: the *underlying* impulses (historical, social, personal) were *shared* ones, relevant to the country as a whole.

It seems not to have occurred to Curnow at the time to challenge his detrac-tors on the ground of their facile definition of myth: to suggest that *indeed* such work might be seen as inventing a myth or series of myths, and that that was *precisely* its value and its achievement, since the elements out of which the myth had been constructed represented a new, perhaps 'truer', certainly more challenging, way of *imagining* the country's past, present and future than had hitherto existed. A poverty-stricken colonialist myth was replaced by a myth which placed the country not on the dependent edge of the British Empire, but at its *own* centre, needing to renegotiate its internal history and rethink its relationship to the rest of the world. To think of myth in this way, however, required recognising that myths play a fundamental role in all human societies, offering culturally distinctive fictive narratives which articulate – always contingently, *because* they are fictive – their particular values and beliefs.

During the 1950s, however, it seems clear that Curnow became increasingly aware of the shakiness of the 'realist' defence he had mounted against detractors who accused him of mythmaking. The introduction to his *Penguin Book of New Zealand Verse* occupies a fascinatingly ambivalent position at this time of transition in his thinking, lending itself to two quite opposed readings: a realist reading, containing a claim to the 'truth' of a touchstone of a distinctively New Zealand 'reality prior to the poem' (which his detractors eagerly seized upon); and a quite different reading, discernible in the wealth of qualifications, counter-statements and ironic gestures that accompany anything which looks like a truth-statement about a 'real' New Zealand, and a constant recourse to vivid and witty *fictive* metaphors which suggest that any notion of 'New Zealand' will invariably be *imagined* (or fantasised), a human invention whose truth status will always be contingent and provisional. It is precisely that dimension of the introduction which links it most closely to the remarkable poems which Curnow wrote in 1955 and 1956 at the same time as he was preparing the anthology and composing its introduction – 'Spectacular Blossom' (the first of his mythmaking tree poems), 'The Eye Is More or Less Satisfied with Seeing' (with its ironic questioning of the capacity of the self or eye/I to transcend the limits of its space-time environment) and 'A Small Room with Large Windows' (with its lively scepticism about any effort to make the world reveal some final truth about its own nature).

In the 1960s Curnow began to read much more deeply in the history of mythologies, in theories of mythic transformation, and in theories about the nature of myth. Some of the books on this subject which he purchased were highly specialised, and he was particularly interested in the intersection between classical mythology and Christian iconography, and in the intersection between classical (Platonic and neo-Platonic) philosophy and Renaissance thinking about art. He annotated in some detail Jean Seznec's *The Survival of the Pagan Gods*, a study of 'the mythological tradition and its place in Renaissance humanism and art'.[17] Like Edgar Wind's *Pagan Mysteries in the Renaissance*,[18] which explored the significance of Renaissance neo-Platonic thinking on the way some great Renaissance paintings might be interpreted, Seznec's study raised fascinating questions about the intersections of myth and philosophical thinking in the work of Renaissance artists and thinkers. Such books provided immediate sources for *The Duke's Miracle* in 1966, and for Curnow's teaching of Edmund Spenser, but they also reinforced his more general interest in what one might call the history of the idea of divinity, and the variety of theogonies, cosmologies and idealist systems – all expressing aspirations for transcendence – which had come and gone.

In the early 1970s Curnow also purchased G.S. Kirk's *Myth: Its Meaning and Functions in Ancient and Other Cultures*, which offered a lively, critical (if sometimes disconcertingly positivistic) account of theories of myth, from Frazer to Levi-Strauss, from the perspective of an anthropologist.[19] Kirk was sceptical of 'universalistic theories', regarding it as 'axiomatic that myths do not have a single form, or act according to one simple set of rules, either from epoch to epoch or from culture to culture',[20] and drew on a variety of examples, with the main aim of 'exploring and to a degree rehabilitating the role of many myths as in some sense speculative, as concerned with problems in society or incompatibilities between culture and nature'.[21] Although he dissented from the view that myth-forming processes in the past were in any way similar to myth-forming processes in the present (except for 'bastard modern forms'),[22] and was not concerned with the literary uses which many myths had later attracted, his study would have strongly reinforced for Curnow a sense of the possibly 'speculative' character of myths as fictive narratives 'concerned with problems in society or incompatibilities between culture and nature'.[23]

Fictions and *Four Plays* (1972)

Wallace Stevens was likely to have been a key figure for Curnow in enabling him to think of myths as 'fictions' whose significance lay not in any absolute truth that they contained but in their purely human effectiveness (or ineffectiveness) as rationalisations of conflict within and between societies, or between culture and nature. Fiction-making, from this point of view, is central to human existence, and accumulates its varied narratives around *all* activities thought to be significant in particular societies. Curnow first used the term in this all-embracing sense in a remarkable passage in the preface to his *Four Plays*, which he wrote during the summer of 1970–71, only a few months before the poems of *Trees, Effigies, Moving Objects* began to find their final shape and order:

It is possible to think that we live by fictions which we tell ourselves about ourselves, by a kind of magic. For most people, or enough people at a time, they are true; and that would be sufficient, if the question of truth were not always open, or on the point of being reopened. It is more than a matter of knowledge, getting facts right, mere truthfulness. Since we are always short of knowledge, and have to speak and act without enough of it, we have to make do with our fictions. This is human existence such as it is.[24]

He went on to indicate the range of human behaviours – from the most common-place to the most seriously held values and beliefs – around which fictions, believed to be 'true', are constructed:

Any daily paper or cheap weekly recites for us the lesser fictions, the sporting successes, the moral and social postures, the current scientific, economic and political oracles. It may be a little frightening to think how much depends, of such common or personal sanity as we possess, on faith in this kind of magic. If today's fiction wears thin, there will be a replacement tomorrow.

On the greater scale, nations find the fiction of their very existence shaken, if not destroyed, by revolution or defeat in war. The experts in a more potent magic have prevailed; the fictions have to be rewritten, in blood, and in another language. Those about youth, the sexes, and race exhibit symptoms of collapse. . . . Family crisis . . . likewise shakes the fictions.[25]

The idea of fictions adumbrated here in fact provided Curnow with his main methodological tool in the preface for linking plays otherwise extremely unalike in their subjects, locations, actions and historical settings. *The Axe*, he argued, offered an example of a clash of fictions 'on the greater scale', between religious-social orders, in which Davida's crusading 'Christian fiction' triumphs over the indigenous Mangaian fiction 'by which [Tereavai] lived, and ruled'.[26] However, such success is always double-edged, since the defeated at last *know* that what they had believed to be an immutable truth *is* a fiction, while the victors remain convinced that their fiction is truth, rewriting history in the light of it. The title of *The Overseas Expert* identified the 'lesser fiction' which was the play's subject, the persistent colonial adulation of the aristocratic trappings of Britishness, and Curnow suggests that in the aftermath of succumbing to Mandragora's deception the gullible, socially climbing Sopers of Remuera might 'resume their roles in the more dependable fiction of their family affections and loyalties'.[27] The dramatic potential of ageing characters facing death, and with this a dawning awareness of the collapse of the fictions by which they have lived, recurs in a number of the plays. Tereavai, Curnow comments, 'living out the day of his exhausted fiction',[28] returns in the characters of Thomas Judd in *Moon Section*, the Duke of Ferrara in *The Duke's Miracle*, and Busby in *Resident of Nowhere* – the Duke driven by a fiction of 'absolute personal power', Busby 'cling[ing] indomitably to the New Zealand of his first dream' and dying 'crying out for an impossible justice'.[29]

'Among the fictions', Curnow concluded, 'it is a matter of success or failure' – a matter, that is, not of 'spiritual' value, but of material power, superior (political or other) skills or technological resources:

> It seems that I have been trying to represent a conflict of this kind. Success defines itself in a completed action, and there is an end of it – as with Davida, so with the Duke, and with George Mandragora, and with the politics that jettisoned a troublesome Busby. The defeated fiction is put to the question and (like Tereavai) it has 'no explanation ready'. But it may be nearer the heart of the matter, and certainly to the condition of every man in the hour of his death, never mind how much success has come his way.[30]

'The heart of the matter', how one copes with the collapse of the beliefs by which one has lived, or when their insufficiency is revealed, is a condition (as Curnow had commented in a crucial extension of his earlier discussion of fictions) in which '*the question of truth*' [author's italics] is *reopened*, or on the point of being reopened. There is a doubleness of perspective – in which fictions are *revealed as such* and their limitations as products of human consciousness acknowledged, but in which, through this very recognition and awareness, the question of truth and value is reopened – and this doubleness lies at the centre of Curnow's aims in *Trees, Effigies, Moving Objects*. The idea of fictions which Curnow adumbrates is not simply a convenient way of dismissing the 'real', of banishing the ideas of truth and belief from his world. It is a means of reopening those questions from a much more complex, sceptical perspective – the kind of perspective which J. Hillis Miller identifies in Stevens's later poetry as 'the idea that all our spiritual height and depth is available here and now or nowhere'.[31]

Nietzsche and the fatality of existence

It was Nietzsche's metaphysical scepticism combined with the most intense, driven search for truth in a world without absolutes which attracted Curnow to his work at this time. As with all of his interests in philosophy during the course of his life, Curnow did not read Nietzsche systematically. More often than not his interest would be sparked by a casual reference in something else he was reading, or by a particular issue that cropped up in a poem he was writing, or by a recommendation from others, and he would not read the whole of a philosopher's works but a particular text that related to his own thinking at the time. He might be described as a 'pragmatic' reader of philosophy, interested in the immediate poetic use of something a philosopher might say. Nevertheless, from the late 1960s onwards he purchased a considerable number of Nietzsche's works and read *in* them intensively and regularly.

Nietzsche is directly referred to in only one of Curnow's poems, 'This Beach Can Be Dangerous' (published in *An Abominable Temper*, 1973), whose epigraph cites a sentence from a famous passage in *Twilight of the Idols*: 'The fatality of his nature cannot be disentangled from the fatality of all that which has been and will be.' The sentence comes from an impassioned statement by Nietzsche about the condition of human life, once it is understood as unsponsored by *any* transcendent agency, and occurs at the conclusion of a section in which Nietzsche attacked 'the four great errors' that proceed from such metaphysical thinking – the error of mistaking cause for consequence, the error of false causality, the error of imaginary causes (a category including religion and morality), and the error of free will ('the most infamous of all the arts of the theologian for making mankind "accountable"', for the purpose of '*punishing and judging*').[32]

In Curnow's poem, set at Karekare, the speaker walks along the beach with its anonymous warning notice offering stern, well-meaning moral instructions about how to behave ('WARNING . . . BATHE BETWEEN THE FLAGS . . . DO NOT BATHE ALONE') – the sign offering an image of efforts to control and protect human life – but as he does so his thoughts are flooded by images of millions of the dead who seem to ride the windswept oceanic horizon, some familiar, some unknown, but all 'familiarly transfigured' by the diseases or violences ('cancer, coronary, burning, mutilation') which carried them away. Nothing, the poem suggests, by way of moral or other efforts to control human behaviour, can 'save' people from the fatality of existence, in which such deaths are the destiny of all, without exception. For the speaker such knowledge, which is literally a knowledge of '*hope*lessness' [author's italics] – no transcendence or escape from such fatality is possible – produces not *despair* but its own kind of happiness, an awareness of the company of the dead as literally making his own existence possible, and an enlarged sense of the richness of even the simplest of his activities of the moment:

> It was their company that made it possible
> for me to walk there, cracking the odd shell

> with the butt of a manuka stick,
> happy to the point of hopelessness.

Curnow does not deal as directly elsewhere with Nietzschean ideas. To a degree, after the 1960s, they became common currency in much intellectual discourse, and Nietzsche's cry, 'God is dead', became a truism. Nevertheless, Nietzsche remained a figure whose liveliness of mind and originality of style continued to interest him, and he was fond of quoting Nietzsche's somewhat rueful acknowledgement that even 'the wisest among us … sometimes consider an idea truer simply because it has a metrical form and presents itself with a divine skip and jump'.[33]

Final drafts 1971–72: myth, metaphysics, politics, language

As Curnow commented about 'fictions' (the myths which take lesser or greater forms in any culture) in his introduction to *Four Plays*, their history – their coming and going, installation and replacement – is simply 'a matter of success or failure', of shifts (often brutal shifts) in political or social power relations. However, the 'question of truth' which myths open up – once they are recognised as fictions, contingent, temporary and provisional – is at least partly a question of value. Are some myths better than others? In the 1930s and 1940s Curnow had vigorously attacked the New Zealand colonial myth expressed in such self-aggrandising phrases as 'outpost of Empire' or 'more British than the British'. In the 'American' poems of *Trees, Effigies, Moving Objects* he addresses a neo-colonial post-war myth which he saw as no less entrenched than the earlier one had been, refusing to remain passive before the influential fiction of an American centre – political, cultural – necessarily imposing itself on a New Zealand periphery. New Zealand's unthinking and wholehearted commitment to support for the United States in Vietnam, its complicity, as he saw it, in America's sense of global mission and crusading anti-communism, its support for American involvement in the Cold War and the planet-threatening nuclear armaments race, provided a key catalyst for the sense of global crisis which permeates the sequence.

In the first of the 'American' poems, 'Do It Yourself', Curnow raises the possibility of constructing an alternative local counter-myth, playing on the New Zealand myth of d.i.y. resourcefulness, after wittily cutting the American effigies down to type-size and divesting them of their capacity to engender any 'religious' feelings of wonder and awe by adopting the language of a do-it-yourself handyman's kit:

Make it what height you like, the
sky will not fall nor will the dead
president rise because of his

        O

        B

        E

        L

        I

        S

        K

        5

        5

        5

        f

        t

        .

nor is it any wonder that it is
one measured mile down river to the

      P I

   A   T

 C   O   L

one measured mile up river to the

   L I N C

   M   O

   E   L

   M   N

   O R I A L I

   N C O L N M E

   M O R I A L I N

With a few simple tools the handyman
Can erect his thought upon Waiheke, volcanic islet,
lat. 37S long. 175E for the time being.

Read the instructions carefully.

The poem's mock-conclusion warns against a botched job: constructing a superior
or adequate counter-fiction is a challenging business, and since myths are always
rooted in the physical world and hence impermanent, Waiheke Island, in the
Auckland harbour, provides a witty example of an especially unsuitable location.
As a volcanic islet it is geologically unusually recent, and unusually unstable.

Undoubtedly the boldest, riskiest and most ambitious of Curnow's moves in *Trees, Effigies, Moving Objects* was his effort to answer the challenge in 'Do It Yourself' and construct his own counter-myth. The poem in which he did so was 'A Four Letter Word', the most remarkable poem in the sequence and one of the major poems of Curnow's career. Curnow asked Dudding not to include this poem in the group he chose for *Islands*, almost certainly because of its centrality to the sequence, and because he was anxious not to have the *Islands* selection pre-empt the full sequence to be published soon afterwards by Glover. The poem's subject is Tane Mahuta ('Lord of the Forest'), the name given by Maori to the huge, now decaying kauri tree in the Waipoua Forest, an 'effigy' of the Maori fertility god, Tane, the original creator of the physical, spatio-temporal world as he forced apart the sexually embracing earth goddess and sky god (Papa and Rangi), letting light into the primordial cosmic darkness.

The myth of Tane, as Curnow reconstructs it, becomes a prototype of *all* myths, and the focus for a reinterpretation of the nature of myth itself. At the centre of the reinterpretation – the 'instruction' Curnow has carefully followed – is a rejection of all transcendentalist or idealist or apriorist thought, the kind of absolutist or essentialist thinking (religious, philosophical or political) premised on belief in hidden Cosmic Dramas, First Causes and Final Truths, Golden Age origins or happy-ever-after paradises, or (in the case of American nationalism) in a sense of divinely appointed global mission and destiny. The mythic prototype represented by Tane is presented as a purely human contrivance (specifically, a creation of language, coeval with the primordial origins of human beings as language-speaking animals) rooted in an obstinately physical, existential world; far from revealing the gods behind events, myths in fact rationalise events, expressing a human need for order and control which events themselves never satisfy. There was 'no nativity ode' for Tane, no pre-existing divine genealogy in terms of which his birth is made meaningful. Tane, in Curnow's redefined mythic narrative, is the four-letter word itself, the di-syllable, born out of the very nature of language, blurted expletively, 'ripped from the tongue's root', at the moment when the world impinges (was primordially created) as an inescapably physical, anarchic, sexual presence.

Tane is the prototype of all such language acts (no matter how complex and ramified the linguistic (philosophic, cosmological, theological) systems and nar-ratives become, in particular cultures), and Curnow's myth thus privileges language as providing the key sign of difference between nature and human nature. However, it is not language as the Logos, as if it pre-existed the world and provided access to some transcendent prior or final truth about its nature (in a sensationally reductive pun Curnow describes the blurted name of Tane as a 'Logos begotten of log'). Language simply *is*, sharing the contingency and unpredictability of the spatio-temporal world in which, alone, it has its being.

For Curnow the simplest form of mythmaking represented by Tane can be observed in expletive acts (spontaneously uttered taboo obscenities and blasphemies, in which gods are named in frustration, anger or despair) expressing a direct response to the unpredictable, 'unspeakable' otherness of events in the physical world. In their most elaborated narratives myths offer complex, 'speculative' explanations designed to control, order and rationalise what is otherwise inexplicable, either 'unspeakably' horrifying or threatening, or 'unspeakably' new, fascinating, exciting beyond words, in our experience of the world. Such elaborated narratives invariably accumulate around the most seemingly inexplicable of experiences of the physical world: time, space, sex and gender, disease, ageing and death; political experiences of war, violence, revolution, nationality; the inner psychic experiences of desire, fear, anxiety and hope.

Why is Curnow's reinvented myth of Tane 'better' than, 'superior' to, others? Because it proposes an imagining of the mythic as that which contains within itself knowledge or 'truth' about its own nature, as contingent, fictional, provisional, contestable. Curnow implies throughout the sequence that whenever myths attract or require belief in themselves as absolute truth, whenever they harden into dogmas and systems, they turn into despotic abstractions justifying 'unspeakable' violence, in the name of whatever god or whatever political ideology is invoked – of which, war and atrocities, the proliferation of weapons of mass destruction, the destruction of natural resources, offer obvious contemporary examples. Despite the difficulty of imagining quite what form(s) such new Tane-informed myths might take, despite the grim sense of contemporary political crisis that permeates the apocalyptic imagery in the sequence, Curnow wishes to at least adumbrate the possibility of change and transformation, a space of freedom in which more adequate myths might replace those that have failed. Wallace Stevens's 'Supreme Fiction' needed to fulfil three requirements: It Must Be Abstract, It Must Change, It Must Give Pleasure.[34] Perhaps Curnow's new mythopoeia also needs three requirements: It Must Be Contestable, It Must Be Adequate, It Must Be Self-conscious. It will never achieve Utopia, but it might secure the planet's survival.

'A Four Letter Word' is the second of a sub-sequence of four deeply con-sidered 'effigy' poems (numbers 12 to 15) in *Trees, Effigies, Moving Objects*, each of them divesting *particular* myths of the transcendental truth-discourse which originally sustained them and reinterpreting them in purely secular terms for their possible bearing on a present in which 'the question of truth is always open, or on the point of being reopened'. In 'Magnificat', the huge statue of the Virgin Mary ('Our Lady of Lourdes') at Waikanae on the Kapiti Coast, with its incised words, 'I am the Immaculate Conception', is ironically reduced to its merely physical dimensions, removing her grandiose claim to embody absolute truth

– pure thought wholly detached from and unstained by the real world. But the issue of truth is reopened, at the end of each stanza, in a series of unanswerable questions which human beings are driven continually to ask precisely *because* consciousness and thought are incorrigibly rooted in the physical world: how far is time? how high is heaven? how quick is death? what is darkness made of? how big is god? where is the world? In 'A Hot Time' the Old Testament story (from Daniel 3) in which Shadrach, Meshach and Abednego refused to worship Nebuchadnezzar's golden image and walked unscathed in the fiery furnace into which they were thrown, is rewritten as a narrative of a contemporary rock party, in which a sexually permissive, drug-fuelled younger generation of 'holy children' dance their defiance against the world inherited from their elders.

The fourth of the sub-sequence of effigy poems was 'Bourdon', which went through many drafts before it found its final form in *Trees, Effigies, Moving Objects*. It was in fact the first-conceived of the effigy poems, and Curnow's decision to excerpt its elements from the early 'Capitoline Spring' – to rework them into a poem wholly focused on the Lincoln Memorial in Washington – was crucial in generating the idea of a number of such effigy poems. The 'question of truth' opened up by this poem has to do with the *historical* origins of the American belief in its own special global mission and destiny.

The immense seated marble figure of Lincoln, throned in a Greek-style temple surrounded by Doric columns – on the walls of which are inscribed the texts of his Second Inaugural Address and his speech at Gettysburg – stares ahead impassively as a spectacular, violent spring thunderstorm bursts over him, sifting its 'slow detritus' of dust and cherry blossom toward the Potomac River nearby. The scene is the birth (or stillbirth) of a national myth, and the poem focuses with grim irony on the idealism which invested American mythic self-conceptions with the force of transcendental truths, turning them into despotic abstractions. Throughout, the stony effigy resists the transcendental idea it is intended to realise, as the annunciatory thunderbolts crack 'the matrix . . . again, again!', but fail to achieve a resurrection of Lincoln, the founding father-god of the nation.

The American national myth explored in this poem conforms to the prototype enunciated in 'A Four Letter Word'. It is born in a historical period of extreme anarchy (a violent civil war, ending with Lincoln's assassination) and rationalises that anarchy, representing the nation as unified, with a cosmic destiny and a grandiose sense of moral mission to humanity. Throughout, the sequence counter-poses this sense of moral mission with its actual aftermath in the post-Second World War world, in which the same grand rhetoric is used to underpin the Cold War, the nuclear arms race, the military intervention in Vietnam. The 1960s, as Curnow presents them in 'A Framed Photograph', represent a tragic recurrence of the events of the Lincoln era: a decade beginning with the seeming new era of the

Kennedy renaissance and ending (after the assassination of the president in 1962 and, in 1967, of his brother) with the mass bombings and napalmings of Vietnam and the massacre of innocent civilians at My Lai in 1968.

For Curnow the idea of myth adumbrated in 'A Four Letter Word', and underpinning his readings of myth in all the effigy poems, has its origins in the limits of language when confronted by the otherness of *everything* to which it refers, even other utterances. 'Look hard at nature', Curnow writes, in a later poem in the sequence, 'There Is a Pleasure in the Pathless Woods': 'It is in the nature / of things to look, and look back, harder.' It is 'natural', that is, to look – to observe, attempt to 'understand' nature – and nature by its 'look' seems to invite such an interaction; however, it is also 'natural', inevitable, that 'things' themselves (objects, events, even people, including one's own impenetrable, unpredictable self) 'look back harder', resist the reductive drive to understand, insist on their separateness and otherness, just as it is natural in turn for the observer to keep looking back at that which looks back at him. It is in this *always* defeated exchange that myth takes root and has its being, offering the illusion of escape from the anguish and anxiety of non-identity, meaninglessness and subjection to the chaos of events which have the capacity, at any moment and in any place, to 'unspeakably supervene'.

The word 'unspeakably' is a recurrent word throughout the sequence, carrying its commonplace emotive sense, as well as a literal sense – that which defies language. Even botany, Curnow concludes (drawing his example from the seemingly unproblematic taxonomic procedures of the natural sciences), 'is panic of another description'. Even mere description, that is – seemingly the least order- and control-driven of responses to nature, the least *self*-imposing of responses – brings us no closer to the things being described (as Nietzsche was at pains to observe), and 'panic', existential anxiety, underlies even the most seemingly objective taxonomies. Moreover, concealed in Curnow's word 'panic' is a pun on the pagan fertility god, Pan, a classical version of the Maori god, Tane. Botany is as much a source of mythic rationalisations of nature as any other system of knowledge. In the opening section of 'A Four Letter Word' a similar perception of the limits of language provided the starting point for the poem's rethinking of the myth of Tane:

> A wood god bothering cantor
> rolls out his call. He names
>
> tanekaha, kaiwaka, taraire.
> Mispronounced, any of these
>
> can strike dead and dumb. Well spoken,
> they are a noise neither of the writhing root

nor glabrous leaf nor staring flower,
all that can unspeakably supervene.

Language itself – its vocabularies, idioms, grammars – because it is part of the physical, material world (sounds uttered, marks on a page), is subject to the same processes of change and decay, and has the same capacity at any or every moment to supervene unspeakably, surprising or appalling us into silence. For most day-to-day purposes we manage adequately with our systems of communication, without worrying too much whether what we think we said is what others thought they heard, or whether the words we repeat five minutes later (let alone a generation later) mean the same thing. But self-conscious reflection on our acts of speech (as on our memories) – especially when we are *anxious* about problems of communication (over generation gaps, or as poets) – always makes us aware of resistances in the things or persons or events or ideas or feelings which provide the subject of our speech, stubbornly refusing the transcendences offered them.

The problematic nature of communication, whether at the simplest level ('We speak only / to each other but *as if* a third were present, / the thing we say') [author's italics], or in the complex utterances we call poems, is a recurrent theme throughout the sequence, and built into its own poetic self-awareness, which draws attention to the complexities underlying even the simplest notions of what it means to 'observe', to 'describe', to 'remember', to 'speak', to 'write' – let alone to 'feel' and to 'think'. Communication is explicitly the subject of the third poem, 'An Upper Room'. The title invokes the biblical myth of Pentecost, in which the Holy Spirit descended to inspire Christ's disciples to communicate in tongues, and the subject is a literature tutorial for students whom the poet envisages 'growing up the stairs' to his university office, as – now in his sixty-first year – he feels the threat of a younger generation, and remembers fragments of the nursery rhyme 'Goosey Goosey Gander', about an old man who refuses to say his prayers and is thrown down the stairs for his refusal to conform. Curnow's text is Milton's 'Lycidas', an elegy to his drowned friend, Edward King, in which Milton invokes 'the dear might of Him that walk'd the waves' to inspire his own wish to make the drowned man survive his death and achieve the 'immortality' of resurrection in the elegy he has written about him. However, the myth (deeply ingrained in classical and romantic thinking about art) that poetry has some special capacity to transcend time – as if walking on water – speaking across generations, across cultures, and over centuries, is subject to the same scepticism as all other forms of mythmaking in the sequence. 'Keep clear of the margins', Curnow writes of his own poems, '*Here* my line starts and it finishes *here*, / no later than the light lasts.' [italics in original]. Beyond the margins are the vast gulfs of time, the darkness of death, offering no guarantee of survival in whatever shorter or longer temporal perspective one takes, to which the poet's mock-despairing response is a deliberate collapse into doggerel:

> Smaller than thought can think
> the hours between us shrink,
> books wink, volcanic islets sink
> below that brink,
> black margin, blind white ink.

Final drafts 1971–72: styles and forms

In the more personal poems of *Trees, Effigies, Moving Objects* (as with its more impersonal, public poems) a sense of crisis and anxiety predominates. In 'Lone Kauri Road' the simple, seemingly leisurely personal act of observing a coastal scene is undermined by the unsettling sensation of everything 'backing away' and the sun visible through moving clouds suddenly generates a grotesque image of an accusing or judgemental eye in the sky, as the darkening cloud transforms itself into a 'black traveller'. In 'Friendship Heights' a hallucinatory experience – a warm personal memory of street scenery in the Washington suburb where Curnow stayed in 1961, sparked by a present-day scene of an underwater fish-tank forest – is suddenly, again, at the end engulfed by images of predatory violence. In the concluding poem, 'Any Time Now', an apparently casual walk down Brighton Road, Parnell, is suddenly interrupted by a macabre fantasy of the ground breaking open, 'disclosing a billion bodies burning under a thin smoke', and the poem concludes with a moving image of the moment of personal death: 'couldn't have picked a better day for it / I was just saying / when the ground closed over the sky / hollow as the cloud was high.'

However, there are two poems at the centre of the sequence, 'The Kitchen Cupboard' and 'A Dead Lamb' – much less anxiety-ridden than the rest – where the *sufficiency* of the present moment is entertained, where the capacity of events and objects in their existential otherness to surprise and fascinate (rather than threaten) is celebrated. 'A Dead Lamb' is one of the most anthologised of the poems from the sequence, perhaps because it is simpler than the others. Despite the warning notes (about the fall of time and the presence of death) at the beginning and end of the poem, at its centre it richly evokes the pleasurable strangeness of every succeeding moment during a beach walk at Karekare:

> Never turn your back on the sea.
> The mumble of the fall of time is continuous.

> A billion billion broken waves deliver
> a coloured glass globe at your feet, intact.
>
> You say it is a Japanese fisherman's float.
> It is a Japanese fisherman's float.
>
> A king tide, a five o'clock low, is perfect
> for picking mussels, picking at your anklebones.
>
> The wind snaps at the yellow-scummed sea-froth,
> so that an evanescence of irised bubbles occurs.
>
> Simply, silverly the waves walk towards you.
> A ship has changed position on the horizon.
>
> The dog lifts a leg against a grass-clump
> on a dune, for the count of three, wetting the sand.
>
> There is standing room and much to be thankful for
> in the present. Look, a dead lamb on the beach.

The same sensuous richness is also felt at the centre of 'The Kitchen Cupboard', as the poet observes the Hobson Bay scene:

> All the bays are empty, a quick-drying wind
> from the south-west browns the grey silt
> the ebb-tide printed sexily, opulently,
> making Nature's *art nouveau*, little as it matters
> to mudlarking crabs and the morning's blue heron.

Despite the grimness of vision in many of the poems, *Trees, Effigies, Moving Objects* continually affirms and celebrates the sheerly pleasurable sensuous vitality, richness and strangeness of the physical world through the precision of the poet's observations of it. The otherness of nature, even when it provides matter for intensely unsettling self-reflection, continually delights and surprises, through the paradoxical *precision* of the poet's observations of it. This is as true of the 'writhing root', 'staring flower' and 'glabrous leaf' of 'A Four Letter Word' as it is of the shifting cloudscape of 'Lone Kauri Road', and the profusion of wittily precise metaphors characterising the native trees in 'There Is a Pleasure in the Pathless Woods' – all of them poems whose 'argument' is the impossibility of such precision:

When the green grenade explodes, does the kauri
experience an orgasm of the spent cone?
What is the king fern doing with its hairy knuckles?
Wildling and epiphyte, do they have problems too?
There's a reason for the spastic elbow of this taraire.

A similar paradox underlies the sheer formal variety and unpredictability of
the sequence – between one poem and the next (and even, on occasion, within
particular poems) – and the linguistic energy and vitality of the poetry, whose
humour and wit, play of puns, ironies, double-meanings and allusions, and supple
(often deliberately ambivalent) syntax challenge readers to an equally pleasurable
alertness of attention, intensifying and underscoring the deeply unsettling nature
of the poems' vision. Above all Curnow develops a rapid movement across lines
and stanzas in many of the poems. Hillis Miller's phrase describing Stevens's later
style – its achievement of a 'flickering mobility', 'a way of matching the fluidity
of time'– comes to mind, except that Curnow's 'mobility' is totally different from
Stevens's. Curnow's verse takes liberties with syntax, plays with 'incomplete' line
endings and variable – often quite unconventional – deployments of stresses and
pauses, inserts fragments of nursery rhymes and occasionally plays typographical
tricks, deliberately juxtaposes formal and informal utterances within poems, and
plays with the variations between metrically regular and quite irregularly structured
poems, in ways which make Stevens's verse seem classically formal and regular.

The most spectacular instance is provided by 'Two Pedestrians with One
Thought', with its breathless evocation of a windswept walk in which even the
most stationary and fixed of objects are caught up in the sensation of chaotic,
uncontrollable and unpredictable flux mimed by the movement of the verse itself:

> hang on there
> as long as you can
> you and your dog before the
> wind skins the water off the
> road and the road off the
> face of the earth.
>
> ...
>
> hang on to your hands
> anything can happen
> once where the wind went
> fingers you feel to be
> nailed so securely
> can come loose too

> hold on to your ears and
> run dog run.
>   . . .

In 'A Hot Time' Curnow uses an anapaestic rhythm with a variable number of stresses in each line to evoke the lurching dance rhythms at the rock party:

> All the holy children were dancing on the needle
> doing nothing but their thing in the burning fiery furnace,
>
> Shadrach and Shakeback and Meshach and Sheshach
> and Abednego and gay to bed we go along and upwards
> of a hundred holy children in the burning fiery furnace.

The effectiveness of 'Magnificat' was also very much a matter of the lines finding their own, utterly distinctive, formal shape. Sister M. Vianney, of the Presentation Convent in Paraparaumu, replied in generous detail to a request from Curnow for architectural information about the statue, and her letter (adding to details in a brochure) provided several phrases eventually used directly in the poem:

> The material is not reinforced concrete – the statue is hollow in the centre having been built on a 2" x 4" scaffolding covered with many layers of scrim and finished off with a 3" plaster. (Incidentally, there are 'steps' inside the statue, and a trap-door through Our Lady's head! This is used for maintenance, painting, electricity, etc.) . . .[35]

In April 1972 Curnow wrote to Glover that 'Our Lady of Kapiti' had 'come right after many drafts',[36] adding – in response to Glover's praise of it ('a triumph'):[37] '*That* metre (which baffles my prosody to describe) without rhyme was a challenge, & I hoped I had won a long & bloody fight with the versification.'[38]

The basic pattern consists of alternating three-stressed and two-stressed lines, unrhymed and with hugely varying numbers of syllables, enabling the poem to contain breathtaking shifts of tone from the most prosaic, descriptive utterance to moments of sustained and moving eloquence. It was crucial to the poem's final form, that it is rhetorically structured not as a litany or monologue or ballad or as informal poetic prose (the modes he initially tried), but as a series of urgent metaphysical questions posed by the statue's physical dimensions. (Curnow was angered by later suggestions (from Bertram and others) that the poem was a series of cheap shots at the Virgin Mary.) The syntactic structure of the poem is *interrogative*, and the questions are not simply ironic, even if they are unanswerable:

Who hasn't sighted Mary
          as he hung hot-paced
by the skin of the humped highway
          south from Waikanae
three hundred feet above the
          only life-size ocean?
Tell me, mother of mysteries,
          how far is time?...

Mary's frame is timbered
          of two-by-four,
lapped with scrim and plastered
          three inches thick.
Westward of Kapiti
the sun is overturned.
Tell me, Star of the Sea,
          what is darkness made of? ...

I AM THE IMMACULATE
          CONCEPTION says
Mary's proud pedestal.
          Her lips concur.
Masterful giantess,
          don't misconceive me,
tell me, mother of the Way,
          where is the world?

During the final period of composition of *Trees, Effigies, Moving Objects* Curnow completed a further 'effigy' poem, a witty deconstruction of theological metaphysics which played typographically with the messages appearing on the back of vehicles. Curnow's earlier titles were 'The Theologian in his New Car' and 'Theology is the Queen of the Sciences', though he eventually settled for 'Eyes Front':

SMILE GOD LOVES YOU
his rear window
menaces I cannot see the
face of the driver for the
back of his head nobody
sees me smile

DON'T FOLLOW ME I'M LOST
his rear window
entices I cannot see the
face of the driver for the
back of his head nobody
sees me follow

IFYOUCANREADTHISYOUARETOODAMNCLOSE
his rear window
argues I cannot see the
face of the driver for the
back of his head nobody
sees if I

4 SALE! 4 SALE! 4 SALE!

Perhaps he decided not to include it because the sequence already contained a 'sufficient' number of instances of typographical play (with the effigies in 'Do It Yourself' and with the inverted apple juice carton blown away in the wind in 'Two Pedestrians with One Thought'). Glover disapproved of Curnow's 'Typological tricks', complaining that they were 'an old device, revived too frequently and even as late as D. Thomas',[39] and prompted Curnow to a defence of them:

> The defence has to be: 1 they are few; 2 they don't (I think) suggest a manifesto for this kind of thing; 3 they please *me*. Not strictly the 'altar poem' kind of thing that Thomas tried out, & Puttenham didn't fancy as early as 1589. Because they occur as distinct detail in poems which aren't otherwise 'shaped' that way. It's really only the Washington/Lincoln piece, where I mean to cut the 'effigies' down to type-size. I hope, by the way, the *real* printer can reproduce the upside-down APPLE JUICE. Some people spit out the pips, others don't mind chewing them; qua pips, they are part of the fruit, even if indigestible to some.[40]

Curnow's many late, small-scale revisions to the poems were almost always stylistic, concerned with what he called the 'plasticity' of the verse, aimed at energising the lines, removing rhythmically inert lines or phrases, adding precision and directness, introducing livelier (often vernacular) words and idioms – in general, adding dramatic force to the encounter between consciousness and its objects, attending to what Nietzsche called the 'divine skip and jump' by which poets made ideas seem 'truer'.

The old firm: Glover, publisher, Curnow, poet

The same meticulous attention to detail marked Glover's design of the text, format and typography of *Trees, Effigies, Moving Objects* for his Catspaw Press, about which he and Curnow conferred regularly during the six months, April to November 1972, between Curnow's sending the manuscript and its publication. Glover consulted Curnow at every stage of the production, patiently including Curnow's last-minute corrections, adding 'Any Time Now' to the design when Curnow sent it to him later in June,[41] sending Curnow a copy of the dummy, and asking him to do his own version of a paste-up from the galleys (which he then worked with). He coordinated the publishing schedule to ensure that Dudding was able to include his selection from the sequence in the first issue of *Islands* in September/October. He also placated Albion Wright at the Pegasus Press, who printed the book ('a prestige job', as he described it to Wright)[42] and had to deal with Glover's exhaustively detailed instructions. 'You have glanced at the copy', he wrote early on to Wright, 'and found that as usual Allen is an exasperating enigma[,] so much so that he demands and commands attention.'[43] Curnow himself contributed $50 towards Glover's production costs.

The result was one of the most impressive of all Glover's productions of Curnow, superior to *Poems 1949–57*, and the equal of *Island and Time* published 30 years before. Amongst his detailed notes to Curnow he mentioned his decision, 'against all the canons', to open the first poem on a verso:

> This I elect to do because I am against the presentation of a poem of which the conclusion is turn-over-the-page. This you will find recurrent. Later on, without more thought than an anxiety for the 32 pp football field, I thought two shorties could go on a page together, with generous space between. But I think my first point the valid one.[44]

No fewer than six of the poems would have had 'turn-over-the-page' endings if Glover had conformed to a conventional beginning on a recto. Curnow was happy about this, but anxious about the problem of having two poems on a page:

> Most important of all – here I positively plead, wheedle, demand, whichever it is – I do most particularly want one poem, one page. The style isn't my business, but the Sequence arrangement is. To me, the whole balance of the numerical order gets upset, if we tuck in short ones like this. Nothing must even *look* as if it is there to justify a page.

Your poems make light of this sort of designing, as do, e.g. William Carlos Williams's, or Wallace Stevens's (in some books). Mine *resist* it (almost to the death), as do Thomas's, Yeats's. Each of mine is a little distinct 'ritual': yours more like 'sentences' in the office of the whole. It's not a question of success or value, but of intention.[45]

In mid-November Curnow received advance copies of the volume. Glover was cautiously optimistic: 'I'm pretty pleased: good understanding between the three of us.'[46] Curnow was, as usual, extremely nervous about their reception:

Of the contents, I have the usual manic-depressive syndromes. . . . The weaknesses – I know where they are – are where almost nobody now living except ourselves is likely to look for them – here and there in the verse dynamics, the plasticity, one daren't say form since that's a dirty word – what WBY meant by 'ice or salt' without which the 'personal soon rots'.* [47]

To Tim he wrote that he did not expect the poems to be popular, since they were 'strictly for reading, not for intravenous injection':

I'm too old to wave a borrowed banner in the outflanked avant garde of the 'sixties. Time the old sniper will pick them off one by one – me too, very likely. It takes a lot of art and a certain amount of luck if a few poems are to survive. The art may be insufficient, and the luck unwilling. I believe they're as good as the best of my old things, & new themselves.[48]

However, he had already received a number of favourable responses to the *Islands* selection, most notably from Lilburn and Brasch, and Stead's response to the sequence was equally positive. Despite Curnow's uncertainties at the time, 1972 turned out in retrospect to be a watershed year for his poetic career. From this time on, his creative energies were to be devoted exclusively to poetry. Already, at the end of the year, he was working on a new collection.

---

* W.B. Yeats, 'A General Introduction for My Work' (1937), reprinted in *Essays and Introductions*, Macmillan, London, 1961, pp. 509–526 at p. 522: '[A]ll that is personal soon rots; it must be packed in ice or salt.'

Chapter Twenty-five

New and Collected Poems, 1973

You may not remember some letter you wrote in the past 18 months,
where you said 'put them all in'. I haven't quite done that, but so nearly,
nobody will notice. Discarding was a habit of years: cowardice, really,
playing safe. Trying to make sure the alter ego (or alter id?) couldn't
embarrass me in company, by his table manners, picking his nose,
passing ignorant remarks.[1]

Leave plans, and extended family changes

Whatever 'manic-depressive syndromes' Curnow felt about the way *Trees, Effigies,*
Moving Objects might be received,[2] by the end of 1972 he felt strongly that his
poetry had at last found a new direction, and with that confidence came a new
energy for projects related to poetry. During 1972, partly prompted by Tim in
Sydney, he agreed to prepare a collected poems for A.H. & A.W. Reed, and spent
much of the summer of 1972–73 working on the manuscript. He had also been
writing other poems, and continued to do so over that summer, so that by May
1973 he felt able to approach Glover, again, to ask about the prospect of publishing
another small collection of new work. The new collection, *An Abominable Temper*
and other poems, appeared in November 1973, exactly a year after *Trees, Effigies,*
Moving Objects. At the suggestion of Robin Dudding, Curnow also agreed to
undertake an interview about his literary career with MacDonald P. Jackson, a
colleague on the staff of the English Department at the University of Auckland,
and this task, which resulted in the most substantial and informative of all the

interviews Curnow gave during his life, was also fitted in between December 1972 and April 1973.

There was some urgency in completing these projects before the end of 1973, since Curnow was due to go on study leave, for a full year, in 1974. He had in fact applied in 1971 for study leave in 1973, but been turned down:

> *We* had made tentative plans for a year's leave abroad (UK/Europe this time) in *1973*; but the University, pleading poverty, has put me off till *1974*, damn them; they argued that my last leave wouldn't be a full six years' past, which I consider a quibble, since I returned in May '67 & my teaching year was squeezed to make it a full academic year.[3]

Technically speaking, the university was correct, but there is not the slightest doubt that such a decision reinforced Curnow's feeling that he was undervalued by the institution. In his view, his reputation as a writer (in New Zealand and overseas) seemed to mean little to it, and certainly counted for nothing as far as his professional career was concerned. Even if he was oversensitive, he had every reason to feel undervalued. The university had never made any gesture to acknowledge the positive effects of his presence over many years: his influence on a new generation of students who developed scholarly and critical interests in New Zealand literature (including Stead, Jackson, Vincent O'Sullivan, William Broughton, Wystan Curnow, Roger Horrocks, Max Richards, this author, Ken Arvidson, and numerous others); his role in reviving Auckland as a live literary centre, and his active promotion of that culture through poetry readings; his liveliness as a publicist, controversialist and satirist on issues ranging from censorship to university salaries.

Over the years, of course, Curnow had hardly endeared himself to the university authorities. He was deeply suspicious of all forms of authority, and rarely – if ever – saw the relationship between academic staff and senior administrators except in 'us–them' terms. He regarded the university authorities as timid in defending the interests of the university when issues of principle were at stake, and unwilling to stand up vigorously to parsimonious governments in support of the professional needs of staff. On several occasions, when university salaries were under consideration by the government, he used his journalistic connections and expertise to write feature articles for newspapers drawing attention to the plight of the universities, but it is by no means clear that the university welcomed such publicity. He was aware, also, that in the later 1950s his outspoken position on the siting of the university, in his *Huckster* broadsheets, had attracted the enmity of some university council members; and that the hostile publicity given to his views by the mayor and some city councillors was likely to have embarrassed university administrators who simply wished for a quieter life. Where issues like

promotion and leave were involved he was thus often dependent on the willingness of individuals on the various central committees (like Stead, Jock Asher of
the German Department, and Jack Northey of the Faculty of Law) to stand up
to his detractors – a situation which never arose with staff who concentrated on
their academic careers and avoided the public spotlight.

During the course of 1972 two family events also impinged heavily on the
lives of both Curnow and Jeny: his mother Jessie's health deteriorated sharply
at midyear, and Jeny's father, George Tole, died suddenly in August. Curnow's
annual trip to Christchurch at the beginning of the year had been a busy one, and
included being a witness at the wedding of his cousin Patricia's daughter, Angela
Harman, with David Bowron. His mother was still adamant that she did not
wish to move from Meadow Street, and Curnow spent time talking to her doctor
and caregivers, then attending to a number of small maintenance tasks and renovations at the house. However, this was to be the last time he saw her at Meadow
Street. In June she was admitted to Princess Margaret Hospital with pneumonia,
and although she gradually recovered from this she was now no longer able to
live without constant nursing care. Curnow visited her in hospital at the end of
June, saddened at her deterioration. The pneumonia had cleared up, he wrote to
Tony, but her mind had been permanently affected:

> Her poor old mind has almost given up – the word is almost, because I think she knew I
> was with her, at moments, though there were moments when she didn't; she is perfectly
> clear about one thing, that she does not like being in hospital; she was more resigned to
> it the second day I went …. the recognition in her eyes is only a trace; she was 'confused'
> (nurses' word) about where you and John were, & once asked me, Where's Daddy?[4]

In August she was moved to the Mary Potter Hospice of Calvary Hospital.
She survived there for another 21 months and was well looked after, though
she remained in her own entirely withdrawn world, and died in May 1974 while
Curnow was overseas, as had happened when his father died 25 years earlier.

A most moving (and most unusual) poem, entitled 'What was That?', probably
written early in 1973, appeared in Curnow's new collection, An Abominable
Temper, published later in the year. The poem had its origins in the poet's
thoughts about his mother, as she faced the fact of death, yet it is not about his
mother, though it contains a brief reference to a ward 'in a hospice for the dying'.
It describes a dream (or nightmare) in which the Last Trump is heard not as a
loud blast awakening the dead to Judgement Day, nor even as a 'vocal murmur'
in which human voices might be recognised, but as a continuous, unbroken hum,
a single sound (a 'uni-son') which is the unison of 'all our deaths'. All individual
deaths, the poem suggests, share in this universal continuum of death:

            Socrates died so
                willingly Jesus
                    not without a struggle
                        gave up the ghost
            and a mother pleases
                to smother her baby
                    in the Bronx or the Urewera
                        some other pillow

            brain-tissue splashed
                fractionally after
                    the bullet-hole appeared
                        in the gib board
            freesias and catheters
                perfumed the ward
                    in a hospice for the dying
                        the jumbo crashed

In a remarkable concluding stanza it is as if the poet had derived from the strength of his empathy with his mother's silence and withdrawal – 'less a collapse', he had commented to Tim, than 'as if (somehow) this were happening by some secret will of her own'[5] – a glimpse of some deeper level of inward being in which the self is submerged in the movement of all things towards death, as of a river flowing into ocean depths:

            the Trump played on
                like a sea in my sleep
                    or the thumb-stopped ear
                        where my blood can listen
            to the river of itself
                nobody rose calling
                    deep to our deep
                        last unison.

    The poem is not a conventional elegy at all, but its feelings run deep, as it attempts to articulate what his mother might have discovered in the silence into which she withdrew for almost two years before her death. It is also a technical triumph, marking Curnow's increasing mastery of rapid momentum between one line and the next, and between one stanza and the next, as if miming the restless backwards-and-forwards interior movement of consciousness withdrawn into itself. Dispensing entirely with punctuation, almost every line has the double effect of completing a syntactic relation with the previous line and initiating a new syntactic relation with the line following.

The sudden death of Jeny's father from heart failure, while she and Curnow were holidaying briefly at Russell, was also a deeply upsetting family event in 1972. Curnow wrote affectionately about him to Tony:

> You know how deep and close the family's affections are, and you must count me too. He was 74, & was his full spirited and wonderful self almost to the last. Indeed, we had the news, how dangerously ill he was, early on Saturday at Russell; Jeny's chartered plane wasn't fast enough to reach Auckland in time to see him. The Requiem Mass was at St Michael's, Remuera, the first church he designed – and I think, the only romanesque church in the country, of beauty and distinction. You might remember his interest in conservation? He helped to found the N.Z. Conservation Society, & was president of the Tree Society. Karekare was always a special joy to him.[6]

Later in the year he sought Glover's advice about appropriate lettering for a bronze plate for George Tole's grave, but it was not for many years, in 2000, that a memory of his father-in-law at Karekare sparked the sonnet 'The Pocket Compass'.

Jeny inherited her father's estate, from which she was able to fund the renovation of the basement at Tohunga Crescent into a small self-contained flat. Her father also owned the Seaview Road house in which his surviving sisters (Margaret and Clare) and brother (Charles) lived, and the sisters were guaranteed the use of it for as long as they lived. Although a great deal of responsibility for her uncle and aunts inevitably fell on Jeny's shoulders from this time on, she and Curnow were at last relieved of constant financial struggle to make ends meet. An immediate effect was that Curnow was able to contemplate spending his leave in Europe and the United Kingdom for the first time, rather than the United States. Jeny was also delighted when her mother, Janet Osborne, widowed for many years, decided to return to New Zealand permanently in February the following year – 'a great repatriation', Curnow wrote to Tony [7] – after 40 years abroad. She had been poorly provided for by Jeny's stepfather, but Jeny was now in a position to assist her financially, and purchased a flat for her in Portland Road, Remuera, not far from the Seaview Road residence of her aunts and uncle.

Throughout the second half of 1972 Tony had also been in touch with Curnow about the prospect of his son, Simon, coming to New Zealand (after completing his secondary schooling in England in that year) to undertake arts studies at the University of Auckland. Curnow was nervous at the prospect of taking on an *in loco parentis* role. He enjoyed his role as grandfather to nine grandsons, and felt that these immediate relationships, and Jeny's increased family responsibilities after her father's death, would leave them little time to devote to Simon. He need not have worried. Simon was independent, personable, and soon after his arrival in 1973 became a welcome member of the extended Curnow family network.

Tony himself at this time had been based in Geneva for five years. He had separated from his second wife, Soo Lan, in 1965, and in 1967 left Bangkok to take up an appointment in the information service of the International Labour Office in Geneva. After five years he transferred to the United Nations Secretariat in Geneva as information officer to the UN Economic Commission for Europe. In 1970, while looking for a weekend retreat in the Mâcon region of France, across the border from Geneva, he had met and married Elisabeth Baehni. They purchased and renovated a house in the tiny village of Pruzilly near Mâcon, looking out on the vine-clad slopes of the Beaujolais hills stretching south, and this eventually, after Tony's retirement in 1983 and a few years spent in New Zealand, became their permanent home until they moved into Mâcon itself in 2000. From the early 1970s Tony and Curnow became much closer, corresponding often and seeing each other regularly during Tony and Elisabeth's trips to New Zealand and whenever Curnow and Jeny travelled to Europe and England, as they did on a number of occasions from 1974 onwards.

'The same animal gnawing the same bone': collected poems

By early December 1972, Curnow had begun the task of getting together a collected volume of his poems for Reed for publication in 1974, working with copies of all the poems in his earlier (now out-of-print) books – ten altogether – prior to *Trees, Effigies, Moving Objects*. It was the first time he had ever forced himself to re-read all his earlier work, and he had resisted all thought of a collected volume until he had new work to show, unwilling to contemplate the idea that his poetic career had finished with *A Small Room with Large Windows*. For Curnow the idea of a collected poems, or even a selected poems, always carried with it the idea of *completion*, the danger of entombing the poet in the past, and in his numerous later selections and collections he adopted various strategies of *incompletion* in the ways he organised and ordered the material.

He hoped to finish the job by the end of February 1973 (in order to be able to check the proofs before departing overseas at the end of the year), and was thinking of a volume 'not too much under 200 pp', as he wrote to Tim, depending on 'how much, & what, precisely, must be discarded':

> Not too much, I hope. Over 40 years, a few poems have had special attention –
> partly, no doubt, because they deserve it; but there has also been a good deal of sheer
> accident, my own caprices & other people's, which has spotlighted some & left others

in shadow. A CP should show everything in an impartial light: tastes change. Besides, even as far back as the 'thirties', I wasn't writing in the current fashion. One may not be good enough to write 'for all time'; but it can still be an advantage, to have written from no time in particular.[8]

By early February he was still somewhat undecided 'what, if anything, is to be preserved from *Valley of Decision* & *Enemies*', his earliest volumes. He wanted 'something' from the 1930s, but was aware of at least a few items which deserved 'only to be dropped & obliterated, so far as a CP can do this'.[9] On 11 March he gave a reading (with nine others) from *Trees, Effigies, Moving Objects* at the Christchurch Arts Festival, which was well received, and as the year went on, with a further performance in Christchurch of 'Landfall in Unknown Seas', a review of his new poems by Ian Wedde in *Islands*[10] which deeply impressed him, and a YC radio programme devoted to his work produced by Alan Roddick, he began to feel more confident that his decision to prepare a collected volume was justified. Moreover, as he read more and more carefully in his own earlier work he was fascinated to discover continuities with his more recent poems which he had never imagined existed.   His solution to the 'headaches' posed by his earliest collections[11] was to revise most of those in his first book (*Valley of Decision*) and some of those in *Enemies* – sometimes lightly, sometimes quite substantially – a time-consuming process which delayed the completion of the manuscript until the end of May. However, the delay also enabled him to complete the manuscript of *An Abominable Temper and other poems* in time to include it in the collected volume. By mid-April he was able to report considerable progress to his cousin, Ted Wall, at Reed:

> At the beginning, I have my very earliest collection *Valley of Decision*, touched up here & there, & one or two pieces dropped. The first inclination was to discard all *juvenilia*. Then I noticed that some of these early gropings make sense in the light of later poems; besides, I think the book should contain evidence that I was writing verse at that time.[12]

However, it was to Glover that Curnow gave his fullest account of the 'curious sensations' he experienced as he went over his earlier work: parts of *Valley of Decision* were 'not nearly so weak' as he had once thought; much of *Enemies* made him 'squirm'; and both *Island and Time* and *Sailing or Drowning* were 'full of pleasant surprises'[13]:

> You may not remember some letter you wrote in the past 18 months, where you said 'put them all in'. I haven't quite done that, but so nearly, nobody will notice. Discarding

was a habit of years: cowardice, really, playing safe. Trying to make sure the alter ego
(or alter id?) couldn't embarrass me in company, by his table manners, picking his
nose, passing ignorant remarks. After months getting copy ready, & days with galleys,
he confronts me,

    The real will from its crude compoundings come,

    Seeming at first a beast disgorged, unlike,

    Warmed by a desperate milk

(Stevens, of course.) He's uncouth in both senses. I've never seen him before, nor
has anyone else. Maybe not fit to be seen, but there's no denying his presence. Back
to Valley of Decision (with revisions), Three Poems (Mrs Minogue & the beetroot
swimming on the sideboard), Enemies (headaches [hangovers] & hang-ups), &
much Island & Time (better than I've supposed these 30 years, never having dared
to look at them). Would you believe it, it's the same animal gnawing the same bone?
It doesn't seem very important, at the moment, whether anyone else will see it; more
important that I do myself.[14]

Curnow made a similar point to Ian Milner, commenting that as he worked
on the collection over months 'early & late were related more closely than I
had imagined, & I simply couldn't see where to draw lines between them', and
comparing the finished product to an artichoke: '[I]t's for people who like
artichokes well enough to put up with buttery fingers, inedible prickles, stringy
bits, for the sake of some flavour & even (with luck) a small heart in the middle.'[15]

Curnow's revisions to the early poems are invariably an improvement on the
original: in most cases eliminating poeticisms, stridencies or awkwardnesses;
substituting, occasionally, a word or phrase which *implies* more in its immediate
context; and in some cases reworking lines to emphasise tensions already present
in the original. However, in at least half a dozen instances the revisions do
represent considerable rewritings of the originals. Such poems inhabit a kind
of limbo in the *Collected Poems*: they are not the original poems, nor poems the
poet would in the 1970s have *chosen* to write, but the early poems as the poet later
felt they might have been written, looking back from the 1970s. Curnow devoted
considerable space to justifying the revisions in the 'Author's Note' to the volume,
emphasising that he was not concerned to correct 'youthful belief or opinions'.
This would in any case, he argued, be 'a futile exercise', since in the earlier versions
of *Valley of Decision*, and after, 'some crisis or change from faith to scepticism may
be read, however perplexed and precarious the faith was, and the scepticism no
less so'.[16] What he could not ignore, he added, were the 'instructions for revision'
carried between or under the earlier poems, arguing that if he did *not* revise he
would in effect be 'concealing something from the reader: some part of his own
better understanding'.[17]

More than twenty years later an article by Hugh Roberts[18] on the similarities between Curnow's earlier and later poetry, which quoted from the *revised* versions of *Valley of Decision*, prompted an exchange in which Curnow publicly defended his revisions again, taking exception to accusations by Janet Hughes that the revisions repeatedly tip 'the speaker's apparent allegiance from belief into scepticism' producing a consistency with the later work which is 'partly imposed' by the revisions. Hughes thought Roberts overstated (or even invented) the similarities because he did not work from the original texts, and she implicated Curnow-as-reviser in an evasive manoeuvre to misrepresent his earlier work. Curnow's comment 'the poetry is all one book', Hughes concluded, was 'an unwarranted triumph of mythmaking of a personal kind'.[19] Curnow replied that he simply did not know 'how to account for such a pile-up of "bad faith" imputations', and insisted that his phrase 'the poetry is all one book' was a *metaphor* for *all* the poetry he had ever written, including the earlier versions, and should not be read simply as a literal-minded reference confined to what was between the covers of the *Collected Poems*.[20] Replying to Curnow's response, Hughes regretted if her remarks implied 'bad faith', claiming that that had not been her intention, but maintained her view that 'only with revision[s] do the sceptics acquire a convincing voice, and the poem[s] a consequent irony'.[21]

One of the things Hughes missed in the author's note from which she quoted, however, was the crucial qualification Curnow added to the sentence suggesting that a 'crisis or change from faith to scepticism' was detectable in *Valley of Decision*, and after it: 'however perplexed and precarious the faith was, *and the scepticism no less so*' [author's italics]. The qualification suggests that he did *not* see his poetry as following some simple linear development from faith to scepticism: as if an early crisis of religious belief had been lived through and surmounted, left behind once and for all, and replaced by a firm assurance that the only tenable position was one of scepticism. On the contrary, his qualification suggests that the 'crisis' may be a continuing one in his poetry, that the question of belief – of 'truth' – *remains* a driving concern of his poetry, and that scepticism *continues* to raise as many perplexing questions as it might seem to answer. Almost certainly this was the source of the surprise Curnow felt when he began to re-read his early poetry written more than three decades earlier, leading to the decision not to exclude it as 'juvenilia' – for his sense, as he wrote to Glover, that the poet he once was is 'the same animal gnawing the same bone'[22] as the poet he now is. 'For the first time', he repeated to Glover a little later, 'I can see that I have been driving (or groping) at the same thoughts for 30/40 years.'[23]

How fully 'collected' was the *Collected Poems*? It was largely complete, once Curnow had made the decision to work only from books published under his own name. He omitted four poems from *Valley of Decision* and one from *Enemies*.

He excluded, or did not consider, some excellent early poems (like 'Doom at Sunrise' and 'Inheritance') which had been published in Glover's small Caxton miscellanies in the 1930s, nor poems published in *Recent Poems* (1941) alongside contributions by Mason, Fairburn and Glover. He excluded his satirical broadsheets. He did not retrieve any poems from magazines (of which there were many, especially in the 1930s and 1940s, and two in the *Cornish Review* in the early 1950s). With one notable exception the ordering of poems within each original volume was preserved. The exception was *Poems 1949–57*, whose poems are ordered quite differently in the *Collected Poems*. When they first appeared Curnow's comments to Glover had suggested a certain arbitrariness of organisation – except for the need to disperse the elegies throughout the book, and to have 'A Small Room with Large Windows' placed last. Although the revised ordering is obviously a considered change, the reasons for it are as hard to fathom as in the original volume. Like *Poems 1949–57* it disperses the elegies throughout, and 'A Small Room with Large Windows' appears under its title volume, published in 1962, but the new ordering is definitely not chronological, whatever suggestiveness Curnow hoped it might carry.

Although Curnow submitted the manuscript to Reed three months later than the deadline he had hoped to meet – at the end of May instead of the end of February – his publishers made remarkably speedy progress and he received the galley proofs in October, followed by the page proofs in instalments from mid-November. He was thus able to complete his work on it before departing overseas at the end of December, anticipating its publication in mid-1974 while he was away. Throughout the production phase there was close consultation between David Elworthy and Ted Wall at Reed and Curnow, and the *Collected Poems* was the first of his books in which Tim played an active role as his father's agent, overseeing the contractual arrangements. On one issue Curnow was adamant. He did not wish the manuscript to be submitted to the New Zealand Literary Fund Advisory Committee for a publishing grant. With his *Four Plays* he had accepted a reduced royalty (of 5 per cent instead of 10 per cent) in exchange for Reed's agreement not to seek a publishing subsidy. In the case of his *Collected Poems* he was not disposed to such an agreement.

As far as the Literary Fund was concerned he wished to remain independent of the taxpayer's bounty, disliked intensely the mendicancy mentality fostered by such 'public charity', and 'would regard the necessary printed acknowledgement as betrayal of my own conscience in the matter'.[24] Furthermore, he did not see that a grant would be good business either: 'If they gave you a hand-out, it would be useless if small – and more damaging to the book, if big.'[25] He followed these comments up with an even stronger enunciation of his views:

1) I will not have my Collected Poems go out, bearing the presumptive, and presumptuous, *imprimatur*, of my inferiors – as committeemen, that is, never mind how they strike me as individuals;

2) I will not have the ms pawed or passed around among them, or put them in a position to do that, whether they choose to or not;

3) I neither fear nor wish this kind of thing; their notions don't matter to me in the slightest; I simply don't wish for the contact;

4) Since I won't have it, there's obviously no room for it in our contract; and if it isn't there, there can be no question of subsequent applications; if I weren't satisfied of this, I would want it specified in the contract.

I can't be more definite than that. Any kind of co-publishing deal with a reputable concern, e.g. OUP, I wouldn't dream of interfering with; but not the Piggy Bank.[26]

Reed acceded, and the firm was also helpful on numerous matters of design. Curnow included a smallish number of notes at the back of the *Collected Poems*, some from the books in which they first appeared (occasionally modified or extended) and others new, after Elworthy agreed to his suggestion that the model for their style and approach would be Yeats's notes in his Macmillan *Collected Poems*. Curnow also suggested James Dickey's *Comprehensive Selection* as a model,* and was interested in having a photograph of himself by John Pettit in some way incorporated into the jacket design (by Trevor Plaisted). The result, a kind of abstract design of yellow and green, in which Curnow's face merges with, and emerges from, its background in a kind of *trompe l'oeil* effect, is strikingly effective. The overall result was a handsome book, generously spaced, with every poem beginning on a new page, its length 268 pages compared with the 200 pages Curnow had initially envisaged. There were delays in the printing of the book, so that it did not appear until October 1974, but Glover immediately wrote to Elworthy to give his verdict:

After the vexations, the Curnow has turned out a tremendous success – and I mean as a book & not only for its uniquely important contents. A solid anathema (the Greek please!) [i.e. a tribute] to Allen's long persistence in achievement. Title page nearly very good – I don't care for the Sans of 1933–1973, when a small Albertus would have been my choice. At short range I thgt the jacket a geographer's dream of Asia Minor and the Greek seaboard with Sicily nuzzling in for comfort: at about two feet I see an idealised impression of Allen, negative glasses. Very very ingenious and

---

* *The Achievement of James Dickey: A Comprehensive Selection of his Poems*, The Modern Poets Series, Scott, Foresman, 1968.

effective, especially for display use . . . . Yes, a great achievement. We must all thank you for it.[27]

New poems, *An Abominable Temper* and other poems

Curnow's appetite for new poems was undiminished after mid-1972, when he completed 'Any Time Now', the last of the new poems for *Trees, Effigies, Moving Objects*. Almost certainly, there were one or two drafts and fragments which were not suitable for that sequence. For a number of years, for example, he had been making notes and drafting fragments for a longish poem he hoped to write about his great-great-grandfather, Peter Monro (Curnow's earliest New Zealand ancestor) based on a letter about him written by his son, Judge H.A.H. Monro, to his own daughter Ada (a sister of Curnow's grandmother, Alice Augusta) – a copy of which Ted Wall had given him in the mid-1960s. In March 1973 he returned to the poem again as he was preparing his *Collected Poems*, and completed it in April, giving it the title (drawing on an epithet used twice by Judge Monro to describe his father) 'An Abominable Temper'. 'I knew about his famous "temper" long before this', Curnow wrote to Wystan. 'He once (according to a story of T's) swept the dinner-table bare, simply by tearing off the table-cloth & everything on it.'[28] It was also the longest poem Curnow had ever written, more than 300 lines in ten uneven blocks of verse deploying a range of verse and stanza schemes, utilising documentary material (direct quotations and lists) from the letter, and aiming, above all, for a readable narrative line which was often close to prose.

He sent it to Dudding to consider for *Islands*, and at the same time began to think of it as forming the centrepiece of a possible new collection, alongside a smallish number of new poems that had been accumulating over the previous months, and including one from the 1960s (his birthday tribute to Lilburn published in 1965) which had not yet appeared in book form. By this time he had written three significant new poems, 'This Beach Can Be Dangerous', 'What was That?' and 'A Window Frame', as well as a handful of slighter pieces. At the end of April he asked Glover if he would consider publishing a small edition of the volume,[29] suggesting that it might take its title from either the long poem ('An Abominable Temper'), or from 'This Beach Can Be Dangerous' or 'Tantalus',[30] and eventually sent him a copy of the manuscript a month later: 'As a collection I think they compare pretty well with the last, & may have less of my damned knottiness?? I don't mind being knotty – your word for it, & I know perfectly well what it means.'[31]

Glover was interested, but needed time to work the production into his own schedule, and it was not until early in July that he was ready to proceed, publishing it under his own Catspaw Press imprint, and engaging Bob Gormack at the Nag's Head Press, Christchurch, as the printer. Production moved ahead quickly, and by mid-September Curnow had received the galley proofs. There were his usual last-minute tinkerings, with Curnow particularly concerned about the placement of 'A Refusal to Read Poems of James K. Baxter at a Performance to Honour his Memory in Cranmer Square, Christchurch':

> If I placed the lines on Baxter, 'A Refusal . . .' *last* in the book, that was a mistake. I want the long poem to go last. The Baxter poem must go after 'To an Unfortunate Young Lady . . .'. I have marked the spot in pencil on Galley 2.

> (My problem was to avoid, if possible, placing two short poems with long wordy titles so close together. I find that I can't avoid this. It is much more important not to place the Baxter lines last in the book – too sensitive a position, which would over-emphasise & distort the sense of this short occasional poem.)[32]

Both the Baxter poem and the poem to the 'Unfortunate Young Lady' resulted from Curnow's attendance at the Christchurch Arts Festival in March. He actually wrote the lines on Baxter (as he later explained to John Pocock) 'on the platform of the old university hall, filling in time while the others (nine of them!) read their poems': '[A]s the show finished, I handed them down to . . . Howard McNaughton, who was covering it for *The Press*. I said, your editor may not be interested, but if he is, *The Press* is welcome to it: they printed it next day, in a prominent place.'* [33]

The poem's title echoes Dylan Thomas's 'A Refusal to Mourn the Death, by Fire, of a Child in London'. Curnow's 'refusal' is a refusal to become part of what he felt to be false in the orgy of retrospective public adulation Baxter received after his early death at the end of 1972. Perhaps, also, it was an expression of his own distaste for the role of Christ-like prophet Baxter seemed to adopt publicly in his later years, as if inviting the ritual elevation which occurred in the wake of his death. But the poem is also a tribute to another Baxter, a friend and poet who never wrote better than when he was younger, and who perhaps *shared* Curnow's quandary in not knowing quite how to understand or reconcile the mixed roles he played ('bays, or myrtles, or thorns' – poet, social crusader, suffering Christ). The poem concludes with an emphasis, again, on Baxter's *poetry*, his 'winged'

* Curnow's reading was on 11 March, and the poem's publication in *The Press* was on the actual day, 12 March, of the memorial celebration in Cranmer Square.

words which fly of their own volition, needing no crutch (his own or others' words) to assist them: 'winged words need no crutch / and I've none for you.'

'To an Unfortunate Young Lady'* – its full title 'To an Unfortunate Young Lady who after attending Six Public Readings by Thirty Poets asked, Does anyone care?'– was a *jeu d'esprit* whose occasion was the same arts festival in Christchurch, and the earnest complaint voiced to Curnow was by a youthful Sue McCauley, later to become a well-known New Zealand novelist. The poem gently mocks the notion that people have some social or moral obligation to read or care about poetry, wittily celebrating its unpredictable motivations and significances, regardless of whether anyone cares to read it, as well as the diversity of the pleasures people take in life (whether these include poetry or not), concluding with a tribute to the energy and liveliness of the Young Lady herself:

> Isn't it the mumble
> of something loose behind,
> or a fumble
> in the back seat of the mind?
> Or an innumerable company
> of the heavenly host crying
> rhubarb rhubarb rhubarb rhubarb
> with *obbligato* innumerable other
> syllables in several languages,
> some dead?
>   Does anyone care?
> One man's rhubarb is another man's
> artichoke and that's the reason why
> the poetry of earth is never dead
> dead dead.
>   Rhubarb to you,
> my dear, with cornflakes and cream,
> every glorious carefree day and night of your life.

'Each man to his own rhubarb. / It's as good as the next man's' he had earlier written,[34] before introducing the artichoke in the final draft in mid-May.

At this time also he reworked his earlier version of 'A Window Frame', which originally had the title 'A Smell of Burning' and was written in couplets. Part one of this poem, which extends the epistemological concerns of poems like 'Lone Kauri Road', dramatises the plight of a consciousness driven by the impossible

---

* This is probably a conscious echo of Pope's 'Elegy to the Memory of an Unfortunate Lady' (1717).

wish to contain the *essence* of the observed world within the static frame imposed by the mind: what might be in the frame will constantly change from moment to moment, and be interrupted by the utterly unpredictable intrusion of objects from outside (a sparrow arriving on one of the twigs of a tree), let alone changes in the perspective, focus, thoughts and memories of the observer. Part two of the poem, much briefer, dramatises a counter-voice, which sees (and *accepts*) the constant, flowing interpenetration of observer and observed, of the world 'outside' and the world 'inside', for all the astonishing Magritte-like strangenesses that it offers:

> Look out the window.
>   It is on the page.
> Examine the page.
>   It is out the window.
> Knuckle the cool pane.
>   It is in the bone.
> Why is the mud glassed,
>   with mangroves
> bedded in the glass?
>   Why is the cloud
> inverted in the glass?
>   Why are islands
> in the Gulf stained blue
>   grained green with
> interior lighting
>   by Hoyte?
>   *Why not?*

Both Curnow and Glover were delighted with the small volume when Gormack completed his printing of it in early November, and Glover was especially moved that Curnow had dedicated the volume to him: 'gratifying to me', he wrote to Gormack, 'because of enduring friendship through thick and thin – books too, I mean.'[35] But his comments to Gormack were focused in detail on the production values of the book, 'the usual Nag's Head triumph', and the typical challenges provided by Curnow's poetry: 'Bloody old Allen makes things hard by varying from a one word title to a four line one. Tough on the typographer, who has to make the one look adequate and the other not a poster.'[36] Curnow liked the production even better than that of *Trees, Effigies, Moving Objects*, and commented to Glover:

[Gormack] said he hoped I wouldn't find it 'too severe and textbooky'. Anything but! It's just the sort of presentation I like to think my verse – meaning the kind of thing it is, not how good it is – requires. As if one put on a new suit, & found it (as one never does) as comfortable & familiar as one's favourite old pants & jersey. I'm not comparing, exactly, but I've not had an experience like it since *Island and Time* & *Jack Without Magic*, & had almost forgotten the pleasure it is.[37]

'The impossibility of speaking truth about oneself': Curnow interviewed by Mac Jackson

In June 1973 the fourth issue of *Islands* appeared, featuring both 'An Abominable Temper' (the cover incorporating a page from Curnow's manuscript and photographs of both Peter Monro and H.A.H. Monro) and an interview with Curnow ('Conversation with Allen Curnow') by MacDonald (Mac) P. Jackson. The interview had taken quite some time, and a good deal of collaborative editing, with Jackson, of the four original tapes (recorded between November 1972 and February 1973) before it reached the form which Curnow sent to Dudding in April. 'I'm delighted you find the Interview readable', Curnow later wrote to Glover: 'It was hell for both me and Jackson. I so much wished to be candid – while realising, in the near-panic any sane man must feel, *the impossibility of speaking truth about oneself*. One would have to know it, first!'[38]

Jackson elicited a remarkable amount of previously unknown – or little-known – information about Curnow (about his family background, his time at St John's College and his career in Christchurch as a journalist, in particular), as well as prompting Curnow to reflect at some length on the motivations and aims of key aspects of his literary career – his earlier and later poetry, his plays, the critical positions espoused in his anthology introductions, the nature of his interest in poets like Eliot, Yeats, Thomas and Stevens, and (more diffidently) on the current literary scene in New Zealand.

The initial length of the interview as it had been hammered out between Curnow and Jackson – 25 pages – was substantially longer than the fifteen pages Dudding had planned for *Islands*, and he edited it judiciously to reduce the original by a quarter to about nineteen pages. Like Brasch before him, Dudding had been unsuccessful in persuading Curnow to contribute an autobiographical piece in the 'Beginnings' series, but Curnow almost certainly saw the format of the 'Conversation', with an interviewer whose critical mind he trusted and admired, as a means of contextualising the whole of his poetic career for readers who would soon, for the first time, encounter almost all of his poetry (most of it long out of print, except for well-known anthology pieces) in his *Collected Poems*. The impulse to speak candidly about himself, despite his scepticism about the possibility of 'speaking truth', was of a piece with the momentous nature (in his view) of the decision to offer an *inclusive* collected, rejecting the habit of 'discarding' which he had developed over the years, perhaps a sign of 'cowardice, really, playing safe'.[39] This interview, and later ones with Harry Ricketts and Peter Simpson, together with the documentary film about himself produced by Shirley Horrocks in the last years of his life, was the closest Curnow ever came to autobiography, a form which he deeply distrusted.

Jackson also persuaded Curnow, somewhat unwillingly, to talk about Whim Wham ('I suppose we have to talk about Whim Wham. I try to suppress this as well as I can.')[40] – the only time, in print, in which he allowed himself to reflect on the relationship between his serious poetry and his light verse:

> [T]he serious, as we call it, poetry is a different area of oneself altogether and Whim Wham is really a kind of persona. It's neither me, nor not me – he's a sort of minor mask. The Whim Wham character makes its own particular demands. One has, as it were, to act the part of Whim Wham – one is the thing for the time being while it's being written. The 'serious poetry' is a very different sort of thing. One is searching oneself and searching the terms of one's very existence in an entirely different spirit. There is another thing here: the important thing is that the serious poem is something one is journeying towards, not something that comes towards one as a kind of message from space and is immediately intelligible. One is working one's way towards the poem. It starts almost as a remote objective and as one gets closer to it, it gets a bit clearer. One finds out what it was one meant to write. The Whim Wham verse is another thing; perhaps just hard work.[41]

Despite the interest of these and other comments about Whim Wham, Curnow came to regret that he had made them, concerned that in the minds of some readers and critics the kind of distinction between his serious poetry and light verse that seemed to him self-evident (and which he had attempted to make in his comments in the interview) would be blurred. For him the difference seemed absolute. He seemed not to be able to imagine any approach to his 'serious poetry' which drew on his light or satirical verse (no matter how sensitive and complex the understanding of the relationship might be) except as potentially *reductive* of the value of the kind of serious poetry he wrote. It was not that he did not regard satire as a serious poetic mode (he regarded both Pope and Byron as truly major poets of the English tradition), and he had been happy to publish a number of satirical broadsheets under his own name, though he did not include them in his *Collected Poems*; rather, it had to do with the kind of serious lyric poet he aspired to be, and the fact that Whim Wham, both by chance and design over the years, had become that poet's polar opposite in nearly every respect. If anything, in the later years of his life, he was even more concerned than he had been earlier to avoid any public identification of Whim Wham, and when the interview with Jackson was later reprinted in a selection of Curnow's critical writings edited by Peter Simpson, *Look Back Harder* (1987), the section relating to Whim Wham was excised.

Effectively, the interview contributed to what Curnow saw as the launching of a new career as a poet – an implicit statement that he was not only not finished as a poet but embarking on new directions as well as rethinking his earlier poetic career, or perhaps – as he wrote to Alan Roddick, mentioning that both the *Collected Poems* and the interview were a 'kind of exposure I have been avoiding most of my life' – a way of clearing the decks 'for new & better things'.[42] In addition to the poetry reading from *Trees, Effigies, Moving Objects* he gave at the Christchurch Arts Festival in March and the reading of 'Landfall in Unknown Seas' in the new Christchurch Town Hall as part of the University of Canterbury centennial celebrations in May, he was pleased to be approached by Roddick, editor of the YC Poetry programme for 1973, for permission to include seven of the ten poems from his reading earlier in the year, which had been tape-recorded by the NZBC. Roddick also asked Curnow to read two or three poems from *Poems 1949–57*, which he planned to use as 'a sort of abutment for a bridge between the two collections'.[43] Curnow suggested 'Spectacular Blossom', with any others to be chosen from 'Jack-in-the-Boat', 'Keep in a Cool Place', 'To Forget Self and All' or 'An Oppressive Climate, a Populous Neighbourhood'. Curnow was extremely pleased with the programme when it was broadcast in early July, including Roddick's commentary on the poems: 'It had the effect of *presenting* me, with an outline of clear ideas: & with what Glover calls my "knottiness", those must have been hard to arrive at!'[44]

It had been a remarkably productive (if exhausting) year devoted to poetic projects, and Curnow looked forward to the prospect of a full year's sabbatical leave in 1974, away from New Zealand. Relieved for the first time of having to earn money overseas to support his leave, his plans were more open and flexible. He had only one fixed commitment, a second reading (this time with the British poet Thom Gunn) at the Library of Congress in Washington in November, for which he would be paid US$1,000. Initially, he and Jeny thought of spending two months in Europe, followed by six months in the United Kingdom, then a final two months in the United States. He wrote to Dan Davin, Leslie Rowse and Jim Walton, hoping to catch up with them, and he also hoped it might be possible to visit Ian and Jarmila Milner in Prague while he was in Europe.

It was to be Curnow's last sabbatical leave from the university, since he was due to retire at the end of 1976. The prospect of visiting Europe (Italy and France) for the first time – he was now in his sixty-third year – was especially exciting, but (since it would also be the first time he had lived in foreign, non-English-speaking countries) also daunting. 'I am scared, & fascinated too, by the idea of being in Europe', he wrote to Milner, 'never having crossed the channel: though Jeny did, some 20 years ago.'[45] In the event, their plans changed dramatically. The European leg of the trip was extended from two to six months, followed by only three months in London, and then six weeks in Washington and New York.

As always, it took some time for the experiences of this trip to be assimilated, but in retrospect it can be seen as a watershed in Curnow's poetic development. From this time onwards the United States receded from the international foreground of his writing and poetic interests, and was gradually replaced by new connections with Europe (especially Italy) as a location, and reforged literary connections with the United Kingdom. The polarity of 'here' and 'there' remained central to his poetry, and his favoured New Zealand locations (Karekare, and the Auckland city- and harbour-scapes observed during his Parnell walks) remained the 'omphalos', the place *in* and *from* which the poetry was generated, but in relation to a new and broadened sense of the global forces of history and contemporary life.

Chapter Twenty-six

Discovering Europe:
Leave, 1974

I have a satchell [sic] stuffed with broken notes, & no idea what poems if any they may suggest later on. At moments, Europe can seem like an exam for which one hadn't done the reading.[1]

Florence, Venice, Ravenna, Sicily, Rome, February–June

Curnow and Jeny travelled to Italy on the *Gugliemo Marconi*, joining it on 2 January 1974 in Sydney, where they stopped to see Tim and his new partner, Lea, in Paddington. The four-and-a-half-week voyage, which included stops at Melbourne, Perth, Cape Town and Tenerife before disembarkation at Genoa on 5 February, was not without its longueurs. There were few passengers with whom they could share their interests, and although they were travelling first class their cabin was small, and they did their best to avoid the regime of games and entertainment. The brief stop at Cape Town reinforced Curnow's detestation of the apartheid system, as did the demeanour of the white South Africans who joined the ship there for the rest of the voyage. The Mediterranean leg of the trip, which included brief stops at Malta, Messina and Naples, however, was full of interest, and at Messina they checked out accommodation options, since they planned at this stage to spend further time in Sicily until the worst of the northern winter was over.

Tony and Elisabeth made a brief trip from Geneva to meet the Curnows at Genoa, driving them to Florence, where they settled into the Hotel Aprile.

They intended to stay in Florence for several weeks before travelling south, and immediately embarked on their own unorthodox brand of casual, leisurely *flânerie*: a great deal of walking and observing, using the local bus system, discovering cafés and bars where they could sample the local cuisine and meet local people. Jeny was interested in the shops and Curnow spent time reading local newspapers to catch the political ambiences of the contemporary scene, finding after a time and with the assistance of a dictionary that he could achieve a reasonable understanding of Italian. They visited Fiesole, in the hills near Florence, and the Duomo and Baptistery, returning there the following Sunday to attend High Mass.

However, within a week of arriving at Florence Tony sent a distressing message from Jeny's lawyer in Auckland, that her mother was seriously ill, and Jeny immediately decided to return. During the time she was away Curnow stayed with Tony and Elisabeth in Geneva. Her mother was heavily sedated through most of Jeny's two-week stay in Auckland, but doctors were confident that she would pull through. It was a frantically busy fortnight. Jeny visited her mother every day (delighted, occasionally, when she recognised and spoke to her), attended to arrangements for her ongoing care until the end of the year, sorted through her belongings at Portland Road and arranged the letting of the flat, as there was no hope of any immediate return there, leaving instructions with her lawyer. She also found that she had to do a great deal to assist her oldest aunt, Marge, who was also unwell and in need of hospitalisation.

The flight back to Geneva on 5 March, via Los Angeles and London, was exhausting, and after her arrival she and Curnow decided to rest for a while and rethink their travel plans, extending their time in Italy. They stayed in Geneva for a further two weeks, and then planned to travel to Venice for a fortnight on 19 March, followed by a week in Ravenna and a further two weeks in Florence. At the end of April they would travel south to Sicily, and after a month there, followed by a week or two in Rome, return to Geneva around mid-June.

Venice turned out to be a delight beyond Curnow's expectations, and he was to return there on numerous later trips to Europe, staying at or near the same pensione, La Calcina (where Ruskin had stayed in 1877) at 780 Zattere, overlooking the Giudecca Canal, and patronising the same small trattoria nearby, Ai Cugnai, where he and Jeny became regular and welcome guests. 'Random and capricious tourists that we are', Curnow wrote,[2] they walked a great deal, and visited the Accademia dell'Galleria on several occasions – Curnow was especially interested in the paintings by Tintoretto, Titian and Giorgione – attended Mass at St Mark's Basilica on their first Sunday there, heard a performance of Beethoven's *Eroica* symphony at the Teatro La Fenice, and arranged for some Venetian glassware to be made and sent directly to Tohunga Crescent. They did not feel the slightest pressure to 'see everything', rested most afternoons, and made a habit of revisiting places which interested them. In pursuit of works by Titian and Tintoretto they discovered the Francisan romanesque-gothic church of Santa Maria (the Basilica dei Frari) – though, as Curnow noted in a later poem, 'Organo ad Libitum', Titian's blockbuster *Assumption of the Virgin* had been removed for restoration – and they also revisited the Scuola of San Rocco, the great site of Tintoretto's work.

Although the weather was often still very cold, there were few tourists about, and Curnow was astonished by the absence of traffic noise, 'the quietness, the presence of *human* sound in public places': 'Can there be another city where the sounds are those of the pre-automobile age?'[3] 'No road traffic!' he wrote to Tony. 'We should have known but that's the most marvellous surprise. Quiet to walk and sleep in. The West (or East) should have tried more cities on the same plan.'[4] Surrounded as they were by so many monuments of the past, such experiences of a human scale – people walking, conversing, laughing – provided an important touchstone of value in Curnow's response to the places he visited.

On 5 April they travelled by train to Ravenna, where they stayed for a week, dividing their time between visits to the Marina di Ravenna a short distance away on the Adriatic coast (whose pines and dunes reminded them of Waikuku, north of Christchurch), and visits to the sixth-century Basilica of San Vitale (with its magnificent Byzantine mosaics of Old Testament scenes and of the Emperor Justinian and the Empress Theodora), and to the fifth-century Mausoleum of Galla Placidia nearby, also a small masterpiece of Byzantine architecture and mosaic art. Its blue dome, studded with stars, provided a motif of magical epiphany in Ezra Pound's *Cantos*, recalled throughout in his phrase 'in the gloom the gold / gathers light against it', and Curnow himself recalled that phrase and its context in one of his best-known later poems, 'You Will Know When You Get There'.

During their stay in Ravenna these Byzantine splendours were bizarrely interrupted by an episode in which they somewhat rashly accepted an invitation from a lively, outgoing man they met in a bar to be driven to the Capanno Garibaldi (the hut in which Garibaldi had been protected by patriots during his flight from the Austrians in 1849), some 8 kilometres from Ravenna. The drive became increasingly hair-raising and dangerous, and they were extremely lucky to escape the generous hospitality without serious accident. Curnow scribbled rough notes throughout his travels in Europe, and the wild drive to Garibaldi's hut was the catalyst for a Ravenna-based poem which he spent considerable time on, fascinated by the curious intersection of history and the present. 'Call this [poem]', he instructed himself in one note, '"A Ride to Ravenna", design it for accelerating speed.' 'The 5th/6th centuries', he also noted, alluding to the Byzantine monuments he had encountered in Ravenna, 'are / an intensely personal poem / which I mean to write some day / when I have finished with my feelings.' The question *how* to include history in his poems, given its overwhelming presence in the

places he was visiting, was a central preoccupation, to be worked into the poem
he had in mind:

> The past is too small for the present,
> We can't all get in.
> The present's too small for the past,
> We can't carry all that.

By April the tourist invasion of Italy had also begun, and the other contemporary element in the poem was an incident in tourist-swarming San Vitale ('We
can't all get in') in which Curnow accidentally backed into the tripod of a huge
camera trained like a blunderbuss by a German tourist on the murky ceiling of
the Basilica:

> Trying to make out exactly what Moses does
> In the murky overhead glint of the mosaic
> Up Sinai fetching the Law
> I heeled the stainless tripod leg
> Of the young German's gun-belled camera,
> Blunderbuss rather, trained on the doves and angels
> And the saints, patriarchs, evangelists
> In the murky overhead glint of the mosaic,
> Crack marksman! Sorry, I said,
> Lying. Swarthy Jesus, golden Jesus, only stared
> Up there in the apse. Our problem, not His.

The poem was never completed, but it had the distinctive elements of Curnow's
later poems about history – a subjective mix of seemingly random contemporary
events and memories, and fragmentary historical observations. The past, these
poems imply, does not embody some abstract, fixed truth that might ever be
finally and fully recovered, cannot be frozen and fixed within a frame, but exists
in a dynamic relationship with the present, whose contingencies, perspectives,
feelings and thoughts, imaginings, continually interact with it. From this
perspective, history – even the most distant past of previous centuries or
millennia – is through-and-through *dynamic* and present. The poems resist the
habit of thinking of history as what occurred up to some arbitrary limit of (would
it be?) a decade or a century ago: every moment is the next moment's history,
every today is tomorrow's yesterday, every this week is next week's previous week.

One remarkable poem which did eventuate – though not immediately – in the
wake of this first trip to Italy was 'In the Duomo', about the Pazzi assassination

conspiracy against Lorenzo and Giuliano de' Medici in fifteenth-century Florence, whose violent location was the Duomo itself during High Mass on 28 April 1478. And it was to Florence, after their week in Ravenna, that the Curnows returned to resume their interrupted stay there of two months earlier. It was Easter Week, and on the day after their arrival, Easter Sunday, they managed to make their way through the huge throng in the Piazza di Duomo into the crowded cathedral, where they observed the vivid theatrical spectacle prior to Mass, beginning with 'a long procession down the aisle which included the police carrying the Italian flag, the Florentines with their flags and trumpets',[5] followed by bishops and priests and the cardinal. At midday, an hour into the service, one of the highlights of the event occurred, for the crowd outside, as Curnow vividly described it to Belinda:

> Easter Mass at the Cathedral in Florence was bound to be spectacular: what one didn't expect was a fireworks dove, mounted on a steel column near the high altar, which at the right moment of the service went off with a tremendous bang and a trail of sparks, flashing along a wire to the west doors and outside to a tall ornamental cart (pulled into the square by white bullocks) – what happened outside, we heard only from inside the Cathedral; it was 'the bursting of the cart', more precisely the blazing dove touched off all the fireworks in the cart, and a quite deafening series of explosions, more like bombs than ordinary fireworks, for the amusement of some thousands gathered in the square: actually, as we saw from photographs, people nearest the cart had hands over their ears. It's a performance that's been repeated every Easter for some centuries.[6]

Bonechi's guide to Florence gave Curnow some of the architectural details of the Duomo and the Baptistery nearby, as well as a first hint about the Pazzi conspiracy – key elements (alongside his discovery that the south cliff face at Karekare where he often fished was locally nicknamed 'the Cathedral') of the powerful poem, in five parts, which he was to write after his return to New Zealand and which eventually provided one of three central pillars in the structure of *An Incorrigible Music*.

The return visit to Florence was much more enjoyable than their earlier stay, as Curnow wrote to Wystan:

> In February, F. was cold, dank, claustrophobic. Take one Ren. walled city, a few squ. miles. Add 10,000 Fiats, VWs, Lancias, etc, public transport and other heavy traffic. Stir with a long memory. Garnish pavements with dog turds. Add viruses, gastric & bronchial. Chill well before serving. The effect couldn't be bettered by the Hell in the ceiling of the Baptistery to which Christ in Judgment consigns the damned. Now, in the mild spring weather, the subjective picture is transformed.[7]

During their fortnight there they visited and revisited some of the main tourist locations (the Uffizi Gallery, the Pitti Palace and the Boboli Gardens), revisited Fiesole, and spent much time engaged in Curnow's favoured form of sightseeing and tourism – simply walking and observing. On the day of their departure on 27 April, by train fourteen hours overnight, from Florence to Messina, Curnow heard from Tony (contacted by his brother John) that his mother was very ill indeed, and wrote to Belinda that 'it sounds as if she must be very near the end of the marvellous long life she has had'.[8] There was little they could do but wait, and keep Tony informed of their contact addresses in Sicily.

Although they did not know what to expect in Sicily, they were hoping to find a place that had the kind of regional distinctiveness that always fascinated Curnow, that was out of the mainstream of Italian culture, and might be less overrun by tourists. They were not sure where, or for how long, they might stay in the south; 'notionally, [until] about end of May or early June', Curnow wrote to Tony. 'Realistically, one can't expect an idyll of one's own, far from the tourist tracks; but perhaps some spot where the tracks aren't too wide or well-beaten.'[9] After a brief foray southwards from Messina they settled on a hotel – Il Capo Skino – at the small, hillside, coastal town of Gioiosa Marea, about 80 kilometres west of Messina on the northern coast of Sicily, arriving there at the beginning of May on a stormy day with a wild sea not unlike – to their delight – a similar day at Karekare. They settled into this small township (with a population, then, of about 7000) for three weeks, returning to Messina at the end of May after spending a week in Stromboli, the remotest of the Aeolian Islands, two hours by hydrofoil from Milazzo on the northern coast.

Il Capo Skino, built directly above the sea, was large and well-appointed, and had few longer-term guests, catering mainly for short-term visits by busloads of German or French tourists. Curnow fished regularly (without much success), and as the changeable weather warmed up, he and Jeny swam and took long walks, and visited neighbouring bays. 'It's possible', Curnow wrote to Belinda, 'to walk goat tracks, among olives & cactuses & scrubby oaks, out of sight of the town, over the Mediterranean, which has been neither as calm nor as blue as they say in the stories.'[10] They also enjoyed meeting locals in the township and getting to know the owners of the hotel – three brothers and their wives – and were fascinated by the Italian political scene, as they came to know it through conversation (usually in French) with people they met, whose left-wing sympathies they found congenial, at a time when strong feelings were aroused by a right-wing-inspired referendum designed to abolish the divorce law:

> The 3 Sicilian brothers & wives who built & own this very large hotel are all sturdy anti-clericals, della *Sinistra* in politics, anti-mafioso, & all voted NO to the abolition

of the divorce law. The Church & the political Right, of course, suffered a big reverse when the vote went so heavily against them. Fanfani, éminence grise of the Right (not to say Fascist) forces, went on TV the night before; but even Sicily, & Palermo itself (the Mafia capital) gave a small majority to *i Divorcisti*, & of course the North did the rest. *Our* contacts have been a middle-aged man of property with whom we have morning coffee in the village; his French is about as good as ours, but sufficient; *and* the wife of one of the hotel-owners – highly intelligent, indeed [a] *cultivated* woman, whose English is as good as our French, & whose French is fluent beyond our range. We learn (not from her) that she is a former Communist Party deputy of the Italian Parliament, which may explain the business on which she is mostly absent in the north (Turin). What we learn here is not 'Godfather' capomafia stories. We *do* learn that the Christian Democrats lean on the Mafia to deliver the Sicilian vote; that the Carabinieri are hand-in-glove with Mafia (both North & South); and, of course, that the Church is not above collusion. . . . You will imagine how all this fascinates us. If only to find ourselves among people of the Left – who are *propertied* & professional.[11]

A week after their arrival at Gioiosa Marea, on 7 May, a telegram arrived from Tony in Geneva (it took four days to reach them, in the chaotic state of the Italian postal services at the time) to say that Jessie had died on 4 May. Curnow telephoned Tony, cabled John, and wrote immediately to Belinda, who attended the funeral and burial service at Halswell Church on the family's behalf. 'We are thinking of nothing else', he wrote, '& Sicily seems anything but the right place to be', adding: 'You will *write*, and tell us all about the funeral? I can see Halswell so clearly.'[12]

Two days later another ominous message arrived from Tony, to telephone him. He had received a cable from Jeny's godmother, Audrie Jacobs, 'Deepest sympathy double loss. Mother knew no-one. Letters in post.' Jeny managed to telephone her Uncle Charles in Auckland, who confirmed that her mother had also died (the day after Jessie), but who had apparently been confused about Jeny's whereabouts and written to London. 'If Audrie hadn't been so kind & sensible I might not have known till June or later', Jeny wrote in her diary, adding: 'I am too shocked today to feel much more than numb, helpless & out of touch. What a hell of a week it has been for both of us.'[13] Janet was only 64, and when Jeny had returned to Europe in March she had every reason to believe that her mother would recover, if slowly. The shock of her death remained for much of the rest of the year she was away, and she was touched that Wystan and Sue attended the funeral service at St Michael's Church, Remuera, on her own and Curnow's behalf.

They both needed quiet during their remaining time (a little less than a fortnight) in Gioiosa Marea, and made only one day-long expedition – by train westwards along the northern coast to the city of Palermo, where they visited the Botanical Garden, and purchased books (including Lampedusa's *The Leopard*) and records of Sicilian music. Back in Gioiosa Marea, both read, and Curnow also worked on notes and drafts of poems. On 22 May they travelled to Milazzo in preparation for their departure for the island of Stromboli the following day. Normally two hours by hydrofoil, the trip across became something of an adventure. The weather was so rough that at Lipari they were transferred to a 40-year-old steamer which wallowed for another four hours before reaching their destination on Stromboli, La Sciara Residence in the tiny northern village of San Vincenzo.

'I could think of plausible reasons why this brief escape to Stromboli was necessary', Curnow wrote later to Ian Milner, 'but none of them occurred to us at the time. Such as insular nostalgia, another "volcanic islet",* its beaches free from plastic containers, beer cans, broken glass & oil sludge, as very few beaches are, on the Mediterranean.'[14] With a permanent population of only 400, and its difficulty of access, 'like our bad West Coast roads at home', Jeny wrote to Wystan and Sue, the unspoilt black sand and black rocks also reminded her of Karekare.[15] After the rigours of their boat trip to the island, the weather was excellent, and they relaxed into a routine of swimming before breakfast, walking, reading, and swimming again later in the day.

The journey back to Milazzo on 30 May was calm, and late the following day they took an overnight train from Messina to Rome, where they now planned to stay for a fortnight before joining Tony and Elisabeth back in Geneva, on 17 June. The Sicilian segment of their trip, despite the personal bereavements both had experienced, had proven a highlight, like their visit to Venice. They had been able to meet local people and glean much from them about their perception of the Italian political scene, the role of the Church, and the mafia. They had enjoyed the local Sicilian cuisine – especially the seafood, and *nespole* ('fresh sweet loquats as big as small apricots')[16] – and ordinary activities (fishing, swimming and walking) which they always enjoyed at Karekare. Other parts of Italy, of course, interested them as well – and generated poems in later years (Florence, Naples, Rome, Rapallo and the Ligurian coast) – but on later visits Venice and Sicily never lost the special, magical lustre which they had on the occasion of this first encounter with them.

Their fortnight in Rome was another small epic of walking and observing, the scale and number of its masterpieces of art and architecture, its famous ruins and monuments, altogether too vast for Curnow to comprehend. The effect, he wrote to Wystan, was a blur of 'closed circuit images in my head'.[17] Their hotel (the Anglo Americano) was central, overlooking the Palazzo Barberini, and they were able to walk to the museums and galleries in the Borghese gardens and

* A reference to Waiheke Island in the poem 'Do It Yourself'.

elsewhere, to the Forum, the Colosseum and the Pantheon – all of it a 'test', he wrote to Wystan, of 'psychic insulation (for want of a better term)':

> I have a few notes & a few notions . . . . I realise that I may have written anything I have to say about Antiquity in my sonnet about the Moa in the Canterbury Museum. Guides are mostly liars. We brush them off & try to use our eyes, for what *they* are worth. The trouble is that one feels Rome should awe, & awe is a word that don't [sic] denote anything any more, whatever it still vaguely connotes. Did it ever? . . . The best reward may be a slight subduing of one's irritable ego, & a moment's holiday from the drudgery of being (unsuccessfully) oneself. Or to discover that circles are better than ellipses, i.e. the Pantheon is greater (though so much smaller) than the Colosseum.[18]

He enjoyed most the manageable pleasures of smaller-scale discoveries – the Pantheon, Holbein's *Henry VIII* and Titian's *Venus and Adonis* in the Barberini Palace, the sculpture of Mastroianni in the National Gallery of Modern Art, a splendidly theatrical procession on Italy's national day, the myth paintings of Veronese in the Capitoline Pinacoteca, the historical ambiences of the letters SPQR on the manhole covers. St Peter's, however, left him unmoved:

> It could make no difference to Rome, or to anyone, if I wrote down: St Peter's is man's worst-made mountain, as profoundly irreligious as Babel, a colossal waste of energy & genius. Like Royalty, its apparent grace & authority owe nearly everything to photography & faith in an institution. San Vitale at Ravenna is everything S. Peter's is not. Did *Rome*, as early as the 16C, know that the Church had already ceased to rule & begun to advertise? How many Banks, etc., then modelled themselves on the West Front of S. Peter's?[19]

Perhaps his response was deeply coloured by his fascinated reactions to the contemporary Italian political scene, as well as by his own deeply ingrained anti-clericalism. There had already been fascist terrorist activities (in Brescia and elsewhere) in the wake of the failure of the anti-divorce referendum, and during his stay in Rome the centre-left government collapsed. He strongly believed that the Vatican, closely linked with the Christian Democrats, was implicated in efforts by the political right to destabilise the government.

Geneva, Paris, London, June–October

After the bewildering kaleidoscope of images and impressions left by Rome the Curnows were glad to spend the rest of June in Geneva. There was a backlog of correspondence about Jessie and Janet to respond to, and they were both especially moved by a long letter from Belinda describing her visit to Christchurch for Jessie's funeral service, about which they had heard very little:

> Jeny and I were both very much moved, and reading it again this morning, we know how well you understand our feelings and how true and real yours were. John wrote very briefly to Tony and me; after all he had been through and done, it was something that he managed to write so soon . . . but until yesterday we could only try to guess what it was really like that day. You were there in my place, and in place of the daughter Muz always wanted – her memories of you, like yours of her, were something special and precious. You bring Halswell so clearly back. It was the Vicar of Styx-Redwood, wasn't it? . . . He arranged for me where Muz was to be buried. I knew it was to be in a newly-opened part of the churchyard, but not very far, I think, from T's grave. I was overseas when he died, too. I could hardly help remembering that, when the news about Muz reached us in Sicily.[20]

During their ten days at Geneva they regularly enjoyed Tony and Elisabeth's warm hospitality, including a weekend visit with them to their *maison de campagne* in the French village of Pruzilly, 13 kilometres from Mâcon, and they also worked on arrangements for the next stage of their travels – a three-week visit to Paris (29 June to 18 July), followed by a further week with Tony and Elisabeth at Pruzilly, before travelling to London for three months on 25 July.

In Paris they stayed at the Hotel d'Orsay, centrally located on the Left Bank across the river from the Place de la Concorde and the Jardin des Tuileries, from which they were able to walk to many of the main tourist spots and galleries, and after they mastered the Metro they found it easy to travel further afield, including to Montmartre, the Bois de Boulogne and the Eiffel Tower. The mass of tourists was again difficult to cope with, and the commercialisation of sites like Montmartre and the Eiffel Tower, but they enjoyed swimming in the Piscine Deligny on the Seine River, near the hotel, and Curnow's particular pleasures were retrospective exhibitions of paintings by Juan Gris at the Orangerie and of Miró's paintings, sculpture and ceramics at the Grand Palais, as well as an exhibition of Hans Arp at the Denise René Gallery. Curnow spent some time in private Left Bank galleries in the streets off the Boulevard St Germain, purchasing a Miró lithograph and prints of posters by the Hungarian op artist Victor Vasarely and by Arp.

However, for much of his stay in Paris Curnow was struggling to cope with a recurrence of a disc injury in his lower back, which occurred when he was lifting baggage during the train trip from Geneva to Paris. Halfway through their stay he contacted the New Zealand ambassador in Paris (Paul Gabites) who recommended a specialist. Improvement was still slow, and shortly before they left Paris the specialist recommended rest and also arranged for his back to be put in a plaster cast for a fortnight. It was fortunate that the week after Paris was spent at Pruzilly with Tony and Elisabeth, since Curnow was able to recuperate for most of the time, but for the first month of their stay in London he had to keep resting, and required further specialist treatment. One casualty of his ill health was the possibility (at the back of their minds) that they might visit the Milners in Prague. '[I]t's the kind of nuisance', he wrote apologetically to Milner, 'that inhibits travel.'[21]

The Curnows left Pruzilly on 24 July and arrived in London by boat-train from Paris the next day, where they stayed until the end of October in a comfortable Nuffield flat in Prince Albert Road overlooking Regent's Park in north London. Until September Curnow's movements were restricted – on his arrival he arranged for twice-weekly treatments of his back by a specialist in Wimpole Street – and Jeny during this time rediscovered London on her own. For Curnow (as for Jeny) London had changed greatly since his previous year-long stay there 25 years earlier, as he discovered when he revisited his old haunts around Fleet Street (the *News Chronicle* no longer existed) and Broadcasting House, and most of the newspaper and radio journalists he knew had died or retired.

In September he made return trips with Jeny to ancestral sites in Norfolk and Cornwall, and during the trip to Cornwall enjoyed catching up with Leslie Rowse (now retired from All Souls' College, Oxford, and living at Trenarren), who advised them to visit the many Curnow gravestones at Towednack. There were also many members of Jeny's mother's family to see in London. Curnow saw Davin in London and visited John Lehmann, as well as catching up regularly with Bill Pearson, also on leave there at this time. Essentially, however, Curnow's three months in London and the UK involved discovering the place anew. He liked being in London again, occasionally accosted by 'some kind of recollective, spectral self',[22] but he was glad that their original plans – to spend only three months on the Continent and six months in England – had changed, since their longer stay in Europe 'corrects the London perspective in all kinds of ways':

> Strange to remember how Anglo oriented NZ was 40, even 25 years ago; one felt it personally too, of course. The change is not complete, neither is it superficial. The feeling of being here has been much modified. Had we scampered round Italy in buses, instead of making longish stops in a few places & had a good deal to do with the people, we mightn't now feel the foreignness of England itself, its identity as just one nation among all the others. There's always been America, yes, but even after 200 years don't they still have traces of our own ambiguous attitude to England? In spite of themselves?[23]

As for London's 'identity', it seemed (especially from the character of its press and media) to be that of 'a Huge City which lacks the sense of a role in the world ... troubled by a suspicion that the World, after all, may be one-up'.[24] They did not find the theatre and arts scene in London especially lively, though they saw many plays and went more than once to an exhibition about Byron at the Victoria and Albert Museum.

Drafts and fragments: 'the present / on which the past depends for its liveliness'*

The day after his arrival in London Curnow purchased a small typewriter. 'I have many notes', he had written to Pearson from Geneva, 'which may be worthless, as such notes so often are, but which I hope to work on in London.'[25] He had materials for eight or ten poems from his time on the Continent, and one of the first he worked on was the Ravenna poem he had tentatively entitled 'A Ride to Ravenna'. From Florence there were notes and verse fragments on the Day of Judgement scene on the ceiling of the Baptistery (especially its depiction of the Devil and Hell), and also some wry verse reflections ('Michelangelo, here we come') on an Open University Foundation course textbook, *Introduction to Art*, left behind, with notes, by a student in the foyer of his hotel. 'I nearly looked inside', he comments: 'Why / Should the Open University remain / A closed book to me?' In a lively irony which conveys his distaste for the tourist- and education-driven public consumption of culture and history in Florence, he resists the temptation, not because he wishes not to intrude on the owner's privacy, but because 'I was thinking about my own'.

> From Sicily there were snatches of scenic impressionism, such as:
> In May the trickle of refugees
> Begins to thicken, by air to Palermo,
> By *wagon lit* to Messina,
> Sicilian sun already a genial fireball
> And July's furnace doors yet locked.
> Half Capo Skino's hundred rooms
> Stare vacantly, high haze blinds,
> Most days, Aeolian cones shadowing,
> Vanish into the haze ....

---

* Editor's note: The drafts and fragments discussed in this section were made available to the author from among the private papers of Jeny Tole since deposited with the Alexander Turnbull Library.

Another draft, more fully worked, evoked the sea and coast where he fished, offering Curnow's distinctive mixture of personal, present observation and historical reflection:

> When I first saw it, how could I know
> What it was? It was the sea.
> It ebbed, it rose, it erected itself like death,
> Or it sloshed an ankle, or a knee
> With a blind, senseless caress,
> Paddler's or swimmer's . . .
>
> Homer can jump into it.
> His islands can empty into the evening fog,
> Vulcano, Lipari, Stromboli.
> A bag of wind for Odysseus.
> Sicily. It has to be me,
> It has to be now, it has to be
> A pair of NZ-made sandals
> Full of genuine Gioiosa Marea gravel,
> A squid-baited rod, small fish biting.
>
> Only the sea, they said,
> What else could it be?
> It ebbed, it rose, it erected itself like death,
> Like it always did.
>   Water rats!
> *Ragazzi*, one Sardinian born
> Tidies the bait on my hook with a boy's deft finger.
> *Prima pescatore nella Sardegna.*
>
> I go on fishing, catch nothing.

From Stromboli there were also many prose fragments noting details of flora and place, impressions of people and their activities, reflections on its unspoilt character, and one verse draft whose subject was the phenomenon of tourism itself. While at Gioiosa Marea Curnow also began a lively satire of Blatty's recently published popular novel *The Exorcist*, sparked by his reaction to its author's note which offered an elaborate series of factual disclaimers, and references to Jesuit authorities, as a device to buttress belief in the novel's fantasy of possession by the Devil. Curnow read the novel as a commercially driven exploitation of sensationalism, masking its motive by deviously protesting its concern for truth. He took the poem no further, but returned to the notion of fiction's power to mask an actual sensationalism beneath a seemingly factual, sophisticated narrative technique in a controversial poem he wrote later in the decade, 'Dichtung und Wahrheit'.

A thread running through many of the drafts, offering an insight into the key significance of Curnow's encounter with Europe for his later poetry, was the sheer scale, magnitude and power with which history, the past, impinged on, 'invaded', and seemed to dwarf the self and the present, through the relentless succession of monuments, excavated and reconstructed ruins, cathedrals and churches, museums and galleries, encountered in all its major cities. The human scale seemed diminished, perpetually visible everywhere in the hordes of commercially exploited, relentlessly camera-clicking busloads of tourists, automatons on a conveyer belt, 'doing' Venice or Florence or Rome in two or three days, that history's most disingenuous victims.

Curnow had experienced nothing like that sense of history in the United States, whose monuments (even in Washington) were (or now seemed) *recent* in comparison with Europe's. In the poems he wrote in *Trees, Effigies, Moving Objects* the Washington monuments had not been quite so intimidating, 'unassimilable', as to rule out the imagining of new and improved local effigies. Europe's 'monumentality' seemed on a different scale altogether. Even in England in 1949 he had not experienced history as relentlessly oppressive – in fact, precisely the opposite. His encounter with his ancestors' graves in the Norman churchyard at Caistor St Edmund *released* him from the dead hand of the past. They were 'real' because they seemed recent, and even Norwich Cathedral, built by Bishop Herbert de Losinga between 1095 and 1145, could be imaginatively assimilated to a New Zealand present in which his father's life was celebrated and his death mourned. Cornish myths, stretching even deeper into the past, could also be 'acclimatised' to a New Zealand childhood in a poem like 'The Changeling'.

'A Ride to Ravenna' had raised these issues, and they recurred in a fragment written at Gioiosa Marea, in a detached, third-person mode:

> Of course, he felt small, cooped up in himself
> While the painted angels of a dozen annunciations,
> Resurrections, transfigurations, visitations, agonies,
> And the putti, cooing doves, pampered dogs
> Had Venus all to themselves,
> Everyone looked at everything but him;
> The galleries were cruel punishments for an ego
> Not much accustomed to second place –

It was only when the past began to shrink,
And look smaller even than he felt himself
That he genuinely took fright, & fled to Messina,
Grateful for earthquakes & American bombs,
The unhistoric present, the cruise ships at the quay . . . .

In many of the drafts, the theme might be described as the restoration of human scale through the discovery and celebration of simple, commonplace events and encounters, a celebration of presentness other than that provided by tourism. In Gioiosa Marea the present pleasures of conversation with ordinary people (about food, politics, current affairs), of fishing, of the *ragazzi* (boys) who show him how to bait his fishing rod with squid, of walking, provide examples of a human resistance to the encroachments of history. In one of the drafts from his stay in Rome ('Hot June in Rome'), the commonplace is restored through his thoughts about the fate of fish in a drained fountain, against the background of the grandeur of the Barberini Palace:

This morning I was afraid they were emptying the fountain
In the Barbarini [sic] Palace yard.
I was worried about the fish.
Yesterday they sought the shade under the
Collar of coarse green growth
In the centre of the basin.
A Roman is washing his Fiat at the fountain
With what remains in the basin.
Where are the fish?
I am dressing, watching from my window
Of the Albergo Anglo Americano.
I am relieved to see that the basin is brimming now,
Because of the fish.
Their only home, in the high blue heat of summer.
This is mine, my window, as I call it,
For the time being, three weeks, that is,
In the basin of the fountain they have not really emptied yet.
The Roman is driving his Fiat, his *shining machine*,
Past fountains, fish out of water,
In the Street of the Four Fountains.

On the pavement, a bluejeaner American boy
Patches his girlfriend's blistered feet

With band-aids, made by Johnson & Johnson.

I am worried about the fish.

Less shaped than the fish poem, another Rome fragment is sufficiently advanced to indicate the kind of sustained meditation on history and the present Curnow was pondering:

> An Eternal City seems a suitable place for
> Putting in a word for the present
> *It is all we have*, most of the time
>
> [Pick detail:
>> Domenico's enjoyment of his food, his pipe, his big *machine* . . . .
>> Bars?
>> Frankie (fisherman) Stromboli]
>
> No serious risk the past will be overlooked,
> It can take care of itself, for a moment –
> A truancy, an absence in the present –
> The past *is* present, come to that.
> Trajan's Column, & other more broken columns
> (*Sunlight on a broken column* (Eliot))
> Are *present*.
>
> So are the girls' arses nipping & the boys' eyes turning. . . .
> And my feet, a bit sore with the heat,
> & the shaded pavement of the via Nazionale
> And the Quirinale. . . .
>
> *The present*
> On which the past depends for its livelihood,
> It's beggar's crumb or coin.
> The waiter leans, props up the Coliseum. . . .

'Maison de Campagne', a piece based on his stay at Tony and Elisabeth's weekend house at Pruzilly, continued the impressionism of a number of the Italian pieces, and his experience of Paris produced two drafts, one ('Doubting Thomas') a lively comment on the issue of belief, based on a painting in the Louvre, the second another edged meditation on history, on what he calls (with a degree of black humour) the *intellectual* ruins of Paris. He prefaces the poem with a comment about the city from the location, near the Pont de la Concorde, where they were staying: 'Paris from Pont de la Concorde under a dark blue cloud & a brighter white sky down river . . . it has a skyline, not so many great cities have(?).'

> Nobody discovers Paris any more,
> Or any of the great cities,
> Too many people are discovering Paris
> All at once, the fumes are oppressive,
> One is glad for the cloud, & a drop of rain.
> It lays the dust of all those hungry heels, for one thing.
>
> Nobody discovers Paris any more,
> Except the visitors from distant places,
> In search, not of Paris, but of something
> Hazlitt said, or Balzac, or H. James
>   Or Joyce or Fitzgerald or Henry Miller,
>   Or Chevalier, or . . .
>
> And nobody who discovers Paris
> Wants to open his open mouth wide enough
> To swallow his wandering foot.
> The awful ruins of Paris are intellectual,
> A mortified silence is a not unsuitable response.
>
> Nobody thinks of drowning, in modern dress,
> In the Tiber, but there's more than one good reason
> For the police telephones on the bridges of the Seine
> Where it is possible to drown, if the thought occurs to you.

Curnow worked on these and other drafts and fragments during his time in London, as well as two whose location was London itself (one about a painted, postcard scene of Milford Sound in a London pub, the other the brief beginnings of a pantoum contrasting the distinctness of remembered scenes against the blurred character of the self who has such distinct memories of place). None of them ever reached the kind of 'completion' that satisfied him, despite the liveliness and interest of many of their lines and phrases, their images and ideas.

What they reveal, however, is the emergence of a new way of writing poetically about history which was crucial to many of Curnow's later poems, beginning with the sequence *An Incorrigible Music* later in the decade. It involved the articulation of what he called (in 'Moro Assassinato'[26]) 'the moment's mixture' – a momentarily contained image drawn from the flux of seemingly random, present observations and sensations, subjective thoughts, dreams, memories, into which history is dispersed and fragmented. The effect is to make history a mode of *present* experience, and present experience a mode of history: past and present interact and intersect, every present carrying within it, inseparably, traces of a past, and every past inseparable from the present in which, alone and always contingently, it has its being. The effect of such a poetry is that history is deprived, during the 'moment' of the poem, of its despotic power as an abstraction, and the present moment deprived of its randomness and contingency. It required a technique and a flexible language maintaining a rapid, fluid, continually surprising movement between past and present. Often, indeed, there is a strange *doubleness* of effect, as of present becoming past and past becoming present *at the same time*. At such moments, of which the later poem 'An Evening Light' is one of his finest examples, Curnow comes close to articulating a moving *visionary* impulse.

'Home is the place, if there is one': returning via the USA, November–December 1974

After an enjoyable week in Dublin, where they stayed with Jim Walton (professor of English at Trinity College) and his family, the Curnows flew to Washington to begin the final five-week segment of their overseas trip. In Washington they stayed with Milton and Zaro Starr, caught up with the Baslers again, and on 4 November Curnow gave a poetry reading with Thom Gunn at the Library of Congress, to an audience of 300. Gunn read first, and intrigued Curnow: 'Nice boy, but at 45 (!) a bit dated in jacket & leather pants. A curious mésalliance of Yvor Winters (his confessed guru at Stanford) and Acid.'[27] He was extremely pleased with his own reading, which was also broadcast on the National Education TV network. He read from the late work only (*Trees, Effigies, Moving Objects* and *An Abominable Temper*), including – in the wake of the Watergate scandal and Nixon's resignation a few months earlier – two of his Washington poems, 'A Framed Photograph' and 'Friendship Heights', and found himself 'beset by a gratifying, if fatiguing, swarm of admirers at the ensuing wine-&-cheese'.[28] Stanley Kunitz, Consultant in Poetry at the Library of Congress at the time, chaired the reading, greatly admired Curnow's poetry, and offered to try to assist with the publication of an American edition of the *Collected Poems*. The book had finally appeared in early October (unfortunately, too late in Curnow's stay in England for him to be able to pursue avenues of publicity there) after a printers' botch-up which meant that the whole print run had to be redone.

From 7 to 30 November the Curnows were based in New York, visiting old haunts, seeing a great deal of theatre, and spending time at the Metropolitan Museum of Art. They were especially interested in the op art and kinetic art works of the Venezuelan sculptor and painter Jesús Soto, in a retrospective exhibition at the Guggenheim Museum. Curnow revisited Stanley Kunitz, and also approached John Cushman Associates (the US branch of Curtis Brown) about possible American publication of his *Collected Poems*. He was also pleased that his old bookshop haunt, the Gotham Book Mart, was keen to stock copies of it. There was an emotionally exhausting trip, especially for Jeny, to Auburn, to see many of her mother's relatives, and in New York a warm catch-up with their old friends Cree and Bruce Harland. By the end of the month they were beginning to look forward to their return to New Zealand. On this fourth visit to the United States Curnow summed up his feelings to Stead:

> NY, as you know, caught me first at the impressionable age of 38. This is the fourth exposure. The best to be said for the past, is that it gets easier not to waste time here. But this voice, 'cracked & harsh', won't sing in exile. Home is the place, if there is one.[29]

They left New York on 30 November and after a few days in San Francisco and (with Jeny's Osborne step-relatives) in Hawai'i, arrived back in Auckland on 8 December 1974.

Chapter Twenty-seven

Europe revisited, and
An Incorrigible Music, 1975–78

I continue disengaging myself from university, this last year. Not that I have ever been 'engaged' the way some people are: but it tends to stick to the mind like some invisible tacky substance.[1]

Last years at university, 1975–1976

After his return from leave at the end of 1974 Curnow had only two years of 'honest toil' remaining before retirement from the University of Auckland. He wished for as little notice of the event as possible, regarding 'the completion of my university service [as] incidental to my work',[2] though he enjoyed his retirement farewell in the Department of English, at which he received 'a really fine bowl potted by one of the best local potters'.*[3] To Lilburn he described how eagerly he was looking forward to the challenge of a 'fresh start':

Of course, this has to mean a fresh start (not that I consider I ever stopped) in poetry; lucky for me that every poem has always been a fresh start; & I can take no credit for not repeating myself, because I don't know how. I suppose one could 'repeat oneself', if one knew 'oneself' even half well enough; but there's always the 99.9% still unknown. Why, I've just brought home from univ. my old Book of Common Prayer *with* Hymns

---

* Len Castle.

> A[ncient] & M[odern]; not for churchgoing use, but because there's so much here that
> has lain obscured or mentally censored, & must have to do with such mind as I possess.[4]

At the end of 1975 he was delighted to be awarded an honorary DLitt at
the University of Canterbury, at a ceremony in which his long-standing mentor
John Schroder also received the degree. Such recognition from Canterbury to a
certain extent compensated for his ongoing feeling of being undervalued at the
University of Auckland. In April the previous year, with his retirement not far
away, he had written to Stead from Florence asking for his advice about applying
for a personal chair at Auckland, after initially receiving a polite brush-off,
commenting that he 'felt a taste of relegation' in the fact that he had not been
included in the numerous appointments to personal chairs in the department,
and 'especially with younger men coming up'.[5] Stead seems to have been taken
by surprise, writing a personally supportive reply but hinting at other behind-
the-scenes developments which would make Curnow's appointment unlikely.[6]
Curnow was grateful for Stead's support, and tried to understand the depth of
feeling aroused in him by what he saw as yet another institutional rebuff:

> I expect my feeling goes right back to the 'fifties – undergraduate awe of those towering
> intellects never had a chance to unfreeze during all those 15 years in newspapers . . . .
> It's possibly not farfetched to guess that the Church with its orders & trappings was
> at the bottom of all this. Besides, I was genuinely thankful to escape from a profession
> I never loved much & had come to detest.[7]

In effect, he added, he had always been regarded as 'a 2nd class citizen of civis
academicus [sic]', someone who should be 'content with his station, underpaid
but permissively (even enviably) a bit irresponsible in the serious intellectual
business of a university department'.[8]

However, he had numerous other interests to occupy him during his final
two years of academic life. In 1975 the bach at Karekare was enlarged (making it
easier to invite visitors to stay); there were trips to Wellington and Christchurch
(where Curnow attended to the sale of his mother's house at Meadow Street)
and brief holidays in Rotorua and Russell; and at the end of the year Jeny decided
to retire from Selwyn College, where she had been a teacher and school counsellor since 1967. She enrolled part-time in Maori-language papers, under Professor
Bruce Biggs, in the Department of Anthropology at the University of Auckland,
marking the beginning of a significant new career as a freelance research scholar
working on Maori-language projects.

In 1975 Tim had arranged with the Australian Broadcasting Corporation for
a new production of *The Duke's Miracle* – broadcast in January 1976 – for which

Curnow pre-recorded some introductory comments (making it clear, as he wrote to Tim, that 'Browning provides the *scenario* only. The play starts there, & goes its own way.')[9] – and during the August vacation of 1976 the Curnows also spent two weeks in Sydney, meeting up with Tim and Lea, who had married at the end of 1974. By this time Tim was agent to numerous major writers in Australia and New Zealand, and his work for his father also kept him busy. The poetry was increasingly in demand for anthologies, requests for quotations in a wide range of books and on the media were numerous, and Tim also advised his father about contracts, suitable fees, and the placement and promotion of his work overseas.

Publishers often thought Curnow made unreasonable demands for fees, but they were based on Tim's advice about fees for poetry in Australia, reduced to take into account the smaller market in New Zealand, and on his own considered assessment of print runs, especially where anthologies were involved. Curnow took a thoroughly professional view of his relations with the publishing industry, refusing to accept that because of the smaller market for poetry in New Zealand, poets (as was often the case) should be grateful to be published at all, with little or no recompense – a hangover, in his view, from the colonial habit of regarding poetry as a spare-time, recreational hobby. Even where print runs were small he insisted on the principle of some payment, and he adjusted his scale of fees over the years to include inflation. He also did not accept the so-called 'democratic' principle that all poets should necessarily be paid the same, arguing that differences in quality, reputation, market value, should be reflected in fees. If this often made the business of producing an anthology awkward for publishers, since he was requesting higher fees than others, on balance his position supported all writers, since he was insisting on the principle of professional recognition.

Throughout 1975 there were many reviews of the *Collected Poems*. Somewhat unreasonably, since almost all of them were positive, Curnow was disappointed with the response, feeling that (with only one or two exceptions) the book had failed to make the substantial impact which he hoped for. He was particularly disappointed that by 31 March (the first royalty period) only 674 copies had been sold, and that by June – nine months after publication – no notice had appeared in the *New Zealand Listener* and nothing on any of the radio arts programmes:

Personally I regard the figures as bad – bad. In part, they reflect a bad & silly poesy period in NZ. I've seldom felt the pettiness of the place more: not since about 1935. 'Poetry' is a sub-sub-culture . . . . Nearly all of it is flimsy, trendy – the trendiness of, say, California ten years ago – & disgustingly soulful . . . . Since last October when CP came out, [the *New Zealand Listener*] has printed not a line of a notice: while puffing every bleating little bard in the nation . . . . Really, the author of CP is a Missing Person. I know I'm read. But this is different from the perennial flood of little books of poems, the world over. For NZ, right now, an unhappy mutation has occurred, of the public idea of *what a poet is* . . . . In the meantime, the home truth for me . . . is that the climate is not good for a book like CP.[10]

He added a mollified postscript to this 'bilious' letter three days later, having just heard that he had been awarded the New Zealand Poetry Award for 1974,[11] but was to be disappointed again when the book was not shortlisted for the Goodman Fielder Wattie Book Awards. There is no doubt that he felt increasingly isolated from, and antipathetic to, what he saw as a trendy mainstream seventies poetry culture which he felt had easy access to publication and the media, and this feeling of isolation influenced him later in the decade to seek publication outlets elsewhere, especially in the United Kingdom. Quite simply, he felt that (with the exception of *Islands*) magazines like *Encounter*, the *London Magazine*, *PN Review*, and later the *London Review of Books*, offered a more rigorous, more reliable testing of the value of what he wrote.

Towards *An Incorrigible Music*

'An Incorrigible Music' was the last of a group of poems on which Curnow worked intensively for some nine months, from May 1977 to February 1978. During the previous two years, his last before retirement, he also worked on other drafts of poems, though none of them came to anything. They included two longish poems entitled 'Adam was never born' and 'Hyperkinesis' (the latter based on a Renaissance painting). For the first few months of his retirement he had much to do to organise his books and clear the decks of business and correspondence, writing to Tony that 'what the world calls retirement has only begun for me':

> Any amount of reading, of course: with the difference that one reads for one's own purposes, & must decide what one's purposes are! I discover that what the 'retired' really miss is less the real work than the mere mechanics of the occupation, the common drudgery details, & the sense of being a working part. One simply has to ignore the alteration of one's 'social image' in the eyes of other people, & get on with one's tasks.[12]

The routine he gradually settled into involved writing in the mornings and purposeful reading in the afternoons. Whim Wham remained a Thursday chore. He also had significant amounts of correspondence to attend to most days, walked the dog (Bounce) regularly every day, and was able to devote more time to household tasks. His main reading at this time – though he said little about it to others – was Nietzsche, but he also read the historian Burckhardt on Italian

Renaissance history, seeking historical background to the Pazzi conspiracy against the Medici, and caught up with a novel, *A Soldier's Tale*, published the previous year by his English Department colleague M.K. Joseph.

It was in May 1977 that the idea of a group of related poems (the germ of *An Incorrigible Music*) began to form in his mind, in the wake of completing a poem which he described as his 'fishing-knife poem' in a letter to Wystan hinting cryptically at other possibilities: 'it seems possible that my fishing-knife poem may lead to others, & some unforeseen & perhaps surprising possibilities'.[13] The title of the fishing-knife poem was taken from God's mocking words to Job in the Old Testament Book of Job (41:1) – 'Canst Thou Draw out Leviathan with an Hook?' It was set at Karekare, vividly evoking the activity of hooking, landing and gutting a big kahawai as heavy seas pound the rocks below the cliff face known as 'the Cathedral'. The most striking aspect of the poem is the dispassionate, unsentimental emphasis on the violence involved in so seemingly harmless a recreational activity: the preparatory sharpening of the knife, the splitting of the fish's belly and severing of its spine, the need to bleed the fish quickly to preserve its flavour, the details of the gobstick working on the hook stuck in the fish's gullet, its barb fastened to the root of the tongue. The broader setting is also suffused with 'natural' violence, the rocks 'kicking' and 'raging' at the sea 'which rears up green roars down white' against them, and there is the grim image of a drowned man 'fished' by helicopter out of the rip, 'swung copular / under the winching chopper's bubble / too late for vomiting salt but fluent at last / in the languages of the sea.'

The poem's title sets up a puzzle about its relation to the setting and events at Karekare. In the Book of Job, God *taunts* Job with his rhetorical question: unlike God, who is all-powerful and plays with Leviathan as if he is a domestic pet, Job is powerless to catch the mythological sea beast with a mere hook. One of the implications of God's assertion of his omnipotence over nature is that Job, in wishing to be released from his undeserved suffering, in seeking reasons for his being unfairly chosen as a victim, aspires to that omnipotence himself. Throughout the poem there is a suggestion that the fisherman is playing God, callously inflicting pain on an innocent creature in order to satisfy his desire to land (in the vernacular fishing parlance of the poem's final line) his ever-elusive Leviathan, '*A big one! A big one!*' The sharpened, death-dealing knife is a 'steely cloud' held god-like in his hand, 'hung blue dark over the waves' where the kahawai swims to the lure, and it later hovers over the bloodied rock pool in which the hooked fish struggles in its death throes. Two brass rivets, the poet notes, keep 'body and blade together': not simply the body and blade of the knife, but the knife and the body of the fisherman, as if identified bodily with his role as a knife-wielding killer. The 'real' Leviathan, however, is always the 'big one' that got away, and at the end the poet is left with a conscience-driven sense of identification with the suffering he has inflicted on the fish.

The sequence which this poem eventually introduced is grim indeed in its suggestion that violence is endemic to nature and human nature, not only in its more obvious manifestations of killing, murder, maiming and torture, but in the most commonplace activities – indeed, as another poem in the sequence puts it, in the very fact of existence itself, 'merely to exist being even for the gentlest / the rape of another's breath and bread.' 'Life lives on death's dead', Curnow wrote in one of the many drafts for this and other poems.[14] Introducing a number of the poems in a radio programme on the ABC a few years later ('The Poet's Tongue'), he mentioned that in the later 1970s 'I began to see myself as one of a species, our human species, who are killers by nature and necessity. Even by being born, by existing, we kill over again all the dead who died before us; and we survive by acts of violence, our own or somebody else's.'[15] Violence is thus part of the 'incorrigibility' of existence, neither atoned for nor mitigated at the human level by an 'apology' ('An insult in the form of an apology / is the human answer to the inhuman / which rears up green roars down white / and to the fish which is fearless'), nor by 'compassion' for victims (which always, because it is *after* the event, merely 'sings to itself'), nor even by the operations of 'conscience', in which the self feels guilt for the violence it contemplates or inflicts on others.

'Conscience' is the implicit subject of the final section of 'Leviathan', in which the pain experienced by the tortured fish is internally felt by the fisherman and the reader hooked into the poem ('you're caught, mate, you're caught') as a matching self-torture – the whole transaction making 'no sense whatever'. 'Somewhere in one's consciousness, impossible to locate, something twitches in blood sympathy with the fish', Curnow commented, which 'doesn't spoil the sport, in fact it's part of it':[16]

> Fingers and gobstick fail,
> the hook's fast in the gullet,
> the barb's behind the root
> of the tongue and the tight
> fibre is tearing the mouth
> and you're caught, mate, you're caught,
> the harder you pull it
> the worse it hurts, and it makes
> no sense whatever in the air
> or the seas or the rocks
> how you kick or cry, or sleeplessly
> dream as you drown.

When Glover first read the poem he was immediately won over, addressing his response 'Dear Hobbes', 'This Leviathan took the hook in one swallow . . . *a great achievement*. Knowing the coastline, and your Walton mind while you are dangling and angling, I see the sequence clearly.'[17] Perhaps, in invoking Thomas Hobbes's *Leviathan*, Glover saw in the poem a Hobbes-like perception of human life as 'nasty, brutish and short', but his more acute reference is to Izaak Walton's philosophising bent in *The Compleat Angler* (1653). Curnow's poem (like all the poems of *An Incorrigible Music*) is initially accessible through its vivid evocation of an outward scene, but its more profound – and disturbing – resonances are internal, the poet's mind providing the *mise-en-scène* for a self-searching religious, philosophical and moral drama whose subject is the pervasiveness of evil, violence and suffering in human history.

Over the next six months – from July 1977 to early 1978 – Curnow's letters occasionally refer cryptically to other poems he was intensively working on. In August he wrote to Lilburn:

> I'm working on a number of new poems, which ought to have a common theme, but one implied rather than stated; if it could be stated there wld be no need for the poems. Slug pellets are important in one of them, a big kahawai in another; & it's now clear that I have to worry a poem into existence (or myself out of it) touching the Pazzi conspiracy (Florence 1478). It's hard work, & the hardest parts to come. Nearly all new verse these days is so innocuous, poetry has become such a fashionable hobby. If these are any good, they won't be innocuous.[18]

In September he wrote to Tim that he was working on a 'batch of difficult new poems: three almost complete, about 100 lines in all, & several others in the chaotic drafting stages'.[19] In October he wrote to Eric McCormick:

> *I have been putting my own tender nose to the same grindstone most of this year. A group of about a dozen new poems is under way; the words are 'group' and 'new'. With poems – this really is a discovery – daily regular hours are possible, but one has to know when to stop; otherwise drafts multiply, or the poem picks up its pace, or loses it, or one loses sight of the poem. It's when a poem looks close to finishing, in the last draft but one or two, that the regular hours pay off – because there is something to revise . . . . I still spend weeks, months, trying to get a dozen quatrains right, & I can't promise that the product is 'a poem'. I am trying to write the kind of thing that people who don't love poetry will not despise – & how's that for conceit?[20]*

By the end of October something like the shape of the final sequence began to emerge (with the tentative title at this stage of *Expiations*), as he wrote to Stead:

> I shall be a little slower than I hoped, passing over the poems which I so much want you to see. Without others (one in particular) for context, the MKJ [M.K. Joseph] piece ['Dichtung und Wahrheit'] might miss what I am after. At the moment I'm working over a passage in a terza rima ['Recitative'], a little irregular in scansion & dissonantly rhymed, but otherwise strict – you'll imagine the difficulty, which is just what the piece needs; besides a sort of decorum in lines which have to do with Florence.[21]

Reading them six weeks later, now with a title taken from the last poem in the sequence, 'An Incorrigible Music', Stead was immediately impressed: 'I'm convinced this is the best you've done since Trees, Effigies . . . and as good.'[22] As so often in later years his tactful queries about details in the poems prompted clarifying responses, either in agreement or disagreement. Stead was a little puzzled by Curnow' deployment of 'had to' syntax in a number of poems about the suffering of victims of violence, as if there was a shocking necessity in the suffering. Giuliano de' Medici, for example, 'bled where *he had* to bleed', was 'dead / where he *had to* die', the big kahawai in 'Leviathan' '*had to* swim close / to the rocks' as if inviting its own destruction, and Curnow deployed the same 'had to' syntax later throughout 'Moro Assassinato'. Curnow's reply in defence was revealing about his intentions in the sequence as a whole: 'The phrase itself pleases me, besides seeming to generalise what I hope is the effect of them all – all that "had to" syntax, *the "incorrigibleness" of existence.*' [author's italics][23]

He continued to work on the poems during the summer of 1977–78, and in early March sent them to Dudding at *Islands*, who published 'Canst Thou Draw out Leviathan with an Hook?', 'In the Duomo' and 'Bring Your Own Victim' in the May 1978 issue. He also sent a selection from them to *Meanjin* in Australia, but although *Trees, Effigies, Moving Objects* had attracted high praise there from A.D. Hope and Bruce Beaver, the new poems (perhaps predictably) did not impress the young Melbourne poet Kris Hemensley, who was *Meanjin*'s reader. In early April Curnow took the poems with him when he and Jeny made their second overseas trip (for six months) to Europe and London, intending to finalise their preparation for publication. One poem in particular, about Descartes ('Things to Do with Moonlight'), needed further work. He had been grateful to Stead for suggestions to correct it, 'cutting out the pastiche stanza, & mending the preceding one to "best bond for body & soul"', adding, 'those excrescent lines were left-over from the earliest draft of a piece about Descartes'.[24] To Tim he wrote that the sequence 'can't be finished until I have re-read Descartes' famous *Discourse*, not exactly the best assignment in these final days before travelling'.[25]

The sequence sparked off by the fishing-knife poem was a remarkable group of poems, exploring the ramifications of the self's seemingly inherent, ruthless drive to assert control and order over a spatio-temporal world whose constant, obstinate, resistant otherness, its 'incorrigibility', both frustrates and reinforces that drive. The occasion of 'A Balanced Bait in Handy Pellet Form' is a scene of carnage resulting from the commonplace activity of killing slugs and snails by randomly scattering poison pellets. Both the title (with its neat onomatopoeia and metrical precision, and its casual epithet, 'handy', implying special ease of use for killing) and the poem's final line (with its scientific description of the poison, 'active ingredient / 30 g/kg (3%) Metaldehyde, in the form of a pellet') are lifted directly from the product's own packaging, offering a chilling – if small-scale – image of the capacity of language to disguise or rationalise death-dealing intentions and actions. Surveying the aftermath, in which 'Dead snails / have left shells, trails, baffled epigraphy / and excreta of such slow short lives, / cut shorter by the pellets I "scatter freely"', the poet reflects on lines from Byron's *Childe Harold* which lament the absence of harmony between human life and nature ('*Our life is a false nature 'tis not in the harmony of things*'). For Curnow such a lament is misplaced: 'There we go again, worrying / the concentric, the one and identical, to the bone / that's none of ours, eccentric to each other.'

'A Balanced Bait' also suggests, throughout, that any sense of 'the harmony of things', of unity between the self and the world, depends, precariously, on belief that there is a 'natural' correspondence or fit between the world and language. Quite how precarious that naturalness of fit is provides the subject of 'A Cool Head in an Emergency'. At this early stage the poem had the title 'An Anxious Moment'. It begins with what seems to be a public scene of panic-stricken mayhem in the streets as police, army, fire and ambulance services are suddenly mobilised to apprehend a dangerous prisoner on the loose. There is then a sensational double-anticlimax, as the public emergency turns out, embarrassingly, to be a false alarm, and reveals itself also, 'merely' as a metaphor – an extended metaphor – for a personal emergency: a simple lapse of memory, during a walk, when the name of a tree is forgotten. It is not until late in the poem (in the third of its three sections) that the poet finally relieves the readers' frustration at not knowing what the 'wanted word' is which has been 'let slip to the dark, / where the tip of the tongue plays blind / man's buff and the wanted word / baffles the breath.' The word is *gingko*, the name of an exotic Japanese tree (perhaps Curnow intended an irony in its reputation for memory-enhancing herbal properties), of which a splendid example grew in Tohunga Crescent (the unstated location of the poet's walk), covered with spectacular autumnal yellowing leaves. Despite the poem's scintillating wit ('What's death / but a defect of memory?'), and its brilliant miming of the frustrations of memory loss so that the reader experiences a parallel frustration, it is uncompromising in its characterisation of language as an act of violence committed on the world (things, objects, events) to which it refers. In his jacket note to the published volume Curnow referred to 'the death-struggle of mind and matter' by way of relating its concerns to the broader exploration of violence in the sequence.

'Leviathan', 'A Balanced Bait' and 'A Cool Head in an Emergency' offer the poet himself as everyman or everywoman: all of us, the poems imply, are perpetrators of violence in our most commonplace interactions with the world. Curnow's aim, in beginning the sequence with the fishing and gardening poems, was to anticipate and destabilise the self-righteous habit of regarding violence as something others engage in. Much of our behaviour consists of rationalising after the event or setting up motives before it in order to excuse ourselves afterwards.

'In the Duomo' was the longest poem in the sequence at this time, and turned to a spectacularly violent event in Italian history, strikingly distant in place and time from Karekare. Its subject was the assassination plot (known as the Pazzi conspiracy) against the powerful Renaissance Florentine rulers, Lorenzo and Giuliano de' Medici, which had occurred almost exactly half a millennium earlier in April 1478. The reasons for the conspiracy – the wealthy Florentine Pazzi family's jealousy of the power of the Medici, the rivalry of neighbouring city-states, and the murky role of Pope Sixtus IV, whose secular ambitions included the expansion of the Papal States on Florence's border – are hinted at in the poem, as well as the failure of the plot: although Giuliano was murdered, his brother Lorenzo – the bigger fish – escaped.

In the five poems of 'In the Duomo' the key historical events assume centre stage in the three central poems. The introductory and concluding poems are set at Karekare. The effect at one level is to encounter history through Karekare, which provides both a point of entry and a point of departure, but at another level (in the *mise-en-scène* of the poet's intense meditation on the events) a transference of locations occurs: poet and reader are in both places at the same time, and history – without losing its brutal specificity – becomes present. In the poem's final lines the poet imaginatively confirms the link between the sacrifice/murder scene in the Duomo and the spot to which he himself, fishing for a big one, had brought 'the blooding hand, the scaling, / the scarlet clouded pool, / the necessary knife.'

The sea which pounds the rocks ceaselessly at Karekare, rearing up green roaring down white, carries this grim history of repetitions and re-enactments, making *An Incorrigible Music* one of the richest examples of the 'oceanic imagination' in Curnow's poetry. It is the same sea as washes the coastlines of Europe and all other global landmasses. It is the same sea as 500 years ago, and will be the same sea as long as the planet survives. In one early draft Curnow contemplated our incorrigibly anthropomorphic habit of assigning feelings to the sea, speaking of its 'rage' and 'fury', as if it were an active, malign force, and went on to ask playfully why we don't describe it as mad or insane. Rather, he went on, the sea is 'a helpless power', 'a power helpless to restrain itself'. In a remarkable descriptive passage expressing this idea in 'Leviathan' he describes the 'rage' of the sea as 'all an act', a projection of a rage which 'actually' belongs to the rocks which 'kicked angrily' and 'hurt only themselves', expressing 'the self-lacerating hurt of the land'. The rocks and land here are the location of the human, the sea the realm of the incorrigibly inhuman: ongoing, permanent, oblivious of and indifferent to human desires and ambitions, the carrier of history, the source of life but just as surely and inevitably the repository, the 'receptacle', of the dead.

In *Trees, Effigies, Moving Objects*, one poem, 'A Four Letter Word', played a key role in articulating the core ideas of the sequence as a whole. In *An Incorrigible Music* a similar role was played by the poem 'Bring Your Own Victim'. Playing blackly on the vernacular party-phrase 'BYOG' ('Bring Your Own Grog'), the poem offers – in its three parts – a kind of history of the idea of divinity, and of the attitudes to violence entailed in that history. It invents a historical frame within which the particular instances of violence discussed elsewhere might be contextualised. In part one, drawing on examples from Old Testament and classical mythology (Abraham's willingness to sacrifice his son Isaac to God, and Agamemnon's willingness to sacrifice his daughter Iphigenia to the goddess Diana), Curnow posits an earliest dispensation of divinity in which gods and goddesses exercise a transcendent, arbitrary, remote power over nature and human destinies, exacting unquestioning obedience and absolute faith. In part two this absolute order of divinity, entirely separate from the human/natural world, is challenged and replaced by an 'incarnational' idea of divinity ('The gods got into the act / and they played our game'), which in turn reconstitutes the relationship between the human and the divine. The notion of a God who is both divine and part-human (as in the Christian dispensation, though for Curnow the shift is reflected across theogonies, in the widespread mythic phenomenon of the *demi-urgos* or demigod) prompted the notion of the human as (at least potentially) sharing and aspiring to the divine, becoming a responsible agent capable of transcending his or her natural/human nature and fulfilling the divinity within – capable, that is, of exercising some control over destiny.

However, the consequences of this new duality in human nature are double-edged. If incarnated gods enter history, human beings also conceive the possibility of their transcending history, manifesting the divinity within. If they now have a degree of free will, and of self-agency, they also carry responsibility for the mistakes and blunders they make, and a new psychic constitution emerges. The pangs of individual 'conscience' are born of this doubleness: anxiety and guilt about the motivations and effects of one's behaviour, uncertainty and doubt about whether a course of action expresses the divine or simply manifests self-interest, the ever-present temptation to rationalise, or invent 'divine' justifications for, base behaviour. The concluding stanzas brilliantly characterise this new dispensation:

> Bring your own victim
>   ruled from then on,
> conscience cut its milk teeth
>   on the live bone.
>
> Brutus knew that the blood
>   had to be Caesar's,
> Caiaphas and Pilate found
>   no proxy for Jesus.
>
> You sharpened your knife, you steeled
>   yourself, the wound
> twisted the knife in the hand,
>   the knife in the mind.
>
> Man or beast you bought
>   on the hoof hung dead,
> neither the cloud nor the covert sun
>   commented,
>
> and you never knew
>   what hung by the other hook
> in the heart, your blessed sacrifice
>   or your damned mistake.

Part three is a bleak and bitter characterisation of a post-Nietzschean, purely secular era from which God has absconded entirely. Lacking either the arbitrary sanctions of an absolute deity or the inner sanctions and promptings (no matter how flawed) of conscience, human beings are now entirely 'free', unsponsored, 'alone with your life, alone / with your politics', randomly located 'in a galaxy . . . / among the spitting and the shitting stars', solely responsible for their own destinies. No poem Curnow had ever written expressed so grim a prophetic sense of the fate of a world entirely at the mercy of a never-satiated, murderous hubris in which human violence knows no constraints, imagining that even time itself can be exorcised from the human condition. In the poem's shockingly ironic final stanza, the death-dealing 'steeled thumb' is not that of the knife-wielding recreational fisherman in 'Leviathan' nor of the assassins in the Duomo, but the scalpel of a professional ('eminent') medical surgeon, the poem's concluding metaphor for the new post-Nietzschean operators wielding godlike power of life or death over the body politic:

> You knew there was never nothing
> > miracles wouldn't fix,
> alone with your life, alone
> > with your politics;
>
> alive, alone, one-upping
> > war, pestilence, famine,
> happy in your Jonestowns, Hiroshimas,
> > happy to be human,
>
> happy to be history . . . .
>
> Spillage of bird blood,
> > fish, and flesh went,
> the spoonful in the womb, the aged,
> > and incontinent,
>
> under your steeled thumb:
> > so to imagine
> slaughterman, overman, everyman,
> > time's eminent surgeon.

There were three other poems in the sequence as Curnow completed it at this time, each exploring particular aspects of violence. 'Dichtung und Wahrheit' lampoons an imagined novel,* in which a particularly ugly wartime episode of violence and sexuality is transformed into literary entertainment, by reducing and simplifying its events to the grossest, most explicit sexual obscenities. 'Things to Do with Moonlight', which Curnow at this time called 'Doppelgänger at Karekare', is a much more complex poem, demythologising the Christian theology surrounding Easter (the Crucifixion and Resurrection), by sceptically exploring the idea of resurrection after death as a purely mental operation. 'An Incorrigible Music', the title poem of the sequence, offers a delightful coda in which the poet

---

* Occasioned, in fact, by a real novel, M.K. Joseph's *A Soldier's Tale* (1976).

observes herons arriving and departing from a scene of mangroves and mudflats at Hobson Bay, reaffirming (and celebrating) the rich otherness of the world. The herons are resistant to his most strenuous attempts even to count them, let alone contain the scene in its totality: not only do the numbers constantly change, as birds arrive and depart and change position, but as the water surface calms (but only momentarily), 'each heron is four herons, / one right-side-up in the air, / one upside-down in the tide, / and these two doubled by looking at.' Furthermore, 'the mudbacked mirrors in your head / multiply the possibilities of human / error'. 'What's the alternative?' the poet asks, and offers an image of the unique sound produced by 'the small wind-instruments in the herons' throats'. Like the rich autumn colours of the gingko tree, the heron's sound is simply, indescribably itself, irreducible to any other sound. The poem concludes by insisting on the paradoxical doubleness of the mind's constantly changing interactions with this rich, constantly changing physical world. 'Punctually' (that is, at any moment one might care to nominate, but always retrospectively) 'the picture completes itself / and is never complete.' At every moment when the 'completed picture' is arrested, contained 'accurately' within the fixed forms of language, the world itself has moved on, rendering that utterance a 'misquotation':

> There's only one book in the world, and that's the one
> everyone accurately misquotes.

> *A big one! A big one!*

Leviathan, the 'big one', emerges here as the name for that ever-elusive 'other-ness' of the world, beyond human control or power or language, which has its own 'incorrigible music'. It is the monster, 'the lion locked in stone' of Stevens's poem in *The Man with the Blue Guitar*, which the poems have attempted to match with the music of 'the lion in the lute'. Perhaps Curnow intends an echo of Wordsworth's famous characterisation (in 'Tintern Abbey') of the mystery he perceived at the heart of human experience of the world in the phrase 'the still, sad music of humanity'. Curnow's music, however, is anything but sad or still: it arouses the whole gamut of human emotions, from fear, terror and anxiety to elation, astonishment and delight; it is a spur not to resignation and sadness but offers a Nietzschean challenge to the most vigorous, dynamic efforts to produce a matching utterance, perhaps with something of Nietzsche's 'divine hop, skip and jump'. It is the music of a world in which violence and death are inherent and inescapable, where 'merely to exist [is] even for the gentlest / the rape of another's breath or bread'. The sequence, throughout, is uncompromising in its refusal to settle for sentimental illusions, refusing to exempt the self from the implications of the poetic vision, and it is acutely aware of the subterfuges, platitudes and rationalisations with which people (including Curnow himself) evade the fact of violence at the core of their lives.

Interlude: Italy and London, April–October 1978

Curnow's retirement gratuity from the University of Auckland had made it possible for him to think of an immediate return trip to Europe, but he postponed the trip until 1978 after he had had time to establish a new routine in his life. He and Jeny planned a six-month trip, flying via Los Angeles and London to Milan in early April, spending two and a half months in Italy (until mid-June) followed by a fortnight with Tony and Elisabeth in Geneva and a week in Paris, then spending the remaining three months in London. They were not in the least interested in pursuing an entirely new itinerary. Rather, they returned to the main places they had visited in 1974 (Venice, Sicily, Rome, Paris), with the aim of getting to know them better, while adding a small number of new places to their itinerary – a few days each in Milan and Bologna (instead of Florence) and a week in Naples.

Within a few days of arriving for their three-week stay in Venice Curnow wrote to Pearson that 'Already we are glad of the decision to return'.[26] They stayed at Hotel Agli Alboretti, close to La Calcina (where they had stayed in 1974), and were delighted to find that they were well remembered at their favourite trattoria, Ai Cugnai, nearby. They were also warmly remembered by the waiter Domenico at his café on the Zattere, where they regularly had morning coffee, watching the huge ships pass through the Giudecca Canal, with a view across the canal to the tall bell tower of the church of San Giorgio Maggiore. Here Curnow worked at deciphering the latest news in *La Corriere della Sera* and *La Stampa* about the kidnap of Aldo Moro, five times Italian prime minister and president of the National Council of Christian Democrats. Moro's abduction in Rome by the *Brigate Rosse* (Red Brigades) on 16 March had plunged Italy into political turmoil, and like millions of Italians Curnow and Jeny could only watch helplessly as the paralysing crisis deepened throughout April and early May. 'It was impossible', Curnow wrote later, 'to live in Italy from early April through June, reading the newspapers, catching the mood of chance remarks or no remarks at all, and not to be affected.'[27]

As usual they walked a great deal in Venice, revisiting old haunts (including San Rocco and the Church of the Friars, where Titian's celebrated altarpiece, *Assumption of the Virgin*, was now back in place). They made several visits to the Correr Museum as well as to the church of Santa Maria della Salute, where

Titian's paintings on the ceiling of the sacristy – of Abraham and Isaac, Cain and Abel, and David and Goliath – were 'so near the subject of my latest verses' (no doubt recalling 'Bring Your Own Victim' in particular) that 'it was uncanny to look up at them'.[28] Close to the Zattere itself they also visited the church of San Sebastiano (attracted by its collection of Veronese's paintings) as well as the Dominican church of I Gesuati. There were day trips to Padua and to the island village of Torcello, where a twelfth-century mosaic representation of the Last Judgement (with fire coming from Christ's left foot) was to prompt a revision to the already published *Islands* version of Montesecco's description of the damned in the third poem of 'In the Duomo'. Tony and Elisabeth also joined them for four days, where they celebrated Tony's recent appointment to the highly prestigious post of Director of Information Services at the Palais des Nations in Geneva, the headquarters of the United Nations in Europe.

After four days in Bologna the Curnows spent the week of 4 to 11 May in Naples, which 'was nightmarish for a couple of days, till we could read the mind of its demented traffic, & mastered the public transport'.[29] They made day trips by electric rail (the Ferrovia Circumvesuviana), to Pompeii, then Herculaneum, and on 9 May to Sorrento, the latter much disfigured – like, increasingly, the whole Calabrian coast – by vacation developers. On their return to their hotel later in the day, they read at the reception desk the huge headlines in a special edition of *Il Mattino*, the Naples daily: 'MORO ASSASSINATO'. 'The faces, & the words, of the hotel people could almost have told the story', Curnow wrote to Tony.[30] The man at the reception desk typified the sense of shock and grief: 'I never supported his party, but I say to you: they have killed the wrong man. The wrong man!'[31] 'You're a guest, in a stricken house, / eavesdropper, easy tourist', Curnow later wrote of that day and those following.

The day after the assassination they travelled to Messina in Sicily, where they arranged to stay – as they had in 1974 – on the northern coast, spending a week at Milazzo followed by a fortnight at Cefalù, further west than they had stayed in 1974 and closer to Palermo, an hour's travel away. 'So far, the country's political nerves are holding well', Curnow wrote to Tim from Cefalù ten days after the assassination.[32] Very tentatively and diffidently, at this time, the notion of a poem about Moro had occurred to him: 'M's death, & the way of it touched me in another way; can I perhaps abstract it into a poem for my new sequence? A notion merely. Perhaps a poet should leave it alone – and to the journalists.'[33]

In the meantime Curnow and Jeny settled in to enjoying their three weeks in Sicily. During their week in Milazzo they made a day trip by hydrofoil to the island of Lipari, where they heard a shuddering detonation from Mt Etna and were glad to be 30 miles away.[34] In Cefalù at the Hotel Kalura (a short bus trip from the township, and with a beach of its own) they found 'an ideal place for mere sun & sea, & a rest from sightseeing', and made two day trips to Palermo.[35] Although Cefalù was 'a minor suburb of vacationland', in May there were not a great many tourists, and they especially enjoyed their contact with local people: 'Poor as people are in these parts, every contact, in a bar, a shop, or the street, is an exercise in civility.'[36]

After leaving Cefalù in early June the Curnows spent nine days in Rome, staying at the Hotel Quattro Fontane in the same part of the city as they had stayed in 1974, revisiting their favourite haunts and finding new places, and also visiting Via Caetani, where Moro's body had been discovered in the Renault 4. They were deeply affected by signs of grief at the site, even though it was a month since the assassination:

> At the spot in Via Caetani Rome, where the murdered man's body was left, in the Renault 4, about a dozen metres of wall were covered with private tokens of respect – handwritten papers, placards, flowers – from the ground to above head height. People came and went, or stood silently. That was mid-June, a full month later.[37]

After enjoying the hospitality of Tony and Elisabeth at Geneva and Pruzilly for twelve days (15 to 27 June), the Curnows spent a week in Paris (staying at the Hotel Solferino) where the highlights were a Cézanne exhibition at the Grand Palais and a visit to the modern art collection at the Beaubourg museum. On 5 July they arrived in London, which was to be their base for the remaining three months of their trip.

Curnow had booked a flat, sight unseen, at 4A Devonshire Hill, Hampstead, which 'turned out to be extremely disappointing – dirty, cramped, ill-furnished and ill-equipped',[38] though the environs were pleasant and the flat was cheap compared with other accommodation in the area. It took ten days – and vigorous complaints about the state of the flat to the landlord – before it began to seem like a home. Jeny had picked up a cough in Paris which quickly worsened into severe bronchitis, eventually requiring specialist care, and for at least a month she had to take things carefully.

Within a week of arrival, however, Curnow began to pick over his Moro materials, hoping for a start on 'the most difficult verse I have ever attempted'.[39] He also worked on a number of other drafts and fragments from his stay at Cefalù, and returned to the poems of *An Incorrigible Music* with a view to trying to place some of them in the *Times Literary Supplement* and *Encounter*, and submit a final manuscript to Auckland University Press. In early August he sent the manuscript off – with quite a few revisions, especially to 'In the Duomo' in the wake of his second trip to Italy, and including careful attention to punctuation, which had been entirely omitted in the earlier versions published in *Islands*. At this stage the question of a Moro poem was left in abeyance and he did not mention the possibility to AUP's editor Dennis McEldowney, anxious (as he wrote to Stead) to insist that the sequence had its integrity quite independently of whether a Moro poem was added or not.[40]

In the meantime he sent selections from the poems to the *Times Literary Supplement* and *Encounter*. At the time the former had temporarily ceased publishing because of a printers' strike, and returned the poems to him, but the editor singled out 'Dichtung und Wahrheit' for praise and asked him to send more when publication resumed. Anthony Thwaite, the literary editor of *Encounter*, an important avenue for literary publication in the UK, immediately accepted 'A Balanced Bait in Handy Pellet Form' for the December issue, adding that he liked several of the poems Curnow had sent and had 'admired some of your work for a long time'.[41] Curnow was greatly encouraged by this small sign of acceptance in the United Kingdom: 'It's something to be just visible outside NZ, & indeed I've felt my invisibility now & again in the last 3 months.'[42] Throughout the rest of his stay in London, however, his work on Moro remained primarily at the briefing and note-making stage.

Working regularly on poems kept Curnow busy for much of his time in London, but after Jeny's health began to improve they made time for casual visits to galleries (especially a new collection of Henry Moore sculpture at the Tate Gallery as well as its Turner collection), and to the theatre and opera, as well as trying out numerous pubs recommended by Glover and Pearson. Jeny worked regularly at the local Citizens Advice Bureau, and there were also social gatherings with her extended family in London, and long-weekend trips to Bath and Salisbury, to Dover and Canterbury, and to Cambridge. Towards the end of their stay Tony and Elisabeth visited for a long weekend, and on the day of their departure (1 October) they were fortunate to see Tim (just arrived from New York, on a business trip) who was able to show them photographs of his recently born son, Mark. Within a month Tim was to write that he had arranged with BBC radio for a new production of *The Duke's Miracle* (broadcast sixteen months later in April 1980), a further welcome sign that Curnow's later work was beginning to find acceptance in the United Kingdom.

Chapter Twenty-eight

Return to New Zealand, 'Moro Assassinato', 1978–79

Moro goes forward, though still in the briefing (not writing) stages. What a victim! His shirt & other linen were washed & ironed, not a button of the 20 in his clothing out of place.[1]

'Moro Assassinato', summer 1978–79

For the first month after their return to Auckland the Curnows were based at Karekare, since the house at Tohunga Crescent had been rented until the end of October; and Curnow worked hard on the Moro poem during that and the following months. At the end of October Dennis McEldowney sent him a draft contract for *An Incorrigible Music* and agreed to the idea of adding a Moro poem if it eventuated. Later in November Curnow mentioned to Tim that 'there's still a little work on the new poems' (adjustments that would be required in the light of the attention he was giving to Moro), and 'much more than a little' work needed on the planned Aldo Moro poem, indicating for the first time that he was thinking of a substantial work, 'on a big scale, & for which I feel underprepared'.[2]

In fact, the Moro poem turned out to be *much* longer than he anticipated – a nine-part sequence of 360 lines, which added sixteen pages to the 26 occupied by the other poems – and it was not until later in February that he sent the completed poem to McEldowney, who 'was evidently keen to waste no time, & has been so patient with me'.[3] 'After 4 months' hard labour I can't make it any

517

better', he wrote to Tim,[4] though he expressed typical uncertainties about the completed product to Stead:

> The *form* (to dignify it) simply grew out of the material & the stress of containing it in a poem, or poems. It's a good deal more, in some ways, & of course less in others, than I hoped when I first thought of it. Perhaps it looks like a modern mirror of 'In the Duomo'?[5]

'Moro Assassinato' was the most ambitious long poem Curnow had ever attempted, and his most impressive, adding a contemporary political dimension to the historical and local concerns of the rest of the sequence, with which it was carefully integrated, while retaining its own integrity and immediacy as a profound analysis and insight into the events themselves and the phenomenon of terrorist violence in the contemporary world. In the period leading up to the abduction – a time of serious economic, political and social crisis in Italy – Moro had been the prime mover of a strategic political compromise, which deeply alarmed both the extreme left and the extreme right, aimed at bringing the Christian Democrats and the Communist Party together to form a government of national solidarity. There was a terrible irony in the fact that, later on the very day of his abduction (he was seized and his bodyguards killed, on his way to a session of the House of Representatives when a crucial vote would be taken), the first stage of his vision was achieved when Giulio Andreotti (of the Christian Democrats) was voted into power with the support of the Communist Party.

Curnow was also struck by the sense of history repeating itself, 500 years ('a half chiliad'[6]) to the month after the conspiracy to assassinate the Medici in 1478, and the extraordinary coincidence of his being in Italy as the Moro crisis unfolded to its brutal conclusion. Interwoven with poems about Moro, about his abductors, about the machinations and power plays of political rivals and the betrayal of those he regarded as his political friends and allies, and about the anguish of his wife and family, Curnow also included connecting references to Karekare, to 'In the Duomo', and to his own presence as a traveller ('a guest, in a stricken house, / eavesdropper, easy tourist') in Venice, Naples, Sicily, and central Rome. The site where Moro's body was discovered in Via Caetani was almost exactly (as some commentators noted) halfway between the headquarters of the two political parties (the Christian Democrats and the PCI (Communist Party)) who had been united in refusing to negotiate with the *Brigate Rosse* for his release.

The first poem in the sequence, 'The Traveller', is set in Venice on the Zattere on the Giudecca Canal, the bell tower of the church of San Giorgio Maggiore reminding the poet of Paratohi rock at Karekare. Written in tercets to suggest a link with the opening poem ('Recitative') of 'In the Duomo', the poem introduces the theme of violent history repeating itself across times and places, as if endemic in human behaviour:

> All the seas are one sea,
> The blood one blood
> And the hands one hand.
>
> Ever is always today . . . .
>
> . . . . . . the obliterations
> are one obliteration
>
> of last year's Adriatic,
> yesterday's Pacific . . . .
>
> the tales are all one tale
> dead men tell, the minor
> characters the living.

The next six poems, written in a variety of forms suggested by the material itself, explore the motives and behaviour of the main protagonists in the drama, beginning with a study of the mind of the 'urban guerilla', and tracing the increasing tension as the abductors live with the logic of their credo that 'we had to be / terrible news, or die.' 'Lampoon', the brief third poem, parodies the dehumanising political language of those justifying the abduction, their contempt for Moro's efforts to achieve a rapprochement between the right-wing Christian Democrats and the Communist Party; and the fourth poem, '16 March 1978', turns to Moro himself, and the moment when 'normality', as he travels (accompanied by security guards) to a meeting, is violently disrupted by the murder of the security guards and the abduction.

It is a violent disruption, but in a world where such events recur, such violence is also part of the 'normality' of 'the moment's mixture', and the poem insists – disturbingly and powerfully – on its commonplace nature. In the moving conclusion Curnow (perhaps remembering an incident from his own childhood Sheffield days) has Moro recall an example of mindlessly cruel, seemingly motiveless bullying he suffered as a child, as he attempts to accept that his case 'was not so special':

> The child I was would have known
> better than the man I am,

when they tripped him, trapped him,
ripped his shirt, emptied his bag,

caught him, laughed him to tears,
rubbed cowshit into his hair,

the irreversible justice
of the wrong once done, the victim's

yes to the crime. Who knows
he had to be punished knows

how the women who wipe away
the tears and the shit

heal no hurt but their own.
Tell the bullet to climb

back up the barrel and close
the wound behind it. They carried me,

carrying the child who could teach me
my case was not so special.

The fifth and sixth poems, 'The Prison of the People' and 'The Letters', are written in a more flexible language often close to prose, and these poems present much of the detail of what actually occurred in the public arena during the 54 days of Moro's captivity. The fifth poem presents the political manoeuvrings of the main political parties and their leaders from the often incredulous perspective of the abductors themselves, who are initially astonished and buoyed by the 'compliance' of the press in publicising their communiqués and Moro's letters ('Christ! They printed it all. Next thing / we sentenced him to death. They printed this.'), but gradually disillusioned as their hopes for a political deal ('the exchange for our comrades / gaoled by the State, their liberty for his life') fade, and they become locked into the inexorable logic requiring the killing of Moro. In the case of Moro the media not only ensured continuing, sensational publicity of every rumour and speculation during the crisis, but effectively collaborated with the state authorities in their branding of Moro's letters as inauthentic.

In the end Curnow did not include any poem written from the perspective of the state and its political leaders, though his early jottings about 'sympathies' raised that possibility.[7] Quite simply, his sympathies failed him, as he became aware of the extent of the betrayals, rivalries, devious back-room dealings, and sheer callousness with which the authorities treated Moro – whose behaviour, in adamantly refusing 'for reasons of state' to negotiate the release of *Brigate Rosse* prisoners in exchange for Moro's life, effectively sealed his fate, making his murder inevitable. Even the Pope, offering himself as a substitute in an appeal to the terrorists for Moro's release, required it to be 'unconditional', effectively aligning himself with the position of the state; and the nadir of Moro's betrayal was reached on 25 April when 50 individuals (politicians, intellectuals, scholars), describing themselves as 'old friends', signed a document for publication declaring that the Moro who in his letters was desperately arguing the political and personal case for his release was 'not the man they knew', whose 'spiritual, political and juridical vision' had once inspired them.[8] Curnow has the abductors themselves make the link between Moro's situation and the multiple betrayals by friends and the Roman authorities leading to Christ's crucifixion:

> Did we seriously expect these [Moro's letters] would procure
> the political deal, the exchange for our comrades
>
> gaoled by the State, their liberty for his life?
> 'An episode in a war', terror for terror,
> an honourable swap. So his letters argued.
>
> He knew us better than they, adduced Palestinian
> precedent, humane principle, the party interest,
> all that shit. What did he, or we, expect?
>
> Jesus wrote no letters to Judas or Caiaphas.
> It was he or Barabbas, and that was another Rome.
> *Not known at this address. Try Simon Peter.*
>
> Silence in Jesus Square, his Demo-Christians
> denied him by protocol, *il vero Moro è morto*
> *il 16 Marzo, ultimo suo giorno di libertà.**
>
> Consenting silence in the house of the Left,
> Christ's communist other woman, three in a bed
> With Rome, last word of his long clever speeches,

---

* 'the true Moro died on 16 March, his last day of freedom'.

Grosso orchestratore. And among themselves
read in his letters forgery, torture, drugs,
practices in the Prison of the People

Which 30,000 police, etc., could never locate.
Dead, by the party line, a just man we once knew,
of whose visible blood we shall be innocent.

See ye to it.

The sixth poem ('The Letters') asks the question, 'How can we know / who it is that speaks?', allowing passages from Moro's letters to speak for themselves, movingly, as he refutes the allegations of coercion, expresses the deepest love and concern for his wife Noretta and their children, and at the end – knowing that his death is inevitable – angrily denounces to Benigno Zaccagnini (secretary of the Demo-Christian Party) the failures, of humanity and judgement, that have sealed his fate:

I repeat, I do not accept
the unjust, ungrateful judgment of the party.
I absolve, I excuse nobody.
My cry is the cry of my family, wounded to death.
I request that at my funeral, nobody
representing the State, nor men of the Party,
take part, I ask to be followed by the few
who have truly wished me well and are therefore worthy
to go with me in their prayers, and in their love.

Moro was buried in the local cemetery after a small private funeral in the village of Torrita Tiberina. Despite his wishes there was a full state funeral ceremony in Rome, presided over by the Pope. Noretta and their children did not attend.

The seventh poem, 'The Executioners', describes in brutally specific detail the murder of Moro, beginning with an allusion to the second part of 'Bring Your Own Victim', in which God enters human history, and real victims like Moro (not substitutes) are required: 'Christ set it going and ascended, / leaving the engine running'. The poem insists on the ordinary details of 'the moment's mixture' – the impeccable attention of the 'girl comrade' to Moro's dress, except for the socks ('wrong-side out') – followed immediately by the atrocity of the eleven bullets

* 'Big orchestrator'.

fired into the 'doubled-up foetus' Moro's body made in the baggage end of the Renault 4. At the end (in a horrifying visual miming of the gun from which each bullet is fired), Moro's grotesquely nodding head (from the whiplash effect of each bullet) recalls his childhood memory in the fourth poem, 'the victim's yes to the crime' at the moment, irretrievable and incorrigible, when the atrocity is committed:

> *yes yes yes yes*
>   *yes yes yes*
> *yes yes yes yes*

The last two poems of the sequence return to the personal context of the traveller, as in the first poem: '9 May 1978' recalls the moment when Curnow first heard of the assassination in Naples, after returning from a visit to Pompeii and elsewhere, connecting and contrasting the many unremembered, unknown dead buried under the violent eruptions with Moro's recent death:

> They are all as dead as nineteen hundred
> years or the moment after.
> They do not live in memory or imagination
> or history, or any other
> of death's entertainments.

'Poems' /, he adds, 'don't work any more'. 'The poetry of tears is a dead cuckoo', he had written in *Trees, Effigies, Moving Objects*. The individual finality of death is a finality (whether of a moment ago or millennia ago) beyond any momentary transcendence its remembering in a poem might offer, of no consolation to the dead. 'Compassion' – even the huge compassion which informs Curnow's imagining of Moro's 54-day agon – in the end, 'always sings to itself'.

Curnow's earliest draft of the final poem, 'The Poor', is dated 'Cefalù, May 1978', suggesting that it was the first of the poems to be written. It is one of the most moving in the sequence, placing Moro's death in an age-old tradition amongst the poor of 'publishing' their grief at the death of a husband or a wife or a brother, on a 'scrap of newsprint' attached to doors and doorways: *'per mio marito, mia moglie, / mio fratello'*.* The guardian of this tradition at the conclusion of the poem is a grandmother, into her ninetieth year, who sits 'catching the sun' in her doorway. Indomitably, she represents ongoing life, something of an acceptance of the incorrigibility of the world. And on the lintel above, sign of Moro's presence

---

* 'for my husband, my wife, / my brother'.

as one of the family of the poor, is the simple newsprint message, one of many observed then and later in the poorer areas, 'Per Aldo Moro'.

Whim Wham: the darker note, 1970s

As anxious as ever to preserve an absolute distinction between his poetry and his work as Whim Wham, Curnow asked Allan Cole, assistant editor of the *New Zealand Herald* at the time of the publication of *An Incorrigible Music*, to ensure that any review did not mention his identity as Whim Wham: 'The weekly column has its own integrity, & so has the poet who takes a few years to get his lines right.'[9]

Despite the differences between 'weekly columnist' and 'poet', Whim Wham clearly shared with Curnow the much darker tone which entered the poetry in the 1970s, in both *Trees, Effigies, Moving Objects* and *An Incorrigible Music*. In the case of Whim Wham it is strongly reflected in the subject matter, in the weighting given to serious topics compared with light topics. There were many satiric pieces on the Vietnam War, as well as at least six or eight pieces each year through the 1970s – increasingly angry and despairing – about the gathering social and political crisis for New Zealand of its involvement in racially based Springbok rugby tours. There were also many pieces on the heightening inter-national crises in the Middle East, French nuclear tests in the Pacific Ocean, armaments stockpiling, and the failure of Cold War diplomacy. A new kind of piece, offering a bleak, generalised indictment of humanity, entered Whim Wham's repertoire. 'It's a Sick Beast',[10] sparked by anti-abortion rhetoric (though Curnow was equally troubled by pro-abortion rhetoric) and a news report of the mass poisoning of '1.5 million disease carrying blackbirds' in Kentucky, might be read as Whim Wham's twentieth-century gloss on the grim subject matter, later, of *An Incorrigible Music*. A similar gloss on the religious and political concerns of some of Curnow's seventies poems might be read into Whim Wham's 'By Their Fruits',[11] one of his Vietnam pieces sparked by US President Richard Nixon's invoking of God's blessing on new military initiatives.

The dark thread running through such verse was not simply a consequence of its subject matter. It had a great deal to do with the *kind* of satire Whim Wham deployed, with the balance shifting away from the genial Horatian mode of so many of his earlier lighter pieces to the more corrosive mode of Juvenalian satire, striking fiercely, sometimes despairingly, at the stupidity, arrogance and callousness of the powerful – as well as at the apathy of people in accepting the abuses and self-justifications of political and bureaucratic power. When he wrote his half tongue-in-cheek introduction to *Whim Wham Land* in the mid-1960s

Whim Wham was able to speak 'genially' – with fondness and affection – about the habits and foibles of the ordinary New Zealanders whose 'ethnography' his verses mapped. But from this time onwards he found it increasingly difficult to sustain the kinds of identification which had underpinned his earlier genial satire of the 'average Kiwi'. Perhaps the Vietnam War was as significant, in this local respect, as it was in deepening his anxieties about the international scene.

Apathy was also a key theme of many of the pieces lampooning Robert Muldoon after his election as prime minister at the end of 1975. Curnow was shocked by the electorate's embracing of a man whose abrasive, 'dictatorial style' and 'contempt of Parliament' he detested,[12] whose politics of denigration of any who expressed dissent created (in Curnow's view) an unprecedented climate of fear. In 'And a Very New Year It Was' (December 1975), set in an imaginary future, historians characterise Muldoon ('Ironlips') as exploiting 'the guilty Mind of a sick / People who cried for the Rule of a Rod', while 'Learning the Language' (May 1976) offered a bitter comment on Muldoon's 'climate of fear' politics. Throughout this period newspapers (and the media generally) were extremely nervous about defamation writs from Muldoon if they published even slightly critical opinions, and Curnow was not immune from the *New Zealand Herald*'s lawyers, who were nervous about 'Legerdemain', a lively squib about Muldoon's less than wholehearted protest to the French government about their resumed Pacific nuclear testing programme, because of the possible repercussions of a strong protest on the country's primary produce trade with France. Legal advice to John Hardingham, the *Herald*'s editor, suggested that the final two lines ('Where is the Nation, and where's the Man / Who doesn't have his Price?')[13] might be read by Muldoon as alleging 'personal venality' and attract a writ. Curnow changed them to 'Like a proper Ledger, it's got two Sides, / the Policy, and the Price', commenting to Tony: 'If I hadn't been able to tinker the lines so as to sharpen my point & relieve the editor's mind at the same time, I would have had to withdraw the whole piece.'[14]

However, throughout the later 1960s and 1970s both the *New Zealand Herald* and *The Press* continued to value Whim Wham's weekly contributions, and after his return from Europe at the end of 1974 he was able to negotiate an increase in his weekly fee from $15 to $20. There were very occasional rejections. In 1973 neither newspaper used an anti-Springbok tour piece ('Time Off for Injuries') because it might inflame opinion at a time when a partial boycott of the Commonwealth Games in Christchurch early the following year was a possibility. Norman Macbeth at *The Press* couched his rejection diplomatically, describing the piece (which has not survived) as 'one of your more savage lunges', and mentioning that he was thinking of sending 'The Man with a Stomach Pump'[15] to the *New York Times* or *Washington Post* after receiving an opinion that it was 'wittier than any commentary on the Watergate affair' in United States newspapers.[16] Macbeth was also interested in sponsoring a new selection of Whim Wham's verses. Nothing came of the proposal, though Whim Wham's weekly contributions, with their many savage lunges at ignorance, stupidity, violence and the abuse of power, continued until he bowed out towards the end of the 1980s.

Reaction to 'Dichtung und Wahrheit'

An Incorrigible Music eventually appeared in July 1979, under the joint imprint of Auckland University Press and Oxford University Press, and Curnow was delighted with Dennis McEldowney's oversight of the book's design and typography, modelled on Wallace Stevens's *Harmonium* (1923). The book attracted some unusually lively reviews in New Zealand – especially by Bill Manhire in the *New Zealand Listener*,[17] and Peter Simpson in *Islands*[18] – as well as, eventually, in Australia and the UK, including one by Desmond Graham in *Stand*, entitled 'Mudbacked Mirrors', which so impressed Curnow that he took the unusual step of writing to him: 'it makes the kind of sense about the poems that touches my own, quite uncannily in places'.[19] The book appeared in time for Curnow to read from and speak about at a lecture and public reading at Victoria University on 31 August as well as at a session, on the long poem, of the PEN Writers' Conference held at the university immediately afterwards. Despite his misgivings about the conference ('Curious, but true', he wrote to Tony, 'this kind of public exposure on the small & bloodyminded NZ literary scene is much more trying than in, say, Washington, among strangers.'),[20] his readings were extremely well received, and on the same weekend he was interviewed about the book by Elizabeth Alley for the Radio New Zealand Concert Programme, whose talks editor at this time was Fiona Kidman.[21] Later in the year he returned to Wellington to read at the Poetry Society, and the following year the volume won the New Zealand Poetry Book Award for 1979.

There was one particular poem in the sequence, however, which a number of readers and commentators found highly offensive. The occasion of 'Dichtung und Wahreit' (a title drawing attention to Goethe's discussion of the relationship between poetry and truth) was a recently published novel by M.K. Joseph, entitled *A Soldier's Tale* (1976), whose literary-minded narrator – known simply as Bom – told the story of a rough, working-class British soldier Saul Scourby (using a mixture of Scourby's words and Bom's own educated gloss on them) which had exercised a compulsive fascination on him since Scourby had first told it to him nearly three decades earlier. In an incident in France towards the end of the Second World War Scourby had 'saved' a desperate young French woman (Belle) from partisans seeking revenge for her betrayal of fellow partisans to the Gestapo, by murdering her himself. During the course of a weekend, as the partisans wait for his unit to move on, he forces himself violently on the woman, who gradually (in what is presented as a kind of love story) yields to his advances, but when he realises that there is no way he can save her from the atrocities she will suffer under the partisans he cuts her throat, leaving her draped on her bed with candles and a crucifix, for the enraged partisans, cheated of their revenge, to discover.

Curnow found the novel personally repellent because it struck him as a 'sentimentally fudged'[22] presentation of sex, rape and murder, and anticipated that some amongst those local readers who recognised Joseph's novel behind the poem's savage reduction of its narrator's 'literariness' to the crude and violent obscenity of the events themselves might read it as an unfair and gratuitous insult to a colleague widely respected as a gentle, humane scholar.

> What a fucking shame, this man the one the man
> I know knew decided, if you want a job done well
> do it yourself, and he did and he left her in a bath
> of blood from the hole in her neck which he carved
> in soldierly fashion, a way we have in the commandos,
> after the fuck he knew she didn't of course
> was her last, and a far far better thing, wasn't it?
> than the bloody fuckup it would have been if he'd left her
> to be unzipped and jack-the-rippered by a bunch
> Of scabby patriots with no regimental pride.

However, he did not identify either the novel or its author in the poem, seeing its relevance to *An Incorrigible Music* (as a poetic sequence about violence in human nature and history) as more general: it enabled him to explore 'the aspect of homicidal violence as entertainment'.[23] The poem from this point of view was closely related to poems like 'Leviathan' and 'A Balanced Bait' which explored the aspect of violence as recreation, the poet himself implicated in such violence as he enjoys the everyday activities of fishing and gardening.

Despite the contretemps over 'Dichtung und Wahrheit' Curnow was buoyed by the impact which *An Incorrigible Music* made at the PEN conference in Wellington and in other public readings, and he was pleased with the interview about it with Elizabeth Alley. Younger poets had taken notice of it. He felt that he had now definitely re-established himself as a significant contemporary presence in the local scene, and that he was beginning to be noticed again overseas, in the UK in particular. By the end of October, he was writing confidently to Tim, 'Make no mistake, I have new things on the way.'[24] By the end of the following year, 1980, he was well on the way towards a new collection.

Chapter Twenty-nine

A Growing UK Reputation,
You Will Know When You Get There,
1980–81

I promise myself [to catch up on local books] when one or two philosophers
& poets permit. Most of my reading is a sort of composting for poems, &
digging over my own patch for the next crop. Either side of the puddle
[the Tasman Sea], the taste is for fast foods. My things don't smell of the
takeaway bar, either.[1]

'The next crop': new poems, 1980

Early in 1980 Curnow began an eighteen-month period of concentrated creative
writing reminiscent of the earlier periods 1955–56, 1970–71 and 1977 which had
produced the major poems of *Poems 1949–57* (1958), *Trees, Effigies, Moving Objects*
(1972) and *An Incorrigible Music* (1979), and by mid-1981 he had largely completed
a new collection – *You Will Know When You Get There* – which was published a year
later in 1982. It contained some of what were to become his best-known shorter
philosophical lyrics ('You Will Know When You Get There', 'The Parakeets at
Karekare' and 'The Weather in Tohunga Crescent'), as well as three major longer
poems remarkably different in style and tone – the philosophically dense and
challenging 'Dialogue with Four Rocks', a virtuoso surrealist fantasy ('Organo ad
Libitum'), and a free-flowing historical narrative poem (entitled 'A Fellow Being')
about a flamboyant early twentieth-century Auckland entrepreneur, Dr F.J. Rayner.

Curnow certainly thought of his new collection (there were fourteen poems altogether) as possessing 'a unity of mood and purpose',[2] and even briefly contemplated declaring it 'a sequence', as he had *Trees, Effigies, Moving Objects* and *An Incorrigible Music*, but though it often drew on familiar locations (Karekare, Washington, Sicily) it did not deploy them as a structuring device to generate large-scale political and historical polarities as the earlier volumes had done. The shift that occurs in these new poems of the 1980s is reminiscent of the shift that occurred in the 1940s from the public poetry of *Island and Time* and *Sailing or Drowning* to the more personal vision of the poems of *At Dead Low Water*, though it is less dramatic, more a matter of the personal displacing the political in the foreground of the poems, of the political receding to the background. This shift of perspective is also reflected in the variety of tone and subject matter of these later poems – especially in the humour and playfulness that accompanies their more sombre moments – and in the newly energising force of Curnow's use of syllabic measures, which from this time on become his preferred mode of versification. A much freer deployment of enjambment, across lines and stanzas, gives a distinctive mobility, an often breathless rapidity, to the movement of the verse and this is reinforced by a distinctive prosody that plays with multiple ambiguities of syntax and punctuation. 'De-punctuate' is an instruction Curnow often writes to himself across early drafts of the poems of *You Will Know When You Get There*, accompanying his reworking of conventional metres and stanzas as he tries out a variety of syllabic patterns.

Perhaps the most notable change in a number of the poems of *You Will Know When Get There*, after the deeply pessimistic vision of human violence in so much of *Trees, Effigies, Moving Objects* and *An Incorrigible Music*, is their changing perspective on death. It would be putting it too simply to generalise that Curnow's poems after the 1970s are more 'accepting' of death (a poem like 'Dialogue with Four Rocks', for example, contains a grimness of vision continuous with poems of the 1970s), but again and again in the late work the fact of death, pain and loss underpins awareness of the pleasures offered by the 'continuum' of the transient, ongoing physical world – of commonplace natural objects and events, ordinary human activities (walking, observing, thinking, dreaming, remembering), and of the astonishing world of imaginative language itself. The Australian poet and critic Chris Wallace-Crabbe spoke of a 'new joyousness mak[ing] itself felt in the poetry' in the 1980s, 'an air which I would call', he went on, 'at the risk of sentimentality, falling in love with life all over again'.[3] It would be going too far to claim that the late poems articulate (like Ezra Pound's late *Cantos*) an earthly paradise in such terms, but the poems repeatedly discover, in their acts of reflection on objects, events and people, moments of delight and astonishment in their saving otherness and uniqueness – in the spectacular colours of the gingko tree, the uniqueness of the reef heron's sound, the resilience of the individuals who populate the poems. Death presides over such a world, is a condition of its existence. But if the theology of Original Sin lurks behind the image of man as by nature a killer in *An Incorrigible Music*, the theology behind the vision in Curnow's late poems might best be described in the paradox of the Fortunate Fall. The 'continuum', one of Curnow's favourite later terms for the world of spatio-temporal contingency, is a saving order, protecting consciousness from the nightmare of non-existence or total solipsistic self-absorption.

The earliest of the poems Curnow wrote for *You Will Know When You Get There* revealed the lighter, more casual elements of humour and play that entered the poetry at this point. 'The Ocean Is a Jam Jar' was a *jeu d'esprit*, comparing poetic reputation with the size of fish, which he tossed off for the editor of *London Magazine*, Alan Ross, then visiting New Zealand, after meeting him at the Steads' in March 1980. 'It's not often', Curnow wrote to Tim, 'that a poem gets written before breakfast – after a late night – revised after breakfast, & placed so nicely by dinner time.'[4]

'A Passion for Travel', drawing on memories of visits to Sicily in 1974 and 1978, offered a witty linguistic excursus on the textual difference between the words 'erotic' and 'exotic' and the promiscuous couplings of the worlds they refer to 'after dark' (outside, that is, the printed page). Based on a proofreader's textual correction, cancelling the 'r' in erotic and substituting an 'x' to make the word exotic, it is the inextricable mingling of the erotic and the exotic in the actual world to which the words refer, which generates the wit and play of the poem, including delighted plays on the letters (and syllables) 'ex' and 'ar' throughout.

'An Excellent Memory' contained an affectionate memory of a reception in Washington at which the New Zealand ambassador's wife, Pat Laking, recited the whole of Charles Brasch's 'Parting' (with its memorable concluding line, 'Distance looks our way') by heart.* 'After Dinner', a poignant 'familial poem',[5] in memory of Curnow's uncle, Arnold Wall, offered an economical character portrait, charac- terising Wall at the end of his long life after his own dry, scholar's fashion, and through images derived from his conversation and appearance. A comment on D.H. Lawrence ('Terrible young man. / Ran away with my friend Weekley's wife.') places Wall humorously in a much earlier generation, and an image of the white bandage covering his left foot (gangrene 'in the door / and pressing hard') gener- ates a tribute to his mountaineering feats. Death is the last of the icy challenges he

---

* Although Curnow dates the occasion in the poem itself as '8 November 1974, just about / midnight, give or take a few minutes', his own memory failed him on this occasion, since the event actually took place during his trip to Washington in 1966. Curnow later confirmed the mistake to Peter Simpson, who was editing a collection of Curnow's critical writings. He did not later correct the mistake when the poem was reprinted, however, allowing the precision of the notation to stand, notwithstanding its inaccuracy.

will be facing, compared with the 'whitenesses' he had conquered throughout his life as a mountaineer ('Other whitenesses / were summits, mountain faces, / alps both Southern and Swiss, / Tibet, one icy toehold / after another, still climbing now / in the thinnest air.'). Wall's son Ted was deeply moved by the poem, by the humane image it created of Wall's civility and unsentimental acceptance of the fact of impending death.

'A Reliable Service', remembering a fifteen-minute ferry trip between Paihia and Russell in the Bay of Islands, offered yet another of the seemingly more casual and varied occasions that often sparked poems from this time onwards, hinting at personal death but without any of the larger historical and political resonances of the poems of the 1970s. In the poem, Chris Miller suggested, 'Curnow makes of his own hypothetical death a solipsistic metaphor for the end of the world. The world, perceiving the fallacy, continues unabashed.'⁶ The transient 'moment's mixture' of the scene observed from the *Bay Belle* is presented as if freeze-framed in a vividly coloured picture postcard – as if, that is, time has suddenly stopped. The ensign on a ketch observed slogging seaward is suddenly arrested 'mid-flap', as if 'printed and / pinned on a wall at the end / of the world.' In the light of such possibilities of meaning, other commonplace details in the poem also become strangely suggestive. '[T]he white water / shoves Paihia jetty back' gives a sensation not of the forward momentum of the ferry but of the land retreating, backing away. 'Nobody aboard but the two of us' perhaps invites the question, who is the second person referred to here? If he is the 'boatmaster', might he not also suggest Charon, the figure of classical mythology who ferried the dead across the River Styx to the underworld? Other resonances attach to the reference to the ferry's ostensible but unnamed destination, Russell ('No lunch / over there either, the place / at the beach is closed.'), and even more so to the seeming anti-climax of the poem's concluding sentence: 'That / will be all, I suppose.' If the poem is read not simply as the depiction of an outward scene but as an inward scenario, involving a mind and feelings preoccupied with death, the final sentence becomes a poignant statement about its finality and ultimate mystery, and about the limits of what might be said about it.

By the mid-1980s these and one or two other shorter poems had been accepted by *Encounter* and *London Magazine* for publication in the UK, and alongside them Curnow had embarked on a number of more ambitious landscape-based philosophical lyrics, extending themes in his poetry of the 1970s. 'The Parakeets at Karekare' and 'You Will Know When You Get There' were both Karekare-based, deeply considered meditations on language and the dilemma of representation, on ageing and personal death. 'The Weather in Tohunga Crescent', exploring the same rich vein of ideas and personal experience, 'digging over my own patch for the next crop',⁷ also revisited his long-standing interest in the nature of art itself.

'The Parakeets at Karekare', like 'An Incorrigible Music', attempts to characterise the sound made by a group of brightly coloured parakeets (Australian
rosellas) in brief flight before they suddenly disappear, in the space of 'less than
a step and a wink', into the darkness and silence at the base of an overhanging
cliff face. The raucous sound of these birds is anything but like that of 'the small
wind-instruments' in the throats of the reef herons in the earlier poem, and the
poet's initial painterly characterisation, in a kind of synaesthesia, is in terms of
the vividly expressive colours of the birds' plumage, by way of contrast with the
monotonous 'sounds' of the scene (the 'monologue' of the sun, the 'long winded
sea', the silence at the base of the cliffs) around them:

> The feathers and the colours cry
> on a high note which ricochets
> off the monologue of the morning sun
> the long winded sea, off Paratohi posturing
> on a scene waiting to be painted.
>
> Scarlet is a squawk, the green
> yelps, yellow is the tightest cord
> near snapping, the one high note, a sweet-sour
> music not for listening.

As this 'moment's mixture' suddenly collapses into silence ('Darkness and a
kind of silence under / the cliff cuts the performance') the speaker is left, as if
stranded, with the problem of representation, which is always *after* the event:
how to recall the unique spatio-temporal singularity of the parakeets' colourful
visitation. 'Can scavenging memory help itself?' he asks. Can memory assist to
retrieve that brief passage of spectacular, cacophonous flight? Perhaps memory
cannot *but* make such an effort (it can't 'help itself'), but what kind of operation
does it perform on 'the moment's mixture'? Does it simply 'help itself', pick
and choose whatever it likes? And if memory 'scavenges' on the scene, like a
hawk on offal, how can such an act even remotely be said to 'recover' or represent
the original moment? The multiple meanings of 'help itself', played off against
each other, thoroughly destabilise the idea that there is any simple relationship
between memory and the event.

The same luminosity of detail occurs in 'You Will Know When You Get There',
one of Curnow's most widely anthologised later poems. The scene is Karekare,
the time late afternoon as the sun pours the last of its light 'out of its tank in the
sky' onto the glinting wet-metalled road winding down to the beach and over
the sea (which 'gathers the gold against it', as Pound in his *Cantos* envisioned

the light absorbed into and intensified by the beautiful, star-studded mosaic ceiling of Galla Placidia's tomb in Ravenna). The speaker, walking 'the last steep kilometre' to the beach with a bag to collect mussels, is wholly alone because of the lateness of the day and the season ('Nobody else comes up from the sea . . . and nobody else goes down'), and has 'an arrangement with the tide' – 'the ocean to be shallowed three point seven metres, / one hour's light to be left'. He passes two boys with a campfire on the beach, but no one speaks, the 'hesitancy to speak' being 'a hesitancy of the earth rolling back and away / behind this man', as if the speaker is an apparition, somehow disembodied from the physical setting from which he emerges. As he descends the beach towards the receding surf, heavy waves pound the sea-floor: 'A door / slams, a heavy wave, a door, the sea-floor shudders. / Down you go alone, so late, into the surge-black fissure.'

Wonderfully rich in its particulars ('You've never got the feeling of Karekare better', Stead commented),[8] the poem also creates a heightened, almost preter-natural aura of mystery around the commonplace events it describes. The profuse light shed by the setting sun – in so many of Curnow's poems a prelude to vision (introducing a moment of visionary identification with the poet's father in 'An Evening Light', for example) – leaves the speaker poised between belief and unbelief in the possibility of a spiritual or divine presence 'sponsoring' or sustaining the scene. The 'dammed reservoir' (damned?) in the sky from which the light pours is 'Too / credibly by half celestial', seeming to half-invite belief in its otherworldly origin (and perhaps alluding to Milton's passionate address to 'Celestial Light' in the opening lines of Book III of *Paradise Lost*). However, this mental gesture is counterposed to the colloquial meaning of the phrase 'too . . . by half' (as in 'too clever by half', so clever as *not* to be clever at all), which negates any suggestion that the light has a spiritual source and insists on its purely *given*, physical character, manifest (as Curnow put it in 'A Balanced Bait') only by *what* it lights – the glinting metal on the road, the shimmering sea surface, the varying opacities of the summits, trees and cloud formations – and by the explicitly physical character of the images (tank and reservoir) describing it. The vision at the end of the poem, as the light vanishes, is of a sudden, overwhelming engulfment by blackness: a crashing wave as of a door abruptly slamming, and a shuddering sea-floor as the wave recedes, opening up a 'surge-black fissure' into which the speaker, alone, 'goes down'.

'The Weather in Tohunga Crescent', completed early in 1981, is perhaps the most 'breathless' of all the poems in *You Will Know When You Get There*, a triumph of syllabic versification, and almost entirely 'de-punctuated' throughout its fourteen quatrains. In fact the subject itself might be literally described as 'breath-lessness', the evocation of a moment (as the poet sits in his 'usual chair' at Tohunga Crescent, pen in hand as if poised to write a poem, observing the scene across

Hobson Bay) when the wind suddenly drops and the scene becomes 'unnatu-
rally' calm, as if the '"life support system"' of the time- and wind-energised visible
material world had suddenly been switched off. It is as if the sheer, breathless
momentum of the lines, in which almost every line and stanza runs over into the
next, itself struggles to break the overwhelming sense of stasis and entrapment
in the static 'moment's mixture' the poem struggles retrospectively to articulate.
One of these images (recalling the spectacular dive of the 'gannet impacting / on
a wire' in 'A Small Room with Large Windows') is of a 'single gull' which 'steeply
/ stalling' – as if its engine had suddenly cut out – 'dead-centred the hole // in a
zero the stillest abeyance / and vanished into the morning's / expressionless waterface' in Hobson Bay. Another, recalling Hobson Bay's herons in 'The Kitchen
Cupboard' and 'An Incorrigible Music', describes 'Seven stilts / at a standstill',
as if posed formally for one of Audubon's superb paintings in his classic *Birds of
America* (1840): 'a study in black // and red beaks all the better to / stab with are
modelling for Audubon / mounted on sand in the frame of your / own choice'.

Towards the conclusion of the poem, as 'the world you // didn't switch off'
reasserts itself, the wind returns, and the static cloud cover (now a 'spongy firma-
ment') begins to drizzle, wetting the paper over which the speaker's pen has been
poised. The poetic impulse dissipates as suddenly as it appeared: 'put the pen
down go indoors'. '[T]here's evidently something / up there', the speaker adds,
'and the thing is the spirit', a 'thing' as unpredictable in its comings and goings as
the breath of life itself or the breath of poetic inspiration:

> whistle for it wait for it
> one moment the one that's one too
> many is the glassiest calm an
> 'intimate question' for the asking.

The '"intimate question"' raised by this particular paused moment – which
is 'one too many', producing a calm glassier than any other – will never actually
be asked (hence its inverted commas) since it is the final 'pause' (a pause *without*
the resumption that enables consciousness to ask questions about it) of personal
death. The perception here is of a piece with 'the shot / in the dark I shall not
hear' at the conclusion of 'Dialogue with Four Rocks', or the always-withheld-
from-consciousness final knowledge implied in the sentence 'You will know when
you get there'. The imminence of personal death shadows the poem throughout,
producing a kind of parallel meta-discourse to that about the relation between
art and the world. The recurrent references to the world as if it were an intensive
care ward of a hospital, with a life-support system to be switched on or off, signify
the sheer fragility of individual consciousness in the face of a pause as arbitrary,

unpredictable and final as death. The mid-flight engine failure that produces the unpremeditated vanishing of the gull into the 'expressionless waterface' as it dives into the abyss of 'the hole in the zero' occurs 'when it's your *turn* in the usual / chair to stare up into the cloud-cover' [author's italics]. 'Turn' is wonderfully expressive: death is inescapable, unpredictable, hanging on a thread as fragile as a heart attack or a stroke.

Yet, despite the personal preoccupation with death, poems like 'You Will Know When You Get There' and 'The Weather in Tohunga Crescent' are not grim or pessimistic as many in the previous decade were. The sheer energy and momentum and wit of the writing, and the vivid, unpredictable play of imagination with ideas, with fantasies, with puns and word plays, and with the 'phenomenological welter' of the physical world, convey something of the 'divine hop, skip and jump' which Nietzsche saw as the envy of philosophers stuck with the leaden discourses of metaphysics, ethics and aesthetics. Whatever the limitations of consciousness and the world in which it is rooted, the poems invite readers to celebrate (in Stevens's terms) 'the lion in the lute', their achievement as an imaginative statement matching 'the lion locked in stone', the sheer, ongoing, given, time-bound and death-bound reality of existence.

By October 1980 Curnow felt confident enough to write to Tony that: 'If the summer is productive, I should have enough for a new small book.'[9] By mid-January he had written another major new poem, 'Dialogue with Four Rocks', and revised 'Organo ad Libitum', whose earliest version he had tried unsuccessfully to place with *London Magazine* and *Encounter* in mid-1980. Then between February and April 1981 he worked on a long, nineteen-page narrative poem ('A Fellow Being') about the life of Dr F.J. Rayner (1875–1931). With the completion of these three long poems, the new collection was substantially in place, and 'A Fellow Being' provided the initial title of the manuscript which he eventually sent to Dennis McEldowney at Auckland University Press in August.

In 1980, however, as the new crop of poems began to emerge, Curnow's interest had also been drawn, for the first time in nearly two decades, to new developments in critical discussion about New Zealand poetry.

'Brand-name poetics': Stead's 'From Wystan to Carlos' and 'open form'

The relationship between Curnow and Stead was important to both during the writing of *You Will Know When You Get There*. Curnow showed most of the poems to Stead, and he appreciated Stead's always tactful general appraisals and his acute comments on points of detail. Stead at this time was also working on a significant new collection of his own, *Geographies*, and Curnow in turn often commented at length, equally tactfully, on drafts of the poems which Stead showed him, including sending him five pages of notes on 'Yes T.S.', one of the long poems in *Geographies* which he particularly liked.

However, there were also tensions in the relationship with Stead at this time. In 1979 Stead published a lively polemical article in *Islands* 27,[10] the text of an address he had given to the Writers' Conference in Wellington in August of that year. Its title, 'From Wystan to Carlos: Modern and Modernism in Recent New Zealand Poetry', played on the coincidence that the first-born sons of Curnow and one of the main later-generation figures in New Zealand poetry – Ian Wedde – had the same Christian names, respectively, as W.H. Auden and William Carlos Williams. Auden and Williams, Stead went on to argue, were representative of earlier and later twentieth-century movements in poetry in English, including in New Zealand: a 1930s 'truth-telling' realist (or 'modern') Auden generation who were inheritors of the Georgian realism of poets like Sassoon and Owen, and a 'modernist' generation (its founding figures Ezra Pound and Eliot of *The Waste Land*, as well as Williams) whose poetics – formal openness, emphasis on 'maximising . . . linguistic energy',[11] freedom from traditional prosodies and logical narratives, and an emphasis on enacting experience as a process rather than encapsulating it in a closed, end-driven product – rejected the notion that poems were simply truth-telling vehicles for the proposition of ideas and beliefs (moral, political, religious, nationalist, or otherwise). Turning to New Zealand he argued that poets from the 1930s to the 1950s, including Curnow, were affiliated to the Georgian-derived realist mode of the Auden generation, aiming to make poems the vehicles of 'the truths of history, politics, economics'[12] – from this perspective there was no fundamental distinction between the 'Curnow' and 'Baxter' generations of poets of the 1930s and 1950s, merely a difference of subject matter – and that it was not until the 1960s that '[a] new wave of young New Zealand poets discovered what I'm calling the Modernist tradition'.[13] The particular contemporary poets he had in mind, in addition to Wedde, were David Mitchell, Alan Loney, Murray Edmond, Alan Brunton and Bill Manhire.

Stead reiterated throughout that although he had a personal preference for modernist poetics it was not his purpose to argue that modernism was better than the earlier tradition of post-Georgian realism (good and bad poems could be written in both modes), but nevertheless insisted that what he called 'the tide of literary history'[14] was towards 'all that is characteristic of Modernism at its best'.[15] Furthermore (whether deliberately or not) the rhetorical frame of his article loaded the vocabulary in which he discussed modernism with positive connotations, and Georgian realism (the 'modern') with negative. Curnow was featured strongly, not only as the main critical voice of realism, placing great emphasis on 'truth' and 'reality' in his anthology introductions, but as one of the leading practitioners from the 1930s to the 1950s (along with Fairburn, Glover and Baxter) of poetry written according to its principles. Curnow's more 'open' later poetry, Stead went on to argue, illustrated the new literary history he was himself proposing, though the shift in his verse had occurred 'without [his] being aware of it'. Curnow's poetic 'silence' from the end of the 1950s until *Trees, Effigies, Moving Objects* in 1972, he argued, when his poetry assumed 'at least some of the features . . . of Modernism',[16] was clear evidence of the exhaustion of the earlier 'realist' phase in his own and New Zealand poetry generally.

It is difficult to know quite how Stead thought Curnow would react to the way his poetry and critical thinking were recontextualised and reinterpreted in the article. Curnow did not directly engage with Stead about the 'shaky premises' and 'wrong conclusions' which he detected in it,[17] though he made highly critical annotations in his copy of *Islands*, and drafted copious notes about it. Listing at length Stead's vocabulary of good (modernist) terms and bad (realist) terms ('closed, conceptual, narrative, logical, moral, artificial, organized abstraction, "mental structures" and so on') he noted that 'the whole discourse is loaded with morally arm-twisting terms', and repeatedly used the term 'mystification' to describe the 'touch of religious "uplift"'[18] he detected in Stead's account of modernist 'open form' as aiming 'to invade, to absorb life, almost to become indistinguishable from it, to collapse conceptual distinctions . . . to get nearer to the true feel of experience'.[19] For Curnow, Stead's notion of a modernist, 'open form' poem as attaining a 'life-likeness in the very absence of those mental structures which life as we live it moment by moment doesn't have'[20] was quite simply a contradiction. Unless one is a Platonist 'mental structures' are inevitably part of 'life as we live it moment by moment'; they cannot be divorced from it.

As might be expected, given the constant emphasis Curnow had given to aesthetic issues relating to language and poetic form throughout the 1930s and 1940s – indeed, from the time of *Poetry and Language* (1935) onwards this provided the single most distinctive contribution he made to thinking about New Zealand poetry in those decades (and after), and was at the forefront of his own poetic practice – he was also hardly likely to be impressed by Stead's argument that in this period 'technical problems were glossed over or brushed aside'.[21] 'Nearly every poem in "Island & Time"', Curnow noted privately to himself, 'is a formal experiment':

CKS will not disagree, that the variety of stanzaic & prosodic forms here speaks for itself. At least five of the stanzas were my own invention. The metres, mostly I think, are not at all mechanical. The art of metrical verse, with or without rhyme (& I did a lot of quite elaborate rhyming) consists in marrying both the metre & rhyme with the language as spoken, 'natural momentum of the syntax' (Yeats). Where CKS will part company with me, is (1) in refusing to recognize all this as 'technical problems'; for him, questions of prosody are irrelevant; (2) in his insistence that 'an uncertainty about the fundamental techniques and purposes of poetry' remained, since 'technical problems' had been 'glossed over or brushed aside'.[22]

Curnow did not raise any of these issues directly with Stead, but he did publish a brief letter in *Islands* responding to a footnote in 'From Wystan to Carlos'[23] in which Stead conjectured that Curnow might have 'consciously or unconsciously' derived his vertical arrangement of the word 'obelisk' – a modernist device – in 'Do It Yourself' (in *Trees, Effigies, Moving Objects*) from the back cover of *Freed* 4, one of the 'new wave' poetry magazines of the late 1960s. It was a seemingly minor point, and Stead had mentioned it as 'I suppose, no more than idle speculation', but its gist was to suggest that Curnow had been influenced into modernism by the 'new wave' of younger poets.

Curnow was unimpressed by Stead's interpretation of his silence, by the implication that he had been saved from oblivion by the zeitgeist, and through sheer luck (rather than through efforts of his own) been swept back into the progressive tide of literary history, 'illustrating it without being aware of it'. His career had in fact been punctuated by numerous such gaps since the 1930s, during which he felt constantly challenged to rethink his aims and directions as a poet, to 'make it new', and the process invariably involved consciously rejecting the zeitgeist, the 'tide of literary history'. He may have been deluded in believing this, or mistaken in the kinds of reading he gave to the zeitgeist, but it is not difficult to see why he would have felt that Stead's interpretation went to the core of his own self-belief as a poet, his long-held motives for being a poet at all.

In his letter to *Islands* about Stead's footnote – his only public comment on the article – Curnow insisted that 'the brief existence of *Freed* in the years 1969–72 passed unnoticed by me',[24] adding:

> It is nice to be credited with 'features of Modernism', if that is what they are; but really I was too ignorant of what the 'Freed poets' were up to, to profit in the slightest by their example. I think chronology is against the supposition, to say nothing of internal evidence in the poems themselves.[25]

In a brief concluding paragraph he allowed himself an ironic, glancing reference to the article as a whole, to its reconstruction of his own work to make it fit into the historical pattern proposed:

I see that Stead has anticipated what I might have said about literary history and poetic movements if he had 'discussed these matters' with me. I might not have put it as well as he has. I might have tried to add that one of the arts of literary history is making fits out of misfits, and that in 'poetic movements' it's often the misfits that matter.[26]

Writing to Stead himself in advance of the letter's publication, Curnow commented that he did not think there was anything 'seriously or personally contentious' in it, though he took objection to the spirit of religious zealotry he associated with the practitioners of 'open form', as Stead had characterised the movement:

[I]t wld be an indecency to air an objection, that the New Wave (pace one or two individuals) look to me a bit less interesting than you let them appear. May the Lord make them truly thankful.

I suspect (don't you?) that some of the Open Brethren would prefer the *end* of literary history to any other place in it? Every man his own messiah. When I'm burned for heresy I shall offer you the up-wind side of my stake.[27]

'If there's an Open Brethren', Stead replied, 'I suppose there's also a Closed Brethren – and one with similar anxieties about its place in history', adding, 'I think you possibly suffer from a sort of critical agoraphobia'.[28] The exchanges continued throughout May, politely, but with an edge on both sides. 'Do I simply find the "steady gaze" of the lit historian rather chilling to my preconceptions?' Curnow commented. '[The historian] is busy ridding himself of his own, while I'm busy (if at all) trying to make sense of almost everything except literature, & extract a poem or two with the tools I have learned to use.'[29] Again, '[p]erhaps I shall get used to being both a historical object & one who feels all the work has yet to be done, or done again', he wrote later.[30] In fact Curnow never resolved that conflict, and Stead does not seem to have been aware – or not wished to acknowledge – how deeply internal it was for Curnow, how little it had to do with where, precisely, the poet was placed within the literary historian's frame and terminology, and how much it had to do with belief in the freedom continually to make oneself and one's poetry anew.

Stead, on his side, seems to have been surprised at the strength of feeling he detected in Curnow's response to the article, and insisted that when the literary historian considered the landscape at large there was no reason why any feature – 'even a large and dominant one' (like Curnow) – should expect 'a friendly nod and a wave'.[31] However, his further explanation of the article's genesis was more personal: Curnow, it seems, had earlier criticised Stead's 'Scoria' for making 'too many concessions to the Poundian mode', a comment which in Stead's view showed so little understanding about 'what "open form" means and implies' that he decided that it was time 'to put some ideas about':[32]

> When you wrote your anthology introductions one thing you did (an important part of it) was to offer a set of criteria by which your own poetry might be seen and judged to advantage .... I think in your reaction to my Wgtn piece you don't take sufficiently into account that I'm quite as serious about my poetry as you are about yours (why pretend otherwise?). That means one is drawn to describe the landscape in terms which show one's own work to advantage – just as you did in your intros.[33]

It was Curnow, in response to this personal note in Stead's letter, who moved to heal the rift that had opened up, citing 'by way of self-reproach' Boileau's *'Que les vers ne soient pas votre eternal emploi / Cultivez vos amis'* ('Lest poetry permanently preoccupy you, cultivate your friends').[34] 'Yes, indeed I might have remembered better', he added, 'that you, no less than I, are concerned in all this as a poet, & how the history, the practice & the history are inseparables.' He apologised that he had not sent a copy of his *Islands* letter to Stead beforehand, 'not caring to invite, or seem to invite complicity', and asked if Stead would care to see some new poems of his.[35] Despite the apology Stead was upset when the *Islands* letter did appear in July, accusing Curnow of 'sniping' at him, and prompting another apology:

> Sniping at you was, & is, as far from my mind as from my heart, & the latter has been much troubled by [?] feeling that so it must appear. I *hoped* it could seem a civil exchange between equals (not to flatter myself!) & at least serve notice that you & I don't automatically agree about everything.[36]

The awkwardness between Curnow and Stead subsided at this point. The respect each had for the other, Stead for Curnow's poetry and Curnow for Stead's critical judgement, remained, but the potential for conflict also remained. In psychoanalytic terms Stead's relation to Curnow might be seen as a classic instance of what Harold Bloom called the 'anxiety of influence' – the need of a younger poet to assert himself against the influence of a powerful poetic forebear – and 'From Wystan to Carlos' might be read as a textbook example of what Bloom called 'misprision' – a misreading of Curnow (either deliberate or unconscious) with a view to displacing him from the centre and creating a space in the present in which his own work can be seen as its true inheritor.* Curnow, on the other hand, feared

---

* Harold Bloom, *The Anxiety of Influence: A Theory of Poetry* (1973).

being locked into the agendas of others, and resented the kind of co-option of himself that he read into Stead's article (as a kind of modernist *manqué*, in Stead's redefinition of the term).

The weakness in Curnow's 'position', during these exchanges, was quite simply that he was not especially familiar with the younger New Zealand poets whom Stead defined as introducing modernism to the country. Stead was far more widely read in contemporary New Zealand poetry (and fiction) than Curnow, and had continued to write a great deal about it – criticism which Curnow admired though he disagreed with its assessments of figures like Fairburn and Baxter. However, from the 1960s onwards Curnow ceased to read New Zealand poetry in a systematic way at all, though he picked up quite a lot in the casual course of his reading of magazines. One positive effect of 'From Wystan to Carlos' and of his exchanges about it with Stead was that he felt he needed to know more about the poetics of 'open form'.

By coincidence, the article appeared at the same time as a new anthology, *15 Contemporary Poets*, edited by a close friend of Stead's at the time, the poet Alistair Paterson, in which Curnow found himself prominently featured. The anthology – published by Grove Press in the United States, as well as in New Zealand – turned out to be a vigorous manifesto for 'open form' poetry (describing 'the traditional direction of poetry' as having 'undergone a permanent change' and *An Incorrigible Music* as placing Curnow 'immediately in the vanguard' of the new movement'),[37] though Curnow had been unaware – or not taken sufficient trouble to inform himself – of the fact. It is hardly surprising that he felt the pressure of co-option at the time, describing the anthology as a 'rather bizarre volume' to Tim:

> I'm a bit sore with Paterson (& maybe one or two others) who could have been more *open* with me when they negotiated for poems last year. The last thing I wish is to be identified with *brand-name* poetics of this dubious description. It's the Olson / Creeley / Duncan school – USA, Black Mountain College & all that – which is pandemic, of course . . . . I have the feeling of having been kidnapped by the wrong party.[38]

When he was opportunely asked to participate in the Turnbull Winter Lecture series in 1981, on the general topic 'New Zealand Through the Arts: Past and Present', Curnow broke a long critical silence to venture again into the field of poetics, engaging with what he took to be one of the key sources of 'open form' proselytising in New Zealand, the American poet Charles Olson's 1950 essay/manifesto 'Projective Verse'. His address, 'Olson as Oracle: "Projective Verse" Thirty Years On', published in 1982, was to be his last substantive involvement in

public debate about poetry in New Zealand. Apart from its immediate engagement with Olson and the discourse of 'open form' it was to provide invaluable
insights into his own later poetic thinking and practice.[39]

Death of Denis Glover, August 1980: 'my oldest, closest and best-loved friend'

Denis Glover's death, at 68, was sudden, after a fall while he and his new wife,
Lyn, were shifting house from Strathmore, overlooking Wellington harbour,
to Breaker Bay. Curnow wrote an obituary article in the *New Zealand Herald*,
and he and Albion Wright gave funeral addresses to the large gathering at the
chapel of the Karori Crematorium, at the request of Glover's son, Rupert. 'How
I got through the day, I hardly know', he wrote to Stead,[40] but his funeral tribute
was one of the most moving and eloquent he ever wrote, laced with personal
comments about his 'oldest, closest and best-loved friend' and singling out the
'passion for excellence' as the defining motive of his life – as poet and printer, and
man of action:

> I learned something from Denis, which death does not take away. Something –
> I hardly know what to call it, but I am *going* to call it the meaning of excellence. That
> will have to do. The meaning of excellence, and that nothing less is good enough. I am
> saying now, that he was my teacher, and my example, for nearly 50 years. I am saying
> this now. Before now, there was no need to say it. Denis would have laughed at the
> idea, which could never have crossed his mind. Nor did it ever cross mine. Not until
> now, while I am trying to tell my scrap of truth about him, in the presence of so many
> who knew him too.[41]

As for the public myth of Glover in later life as a boisterous, obstreperous
joker and womaniser who could never take himself or others seriously, offering
the spectacle, as Stead put it, of 'a good man destroying himself with booze, and
of a good poet publishing drivel',[42] Curnow emphasised the 'impatience' that
underpinned so much that seemed erratic in Glover's behaviour. He was 'impatient
with himself, impatient with the necessary second-rateness and third-rateness of
people and public affairs, impatient with the inescapable vulgarities and fatuities,
all the nonsense and inconsequence of our lives'. 'It was a splendid impatience',
he added. 'We owe it some fine examples of his wit and irony.' However, '[i]t was
also part of the price, for him, *of being himself*'. Behind his public 'comedian's
mask', which Curnow believed many 'mistook . . . for the man', was an elusive,
complex figure, perhaps an essentially solitary figure, like those Glover wrote

about in some of his finest poetry. 'He was more solitary in the later years than a few Wellington friends could have guessed', Curnow wrote to Stead, 'sighting him *only* on occasions when they picked him up & took him out.'[43]

'It was a great solitude which you made a society for me',[44] he had written to him 40 years earlier while he was overseas on naval service during the Second World War, and the personal gap created by Glover's death could never be filled. The gap was also a generational one, since Curnow was now the sole survivor of the thirties poets with whom his own beginnings as a poet were so closely linked. He enjoyed a clever couplet (parodying Mason's 'The Lesser Stars') which Lilburn sent to him ('Mason, Fairburn, Glover, are dead – / You're left with me and C.K. Stead'),[45] but Lilburn – also closely linked with his own earlier poetic endeavours – had himself by this time ceased composing music. For the last two decades of his life Curnow's was the solitary, still-creative voice of the 1930s generation, and his loyalties remained absolute. In 1981 he spoke at the launching of *The Letters of A.R.D. Fairburn*, selected and edited by Lauris Edmond, a long-delayed project initiated and pursued by Glover, and in the same year he saw Glover's Penguin *Selected Poems* through the press, proofreading the poems (which Glover had chosen before his death), and writing a 5000-word introduction, the last critical study of a particular author which he ever wrote.

Glover's last letter to Curnow, speaking of old friends, had mentioned John Schroder's recent death and Ngaio Marsh's failing health.[46] To Stead, Curnow spoke of these events as 'crumblings at the edge of one's small property in time. I don't dwell on them.'[47] In later years he did not dwell publicly on Glover's death either, but his eyes often brimmed when Glover's name was mentioned. In his interior world a portion of the land had slipped irrevocably.

The later poems of *You Will Know When You Get There*, 1981

After he returned to Auckland Curnow began work on one of the most challenging and demanding of the poems of *You Will Know When You Get There*, entitled 'Dialogue with Four Rocks'. In early October 1980 he wrote to Tony that the poem, at that stage 'about 60 lines', was 'still causing me headaches',[48] and to Stead, at the end of the month, that he was still 'quietly sweating out another 80 ll. poem'.[49] It was not until January the following year that he sent the completed poem (now 90 lines, in four sections) to Stead.

Even more uncompromisingly than the forbidding, alien tree presences in *Trees, Effigies, Moving Objects*, the rock formations in 'Dialogue with Four Rocks' prompted the poet into an encounter with otherness – with sheer, bedrock, unmediated, extra-linguistic reality – in its most seemingly obstinate and resistant manifestations, and the poem is driven by its awareness of the deeply paradoxical nature of the enterprise in which he is engaged, since imagination has nothing *but* language with which to engage with that otherness. In each of the four sections his primary approach is to offer vividly particularised images of rock formations, conducting his interrogations *within* the always already linguistically mediated details of the scene. In the first a storm-exposed rock-reef the size of 'a visiting beast' suddenly emerges on the beach at Karekare as the sand's level dramatically sinks – a 'thing' which confronts the poet with the unan-swerable question, 'I know you do you know me?' 'Nothing's either / covered or uncovered for ever', the poet responds enigmatically, as he imagines the rock-ap-parition disappearing in time, covered over again, as if naturally, by wind- and tide-driven sand and spinifex and lupin.

Nevertheless, the second section turns to another rock, as if attempting to answer the question posed in the first – this time, a huge, ominously overhanging rock at Karekare, 'the size of a small church', within whose skull-like 'wall of human bone' with its 'wig' of wind-blown trees and wreath-like chaplet of white-flowering clematis and gold-flowering kowhai, the poet imagines a colossal cerebrum 'thinking big'. What would the primordial utterance of this Big Wig be, *if* it were to speak? – what 'stony secret' about the nature of its own being would it dislodge? – the poem asks. The 'argument' of this section, rooted as it is in the vivid anthropomorphism of its description of the rock, remains unresolved. The rock remains irreducibly itself, refuses to dislodge its 'stony secret', and when it 'speaks' merely gives back to the questioning consciousness the same words and thoughts that consciousness brought to it. However, by remaining itself, it confirms a sense of self and identity for the speaker. And the 'unknowability' of the rock, its obstinate otherness, also confirms for the speaker the multiplicity of the world of time and change to which both it and the self belong – generating the multiplicity of the individual languages human beings bring to its understanding, and of the 'languages' of nature, 'the parakeet's brilliant remarks / the fluent silences of the / eel in the pool'.

However, this world of time and change (as Curnow's poetry never ceases to remind us) also has death at its centre – and death (and disease) are significant attributes of the complex symbolism the poet develops in his imagining of the rock. In the third section a rock face is imagined as a vivid female presence, its mouth a cave which children playfully clamber up to, but the speaker's sight is drawn to the macabre signs of disease and ageing in the 'creased' and 'cracked' complexion: 'yellow lichens ashy / patches thicken sicken / on the skin of the face / of the rock from spots the / size of the iris of a / mouse's eye to a smashed / egg the rock is wetted / by a weeping lesion'. This aged, ailing, weeping mother is anything but a *pietà* figure, or cleft Rock of Ages offering consolation to the dying, and speaks all too 'fluently' of disease and death as a given condition of life. '[I]t looks down I look up', the section concludes, 'a wink is sufficient.' A wink, a moment only – perhaps because to dwell on such a sight is intolerable, but also, perhaps, because such a grotesquely playful gesture is the only tolerable response to such suffering.

The fourth rock, also a 'mother rock', vividly recalls (from a shooting expedition in the 1940s) a scene in which the poet crawled through a blackberry-infested recess underneath a large rock seeking to put a wounded hare out of its misery. Identifying with the hare, he imagines himself now as listening for 'the shot / in the dark I shall not hear'. Death is 'the oldest-fashioned fate, / which never answers back', and this vision of personal death is the last of the speaker's imaginings sparked by the four rocks. The rock has the first word in the poem, as well as the last, unanswerable word.

The poem seems to have begun with what became its second section, with its dominating image of the silent rock-colossus (though both the self and the rock are in turn dominated, 'overhung', by the uproar of the sea, 'cupped' by the dense cloud above, and beyond that by 'the hot star' which 'nothing overhangs') suggesting the primordial (and non-spiritual) origins of the physical world. The other three sections emerged as spin-offs during the poet's 'dialogue' with this rock. The poem also went through multiple stanza rearrangements, ranging from three to six lines in length, before reaching its final form, in which the first two sections consist of seemingly randomly numbered blocks of lines broken up (again randomly) by mid-line spacings, and the third and fourth sections consist, respectively, of strict three- and four-line stanzas. Perhaps the single most important – certainly, the boldest – formal decision Curnow made, however, was to recast and revise the lines on syllabic principles: nine-syllable lines in the first section, eight- in the second, six- in the third and seven- in the fourth. No poem illustrates more clearly why Curnow was so uneasy about being identified with the practice of 'open form'. The poem is open in many respects but its openness is in a constant tension with the rigorous formal and prosodic requirements of the syllabic measures.

The poem also seems more 'open', seems to move much more freely, because so many of its lines had been 'de-punctuated' during revision, though earlier poems like 'Two Pedestrians with One Thought' and 'What Was That?' had already deployed the technique very effectively. He had firmly defended the practice to Glover – who criticised the omission of punctuation marks in the selections from An Incorrigible Music which Dudding published in Islands in 1978 – on the ground that 'I wanted syntax to justify itself without the aid of punctuation marks'. 'Tis syntax, syntax, that hath ravished me!' he added, alluding to Dr Faustus's ravishment by the charms of magic in Marlowe's play.[50] He also returned to this issue when he sent the manuscript of You Will Know When You Get There to

McEldowney, emphasising that it was primarily a means of disciplining his syntax, making the syntax work harder and more precisely to achieve his aims:

> Your editorial eye will notice that I have discarded punctuation to a great extent. But not entirely consistently, as a few of the shorter poems will show. This does become a matter of composition – a discipline of my syntax, as e.g. in the whole of the long title poem. I have discarded the convention where it has been no help to me; but there is minimal punctuation in places where otherwise its absence would look like affectation. If only orthodox punctuation were as well understood & unambiguous as it was to Browning's readers, there might be no such problems![51]

Nothing illustrates the 'disciplining' effect of 'de-punctuation' more clearly than the concluding lines of the second section of 'Dialogue', where the poet implores the rock to speak 'the word of a stony secret' (the 'primordial grunt / of the demiurgos', as he put it in an earlier draft),[52] a primal word which might establish a link between self/creator and world, providing the foundation or proto-type of all human consciousness of kinship with the natural world and with other human beings:

> I think the rock
> thinks and my thought is what it thinks.

The absence of punctuation in these lines compels the reader to consider, and hold in balance, various syntactic options. 'I think that the rock thinks' (that is, I'm not sure; I may be 'imagining' what is simply an absurdity; rocks can't think) is one option. 'I think. The rock thinks.' – is another, altogether a more declaratory statement that the self and the rock are two separate consciousnesses. The syntax of the next clause, 'and my thought is what it thinks', is also double, depending on the previous options: the substance of *my* thought is 'what the rock thinks', or, in a reverse transference, the *substance* of what the *rock* thinks is what I think. The conclusion thus holds in tension both the separateness and the inseparability of consciousness and world, self and rock, and the ground of that always ambiguous doubleness is the *word*, language itself.

In February 1981 Curnow wrote to Pearson that he was working hard on a long poem about F.J. [Frederick John] Rayner (1875–1931), the flamboyant Canadian-born entrepreneur who married the wealthy heiress of a Chicago meat-packing business. Rayner immigrated to Auckland in 1900, developed a successful business as a dental surgeon in Queen Street using new American electrical techniques, and became a wealthy property magnate in central Auckland with a palatial property on the lower slopes of Mt Eden in Epsom. He also built a fishing lodge at Lake

Above: With Douglas Lilburn (left) in Wellington in 1979. They first met in 1934, marking the beginning of a close friendship that lasted until Lilburn's death in 2001. Lilburn's setting of Curnow's poem 'Landfall in Unknown Seas', commissioned in 1942 to commemorate the three hundredth anniversary of Abel Tasman's arrival in New Zealand, has become part of New Zealand's classical music repertoire. This Jane Ussher photograph dates from a writers' festival in Wellington in 1979. (*NZ Listener, courtesy Philip Norman*)

Below: Curnow and Jeny at Tohunga Crescent, 1983. (*Bruce Connew*)

Above: With Anthony Thwaite at Karekare in 1986. From 1973 to 1985 Thwaite was literary editor of *Encounter* magazine, which had become an important avenue for Curnow's literary publication in the UK. (*Privately held*)

Below: With English author and academic Malcolm Bradbury at Karekare in 1989. They had first met in 1985 at the Toronto Festival. (*Privately held*)

Above: Curnow received the CBE for services to literature in June 1986. Shown here with Jeny after his investiture by the then Governor-General Sir Paul Reeves. (*Privately held*)

Below: Receiving the Queen's Gold Medal for Poetry from Queen Elizabeth II in 1990 during New Zealand's sesquicentennial celebrations. The award is offered irregularly on the recommendation of the Poet Laureate in the United Kingdom, who at that time was Ted Hughes. Curnow had also been awarded the Commonwealth Poetry Prize in 1989. (*Fairfax Media NZ EP/1990/0604/8A-F*)

Right: The Curnows stayed once again in Venice in 1988, on their fifth visit to Europe since 1978. This photo, by Jeny, was taken from their room at La Calcina on the Zattere, overlooking the Giudecca Canal with the bell tower and dome of San Giorgio Maggiore in the distance. It was used in a full-page presentation of Curnow in *Die Tageszeitung*, July 1992, featuring three poems translated by Joachim Sartorius. (*Privately held*)

Below: The Curnows were joined for the last four days of their stay in Venice by poet and critic Michael Hulse, visiting from Cologne. Hulse had avidly pursued publication possibilities for Curnow in Germany. (*Privately held*)

Above: At lunch with Anthony Thwaite (left) and fellow poet Peter Porter (right) at the British Library, a few days after his reading at the Poetry International Festival at the Royal Festival Hall in October 1998, during his last trip to London. (*Privately held*)

Below: Curnow and Jeny at Karekare, late 1990s. (*Privately held*)

Right: Curnow in 1997, photographed at home in Tohunga Crescent, Parnell. (New Zealand Herald/*newspix.co.nz*)

Below: Curnow surrounded by fellow writers at the Going West Books and Writers Festival in 1999, flanked far left by Vincent O'Sullivan and Hone Tuwhare (pointing) and far right by Maurice Shadbolt and Marilyn Duckworth, with historian Michael King holding the umbrella. A reading in Curnow's name is now offered every year at the festival. (*Courtesy the Gerrard and Marti Friedlander Charitable Trust*)

At the launch of Curnow's final volume of poetry, *The Bells of Saint Babel's*, in March 2001, at the home of publisher Elizabeth Caffin. Above: In conversation with C.K. Stead. A neighbour for many years in Tohunga Crescent, Stead was a long-standing literary friend whose response Curnow would often seek to a newly written poem. (*Privately held*)

Below: Before the speeches, from right, Elizabeth Caffin with Curnow's brother Tony and wife Elisabeth, Mattie Wall (daughter of Curnow's cousin Arnold Wall), centre, and Jeny in the foreground. (*Privately held*)

A photographic portrait of Curnow by Marti Friedlander, used on the Order of Service for his funeral in September 2001. As Terry Sturm commented in his speech to the University of Auckland Senate on Curnow's death, '[Curnow] received numerous awards for his work during his lifetime, though these mattered less to him than the next poem he hoped to write.' (*Courtesy the Gerrard and Marti Friedlander Charitable Trust*)

Rotoiti in the Bay of Plenty, and owned an expensive launch and numerous automobiles. In 1907 he purchased cheaply a large block of kauri-forested land on the west coast (an area on the westward side of the Waitakere Ranges from Anawhata southwards through Piha and Karekare to Whatipu) and for six years extracted and milled large quantities of kauri before selling out profitably in 1913 to the Government Railways Department. The last kauri in what had once been a magnificent forest was felled in 1921.

On the surface it would be difficult to imagine two individuals as different in their lives and careers as Curnow and Rayner. Yet in calling his poem 'A Fellow Being', Curnow set himself the provocative challenge of exploring similarities as well as differences between Rayner and himself – initially intrigued by the coincidence that the year of Rayner's death, 1931, was the year in which he himself had first visited the west coast as a young university student. In the poem's final section he imagines that their paths might have crossed on 'collusion course', 'your life-cycle and mine / humming the tune of it's finished / to the tune of it's just begun'.

Like 'An Abominable Temper' and 'Moro Assassinato', the poem drew on the Browningesque convention not of plotted narrative but character portraiture, in which Rayner's personality and the circumstances which shaped it are filtered through a variety of different perspectives. Like 'An Abominable Temper' also, 'A Fellow Being' is a self-portrait, integrating the poet's personal and historical concerns much more seamlessly, it might be argued, than the earlier poem, though it resembles 'Moro Assassinato' in its attention to the broader historical and political context of the protagonist's actions. 'A Fellow Being' evokes not only a largely forgotten actor in a piece of long-forgotten west coast history but the social and commercial context of Rayner's life in turn-of-the-century entrepreneurial Auckland.

For information about Rayner himself Curnow had few sources to draw on: some brief comments in the rambling reminiscences of one of Rayner's friends, the wealthy Auckland businessman and philanthropist Eliot R. Davis, *A Link With the Past*,[53] and a lively ten-page sketch of Rayner in a chapter entitled 'Audacious Pigmies, Ancient Giants' in Dick Scott's *Fire on the Clay: The Pakeha Comes to West Auckland*.[54] Throughout, the poem quotes directly from both sources, as well as drawing on the illustrative materials (photographs, advertisements and inscriptions) in Scott's narrative, and the effect (as with 'Moro Assassinato') is to give parts of the poem a strong documentary feel.

During the earlier stages of composition Curnow had written to Pearson about his efforts to find 'a grip (which still eludes me) on the subject of Dr Rayner .... He intrigues me in a personal way; the difficulty is to discover *why*.'[55] He builds this elusiveness into his development of the poem. It was Wallace Stevens, whose career as a legal partner in an insurance firm involved him in the world of business, who in one of his most provocative and enigmatic aphorisms wrote 'Money is a kind of poetry'. Provocative, because he knew that in the minds of most of his readers, brought up on romantic notions of poetry, the notion that making poems is in some way akin to making money would have seemed scandalous. However, it is precisely this possibility which 'A Fellow Being' entertains as a key to the kinship, 'the collusion course', between Rayner and the poet.

The phrase 'poetry of wealth' occurs in the poem's sixth section, in which Curnow dissolved what he called an *abstraction* – Rayner's huge wealth – into the many particulars of his business dealings in the dental profession, property speculation, the film industry and timber-milling ('if anything bothered me / I could just eat it'), and his lavish expenditure on luxury material goods, even (as 'a splendid cook') his pleasure in producing 'the finest grilled trout imaginable' caught from his launch at Lake Rotoiti. Such particulars – including 'Ethel his wife a lyric in her own right' – constituted the *poetry* of Rayner's wealth, his creative achievements as an entrepreneur. The notion that Rayner's wealth might be described as a kind of poetry became 'a bit of a crux', as Curnow wrote to Stead,[56] because it went to the heart of his unconventional identification with Rayner as 'a fellow being'.

Curnow seems to have been attracted by Rayner's flamboyance, by the bohemianism that Eliot Davis detected in him, by the sheer energy with which he pursued his goals, dubious as many of them were. Stead's description of the poem as 'buoyant' (its 'affirmative' tone making it 'a marvellous light and shade pair' with 'Moro Assassinato')[57] is also highly apposite. Much of it is playful, as if aiming to match the liveliness of its subject. Throughout, there are recurrent tongue-in-cheek allusions to Rayner's 'soul' being reincarnated in the poet, as if the coincidence of their 'crossing paths' at Karekare in 1931 had effected a rebirth. Throughout, also, there is Curnow's vivid sense of a world of nature which renews itself inexhaustibly, whatever destructions are wreaked by Rayner, by later equally entrepreneurial and consumerist generations, or by the poet himself. The poem ends on this affirmative note, with an image of a kauri cone from a regenerated tree bursting on the roof of the poet's bach at Karekare, 'where the paths cross and the / young trees know only how to grow.'

In June 1981 Curnow returned yet again to 'Organo ad Libitum', that strange, phantasmagoric, fast-moving piece blending outrageous humour and macabre images, in which the details of a funeral rite are juxtaposed and interwoven with a fantastic range of fables, fictions and myths celebrating the vitality of life. The poem is a kind of jazzed-up version of a Dance of Death. Curnow had sent his first version of it – written in a single movement, in three-line stanzas – to Stead in June the previous year,[58] then worked on it again over the summer of 1980–81, expanding it substantially, freeing up the lines and recasting it into nine sections of varying lengths, and interspersing more formally constructed sections (in strict four-, three- and two-line stanzas) with free-flowing 'ad libbed' blocks of verse utilising a variety of spatial arrangements on the page. Stead liked all versions of the poem as he read them (describing it as 'a marvellous performance' and 'one of my favourite Curnow poems'),[59] but it remained the one poem in *You Will Know When You Get There* which did not appeal to the magazine editors to whom Curnow sent it. 'It may turn out to be one of those works which the author likes better than anyone else does', he wrote to Pearson,[60] and at the time of the publication of the collection the following year was 'prepared for a few bewildered remarks about "Organo ad Libitum" (which pleases me)' while hoping that these might be balanced by the reception of his Rayner poem.[61]

'Somewhere behind the "Organo ad Libitum" poem', Curnow later wrote to Lilburn, 'was the Crem. service over dear Kathleen Alison, late university bursar here (full of your sound system stuff, as at Karori); but the organ, one of several, might be in S. Michael's RC, Remuera.'[62] The basic funereal and burial theme of the poem is announced in the opening stanzas, evoking the moment at the end of a funeral service when the coffin is solemnly carried out of the church towards a waiting hearse, to the accompaniment of (in this instance) Handel-like organ music ('*largo* it says / *e grave*'), and the poem returns to this base theme in the third section (the procession of cars to the crematorium and cemetery), in a brief sixth section (the departure of cars after the interment), and in the seventh section (the imagined thoughts of passengers, 'reprieved into the time of day', in the wake of the funeral rite).

Curnow's presentation of the ritual of burial in these sections, however, carries anything but the expected aura of solemn, religious formality. The ritual is less a sacred event than a profane, *human* event, merely. 'Time's up you're got up to kill', the poem's opening line, suggests that the ritual is a formal *re-enactment* of the deceased person's death, the vernacular 'you' (as throughout the poem) addressing both the formally arrayed corpse and the mourners themselves, who include the poet. The coffin, hoisted on the shoulders of its pallbearers, is described memorably as a 'black twelve-legged beast', carried with 'hobbling pomp', out of step with the rhythm of the organist's solemn music; and the ordinary, physical character of the organist's activities – whatever sacred mood he tries to create – is insisted on throughout, as 'he polishes the stool he rocks on / the bones of his arse / he reaches / for a handful of stops he's nodding / yes to your proceeding'.

At this point, in the middle of the first section, the poem makes the first of a series of virtuoso ad libbing leaps from the immediate scene to an imagined one which are astonishing in their variety and vitality, in this case to a famous passage in chapter four of Samuel Butler's New Zealand-based satirical utopia,

Erewhon (1872). In this scene Butler's narrator, lost amongst the towering terraces and glaciers of the Southern Alps, 'cut off from all one's kind' and beginning to doubt his own identity, dreams that the cliffs and precipices on a mountainside have been transformed into a vast organ at the top of which the gigantic form of Handel is seated, 'his head buried forwards towards a keyboard, and his body swaying from side to side amid the storm of huge arpeggioed harmonies that came crashing overhead and around' as if 'drowning out' with the power of his music the terrifying, identity-threatening otherness of the vast ice-bound alpine wilderness in which the narrator is lost.

The intensity of Butler's Handelian dream-sequence (so different from the awkwardly human trappings of the actual funeral service of the poem) is then followed by another breathtaking leap of imagination, in the poem's second section, to a memory of a hilariously raunchy scene from a blue movie by Walerian Borowczyk, *L'Intérieur d'un Couvent*, which Curnow had seen at Montparnasse in Paris during his visit to Europe in 1978. Like the funeral rite this scene also involves a chapel, a corpse and organ music. Released from their sexual inhibitions after poisoning the mother superior a bevy of nuns wildly celebrate their freedom by dancing naked in the chapel — a response to death which takes the form of an abandoned, orgiastic celebration of life:

> and they danced
> their hot pants down on the stony
> gallery for joy of their nubility
> crying 'La Mère est morte!' they
> swung on the bellrope naked making the
> bell-mouth boom at the sun
>   one
> sneeze of the gusting equinox
> whipped the doors from the bolts and up
> went the scarlet skirts of the cardinal
> dead leaves and fingers
>   flying
> to the roaring organ the guffaw
> of the daylight and the rain pouring
> from the outside in
>   the movie's
> over
>   will you get up and go?

'I suppose the test has been that the more death there is in a poem the more life it needs,' Curnow wrote to Stead:

No problem while Xtian afterlife was the general assumption. Was it beginning as early as 'Lycidas' – though Gray's 'elegy' hardly leans on religion, except that it's in a 'churchyard'. Not to dodge the existential dilemma, by what Camus calls the 'leap' sideways into faith or any other transcendence. So much for the 'serious'.[63]

In the poem's final section Curnow remembers a conversation with Domenico (the waiter he and Jeny had come to know at the café on the Zattere in Venice where they regularly had their morning coffee) in which the same sentiment is expressed: 'Domenico's / mother said and he quoted "life / is bitter we must sweeten the coffee" / shovelling the sugar'. Throughout, the 'life' in the poem is provided by its virtuoso ad lib imaginative flights which form a kind of counter-statement to the base theme of death's finality, in a formal musical pattern which is less that of a classical 'theme with variations' (where the scope of the variations is always formally controlled by the basic theme) than of a jam session in jazz, where each solo performer improvises freely from an initial musical 'statement' before returning to it and passing the performance on to the next solo improviser.

Curnow's improvisatory flights are astonishing in their variety and vitality. In the fourth section the scene is a hotel room in which the obligatory 'black book' ('the Gideons' bible') is contrasted with the life-affirming prismatic colours of the poet's own bedside paperbacks. In his earliest draft Curnow provides a formidable list of the philosophical authors concerned ('Plato / Schopenhauer Kierkegaard Nietzsche Husserl / Camus' – very much a list of those he had been reading as 'compost' for his poems at this time), but 'dissolves' them in his final version into a single striking image from one of the paperback covers ('there's this marvellous / meteorite or enormous / boulder of Magritte a motto for / Sisyphus …'). In the moving fifth section, the aircraft captain at the controls of the Air Zealand jet which crashed into Mt Erebus in the Antarctic is figured as an organist at his console, and the catastrophic moment of the crash itself linked to Butler's terrifying experience of 'dissolution of the self' in the Southern Alps:

                    mark
        the exits fasten your bible-belt
        or take-off
                        'the unlikely event
        'of an emergency'
                    he sits with his

> back to you 'busier than God' his
> instrument flashes the crash is
> programmed the music is magnified the
> size of the side of an Antarctic
> volcano
>   you disintegrate there
> *buzz buzz*
>   with or without your
> loved ones and a face the mirror has
> forgotten.

Perhaps the boldest of the ad libbed flights Curnow risks in the poem is the eighth section, whose first word – perhaps intended as a subtitle – is *'palingenesis'*. Curnow derived the term from the philosopher Arthur Schopenhauer, for whom it carried a specialised meaning, referring to a kind of metempsychosis (reincarnation of the soul) in which at death the body and individual consciousness are extinguished but the universal will-to-live (of which body, self and consciousness have been mere temporal embodiments) survives, generating a new, distinct temporal embodiment. Traditional theories of metempsychosis envisaged 'the transference of the entire so-called soul into another body', whereas palingenesis involved 'the *decomposition* and reconstruction of the individual in which *will* alone persists and, assuming the shape of a new being, receives a new intellect'.[64]

Curnow encountered the idea in Schopenhauer's major work, *The World as Will and Representation*, in a chapter entitled 'On Death and Its Relation to the Indestructibility of Our Inner Nature' as well as – expressed more simply and eloquently – in one of the essays in Schopenhauer's late *Parerga and Paralipomena*, 'On the Indestructibility of our Essential Being by Death':

> What dies goes to where all life originates, its own included. From this point of view our life is to be regarded as a loan received from death, with sleep as the daily interest on this loan. Death announces itself frankly as the end of the individual, but in this individual is the germ of a new being. Thus nothing that dies dies forever; but nothing that is born receives a fundamentally new existence. That which dies is destroyed; but a germ remains over out of which there proceeds a new being, which then enters into existence without knowing whence it has come nor why it is as it is. This is the mystery of *palingenesis*.*

---

* Arthur Schopenhauer, *Essays and Aphorisms*, trans. R.J. Hollingdale, Penguin, 1970, p. 72. Curnow's copy of this book was annotated at some length.

In his first draft Curnow confined himself to playing sceptically with the more specialised, abstract, post-Kantian vocabulary of Schopenhauer's meta-physics, with its opposition between pure, transcendental *Will* on the one hand (in which nature and human nature share in the unknowable being of the world as a numinous, will-driven 'thing-in-itself'), and *Idea* on the other hand – the merely phenomenal appearance (or representation) of that world under the guise of time, space and causation:

> your replacement's
>
> on his way the thing-in-yourself after the
> inconvenience of existence resumes its
> thing-in-itselfhood the biodegradable
>
> part recycles its degradations the
> resurrection's a fresh wreath every time . . . .

In the final version the abstractions disappear and are replaced by an extended 'beach scene' at Karekare, a *tour de force* (surely one of the strangest of the mythic visitations Curnow ever imagined at Karekare) in which the 'actual' recycling of the 'biodegradable part' into a new individual self occurs while the indestructible 'thing-in-itself' latent in the old self is spirited away into the elements of sun and sea. The organ which accompanies death achieves its last metamorphosis here into the storm-wracked sea itself, and the beach – curiously curtained off from the land by gauze-like mist – becomes a kind of chapel in which the rite of reincarnation occurs:

> naked on the beach
>   now storms from the west
> stand the sea on end
>   it's an instrument
> big enough to drown
>   accompanies you
> all the way down the
>   'cold front' feathering
> inland hanging its
>   gauzes uncloses
> closes teases you
>   don't see anything
> clearly

taihoa!
                your replacement's on
his way
        you're naked
                as the fish bottled
'in its element'
                lifted to the sun
and it's the same wave
                spirits you away
out to sea while the
                biodegradable
part picks up its heels
                recycles all its
degradations
        fresh
                wreaths every time and
no resurrections.

If Curnow takes a sceptical pleasure in Schopenhauer's idealistic notion of a primal will-to-life which survives its particular embodiments in individual selves and the phenomenal world – both in 'Organo ad Libitum' and in the playful idea of Rayner's essential 'being' undergoing a reincarnation in the poet himself – Schopenhauer might also be seen as one of the presiding philosophical influences, more generally, on the poems of *You Will Know When You Get There*. Poems like 'The Parakeets at Karekare' and 'Dialogue with Four Rocks' might be described as meditations on Schopenhauerian ideas in which particular phenomenal worlds are brilliantly captured by the poet's imagination, but their essential will-driven being as 'things-in-themselves' always remains elusive, teasingly alien to every effort of consciousness (driven by desire, regret, anxiety, anticipation) to elicit and articulate such being. Such poems offer a critique of Schopenhauer's idealism, but they reveal a fascination with the philosopher's efforts to explain the dilemma of the self's relation to the phenomenal world and to otherness without recourse to Christian ideas of transcendence, just as Freud found in Schopenhauer's notion of the Will a secular prefiguring of his own idea of the Unconscious.

In July 1981, at Stead's prompting, Curnow sent Donald Davie, co-editor of the *PN Review*,[*][65] his revised 'Organo ad Libitum', as well as 'Dialogue with Four

---

* Davie, a distinguished poet himself and author of a number of influential books on twentieth-century British and American poetry, replied to Curnow that he was 'delighted to be in touch with one of the rather few poets of the English-speaking world whom I am prepared to respect', recalling a first encounter with Curnow's poems, many years earlier, as a co-contributor to the *London Magazine* in the late 1940s.

Rocks', 'The Weather in Tohunga Crescent' and a slighter piece, 'You Get What You Pay For'. Davie, who greatly admired the new poems, sending them on to the general editor Michael Schmidt, who eventually chose all but 'Organo ad Libitum' for the magazine.[66] Apart from Davie's accolade, Curnow was especially pleased with *PN Review* as a venue, he wrote to Tony, 'because it has a transatlantic readership, and contributors, incl. old acquaintances like Richard Eberhart and Richard Wilbur'.[67]

He also held high hopes for the new collection of which these poems would be a part. None of his earlier collections – except perhaps *Sailing or Drowning* in 1943 – had had quite such a distinguished array of prior magazine credits, and the volume marked a breakthrough for the later work into the UK poetry scene, with no fewer than eleven of its fourteen poems appearing initially in *Encounter*, *London Magazine* and *PN Review*. He also thought carefully about the title of the new collection, eventually choosing 'You Will Know When You Get There' as the title poem, instead of 'A Fellow Being':

> Of all the poem-titles this is the one which suggests the character of the collection without interfering in the special business of any poem taken by itself. Or so it seems to me. None of the shorter titles does this. The next-best wld have been *Organo ad Libitum*, perhaps intriguing & suggestive, but for the few readers who wld get it in one, there might be many who would find a double-take or suspect some kind of erudite purpose. I hope you agree that it does have to be one of the poem-titles. I'm sure a good title cld be invented for the whole book, tho terribly hard to do this without seeming to prescribe over the heads of the poems; & such titles always (to me) look pasted-on.[68]

Curnow's concern was to avoid a title which might be reductive of the distinctive 'business' of individual poems, 'prescribing' how the poems might be read and depriving readers of the freedom to make their own discoveries of the links and differences between one poem and the next. With the exception of *Poems 1949–57* and *Trees, Effigies, Moving Objects*, this had been Curnow's habitual practice from his earliest collection, *Valley of Decision*, and was to remain so until his last, *The Bells of Saint Babel's*.

Chapter Thirty

Curnow and the Theory of 'Open Form', Apartheid, Brisbane Writers' Week, 1981–82

The phenomenological teaching is no better guarantee of art than the dogmas of Marxism, psycho-analysis, Catholic orthodoxy, or existentialism.[1]

Turnbull Winter Lecture series 1981: 'Olson as Oracle: "Projective Verse" Thirty Years On'

In May 1981, after he had completed the Rayner poem, 'A Fellow Being', and before he began his final revisions to 'Organo ad Libitum', Curnow turned his attention to the paper on Charles Olson's 'Projective Verse' which he was due to give at Turnbull House in Wellington in June. 'I suppose it's like me (as they say)', he wrote to Lilburn, 'to choose the most difficult & worrying subject in the whole poetical agenda – "open form" or "projective" verse – not so much the product as the theory of the thing. I don't know whether to expect a lynching party or dumb disdain from among the discipleship, if & when it reaches print.'[2] Writing guardedly to Stead, who asked to see a copy, he acknowledged that its subject was close to that of 'From Wystan to Carlos', but commented that the 'irritant' had been provided not by that article but by Alan Loney and 'one or two others': 'Yes, I think perhaps it *would* interest you, & I should be able to bear it if you find any of it, or even the whole of it, ill-considered.'[3]

Loney had recently published a negative review of Stead's collection *Walking Westward* (1979)[4] in which he referred briefly to 'Projective Verse' as a 'ground-breaking' essay – perhaps sufficiently for Curnow to think of him as one of Olson's 'discipleship' – but Curnow had chosen Olson's 1950 manifesto as his topic long before Loney's article appeared. The 'real' irritant (though the address included complimentary remarks about Stead and criticisms of Loney) was 'the shaky premises' of some elements in Stead's own essay,[5] and perhaps Paterson's claims for 'open form' in his anthology, *15 Contemporary New Zealand Poets*.[6] Writing the lecture 'took weeks of work & a lot of worry', he wrote to Pearson.[7]

Apart from a vein of running jibes at the 'proselytising' character of the projective verse movement – with its 'doctrinaire attitudinizing', its 'nervous nose for heresy', its 'born-again young poets', and its 'evangelical enthusiasm'[8] – the lecture's basic procedure was an attempt to unpack a number of key terms in Olson's essay, emphasising the differences between Olson's thinking and that of his supposed forerunners (especially Ezra Pound), and identifying what Curnow saw as largely 'traditional' or 'truistic' in terms like 'high energy-construct', 'composition by field' and 'form is never more than an extension of content'. His most sustained critique, however – the point at which the lecture relates most relevantly to Curnow's own practice as a poet and to his disagreement with Stead – was of Olson's instructional underpinning of the idea of the poem as a process:

ONE PERCEPTION MUST IMMEDIATELY AND DIRECTLY LEAD TO A FURTHER PERCEP-TION . . . . [G]et on with it, keep moving, keep in, speed, the nerves, their speed, the perceptions, theirs, the acts, the split-second acts, the whole business, keep it moving as fast as you can, citizen . . . . [A]lways, always one perception must must must MOVE, INSTANTER, ON ANOTHER.

'He says [perception] *must* do this, as if perception could possibly be followed by anything else', Curnow commented, adding: 'We don't just stop perceiving, one way or another, one thing or another, so long as we are conscious.'[9] What he detected here was the 'arbitrary conversion of a philosophical position into a system of poetics'.[10] That philosophical position was phenomenology, which Curnow presents by quoting at some length from Camus's comments (in *The Myth of Sisyphus*) on Edmund Husserl, its originator. Immensely attractive as a way of drawing attention to the richness of the world delivered to the mind by sense-perception, phenomenology in Curnow's view was simply insufficient as the basis of a poetic system, and his account of its insufficiency might serve as an epigraph to every poem he wrote from the time of *Trees, Effigies, Moving Objects* onwards:

That 'shimmering of phenomenological thought' is always disturbed, interrupted, accompanied by conceptions of all sorts; by aberrations, nightmares, daydreams, fantasies; even the phenomena, the perceptions – so far as we can focus and fix them – keep on joining, disjoining, connecting, conflicting, relating, failing to relate. Poetic order is still *order* of a special kind. Something has to hold the bits and pieces together, they won't do it of themselves. Even logic and classification are *human*. An enormous part of language has directly to do with this; far too much of it to be disregarded by poets, whose material it is.[11]

It was precisely phenomenology's rejection of reason and logic which Curnow had most objected to in Stead's characterisation of 'open form' in 'From Wystan to Carlos' as attaining 'a life-likeness in the very absence of those mental structures which life as we live it moment by moment doesn't have'.[12] In an earlier draft of the passage above Curnow was even more expansive on the subject:

It's one thing to call the attention of poetry to the concrete, to the 'thing' present to our senses, to the realm of 'phenomena'. When art gets over-rationalised, over-moralised, and over-literary, it's a great refreshment to insist on the sensations, the perceptions, the *things*. This doesn't, & can't, mean that poetry limits itself to a philosophical system of this description. Language in *all* its operations is our material. Language is *not* a phenomenological vocabulary. It's *not* a mere means of recording *instants*. It embraces logic, rhetoric, discourse of any sort, *concepts*, dreams, hallucinations, fantasies, fictions, ideologies – briefly, the lot! There's nothing language does, or can do, or is expected to do, which doesn't one way or another prompt a poet to provide him with poems. A *poetic can't* be fabricated out of the leftovers of philosophers. The phenomenological teaching is no better guarantee of art than the dogmas of Marxism, psycho-analysis, Catholic orthodoxy, or existentialism. 'Good dogma makes bad doggerel'.[13]

Stead's response to the lecture, after Curnow had sent him a copy, was a tactfully phrased disagreement with its negative approach ('if you don't like [a theory] it's hardly worth saying so because, of course, any theory will be full of holes and never comprehensive enough'), and an ambivalent comment of his own about Olson's essay: 'The theory strikes me as pretentious in presentation, but I do respond, more I think than you do, to the idea of a momentum, keeping it moving, keeping the pressure going forward.'[14]

'My trouble was', Curnow replied, 'that [the theory] didn't (altogether) leave *me* alone & I *was* trying to sort myself out in sorting it out.'[15] He nevertheless continued to think highly of the address, and after it appeared in the *Turnbull Library Record* in May the following year sent a copy to Michael Schmidt for consideration for the *PN Review*.[16] Schmidt did not reprint the piece, but it continued to attract the interest (if not the assent) of younger poets and critics in New Zealand, who tended to 'anxiously disclaim discipleship, and then fall back on terms which are his [Olson's] and only his, e.g. "Field"'.[17]

'One of the vilest systems of oppression ever devised by man's inhumanity to man': apartheid and the Springbok rugby tour, 1981

It was an exceptionally busy year for writing projects. In 1981, in addition to his own new poems and the preparation of the manuscript of *You Will Know When You Get There* for Dennis McEldowney at Auckland University Press, as well as his work on the introduction and proofs of Glover's *Selected Poems* and his Turnbull lecture, Curnow had also contracted with Penguin Books to prepare a new *Selected Poems* of his own by September for publication in November the following year. The *Collected Poems* published by Reed in 1974 was now out of print and *An Incorrigible Music* was close to selling out, and he was particularly attracted by the prospect of overseas distribution of his poems, especially in the UK, because of Penguin's international imprint. The selection was reasonably generous, beginning with *Not in Narrow Seas* and including all poems from his three 1970s volumes. It was also 'not entirely free from a few revisions in places which have worried me'.[18] Curnow was pleased with the photograph used on the front cover (showing the poet in reflective mood in his study at Tohunga Crescent, lighting his pipe), commenting to Tim: 'I suppose if we must have faces on jackets, the thinking-man's poet is as good an image as the hollow-eyed mystic or dishevelled sorcerer.'[19]

It was also the year of a rugby tour of New Zealand by the South African Springboks, which plunged the country into a deeply divisive political and moral crisis. The South African team had excluded black players, in accordance with the country's apartheid sporting policy, and for Curnow (as for many others) the tour was a key test of race relations within New Zealand, as well as a test of the country's willingness to act in a principled way against apartheid, in one of the few areas in which it could be effective on the international stage. As Whim Wham, he had written scores of anti-Springbok tour satirical pieces from the late 1950s onwards, a period during which – with the honourable exception of Prime Minister Norman Kirk in 1973 – governments temporised, played electoral politics with pro-rugby public opinion, and allowed an increasingly obdurate New Zealand Rugby Football Union (NZRFU) to dictate the country's foreign policy.[20] In 1981 Whim Wham produced a dozen such pieces, leading up to and during the months (July to September) of the tour itself – the largest concentration of pieces on a single topic since his attacks on Hitler and Nazism.

Curnow (now 70) and Jeny strongly supported the protest movement and its two main sponsoring organisations, HART (Halt All Racist Tours) and CARE (Citizens' Association for Racial Equality), and took part in all of the protest demonstrations which occurred in Auckland. In addition to his regular contributions as Whim Wham, Curnow wrote detailed and vivid accounts of the events of the tour to Pearson (on sabbatical leave in London) and to Tony. As the months leading up to it passed, it became clear that neither the government (led by Robert Muldoon) nor the NZRFU (led by Ces Blazey) was prepared to cancel it. This was despite the government's being a signatory to the Commonwealth Gleneagles Agreement in 1977 (under which it was required 'to take every practical step to discourage' sporting contacts with South Africa), and despite mounting opposition from a wide cross-section of the country and widespread condemnation abroad (from the United Nations and the Organization of African Unity especially). Curnow became increasingly certain that confrontation was inevitable and its nature and consequences ominously unpredictable. 'One way or another, one's only satisfaction', he wrote to Pearson, 'is that a "moment of truth" may well be imminent, after years of ignorance & double-talk in N.Z.'[21] On the eve of the arrival of the Springboks, 'Learn Your Alphabet' was one of the bitterest pieces Whim Wham ever wrote, its focus the shameful, humiliating capitulation to racism to which government and rugby union were privy. It concluded: 'Y is for the Year and the Year's Degradations, / Z is for our Zero, on the Scale of Nations.'[22]

Curnow and Jeny participated in eight demonstrations organised in Auckland during the two months of the tour, two of them at Eden Park itself where the last two games were played, the others at strategic targets (NZRFU headquarters and buildings and organisations associated with support for the tour) chosen to tie up police numbers and resources when games were being played elsewhere in the country. The intimidating presence of massed police forces (including elite squads of specially trained police in full riot gear), the use of army resources to create barbed-wire and other defences around all grounds and the approaches to them, and the actual threat of violence from enraged or drunken rugby supporters, created an atmosphere reminiscent of a battle zone. 'One could, of course', he wrote to Tony, 'do nothing but sit at home grieving over the failure of "law and order", etc, and the absurdity of it all. In that case, one would only be aiding Rugby, [South African Prime Minister P.W.] Botha, & apartheid – & supporting the worst kinds of illiberal opinion.'[23]

Curnow was arrested for an act of civil disobedience on the day of the last game of the tour (a test match at Eden Park) – one of the numerous small-scale diversionary activities away from the main protest at the test venue itself – and charged that 'On the 12th day of September 1981 at Mangere [he] trespassed on the taxi way at Auckland International Airport and refused to leave after being warned to do so by the occupier of that place'.[24] He described the event (at which Wystan was also arrested and similarly charged) to Tim:

My meritorious arrest is hardly news among the catch of 205 (Auckland alone) for the day. Forty of us, nine cars, drove from Western Springs to airport: a sprint from carpark to wire barriers along domestic tarmac: the young & active went up & over, & pulled down a few sections of fence; no trouble for me to scramble over. A fool of an airport security van driver tried a bit of drag-strip driving, but nobody was bumped. All we did was form a tight linked bunch, with a couple of banners round it, FLY APARTHEID WITH AIR NZ, while about 30 Johns solemnly surrounded us (about 20 males & the same number of females, we were): no angry words or blows. It took them nearly 2 hours to arrest us all ('wilful trespass'), photograph, finger-print, & load us into paddy-wagons for Otahuhu police station. Four hours in a cell there, but the company was excellent: W & I got through more good talk than we've had together in years: others present incl. Oliver Stead (Karl's eldest, 18) & a DSIR geothermal chemist from Taupo, teachers, etc. By 7 pm our drivers had their cars back from airport – & so home. My only complaint is against the dumb sergeant, who had the cheek to say, 'it's the *young* fellow', his idea of a joke. Well, it all helped to stretch the police, along with other such sideshows like blocking the Harbour Bridge.[25]

Curnow appeared at the Otahuhu District Court, along with two others from the forty or so arrested, on 15 October, and was pleasantly surprised when the charge was dismissed, on the purely technical and procedural grounds that he had not been subject to a 'positive identification' at the time of his arrest. He had expected a conviction (which carried a fine of up to $150), conducted his own defence, and prepared an ingenious submission based on a section of the Trespass Act which required a warning to be given to 'the individual person' at the time of the trespass, questioning whether such a requirement had been met by the airport security van's loudhailer general address ('please leave immediately') to the group as a whole. According to Curnow the thick Glaswegian accent of the security guard, the noise of the vehicle and the demonstration itself, and the imperfect use of the loudhailer, had made it impossible to understand the words in any case, but his main submission consisted of a detailed account of the meanings of the word 'individual' (and all its siblings) in the *Shorter Oxford Dictionary*, from which he concluded that the Act's reference to the individual person could only mean that alleged trespassers had to be warned *individually*, 'singly, one at a time', as none of those charged had been.

'The Judge – a piece of luck – was altogether admirable', Curnow wrote to Pearson, 'relaxed, knew "who" I was, & gave me all the help & consideration & courtesy I could have hoped for':

I began in some trepidation – not showing any – but was at once aware that Judge Nicolson was listening & following every word, with interest. More than that – when I ended & began to recount a few facts of what actually happened, he stopped me most civilly, pointing out that these had no place in a 'submission', only if I'd been a witness, not my own counsel. I was quite happy to stop with an 'as your honour pleases'! When he finally came to give his decision 'no case to answer' – of course, on the ground of failure to identify, not my particular submission – he added an 'aside' addressed to me as between friends, 'Now you see what I meant, Mr Curnow, about keeping facts out of legal submissions'.[26]

In other words, if Curnow had been allowed to continue with his account of 'facts' – by implication admitting his presence at the airport – it would have made it impossible, or at least much more difficult, for the judge to dismiss the charge on the grounds of failure to identify. Other defendants from the Mangere protest were less fortunate in the judges assigned to their cases. Wystan, ten days later, was convicted on the same charge and fined $125.

Brisbane Writers' Week, September–October 1982

The Springbok tour did not prompt any poems (perhaps because so many of Whim Wham's pieces at the time dealt directly with the topic), though there was a brief, unbidden reference in a poem written on an entirely different topic in August, 'Impromptu in a Low Key', which was a late inclusion in *You Will Know When You Get There*. 'Things get in, somehow unauthorised', he wrote to Stead,[27] after noticing that in lines he wrote about the site, in Milazzo, Sicily, of what was reputed to be Homer's Cave of Cyclops ('grotto di / polyfemo'), he had recalled that 'the / town football pitch / is netted all round with / rusty wire' – as if transferring the barbed-wire-ringed perimeters of New Zealand's football grounds where the Springboks played. The poem had nothing whatever to do with the tour, however, and lightly recalled the 'essential / onceness' – the transitoriness – of personal experiences of Edenic moments during the course of his life, experiences from his 'personal infancy' in the garden orchard at the Belfast vicarage, swimming at Corsair Bay and 'the summer come / of sex' during his adolescent West Lyttelton years a decade later, and his 'visitor's' interest in the Edens of others, like Homer's Odyssean locations in Sicily:

It's all very Homeric round that NE corner of Sicily, Aeolian Islands off shore & Scylla & Charybdis reputedly in Messina Straits. I thought, then *here's* the Cyclops, & of [J.M.W.] Turner's picture! And all I found was a rather neglected football park,

& what might be the remains of some World War II concreting. Not an 'Eden' but a
sort of disenchantment.[28]

At this time Curnow and Jeny were thinking of making another trip to
Europe and the UK the following year, with the hope that costs might be assisted
if Curnow received a Katherine Mansfield Memorial Fellowship, an annual
award which provided for six months devoted to writing projects, based at
Menton in the south of France. However, they decided to delay any application
for the award until the following year, 1982, with a view to making the trip the
year after that. Jeny was in the final year of her Master's papers in Maori studies,
but had yet to write her thesis, and Curnow was also heavily involved in super-
vising the construction of a house for Tony and Elisabeth on a section adjacent
to their own bach at Karekare, where they planned to live after Tony's retirement
from the UN Secretariat at Geneva.

After the exhausting pace he had set himself in 1981 Curnow was able to live
a more relaxed life during the summer and autumn of 1982, without the pressure
of deadlines except for proofreading his new collection and his *Selected Poems* in
January. He enjoyed Alan Roddick's astute study of his work in the New Zealand
Writers and their Work series published by Oxford University Press,[29] which
despite Roddick's efforts to persuade him otherwise had had to be written without
any reference to Whim Wham. In November 1981 he spoke at the launch of Lauris
Edmond's edition of Fairburn's letters.[30] 'In the light of it', he wrote to Pearson,
'almost everything that's been written about Rex and Ron Mason (fortunate
there's so little of it) has to be reviewed.'[31]

In April 1982 he sent copies of a new poem – the first since 'Impromptu in a
Low Key' in August the previous year – to Stead and Tim. Entitled 'You Can't be
Too Careful', it was a first draft of what was to become 'Moules à la Marinière',
about 'being picked off the rocks by an unexpected swell while picking mussels',
he wrote to Tim. 'Not a very serious fight. It's possible to swim, long enough, in
jeans. But a bagful of excellent mussels went off into the tide. I felt a bit excited,
if a fool for giving the sea its chance.'[32] Alan Ross later accepted the poem for the
London Magazine.

The following month he sent another, entitled 'Another Calm Day', to Stead,
one of his finest 'pedestrian' or 'walking picture' poems sparked by a walk down
Brighton Road in Parnell. Carefully reworked during the next two months in the
light of Stead's thoughtful comments, the poem was published later in the year
by Geoffrey Dutton, editor of a literary supplement for the Sydney *Bulletin*, with
the title 'Canto of Signs without Wonders'. The poem is rich in its observation of
physical particulars and of the many signs of human presence – a pianist playing
Mendelssohn, the carefully tended swimming pools of the affluent, a rusted VW

with a sticker advertising 'my other car is a Rolls', a young lover fondling the 'stitched name of Levi Strauss' on his girlfriend's jeans – as the poet walks with his 'feet falling in turn / on the pavement which is falling away'. However, in counterpoint to the steady downwards momentum of the poet's walk (the poem's title and versification in tercets suggesting a comparison with Dante's downward progression in the *Inferno*), his eyes are continually drawn upwards, as if walking a tight wire, to the scene above the city, a middle-distance prospect over Remuera and the eastern bays suburbs above which white clouds constantly shape-shift against the background of the deep blueness of the sky – a scene so sensuously charged that it suggests the painterly effect of the technique of impasto: 'the clouds lay the whitenesses on thick / over the bluenesses.'

Furthermore, unlike the visible signs that everywhere map and delineate the objects in the street scene through which the poet walks (the Steinway piano, the VW and Rolls-Royce cars, the Levi Strauss jeans) – constituting the signature of human occupation and presence not only in the suburban present but throughout history ('as far as the bluest // dilations of clouds and seas and names / to call islands by') – the constantly changing skyscape remains tantalisingly unsigned. It yields only 'a kind of an impression / of lettering rapidly rubbed out / before I can read, pasted over again // and rewritten', hinting at the possibility of transcendence – of a divine author or maker sponsoring the universe and branding it with his presence, a heavenly sign-writer – only to withhold any such religious certainty. Literary allusions in the poem – to Dante's *Divine Comedy*, to biblical texts linking religious belief with signs that guarantee the wonder of God's presence, to T.S. Eliot's 'Gerontion', and to Blake's assertion that the true authors of his epic *Jerusalem* are 'in eternity' – carry its transcendental speculations, but the 'system' of signs which the poet sees himself as inhabiting remains obstinately 'without wonders' – without hint of spiritual agency or origin – immersing him in the sensuous, if time- and death-bound, continuum of the physical world.

The balance of feelings in the poem (despite an enigmatic comment to Stead that the poem is 'personal in ways that have given me one or two frights (I hope salutary)')[33] falls much more strongly on the unpredictable pleasures offered by the contingent world of nature with its ubiquitous signatures of ordinary human presence, than on anxiety and anguish at the prospect of loss of belief. The poem provided yet another example of the shift in tone and register, after the 1970s, to a poetry celebrating the continually surprising diversity of commonplace experiences and sensations. At its simplest level, 'Canto of Signs without Wonders' encapsulates the sights and sounds and atmosphere of Auckland, its changeable, cloud-swept skyscapes, its fragile volcanic geology, its affluent inner-suburban streetscapes.

In May Curnow received an invitation from the Department of Internal Affairs to attend the Brisbane Writers' Week festival (coinciding with the 1982

Commonwealth Games there) from 27 September to 3 October. He participated in two sessions, a reading with A.D. Hope, Mark O'Connor and E.K. Brathwaite (for which he chose to read the whole of 'A Fellow Being'), and a discussion of poetry in Australia and New Zealand in which the other participants were Tom Shapcott, John Blight and Judith Rodriguez.

In Brisbane there was also a small launch of *You Will Know When You Get There* and of his Penguin *Selected Poems*, and Tim was active in building a programme of literary activities in Sydney around Curnow's visit. These included readings at the University of Sydney and Macquarie University, an interview with the ABC for its Books and Writing programme, and recording a programme in the ABC's *The Poet's Tongue* series, for which he introduced and read sections of 'Canst Thou Draw Out Leviathan with an Hook?' and 'Moro Assassinato' as well as the whole of his recently finished 'Moules à la Marinière'. Curnow put considerable care into the drafting of his 20-minute Poet's Tongue script, which was later rebroadcast by Elizabeth Alley on Radio New Zealand's Concert Programme in October 1983, after he had agreed to remove one line ('and the cameras in at the fuck') from 'The Prison of the People' in 'Moro Assassinato'. 'Scripts of this sort are difficult', Curnow wrote to Tim:

> They might keep in mind that my delivery tends to be a bit more rapid than that of some readers. This is *not* because I hurry, but because I'm distinct, & I don't have to drag or labour my lines. I feel it doesn't do to tack together more or less loosely a few poems that otherwise don't *belong* together. It puts too much burden of connecting on to the listener. That's why I use nothing from 'A Fellow Being', or any short things which won't bear any fussy introduction by the author. I think I need the new poem ['Moules à la Marinière'] at the end. Alan Ross likes it, and so do I. It looks longer than it actually is, when properly read.[34]

Curnow was pleased with his trip to Australia, which contributed significantly to the growth of his poetic reputation there, as was also occurring in the UK. 'The whole visit was refreshing', he wrote to Stead. 'I had to pick up my heels & run with the fast pack, if only to keep up with the things I was reading.'[35] 'I'd always imagined myself invisible in Australia – in the poetic scene, that is – and found myself both known & welcome', he wrote to Lilburn. At Brisbane he met and particularly enjoyed the company of Peter Porter, 'a good & successful poet in UK, Queensland expatriate, but neither too happy nor too doctrinaire about it'.[36] The meeting with Porter, a close friend of Anthony Thwaite, was the beginning of a friendship that lasted during all Curnow's subsequent trips to London.

In July 1982 Curnow applied for the Katherine Mansfield Memorial Fellowship, worth $9,000, with plans, he wrote in his application, 'for a major new work, poetic and (in part only) autobiographical',[37] and was delighted to learn later in September that he had been successful. During the next few months he and Jeny worked on plans for the trip, with a view to basing themselves in Menton from April to June 1983 (including time in Italy during that period), and then spending a further three months (July to early October) in London. Anton and Birgitte Vogt, living in Menton, were helpful in arranging accommodation there, and for their London stay they arranged accommodation in a Nuffield Foundation flat, as they had in 1974. There were literary contacts which Curnow hoped to follow up in London, with the magazine editors Ross, Thwaite and Schmidt, and with Peter Porter; and Donald Davie invited the Curnows to visit his home in Silverton near Exeter in Devon. He also hoped to pursue whatever opportunities emerged for promoting his own work in London, after the recent publication of both his Penguin *Selected Poems* and *You Will Know When You Get There*. Remarkably, the latter's edition of 1000 copies had sold out by November (after five months), and a reprint of 800 copies was in the offing.

Soon after his return from Brisbane in October Curnow decided to deposit many of his literary and personal papers in the Alexander Turnbull Library. They made a total of 71 files, and he was pleasantly surprised to be offered $6,500. There were not a great many from the Christchurch period of his life, and it had never occurred to him that his papers might have any archival value, but from the later 1950s onwards he began to keep some papers on a regular basis – a complete file of the correspondence relating to his edition of *The Penguin Book of New Zealand Verse*, for example, as well as correspondence with Glover and Lilburn, drafts of poems written in the 1960s, and papers relating to his trips to the United States. His main reason for keeping papers at this time (like manu-scripts of *Moon Section* and *Dr Pom* and a large file of drafts and papers relating to Dylan Thomas) was that they represented *unfinished* projects, materials which he felt he might come back to at some time in the future. It was only in the 1970s that he adopted the habit of keeping literary papers on a more systematic basis. By this time there was an increasing stream of business correspondence with publishers, and an increasing number of requests for permissions to publish or quote from his work in anthologies, histories and educational books.

The immediate trigger for his decision to contact the Turnbull Library in 1982, however, was an approach by a doctoral student seeking background information about the 1960 Penguin anthology.* Curnow replied in detail, confidentially, but was unhappy about misinformation provided by other interviewees, and about the (inevitably) partial nature of the information about the Penguin episode, from people who knew only a small portion of the total story, in other sets of

---

* The PhD student was Simon Garrett of the University of Canterbury.

deposited papers. To accompany the file of Penguin papers he deposited in the Turnbull Library he appended a long narrative explaining the sequence of events with a view, as he saw it, to correcting the many inaccuracies and misreadings which had found their way into the public record. Elaborating on his reasons to W.H. Oliver, who had been in touch about permissions for a book on Baxter which he was writing, Curnow commented:

> It wasn't so much your writing [to me] about the Baxter book that hurried me up. I was favoured lately with some examples of oral testimony about the same matter, one of which contained a serious misstatement of fact; another was so vague that almost any conclusion could be drawn. People's memories can be so unreliable. The complete story is in that folder of mine.[38]

In November Curnow wrote a longish piece for the *New Zealand Listener* about his meetings with Dylan Thomas in 1949 and 1950 – the only piece he ever put into print on the subject, despite his numerous efforts over the years – by way of background (and implicit corrective) to a new BBC documentary on the Welsh poet which was to be broadcast in New Zealand. The *'essential untruth* of the film', in Curnow's opinion, was contained in its advertised aim to depict the poet surviving 'in his own bizarre terms as an archetypal poet': 'I don't believe he had any such conception of how a poet "should" or shouldn't live, he just survived as best he could, & never found anything specially poetic in the muddles he got into.'[39]

The prospect of a relaxing Christmas, with a visit from Tony and Elisabeth to see their by now almost completed house at Karekare, was disrupted in mid-December when he suffered a recurrence of his old back trouble, a violent attack which left him prostrate and in extreme pain. He was taken by ambulance from Karekare to Greenlane Hospital, and the next day transferred to Middlemore Hospital for several days. Over the next two months he gradually recovered, but the excruciating pain he suffered was not an experience he forgot. 'I could have done with a helicopter instead of ambulance and overnight stop at Green Lane [sic]', he wrote to Stead, adding, 'I've been trying to get a few lines on paper, to do with some odd experiences at Middlemore, but it won't work.'[40] It was not for two years, late in 1984, that he came back to and completed one of his most original poems, 'Blind Man's Holiday', which began with memories of the episode of December 1982.

The early months of 1983 were spent quietly. The *New Zealand Listener* devoted two pages to a long interview with Curnow by Tony Reid (to mark the appearance of his *Selected Poems*), which elicited some revealing comments about his later poetry.[41] He spent time finalising accommodation and travel arrangements for the trip to Menton and London, and tried to ensure that copies of both his new books would be available in the UK during his time there later in the year. For Jeny, however, these were extremely busy months, as she worked to complete her thesis on previously untranslated manuscripts by Te Rangikaheke, an advisor to George Grey. She finished it a fortnight before she and Curnow flew out to London on 26 March, and six weeks later (in Menton) heard that she had been awarded her Master's degree with first-class honours.

Chapter Thirty-one

Menton, London and Toronto, *The Loop in Lone Kauri Road*, 1983–86

> [T]hey are great poems of the human disposition and ... he's using all
> the resources he's ever known as a poet, and making these exceptionally
> powerful statements of that disposition at a point of age and in a
> particular place. Those poems are adamantly New Zealand – that's
> what's so forceful about them.
>
> *Robert Creeley[1]*

Menton and London, April–October 1983: an autobiographical impulse

The Curnows spent five days travelling from Auckland to Menton, with stop-overs of two nights in London and Paris and a further night in Marseilles, before arriving at their destination on Good Friday (1 April). It was a tiring trip, the weather was wet and windy and Curnow was unwell with flu, and it took a little time for them to settle in and establish a routine for their three-month stay there. They were pleased with their accommodation, a small first-floor apartment, 'Villa Quieta', 49 Avenue Porte de France, 'directly on the seafront, with 2 large French doors and a balcony overlooking the sea, the port & the old town',[2] only a short walk from the Villa Isola Bella where Mansfield had stayed between September 1920 and May 1921. Here, what had originally been a street-level cellar with its own small garden and separate entrance had been converted into a room for use by Katherine Mansfield Fellows during their tenure. 'It's a monkish cell, with

569

table, chairs, & a bed, & escritoire', Curnow wrote to Tony,[3] and he used it regularly in the mornings to read and make notes.

It did not escape his notice on this first visit, that a memorial plaque near the door had mistranslated a comment Mansfield had made to John Middleton Murry about Isola Bella ('You will find Isola Bella graven in pokerwork on my heart') as 'Vous trouvez Isola Bella gravée sur mon coeur', omitting the ironic, punning reference to the burning pain of consumption in the metaphor of 'pokerwork' and turning her words instead into a statement of sentimental attachment. Curnow used the mistranslation as a starting point for numerous of the drafts he wrote about Mansfield at this time. During his first days there he also reread Antony Alpers's biography of Mansfield – 'enough . . . to get her out of my mind, or at least the cult that some of our literary cannibals make of her'.[4] Despite this early comment he seems to have had in mind a longish, free-flowing poem about her along the lines of 'A Fellow Being', but achieved nothing that satisfied him. It was not until the summer of 2000–2001 that he returned to the scene and to Mansfield in the last poem he ever wrote, 'A Nice Place on the Riviera'.

Menton was not a place which either Curnow or Jeny especially warmed to during their stay there. To Tim he described it as 'full of the aged, the sick, & other sun-starved northerners & the hard-nosed developers & shopkeepers who sell the climate the way Arabs sell oil'.[5] A visit to Monaco nearby also left them unimpressed. However, as the weather gradually improved they were able to enjoy swimming on the small, crowded section of beach available for public use at Menton. They also discovered that the Italian border was only 20 minutes' walk away along the coast to the east, and the small Italian coastal town of Ventimiglia only ten minutes by train from the Menton railway station, Gare SNCF Garavan. They made a regular habit of visiting Ventimiglia on Friday mornings, shopping for food and enjoying coffee or amaro (a herbal liqueur) at an unpretentious café, where they encountered the same Italian hospitality and friendliness as they had discovered in Venice and Sicily on earlier trips.

The Curnows had planned to make two visits to Italy during their stay at Menton, to Venice and to Rome, and the first of these (to Venice) took place over the fortnight 23 April to 8 May. It was their third visit to Venice, and as much a pleasure as the previous two. Their accommodation in Dorsoduro (at Hotel Agli Alboretti) was the same as in 1978, and they renewed their earlier friendships in the neighbourhood of the Zattere – with Domenico at his café on the Zattere, and with the family who ran the trattoria Ai Cugnai – as well as discovering another friendly trattoria in the same area, Da Rino. They revisited numerous of their favourite places from the previous trips (the Basilica dei Frari with its large *Assumption of the Virgin* by Titian, San Rocco, St Mark's for Sunday High Mass, Teatro La Fenice for a lieder concert), as well as exploring new rooms at the Accademia and the Doges' Palace. They also revisited the Lido, shopped at the Rialto and (for glassware) at Cenedese's, discovered other churches, and saw exhibitions of modern Italian art. They twice visited the Casa Frollo, on Giudecca Island, to take photographs of its garden for Elizabeth Sheppard, who was researching the life and art of Frances Hodgkins.

The trip to Rome, from 4 to 12 June, was equally pleasurable, despite a heatwave and the noticeably increased noise and fumes of traffic. As in Venice they stayed in the same vicinity as their earlier visits (at the Hotel d'Italia,* [6] Via Quattro Fontane, opposite the Barberini Palace), and combined remembered walks and visits to favourite haunts – the Borghese Gallery and gardens, the Barberini Palace, an outdoors dinner at the Piazza de Mercanti in Trastevere with lively folk musicians and singers as in 1974 and 1978 – with new discoveries such as the Chiesa di Sant'Ignazio where they attended a Vivaldi concert.

The highlight of this trip, however, was their discovery of the coastal township of Rapallo on their way back to Menton – a location associated with a great deal of Ezra Pound's Italian life and poetry before and during the Second World War and after his return to Italy in the later 1950s. The place 'can't have changed, at least in the last 100 years', Curnow wrote to Pearson, '& has the secret of *living* with tourism & hasn't *died* of it like the Côte d'Azur'.[7] They stayed an extra night at the Albergo Marsala, Curnow purchased a prized, numbered copy of *Ieri a Rapallo* (*Yesterday at Rapallo*), a private-press, limited-edition book by G. Bacigalupo which contained essays on Pound's and Yeats's lives there, and on their second morning took a memorable boat trip across the gulf to Portofino, before departing by train for Menton, with late-afternoon seaward glimpses as the train wound its way in and out of tunnels along the Ligurian coast. This train journey provided a vividly remembered scenario for 'Do Not Touch the Exhibits', which Curnow completed early the following year.

Apart from the 60 pages of drafts for a poem about Mansfield, Curnow worked on drafts dealing with other aspects of the Menton location, with the philosopher Blaise Pascal (whose *Pensées* he took with him during the trip), and with Rapallo. However, by far the most significant of the drafts and notes Curnow made at Menton – significant for the later development of his poetry – related to his own early childhood at Belfast and Sheffield, and to memories of his father and grandmother during the years of the First World War. The numerous fragments he drafted at this time constituted his earliest work on the plan he had outlined in his application for the fellowship.[8] Although a *single* work incorporating auto-biographical elements, on the large scale suggested by his application, did not

---

*   The same hotel, Jeny later noted, 'from where Ezra Pound had made his infamous [propaganda] broadcasts' on Radio Rome during the Second World War.

eventuate, what did emerge was an interest in the possibilities of a new kind of autobiographical lyric: memory-based, reaching back to formative childhood and familial experiences, revisiting history not through large-scale abstractions but through densely textured, small-scale, locally focused observations of the social, political, geographical and domestic contexts in which it occurred. Numerous of the autobiographical verse and prose fragments drafted at Menton subsequently found their way into poems completed during the rest of his career. In fact more than a third of the 40 poems he was still to write – many of them amongst his very best – were written in this new mode, and memory in the broadest sense from this point on became the single most important source of inspiration for his poetry.

Aspects of the Menton environment itself also assisted in drawing Curnow back into himself at this time, as if engaged on a pilgrimage into memory. In one fragment he writes, simply, 'The sun / follows me round / you can't get away from it / 'Belfast' / – – – [places] to / Côte d'Azur', anticipating, it seems, writing about a succession of intermediate locations which might link his earliest memories of place in New Zealand with his current location. Furthermore, whereas his previous visit to Europe in 1978 had been dominated by the pressure of external events, by the political crisis into which Italy had been plunged by the abduction and murder of Aldo Moro, in Menton he was much more isolated from contemporary events than he had been in 1978, thrust more strongly onto his own resources. Almost certainly his thinking about Mansfield also reinforced the inwards turn his imagination took, prompting him to begin to think of his own life during the second decade of the century, and of the ways in which childhood experience was formative for his later life, as it had been for Mansfield.

Over the years, Curnow had very occasionally written poems which drew on childhood experience (with his father at Governor's Bay in 'At Dead Low Water', for example, or walking to school at Sheffield in 'A Balanced Bait in Handy Pellet Form'), but with nothing like the concentration of focus which occurred after his trip to Menton. Although no completed 'childhood' poems emerged during the trip itself, he kept working on the notes and fragments after his return to New Zealand, the first fruits of which – the following year – were two 'Belfast' poems, 'A Raised Voice' and 'A Sight for Sore Eyes'.

On 30 June the Curnows left Menton for London, enjoying three nights' hospitality in an apartment at the New Zealand Embassy in Paris, as guests of the ambassador John McArthur and his wife, before arriving on 4 July at their Nuffield Foundation flat at 6 Prince Albert Road in the area of London – Regent's Park, Primrose Hill and Camden – whose character and familiarity they always enjoyed. Curnow immediately hired a typewriter and began further work on the notes and drafts he had accumulated in Menton. In August he completed a Menton-based poem, 'Gare SNCF Garavan', which Alan Ross accepted for

London Magazine. Initially entitled 'A Frequent Service', the poem's setting is the local railway station (the poet awaiting a train, presumably on one of his and Jeny's numerous trips to Ventimiglia), its occasion one of those misty, hazy days in which objects lose their distinctness, boundaries become blurred, and even the smallest events seem to occur in a vacuum, without connectedness.

> A frequent service. Madame emerges, bearing her
> official baton, producing a train from Nice,
> Italy's minutes away, an old-fashioned thought,
>
> an old-fashioned iron expostulation of
> wheels, fluttering doors, interrupts nothing.
> So much at risk, a miracle that so much gets
> taken care of, Madame picks up her cat from
> the quai and cuddles it, conversing with friends.

Despite Curnow's 'itch to stay put . . . and get new verse under way',[9] he and Jeny managed numerous excursions to the theatre (including *Macbeth* and *The Tempest* at the new Barbican Centre) and twice – through arrangements made by long-standing family friend Catherine Pierard, now making a career for herself in England as an opera singer – visited Glyndebourne, on the first occasion to see a production of Prokofiev's *The Love for Three Oranges*, and on the second to attend a staged rehearsal for a TV production of Strauss's *Intermezzo*. There were visits from Tony and Elisabeth (for a long weekend), and from Wystan (on his way to the Edinburgh Festival), as well as trips to Dover and Canterbury, and for five days in September to Bath, Gloucester and Salisbury – including Nether Stowey, interesting to Curnow because of its associations with Coleridge and Wordsworth. Wordsworth in particular, at this time – in poems like 'Tintern Abbey' (located in the Wye Valley) – was emerging as a key figure in Curnow's thinking about the possibilities of the autobiographical lyric.

Curnow's most important contacts during his London visit, however, were with literary friends. On 18 July he and Jeny travelled to the village of Silverton, in Devon, to stay with Donald Davie (who was soon to retire from his chair at Vanderbilt University, Nashville, Tennessee) and his wife Doreen. It was 'a lovely visit', Jeny noted in her diary, 'especially for Allen whose talks with Donald are the best he's had in years',[10] and Curnow described their discussions about poetry as 'enormously encouraging & stimulating'.[11] In August the Curnows caught up with Alan and Elizabeth Ross, and met the Ross's close friends Peter and Beryl Bland for the first time, whose company they greatly enjoyed.[12] Curnow had never met Bland during the latter's sixteen years in New Zealand from the late

1950s to the 1970s, and Bland was now active in the British theatre and television scene as well as maintaining his poetic interests through his association as an advisor to Ross on *London Magazine*.

In August and September Curnow also saw Peter Porter and Anthony Thwaite on numerous occasions, lunching and dining in each other's company. Curnow found that conversation with Porter could go deeper than on purely literary matters. 'I like PP better & better', he wrote to Stead, '& for all kinds of reasons which have nothing to do with his poems or the *Observer*. Haven't in a long time met anyone, let alone any poet, who talks so freely & trustingly, & unguardedly, rare among either Brits or expatriates, & is capable of questioning the value of his own kind of success.'[13] The last literary-social event of the trip with Porter and Thwaite was a restaurant dinner in Fulham Road with four others (including the English poet Alan Brownjohn and the Australian poet and editor Jamie Grant) after all had attended the opening of a poetry exhibition organised by Thwaite at the Poetry Society in Earls Court on 21 September.

The Curnows arrived back in Auckland – after a week-long stay with Jeny's stepsister and her husband in Hawai'i – on 13 October. The London segment of the trip had been important in cementing a number of literary friendships, and confirming Curnow in his wish to pursue publication opportunities in the UK, 'where nobody minds (much) who I am, or tries to fit me into some sectarian slot, or generation'.[14] In New Zealand he had come increasingly to feel trapped under the 'steady gaze' of the literary historians, made to 'fit' into someone else's historical pattern, locked into others' public image of himself, when he preferred seeing himself as a 'misfit',[15] driven still by a passion to understand the world anew, uncertain what might survive from the things he had written and what might emerge in the future. He was under no illusions about how 'enormously competitive' the British poetry scene was: 'no doubt it always has been, but contacts with people in the thick of it, like Davie & Porter & Ross, bring it home to one especially. I certainly feel what a privilege it is, having a pretty secure name & base in my homeland'.[16] However, his relative anonymity on the large British scene was attractive, as it certainly was a challenge, and he also found the fact of being an outsider, where he was entertained 'as a visitor to the scene, not a candidate for admission to it',[17] equally stimulating. It provided him with the kind of freedom he always needed to 'start again'.

'Spoiling for work', new poems 1984

During his absence overseas Curnow learnt that *You Will Know When You Get There* had shared the New Zealand Poetry Book Award for 1982 (Belinda attended the ceremony in Wellington on his behalf), and he was pleased with the notices it (and his *Selected Poems*) received overseas. In Australia there were laudatory reviews by Geoffrey Dutton in the Sydney *Bulletin*, David Martin in the Melbourne *Age*, and Bruce Beaver in *The Australian*, as well as a long appreciation by Chris Wallace-Crabbe in *Scripsi*. In the United States Robert Creeley, in an interview with Alistair Paterson, spoke warmly of Curnow's new collection, comparing his work with that of Pound and Williams and commenting of his later poems generally:

> [T]hey are great poems of the human disposition and of a necessity that every one of us has to deal with: to break free of any restrictive writing habit . . . . [H]e's using all the resources he's ever known as a poet, and making these exceptionally powerful statements of that disposition at a point of age and in a particular place. Those poems are adamantly New Zealand – that's what's so forceful about them. That's the point for me and that's what's parallel with American writing. . . . [T]he thing that's extremely moving in the poetry of Allen Curnow is that his new writing has an adamant need to be articulate and specific in relation to a particular way in which he feels he ought to be.[18]

In London the *Observer* (whose Books page was edited by Blake Morrison) published an influential review of *You Will Know When You Get There* by Peter Porter, who also took the opportunity to chide British Penguin Books over the unavailability of the *Selected Poems*:

> [T]o experience the full range of his talent, you will have to import his Penguin 'Selected Poems' from New Zealand, since the British mother-firm is not handling the book. I suggest readers ring New Zealand House to ask for details of works by this modern master, whom the Australian poet Chris Wallace-Crabbe has called 'one of the finest and subtlest poets in the world' – great praise, since Australians are not given to lauding New Zealanders.[19]

The hint was taken, and the New Zealand branch was immediately telexed to send 200 copies to London. 'Now, I can feel everything possible has been done for these books', Curnow wrote to Tim, 'they can fend for themselves from now on, or until I write more.'[20]

Poems had been scarce since August 1981, but by the end of 1984 Curnow had completed seven new poems, enough to make a small manuscript of ten which he sent to Dennis McEldowney at Auckland University Press early in 1985, and which appeared early in 1986 under the title *The Loop in Lone Kauri Road*. In February 1984 Curnow revised 'Moules à la Marinière' and resent it to Ross (who had accepted the poem eighteen months earlier, but seems to have mislaid it), who published it in the *London Magazine* at the end of the year. He then went back to the Rapallo fragments drafted at Menton the previous year, and began working on 'Do Not Touch the Exhibits', which he completed in March and sent to Thwaite, who immediately accepted it for *Encounter*. Capturing fragmentarily observed details of the seawards scene as a train moves in out of tunnels along the Ligurian coast, the poem uses the scene as an image of the mind's always piece-meal mode of apprehending an ever-elusive reality: 'Where you're going's never what you see / and what you saw, is that where you went?' A momentary glimpse of a fisherman becomes in retrospect, as the train enters a tunnel, an uncertain memory, and the fish he might have landed (a dorado) becomes an imagined possibility only. The enumeration of objects might go on endlessly, except that the mind in the artificially lit darkness of its tunnel edits and selects from what it has observed, dealing only with 'beachcombings, introjections'. Screwed to the wall of the railway carriage the poet observes one such 'beachcombing', a poster of Botticelli's *Birth of Venus* 'paroled from the Uffizi' – a famous instance, in art, of an image retrieved from the sea coast outside. At the base of his carriage window the poet also notices, 'indelibly incised in steel', the instruction, 'e pericoloso sporgersi' ('it is dangerous to lean outside'). If it is a warning – of a threat to the mind's being and well-being by too great an immersion in the world of things outside itself – it is also perhaps a challenge: the poem itself survives as a vivid 'tunnelling' into reality, a retrieval from the world the other side of the carriage window.

Completing 'Do Not Touch the Exhibits' seems to have tapped a spring in Curnow's imagination. During April and May he worked on three new poems: a Karekare-based poem ('The Loop in Lone Kauri Road'), a poem about his father preaching at St David's Church in Belfast ('A Raised Voice'), and a poem about religious belief ('The Answer Is a Question') which was later considerably expanded to become 'Lo These Are Parts of His Ways'. The subject of 'The Loop in Lone Kauri Road' might be described as a process of 'coaxing' familiar things into the open. The poet walks with his dog down Lone Kauri Road to the beach and doubles back, observing familiar specificities throughout. 'The topography', as Peter Simpson commented, 'is the setting for a powerful if obscure existential drama.'[21] 'Obscure', perhaps, because the poem's drama is so deeply internalised, as the opening lines immediately imply:

> By the same road to the same
> sea, in the same two minds,
> to run the last mile blind or
> save it for later. These
> are not alternatives.
>
> So difficult to concentrate!

Running 'the last mile blind' suggests immersing oneself in the flux of the scene, the 'phenomenological welter' of sensations and events and thoughts, without mental concentration, the alternative being to 'save' such self-conscious reflection 'for later' (to be worked on, mentally digested, as memory, for example. However, this either/or option is not available, the poem argues. As Curnow had insisted in his discussion of Olson, the mind does not allow itself to be turned off, nor does the 'phenomenological welter' cease to impinge on it.

Aware that 'immersion' or 'reflection' are *not* alternatives, the poem then proceeds to offer a 'studied performance', as the speaker strives to 'concentrate', to pay attention, to extract significance, both from what he observes and from the seemingly random thoughts (pleasurable or otherwise) which occur during the walk. One is never 'innocently' in such a landscape. Every sensation carries a thought, or thoughts, and every thought a sensation, or sensations, inextricably. The real 'studied performance' of the poem lies not in the way the concentrating mind reduces the multiplicity of things and thoughts to a single order (a 'theme'), or dissolves the mind into the impressionistic flux of events and sensations, but in the way it *maintains* the free play of its opening paradox, refusing to collapse its alternatives. The poem preserves the paradox (of concentrating and forgetting) in its final stanza, which offers two vividly remembered images from the walk:

> Concentrate! The hawk lifts off
> heavily with an offal of silence.
> Forget that, and how the helicopter
> Clapper-clawed the sea, fire-bucketing
> the forest, the nested flame.

'A Raised Voice', which became the opening poem of *The Loop in Lone Kauri Road*, was the first of the lyrics from this time on in which the poet 'looped back' in time to scenes remembered from his childhood, and it was the first of the completed poems which resulted from the autobiographical turn his thinking had taken at Menton. Its earliest form is found amongst fragments about his father drafted there, where the distinctive merging of past and present which characterises all Curnow's later poems about his childhood is apparent. The poem is written as if from the remembered present perspective of the child 70 years earlier, but also from the present perspective of the *poem*, interpreting the child's thought processes while also probing the poet's own present self, 'looking up into my thought of my father'. Much in the remembered detail of the poem cuts the 'giant in the pulpit' humorously down to life-size. But the effect is not simply to dismiss the child's perspective as a quixotic fantasy which the adult has outgrown: the 'issues' – fear of death, uncertainty about religious belief – remain those of the adult, indeed are seen to have their source in childhood and to provide the motivation of the poem itself.

Memory poems like 'A Raised Voice' explore temporal or historical intersections between a past 'there' and a present 'here', with a refusal to see them as static, mutually exclusive polarities. If there was any particular model for these new familial poems it was a poem which loomed increasingly importantly in later years in Curnow's reading and thinking about how poets might deal with the relationship between the past and the present, Wordsworth's 'Tintern Abbey' – 'his greatest poem, as I sometimes think it is', he commented in an interview with Simpson.[22] In the interview Curnow singled out 'An Evening Light' for its Wordsworthian parallelism, but his comment might apply to all of his poems about childhood, including 'A Raised Voice':

> I like to think poetry can – perhaps even that it does – substitute a kind of simultaneous order for the linear, chronological if you like, order that we assume for most practical purposes. Something of the sort is going on in Wordsworth's famous Tintern Abbey poem, though he gets at it indirectly and circumstantially – what he saw five years earlier and what he sees now are still a then and a now – his calendar still hangs on the wall and his clock still ticks.[23]

Like Curnow's poems, 'Tintern Abbey' maintains a present focus as the poet revisits a remembered scene of vivid natural beauty, is reminded of its significance in following years when, absorbed into memory and consciousness, it shapes his moral and social being, and at the end reasserts its ongoing significance in shaping the life of his sister and his relationship with her. The difference, as Curnow's comment suggests, is that Wordsworth is more explicit and deliberate in his handling of the transitions between past and present: 'his calendar still hangs on the wall and his clock still ticks'.

In Curnow's poems of childhood recollection the transitions and intersections between present and past are less deliberated, much freer and more flexible. The openings of the poems are especially important in conveying this flexibility. 'A Raised Voice' begins, 'Let it be Sunday and the alp-high / summer gale gusting to fifty miles'. The lines could refer to present or past, or to present *and* past (or the future, for that matter), they could be specific (a particular Sunday) or general (any Sunday), and they also signal the *imagined* nature of the scene ('Let it be . . . .'), inferring the present-ness of the poet setting about the creation of the scenario of the poem.

'A Sight for Sore Eyes', written a few months after 'A Raised Voice' and set in the back garden of the vicarage next door to St David's Church, contains the same vivid recollection of a specific scene and events, the child's experience of the

'warm and dry', dust-laden, Canterbury nor'-wester mixed with the adult's interpretation of the memory. What is captured is the four-year-old child's puzzled,
emerging consciousness of how the landscape surrounding him is powerfully
defined by the language he is beginning to learn and how the angle of perception
shapes *what* is seen (by tugging at a nail hole in the galvanised iron fence, he can
make the distant mountains viewed through it shift and 'heave clear' of their
apparently solid moorings). However, the child's understanding of these mysterious processes is unstable, and in this threatening world the one secure, nurturing
presence is his mother, her garden a sign of instinctive human resilience in the
face of the destructive forces of nature.

Because such poems are so rich in detail, they also suggest a different way of
thinking about and understanding history – not in terms of large, abstract, linear
generalisations, but in terms of intimate snapshots of the immediate experience of its participants. History is not something which individuals have to be
slotted into; history is actively or unconsciously made by individuals in the most
commonplace activities they engage in, including the language they speak. 'The
Answer Is a Question' was written at the same time as 'A Raised Voice' and might
be seen as a companion piece to it, since it takes up the question of belief underlying the child's anxious questionings in that poem, offering a witty excursus on
a comment by Wallace Stevens, late in life, that he needed (as Curnow quotes it
in the poem) 'to make up my mind about God / before he makes up his about
me'. Referring to the 'question of belief', choosing between 'the ethereal / and the
dustiest answer', raised by Stevens's comment, Curnow concludes the poem:

> Let it hang! Who's creature, who's
> creator, to believe him into existence
> or disbelieve him out of it?

Is God a being created, believed into existence, by the mind of man, or is man
a being created by the mind of God? Although the poem is playful in tone, the
question it explores, and the agnostic answer it provides, reveals the same anxiety
as is felt by the child in 'A Raised Voice', uncertain if he is 'safe'. The poem at this
time was also quite short, and Curnow returned to it later in the year, expanding
it greatly and eventually settling for the title 'Lo These Are Parts of His Ways' –
interspersing its more abstract, philosophical and theological language with some
remarkable imaginative flights suggestive of 'Organo ad Libitum'.

In early June Stead asked Curnow if he had any new poems to contribute
to a New Zealand issue of the Canadian journal *Ariel*, which he was co-editing
with Mike [Charles] Doyle. 'I'm looking hard at one or two unfinished
things', Curnow replied,[24] and within a month sent 'On the Road to Erewhon'.

Drawing on an episode in Samuel Butler's novel *Erewhon* where the narrator encounters a circle of ten gigantic statues, the poem evokes a mind gripped by fear and panic when confronted by apparitions which express 'superhuman' malevolence, pain, hate and cruelty. In Butler's text two fallen statues guard the summit of the alpine pass between the 'reality' the narrator has left behind and the 'nowhere' he is about to descend into. Curnow was fascinated by Butler's text, at such moments, for its revelation of the repressed psychic fears and anxieties beneath the surface of the narrator's conventional Victorian religious and social beliefs, when their fragile moorings are cast adrift in the icebound wilderness and solitariness of the alpine terrain.

However, the poem's inwardness is not simply a matter of its identification with the narrator's interior thoughts. It is inward in a way which is more personal to the poet himself, raising questions of belief closely related to the two poems which immediately preceded it, 'A Raised Voice' and 'The Question is an Answer'. There is a suggestion the statues are vengeful apparitions, haunting the unconscious of those who have abandoned them. Curnow commented to Lilburn that 'in one or two places [the poem] mystifies *me*',[25] perhaps on the edge of an acknowledgement that it reached back deeply to his own abandonment of the Church, and to the unconscious, still-active sense of the power over him of what he has rejected, even if it survives simply as a 'sudden shiver':

> Physical, *superhumanly*
> *malevolent* faces look back, too
>
> hard for your nature to bear, only
> the legs and how fast they can carry
> you the hell out of here *as though one*
> *of them would rush after me and grip*
> *me* . . . If it were just one of those dreams
>
> where running gets you nowhere! [. . . .]
>
> > > Back there, in
> the cloud the trumpeting heads perform
> their own *Te Deum*. Panicky antiphons
> die down in the blood. You can shiver
> suddenly, for no reason at all.

That there are deeply personal resonances in the poem is confirmed, perhaps, by the note to the poem which Curnow drafted for his next collection. In this he drew attention to its connections with both 'A Raised Voice' and the poem he wrote next, 'A Sight for Sore Eyes', commenting that the 'mountains, rivers, and winds' of those two poems provided 'outdoors bearings', sharing the 'common terrain and climate' of Butler's alpine landscape.[26]

Pain, pornography and metaphysics: 'Blind Man's Holiday'

In July 1984 Curnow felt, writing to Tony, that '[a]nother small collection looks possible, maybe early next year',[27] and after completing 'A Sight for Sore Eyes' in August he began work on 'Blind Man's Holiday', the last, longest, and most remarkable of the poems which were to make up the new collection. For this poem he went back to the 'odd experiences at Middlemore [Hospital]' two years earlier which he had tried unsuccessfully at the time to turn into a poem. Its subject, the difficulty of describing the nature of intense pain, was challenging.

As he later reflected on the pain he had felt during the spinal episode that prostrated him at Karekare and continued during his 1 a.m. ambulance ride to Greenlane Hospital, a number of other things struck him about the experience. Intense pain seemed of its nature to be self-effacing, plunging its victim into a kind of blurred, twilight world in which one lost any sense of time, and the sensory or mental activities by which the self normally interacted with the world went into a kind of suspension. Perhaps this was one explanation for being unable, later, to remember quite what the pain was like. Furthermore, because of the 'self-effacing' effect of intense pain, a wholly personal, self-focused poetic treatment of one's own pain was 'an impossible subject', a contradiction in terms, apart from its dangers of sentimentality, or its 'risk of fatuity',[28] or indeed its risk of 'insult' to the sufferings of others by the personal claims it made.[29] One of the driving motivations of the poem – linking it with the concerns of poems like 'The Parakeets at Karekare', 'The Loop in Lone Kauri Road', and poems exploring childhood memories – is thus the problem of representation itself. Indeed, in the particular case of pain, the inability to remember what it was like might be seen as posing that problem in one of its acutest, most uncompromising forms, since the experience (as he struggled to recall it) was characterised by a radical loss of bearings in the real world.

In the opening section, in addition to speculations about the nature of pornography, metaphysics and theology (the latter, mental disciplines whose 'pensées', like erotic pictures, also 'take the place' of the world they purport to represent), Curnow introduces a series of allusions to Wordsworth's 'Tintern Abbey', evoking Wordsworth's intense mental efforts to 'picture' his earlier transformative experience of nature as he revisits the scene five years later, and these allusions prefigure

Curnow's move to personal experience in the poem's final section. '*The picture in the mind revives*, our poet / noticed, and so do I'. '[A]nd so do I' looks forward to the moment when pain subsides, and sensory and mental faculties revive, bringing with them a recovered awareness of self. The experience itself, however, remains unrepresentable, to be imagined (as Wordsworth put it in 'Tintern Abbey') only in 'gleams of half-extinguished thought'. It belongs, as the first section concludes, in 'a particular darkness' which 'forgets our visits'.

The actual, moment-by-moment experience of the 'pain / journey' is marvellously conveyed throughout, as, at the conclusion of the poem, is his arrival at hospital:

> somebody is brought in dead. I want my shot
>
> and a couple of 50mg
> indocid is all I'm getting if that's true
> about the key to the cupboard where they keep
> the morphine and the sister who comes on duty
>
> at five, that's four hours more of this, the
> bloody sheet keeps slipping off. You get the picture?
> Amnesia, muse of deletions, cancellations
> revives, revises pain, a ride in the dark.

'You get the picture?', addressed to the reader, takes us back ironically to the references to 'picture-pensées' – never adequate to the worlds they depict – in the earlier sections of the poem. And in a final ingenious twist Curnow invents a tenth muse (to be added to the nine of classical mythology) to preside benignly over this dark world of pain – one whose inspiration is most desired by its victims: not Mnemosyne (Wordsworth's saving muse of memory) but her opposite, 'Amnesia' (forgetfulness), a muse of 'deletions' and 'cancellations'. Amnesia's saving 'revival', in the last line, as the painkilling drugs take effect, *revises* pain – deletes it, and the memory of it, from the poet's world – restoring it to the unrepresentable realm of 'a ride in the dark'.

The association of pain with darkness, throughout the poem, in opposition to the poem's association of mental and sensory activity with light, also explains the bearing on the poem of its intriguing title, 'Blind Man's Holiday', a now-obsolete colloquial phrase which referred to the twilight period of near-darkness, with fading remnants of light, just before nightfall. Curnow remembered it as a phrase used at home during his childhood:

I've known the title from childhood – my mother (or grandmother?) used it after nightfall, or just before it, if the light wasn't lit & perhaps only a bit of firelight. I think they rather liked it. The Blind Man has a holiday from being blind, everyone else being the same, we're all playing at blindness.[30]

Pain, one might say, is a great leveller, its victims linked – as, momentarily, are the 'blind' and the 'sighted' at nightfall – in the same common experience of sensory deprivation, the same confrontations with its 'darkness'.

Stead was enthusiastic about the poem: 'A great poem', he wrote. 'Nobody alive is writing such poems anywhere in the English language – I am sure of it.[31] After completing 'Blind Man's Holiday', which Jamie Grant immediately accepted for publication in the *Age Monthly Review* (Melbourne), Curnow wrote to McEldowney in late November that he planned to send the manuscript of his new collection 'within a week or two', to be called either *The Loop in Lone Kauri Road* or, simply, *Ten New Poems*.[32] However, he was at this time still 'itching for something new'[33] – perhaps to expand the slim new collection – and in early January 1985 wrote again to McEldowney to say that he was 'working on something new, to add to what I already have', though 'it's a little soon to know how this will turn out'.[34] The new poem did not materialise, though when he finally sent the collection to McEldowney at the end of February, he had revised and extended 'The Answer Is a Question', giving it the title 'The Acronym is MAD'. The new title was a play on the Cold War phrase 'mutually assured destruction', applied wittily to the equally self-cancelling capacity of the 'two minds' of Stevens and God to believe or disbelieve each other out of existence, the stand-off between them maintaining a fragile 'balance of terror'. However, even this version did not satisfy him, and he began almost immediately to revise and expand the poem again, developing at length the Cold War / nuclear holocaust metaphor implied in the acronym. When he sent this final version to Stead in early April, now with the title 'Lo These Are Parts of His Ways', he commented:

It's been through a dozen versions & versifications & I think discovered itself along the way. Anyway it wouldn't let go. If it's not good, it must be original, to make God a Russian chessmaster in the games room of his own Star Wars system?[35]

The collection in its final form was accepted for publication by Auckland University Press in April 1985, and published in March the following year in an edition of 1200 copies.

'How to be historical and busily alive at once': *Look Back Harder* and 'related doings' 1984–85

In September 1984 Curnow reported to Tony that 'new poems and related doings take most of my time'.[36] Amongst these 'related doings' were his rebuttal of criticisms of 'Dichtung und Wahrheit' in the form of a long letter to *Landfall*,[37] and his role as a consultant for a substantial collection of his own critical writings which Peter Simpson was editing for Auckland University Press. Simpson had approached Curnow and McEldowney early in 1984 about the feasibility of the project, and throughout this and the following year regularly sought Curnow's advice about the selection of items and about the many editorial decisions that needed to be made. These included the eventual title, *Look Back Harder*, of which Curnow approved, though – worried as ever that he did not want the book to be a '*corpus vile*', consigning him to history – he insisted on the addition of the dates '1935–1984' in the subtitle.

For Curnow the project was timely, though it was not something he had the time or inclination to take on himself ('[n]ew poems claimed all my attention, and continue to do so'),[38] and he was quickly impressed by the editorial expertise which Simpson brought to it. Simpson persuaded Curnow to agree to a much fuller selection of his critical writings (33 items altogether) than Curnow had himself contemplated in the later 1960s when he compiled 'Origins' with its dozen or so items compared with the 26 Simpson included from the same period. The 26 items included a small but judicious selection of Curnow's newspaper reviews, mainly New Zealand-focused, and managed a careful compromise between items relating to the literary culture and items related to the poet's own practice as a poet. There was only one significant revision to the originals which Curnow insisted on – the omission of a section on Whim Wham from Jackson's interview with him in *Islands*. Other corrections were minor, confined to matters of fact.

Revisiting the 'past selves' embodied in his earlier critical writings produced 'their uneasy moments' for Curnow.[39] However, it also prompted surprise at how well some early pieces had stood the test of time, and confirmed his sense of the value of the project. He realised that his supposed critical 'nationalism' was a notion which Simpson had to deal with in his introduction – if only because so much discourse by others *about* his critical writings had used it (usually pejoratively) – though he remained uneasy about the term. '[T]he word travesties every idea I ever had on the subject', he wrote,[40] adding later: 'How often I've had to point out (privately) that all I ever wrote in that connection tended to be deprecatory, if not downright pessimistic – insisting only that nationality isn't an option but a circumstance.'[41] Another problematic term for Curnow was 'poetics'. 'My "poetics" (if we have to admit the term)', he insisted, 'are inferential, from my practice: and from a few explanations and rejoinders when challenged, all very thoroughly dealt with in your Intro.'[42]

Re-reading so much of his earlier criticism also served to remind Curnow, uneasily, that whether he liked it or not he had become a 'historical subject', increasingly the subject of historical and critical scrutiny in which he often found it difficult to recognise himself. In addition to Stead's recontextualising of his poetry and criticism in 'From Wystan to Carlos' and Paterson's presentation of him in *15 Contemporary New Zealand Poets*,[43] Leigh Davis offered a provocative new reading of the poetry, in 'Solo Curnow', published in the third issue of the magazine *And* in October 1984, informed by postmodern and poststructuralist perspectives, and Roger Horrocks, in the first issue of the same short-lived magazine (October 1983), offered the first genuinely new reading of Curnow's introduction to his Penguin anthology, in a seminal article entitled 'The Invention of New Zealand'. In this new local critical context of the 1980s Curnow was nervous about how to approach an interview which Harry Ricketts had proposed, for a collection of interviews he was preparing on contemporary New Zealand poets.[44] 'I think CKS might remind me (if it occurred to him) that there's no arguing with "literary history"', he wrote to Ricketts, but 'one's problem is how to be historical and busily alive at once!'[45]

Curnow had engaged tangentially with some aspects of the New Zealand literary scene in his Turnbull paper on Charles Olson, but his own 'poetics', as he wrote to Simpson, were 'inferential', related in that paper to his current, 'busily alive' interest in the relationship between phenomenology and his own practice as a poet. In general, the approach he adopted for the rest of his life was to avoid public intervention in any of the ongoing debates about theory or literary history and about his own placement in such discourses, and to refuse to be drawn into public pronouncements about other poets, while willingly involving himself in readings and interviews which related to his own poetry. He gave numerous such interviews in newspapers and on radio, in New Zealand and overseas, for the rest of his life. They were always generous (and often highly illuminating) about the provenance and context of the poems he was writing himself, but were careful not to make negative judgements on other poets or *ex cathedra* pronouncements about the literary culture at large.

One of the issues he did not wish to be drawn into in his interview with Ricketts was a comparison of his own work with Baxter's. His own view of Baxter clearly separated the poet (at his best) from the myth of the public figure and religious prophet in later life, for which he had little respect:

[I]t's what he does in the Boss's time with the Boss's letterhead that can raise doubts about the honesty of his enterprise. Jimmy didn't make Yeats's famous choice between

'perfection of the life, or of the work' – he used religion to advertise the poetry, and
poetry to advertise the religion, & compromised both.[46]

However, he had an immediate reason to be wary of such comparisons. In October
1984 Jamie Grant had written a piece in the *Age Monthly Review* in which he challenged an opinion that Baxter was New Zealand's 'foremost' poet and suggested
that such an accolade, if it were to be used at all, belonged to Curnow. Curnow
wrote to Tim that 'it was impossible not to welcome a dissenting voice in the
general beatification of Baxter',[47] though he found 'the tendency to compare his
work with mine – the reputations, that is, rather than the work – . . . odious, like
most such comparisons'.[48] This '"rival poets" nonsense' is why he felt that it would
be best if no question of 'me and / or Baxter' came up in the published interview.[49]

Given his frustrations with local literary politics during the first half of the
1980s it was hardly surprising that publication in the UK greatly appealed to
Curnow, and it was a sign of the increasing interest in his poetry there that he
was invited in August 1984 (with Bill Manhire and Lauris Edmond) to read it at
the sixth biennial Cambridge Poetry Festival in June 1985. Assisted by a recently
established New Zealand Literary Fund travel bursary, worth $5,000, he planned a
two-month trip (June to early August) with Jeny, based in London, and a number
of other events were organised, including a reading at the Poetry Society in Earls
Court, a reading (also with Manhire and Edmond) at New Zealand House in
London, and a recording of a 20-minute programme devoted to his work for BBC
Radio 3 (under its features producer, Fraser Steel) in its 'Living Poets' series.

During late 1984 and the early months of 1985 Curnow finalised the
text of *The Loop in Lone Kauri Road*, attended to the interview with Ricketts
(and another, about Ngaio Marsh, with Bruce Harding),[50] and worked on
arrangements for the overseas trip. Such visits had now assumed an increasing
importance for him. Stocks of *You Will Know When You Get There* were still available in the UK, distributed through Oxford University Press, but the 200 copies
of the Penguin *Selected Poems* sent to the UK a year earlier had sold out, and he
was anxious that stocks there be replenished. He replied carefully to a series of
questions about New Zealand poetry and his own work from Robyn Marsack, of
Carcanet Press, who was preparing an article on Curnow, Manhire and Edmond
for a special issue of the *PN Review* timed to coincide with the Cambridge
Poetry Festival. Insisting, in answering one question, that 'isolation is a fact, not
a feeling', he also took the opportunity to clarify his view of the relationship
between poetry and theory:

I think 'theory', whether poets' or critics', is best regarded as systems of apologetics
for practice, as by Spenser, Sidney, Jonson – of course they had their Puttenhams and

Gabriel Harveys too – or Hopkins (funny, how we hear so little of him lately), Yeats, Eliot, Pound. A poet had best keep a safe distance from linguistical namedroppers and self-mystifiers; he can't help being in their world, but he's not of it. His 'theory', if anything, is his own business, which may have more to do with what theory can't account for than with what it can. I don't mean he *despises* it – at least while it's an effective advertisement for poetry, rather than for itself.[51]

Marsack quoted extensively from Curnow's comments in the piece she wrote, 'A Home in Thought: Three New Zealand Poets',[52] which also included three of his most recent poems, 'A Raised Voice', 'On the Road to Erewhon' and 'The Loop in Lone Kauri Road'. While he was making these preparations he was also contacted by Greg Gatenby, the organiser of the Toronto International Festival of Authors, with an invitation to visit in October. The prospect of reopening this wider North American horizon for his work provided further relief from the frustrations he felt in the local literary scene.

London and Toronto, May–August and October 1985

Curnow and Jeny left Auckland on 28 May 1985, travelling via Tokyo, where they stayed for three days. 'What a 12-million megalopolis', he wrote to Stead on a postcard featuring Utamaro's *Fickle Look*, 'all glitter & riches in the middle & 50 miles of industrial disaster all around.'[53] They were met in London on 1 June by Catherine Pierard, who helped them in many ways during their stay there. The Cambridge Poetry Festival ran from 14 to 16 June, and in the meantime they settled in to their studio flat in Chelsea Cloisters in Sloane Avenue, acquainting themselves with their new London location, revisiting the Turner rooms at the Tate Gallery, and seeing a Royal Shakespeare Company production of *Hamlet* at the Barbican. Curnow proofread his latest poem, 'Lo These Are Parts of His Ways', at the offices of *Encounter*, and also spent time preparing for and rehearsing his poetry reading, to be given on the first evening of the festival, Friday 14 June, in which he was to share the platform (half an hour each) with the Northern Irish poet Seamus Heaney, with the American poet Amy Clampitt, and with the French-Canadian poet Anne Hébert.

Curnow's three days at Cambridge were busy and tiring, but extremely enjoyable. He and Jeny were hospitably entertained as house guests by Rosemary Davidson, of the educational division of Cambridge University Press, where they were joined for the second two days by Olga Rudge, Ezra Pound's lifelong friend, then a spry, highly intelligent 91-year-old, a guest of the festival which included a number of events marking the centenary of Pound's birth. On the afternoon of 14 June, prior to his own reading in the evening, he attended a performance in Peterhouse Lodge of Geoffrey Hill's poetic sequence 'The Pentecost Castle', set to music for piano and baritone by Robin Holloway with the title 'The Lover's Well'. It was 'one of the best things to be heard' at the festival, he wrote to Lilburn.[54] Hill's knotty, intellectually challenging poetry interested Curnow greatly, and he was intrigued that the work was performed twice for its audience – a mode of presentation which he later experimented with himself.

Heaney was a big draw card for the reading that evening and there was 'a packed house of 500'.[55] Curnow's selection was designed to include both the local (Karekare) and European range of his later work, comprising 'Canst Thou Draw Out Leviathan with an Hook?' and the sequence 'In the Duomo' from *An Incorrigible Music*, followed by a number of more recent pieces, including 'A Sight for Sore Eyes' and 'Blind Man's Holiday'. He was pleased by the warmth of the comments he received, including from the festival chairman, the poet Peter Robinson, whose own work even at that early stage in his career had been influenced by Curnow and who subsequently became a good friend.

On the following day Curnow made his second contribution, to a panel session on Pound with Charles Tomlinson and Clive Wilmer, intended to be informal and including a brief reading from Pound's poetry. 'I was able to speak briefly', he later reported to the Literary Fund, 'about the literary / political stir in the United States over the 1949 award of the Bollingen Prize to Pound's *Pisan Cantos*: having been there at the time, and personally acquainted with one or two Fellows in Literature of the Library of Congress (who judged the award) I could add a little to the more common knowledge of what happened that year.'[56] His choice of poetry from Pound was the 'Four Poems of Departure' from *Cathay* – brief, richly etched landscape pieces in Pound's imagist mode, whose theme of absence and departure to distant places perhaps resonated with Curnow's own situation as a distant visitor to the festival.

Curnow met Michael Schmidt (editor of *PN Review* and director of Carcanet Press) for the first time at Cambridge, as well as Greg Gatenby and Fraser Steel, the latter covering the festival for BBC radio, with whom Curnow finalised arrangements for his appearance in the 'Living Poets' series on Radio 3. However, the figure who most fascinated both Curnow and Jeny was Olga Rudge, with whom they enjoyed long morning conversations as their fellow house guest. 'Olga is living history', Curnow wrote to Stead, and they heard 'more than she would or could tell a tape-recorder'[57] 'of everything that happened to her and Ez – esp. between Rapallo, Genoa & Pisa at the end of the war – one wanted her to go on, & on'.[58] Rudge lived in Venice on the Zattere, very near where the Curnows had stayed on their numerous visits, and before she left she invited them to stay there at her guest apartment.

Back in London Curnow immediately set to work on his script for the BBC, which he needed to prepare well in advance of the recording session on 10 July, drafting an opening introduction to his work, followed by prefatory comments on each of the poems he selected: in order, 'Any Time Now', 'A Touch of the Hand', 'You Will Know When You Get There', 'Moules à la Marinière', 'The Skeleton of the Great Moa', 'Do Not Touch the Exhibits', 'This Beach Can Be Dangerous' and 'A Raised Voice'. On 20 June they had lunch with Richard and Jocelyn Mayne at their house in Park Village East, Regent's Park. Mayne, amongst his many other activities (historian, translator, editor, broadcaster and journalist), was co-editor of *Encounter* at this time (sitting in as literary editor for Thwaite, who had taken a year's leave, and shortly to take over that role when Thwaite decided not to return to his old position). He and Jocelyn established an instant rapport with the Curnows, offering the use of the house for a fortnight later in July while they holidayed in the Lake District. It was an offer they were delighted to accept, since it not only offered a location in their favourite part of London but enabled them to reciprocate hospitality impossible at Chelsea Cloisters, especially with Jeny's relatives, and including an evening with Alan and Elizabeth Ross and the poet and editor Gavin Ewart.

In the meantime Curnow had other literary engagements to prepare for. On 25 June, again with Edmond and Manhire, he read poetry at an event organised by the New Zealand High Commission at New Zealand House. 'I don't think I've ever felt an audience (around 100) so intensely with me', he wrote to Pearson, describing his reading of 'Moro Assassinato'. 'Perhaps the "hostage drama" character of the poem helped, being so much of the moment.'[59] Ten days later, on 4 July, he gave a solo reading organised by Pamela Clunies-Ross at the Poetry Society in Earls Court, warmly introduced by Fleur Adcock. It was a small audience but he read confidently and effectively, mainly from *You Will Know When You Get There*, including its two 'big' poems, 'Organo ad Libitum' and 'A Fellow Being'. After 10 July, when he recorded his 'Living Poets' programme at Broadcasting House, he felt freer at last to socialise more widely. 'All of these readings', he wrote to Stead, '…make it a strange London visit. It's only the perversity of one's nature to crave attention, & complain of exposure when it comes.'[60]

There had been no time for poems – or even drafts of poems – during the trip, but two ideas for poems were stirring, based on the Tokyo stopover on the way to London. One was focused on Curnow's response to the vast 'geodesic dome' of Narita airport, the other on a long walk during their second day in Tokyo, which took them to the Imperial Gardens and a vista of the Imperial Palace. The shortness of the stay in London also meant, as Curnow commented to Pearson, that he was able to spend less time taking in 'the state of the nation', absorbing the newspapers and weeklies, as was his wont.[61] This trip to London had been very much a working holiday, making his recent work more widely known and expanding his network of literary contacts.

Back in New Zealand Curnow turned his attention to preparations for his trip to the Toronto Festival (18–26 October), for which the cost of his travel and accommodation was shared between the festival itself and the New Zealand Literary Fund. He finalised his involvements in the text of *Look Back Harder*, proofread *The Loop in Lone Kauri Road*, and tried to arrange, again, for copies of his books in print to be available at Toronto. This proved no problem with *You Will Know When You Get There*, but the only arrangement he could make for the Penguin *Selected Poems* – much to his frustration – was to take what copies he could manage in his own flight baggage.

He had three engagements during the festival: a reading (with the Japanese novelist Kenzabue Oe, later awarded the Nobel Prize for Literature, Alice Adams, also a novelist, and Eeva Kilpi, a Finnish poet and novelist) on the evening of 22 October; a panel discussion next day (with Brian Aldiss, Helen Garner, Kilpi and George Lamming) on the theme of 'Writing on the Edge'; and a 30-minute interview with Rick Johnson for a radio documentary (on CJRT-FM) about contemporary poets. 'The Toronto week was worth the effort', he wrote to Lilburn, though with many of the other authors (including 'fellow-Cornishman' William Golding, Angus Wilson, Malcolm Bradbury, Saul Bellow, and his fellow participants) 'it was mostly small-talk & interrupted conversations'.[62] The reading which most impressed him, amongst the poets who participated, was by '30-year-old Michael Hulse, one of the newest & brightest Brit poets, & one of the few whose work I know'.[63] Hulse, a poet, critic and freelance translator (especially of German literature) for Penguin and other publishers, then based at the University of Cologne, was accommodated on the same floor of the Toronto Hilton and they enjoyed a great deal of each other's company during the festival, becoming close friends and regular correspondents.

In the lead-up to his 30-minute reading Curnow was initially unsure whether 'he would be better representing himself with a long poem, which could show what he could turn around in a substantial space, and the different registers he could hit on and so on, or whether he would be better advised to do a reading of shorter poems'.[64] In the end he chose the long poem 'A Fellow Being' – partly because of F.J. Rayner's Toronto connections – together with his most recently completed poem, 'Lo These Are Parts of His Ways', and spent most of the day before preparing and rehearsing for the reading, as well as for the panel session the day after that. Hulse remembered Curnow's reading very distinctly:

> [W]hat struck me was the physical presence of the man and the way that the sinew of the poetry seemed to move almost through his body. There were moments when there

were repeated words, like the word 'columnar'. They stand off on the side in the way the verse is set out, and he would replicate that bodily by seeming to stand suddenly outside the flow of the poem as he spoke, and virtually jolt into an erect 'columnar' position. I don't mean that he was going for any large theatrical manner, but there was something in him that wanted to enact a sense of the physical presence of the poem, and 'A Fellow Being' is a poem with a lot of physical energy.[65]

The day after his panel session Curnow took a long walk into the city, avoiding a programmed trip to the Niagara Falls, and at the end of the week took part in a peace march opposing Canada's participation in NATO. He had taken a great deal of pride in the positive comments from other writers about New Zealand's anti-nuclear stance under David Lange's Labour Government, elected the previous year, and wrote to Lange immediately to inform him of the fact.* [66]

Overseas recognition, retreat into poetry writing

During the years 1983 to 1985 Curnow's reputation overseas developed markedly, and he established a significant network of contacts with a number of people (mainly poets) who thought highly of his work. To those who first brought his later work to the notice of UK readers (Anthony Thwaite and Alan Ross) were added Donald Davie, Peter Porter, Peter Bland and Gavin Ewart, and in 1985 Peter Robinson, Michael Schmidt, Richard Mayne and Michael Hulse. In Australia Chris Wallace-Crabbe, Geoffrey Dutton, David Martin and Jamie Grant were strong admirers. In New Zealand, also, of course, his work continued to attract strong critical interest, even though the poetry scene had become much more diverse and divisive, and dissenting voices about Curnow's poetry began to appear.†

The new *Penguin Book of New Zealand Verse* (1985), edited by Ian Wedde and Harvey McQueen, struggled heroically to negotiate the theoretical minefields, and Curnow in turn (despite his liking for Wedde's poetry) struggled to come to terms with his own 'mixed-up feelings' about what he called the 'Bumper Book of Kiwiverse'.[67] He disagreed with much in Wedde's introduction, which he thought 'affects an openness it in fact denies', and regarded Wedde's thoughtful reassessment of the significance of women's poetry as 'blatant politicking &

---

* 'To hear you, and so many others say how good it makes you feel to be a New Zealander gives me, and all of us I think, great heart', Lange replied, adding, '[it] indicates how we are moving away from our rather sad cringes of the past'. In a postscript Lange mentions that he has met Curnow's niece Mattie Wall (in fact his first cousin once removed) in New York who he thinks 'feels the same'.
† Such as Leigh Davis's 'Solo Curnow', *And* 3, October 1984: 'a kind of poetry on the point of exit, or decline'.

dishonesty of thinking, a gross misstatement of facts'.[68] 'A good anthology can carry a mixed cargo', he added, 'but this one makes me seasick.'[69]

Stead's reaction to much that was happening in the literary culture was to engage publicly on the issues. Although Curnow agreed with much that Stead said, his own strategy was to withdraw from the public arena and to concentrate on his own poetry – much as he had 30 years earlier in response to the so-called Wellington–Auckland poetry wars.

In March 1986 Curnow participated in the Writers' and Readers' Week of the Wellington International Festival of the Arts, appearing alongside Hone Tuwhare, Yvonne du Fresne and the American author Robert Stone on 14 March (when he read 'You Will Know When You Get There', 'A Touch of the Hand', 'Canto of Signs without Wonders', 'The Loop in Lone Kauri Road' and 'Things to Do with Moonlight'), and on 16 March he appeared solo in an hour-long session chaired by Wedde. When he returned to Auckland he and Jeny enjoyed entertaining Anthony and Ann Thwaite on their visit from the UK, including hosting them at Karekare, and towards the end of the month *The Loop in Lone Kauri Road* was published. As usual, Curnow was anxious about its reception, and he was also anxious about the absence of new poems. Leaving aside 'Lo These Are Parts of His Ways', which he had revised in the earlier months of 1985, he had written no new poem since 'Blind Man's Holiday' eighteen months earlier.

Chapter Thirty-two

International Recognition,
Continuum and *Selected Poems*
(Viking), 1986–90

I'm anything but neglected at home. I suppose I pine for the more
rigorous critical climate. Critically, there's not much challenge in NZ,
where poets grow like bean sprouts on wet flannel – do I hear you say,
where do they not?[1]

Reception of *The Loop in Lone Kauri Road*

Curnow's new collection was slim, a mere ten poems which with notes and generous
spacings throughout made for a volume of 38 pages – insufficient for a spine,
but with a striking cover design by Phillip Ridge incorporating a photograph of
Len Lye's kinetic sculpture *Roundhead.** Despite its slimness the volume received
outstanding reviews, in New Zealand in the months after its publication in March
1986 and in the UK after its publication there towards the end of that year. Oxford
University Press's New York branch also took 150 copies, and within eight months
of initial publication 1000 copies had been sold. Like its predecessor, *You Will Know
When You Get There*, the volume shared the New Zealand Book Award for Poetry
in 1986, and it also received the Buckland Memorial Literary Fund Award in 1987.

---

* Suggestive perhaps of American electronic music composer Alvin Lucier's visual/acoustic installation
entitled 'long wire' which provided the catalyst for the third section of 'Blind Man's Holiday'.

It was the overseas reception of the volume which most pleased Curnow, simply because he felt that the critical climate in the UK in the 1980s was more rigorous. 'Your poems don't need my praise', wrote *Encounter's* Richard Mayne, 'but I think they are masterly. I still look jealously at "A Raised Voice". But the title-poem is a winner, too. And in that race, there are no losers either. Hommage au maître.'*[2] The volume was warmly reviewed by John Forth in the *London Magazine* and Jenny Penberthy in the *Times Literary Supplement*, as well as by Bernard O'Donoghue in *Poetry Review*, who wrote that Curnow's 'work stands comparison with any English-writing poet of the century':

> These searching and various poems operate with a small nexus of ideas to do with perception, both ocular and metaphysical. In their different way they are as good as anything he has written and – most astonishingly – more imaginatively ambitious than anything before.[3]

The Loop in Lone Kauri Road also attracted high praise from Michael Hulse, in *PN Review* ('If I had to nominate one poet now writing in English with any true claim to greatness, it would be Allen Curnow'),[4] who was one of the few critics at the time to understand the importance of the shift to syllabic measures in the later poetry:

> *The Loop in Lone Kauri Road* contains ten poems. Rhythmically they are tantalising: Curnow likes to establish a notional syllabic count for the line – nine syllables in one poem, eleven in the next – but he reserves the right to depart from his count as often as he likes; and he knows that even behind the most unbuttoned of his cadences, such are our ears, we may go picking out an iambic metre, so he enjambs heavily, and likes to break his line after prepositions or unstressed verbs in order to punch into the next with a stressed syllable, and he threads exclamatory or interrogatory inflexions, colloquial expressions, in among the more deliberately construed elaborations. The effect is to suggest that a vanquished iambic line is staging an attractively counter-pointed comeback.... There is nothing in the handbook of rhythm that Curnow cannot teach a fellow-poet.[5]

In the wake of the publication of *The Loop in Lone Kauri Road* Curnow was hoping for new poems. 'One of these days there will be new poems', he wrote to Stead in April. 'Not too long (meaning the time not the poems).'[6] However, in May he had to spend several days in the Mater Hospital for prostate treatment

---

*   Mayne had accepted 'A Raised Voice' for *Encounter*, only to discover that Curnow had also sent it by mistake to *PN Review*, which accepted it first.

('an entirely routine prostatectomy by laser', he wrote to Stead), and at the same time Jeny was diagnosed, much more seriously, with a breast cancer requiring a partial mastectomy followed by radiotherapy. The operation (in June) was successful, but for some months both were deeply anxious about the outcome.

In the midst of these anxieties Curnow received the CBE for services to literature in the Queen's Birthday New Zealand Honours List in June 1986, an award which 'seems to have pleased more people than I wld have guessed – including me!' he wrote to Tony.[7] He asked the *New Zealand Herald* and Christchurch *Press* to preserve the anonymity of Whim Wham in any publicity, aware (as he wrote to Tim) that: 'Local media simply don't know what to do with a poet who is precisely a poet, not a hippy barnstormer, a paraplegic, or a mother of eight.'[8] The trip to Wellington for the investiture also entailed a precious catch-up with Lilburn, who was able to bring Curnow up to date with progress on a new LP which was to include a performance of *Prodigal Country* – one of Lilburn's earliest works, written in England, which included voice settings from Curnow's early poem 'Enemies', and from poems by Robin Hyde and Walt Whitman. Lilburn also planned a new recording of 'Landfall in Unknown Seas' to be performed by the Auckland Regional Orchestra in a triptych of his works'.[9]

In August, 'after . . . a long and worrying drought'[10] – nearly two years – a new poem at last arrived. In the draft Curnow sent to Stead, derived from fragments in the autobiographical notes he made at Menton and afterwards, its title was 'All the News', but this soon became – after a number of revisions – 'Survivors', and the poem was accepted by Alan Ross for *London Magazine*. Its location was Hagley Park, Christchurch, on Armistice Day, 1918, when the poet was a child of seven – a scene of public celebration, with the fire brigade spouting jets of rose-coloured water 'ebulliently' into the dark, the whole illuminated by the play of searchlights across Hagley Park's small lake – and it is an unusual 'World War I poem', avoiding any hint of patriotic rhetoric or any notion that the experience was the seedbed of national identity. Hoisted onto his father's shoulders the child is oblivious to the larger meanings carried by the momentous event of the end of the 'war to end all wars', fascinated by the colourful spectacle, of 'people simply enjoying themselves', but his responses nonetheless prefigure something of the pathos with which the poet, in the poem's present, invests the scene.

'Survivors' was one of the more readily accessible of Curnow's later poems, written in what had become by this time a favoured syllabic measure – a hendecasyllabic line of eleven syllables. Two months later, after a great deal of intensive work, he finished a second poem – in much more technically demanding tercets of eleven, nine and seven syllables – which was accepted immediately by Mayne for *Encounter* ('a delight . . . I'll make sure that you jump the queue of worthy work').[11] The poem was 'Narita', a powerful meditation going back to his stopover in Tokyo the previous year, evoking the poet's thoughts as he waits his turn to embark and imagines a horrifying jumbo jet crash. Its central event, the imagining of a last departure for those destined to die in an air crash, is shocking for the casualness with which it initially interrupts the speaker's reflections and fantasies, and for the vividness and immediacy of the moment when the plane's tail section ruptures, with its aftermath of fallen, dismembered bodies and belongings. The tragedy and pathos of the scene are intensified by the 'brightness fallen from the air', the scattered accessories, uniforms and badges of the aircraft crew and passengers:

> . . . the meantime is all there is.
> It passes of itself. Your cabin
> crew girls are for off-duty
>
> fantasies. Abaft the loo the tail section
> ruptures, the sky inhales heavily,
> a change of plan is announced,
>
> all four hundred, some gifted or beautiful
> or with greedy heirs, have to die now,
> only to make sure of you
>
> this instant sooner or later than you think.
> The prettiest accessories, like
> silk scarf, matching lipstick, badge
>
> of rank are brightness fallen from the air, you
> will never see it. The uniformed
> personnel most pitiably
>
> heaped, colours of daedal feathers, the smells of
> burning, a ring'd finger, a baby's
> foot bagged for the mortuary.
>
> No, you will never see it. Wish yourself then
> the best of Lucifer's luck. . . .

'You will never see it.' Accidental death, so horrifyingly illustrated in such a catastrophe, emphasises that the instant of death is never predictable ('sooner or later than you think'), and that its occurrence and nature remains forever beyond the foresight and imagining of its individual victims. Curnow's actual presentation of the moment of the crash, however, reveals imagination moving outside the cocooned world inside the airport, and draws part of its inspiration from a poignant line ('Brightness falls from the air') in Thomas Nashe's moving lyric of death's inevitability in plague-stricken Elizabethan England, 'In Time of Pestilence'. For Nashe the death of beauty carries special tragic pathos:

> Beauty is but a flower
> Which wrinkles will devour;
> Brightness falls from the air;
> Queens have died young and fair;
> Dust hath closed Helen's eye;
> I am sick, I must die –
> *Lord, have mercy on us!*

Unlike Nashe's lyric, however, 'Narita' offers no religious consolations, only the injunction, in a world in which death strikes randomly, to 'Wish yourself then / the best of Lucifer's luck.' Lucifer, Milton's fallen light in *Paradise Lost*, hurled from Heaven by God, miraculously survives his fall. The irony of Curnow's allusion not only rejects any redemptive frame of reference, but also implies that survival in a world whose very condition is the unpredictability of events is only ever a matter of luck, fragile at best. Jeny's and his own brushes with potentially life-threatening illnesses a few months prior to the writing of 'Narita' may well have given a special edge to the poem's awareness of human vulnerability to such accidents of fate.

'There's a philosophical pollution of the poetics . . . . the poetry needs cleaner air': cultural politics, 1986–87

Proofreading the collected critical writings which Peter Simpson had edited, writing a brief author's note to the volume (which went through several anxious drafts), and answering last-minute detailed queries, meant that matters of literary and cultural politics (local and international) were never far from Curnow's thoughts during the mid-1980s, though he did not enter any of the controversies – often personality-focused – which surfaced at the time in magazines, newspapers, radio and television, preferring to express his opinions privately in correspondence with literary friends. While he did not wish to engage publicly in general debates about 'theory', or to challenge the revisionist accounts of New Zealand literature (and his own) which they were producing, he did wish to know enough about the key figures and ideas (about Derrida, in particular, on the notion of authorial agency, and about the Saussurian-derived discourse of semiotics) to be able to defend his own practice as a poet, in his own different terms.

During the summer of 1986–87, perhaps spurred into action by his reading in contemporary literary theory, Curnow firmed up on a decision to publish his later poetry as a collection. Perhaps he hoped, as had happened in the 1950s, the poems might quite simply speak for themselves, challengingly and freshly, in relation to whatever might be made of them from current theoretical perspectives. He had mentioned the possibility of such a volume in April and October 1986 to Tim, but in early January the following year wrote more urgently that it was 'something I want to get on with' and seeking advice about copyright on the five volumes he had published since *Trees, Effigies, Moving Objects*, as well as the choice of a publisher.[12] He was unhappy that Oxford University Press had recently decided to relinquish its co-imprint with Auckland University Press, because he felt that Oxford had handled the distribution of his books very well in the UK, and because he had become increasingly frustrated by what he saw as poor distribution of AUP books in New Zealand. He was also disenchanted with Penguin (NZ), especially after their pulping of 500 copies of the *Selected Poems* in 1985 at the very time when they were unable to arrange for copies to be available for the Toronto International Authors' Festival. The dozen copies he was given, to take in his flight luggage, had sold out immediately, and he believed a major promotional opportunity for his work in North America had been lost.

In the end he decided to stay with AUP and sent a proposal to new managing editor Elizabeth Caffin in April 1987. The volume's proposed title was *Continuum. New and Later Poems 1972–1988*, after a poem he had just completed, which supplanted other possible titles (*Survivors* or *Narita*) he had mentioned to Tim earlier in the year. At this stage he was planning to include a few poems from *A Small Room With Large Windows*, relating to the origins of *Trees Effigies, Moving Objects* in 1961, but decided against it. Presumably, these poems would have included at least the two New York poems of 1961, published under the title 'An Oppressive Climate, a Populous Neighbourhood'. His old Washington friend Zaro Starr had recently sent him a copy of Robert Penn Warren's *New and Selected Poems*, and he was attracted by the way Random House had presented Warren's poems in reverse chronological order. He adopted the same principle, beginning with a section containing his six most recent, uncollected poems (under the subtitle *Continuum and other poems 1986–1988*), then proceeding backwards with the five later volumes, each published in full and with the same internal order as in their original publication. An author's note explained: 'The logic of the collection favours this arrangement; besides, it agrees with my own perspectives over these years, and perhaps with the way past and present things shift about in some of the poems.'[13]

Even more to the point was an epigraph he included from Solzhenitsyn's *The First Circle*, a passage which had touched an immediate chord with Curnow, reflecting his own lifelong attitude that every latest poem had to be – or feel like – a new start:

> There is a law that governs all artistic creation, of which Kondrashov had long been aware, which he tried to resist but to which time after time he feebly submitted. This law said that no previous work of his carried any weight, that it could not be counted to the artist's credit. The focal point of all his past experience was always the canvas on which he was working at the time; for him the work in hand was the ultimate expression of his intellect and skill, the first real test of his gifts . . . only *now* was he really finding out how to paint! . . .[14]

'His "law" answers to my own feeling, & I'm sure to others' who have done enough work to feel the same', he wrote to Caffin.[15]

In mid-May 1987, shortly after AUP had accepted the proposal for *Continuum*, *Look Back Harder* was published, and Simpson arranged, with the University of Canterbury and *The Press* as co-sponsors, for Curnow to visit Christchurch, where the book would be launched. It was a busy visit in the first week of June, accompanied by Jeny – his first visit to Christchurch for ten years – and included two talks and readings at the university, a public reading at the State Trinity Centre (formerly the old Congregational Church) in Manchester Street, and an informal mid-morning reception in his honour hosted by the editor of *The Press*, Binney Lock, who invited former editors and journalistic contemporaries of Curnow, as well as the current literary editor, Naylor Hillary. Norman Macbeth, editor during much of Curnow's time there in the 1940s, was unable to attend, but wrote warmly about Curnow's calibre as a journalist during the war years, his special competence 'on the stone' (his ability to spot or foresee potential difficulties in the layout of lines and columns and make swift adjustments to the text), and his impressive feats of 'instant composition' as Whim Wham.[16]

The publication of *Look Back Harder* was also the occasion of two informative newspaper interviews, in which Curnow took the opportunity to allude briefly to his current reading in literary theory. Speaking to Adrian Blackburn in the *New Zealand Herald*,[17] he emphasised the *ex post facto* character of literary theory, the need (in writing about the past) to avoid 'being trapped by one's own sentiment in remembrance of the past', and the distinctly separate activities of the poet and the critic. In *The Press* Hillary also elicited informative comments about his reading and compositional methods. 'Curnow confesses to an interest . . . in the French theorists or philosophers, or their post-modernist followers', Hillary wrote, 'but he is cautious of poetry as an expression of philosophy':

'The more I try to muddle out their writings, the less it seems to have to do with poetry or literature at all. The philosophical debate is in one world. Matters concerning the poet, busy with his art, take place in another world.'[18]

As for the process of writing poems:

'It's all part of a search – looking for the point where the self and the object you are trying to put together are as close as you can possibly get them. You can never get yourself out of your poems – not that you would want to. Sometimes you may work on a poem until you despair. The urge was a mistake. There isn't a poem there. Just an experiment. One day you may go back to it. Poems require hard work and even agony. It has always been so.'[19]

The trip to Christchurch was also 'not without moments & strangenesses all its own', Curnow wrote to Stead.[20] One of these, triggered by an awareness of the decade-long gap since his previous visit, and his own advancing age, was a curious sense of the *recentness* of the city's architecture, as he wrote to Ian Milner:

Looking at Chch again, I have this curious thought: that I'm now myself older than the oldest buildings were when they looked so venerable to me in my school years. What a subjective (& relative) thing history is, sometimes – one's true Pantheon may be the Museum porch on Rolleston Avenue. Chch has been poking a few timid high-rise blocks into that very open sky. An argument is on, about a 300-metre tower from which (developers claim) restaurant diners will get a grand view of the Southern Alps – it is argued wisely to the contrary, that if this is what they want they can have a much grander one from the Cashmere Hills.[21]

A related moment occurred one evening in Latimer Square (near the junction of Manchester Street and Cambridge Terrace where Curnow's grandmother Curnow and his father, as a child, had lived much of their rives), when he and Jeny were struck by the spectacular light effects generated by the setting sun. A year later these experiences, blending with a memory of his father always referring to Christchurch as if the city had existed long before its recent founding in 1850, only 30 years before his own birth in 1880, provided the starting point for one of Curnow's finest later meditations, 'An Evening Light'.

The Christchurch trip was followed by two further trips to Wellington in the months following – in July to receive the New Zealand Poetry Book Award for *The Loop in Lone Kauri Road*, and in August to participate in a number of events marking the opening of the National Library of New Zealand. These included, on 5 August, a reading of 'Landfall in Unknown Seas' with the Wellington

Regional Orchestra conducted by William Southgate (the first reading he had given it himself for ten years), a poetry reading with Witi Ihimaera and David Eggleton, and a long recording session with Elizabeth Alley, of two programmes subtitled 'Looking Both Ways' for a ten-part Concert Programme series, 'Writers at Work'.* From the 1980s Alley was especially active in promoting Curnow's poetry in her radio programmes, interviewing him as each volume appeared, arranging for the BBC Radio 3 programme which he had made in London in 1985 in its 'Living Poets' series to be broadcast in New Zealand, and in 1985 sponsoring a series of programmes (entitled 'Preferences') on individual poems, which included a discussion of 'A Small Room with Large Windows' by Michael Gifkins (then a writer and literary critic), accompanied by a reading of the poem by Curnow. He was delighted with the 'Looking Both Ways' programmes: 'I marvel, & Jeny too, at the fine skills of your editing. . . . If the readings were better than I expect of myself in a studio, it's because you were my audience.'[22]

Continuum, new poems, 1987

By September 1987 Curnow had almost finalised the manuscript of his later poems, and at this stage had four new poems to add to the five previous volumes. In addition to 'Survivors' and 'Narita' from the previous year these were 'Continuum' and 'The Vespiary'. 'Continuum' was completed in April 1987, providing the title for the proposal he sent at that time to AUP. Like 'The Weather in Tohunga Crescent' and 'Any Time Now' the poem has at its centre a disturbing experience in which the physical world suddenly empties itself out – disappears into nothingness. Unable to sleep, unable to rid himself of the self-consciousness of *thinking* about the world, the poet walks outside onto the porch at Tohunga Crescent seeking to lose himself in the reassuring otherness of the contents of the night sky:

> A long moment stretches, the next one is not
> on time. Not unaccountably the chill of
> the planking underfoot rises
>
> in the throat, for its part the night sky empties
> the whole of its contents down.

---

* The series included five overseas authors, and the other New Zealand contributors were Peter Bland, Ruth Dallas and Margaret Mahy. Curnow devoted his first programme to reading and discussing earlier poems ('Tomb of an Ancestor', 'House and Land', 'The Unhistoric Story' and 'The Skeleton of the Great Moa') and his second to a range of later poems ('A Leaf', 'There Is a Pleasure in the Pathless Woods', 'A Raised Voice' and 'The Loop in Lone Kauri Road').

To Stead, Curnow described the experience that sparked the poem as a 'Solipsist Shock': 'all at once there wasn't any out-there, nothing but in-here. . . . I suppose there's nothing special about the idea (or delusion) that one makes the world by looking at it – but if the world unmakes itself, where's the onlooker then?'[23] 'Something of the little uneasiness or misgiving about whether anything is really to be trusted to stay where it is, or to be firm under our feet is something that's in all of us', he commented of such poems to documentary maker Shirley Horrocks.[24]

The other poem Curnow wrote at this time, 'The Vespiary: A Fable', was one of his strangest and most teasing – 'a sort of fantasia', he wrote to Ted Wall[25] – imagining a post-apocalyptic era during which New Zealand (over the course of millennia) has been taken over by an invasion of wasps, who then mixed symbiotically with human beings ('in an agon of orifices, host and guest / legs, wings, damp secretions') to evolve an entirely alien species. In March 1987, at the prompting of Zaro Starr, Rosanna Warren (Robert Penn Warren's daughter), poetry consultant for *Partisan Review*, had approached Curnow to send some poems:

> At that time my cupboard was absolutely bare, but I sent off the first poem I finished, called 'The Vespiary: a Fable'. . . . For years I've rather felt the loss of the few American friends in poetry I ever had.[26]

He finished the poem in early May, a month after he had completed 'Continuum', and sent a copy to Stead in June, after it had been accepted for *Partisan Review*, explaining the multiple origins of its fantasy of a wasp-takeover of the country: a wasp's nest (vespiary) 'on a shrub in front of the corner house in Tohunga Crescent'; a recent newspaper report of a swarm of wasps in Motueka (in the South Island) which attacked and killed a goat and led to the temporary closure of the local school; and a Karekare memory of his sister-in-law, Elisabeth, using the French words with which the poem concludes to warn her two barefoot boys of wasps 'hovering over the grass' as they come up from the beach.[27]

Although the poem does not lend itself to any simple allegorising of its futuristic narrative, it is suggestive at a number of levels. It taps into earlier poems in which a smugly complacent New Zealand society ('our oceanic nation's / defences in traditional disrepair') is overwhelmed by historical forces over which it has no control. It parodies the notion, built into the utopian genre, that the future is predictable and controllable (as a topic, Curnow wrote to Stead, the post-apocalyptic was 'the property of hacks, bad video and the good Greens', and he hoped to make it work 'more like a *genre* than a topic, if that makes sense').[28] Most powerfully of all, the poem is an expression of Curnow's epistemological scepticism, hinting throughout at the partial, contingent, speculative character of all knowledge of the past. Indeed, the poem may well be deploying a bathetic pun on the words 'gap' / 'guêpe' (wasp) in its concluding line – '*Attention! Les guêpes!*' – a warning to be aware of the 'gaps', the deficiencies, in human knowledge.

A few months later, in September, Curnow began another of what he called his 'septuagenarian poems' – poems (like 'A Raised Voice', 'A Sight for Sore Eyes' and 'Survivors') reaching back 70 years to the second decade of the twentieth century, drawing on 'those things early in your life that hit', as he commented in an interview with Judith Whelan.[29] 'A Time of Day' recalled a memory of Curnow's first half-hour air flight as an eight-year-old child in the rear, open cockpit of a 'dung-green' Avro 504K biplane, brought to Sheffield by touring barnstormers for display and joyrides in the year after the end of the First World War. Designed and built for wartime use when aviation was still in its infancy, the Avro 504K was a joint Anglo-French initiative, 'a triumph of 1915 aeronautical science'[30] – in the imagination of many a miraculous technology opening a new chapter in human mastery of nature and offering the prospect of a new era in human communication. 'Believers only', the poem states in its opening line, characterising the religious aura which this fascination generated. The young child shares the curiosity and excitement of the rural, upcountry crowd who pay an entrance fee to gather in the paddock of a local farm and witness the marvel of manned flight, but the poem takes a characteristically inward turn, bearing on the poet's own present, as he contemplates the event 70 years later.

The biplane itself, once seeming to express the marvels of modern technology and embody the promise of a new age, is now a somewhat grotesque museum piece, offering a sceptical illustration of human credulousness. Furthermore, the plane initially 'descends' out of 'pearl-dipped light', as if 'born' of cloud, a numinous expression of some ethereal 'soul of the world' (*anima mundi*) – as if its origins and destination offered to the imaginations of 'these people waiting to be saved' an enlarged image of the spiritual dimensions of the world in which they live. If flight gets human beings off the ground, however, it does so in order to locate them simply in a larger purely physical world hauled into 'the time of day' – Curnow's beautifully evoked vista, from the cockpit, of mountains, sea and sky looming closer:

> Neither does the soul
> of the world, whatever that is, lose
> hold of the load, the bare blue
>
> mountains and things hauled into the time of day
> up that steep sky deepening from sea-
> level all the way west again,

> this paddock, the weight of everything, these people
> waiting to be saved, without whom there's
> no show, stay in place for ever.

'A Time of Day' was the first of Curnow's poems to be accepted by Karl Miller, editor of the fortnightly *London Review of Books*, which from this time on became the main UK venue in which his poems initially appeared. It was an ideal vehicle from Curnow's perspective: it had a large, international readership and rigorous editorial standards, and it published high-calibre journalism, often of article length, on a range of topics (political, social, historical, cultural) beyond the purely literary. Of the 22 poems he wrote from this time until his death in 2001 no fewer than sixteen appeared first in the *London Review of Books*. None that he sent was ever rejected, and they regularly appeared within a matter of weeks of his sending them. He became the magazine's single most important poetry contributor during this period.

Two months after the completion of 'A Time of Day' Curnow was able to add a sixth new poem at page-proof stage to *Continuum*. 'The Pug-mill' was another memory poem dating from Curnow's West Lyttelton childhood years, presenting the local brick-maker Mr Prisk as an archetypal image of the builder and the poet, his dogged, repetitive labour driven by 'thought' so internalised that it appears instinctual or automatic, 'baked in the bones of his wrist'. It provided a lively companion piece to 'A Time of Day' and 'Survivors' in the half-dozen new poems appearing in *Continuum*. It was also the last of his poems to appear in *Encounter*,[31] which had been struggling with a declining circulation for a number of years and folded in 1990.

London, Venice and Rome, August–October 1988

In February 1988 Jeny's uncle, the painter Charles Tole, died, and a small inheritance made it possible for the Curnows to contemplate another trip to Europe – their fifth, since the first in 1974. 'We have *vague* – or rather very vague – plans to visit London and Venice, possibly in August–September', Jeny wrote to Tony and Elisabeth,[32] who by this time had sold their Karekare property and since 1986 re-established themselves at Pruzilly in France.

The plan to visit Europe became much firmer the following month after Curnow was contacted by the publishing director of Penguin (NZ), Geoff Walker, with the news that the parent firm in London was interested in publishing a selection of his poems under its Viking imprint and in its Penguin International Poets series.[33] With the imminent prospect of the publication of

Continuum in late June, which would make all his later poetry available for the first time overseas (he hoped) as well as in New Zealand, and with invitations to visit the Maynes and the Thwaites, and to meet his newest editor, Karl Miller, it seemed a propitious time – after three years – to re-establish contact with the London literary scene.

The Curnows left New Zealand on 10 August, and after an exhausting trip (the flight was delayed for nearly 24 hours with engine trouble) they arrived in London, 55 hours after leaving Tohunga Crescent, on 12 August. They spent the first few days staying with the Maynes at Regent's Park before shifting to a studio apartment at Nell Gwynn House in Sloane Avenue, Chelsea. On 23 August Curnow met Paul Keegan (editor of the Penguin Classics series) to discuss the prospect of a selected poems, and within a week received a formal letter confirming the project: a manuscript of approximately two hundred pages to be submitted by May the following year (1989) which would be published as a Viking hardback in spring 1990, then in paperback in the Penguin International Poets series in autumn, with an advance royalty of £2,000, half payable on signing the contract, the other half on receipt of the manuscript. Keegan also summarised their discussions about the kind of selection it might be, confirming emphasis on the later poems and agreeing that a strict chronological ordering was not essential:

> I think that the volume would certainly benefit from a very generous inclusion of your later work. Michael Hulse possibly feels the same way. The more I think about the lay-out of the selection, the more convinced I am that the poems can stand without direct reference to the individual volumes from which they are drawn . . . . In any case a Selection is an arrangement of a different kind and, in its own terms, complete. This would also mean that you can follow broadly chronological lines but defy chronology when you want to.[34]

The Viking project was by far the most prestigious of Curnow's career, and at last offered the prospect that his work would be readily available on the international market:

> The fact is that for years I've put up with hard-won notices abroad, & being an almost invisible poet, unavailable at booksellers: this new imprint makes a big difference, it kicks me out into the world, & that's the place to be, let it be as cruel as it likes. It amazes me (just a little) that this has happened at all.[35]

The day after his successful meeting with Keegan the Curnows visited Anthony Thwaite at his home, The Mill House, at Low Tharston near Norwich. Thwaite's good company, Jeny observed, reminded her of the relationship between Curnow and Glover.[36] During their stay they revisited the ancestral house, Markshall (where Curnow's grandmother, Rose Gambling, had been born), at Caistor St Edmund, and also revisited Norwich Cathedral. The following week, back in London, they enjoyed catching up with Jeny's relatives, Wensley and Clare Clarkson and Angus and Yvonal Stewart, and Curnow lunched with Karl Miller, where he was pleased to hear himself described as a 'talented poet'. In the first week of September the Curnows visited two of Jeny's step-cousins in Dover and Edinburgh, and after their return attended (on 8 September) the only formal event of their trip, a luncheon in Allen's honour organised by the Commonwealth Institute, at which there were 20 guests, including Peter Porter, Mayne, the Thwaites, Blake Morrison, Andrew Gurr, Fleur Adcock and Gavin Ewart, with others from the Poetry Society, the British Council and the New Zealand High Commission. By this time the London leg of their trip was coming to an end. There were other meetings, with Alan Ross, with Peter Porter and his partner Christine, and a visit from Rosemary Davidson, and they just managed to catch up with Tony and Elisabeth, visiting London, for an hour, before catching their flight to Venice.

Venice, where they stayed for a fortnight (13–27 September) at their old haunt, La Calcina, in a balconied upstairs room on the Zattere overlooking the Giudecca Canal, more than lived up to their expectations on this, their fourth visit after 1974, 1978 and 1983. For ten days they 'explored old haunts and found a few new ones',[37] and spent time at the Venice Biennale and a large Dali retrospective show, and for the last four days of their stay were joined at La Calcina by Michael Hulse from Cologne. Hulse had been part of the sequence of events which led to the Viking selected poems project, enthusiastically recommending Curnow's poems to his friend Chris Miller, an Oxford-based freelance translator and critic who was immediately impressed and brought it to the attention of Keegan at Penguin Books, who in addition to his work as Penguin Classics editor was editor of its poetry list and looking to develop an international list of modern poets, some in translation. Once Keegan had decided to include Curnow in the series he became the eighth in a very select list comprising the Chilean Pablo Neruda, the Russians Anna Akhmatova and Osip Mandelstam, the Pole Czesław Miłosz, the US-based Russian émigré poet Joseph Brodsky, Derek Mahon from Northern Ireland, and the Frenchman Philippe Jaccottet.

From Venice the Curnows travelled to Rome on 27 September, staying for three days at the Hotel Anglo Americano where they had stayed in 1974, and revisiting some of their favourite spots (the Borghese gardens, the Pantheon, and the restaurant in Trastevere where they could request musicians to play Sicilian folk pieces). On 30 September they began the long haul home, via Singapore, arriving in Auckland on 3 October.

The making of the Viking *Selected Poems*

Reviews of *Continuum* had gradually begun to appear by the time Curnow returned to New Zealand, but the two best – by MacDonald P. Jackson in *Landfall* and Mark Williams in the *New Zealand Listener* – did not appear until a year after publication.[38] Curnow was anxious about how long it took the book to be distributed in Australia and the UK, since he had hoped that there would be close to a two-year gap between its appearance and publication of the Viking *Selected Poems*, due out in March 1990. Lachlan Mackinnon had been given a mere three columns to write about nine volumes of New Zealand verse in the *Times Literary Supplement*, but managed more than the faint praise he reserved for most of them when he wrote of *Continuum* as a 'toughly distinguished . . . exceptional volume', whose 'nervy syntactic uncertainty' and 'jerky technique' 'binds details into poems, poems into sequences, masterfully'.[39] The two best UK notices, however, were by Hulse in *PN Review*,[40] and, especially, by Stead in a long review-article in the *London Review of Books*, his most considered assessment of Curnow's poetry since his seminal article of 1963.[41] Stead himself had a significant reputation in the UK by this time – more especially as a novelist and critic – and his review was likely to have been influential for those readers interested in poetry.

As the reviews of *Continuum* gradually filtered in, Curnow was busy preparing his selected poems. It was indeed 'the hardest [selection] I've had to do', he wrote to Tim,[42] since in jettisoning any idea of chronological order and abandoning any signposting by volume, he had to find some other means of organising the selection without (he hoped) forcing the poems too strongly into a preconceived pattern. He chose 82 poems altogether for this 200-page selection: a dozen from the 1940s, ten from the 1950s and one from the early 1960s, the rest taken entirely from the later poems with the exception of four from the 1973 volume *An Abominable Temper* ('To the Reader', 'To an Unfortunate Young Lady', 'To Douglas Lilburn at Fifty' and 'A Refusal to Read Poems of James K. Baxter . . .') and two from the 1982 collection *You Will Know When You Get There* ('Impromptu in a Low Key' and 'The Ocean Is a Jam Jar'). He grouped them into three numbered sections – beginning with some late poems about early childhood and concluding with late poems about ageing and death with a *memento mori* character, the last his most recent, uncollected poem, 'An Evening Light' – and hinted at his organisational principles in a preface: 'The poems may or may not, as the reader pleases, seem to describe a kind of circle, joining age and youth, a loop in the road.'[43]

The decision to avoid chronology altogether was a bold move, challenging those familiar with his work to rethink the connections between them, to avoid premature historical generalisations about the development of his poetry, and to

see it as a whole from the perspective of the poet's present interests and preoccupations. In the earlier chronologically arranged New Zealand Penguin selection
(1982) readers had been given 'a bus journey through familiar country, where
everyone knew the stops, and who was likely to get on and off', he commented
to Simpson.[44] In the Viking selection it became much more difficult to read
Curnow in terms of a simple binary shift from earlier (nationally focused) verse
to later more personal and international concerns, or indeed to see his work as
falling into two 'earlier' and 'later' phases, however these might be characterised.
Apart from the general three-part pattern, many incidental connections are
suggested through the placement of particular poems, and Curnow seems to have
been deliberately playing with the idea of such chance collisions and overlaps.
On the face of it, for example, it might seem odd that 'Narita' is placed between
two poems of early childhood, 'A Time of Day' and 'A Sight for Sore Eyes', until
one thinks of 'A Time of Day' and 'Narita' as a pair with an imaginary subtitle,
'From biplane to jumbo jet', the two poems spanning a century of aviation technology, the tragedy of the later poem offering an ironic comment on the fresh
hopes of the earlier one. Every placement invites readers to ponder connections
which a chronological presentation would have obscured.

It is hardly surprising that Curnow regarded this selection as the 'hardest' he
had yet attempted, since it involved no less than a complete critical re-reading
and personal reassessment of all his work, not only in the arrangement of the
poems but in the selection of those to be included. He was adamant that the
weighting of the selection so strongly towards the later poems did not mean that
he regarded the later work as superior to the earlier:

> No, it doesn't mean that at all. It means that I found more of the best poems in
> the later collections, as well as some of the very best in quite early ones – poems
> that people still admire and quote nearly 50 year after I wrote them, like 'Landfall in
> Unknown Seas', 'House and Land', and the sonnet about the moa.[45]

However, for readers familiar with the poetry, numerous well-known early
poems were absent. Curnow was probably glad of the opportunity to jettison
'Wild Iron', whose popularity always remained a mystery to him, but others
missing from the 1940s include 'Sailing or Drowning', 'Discovery', 'At Joachim
Khan's', 'Eden Gate', 'The Waking Bird Refutes' and 'A Sonata of Schubert',
and from the 1950s 'To Forget Self and All', 'The Eye Is More or Less Satisfied
with Seeing', 'When the Hulk of the World' and 'A Changeling' – ten poems
which might feature highly on other readers' lists of Curnow's best. Hulse, while
agreeing with the focus on the later poems, had also advanced the merits of
'A Victim', the sequence *Not in Narrow Seas*, 'In Summer Sheeted Under' and the

Curaçao poem from *Poems 1949–57*. Curnow chose none of these. He gave a great deal of thought to his sonnets from the 1940s, and despite encouragement from Stead (who listed 20 from the 29 in *At Dead Low Water and Sonnets* which he thought should be included)[46] to be as generous as possible, in the end Curnow confined himself to a selection of eight only.

Keegan was nevertheless pleased with the draft list of contents which Curnow sent him early in 1989 ('the movement of the whole seems splendid – as well as locally unpredictable'),[47] and in early April the manuscript was complete, including a brief preface, and eight pages of highly informative notes to the poems, some taken directly from earlier volumes but adjusted and expanded for a non-New Zealand readership.

'I feel loaded below my private Plimsoll-line with these things': awards and honours, 1989–90

Almost immediately after completing the manuscript of his selected poems Curnow heard that *Continuum* had won the regional (Australasian and Pacific) award for the best volume of poems published in 1988. The award was the first stage in the selection of the winner of the annual Dillons Commonwealth Poetry Prize – sponsored by the Commonwealth Institute in the UK and (for the first time in 1989) booksellers Dillons, and carrying a prize of £5,000. The winning entries from five regions (Africa, Asia, Canada and the Caribbean, and UK and Europe, in addition to Australasia and the Pacific) were then judged by an international panel (including the regional judges, chaired in this year by Anna Rutherford of Aarhus University) meeting at the Commonwealth Institute in London from 12 to 18 May 1989. The five finalists travelled to London for the announcement of the overall prize, which Curnow also won. The effect on sales of *Continuum* in the UK (like Porter's mention of the Penguin *Selected Poems* in his *Observer* review of *You Will Know When You Get There* in 1983) was immediate. Dillons ordered 82 copies for its bookstores and Oxford University Press asked for 150 copies to supplement the hundred copies they had taken the previous year.

Curnow and Jeny had left Auckland on 14 May, with a one-night stopover at Los Angeles, and Curnow was plunged into a hectic round of media interviews on his arrival, followed by an exhausting week's reading tour with the other finalists, taking in Birmingham, Edinburgh, Stirling, Aberdeen, Liverpool, and finally Cambridge, before returning to London on 26 May. Advance publicity was poor and the audiences were often small, but the Curnows particularly enjoyed the company (and the poetry) of Kofi Awoonor (the Ghanaian poet and diplomat, currently ambassador to Cuba), and managed some pleasurable

sightseeing in Edinburgh and Liverpool. For the readings each poet was allo-
cated a twelve-minute slot, enough for three or four shorter poems. For the
first two readings Curnow chose the two 'Lone Kauri Road' poems from *Trees,
Effigies, Moving Objects*, as well as 'The Loop in Lone Kauri Road' and 'Narita',
but varied his offerings after this, including in one programme 'Lo These are
Parts of His Ways', 'Narita' and 'Continuum', and in another 'A Sight for Sore
Eyes', 'Any Time Now' and 'Survivors'. In Cambridge they met up with Hulse
and his partner Dorle Merkel (who had come to England from Cologne to see
them), as well as, for the first time, Chris Miller, who travelled from Oxford to
meet Curnow.

Back in London the Curnows moved into a flat at 61D Aylesford Street,
Pimlico, within walking distance of the Tate Gallery whose highlight at the time
was a Paul Klee exhibition. Curnow had several meetings with Keegan about the
selected poems project (one of them a lively lunch including Hulse, Merkel and
Miller), threading his way to the Penguin offices through a large protective police
cordon and wooden barriers in the wake of Muslim demonstrations against
Penguin for publishing Salman Rushdie's *The Satanic Verses*. They also visited the
Maynes, and Peter Porter and Christine, spent a relaxing day with Catherine
Pierard, and enjoyed two plays during this brief ten-day period – Wycherley's
The Plain Dealer at the Barbican and Chekhov's *Ivanov* at the Strand Theatre –
before departing London on 7 June and arriving back in Auckland on 11 June.

It had been 'a fantastically busy month', Curnow wrote to Tim,[48] its rigours
ameliorated by the fact that the award provided excellent publicity for *Continuum*
as well as for his forthcoming *Selected Poems*. There had also been considerable
publicity in New Zealand, including an editorial, 'Honoured for his landmarks',
in the *New Zealand Herald* – a '21-gun salute', Curnow added to Tim, '[b]ut
it's the thought that counts',[49] and he wrote appreciatively to the editor, Peter
Scherer, that 'it's so seldom that we're reminded of what poetry can mean to
people – our tiresome poetic ego has to earn its keep, outside the mere aesthetics
of the trade'.[50]

To Tony, Curnow also spoke of wanting to start a new poem, 'but it keeps
eluding me'.[51] At this time Ted Wall, continuing his interest in Monro family
history, had sent to Curnow some notes he had written about a terracotta pot
once belonging to Peter Monro (a prized family relic which Grandmother Alice
Curnow had inherited), and about the life of its original owner, in which he
speculated about the location of 'Mata', where Monro had originally purchased
property in the Hokianga.[52] Curnow replied in detail,[53] describing relevant items
in the dilapidated Monro family scrapbook he had in his possession. On one
of its pages a pious visitor to the Monro house in the Hokianga in 1841, the
Wesleyan missionary William Woon, cited a stanza from a hymn by Charles

Wesley warning against 'the power of sound' and 'music's charms', describing himself (with his son and a Mr Marriner) as 'Detained at the Mata, Mr Munro's [sic], during a gale of wind, Oct. 1, 1841'. Perhaps it was Curnow's recent visit to Edinburgh (from which Peter Monro had originally immigrated to Australia, then New Zealand), as well as Ted Wall's queries, which prompted him to revisit his early Monro history in 'The Scrap-book', a poem quite different in character from 'An Abominable Temper' and very much in the mode of his Canterbury 'familial' poems. However, it was not until November that the 'elusive' poem based on Woon's page in the scrapbook was finally coaxed out into the open and sent off to Miller at the *London Review of Books*, who answered Curnow's 'Will this do?' with, 'Good God, of course it "will do"', and printed the poem within a month of receiving it.[54]

In August 1989, only three months after the award of the Commonwealth Poetry Prize, Curnow received a handwritten letter from the British Poet Laureate, Ted Hughes, inviting him to accept another, even more considerable award, the Queen's Gold Medal for Poetry: 'It would give me great personal pleasure if you would accept. And would also gratify the members of my small Committee. Your support is extremely strong, and most emphatically includes me.'[55] Curnow was astonished, touched, and delighted by the recognition. The Gold Medal for Poetry, awarded every two or three years, had been instituted in 1933 at the suggestion of the then Poet Laureate, John Masefield, and was the highest public accolade in the UK for poetry. Previous recipients had included W.H. Auden (1936), John Betjeman (1960), Philip Larkin (1965), Robert Graves (1968) and Hughes himself (1974), and the year prior to Curnow's award it had been 'liberated' (as Hughes put it) from being restricted to UK residents and made available to all 'the Queen's subjects'. The presentation of the medal would be in New Zealand the following February, 1990, during a visit by the Queen as part of the country's sesquicentennial celebrations marking 150 years since the signing of the Treaty of Waitangi in 1840.

In December 1989 Curnow was invited in confidence to accept yet another award, as an additional member of the Order of New Zealand (ONZ) – the highest New Zealand honour, awarded 'for outstanding service to the Crown and to the people of New Zealand', instituted in 1987 and confined to a maximum of 20 recipients, but with provision for additional members to mark special national occasions (such as the sesquicentenary). Janet Frame also received the ONZ on this occasion, and the awards were announced on Waitangi Day, 6 February 1990. 'I feel loaded below my private Plimsoll-line with these things', Curnow wrote to Tony,[56] and he was nervous about the official ceremonies themselves which were due to take place on 14 February – a private audience with the Queen at Wellington's Government House at 4 p.m., when he would receive the Gold

Medal, and the ONZ investiture event at 5 p.m. 'It will be just the two of us [Jeny and himself] for the Medal presentation', he wrote to Tim, describing a nightmare in which he found himself about to be presented to the Queen 'wearing shabby brown shoes':

> How strange (if you think of it) to meet in the flesh a woman whose sole occupation is being Queen! And that queens meet more poets than poets do queens. QEI never received Spenser, but gave him a pension. Victoria asked Tennyson to sit down and talk about the Hereafter. QEII won't ask me to sit down, and I expect our business will be graciously done in a few minutes . . . . I feel curious about this historic moment. The best model is Dr Johnson, when George III paid him a compliment. Had he anything to reply to it? 'No, Sir. Since the King has said it, it must be so. Who was I to bandy civilities with my Sovereign?' But in 1990, how very strange it all is! Not only that it's happening to me, in Wellington, but that it is happening at all.[57]

He met up with Jeny in Wellington, after fulfilling a long-promised engagement to read at the Aoraki Literary Festival (held inland from the town of his birth, Timaru), and in the event the occasion went smoothly and memorably, the Curnows quickly put at ease by the Queen's 'charming, unaffected, and anything but condescending' manner as she presented both honours.[58]

Whim Wham retires

Throughout the 1980s, until Curnow began the preparation of his Viking *Selected Poems* in 1988, Whim Wham's weekly appearances in the *New Zealand Herald* and *The Press* had continued unabated, though there had been gaps during his overseas visits to Menton and London in 1983 and to London, Europe and Toronto in 1985, by which time his payment for each piece had increased to $56. In August 1988, the week before he and Jeny left for their two-month holiday in London and Venice, Whim Wham announced his temporary departure, and anticipated resuming his weekly verses after his return:

> Sir, by the Time You receive
> These Lines, I'll be away on Leave.
> I've granted my own Application
> For two months' Rest and Recreation.
> I've not declared Myself redundant,
> For which my Gratitude's abundant.
> Blind Followers (and blinder Leaders!),

If Hopes were Drugs, could Fears be worse,
But for that weekly 'Fix', my Verse?[59]

Although it was not his intention at the time, this was to be the last of Curnow's Whim Wham pieces. Other events intervened – the award of the Gold Medal for Poetry, the final, minutely detailed checking of the proofs of the *Selected Poems* – and the effect of being loaded below his 'private Plimsoll-line' with honours and awards was not to rest on his laurels (pleased as he was to receive them) but to spur him into new writing, to begin, yet again, afresh. Moreover, Curnow was now in his eightieth year and had lost much of the stamina needed to meet the weekly deadline Whim Wham demanded. Effectively, though his interest in current affairs, local and global, remained undiminished, Whim Wham retired from his remarkable public life of more than fifty years so that his creator could conserve and concentrate his energies on new poems.

The range of issues on which Whim Wham wrote in the 1980s was similar to that of previous decades, though the emphases and particular topics were different. After the Springbok tour of 1981, rugby occupied less of the foreground. On the global front, the threat to world peace posed by nuclear technology and the Cold War, in the era of Ronald Reagan, Margaret Thatcher, Leonid Brezhnev and Andrei Gromyko, continued as a recurrent theme, of which 'Don't Hurry, History' provided a lively example.[60] Numerous pieces praised the adoption of an anti-nuclear policy by the newly elected New Zealand Labour Government in 1984; and on the occasion of British Foreign Secretary Sir Geoffrey Howe's visit to Wellington, Whim Wham attacked his government's muted criticism of France, after agents of the French secret service bombed the Greenpeace flagship anti-nuclear protest vessel *Rainbow Warrior* in Auckland harbour in July 1985.[61] The catastrophic meltdown of an ageing Soviet nuclear reactor at Chernobyl in the Ukraine in 1986, causing widespread radioactive contamination, provoked an equally strong response.[62]

The biggest shift of satirical emphasis, however, after the departure of Muldoon from the political scene in the mid-1980s, was to the new market-based economics engineered by Roger Douglas, Minister of Finance in the new Lange administration. His radical reforms in the second half of the decade were designed to 'deregulate' the economy, allowing 'market forces', local and global, to dictate whether particular industries survived or went to the wall. 'Corporatisation' introduced new 'user-pays' market principles into state-owned entities which were transformed into profit-oriented state-owned enterprises (SOEs), and 'privatisation' led to the outright sale of state-owned assets, at outrageously cheap prices, to the private sector. 'Rogernomics', as it came to be called in New Zealand, was derived from the Friedman-influenced New Right economics of the Reagan and Thatcher administrations in the US and UK, but was far more thoroughgoing in its implementation, and dramatic in its effects, in a small country like New Zealand, suddenly exposed to the 'free' flow of global capital. Pleased as Curnow was by the Labour Government's foreign policy initiatives, he was appalled by its adoption of economic policies which he saw as deliberately creating unemployment and increasing the gap between rich and poor.

Whole new obfuscating vocabularies were spawned out of the new economics ('restructuring', 'level playing fields', 'human resources', 'nourishment centres' instead of soup kitchens, 'clients' or 'consumers' instead of students, and of course 'user pays') and spread into the core fields of government – education, the social services, health agencies – and whole new industries were spawned (management agencies, consultancy firms, communications companies) all with their jargons derived from thriving American university business schools whose models and curricula New Zealand universities rushed to adopt. All these aspects of Rogernomics provided a fertile field for Whim Wham's corrosive wit during his last years. 'Sales Talk' pilloried the new market jargon around the term 'branding',[63] 'On with the Process' poured scorn on the reformers' euphemistic reference to an ongoing, painful 'adjustment process' in the deluded belief that New Zealanders would discover, 'some Visionary Morning, / The Market Force Millennium dawning',[64] while 'Delivering the Goods' registered blank amaze-ment at the emptiness of the marketplace jargon used by Lange as Minister of Education, a portfolio he took over after his re-election in 1987:

> What can these Present Structures be?
> What are the Goods? The Efficiency?
> These Beehive Buzz-words baffle Me!
> They obfuscate, they don't convey
> The Sense of What he doesn't say –
> Disguised by what he does –
> The Words don't mean, they only buzz,
> The Meaning, such as you can trace,
> Being borrowed from the Marketplace –
> Delivering Goods! Will you be wiser
> For those Groceries? That Fertiliser?
> He's the Headmaster to the Nation,
> Restructuring its Education –
> Perched on the Supermarket Shelf,
> He's an Education in Himself![65]

However, it was Douglas himself, the architect of the new economics, who attracted many of Whim Wham's most barbed satirical shafts, in pieces like

'The Jolly Roger',[66] about farmers forced into bankruptcy by the removal of state subsidies, and 'Fundamental Faith',[67] about small businesses forced to the wall. 'Everything Must Go', written in Wham Wham's last year, summed up his feelings about the country, under 'Richard' [Prebble], Minister of State-Owned Enterprises, 'Roger' [Douglas] and 'Dave' [Lange]:

> When Richard and Roger have flogged
>> Off the last SOEs
> To a Consortium of Oz Wizards, Swiss Pawnbrokers
>> And Hong Kong Gnomes;
> When the last millionaire Boatpeople
>> Or sharemarket Refugees
> Are secure in their Luxury Homes,
>> The Costa Brava, Ibiza, Surfers' –
> One Jump ahead of the Receivers –
>> Leaving our Island State, what's left of It,
> To us miserable Under-achievers,
>> The Remnant or Rump, of the Nation;
> When Corporatisation
>> Becomes Privatisation –
> How many of the Population
>> Have no gainful Occupation?
>
> If we're not on the Dole we'll be taxed
>> To support Those who are –
> Till We too are Restructured – and axed –
>> We've been lucky, so far!
> When Richard and Roger have auctioned
>> The Property, Lot by Lot,
> Is this the Nation we thought we had,
>> A deceased Estate – or What?
> Let's throw in Roger's Beehive Desk
>> And the Carpet on the Floor,
> Tack a Private Sector Managing Director's
>> Name on the Door.
> Let's offer Richard's Talent for Hire
>> To some Private Monopoly,
> With a Job for Dave – if he'll behave –
>> Let's do the Thing properly![68]

Throughout the 1980s there were lighter pieces though, as always throughout Whim Wham's career, a typical example of which is 'Today is a Good Dog', an affectionate account of a walk with Curnow's recently acquired pup, Towser, at Karekare, the versification finely adapted to the relaxed, regular pace of man and dog, in step with each other, as time stealthily pursues them:

> For vacant Minds,
> > Vacation Stuff –
> The hardworked Muse
> > Is out of Puff.
> I walk my Dog,
> > My Dog walks Me,
> I'm in no Hurry,
> > Nor is He,
> We don't look round,
> > Behind our Backs
> Time's padding softly
> > On our Tracks.
> The following Week,
> > The following Day
> Catching us up –
> > We walk, and They
> Follow so close
> > There's not Much in it,
> We lead by a Nose
> > From our next Minute.
> We don't look round,
> > Backs to the Sun
> Which always wins
> > In the long Run –
> Never mind That!
> > We're walking now –
> Am I walking the Sun
> > On its Lead, somehow?
> Feeling, briefly,
> > Time is my Dog,
> On an easy Slope, at
> > A gentle Jog? –
> Instead of a Mountain
> > Insurmountable! –

Just for the Moment
     I'm not Accountable?[69]

It was in the nature of Whim Wham's identity that he should retire without publicity or fanfare, much as he deserved such acknowledgement. After his astonishing weekly performances for more than fifty years the feeling of release, the pleasures of 'unaccountability' – perhaps, also, a tinge of regret – when Curnow finally decided that his alter ego would remain in retirement, remained wholly personal. The decision had 'cleared the decks' for whatever new directions his serious poetry might take from this time on.

Chapter Thirty-three

Expanding Critical
Interest in Curnow, 1990–93

*Allen Curnow shares with Eliot and Rilke the symbolist leaning to the
sacred; with Pound the desire to present larger historical subject matter
alongside the things of the world in all their manifold diversity; with
Williams the democratic love of the things of the world for their own
sake. . . .*

Michael Hulse[1]

Reception of *Selected Poems, 1940–1989*

The Viking *Selected Poems* was very well received, though it produced a noticeable
division between New Zealand reviewers, who were intrigued by the volume's
abandonment of chronological order and concentration on the later poems,
and overseas reviewers, who scarcely mentioned the order and concentrated on
the impact of the poems as a whole. Curnow tended to be impatient with local
suggestions that the organisation and selection had been specifically geared to
an international audience, 'like export quality lamb – or specially slaughtered for
Muslim consumption'.[2] Despite his misgiving that in the UK 'somebody is sure
to be whetting his little hatchet',[3] reviews in the *Financial Times*, *The Literary
Review*, *Poetry Review* and the *London Review of Books* were unanimously favourable, and he received warm compliments from friends like Anthony Thwaite and
Richard Mayne. 'I can only express admiration for a cathedral built over so many

years', Mayne wrote, 'and I appreciate how you've arranged the poems: a full circle, in fact, as memory recreates the earliest years as a porch to the glorious building.'[4]

Max Richards, a former student of Curnow's, now at La Trobe University in Melbourne, commented in *Span* that '[a] slow trot through much early Curnow might have impeded recognition of the versatile and adventurous poet he has become',[5] and Peter Porter wrote a highly intelligent review in the *Sydney Morning Herald*:

> Curnow is a quiet virtuoso whose command of language is so consummate that the reader is in danger of attributing to his or her own quickness insights and satisfactions already plotted exactly by the poet. Whether you are startled, as if by a sequence of peremptory chords, or lulled quietly into the delta of a poem, you may find yourself well into one of Curnow's pieces before you begin to notice its technique. He combines a vernacular diction with a high baroque tone, and never wrenches the tessitura of his language, even over an extended range.[6]

However, 'this beautifully produced volume is not the whole story', Richards warned, and reminded readers of the earlier 1982 New Zealand Penguin *Selected Poems* (which he had also reviewed) which 'contains poems from his earlier books which reveal a more galvanic Curnow'.[7]

Curnow was also pleased with Michael Hulse's review in the wide-circulation UK weekly newspaper *The Independent on Sunday*, which conveyed the broad range of the poet's interests and left it open to readers to come to terms with his achievement as 'arguably one of the finest poets in the English language today'.[8] Yet he was less impressed by a review by Giles Foden in the *Times Literary Supplement*, which was a curious mixture of praise and blame, attacking Curnow's Poundian 'modernism', of which he is seen as a 'brave' inheritor, expressing a 'classic modernist stance' in an age of postmodernism which 'seems largely to have passed [him] by'.[9]

Foden's review had the immediate effect of provoking a lively article in Curnow's defence by Donald Davie, entitled 'Postmodernism and Allen Curnow', which appeared in *PN Review* early in 1991. He agreed with Foden that Pound was 'the presiding presence over Curnow's poetry as we now have it, defined by the poet himself, in this *Selected*', but disagreed strongly that such an affiliation locked Curnow into a superannuated past, as if 'history has moved on [into the postmodernist present] while he, privileged simpleton, hasn't noticed'.[10] Curnow was pleased with Davie's vindication of his work, as well as his 'very civil & authoritative rebuttal of Foden's positions',[11] though he was puzzled by the emphasis Davie gave to Pound while at the same time downplaying the significance of Wallace Stevens. '[O]ne may be a devotee of one of these modern masters or of the other one', Davie had written provocatively, 'but not of both at once.'[12] Curnow would almost certainly have distinguished between the profound relevance of Stevens's *thinking* about poetry to the post-war world, and the fascination of Pound's *practice* as a poet in handling the personal materials of memory, a practice that appealed strongly to Curnow's own interest in such materials in his later poems.

Widening attention in New Zealand and overseas, the early 1990s

After the launch of the *Selected Poems* on 23 September, at the Under Silkwood Bookshop in Parnell, Curnow and Jeny took a fortnight's holiday in Sydney (to mark their twenty-fifth wedding anniversary), where Curnow saw his first Wagner opera (*Lohengrin*) at the Sydney Opera House. On their return Curnow fulfilled his only 'official' 1990 engagement, a reading of 'Landfall in Unknown Seas' with the Wellington Regional Orchestra at the new St Paul's Cathedral in Wellington on 26 October.

Throughout the 1990s, however, Curnow continued to be an object of critical attention in New Zealand as well as in the UK, and was increasingly in demand for interviews and comments about other writers of his generation. In January 1990 Peter Simpson visited Curnow at Karekare and taped an interview which was later published in *Landfall*. In 1990 Curnow also wrote at length to Margaret Lewis about Ngaio Marsh, for Lewis's biography of Marsh, and corresponded with Lawrence Dale – an admirer of Davie and Geoffrey Hill, who was on a visiting fellowship from the UK to Victoria University, Wellington – about possible comparisons between his own poetry and that of Hill. Curnow politely declined the comparisons, describing his first admiring encounter with Hill's work in 1983:

> It was the happy discovery of a poet with whom I find myself purely and solely a *reader*, reminded of nothing I have written myself, or even might wish to have written, or without the least trouble of conscience over writing the way I do. Ideally, I suppose, this ought to be one's relation to any admired poet whatsoever, to take one's place as part of his *public*, neither hopeful follower nor emulous rival.[13]

Hill remained a poet who had 'a more magnetic kind of fascination for me, than almost any of the living poets', Curnow commented later to Shirley Horrocks, despite the 'very enigmatic, cryptic' nature of his writing, offering an example of a poetry which he went back to, inexhaustibly, despite the difficulty of achieving a 'coherent kind of understanding'.[14]

In August 1990 Geoff Walker of Penguin (NZ) approached Curnow to write an autobiography. However, as with Brasch's and Dudding's requests in earlier decades that he contribute a 'Beginnings' piece to *Landfall* and *Islands*, he rejected the proposal firmly.[15] He was not averse at this time, however, to the idea of a critical biography and discussed such a project with Michael Hulse. Hulse had applied unsuccessfully in 1989 for the 1990 Turnbull Library Fellowship, which would enable him to work on Curnow's papers in the Turnbull Library, and he applied again the following year, with Curnow's warm support. In the meantime he busied himself guest-editing a special 40-page section of poems, essays and memoirs devoted to Curnow, of an issue of the Scottish-American poetry magazine *Verse* (one of whose editors, the poet Robert Crawford, was an admirer of Curnow's poetry) to mark Curnow's eightieth birthday in 1991.[16] Chris Miller's piece on Curnow's development towards postmodernism was subsequently developed into a fuller, more persuasive engagement with the ways in which aspects of the later work might be described as postmodernist in a provocatively entitled article published in 1995, 'Allen Curnow as Post-Modern Metaphysical'.[17]

Hulse's second application for the Turnbull Library Fellowship was also unsuccessful. He then made alternative arrangements through the British Council to visit New Zealand in 1991. However, the time available to him – a month only, from late August to late September – made the prospect of undertaking the breadth and depth of research necessary for a critical biography difficult. Curnow's strong instinct to maintain the privacy of his personal life meanwhile reasserted itself, and before Hulse left New Zealand they both agreed – though remaining on the best of terms – that the project was not feasible at this time and should be abandoned.

Curnow could take some pleasure in the growing critical interest in his poetry overseas, but in New Zealand critical readings of his work were becoming more diverse and in some instances distinctly negative. In 1990 *The Penguin History of New Zealand Literature* by Patrick Evans was published, its centrepiece a group of chapters in which Curnow featured strongly as the prime target of a provocative revisionist critique of New Zealand literature from the 1930s to the 1960s. For Evans, Curnow was the figure who had most powerfully articulated a narrow, nationalist, monocultural construction of the literary tradition privileging a small number of white, middle-class, male writers. Although Curnow made many pages of notes about what he took to be Evans's misreadings of his own work and attitudes, he decided in the end not to respond publicly.* [18]

---

* *The Oxford History of New Zealand Literature in English*, genre-based and written by a team of eleven scholars, appeared only nine months after Evans's history, and fared somewhat better in Curnow's estimation. He agreed to launch the book, in March 1991, and while praising in his speech the poetry sections written by Jackson and Caffin, the section on Maori Literature by Jane McRae, and the bibliography by John Thomson, alluded with a degree of distanced tact to the contemporary theoretical frameworks used by other contributors (and, in part, by the general editor, Terry Sturm).

To Pearson, he described the book as 'a fair sample of what [George] Steiner calls "the low quality of deconstructive work being turned out by the academic mills"'.[19] Curnow was especially impressed by the Cambridge- and Geneva-based literary critic's most recent study, *Real Presences: Is there anything in what we say?* (1989), which confirmed his own distrust of the deconstructionist's scepticism about authorial agency and the capacity of language to refer to anything beyond itself. Curnow was also astonished by many passages in *Real Presences* which read like glosses on his intentions in poems he had written long before he had encountered Steiner's work. Steiner's book was unpopular in the literary academies, but for Curnow, as a practising poet, it offered a deeply attractive defence of authorial agency, and appealed deeply to those traces from his earlier religious formation which haunted his abiding fascination with the discourses of metaphysics, theology, and the mythic. Curnow also tried to interest Stead in the book: 'You mightn't agree with the theologian *manqué* in Steiner, but on the pretensions (& weakness) of the theory you must have a lot in common.'[20]

An Italian translation of *The Duke's Miracle*, and new poems, 1991

In October 1990 Curnow was approached by a lecturer in English at the University of Ferrara, Italo Verri, for permission to photocopy his play *The Duke's Miracle*. Verri had been interested in the play ever since first hearing its BBC radio production in 1980, partly because of its Ferrarese background as well as because of its relationship to Browning's 'My Last Duchess', which he regularly taught to his students. However, Verri also had a larger project in mind – a translation of the play for publication in a series of literary editions of famous authors who had featured Ferrara and its culture in their works – the series title, 'I Suppositi', taken from the title of a play by Ariosto.

Throughout 1991 Verri and Curnow corresponded regularly about the translation, and Curnow sent detailed and highly illuminating responses to numerous questions about the meaning of particular references and phrases. Verri drew strongly on these responses, as well as on his own scholarly inquiries, in thirteen pages of explanatory notes to the play, and the fine published text in both English and Italian also included a translation of Browning's 'My Last Duchess', an introduction to the play by Professor Guido Fink, of the Department of English and American Studies at the University of Florence, and a longish biographical note drafted by Curnow himself and translated by Verri. The book – *Il Miraculo del Duca* – was published in December 1993, and a formal launch took place the following February in the Biblioteca Comunale Ariostea. Nothing came of the performance possibility, but given the significance of Italy in Curnow's life and poetry since his first visit in 1974, he was delighted with this first translation of any of his work into Italian.

New poems had been elusive since 'A Scrap-book' at the end of 1989, but towards the end of 1990 Curnow completed 'A Busy Port', the first of four poems (the other three were 'The Unclosed Door', 'A Facing Page' and 'Investigations at the Public Baths') which appeared at regular intervals over the next nine months. 'A Busy Port' was several months in the writing. In July 1990 he wrote to Hulse that '[a] new poem comes very slowly',[21] but it was not until Christmas Day that he was able to send the poem, to be included in the issue of *Verse* which Hulse was planning for early the following year.[22] Curnow also sent the poem to Fergus Barrowman, editor of the New Zealand literary periodical *Sport*, whose first issue had appeared in 1988 – the first of his poems to appear in a New Zealand venue since 'The Loop in Lone Kauri Road' in *Islands* in 1985.*[23] Barrowman thought the poem 'superb',[24] and also published the three other poems Curnow wrote later in 1991. Curnow was pleased, after six years, to be able to reconnect with a magazine readership in New Zealand, in a finely produced journal with an editor whose judgement he respected. *Sport* remained his main New Zealand magazine venue for the rest of his life.

The 'busy port' of the poem's title was Lyttelton, and the poem a recollection of the eleventh-birthday treat promised by Curnow's father, to accompany him (in his role as port chaplain) on a small steamship, the SS *John Anderson*, which serviced the more remote settlements of the Lyttelton Harbour and Banks Peninsula with goods and provisions. Curnow had recalled the event to Glover a dozen years earlier after reading Glover's *Banks Peninsula* poems, commenting, on his own memories of the place, 'If I were not so short on fact & so ungifted for fiction, what a subject Lyttelton of the 'twenties might be':

> Master of the J[ohn] A[nderson] was a rotund chap named Bob Hempstalk. Why do I remember that one of those mornings was sunny; & seeing this fat man, busy in the little bridge (like a Punch-&-Judy theatre & not much bigger) & visibly weeping, & overhearing someone on the wharf remarking that his wife had died. Aft of the bridge, one looked down into the engine-room, & Darky Adams – stoker, engineer, deckhand – shovelling slack into the furnace. Off the Heads that day (or another day) seas were rough for the JA – . . . – allowed to stand up there beside the wheel, I can see the JA's bows actually dipping & rising into waves which looked enormous to me.[25]

The poem is organised into two sections, the first at the quayside as the ship prepares to embark, and the second as the ship gets under way towards the

---

* The last issue of *Islands* appeared in 1987.

Lyttelton Heads, 'pitching like a beer-can' into a strong wind and heavy seas. Stead remarked acutely (perhaps noticing the poem's unusual deployment of short sentences and latent narrative elements) that the poem reminded him of 'fiction at its very best', in particular of Mansfield's 'The Voyage',[26] and at the heart of 'A Busy Port' is a birthday event the child could never have predicted as he accompanied his father down the 'steep gangplank' onto the ship – his shocked encounter (in the form of little more than a sideways glimpse into the ship's wheelhouse) with the ship's captain, Hempstalk, weeping: 'A man's tears, obscene to me // caught looking.' The poem's real subject (like Mansfield's 'The Voyage') is the child's encounter with death and adult grief, and all of its descriptive details are coloured by the momentousness of this discovery. The destabilising feelings associated with it remain entirely *inward* to the child: 'Quayside voices (not for my ears) / discuss the dead, bells repeat // *ding-ding* across the wharf.' He says nothing to his father, even though his father's death and the prospect of his own are caught up into the conflicted feelings of the young child (*and* of the poet in the poem's present) as one re-reads the deceptively simple opening lines in the light of the glimpse of Hempstalk in tears later:

> My turn to embark. A steep gangplank
> expects me. An obedient child,
> I follow my father down.

In this opening tercet the tense moves from the poet's present to the historic present, so that the embarkation, beyond its literal occurrence, becomes an embarkation from innocence into experience, informed by the knowledge that the voyage is death-bound. After his shocked glimpse of 'the spot of a fresh // tear on Bob Hempstalk's cheekbone, whose wet / red eyes blink back seaward', the same reference (past and present) to following his father down recurs, in a context of general mortality. The child's voyage is one of many 'frequent sailings' from a 'busy port':

>   Brightwork traps
> the sun in brass when I next look up,
> following my father down,
>
> who made the trip himself many years
> past. The old rust-bucket gets up steam.
> Frequent sailings from where we live.

The second section of the poem deals with the child's capacity to cope with these thoroughly destabilising insights, with the 'forbidden knowledge' to which he has suddenly become guiltily privy. The sea is rough as the ship embarks in a heavy wind, the boarding plank dipping '*with a short uneasy motion*', like Coleridge's menacingly becalmed ship in *The Rime of the Ancient Mariner*, making the child feel that he is moving out of his depth. However, 'I'm hanging on tight', he comments, and in the concluding stanza Hempstalk reappears in the context of an allusion to T.S. Eliot's phrase, 'Eyes that last I saw in tears', a moving image here of endurance and survival in the face of death and loss. If the bereavement Hempstalk struggles to cope with remains beyond words, reducing him to tears, he is expert in deciphering the ongoing, 'abstruse' (or inexplicable) text of the world itself, expert at remaining 'on course':

> *Eyes that last I saw in tears* can read
> abstruse characters of waves, on course
> between them, our plunging bows.

In mid-March 1991 Curnow wrote to Stead that another new poem was under way, its 'prognosis uncertain',[27] but by the end of April it was complete, except for its title, which in the version he sent to Stead was 'The Abattoir'. 'The Unclosed Door', as it finally became, was another 're-visit poem', as Curnow described it to Stead,[28] recalling a time and place close to that of its predecessor, 'A Busy Port', with a similar focus on the child's sudden discovery of 'forbidden knowledge' about the adult world: a glimpse with a schoolboy friend (Bob Crawford) through the unclosed door of the Lyttelton abattoir at a moment when a lamb's throat is being cut. This gross instance of 'the incorrigible music' of violence in man's relationship with nature – as if endemic in human behaviour – is conveyed through a careful deployment of tenses, mixing the present historic (of the children's actual observations of the traumatising event) with the poet's later reflection (in the future perfect tense) on what was *and always will* be inevitable and unchanging in the scene:

> They're all busy now, the hosing down
> will have started. Add water and sweep
>
> shit pellets puddled blood, the outfall
> gulps, discharges over the rock-face
>
> misting all the way to the green bay
> water, with a noise of waters, where
>
> the round stain dilates. An enrichment.
> I think the children had been silent, all

> this time. I will have pulled my bike, off
> his, on the tree. Nothing alters this.

'Nothing alters this.' The memory remains, fixed and permanent, in the poet's mind, and in the poem he has constructed. Furthermore, grimly, nothing can be done to alter the image of human nature captured in the poem: we are still (and always will be) creatures '*in blood stepped in so far* will up / to the eyes or the ears be enough?' Curnow linked the significance of the final line with his decision to change its title from 'The Abattoir' to 'The Unclosed Door': 'That door *was* unclosed & stays that way, & the poem can't / won't close it – the word seems to suggest that, doesn't it? Perhaps it's why "nothing alters this", viz, all I saw through the opening.'[29]

The other striking aspect of Curnow's imagining of the scene is the utter silence in which its events take place, its emphasis on the purely visual. The silence conveys, from the perspective of the boys themselves, their traumatised reaction to the brutal scene they have observed. They remain silent as they retrieve their bikes and leave that scene, going their separate ways, and the impli-cation is that it is a scene neither will ever speak of, either to their parents or to each other, as it becomes deeply embedded in their unconscious minds, beyond speech. Furthermore, the silence the poet builds into the poem, from his *present* perspective, is – also paradoxically – a 'statement' about the sheer inadequacy of language to convey, explain or mitigate the horrors the poem discloses. 'The Unclosed Door' might well have taken its place in *Trees, Effigies, Moving Objects* or *An Incorrigible Music* as a poem about that which, ever unpredictably, '*unspeak-ably* supervene[s]'[30] [author's italics] in our experience of the human and natural worlds.

Karl Miller at the *London Review of Books* was so impressed by the poem, which he found 'adrift in a mountain of letters' without its accompanying note but immediately recognised as a 'Curnow poem',[31] that he immediately printed it, and in August and September Curnow had completed two more poems – 'A Facing Page', which he sent to Alan Ross for *London Magazine*, and 'Investigations at the Public Baths', which impressed Miller even more than 'The Unclosed Door'. 'A Facing Page', originally entitled 'A Bedtime Story', was a relatively slight poem, a hendecasyllabic sonnet recalling a striking engraved pictorial image in a children's storybook once belonging to his mother, *Under the Sunset* by Bram Stoker – the author, later, of *Count Dracula*. The image illustrated a grim story entitled 'The Invisible Giant', in which a blind giant – visible only to the child-heroine of the story – a vast, black-robed, spectral figure, its fingers pointing downwards, advances through the sky to a city which, since its inhabi-tants have long ceased to believe in giants (believing, instead, only in themselves), is to suffer a catastrophic visitation by a devastating plague. The poem came out of 'memory's litter-basket', he wrote to Pocock:

> [I]t must be nearly 70 years since I saw the book, as described. In the same basket, I uncrumple the blind Giant picture intact, along with another that has lost any clear definition. I *think* he is smiting the city with the Plague, in the story, but that's not to the purpose of the poem. I now see that *Dracula* appeared in 1897, which means that my father, who was fascinated by it, probably read it in his student years, as I did in my turn, in a cheap reprint.[32]

The sonnet evokes the child's terror-filled nightmares about the giant – a figure of blind, merciless, retributive authority – and sets against it a memory of the security his mother provided against such terrors, as she warms his night-gown by the fire, then tucks him into bed and kisses him in readiness 'for the dark'. But it concludes with a veiled warning about *contemporary* secular society (in which, like the inhabitants of Stoker's godless city, people 'believe' only 'in themselves'), and the possibility of 'retribution'. The 'facing page' retains its hold on the poet's imagination, a tribute to the power of images themselves to lock deeply and permanently into the unconscious:

> I shut my eyes too tight on a picture-book
>
> for waking to loosen. Locked on to where people
> believe in themselves, engraved fingers point down.

Nineteen ninety-one was the year of Curnow's eightieth birthday, and he was extremely anxious that there be no public fuss about it. Indeed, on a file of correspondence with the media which he deposited in the Turnbull Library he wrote, 'Efforts of A.C. to prevent undue media notice of his birthday'.[33] At the centre of his concern, as so often in the way he reacted to media interest in his life, was an anxiety about the integrity of his poetry. The last thing he wanted was some special case to be made for the significance of his poetry on the basis of his age: age, for him, was as irrelevant to the quality of his work as his gender, race, political or other beliefs. He raised the issue with Peter Bland in a letter thanking him for his contribution (a poem entitled 'Seeing') to the festschrift in *Verse*:

> You save me by Grace and let Works take care of themselves. *Thanks!* You'll imagine my mixed feelings about this anniversary. A festschrift *Verse* seemed a safe distance from home, where I refused interviews, and managed to kill a stupid piece proposed by *Listener*. Family zeal for parties was firmly damped, Jeny and I feasted at home,

enjoying each other's company. Next morning, our usual (twice weekly) 600m swim in the Tepid Baths. I wallow up and down the Slow Lane, in what I politely call free-style. This morning I saw a girl in the Medium Lane, at least 6–7 months pregnant, drop down into the pool and swim like a champion, which perhaps she was.[34]

In the poem Curnow wrote at this time about his eightieth birthday, 'Investigations at the Public Baths', based on that day-after swim in Auckland's Tepid Baths which he had mentioned to Bland, the question of how to write about himself provided a key starting point:

> At nine fifteen a.m.
> on the first day of his eighty-
> first year. Why don't I
>
> first-person myself?
> I was hoping nobody would ask
> me that question
>
> yet. The strong smell of
> chlorine, for one thing, one thing
> at a time, please.

Quite simply, other things (other *things*, in a world of inexhaustible objects, sensations and thoughts) always seem to take precedence over the thought of one's self. In his initial conception of the poem, that other focus was to be provided by the pregnant woman swimming effortlessly and expertly (as natu-rally as the foetus swimming in the amniotic fluid of her womb), but this was quickly displaced by a different 'other' world, a different 'instance', as he puts it – as his attention is caught by a file of exercyclists going through their fitness routines in a gallery above the pool where he is swimming. What follows is a minutely detailed, vividly physical evocation of the cyclists:

> Bums
> on saddles, pommelled crotches.
> The feet rotate, the
>
> hands grip, or hang
> free, or hold open a book,
> demonstrating how

the mind is improved
without progression, if not without
rumbling noises and

lascivious absences.

This seemingly other scene then returns the poet to his own fitness routine in the
pool, an exercise that in fact mimics the exercyclists in its mechanical automa-
tism, in the way in which the mind is never detached from the active, physical,
bodily world in which thoughts are immersed:

There's also the deep
and the shallow end

between which the body
swims and the mind, totally
immersed, counts

and keeps count. I think
sixteen, touch tiles, turn again,
with underwater eyes

follow the black line.
Touch, thinking seventeen, turn
thinking eighteen

and enough.

Something like an answer to the opening Cartesian question, 'Why don't I
first-person myself?', is beginning to emerge at this point: there is no such thing
as a 'personal self' that can be invoked separately from and prior to the world in
which it is immersed. The self is contingent, its traces gleaned only as a speculative abstraction from its interactions with the world of objects and events. The
poem's own sense of such a self is gleaned in this way – as if while the poet is
focused on something altogether other – through its observations, and thoughts
and interactions with the surrounding scene and people. At the conclusion the
poem returns again to the exercyclists, as if acknowledging the link between his
own situation and theirs:

The gallery rumble-trembles, the riders
always up there were

an *abstraction blooded*, a
frieze the wrong side of the urn.
One grins, catching

me looking, lifts
a tattooed hand. I wave back. So.
You know how it is.

Keats's famous urn embodied the wish for a perfected object, lifted out of time into the transcendent permanence of final truth and beauty. Curnow's frieze, by contrast, is 'the wrong side of the urn', witnessing to the incorrigibly temporal, incomplete nature of life, bringing with it a fleeting moment of human companionship as rider and swimmer (anonymous selves) wave to each other. The self the poet offers to us is an abstraction blooded throughout by his inter-actions (mental and physical) with the scene he evokes.

It was a 'wonderful poem', Miller wrote, accepting it for publication in the *London Review of Books*: 'I hope you know how much I value being able to publish your work.'[35] Curnow was also pleased that it appeared in the *Weekend Australian* for 18–19 January 1992, keeping his name visible in Australia. 'Those "relaxed" verses', he wrote to Lilburn, 'are damned hard writing too, & you didn't fail to notice my "occult muse" haunting the Tepid Baths. By the way, Jeny & I did another 18 lengths yesterday, & the same again tomorrow. If it weren't for the bloody unseasonably chilly March, we'd be in the sea, Judge's or Okahu Bay.'[36]

Italy, Seville and London, June–July 1992

In 1991 Curnow was invited to participate as a distinguished guest at the New Zealand government's exhibition at the 1992 World Expo in Seville, Spain. He and Jeny worked on an itinerary which would give them two months away, with two and a half weeks in Italy before the formalities later in the month in Seville, followed by a few days in Madrid and a fortnight (2–16 July) in London, return-ing via the United States.

Once it was known that Curnow was travelling again to Europe, numerous invitations arrived. Italo Verri (who was completing his translation of *The Duke's Miracle*) offered a warm welcome to his family home in Ferrara. Curnow received invitations to read at the 'Voice Box' at the Southbank Centre and at the King's Lynn Poetry Festival in Norfolk, but an invitation to record a radio programme in the BBC's 'Poet of the Month' series was sent by surface mail and did not reach him until after his return to New Zealand. Michael Hulse, who instigated many of these arrangements, also busied himself writing a piece on Curnow for *The Spectator*, timed to appear when Curnow was in London.[37]

The Curnows left Auckland on 1 June, stopping en route in Bangkok, and after four days in Rome (staying, as before, at the Hotel Quattro Fontane) they visited Italo Verri in Ferrara, whose family hospitality and fine cuisine they hugely enjoyed. Verri took them on tours of the medieval city, the Renaissance city, and the Palazzo Schifanoia, and they also spent time at the Duke's castle, site of the powerful Italian Este dynasty and the imaginary setting of Curnow's play, as well as meeting Lucio Scardino, the play's publisher.

From Ferrara the Curnows travelled to Venice (staying again at La Calcina) for ten days, the fifth and shortest of their stays there during nearly twenty years. They enjoyed familiar walks, revisiting many of their favourite locations, and attended a 'superb exhibition' of paintings by Canova and an organ concert in the Basilica dei Frari.[38] Curnow had suffered a bronchial cough during the first weeks of their trip, but by the time they reached Seville on 25 June, after a further two days in Rome, he had recovered sufficiently to participate in the formalities arranged for him, including a talk on 'Landfall in Unknown Seas' for a reception in his honour at the New Zealand Pavilion at 9 p.m. that evening, during which Ian Fraser read the poem accompanied by the chamber sections of the New Zealand Symphony Orchestra. Apart from providing information about the work's composition history, Curnow also managed some considered reflections about the poem's exploration of 'the meaning of that word "discovery"':

> What a paradoxical word it is. It means one thing to the discoverers, and something very different to the people and places they discovered. The moment in history that really matters for my poem, is the moment when the voyages have all finished. There is nothing left to be 'discovered'. We know the limits of our small globe. For mankind, it is a tragic moment.[39]

The following evening they attended a concert by the NZSO at the Teatro de la Maestranza, including Lilburn's *Aotearoa* overture and Kiri Te Kanawa as the special guest-performer singing Mozart's *Exsultate, Jubilate* and Strauss's *Four Last Songs*. The last of their formal engagements the next day included attending the official 'New Zealand Day' parade, followed by a formal luncheon at the Spanish Pavilion and an evening reception for the New Zealand Prime Minister, Jim Bolger. During the day they visited the 'walk-through theatre' attached to the New Zealand Pavilion, at which an eight-minute film-and-music 'cantata', entitled 'Voyages', produced by Don McGlashan and Wayne Laird, screened continuously. Deploying Maori/Polynesian and European characters, images and musical instruments, 'Voyages' also included passages from the opening section of 'Landfall in Unknown Seas', sung by Kiri Te Kanawa to music composed by McGlashan and played by the NZSO, aiming to represent the past 'voyages' of Polynesians and Europeans to New Zealand, and the present 'voyage' of identity as a multicultural Pacific nation.

On 28 June the Curnows travelled to Madrid for a relaxing four days and arrived for their fortnight in London on 2 July, where they rented a small top-floor apartment in the Clearlake Hotel in Kensington. With the fatigue of so much travel and the stress of two significant readings scheduled for the first week, Curnow's voice began to trouble him again. However, both readings went extremely well. At the Southbank on the evening of 7 July he read 'A Reliable Service', 'A Busy Port', 'Continuum', 'A Fellow Being' and 'Lo These Are Parts of His Ways' to a nearly full auditorium which included many of the friends he had made in London over the years. The intimacy of the location appealed greatly to him, as he wrote later to Mayne:

> [I] haven't enjoyed a platform job so much since Library of Congress nearly 20 years
> ago – no, it was nicer than that, being less formal. Voice Box holds only 77, but I can
> call it a full house, only one or two seats being without bums. One or two good young
> poets of Michael Hulse's year came along, and one or two NZ expats, including Fleur
> Adcock, whose support I value a lot.[40]

Two days later they travelled by train to Norfolk, where they stayed the night with the Thwaites at Low Tharston, before being driven by Thwaite to King's Lynn for Curnow's second reading on 10 July, this time with Hulse, as part of its July programme. Again, there was a receptive audience in a small, almost-full auditorium, at which Curnow read 'A Scrap-book', 'Canst Thou Draw out Leviathan with an Hook?', 'In the Duomo' and 'An Evening Light'.

After these events there was barely a week left to see people in London. There were brief meetings with Alan Ross and Paul Keegan, lunch with Karl Miller (who was soon to announce his resignation from the *London Review of Books*) and a much-enjoyed dinner out with Peter and Christine Porter. Shortly before he left New Zealand Curnow heard that he had received the 1992 Cholmondeley Award for poets, jointly with Donald Davie, which he collected from the Society of Authors in Kensington, not being in the UK at the time of the awards ceremony itself on 1 June.* [41] The last days of their stay in London included rounds of social-ising with Jeny's relatives, as well as with Catherine Pierard. The trip home via Zaro Starr's beach house at Cape Cod and Jeny's stepsister Olivia Kahalewai's home at Kailua in Hawai'i was similarly busy. However, they enjoyed the warm hospitality they received from their old American friends, on what was to be their last visit to the United States, and Curnow was touched that Rosanna Warren made a special effort to come to Cape Cod from Boston to visit him, with remi-niscences of the poets he had met during earlier decades.

In retrospect Curnow described the trip as a 'rather harebrained round-world journey', despite the pleasures it had provided.[42] More to the point, perhaps, was the physical toll such a long trip exacted, as Curnow moved into his eighties, and he simply could not have coped unless Jeny had accompanied him. Mindful of the demands on Curnow's stamina, they were to make only one further long-distance trip to the UK, in 1998, confining their trips away to shorter, purely holiday-orientated stays in warmer Pacific climates where they could escape the New Zealand winter – to Sydney in 1990, Nouméa in 1991, to Noosa Heads in Queensland twice (on the recommendation of Pearson) in 1993 and again in 1995, and to Moorea in Tahiti in 1994.

German translations

After his return to Cologne from New Zealand in 1991 Michael Hulse also pursued translation and publication possibilities for Curnow in Germany. In particular he interested Joachim Sartorius, a highly regarded Berlin-based poet, journalist and translator (of Wallace Stevens, William Carlos Williams and John Ashbery, amongst others), in Curnow's poetry. The first fruit of Sartorius's interest was a full-page presentation of Curnow in the newspaper *Die Tageszeitung*, on 2 July 1992. The presentation featured three translated poems from the Viking *Selected Poems* ('Blind Man's Holiday', 'Keep in a Cool Place' and 'The Loop in Lone Kauri Road'), a brief literary and biographical introduction to his work with explanatory comments on 'Blind Man's Holiday', whose title had been translated as 'Zwielicht' ('Twilight'), and an excellent photograph of

* Soon after his return to New Zealand Curnow was contacted by Davie asking if he had ever alluded to the Psalmist, 'however glancingly', in his poetry. 'I'm doing a Penguin anthology about the Psalms in English, and badly want to include you.' Curnow came up with only 'the merest of glances', except for the third and fourth poems in the early sequence *Not in Narrow Seas*, with their direct allusion to Psalm 122 in the lines 'Jerusalem is built as a city / That is at unity with itself'. Davie included the two poems in his anthology (*The Psalms in English*) which was published in the Penguin Classics series in 1996, the year after his death, but he found nothing in Australian, Canadian and South African poetry. 'An irreligious lot, you colonials', he commented to Curnow.

Curnow taken by Jeny from their apartment balcony at La Calcina, overlooking the Giudecca Canal in Venice, with the façade, bell tower and dome of San Giorgio Maggiore in the distance.

Shortly afterwards, also at Hulse's behest, Michael Kruger, director of the Munich-based publishing house of Carl Hauser, and editor of *Akzente*, a prestigious quarterly devoted to international poetry, sought Curnow's permission to feature his work in the first issue for February 1993. The magazine provided an excellent, wide-ranging selection of thirteen translations, five by Sartorius (including the three poems he had published in *Die Tageszeitung* as well as 'The Skeleton of the Great Moa' and 'He Cracked a Word'), and eight by Elmar Schenkel, including the earlier pieces 'Wild Iron', House and Land', 'The Unhistoric Story' and 'Tomb of an Ancestor', and the later poems 'Dialogue with Four Rocks' and 'You Will Know When You Get There'. Schenkel also translated a poem *not* in the *Selected Poems*, 'The Eye Is More or Less Satisfied with Seeing', and (in an intriguing editorial move) Kruger included a second translation of 'He Cracked a Word'.

This poem from the 1950s appears to have interested both translators because of its insights into the way Curnow deployed language in his poems: describing the process as a kind of stripping away of the outer shells of words (the conventional, clichéd layers of meaning they accumulate over time) and waiting patiently for the exposed kernels to shape (or seed) themselves into new linguistic patterns whose origins are deeply rooted in the 'wishes and memories' of the unconscious. Poetic language, from this perspective, is specially distinguished by its complex use of the associative, connotative qualities of words, its deployment of multiple registers and of the resources of wit and irony, word play and puns, syntactic ambiguity, and dense or unusual metaphorical textures – the means by which the poet refreshes and renews the language. Such an approach to language also offers a special challenge to translators.

Sartorius's translation of 'He Cracked a Word' is a plainer, more literally and grammatically faithful rendition of the original than Schenkel's, but on occasion introduces associations not in the original. His title ('Er brach ein Wort') translates 'cracked', plainly, as 'broke', but does not avoid the possible connection (common to both English and German) of 'breaking one's word' with 'breaking a promise', an association not in Curnow's original. Schenkel's title ('Er knackte ein Wort') preserves the nut-cracking metaphor in the original (as she does throughout), as well as preserving the connotation of 'solving a problem' in Curnow's title, though neither is able to include the playful connotation, 'cracking a joke'. Schenkel focuses more on conveying the associative richness of the original. Her translation of Curnow's 'wagging wisdom' – a metaphor suggesting both 'tongue-wagging' (gossipy) and 'finger-wagging' (moralistic) clichés, mere empty shells of words – is 'Narrenweisheit' ('fool's wisdom'), semantically closer to the original than Sartorius's 'wackliger Weisheit' ('wavering wisdom'), which by contrast preserves the sarcastic onomatopoeia of Curnow's phrase. Neither, however, is able to include the metaphorical connotations of 'wagging' in their translations. For Curnow's German readers, encountering his work for the first time in *Akzente*, the experiment of including two translations of the same poem – both, in their different ways, conveying aspects of the original – would have provided a fascinating instance of the necessary 'incompleteness' of any translation as well as an insight into the particular qualities of Curnow's style.*

In the wake of the presentation in *Akzente* in February, Sartorius, with his wife Karin Graf (also a translator), became interested in translating a volume by Curnow to be published by the Göttingen-based publishing house of Steidl Verlag, and approached Curnow for permission. Steidl specialised in high-quality publications of literature (including Günter Grass) as well as in the fields of architecture, photography and the fine arts. Tim advised his father on the contractual arrangements, liaising with Curtis Brown's London office, and these were finalised in August 1993, the book (*Bäume, Bildnisse, bewegliche Dinge*) appearing in April the following year – a splendid production with a striking cover illustration by Klaus Detjen of an abstract figure in motion, suggestive of both a tree's bole (in green) and a 'human' effigy with plinth-like raised arms (in orange) growing out of or superimposed on the bole. The book also had an elegant afterword by Hulse, introducing Curnow, within the broader context of twentieth-century poetry, to a German readership for the first time:

> Allen Curnow shares with Eliot and Rilke the symbolist leaning to the sacred; with Pound the desire to present larger historical subject matter alongside the things of the world in all their manifold diversity; with Williams the democratic love of the things of the world for their own sake. He has inherited the great developments of 20th century poetry and occupies a position simultaneously in both traditions, as it were – in the encyclopaedist and in the symbolist.[43]

Arrangements for the translation were complicated a little by yet another approach to Curnow, in May 1993, this time from the Salzburg-based publishing firm of Residenz Verlag, which was interested in publishing a German edition of the Viking *Selected Poems*. Curnow hoped that both projects would go ahead, despite a degree of overlap between them (*Trees, Effigies, Moving Objects* was already included in the Viking *Selected Poems*, though the Steidl project was for

---

* The author is indebted to Alan Kirkness (Emeritus Professor of German, University of Auckland) and Dr Linda Cassells for their information about the German translations.

a bilingual edition, with the original English-language versions and the German translations on facing pages, and the Residenz proposal was for a German-language edition only). However, in the wake of Steidl's decision to press ahead, Residenz Verlag put their proposal on hold, at least partly to see how the Steidl edition was received, and it was never revived.

Reviews of *Bäume, Bildnisse, bewegliche Dinge* were slow to appear, but a significant exception was the large-circulation daily newspaper *Frankfurter Allgemeine Zeitung*, which published translations of 'He Cracked a Word' and 'A Dead Lamb' on successive weeks (2 and 8 April 1994) at the time of the book's publication, followed later by a highly laudatory review by Harold Hartung ('our finest poetry critic', according to Sartorius)[44] whose title was arresting: 'Mit den Augen des Dompteurs: Der neuseeländische Lyriker Allen Curnow zähmt die Ideen in den Dingen' ('With the Eyes of the Tamer: The New Zealand lyric poet Allen Curnow tames the ideas in things'), linking Curnow's art to W.C. Williams's maxim 'No ideas but in things'. Praising the translation for 'rendering very felicitously Curnow's dry, ironic tone and his unsentimental freshness', Hartung emphasised the sequence's 'openness of regard and rejection of premature syntheses':

> It is something like a duel between World and I – the world as a beast of prey and the poet with the look of a tamer. Yet ... Curnow reveals himself to be a lyrical pragmatist who accepts language and lets things be themselves.[45]

Sartorius was also pleased with the review, and hoped that Steidl might consider another of Curnow's volumes for translation. However, there was no further project, and in the meantime Sartorius completed a substantial inter-national anthology of new poetry in translation (*Atlas der neuen Poesie*) for the Reinbek-based publishing firm of Rowohlt Verlag, in which Curnow was gener-ously represented by five poems: 'Blind Man's Holiday', 'Keep in a Cool Place', 'The Loop in Lone Kauri Road', 'He Cracked a Word' and 'The Skeleton of the Great Moa'. The volume appeared the following year, 1995.

Chapter Thirty-four

Early Days Yet, 1993–96

[I]f only a recognisable new poem would emerge from a heap of more or less directionless & formless drafts & false starts . . .[1]

Five new poems, 1993–94

In February 1993, eighteen months after completing 'Investigations at the Public Baths' in 1991, Curnow began drafting lines towards a new poem set at Karekare. 'I'm persevering with a shot at something quite new', he wrote to Stead, 'but it won't work out – yet.'[2] In the end two poems resulted. The first – 'Another Weekend at the Beach' – was completed by the end of March; the second – 'Looking West, Late Afternoon, Low Water' – was a much more ambitious poem which began as a spin-off from the first and preoccupied him throughout the winter and spring of 1993.

The immediate event which appears to have sparked 'Another Weekend at the Beach' was the sudden, invasive phenomenon of toxic algal bloom, a species of phytoplankton which contaminated shellfish around much of the coastline of New Zealand (including at Karekare) during the summer months of 1992–93, creating a significant threat to public health as well as to one of the country's export industries. Curnow does not introduce this disruptive event, however, until later in the poem, which begins by evoking the predictable, routine features of the natural scene as the speaker casually lists them on one of his many regular walks down Lone Kauri Road to the beach:

637

Turn left at the sign. Lone Kauri Road
winds down to the coast. That's a drop
of about five hundred feet. Look out
for the waterfall, the wooden bridge,
the mown grass, the pohutukawa glade.

The western horizon will have slid
behind the mask of an eye-levelled
next eyeballing wave. Park here. Proceed
on foot. The spot has barbecues with
MALE and FEMALE dunnies in a figtree

thicket, wrong hemisphere, implausibly
fruiting. Tracks cross the wind-sifting dune
skyline of unkempt lupin, marram,
spinifex's incontinent seed-
vessels bowling downwind, the way I've

come and come, how many thousand times
to no other conclusion, the back
of a broken wave, and found no word
or forgot or omitted to write
it down . . . .

The 'reality' of the coastal scene as Curnow presents it in this poem, its physical *givenness* and sameness day-by-day (or weekend-by-weekend), is not dependent on or constituted by language. 'It's all there whether or not it gets written', Curnow explained to Hulse, 'that's all the "text" there is.'[3] The poem suddenly takes an inward metaphorical turn at this point, as the toxic algal bloom secreted by the tides invades the scene, 'deadly to the text', introducing something akin to a metaphysical conceit whose substance is the theoretical discourse of deconstruction. The metaphor carries with it a witty dissenting from 'all [the] rigmarole – and much, much more – about linguistic theory, à la Derrida, lurking behind that "écriture de la différance" – the scripture of words pointing at words only, none of our *signifiants* having any *signifiés*'.[4] '*Ah, quelle écriture de la // différance! l'orthographe derridienne / for every thing's everything*', the poem continues, the algal bloom functioning as 'some sort of metonymous [sic] allusion to the deconstruction pestilence or pandemic':[5]

> Then why
> not phytoplankton, the algoid bloom
> any less than those offshore purples, this
> beached medusa, polythene waste, bubbled
>
> sea-froth, tincture of a present spume
> spattered up the sands? Mind where you pick
> your mussels and *kina*, these tides may
> secrete indigenous toxins. Deadly
> to the text. Shall I copy it again?

To Tim, Curnow wrote that the poem contained 'just a light swipe at that charlatan Jacques Derrida',[6] but his purpose was more thoroughgoing, as he wrote to Stead, explaining that he was initially undecided about the inclusion of Derrida's famous neologism ('différance'), the key term underpinning his sense of the inherent instability of texts, their groundlessness, corresponding neither to any *a priori* 'reality' of or in the world to which they relate nor to any supposed purity of intended meaning on the part of their authors: 'When Derrida turned up, I tried to throw him out, but he hung around. I'm glad you read irony in those lines.'[7] Behind the acerbic wit of 'Another Weekend at the Beach' Curnow was possibly venting a degree of frustration at deconstructive readings of his own poetry.

The poem was accepted by the new editor of the *London Review of Books*, Mary-Kay Wilmers, and Curnow hoped that it might kick-start a number of new poems, writing to Stead in May that he was attempting a sequel to it.[8] However, by September nothing finished had emerged: 'if only a recognisable new poem would emerge from a heap of more or less directionless & formless drafts & false starts'.[9] It was not until early November that he was able to send the new poem, 'Looking West, Late Afternoon, Low Water', to Wilmers.

The motivation and aims of this poem are directly opposite to those of 'Another Weekend at the Beach' – not the notation of samenesses in a repeatedly visited scene but the 'one-off' visionary imagining of a scene unique and disturbing in the experiences it offers. 'Looking West, Late Afternoon, Low Water' is perhaps the richest of all Curnow's poems of the littoral – and certainly a poem which reveals how deeply embedded in his unconscious, from the early 1940s, the 'oceanic' remained as a dynamic arena of change, transformation, the flow of memory and history, the mysterious source of life and receptacle of the dead. The poem offers a spectacular visual scene whose events suggest psychic 'frights' (like the sudden 'solipsistic shock' of the emptying-out of the night sky in 'Continuum') in which the 'blood-orange' sun is drowned overboard from the horizon's 'boat' and the horizon itself seems to detach from its moorings and invade the coast, tsunami-like, bringing huge, pounding waves, and unprecedented low-tide seabed exposures: a cacophonous orchestration of violent natural events.

As the poem's 'tripartite' title might suggest, it reaches back to numerous earlier poems, and brings together many of their motifs: the 'looking west' scenario of 'Lone Kauri Road' with its disturbing 'black traveller'; the 'late afternoon' visionary perspectives of poems like 'An Evening Light' and 'You Will Know When You Get There'; and especially the mysteriously exposed, subterranean oceanic or low-tide scenarios of 'At Dead Low Water', 'This Beach Can be Dangerous', 'Dialogue with Four Rocks' and 'Moules à la Marinière'. If the poem's immediate coastal location is Karekare, its meditative range also takes in multiple other remembered coastal locations and events, including a memory of a beached whale at Waikuku on the Canterbury coast from the 1940s. 'Most of it is "on location" at Karekare', Curnow wrote to Pearson, 'though other beaches may be there too, like New Brighton, Mokau, Otaki – and the whale was at Waikuku (I think) & very likely wasn't a sperm whale.'[10]

The three motifs carried by the title all suggest mortality, and personal mortality and a sense of loss – the death of friends who 'call out / not to be heard' as the shoreline shakes with the pounding of huge breakers – pervade the poem's memory-consciousness. The scenarios evoked by the title are also, recurrently throughout Curnow's poetry, ones of intense mythic and visionary energy. A fish glimpsed swimming in one of the huge walls of water before it crashes on the beach is identified with Leviathan, and at the centre of the poem Curnow evokes the mythic resonances of the scene as a sexual union of the primordial Greek male and female deities of the ocean, the Titans Okeanos and Tethys. He introduces the mythic scene casually, inviting fellow visitors simply to enjoy the beach for its present pleasures ('Come down, this is today // delivered factory fresh, in colour / heated by the late sun.'), then invokes Wordsworth's 'The World Is Too Much With Us', in which the poet wishes to be identified with 'a Pagan suckled in a creed outworn', to be lifted out of the quotidian into a visionary oceanic scenario energised by myth: to '[h]ave sight of Proteus rising from the sea; / Or hear old Triton blow his wreathed horn.' Curnow half-mocks the wish ('but whose / cast-off cult's to be the lucky one?'), before introducing his own much more charged vision, prefaced by lines ('Great waters, unfinished business, done / blind to the deadline.') which he hoped, he wrote to Pocock in December, might contain 'something a bit sibylline', prophetic and mysterious:[11]

From that rock to

this tree was *tapu* and it sticks. Thin
pickings, Tangaroa, this is *pakeha*

story time, only Okeanos and
sister Tethys having it off: the way

they love makes hairy cliff-hanging seas
roll drums on the sand, the three-metre swell

flat on the seabed bangs the pubes,
very ancient and fishlike they smell

close to. Divine all the same. Dangerous,
not to be approached, least of all by

mortal man whose years are four-score plus
tomorrow night. . . .

'*Divine all the same.*' Despite the physicality of the imagined scene (of Okeanos and Tethys 'having it off'), the assertion of divinity embodied and enacting itself in the physical world is equally direct, offering as strong an intuition of immanent sacrality as anything in Curnow's later poems. The purpose of the passage (like the opening section of 'At Dead Low Water' with its Christian symbolism) is to associate the underwater, seabed world with a primordial sexuality at the core of all human and natural life.

Not surprisingly, perhaps, in a poem as intense and 'sybilline' as 'Looking West, Late Afternoon, Low Water' is, a number of references and memories seem to be purely private to the poet. Later in the poem the speaker counts 'three // strong swimmers carried past out of sight / round the North Rocks'. The lines invite (though without answering) the question who the 'three strong swimmers' might be, struggling with – perhaps swept away by – the huge tide. In one earlier version, a handwritten annotation contains the phrase 'Brasch folded in the roll of waves',[12] perhaps suggesting that the other three – stronger swimmers – might be Curnow's dead contemporaries, Glover, Fairburn and Mason. The same general allusion to poetry – this time to his own career and 'craft' as a poet – seems to be invoked in the poem's concluding references to boats:

tsunami!
tsunami! splintering deadwood of the boat

I lost half a life ago, swept
away with a judgment on the work

> *she's amateur built but your friends won't know.*
> Last seen, one inflatable rescue
>
> craft stood on its tuck, bows to skyward
> in fast failing light, a turning tide.

The particular memory here belongs to the 1950s, to a scenario at Ngataringa Bay on the inner northern reaches of Auckland harbour, when a small boat Curnow had purchased from his next-door neighbour got into trouble in a heavy wind. Curnow reminded Pocock of the event:

> You did put to sea with me in that very same boat – 'amateur built, but your friends won't know' – that judgment was neighbour Brian Donovan's, he a naval architect & boatbuilder. Her kauri timbers were too heavy, she was 10 ft long & 5 ft (nearly) wide, and (I suppose) cranky to handle. If you remember (?) the wind blew up from NE as we came home; not trusting the dinghy in seas dead abeam, I turned up Ngataringa Bay (towards the old Devonport Gasworks), & shipped a bucketful of green water over the tuck; mercifully for posterity, the old Seagull [motor] kept firing on its one cylinder, & we made it back, up the creek past the mangroves, on the last spoonful of the falling tide.[13]

In the poem the boat seems to figure as a deeply self-critical image of the poet's earlier 'amateur-built' art, its 'deadwood' splintered and lost 'half a life ago', 'swept / away with a judgment on the work'. What has replaced the earlier amateur-built craft, in the poet's present, is an inflatable rescue craft which stands on its tuck, 'bows to skyward / in fast failing light, a turning tide.' Maybe the inflatable craft has set out to try to rescue 'the three strong swimmers', but it also functions, perhaps, as a metaphor for Curnow's later conception of his art, confronting sky, failing light, and tide, perhaps versatile enough to ensure some kind of survival. At least, at the end of the poem, the tide is 'turning' – returning to 'normal' – suggesting that for the time being the poet has survived the 'freak' tsunami which has threatened to overwhelm him.

Perhaps because 'Looking West, Late Afternoon, Low Water' was so ambitious a poem, Curnow was especially anxious about its reception, and delighted when it was selected by Alan Loney at the Holloway Press, University of Auckland, for a beautifully produced, special edition of 75 copies later in the year. Aspects of its scenario – in particular the 'freak tide' which caused the beach to be 'peeled bare / back to the never quite uttermost / private parts the deep-sea smells beyond / mean low water'[14] – originally occurred in drafts of 'Another Weekend at the Beach', before generating a separate poem. In one instance the proposed title, 'Another Weekend at the Beach (II)',[15] deliberately emphasised the aspect of 'Looking West, Late Afternoon, Low Water's as a sequel to (or commentary on) the earlier poem, an imaginative assertion not of the Derridaean emptiness of the scene but of its mythic plenitude and deeply personal, psychic resonances.

During the next nine months to September 1994 Curnow produced another three poems – a productive period, given the scarcity of poems during the previous three years – and began to think of a new volume. The new poems were 'Early Days Yet', finished in March, 'A South Island Night's Entertainment', finished in June, and 'The Game of Tag' – an especially 'recalcitrant poem'[16] – finished in early September. All were marked by a shift to a much shorter, four- or five-syllabled line – a break from the longer nine- and eleven-syllabled lines he had mainly deployed up to this time. The first two were familial memory poems, set in Curnow's childhood years at Sheffield, and for 'Early Days Yet' – a moving elegy to his father Tremayne – he returned to rough drafts and notes he had made a decade earlier during and after his trip to Menton. It was a more readily accessible poem than its two Karekare-based predecessors, like 'A Time of Day' lovingly reconstructing the antiquated mechanical details of what had once been a 'New Age' mode of transport, the Model T Ford.

The poem's three parts were organised in terms of the distinctive, now outdated, mechanical functioning of the vehicle: fuelling it 'for the week's pastoral mileage' with Big Tree motor spirit in the first section, crank-starting it in the second, and in the third backing the vehicle out of its garage and setting off westward along a 'straight / lonely road' into a 'high / head wind', a dust-laden 'unhinge-ing / nor'west slammer.' The word 'spirit', which recurs throughout the poem, links its multiple levels of reference. There is the mundane 'Big Tree' fuel that powers the Model T, and the individual spirit that 'fires' Tremayne's character and personality – his energy and liveliness dominating the environment in which he pursues his clergyman's routines. The spirit of the age – more particularly its now superannuated 'New Age' technology,*[17] providing its own satirical comment on 1990s new-age, millennial hype – expands to include the spirit of time and history, encompassing the Big Bang origins of the planet in the remote past, the energies of life in the remote Canterbury hinterland in the early twentieth century, and the poet's moving sense of loss as his memories of them fade with his own encroaching death three quarters of a century later. Then there is the poem's spirit of imagination, driving the poet's own recollection of the past, his sympathetic identification with its people and events (including homely memories of the funeral of 'old Mrs. Hole', and of his mother milking the family's cow, Beauty), and the sheer liveliness of the poem's form and syllabic prosody. 'I meant to make

---

* 'How young the century was then', Curnow wrote to Pearson, 'now in its nineties!'

difficulties *for* myself with the tight little tercets – & I did!' Curnow wrote to Pearson, 'though not, I hope, for you.'[18] Finally, beyond these secular ideas of spirit, there is a sense of spirit, throughout, as numinous, mysterious and metaphysical, a ground or presence underpinning the poem's creative connection of its personal, socio-political, and historical concerns, of memory and the present.

'A South Island Night's Entertainment', completed in June 1994, was always – in Curnow's mind – regarded as a companion piece to its predecessor, 'Early Days Yet', linked by its location, and its similar take on the way in which one generation's hyped new age becomes the next generation's old hat, in this case the superan-nuated technology of the silent film era. It is also linked formally with 'Early Days Yet' in its experimentation with a brief, compacted syllabic line – five-syllabled tercets in 'Early Days Yet' and 'tetrasyllabic couplets' (as Curnow described them)[19] in 'A South Island Night's Entertainment', the same challenging form he used in the poem's immediate successor, 'The Game of Tag'. Mary-Kay Wilmers at *London Review of Books* printed it immediately (7 July 1994), announcing 'A new poem by Allen Curnow' on the front page of the magazine.

Throughout 1994, while working on 'Early Days Yet' and 'A South Island Night's Entertainment', Curnow was 'bothered off and on'[20] by another possible poem, based on the enigmatic *trouvaille* of a graffito which had been spray-painted on a timbered roadside crash-barrier in Lone Kauri Road the year before: 'AFRIKA POET HERO DODGER FELIX DEVOE CURSE EXIT / CICERO BEASTIE SAINT THANKS FOR THE TAG AFRIKA POET '93'. 'There's a good deal to do with the New Age of 70 years ago', he wrote to Tim of the poem, 'The Game of Tag', 'as well as this one where the poems have to happen.'[21] Economy of utterance was also closely linked, in this and the two previous poems, to the adoption of brief four- or five-syllabled lines: 'I badly needed a change', Curnow wrote to Lilburn, 'from hendecasyllables & 9-syll (anything but 10!) & wanted something as far as possible from the kind of "poem" that is all slabs & slivers of print to fill the spaces between the "graphics".'[22]

'The Game of Tag', which Curnow originally called 'Rivals', develops a witty comparison between the poet and a youthful tagger who is a kind of surrogate or doppelgänger of the older poet, as well as a poetic rival from a younger generation reminding the older poet that all poetry worth the effort is a kind of risk-taking, whose survival is unpredictable. The speaker both envies, and distances himself from, his exhibitionistic, risk-taking rival, with his uninhibited drive to imprint his unique identity on the world around him. However, both wordsmiths are subject to the sheer unpredictability and finality of death. In a breathtaking mid-poem shift of gear the tagger, giving 'death the fingers' as he accelerates into a wheelie on the road's gravel, plunges into the forest below, 'to be wrapped / round a bole two // hundred years thick, / two hundred feet // below.', leaving – after forest growth and rust have done their job – only 'One chip / of red Perspex // under a stone / in the stream . . . // his (whose?) taillight.' The plunge might also be the older poet's fate: 'Where have they all / gone, with CICERO // BEASTIE, and me / and which of us // leads the way down / post and plank not- // withstanding, car- / apaced in Korean // steel'. 'THANKS FOR THE TAG.', the poem quotes in conclusion, acknowledging the message he has received from his rival – never to lose sight of the individualistic, risk-taking energy that the writing of poems involves, or of the sheer unpredictability surrounding the terms on which one's art (a fragment of tail-light?) might survive.

Penguin Modern Poets No. 7, and The Game of Tag, 1994–95

As the new poems began to appear in 1994 Curnow started to think of getting another collection together. It would be his first new collection since 'Continuum', the group of poems which opened his selected later poems (*Continuum*) in 1988, and with the completion of 'The Game of Tag' in September he now had eleven new poems, enough for a small volume about the size of *The Loop in Lone Kauri Road*. Before finalising the new collection, however, he needed to work on another project.

At the end of June 1994 Paul Keegan, editor at Penguin Books (UK), approached Curnow to include his work in the seventh volume of the Penguin Modern Poets series, which focused mostly on contemporary British and American poets. Curnow was to select 50 pages of poetry, which he worked on until November. He submitted 27 poems, including all five parts of 'In the Duomo', and as in the Viking Selected Poems, avoided chronological ordering. Almost all the poems belonged to the decade framed by An Incorrigible Music (1979) and Continuum (1988), whereas his fellow contributors (Donald Davie and Samuel Menashe), selected broadly from all their published work. The volume was originally scheduled for publication in 1995, but was delayed until June 1996, when others in the series would be ready: 'We are trying to publish in batches to gain the maximum publicity / impact for each title', Tim Bates, Penguin Books' new poetry editor, wrote to Curnow.[23] In the meantime, in September 1995, Curnow was saddened to learn of the death of Donald Davie.

By March 1995 Curnow had finalised the manuscript of his new collection, *The Game of Tag: Poems 1990–1995*, which he sent to Tim to pursue publishing options in the UK*. Keegan, who retained an advisory role to Penguin Classics after his retirement from the firm at the end of 1994, advised that Penguin was

---

* Editor's note: *The Game of Tag* was never published as a separate book; the sequence eventually became part of the collection *Early Days Yet*.

not publishing such individual volumes, and Tim then tried Faber (also unsuccessfully), before sending the manuscript to Michael Schmidt at Carcanet Press, who was enthusiastic except for the problem of its brevity: '[T]here are simply not enough poems to make a *book*. Even the most generous cast-off brings this to only just 32 pages. We could not get a spine, and without a spine we could not sell it.'[24] Curnow responded immediately by proposing an expanded volume including 30 pages of additional poems *not* in the Penguin *Selected Poems* or the Penguin Modern Poets selection. He also considered the possibility of simply adding four longer poems ('In the Duomo', 'Moro Assassinato', 'A Fellow Being' and 'Organo ad Libitum') to the recent ones, with a new title, *The Game of Tag: New and Selected Longer Poems, 1979–1995*.

At the same time, Curnow contacted Penguin about the status of the 1990 *Selected Poems*. The hard-covered Viking volume had sold 900 of its 1000 print run, and was effectively out of print. The paperback Penguin volume had sold 1800 of its 4000 print run, and Penguin was willing to agree to a reversion of rights, leaving Curnow free to negotiate a new collection with Carcanet – clearly its preferred option – to be published in 1997, which included all poems from *Trees, Effigies, Moving Objects* onwards, and selections from *Island and Time, Sailing or Drowning, At Dead Low Water, Poems 1949–57* and *A Small Room with Large Windows*, the whole presented in reverse chronological order. By the end of 1995 Curnow had sent off to Schmidt his completed manuscript of *Early Days Yet: New and Collected Poems*, though at this stage his preferred title was that of the opening poem in the collection, 'The Unclosed Door'.

In early September 1995, while he was still thinking about possible poems (not published in the Viking *Selected Poems*) which might be added to *The Game of Tag* to extend its length from 32 to 64 pages, Curnow was contacted by Ambury Hall, an English emigrant and schoolteacher in Auckland, seeking a contribution to an anthology of poems and images which he was editing to protest against the French government's resumption of nuclear testing at Moruroa Atoll in the Pacific. The book he planned, *Below the Surface: Words and Images in Protest at French Testing on Moruroa*, was to be published in November by Random House, and proceeds were to be donated in support of the international Moruroa Pacific Peace Flotilla (including fourteen New Zealand yachts) which confronted the French authorities in the test zone itself. By sheer coincidence Curnow at the time was tinkering with a pantoum he had written in the 1940s ('Pantoum of War in the Pacific') with a view to including it in his expanded *Game of Tag* collection, and the poem provided an immediate spark for the new protest poem which he completed within ten days in September, 'Pacific 1945–1995: A Pantoum'.

Curnow was anxious that the new poem not be seen simply as a revision or rewriting of the earlier pantoum. '[I]t's *not* a revision of the earlier piece, which grew out of the island-hopping stage of the war with Japan', he wrote to Pocock, 'but something more ambitious.'[25] The new poem has a historical dimension not in the original, spanning half a century of Big Power intervention in the Pacific region, offering a bleak comment on human failure to learn from the past, as well as on the hubris which has repeatedly turned the Pacific into a playground for the imperial ambitions of global powers (Japan, the United States, France) during that same half-century. Above all, Curnow returned to the extremely challenging Malay-based form of the pantoum, in which the second and fourth lines of each quatrain are reproduced identically as the first and third lines of the quatrain following, and he liked to imagine that in sustaining such a roll-over momentum through no fewer than '18 diabolical quatrains'[26] he had produced the longest pantoum in the language. It was the extreme technical discipline required by the form, which created 'a curious effect of the leapfrogging of lines from one quatrain to the next', which appealed to Curnow as a means of avoiding the pitfalls – moralism or sentimentality – of writing a political poem to order.

Wilmers at *London Review of Books* again published the poem very quickly, and quoted provocatively from it on the magazine's front cover ('Chirac's thermonuclear hard-on'). It was also reprinted in *The Forward Book of Poetry*, a selection of the best poems published in Great Britain and Ireland the previous year, and Curnow was pleased to have a new poem to add to *The Game of Tag*, in his new collection. He was also relieved to feel, after he read the poem at the book's launching in November, that the roll-over of identical lines from quatrain to quatrain had a clarifying effect on the poem as a whole, 'of making discursive sense of it all': 'Did the ancient Malay intend the thing for oral performance?'[27]

Interviews, exhibitions, events, 1996–97

'[I]f only one could give interviews under a gen[eral] anaesthetic', Curnow had complained to Tony in the early 1980s,[28] and in the mid-1990s Curnow continued to be plagued by interviewers. In April 1996 Auckland's *Metro* magazine published a profile ('Sweating Poesy') by Steve Braunias, based on comments by many who knew Curnow, which he felt misrepresented much in his life and poetic career. In 1994 he had also been contacted by Gordon Ogilvie, Glover's biographer – whose aim was to present a 'multi-faceted Denis ... seen from all angles', 'honest, unsanitised, warts and all'[29] – but remained anxious about the outcome: 'I know, "warts and all" sounds so brave and right-minded – any fool can spot warts, but "and all" is a job for Socrates, not Mr Pecksniff, isn't it?' he replied.[30]

There was one event in 1995 which gave him particular pleasure, however, an exhibition in his honour, entitled *The Loop in Lone Kauri Road*, mounted at the

Lopdell House Gallery, Titirangi, during the month of June. Curnow's poems were transformed into 'an installation of sorts'[31] for the exhibition. The artist Gail Halfern and the graphic designer Douglas Hawkins filled the gallery with large manuscript-like displays of a number of Karekare poems ('The Loop in Lone Kauri Road', 'You Will Know When You Get There', 'Things to Do with Moonlight', 'This Beach Can Be Dangerous', as well as, on all four walls of a room off the main gallery space, the whole of 'A Fellow Being'), 'creating the effect', Lopdell House curator/director Kate Darrow wrote, 'of being surrounded or engulfed by the text'.[32] 'The poems, blown up big', Curnow wrote to Hulse, 'are hung on panels about 6ft x 3ft, made of some sort of transparent stuff laminated, with shadowy graphics of sea or bush behind or between the lines . . .'.[33] In addition there was a limited-edition print of 'You Will Know When You Get There', hand-printed by Tara McLeod, and an exhibition booklet including an essay on Curnow's Karekare poems by Peter Simpson. A ten-minute TV3 television programme was made to mark the exhibition – Curnow's longest appearance in this medium up to that time – including footage of the poet reading 'The Loop in Lone Kauri Road', of the exhibition itself, and of Lone Kauri Road in fading light.

The following year the installation was exhibited at the National Library Gallery in Wellington, and Curnow gave a reading at the National Library auditorium on 14 March, while he was in Wellington to offer 'An Hour With Allen Curnow' at the International Festival of the Arts. During his festival session Curnow read 'The Scrap-book', for which Chris Price, editor of *Landfall* at the time, had arranged a special limited edition published by Sydney Shep at Wai-te-ata Press.[34] Price also brought out a special issue of that literary journal to mark the festival, including two of Curnow's poems, 'The Game of Tag' and 'Early Days Yet'.[35] However, Curnow was much less impressed by another installation involving his work, constructed at the Auckland Society of Arts gallery without consultation and permission, at the same time as the National Gallery exhibition. He described the installation to Hulse:

> It is made of 623 jam jars, each filled with a fruit jelly made to the recipe of the Artist's Granny, cooked by a team of 30 of the Artist's pupils: sandblasted on each jar, a single word of my 'Spectacular Blossom', and the jars shelved so that each shelf holds a complete line of the poem. That required 220 jars: the remaining 400 are devoted to writings of the late Bruce Mason, and Katherine Mansfield, similarly sandblasted. The whole contrivance is entitled 'Spectacular Blossom' and said to 'preserve' the domestic labours of women down the ages. Now, my first knowledge of this gross abuse of my intellectual property rights was a large coloured picture in the *NZ Herald* followed by an approving notice from that journal's deranged art critic.[36]

Curnow broke what he called 'my rule of half a lifetime' (remaining publicly silent on matters of controversy to do with his own work) and wrote to the *Herald*, dissociating himself from the installation, which was the work of an Auckland Institute of Technology art lecturer Monique Redmond:

> I am fairly sure I would have refused permission for this kind of treatment of my lines, had it been sought. The sole purpose of this letter is to correct any impression that I was compliant in this use of my name, my poem's title, and my text, or that it has my authority.[37]

However, at this time two much more substantial critical projects relating to Curnow's poetry, one New Zealand-based, the other internationally based, were under way. At the end of 1995 Janet Wilson (a New Zealand-born academic then lecturing at Oxford Brookes University), together with Michael Hulse and Chris Miller, decided to co-edit a volume of a dozen or so newly solicited essays on Curnow's poetry, its objectives 'to assert and substantiate an international stature for Curnow's later poetry' and 'to provide a broader perspective on his work which has so far been lacking and which we feel would illuminate his achievement'.[38] Contributions came in irregularly, and the project eventually went into cold storage, though a number of excellent pieces designed for the book (including by Miller himself on *Trees, Effigies, Moving Objects*, Peter Robinson on Curnow's overseas travels, and Philip Armstrong on the relevance of Lacan to the poetry) subsequently found publication in literary magazines. The second project was a conference convened by Professor Lawrence Jones and Dr Heather Murray at the University of Otago, 30 August to 1 September 1996, entitled 'Curnow, Caxton, and the Canon: The Making of a New Zealand Literary Culture 1932–1963', the third biennial conference of the Association of New Zealand Literature, which attracted twelve papers on different aspects of Curnow's work. Many of the essays were subsequently published in two issues of the annual *Journal of New Zealand Literature*,[39] as well as two additional essays, by John Bayley ('A Count of Three') and Alan Roddick ('Dead on Time: "A Reliable Service"'), originally intended for the volume edited by Wilson, Miller and Hulse.

Curnow himself did not attend the conference but was pleased to be kept informed about its programme by Jones. His attention at the time was focused more on the fate of *Early Days Yet*. On 14 June 1996 an IRA bomb was detonated in the centre of Manchester, injuring more than 200 people and causing widespread damage to buildings. Amongst the wreckage were the Corn Exchange offices of Carcanet Press. A week later Schmidt wrote a general letter to authors and others informing them that Carcanet would not have access to what was left of the building for some time and that a replacement manuscript might be needed for all works scheduled for publication in 1997 (as was *Early Days Yet*).[40] Curnow immediately set to work on a replacement, and it was not until mid-July that Schmidt was able to inform him that he had been allowed brief access to the damaged premises and discovered that the original had in fact survived the bombing – the only one to do so – and that Carcanet was working hard in temporary premises to maintain its publishing schedule.

In December Schmidt also asked Curnow to choose 240 lines from pre-twentieth-century New Zealand poets, with a headnote of 300 words, for an anthology of English poetry, *Poets on Poets* (in which contemporary poets nominated pre-twentieth-century poems of their own choosing), which he was co-editing with Nick Rennison and publishing in association with the British bookseller Waterstone's. Curnow completed this task in time for Schmidt's deadline of March 1997, though he found it a difficult chore, eventually choosing four poems: an early anonymous ballad about sealing, 'David Lowston', which Wedde and McQueen had discovered for their Penguin anthology in 1985; lines from William Pember Reeves's 'A Colonist in his Garden'; Blanche Baughan's 'The Old Place'; and a substantial excerpt from a largely forgotten poem by Arnold Wall, entitled 'The Ballad of Pope Joan'.* [41]

Schmidt was pleased with Curnow's contribution,[42] and in late March Curnow also received the page proofs of the collected poems from Carcanet, which he went through carefully, making a small number of late revisions. The book, much to his relief, was now on target to be published in the UK in June, and in Auckland (as part of a co-publication venture with Auckland University Press) two months later, in August. As always, Curnow was anxious and expectant about how it might be received – both the new poems and the wider selection of his earlier poems than he had included in the Viking *Selected Poems* seven years earlier. It was a particular pleasure, also, that as seemed to happen so often when new collections were on the point of being published, he completed a new poem in May, after a gap of 20 months. Wilmers immediately accepted 'the wonderful poem'[43] – 'The Kindest Thing' – and Curnow was buoyed to think that he was not finished yet. It gave an additional resonance to the title he had chosen for his new volume, *Early Days Yet*.

---

* The last was a surprising (and perhaps defiant) choice, given that Curnow's earlier anthologies had been criticised for favouritism towards Wall, and he devoted considerable space in his headnote to the poet's defence, albeit cryptic in its comments on the poem itself.

Chapter Thirty-five

Last Poems, *The Bells*
of Saint Babel's, 1997–2001

None of us [poets] can say who will succeed, or even who has or has not
talent. The only thing certain about us is that we are too many.

W.B. Yeats[1]

Reception of *Early Days Yet*

Early Days Yet appeared in the United Kingdom at the end of June 1997 and
was launched in New Zealand in August at a festival of New Zealand poetry,
entitled 'Seeing Voices', organised by Elizabeth Caffin of Auckland University
Press. There was a busy programme of promotional events for the book in
New Zealand, including an interview with Gordon McLauchlan in the
New Zealand Herald[2] and an hour-long interview with Brian Edwards on his
'Top o' the Morning' Saturday National Radio programme,[3] and the performance poet David Eggleton reviewed the volume at length in the *New Zealand*
Listener, blending insights into some aspects of the way the poetry worked with
over-the-top clichés.[4] Reading the review, Curnow felt that it was 'a bit like being
choked with cream'.[5] However, he chose lines from Eggleton's review for the
back-cover blurb of his next collection (*The Bells of Saint Babel's*): '. . . the poet of
multiplicity – of the life lived at different levels and the poet of high seriousness
who can see the joke – . . . celebrating the sacred text that is the world with all its
signs and wonders'.

Reviews in Australia and the UK appeared more sporadically than in New Zealand, where after three months all but 75 of the AUP edition of 500 copies had sold. An enthusiastic review by the poet Alan Wearne in the *Sydney Morning Herald* singled out the pantoum 'Pacific 1945–95' as 'a fine example' of Curnow's urge to 'make it new', 'his obvious belief that boundaries have to be extended', and compared him with the American poet Elizabeth Bishop: 'both are poets who never need to "improve" but rather who searched constantly for new things to write about, new things to say and new ways of saying them'.[6] Geoffrey Dutton, a long-time admirer of Curnow's poetry, wrote handsomely about the collection in *The Australian*, mentioning 'a superb new poem' recently published in the *London Review of Books* ('The Kindest Thing'), and compared Curnow with the Italian poet Eugenio Montale.

In the UK the collection attracted a long review in the *Times Literary Supplement*, by Elizabeth Lowry, offering a considered assessment of his career, and (somewhat oddly) praising the recent poems in the collection (those in *The Game of Tag*) for their difference from the 'curiously static' 'abstraction' and 'impersonality' of his poems from the 1960s to the 1980s, and for their rediscovery of 'a genuine emotional urgency unmatched by anything written since the 1940s'.[7] In a somewhat parallel vein Sean O'Brien in the *Sunday Times* praised the 'impressive and attractive formalism' of Curnow's 1940s poetry, compared with the florid, over-written manner of the 1950s and 'the open, unbuttoned forms which were to follow'.[8] Curnow was presumably somewhat taken aback by such unstinting praise of the earlier poetry in comparison with his later work. However, as with Eggleton's review he also chose lines from Lowry for the blurb of his next collection – her praise of Curnow's late familial poems as 'brilliantly realised dioramas . . . which manage to suggest that fusion of place and self . . . that is surely the secret of all poetry'.

At the end of September Curnow and Jeny spent a week on holiday in Nouméa, New Caledonia. For Curnow it was a welcome respite from his busy promotional and other activities over the previous few months. During June he had spent considerable time annotating a draft by Peter Simpson of the entry on him for *The Oxford Companion to New Zealand Literature* (edited by Roger Robinson and Nelson Wattie). In particular he expanded a great deal on what Simpson had written about intergenerational and interregional conflicts in the 1950s as these were expressed at the time of the publication of the 1960 *Penguin Book of New Zealand Verse*, and provided a considerable amount of behind-the-scenes information that had not been publicly available up to this time. In one respect, however, his revised account is misleading. Mention of Eileen Duggan was omitted, after Curnow informed Simpson that: 'It was all over between her and me and Penguin, and the book on its way to the press, *before* Baxter, Campbell et al planted their bomb.'⁹ Curnow clearly misremembered the sequence of events, and the fact that it was the disagreements with Duggan which delayed the Penguin's publication for a further eighteen months after the six-month delay caused by the intervention of Baxter, Campbell and Johnson.

The first of Curnow's new poems, 'The Kindest Thing' – written 20 months after 'Pacific 1945–1995' – appeared in the *London Review of Books*¹⁰ in the same week that *Early Days Yet* was officially released in the UK, and is an example of a number of his poems (like 'A Busy Port', and 'The Cake Uncut', which he was to write the following year) in which there is a strongly underpinning narrative element. The poem evoked a horrifying event on one of the Curnows' trips to Russell, during which, motoring near Kawakawa on 'one of those bright / spring mornings', their vehicle was suddenly overtaken at great speed, out of the blue as if from a 'concealed exit', by a Land Rover (in the poem Curnow changed the vehicle to the more generic, and colloquial, 'ute') dragging a dog behind it:

> the dog
> half-hanged, roped
>
> by the neck, raving,
>   clawing at the tailboard
>
> forefeet can't climb
>   back over, hind
>
> legs cruelly danced
>   off the tar-seal.

Curnow stops the car to offer what assistance he can to the dog, convulsing on the road after the rope has broken, but the animal can't survive its appalling injuries: '*These hurts can't heal.*' The hurts experienced by the human protagonists on the scene ('the Maori boy who / saw it all, from / that house', the vet, the poet himself), taking what clumsy, practical steps they can to help the dog and to identify the driver, can't ever heal either. Violence and suffering – deliberately inflicted or accidental – are incorrigibly part of the world in which we all live, as are acts of kindness which involve assisting the death of those ('strays') whose agony, unrelieved, would only otherwise be prolonged.

Soon after his return from Nouméa at the end of September Curnow began work on another poem, 'Ten Steps to the Sea', the last of his 'big' Karekare-based meditative observational poems and another of his 'walking poems' as he strolls with his dog to the beach. He finished it in mid-November and sent it straight

to Mary-Kay Wilmers at the *London Review of Books*. 'It will be such a pleasure
to see it in the paper', she replied immediately,[11] and Curnow was later to use it
as the opening poem of his last volume, *The Bells of Saint Babel's*. In its earliest
drafts it was conceived of in a single meditative movement, but gradually took the
form of ten short numbered blocks, each block (as in some of Stevens's poems)
containing a vivid observation or notation of the scene as it unfolds, or a thought
sparked by (or imposed on) the scene – each of the 'steps' marking a steady physical
and mental progression towards death, accompanied by the perpetual music (in a
wonderful onomatopoeia of gathering, breaking and receding waves) of 'the sea's
habitual heave / sprawl, grumble, hiss.'

The poem, throughout, is full of lively intimations of 'reality' – observed (as
in 'Kikuyu grass / underfoot, thunderheads, purple- / patched sunshine offshore,
onshore / the high dunes, the hollows of / wetted sand, rabbit shit.'), or remembered, as in the memory of a flash flood which once destroyed the small bridge
on the approach to the beach ('stringers, planks, / gadarening down into the tide
. . . . How the upstream / railing splintered, the deck duck- / diving, you'd never
know now. Good as new.'). But the poem returns, movingly, to the speaker's sole
self, to his own efforts to balance the indissoluble connection between reality and
pain, imaged in the force of the wind which blows uncontrollably in his face:

> In reality,
> no. A step in the right direction.
> The pain is this wind, which blows the whole
> time, uncontrollably.
> In your face.

In the last few months of 1997 Curnow and Jeny became involved in a major
new project relating to his work, the making of a documentary video film by
the filmmaker Shirley Horrocks (director of Point of View Productions, whose
most recent work in the field had been an award-winning documentary about
the artist Len Lye), with one of New Zealand's leading cinematographers, Leon
Narbey, as cameraman.* Curnow was nervous about undertaking such a project,
concerned as always to preserve the privacy of his personal and family life and
unsure of his capacity to do justice to himself and his work in so unfamiliar a
medium, but he came to see it as perhaps his best opportunity to make the kind

---

* Over the next three years Horrocks worked hard to secure funding for the project. In 1998 a small but
welcome grant from Creative New Zealand enabled her to keep going. NZ On Air was also supportive,
but constrained by being unable to fund a documentary until a broadcaster had agreed to screen it, and
it was not until September 2000 that TVNZ finally signed a contract for the documentary, enabling the
necessary release of funds.

of personal statement about his life and art that had always eluded him when asked to write, autobiographically, about himself.

Horrocks's first filming for the project (eventually 73 minutes long) provided footage of the launch of *Early Days Yet* in the 'Seeing Voices' festival of New Zealand poetry at the Jubilee Building in Parnell on 22 August 1997, and in November and December of that year the first of at least five or six filming sessions during the next three and a half years occurred at Tohunga Crescent and at Karekare. At the end of 1999 Curnow and Jeny travelled with the film crew to the South Island, where he revisited some of his childhood haunts (including St David's Church at Belfast, the vicarage at Sheffield, and locations at Lyttelton and Governor's Bay), the film visually retracing memories which had become so important a part of his later poetry. Horrocks also took footage of Curnow reading 'The Bells of Saint Babel's' at the Going West Books and Writers Festival in September 1999, at Karekare in September 2000 when he read 'The Pocket Compass' for a BBC International Poetry Day programme, and at the launch of *The Bells of Saint Babel's* in February 2001. He was extremely pleased with the final result, and personally moved by the memories many of its scenes evoked, when it was launched at the Auckland International Film Festival in July 2001.

Perhaps one of the more significant consequences of the publication of *Early Days Yet* in the UK was an invitation to Curnow in January 1998 from Antonia Byatt (daughter of the novelist A.S. Byatt), who was head of literature at the Southbank Centre in London, to read his poems in the Royal Festival Hall's Purcell Room, at its prestigious biennial Poetry International Festival in November later that year. Curnow agreed to make the trip, provided travel funding was forthcoming (which it eventually was), and provided Jeny, of course, could accompany him. It was an event to look forward to, and plan for, during the course of the year.

Two new commissions, 1998

In July 1997 Anthony Thwaite invited Curnow to contribute a poem to a collection by fellow poets to mark Peter Porter's seventieth birthday in 1999.[12] Knowing of Porter's pleasure in poetic forms requiring dexterity and ingenuity, Curnow embarked on another pantoum. Thwaite thought the poem ('For Peter Porter at Seventy') 'a wonderful *tour de force*',[13] and Porter himself was delighted: 'I am proud to have so fine a poem written to me.'[14]

The poem's ingenuity consists in its play with the number 'seventy' and the traditional notion of life proceeding in seven-year cycles. At its centre Curnow affectionately recalls his own first meeting with Porter at the Brisbane Writers'

Week festival in 1982, when he had himself recently turned 70 and Porter was in his fifties, and at this point moves to an elegant tribute to Porter's poetry, through which can be heard a distinctive '*continuo*' derived from 'the high outback sound, / ciphering note of an organ-pipe high wind' in his 'native Brisbane sky'. The *continuo* Curnow sensed in Porter's poems links to Curnow's abiding sense of life as a 'continuum' with its own incorrigible music and its own inescapable mortality, as the 'digits tick' away.

A month after he had completed the pantoum Curnow was approached by the British poet and critic Elaine Feinstein, inviting him to contribute translations of poems of his choice by Pushkin for a volume which she was editing, to be published by The Folio Society and Carcanet Press to mark the bicentenary of Pushkin's birth in 1799. Curnow was intrigued by the prospect, and 'willing to try', though he confessed to having no knowledge of Russian, suggesting that poems 'after' Pushkin might be a suitable way of describing the exercise.[15] To assist poets in their choice Feinstein sent them copies of Walter Arndt's 1972 translation of Pushkin, *Pushkin Threefold*, which offered literal versions with facing Russian text.

Over the next three months Curnow worked steadily on this project, choosing four poems altogether, completing two of them ('The Talisman' and 'When and Where') in June 1998, and the other two ('Winter Evening' and 'The Upas Tree') in August. *After Pushkin: Versions of the poems of Alexander Sergeevich Pushkin by contemporary poets* appeared late in 1999 and included, as well as three poems by Curnow ('Winter Evening' was excluded), contributions by Ted Hughes, Seamus Heaney, Charles Tomlinson, Dannie Abse, Edwin Morgan and Patricia Beer, as well as by fellow New Zealander Bill Manhire, and by Feinstein herself. Stead, highly accomplished himself (in his many poems after Catullus) in the art of making versions derived from originals in another language, thought Curnow's contributions 'awfully good', and offered a practitioner's reasons for his assessment: '[They are] Curnow poems, and that's the only way it can be with translations. Either it's a poem by the translator or it's not a poem – it's a translation. Yours are poems.'[16]

'When and Where', finished a fortnight after 'The Talisman', was from an untitled original, and was selected by the *Times Literary Supplement*,[17] along with other versions by Heaney, Beer, Carol Ann Duffy and Christopher Reid, for reprinting to mark the publication of the book in October 1999. Curnow also regarded it as his best, and was especially pleased to have preserved Pushkin's alternate rhyme scheme (unlike Arndt). His way of presenting Pushkin's concern with mortality and personal death in this poem suggests many links with this theme in his own later poems. 'Someone's last // hour's always next, right here and now' is a typical late Curnow cadence, as is his rendering of Pushkin's meditations about the time and place of his death:

And which day of which year
to come will turn out to have been
the anniversary, distant or near,
of my death? Good question. The scene,
will it be wartime, on a trip,
or at home or in some nearby
street, crashed coach or a ship-
wreck that I'm to die?

'Good question.' – inserted bluntly into the flow of notations of time and place
– is also vintage Curnow, a substitution for Arndt's pedestrian 'intent to guess
among them', capturing something of the ironic self-consciousness which he
conjectures might be in Pushkin's reflections on death.

Last trip to London, October–November, 1998

'Those Pushkins, at moments,' Curnow wrote to Stead in October 1998, 'could
feel like a kind of schizoid game, but on the whole I'm glad to have done them.'[18]
He and Jeny were now beginning to look forward to their trip to London, where
Curnow was scheduled to read at the biennial Poetry International Festival on
1 November, but the trip needed a great deal more care in the planning than in
the past. Curnow was now 87, and he had had a difficult winter, suffering badly
from influenza in July, and being diagnosed with a slow-moving form of prostate
cancer. In the same month he learnt of the death of much-loved cousin Arnold
(Ted) Wall at the age of 90. For several years Wall had lived in a rest home in
Nelson after losing the sight of his remaining eye, and Curnow had been deeply
affected by the dignity and courage with which he accepted his impending blindness, in a letter he wrote announcing that it would be his last.

They planned to be away for a month, from 21 October to 20 November,
breaking the trip each way with two nights at Bangkok, and allowing a week in
London for recovery from jet lag prior to the reading. Arriving in wet and gloomy
London on 24 October (the first time either of them had stayed there at that
time of the year since their first visits in 1949), they stayed at an apartment in
Bloomsbury Street for a week. On the evening of 30 October they attended the
opening event of the festival – a reading by Czesław Miłosz, followed by a reception for participating poets and other guests – and the next day shifted into the
Hotel Russell for four nights (accommodation provided by the festival organisers),
attending the second of the two 'heavyweight' events of the festival that evening,
a reading by the Nobel Prize-winning West Indian poet Derek Walcott.

Curnow's own half-hour reading the following evening was in a programme of four poets, the others being the Canadian poet Anne Carson, the English poet Alice Oswald, and the Canadian novelist and poet Michael Ondaatje. The 300-seat Purcell Room in the Royal Festival Hall was full for the occasion, and Curnow (having rehearsed the timing with Jeny during the previous week) read seven poems, in the order: 'Continuum', 'Things to Do with Moonlight', 'Early Days Yet', 'Looking West, Late Afternoon, Low Water', 'A South Island Night's Entertainment', 'A Busy Port', and (from his most recent work) 'The Kindest Thing'. Chris Miller, who travelled from Oxford to listen to the reading, was struck by the contrast between the elegance and civility of Curnow's presence and the sheer visceral energy emerging from the poems as he read them. Curnow was touched that so many of his London friends came to the event, including Porter and Thwaite, Richard and Jocelyn Mayne, and Fleur Adcock, and especially pleased that Tony and Elisabeth had also travelled from Pruzilly for the weekend, in order to attend the reading and catch up with them.

The reading left Curnow exhausted for the next day or so, but on 3 November he and Jeny had a lively luncheon meeting with Porter and the Thwaites at the British Library, and on the following day they shifted from the Hotel Russell to stay for the rest of their time in London with their old friends Richard and Jocelyn Mayne at Albany Cottage, Regent's Park. This memorable stay was the personal highlight of their trip, though tinged with sadness since all knew that this was likely to be the last of Curnow's trips away. The Maynes were warm and generous hosts, the conversation varied and effortless, and the Curnows were free (on days when the Maynes were away at work) to come and go as they pleased. They visited old haunts like the Tate Gallery, met Elaine Feinstein (with whom Curnow was able to discuss the Pushkin project), and were much impressed by a production of Peter Schaffer's *Amadeus* at the Old Vic. Michael Hulse visited Curnow (the last time they were to see each other), and both Curnow and Jeny enjoyed the warm company of the Maynes' daughters, Zoe and Alice.

Despite the sadness of their parting from the Maynes on 16 November both were looking forward to arriving home, after their Bangkok stopover, on 20 November. 'Home will be good – to unpack, to have summer, our own place, the family & my new work', Jeny wrote in her diary. 'Today is the 44th anniversary of our meeting.'* [19] Those securities had always been precious to both, and were to remain so, during the last years of Curnow's life.

---

* Jeny's 'new work', which was to occupy her for a number of years, was as a member of a research team (led by Maori scholars from the universities of Auckland and Waikato, and in collaboration with the Alexander Turnbull Library) which had been awarded a major three-year Marsden Fund grant to investigate Maori-language newspapers in the nineteenth century, and involved not only working directly on the newspapers herself but assisting in the training of younger scholars in research techniques and methods.

Last poems, 1999–2000

A major poem about the founding of Christchurch and Canterbury Province, 'The Bells of Saint Babel's', which was to become the title poem of Curnow's next and last collection, preoccupied him during the early months of 1999. 'I've dropped so many hints about [it]', he wrote to Pearson – enclosing a copy of it at the end of March – adding: 'It has extended me in more than one way, at least I hope so.'[20] At the same time he sent a copy to Wilmers, with a characteristically short and modest note – 'Will you perhaps find room for this?'[21] – though he was privately aware that the poem was 'a lot longer, & more ambitious than most I've sent to *LRB*. A sort of private wager with myself.'[22] Perhaps the 'private wager' had to do not simply with the length of the poem but with the challenge of reaching a wider international audience with a poem so dense in the particulars of New Zealand's place and history. Ever since Lehmann had reprinted 'The Unhistoric Story' and 'Landfall in Unknown Seas' in his *Penguin New Writing* in the 1940s, it had been an article of faith with Curnow that local reference need never be a barrier to an international readership. It all depended on the *poetic* deployment of the material. Stead was much impressed with Curnow's achievement in this respect: 'It has so much – wit, particularity, history, and the concluding anecdote – and another statement about "us": "Nothing changes".'[23] So, too, was the *London Review of Books*, where the poem appeared in June.[24]

Replying to Stead, Curnow remarked: 'No way of saying, either (is there?) how such a heap of particulars can become a sort of order personal to oneself – those "unexpected favours" Stevens talked about, from working on a long poem.'[25] Those particulars had shaped themselves into a long poem consisting of 150 four-syllabled lines in pairs organised into five numbered sections, revisiting his own earlier poetry (in *Not in Narrow Seas* and elsewhere) in which he explored the colonial origins of the province of Canterbury and the cultural schizophrenia of its aftermath, manifested in the obsessiveness of its mimic British pretensions. The later poem, however, is altogether less impersonal, less narrowly political in its focus (though colonialism remains an implicit theme), much freer, wittier and more variable in its use of story, anecdote, myth and personal memory, and much more wide-ranging in the global (rather than narrowly Anglo-imperial) framework within which he places Canterbury history.

The final section of the poem, recounting a humorous anecdote in which the 'divine' bells drown out a conversation between the Dean of the Cathedral and his elegantly attired colonist-friend, during their morning walk in the Square outside, provides a hilarious example of Curnow's ability to locate (and enact) the mythic in the ordinary, quotidian particulars of a comically confused conversation:

Their morning walk.
What makes the tower

burst but thunderclappers
newly hung, high

peal deafeningly
detonating,

the Dean's delight,
Are not those bells

Divine?
Silk hat,
hand cupped on ear,

shouts back, What's that?
and Gaiters, Divine!

And he, What? What?
Can't make it out –

Sorry, Mister Dean,
can't hear a word

for those DAMNED BELLS.

Perhaps thinking especially of that final section, Curnow commented to Caffin that the poem was 'a *devil* to perform, & get somewhere near the credible *speech* it needs',[26] and when his first opportunity to read it publicly occurred (at the Going West Books and Writers Festival in 1999) he decided to read it twice, remembering the effect of a double performance of Geoffrey Hill's 'The Pentecost Castle' at Peterhouse Hall when he visited Cambridge in 1985.

In October and November 1999 Curnow began work on a new poem, based on newspaper reports of an eleven-year-old boy's death from cancer after his parents – members of an extreme religious sect – refused orthodox medical treatment, relying on the 'will of God' to decide the boy's fate. In particular, he was fascinated by the mother's comment – in a newspaper report of her conversation with the boy's headmaster – that 'the wonderful thing' about his death was that the child seemed to predict its precise moment, as if aware of and acquiescent in God's will. In early drafts Curnow included that phrase, in fact naming the poem after it, but later omitted it (perhaps because it made for too simple a judgement of the mother's credulity or fanaticism), substituting the title 'The Cake Uncut'.

Told largely from the mother's point of view, the poem is remarkable for its humane, non-judgemental view of the parents' actions, insisting on the love they had for their son. Where the media sensationalised the event, seeing a black-and-white moral issue to be dealt with by subjecting the parents to the law, Curnow could only see shades of grey: the cruelty of a world which deals such killer diseases to children, the unpredictable ways in which human beings try to cope with, rationalise and accept such cruelty:

> Shame not to cut the
> cake with his twelve
>
> candles on. God'll
> have you up and running
>
> again, for your
> birthday, I'm saying
>
> and we'll all see
> the Millennium in –
>
> he'd've loved that so,
> every minute, even
>
> knowing, all along,
> what never was meant.

Curnow completed the poem in time for it to appear in a '2000 AD' millennial literary supplement edited by Anthony Hubbard and published by the *Sunday Star-Times* on 2 January 2000, alongside poems, fiction and non-fiction by sixteen other New Zealand writers. The writers had been given a 'relatively free rein', though asked to 'bear in mind the millennium',[27] and numerous of them geared their contributions directly to its significance. Curnow's approach was altogether more oblique – a brief reference to the millennial birthday celebrations which the dead child will miss: whatever miracles of human progress might be celebrated or looked forward to, the circumstances of the child's death are a reminder of events incorrigibly beyond human control – beyond the power of medical science, and beyond the scope of any kind of legal rush to judgment.* [28]

With the 'The Cake Uncut' Curnow had now completed five new poems since *Early Days Yet*, in addition to his four versions of Pushkin, and began to think of a new collection, 'a possible ultra-slim book', he wrote to Caffin at Auckland University Press, 'perhaps 30–40 pp (containing everything) though there are no more than 500 lines of verse all told'.[29] In the meantime he and Jeny travelled to Adelaide where Curnow had been invited to participate in the Adelaide Festival's Writers' Week from 2 to 8 March 2000. It was to be the last time he travelled abroad. For the first two days all of the invited writers (approximately thirty) were hosted at a retreat in the McLaren Vale wine region 45 minutes from Adelaide, where Curnow especially enjoyed meeting fellow participants Fay Weldon, Thomas Keneally and the Irish poet Matthew Sweeney. Tim and Lea drove down from Sydney to be with Allen and Jeny in Adelaide and were able to drive them from place to place. The Adelaide writer Peter Goldsworthy organised an intimate dinner party in Curnow's honour which included Sweeney. After the retreat the writers then returned to Adelaide on 4 March for the public events of the festival. During his solo reading on 7 March Curnow read 'Gare SNCF Garavan', 'A Fellow Being', 'Do Not Touch the Exhibits' and 'An Evening Light', and the following evening participated in a session entitled 'Poets – Home and Away' with Robert Adamson, Rosemary Dobson, Emmanuel Moses, Gig Ryan, Sweeney and Thomas Lynch, during which he read 'The Cake Uncut'.

Soon after his return Curnow began working on 'Fantasia and Fugue for Pan-pipe', one of his most challenging poems – reaching back to early family history, and re-exploring his long-standing interest in myth, in the nature of language, and in the relationship between words and the things or events to which they refer. The immediate subject of the poem had intrigued Curnow for some time – the apparently coincidental appearance of two deeply felt but highly generalised romantic lyric poems on the theme of lost love, one by his father Tremayne and the other by Maud Goodenough Hayter, in Alexander and Currie's 1906 anthology, *New Zealand Verse*. Family tradition had it that Tremayne and Maud had been engaged for a time before Hayter broke the engagement. Tremayne's poem was entitled 'Pan', and evoked a lovelorn Pan plaintively lamenting on his reed-pipes his abandonment by the chaste nymph Syrinx.[30] Hayter's was simply called 'Song', describing the overnight

---

* Because the poem first appeared in the *Sunday Star-Times* Curnow was uncertain whether to send it to the *London Review of Books*, but eventually did so in early February 2000 after adding a brief section in which the mother dreamt of winning Lotto and taking the child to Mexico for alternative treatment of his cancer ('something about / apricot stones'). Wilmers, however, was not in the least bothered by the poem's prior publication and included it in the current issue.

transformation of a 'flaming gold' sunset to a desolate snowbound landscape.[31] For Curnow the speculation that the poems represented 'actual' personal events – or two versions of the same event – albeit displaced into myth (with Tremayne figuring as Pan and Maud as Syrinx) – was irresistible. However, Curnow was also fascinated by the fact of biographical speculation itself, which becomes as much the poem's subject as the 'truth' behind Tremayne's and Maud's relationship and its breakdown.

There is nothing in the poems themselves which explicitly links them to specific events in their authors' lives, and the fact that the two poems appear in the same anthology, separated by 'twenty-odd pages', might be pure coincidence; nor is there anything that explicitly links the two poems, apart from their very general, utterly conventional theme of romantic loss, which they share with many other of the late Victorian lyrics in the anthology. Throughout the poem's first section, which is devoted to the two poems, the speculative impulse to read and decode the texts as autobiographical (as describing a love affair that collapses under the repressive Victorian conventions of chastity and self-denial) is countered by a 'factual' or documentary impulse (providing the name, date, publisher and place of publication of the anthology, as well as direct quotations of lines from the poems) which has the effect of undermining the very notion of arriving at any such final statement of the truth. Neither the bare prosaic facts that he can muster (and there are few of these) nor the poetic descriptions provided by Tremayne and Maud themselves provide sufficient evidence. At the conclusion of the first section Curnow alludes to a dimly remembered family rumour that Maud subsequently married a travelling salesman, but he does so by subsuming the rumour into a quotation from Blake's 'Never seek to tell thy love', with its reference to a 'traveller' who 'came by . . . [and] took her with a sigh'. Whose sigh, Curnow asks, drawing attention even to the ambiguities of Blake's grammar: 'his? / hers? or theirs?' Even at the simplest referential/descriptive level the relationship between language and events remains uncertain.

In the third section of the poem, as he pursues his improvised 'fantasia' about the relationship between Tremayne and Maud, Curnow introduces a second body of 'facts' about Maud, this time from his own past: his memory of a brief visit from her ('Not any more / the slender reed, / fifty-something Syrinx') at the time of his own wedding 30 years later, when he noticed her 'hands / compress the ball / of a hanky, damp / from dabbing tear- / ducts', as she sat on the foot of the bed in his small flat. Asked if she wanted more tea, she declined and left quickly. The pathos in Curnow's narrative suggests a link with his earlier 'fantasia' about the relationship between Tremayne and Maud – that the marriage of her ex-lover's son many years later reactivated a long-lasting nostalgia and regret for what might have been if she had married Tremayne. However, Curnow's speculation remains just that – a description and interpretation of an event which might carry many other possible interpretations, including bearing no connection at all to the supposed earlier relationship between Tremayne and Maud. His own poetic fiction carries the same purely contingent relationship to the actuality of events as Tremayne's and Maud's anthology poems 30 years earlier.

Whatever the explanation for Tremayne's and Maud's poems of thwarted love, the fact of loss (real or imagined) is part of their world. Whatever the causes of Maud's tears at the time of the wedding of Tremayne's son, the pathos of her grief is emphasised in the way Curnow attends to the factual details of the scene. In the final section, whose subject is the death of Pan (a 'fugue' both in the sense of 'flight', and in the musical sense of a counterpoint to the earlier sections), the description brings Curnow back to the pathos of Tremayne's (and Maud's) own deaths, and to the transience and impermanence of their words, as well as those of his own poem, subject to time and chance (like the survival of a message cast overboard in a bottle), and (like Pan's goat-foot prints) constantly threatened with erasure:

> Rolled up the beach
>
> in a bottle, rolled
> back into the surf.
>
> Hoofprints in soft
> and softening sand.

'The poem is great. Many, many thanks', Wilmers wrote to Curnow,[32] publishing it in the *London Review of Books* six weeks later on 6 July,[33] and with this additional longish poem Curnow now felt confident to press ahead with his new collection, supplemented with notes which he felt would be helpful to readers in connection with the background of three of the poems, 'The Upas Tree', 'The Bells of Saint Babel's' and 'Fantasia and Fugue for Pan-pipe'. As with *Early Days Yet* he was especially keen that the collection be published in the UK as well as in New Zealand. Both Elizabeth Caffin at Auckland University Press and Michael Schmidt at Carcanet Press were highly impressed with the manuscript (though Schmidt was concerned that even with the new poem the volume would be a little thin), and during July and August 2000 Tim negotiated contracts with both publishers on the same terms as *Early Days Yet*, with a publication date in New Zealand (and Australia) of February the following year, and in the UK in September six months later.

In August Curnow and Jeny were invited to Christchurch for the 2000 Montana Book Awards, where Curnow received the A.W. Reed Lifetime Achievement

Award. Tim had flown into Christchurch the same day on a business trip and shared the evening with them – it was the last time he would see his father alive. In the meantime work on the notes – especially on the references to Pan in the 'Fantasia' – was interrupted by an invitation from Kirsty Pope at BBC Radio 4 to contribute a sonnet 'having some connection with a point of the compass'[34] as part of a sequence of 'round-the-clock' commissioned sonnets to be broadcast on the UK's National Poetry Day planned for 5 October. 'I tried first with the Petrarchan abba', Curnow wrote to Stead, but 'found myself choking, & invented a new one – not end-rhymes but syllable counts – 11 / 9 / 9 / 11, which nobody will notice, I expect':

> There was once a compass rose drawn elegantly on our railing at Karekare by George Tole (Jeny's father), with his pocket compass beside him to get the points right. I chipped it into the timber, & was sorry to lose it when the rotting rail had to be replaced – and that's what the sonnet is about.[35]

He sent the poem to Pope at the end of August, and she arranged for it to be read and recorded on 10 September 'on location' on the deck at Karekare, with 'appropriate non-verbal sound', though she asked Curnow to provide a different, more readable title from his own awkward first choice, 'i.m.G.E.T'. Curnow sent two alternatives, 'The Pocket Compass' or 'The Right Way Round', and Pope chose the former.

After the diversion of 'The Pocket Compass' Curnow returned painstakingly to the notes he was drafting for the new collection, and at the same time began, or returned to, a poem about the death of Katherine Mansfield which he had first attempted during his tenure of the Menton fellowship in 1983 but set aside. Discussing the time it took to complete his notes to his satisfaction he commented to Stead, towards the end of November, 'I begin to suspect myself of dodging work on a new poem out of the too-hard folder.'[36] In fact, by this time, the longish new poem, 'A Nice Place on the Riviera', was substantially advanced, and before Christmas he was able to send it to Wilmers at the *London Review of Books*,[37] as well as to have confirmation from Caffin that the poem could be included in *The Bells of Saint Babel's*, which was now at page-proof stage.

'A Nice Place on the Riviera' was Curnow's last poem, evoking the period 1920–21 during which Mansfield, ill with consumption, lived in the south of France. Curnow also recalled his own memories of Villa Isola Bella and its setting during his tenure of the Katherine Mansfield Memorial Fellowship in 1983, and compared selected events in Mansfield's life at this time with events in the life of Blaise Pascal, the French mathematician, philosopher and religious thinker, author of the *Pensées*, born in 1623 exactly 300 years before the year of

Mansfield's death in 1923. The poem Curnow wrote, he commented to Stead, has 'much to do with mortality, though my chosen surrogates may surprise a little – or perhaps not at all'.[38]

If Mansfield was one of his surrogates, through whom he could confront, impersonally, his own sense of mortality and physical frailty, and the questions it prompted about the relationship between life, art and spiritual belief, the other was Pascal, who provided the epigraph for the poem, with its image of death as a brutal physical fact of existence: 'The last act is bloody, however fine the rest of the play. They throw earth over your head and it is finished for ever.'[39] Pascal's metaphor also foreshadows the final moments of Mansfield's death at the Gurdjieff Institute, 'that // fatal torrential / haemorrhage, at // Fontainebleau, // stumbling upstairs.'

Like Mansfield, Pascal suffered from debilitating illness throughout his life, a prey to increasingly intolerable headaches probably caused by a malformation of his skull from birth, and he died at the relatively youthful age of 39. Unlike Mansfield, however, he claimed to experience a direct, life-transforming personal revelation of God, lasting two hours, on the night of 23 November 1654, whose visionary contents he memorialised on a parchment which he wore around his neck for the remaining eight years of his life while he worked on the *Pensées*, the passionate but never finally completed *apologium* for religious belief, in the form of hundreds of reflections or 'thoughts' (aphorisms and jottings, paragraphs, short essays) on nature, the mind and feelings, the soul, and Christian life and theology.

In 1983 it was 'without much thought' that Curnow had taken his copy of the *Pensées* overseas – it was small enough to fit into his hand luggage for in-flight reading during the trip to Europe. However, its grotesque cover image of Pascal's death-mask with eyes (lifted from a portrait) poked into the eye sockets and staring directly at the reader also provided the poem, by chance, later, with another powerful image of the brute physical fact of death. There was much else that was serendipitous in the process by which Curnow's two surrogates came together in the poem. A number of early drafts contain mathematical lists of dates relating to events in Mansfield's and Pascal's lives as well as to Curnow's own, as if searching for chance correlations, as he had with F.J. Rayner in 'A Fellow Being'. He worked out that Pascal was 31 years old (in 1654) when he received the vision that convinced him of the existence of a personal God, the same age as Mansfield was (in 1920) when she reached the opposite conclusion, that there was no 'personal God or any such nonsense'.[40] In fact it was with this sheerly random coincidence that Curnow introduced Pascal into the poem in its second section.

Curnow's method in the poem was to juxtapose aspects of the lives (and deaths) of Mansfield and Pascal throughout its nine sections, occasionally obliquely inter-weaving elements of his own experience of Menton – its sirocco-swept landscape dominated by the brooding, sky-obscuring Alpes Maritimes (a bleaker setting than had appeared in 'Gare SNCF Garavan', its mood reflecting the grim experiences of Mansfield and Pascal, confronting disease and death), as well as his memories (in the third section) of the Katherine Mansfield Room used by Literary Fellows, originally the basement to the Villa Isola Bella. It is tempting to see in Curnow's two surrogates – the one a stubborn sceptic about Christianity and the other a passionate, tormented believer, the one committed in her last great works to an impersonal perfection of form, the other (as Curnow presents him in the sixth section) producing a never-completed work of intense, disordered, radioactive fragments: 'Pieces of his mind / by the thousand, // jottings on jumbo- / size sheets. Pierced // For threading string. / Tied in liasses. // Too sick, or just / ran out of time // sorting the huge heap.' – the stubborn persistence of unresolved polarities that had driven his own thinking and feeling about life and art and belief throughout his poetic career. In the brief final section of the poem Curnow 'fast-forwards' to an imagined present – everyone's present, including his own, though he does not name himself – in which the scene at Menton repeats itself:

> Fast forward again
> top-heavy *Alpes*
>
> *Maritimes* grind
> the sky small. One
>
> more dull day scraped
> off a slaty sea.

They were the last lines Curnow ever wrote. Time races forward, as it had for Mansfield and Pascal; the sky contracts as the mountains seem to loom ever-threateningly over the scene; the day is dull and the sea slaty. There are no revelations. Though unspoken, the poet's own life, approaching its end, is linked in these lines with the intellectual and emotional struggles and aspirations of his surrogates.

Last months, 2001

With the publication of *The Bells of Saint Babel's* in late February 2001 (launched at the home of Elizabeth Caffin, with a speech by Stead) Curnow undertook a busy schedule of interviews and readings, and there were visits at this time to

New Zealand by Tony and Elisabeth, and by the Thwaites, the last occasions on which he was to see them. In March, also, he was approached to record poems for the Poetry Archive in the UK (a project initiated in 1999 by the British Poet Laureate, Andrew Motion, together with the recording producer Richard Carrington, and which eventually became established as a website in 2005), and on 27 May he read and discussed his poems with Stead at the Auckland Writers and Readers Festival, speaking to a packed auditorium.

However, Curnow's personal world was also contracting at this time. In April he accompanied Jeny for a week to Wellington, where she was researching archives of Maori newspapers. He had hoped to visit Lilburn, always a first port of call on his visits there, but Lilburn was not well enough to see him. On 6 June Lilburn died, ending a friendship which had lasted 67 years. Asked by Lilburn's niece-in-law, Jeannie Lilburn, for an appropriate form of wording for a headstone, Curnow drew on his own fiftieth-birthday poetic tribute, 'To Douglas Lilburn at Fifty' ('the music affirms, makes room at least / for silence to loom in // larger than in the hills . . .'), though it turned out that Lilburn had left his own, plain and factual, instructions for the stonemason.

Though Curnow never referred to his own health in public, and seemed well (if fragile) to others – his most noticeable handicap being increasing deafness – numerous ailments were beginning to take their toll. Later in June he underwent a cataract operation in order to renew his driver's licence. The operation was successful, though recuperation took the best part of a month, and he was upset to fail his driver's test on his first attempt. He was also distressed by the death after fifteen years of the family dog, Bounce, run over by a car in Brighton Road. 'How I miss the traction of those four feet on the uphill parts of the street, only one dogpower, but enough to pull a small cart', he wrote to Tony:

> It's hard, ambiguously – not to see little Bounce in any of his usual places in the house – curled up against the hall heater or stretched out in the sun, or waiting hopefully at the kitchen bench – just in case something edible dropped. He knew every moment and every movement of the day's routine – quite uncanny sometimes, the way he made his needs / wishes known, e.g. his water dish topped up, or radiator switched on. If I picked up car keys, that meant his lead had to be clipped on, and he'd run down to the car with lead looped in his mouth (a trick he taught himself), then into car and off to the park for our walk. The day he was killed, I let him run off without lead – hoping he would stay with me for a run round the bay at the foot of the street – fatal mistake.[41]

From mid-July to mid-September Curnow again kept up a steady schedule of public engagements. On 17 July he went to the first of four screenings of Horrocks's documentary, *Early Days Yet*, at the Auckland International Film

Festival, and was delighted by the film's warm general reception by the festival audience. A week later, on 22–23 July, he and Jeny travelled to Christchurch, where Curnow read at the Writers' Festival there, and on 31 July they travelled to Napier for the Montana Book Awards, in which *The Bells of Saint Babel's* had been shortlisted. '[F]or the hapless authors it's an unrefined form of torture, with trumpets, drums, and flashing lights', Curnow wrote in advance of the event to Tony, but on the evening itself after what seemed an interminable wait his collection was announced winner of the Poetry Award, and 'with so many friends coming up to rejoice with us, it wasn't (too) hard to see it through'.[42] In August the page proofs of the Carcanet edition of *The Bells of Saint Babel's* arrived, and on 21 August and 6 September he did two three-hour recording sessions for the Poetry Archive at Auckland Audio, produced by Paul Stent, resulting in a 56-minute CD which contained 17 poems altogether, mostly chosen from *The Loop in Lone Kauri Road*, *Continuum* and *The Bells of Saint Babel's*, but also including (a late request from Motion) 'A Passion for Travel'. Carrington was pleased with Curnow's 'magnificently powerful reading',[43] and the website commentary added:

Curnow's reading belies his ninety years, sounding positively youthful in his enjoyment of language and the intellectual paradoxes of his poems. The title of one of his collections seems particularly apt when listening to the accented bite of his words: *An Incorrigible Music*.

Curnow's death on 23 September was unexpected. A week earlier (on 16 September) he had read at the Going West Books and Writers Festival. The following Wednesday, 19 September, he resat his driving test and was hugely relieved to pass, but immediately afterwards suffered a bad bout of his cough syndrome and 'uncharacteristically complained of feeling exhausted'. Jeny described his last few days in her biographical account:

I wasn't unduly alarmed and felt that he had survived many illnesses, that is, until the Saturday morning, 22 September, when he was hyperventilating. An emergency doctor came and recorded very high blood pressure and pneumonia and ordered hospital. We spent the day being admitted but by the time he was in a ward all was ok. I left and returned next morning, staying till about 3. He seemed comfortable and staff were unworried. I decided not to visit in the evening but to be there first thing in the morning when the consultants were doing their rounds. Just after 7 pm the hospital phoned to tell me Allen had 'taken a turn for the worse' and that I should come immediately. I came straight away by taxi, but was too late. He had collapsed and failed to respond to resuscitation. It was comforting to hear from [Bill Pearson's long-time partner] Donald Stenhouse that Allen's long-diagnosed heart-murmur would have been the cause of his enlarged heart and that revival after such a collapse is unlikely. This was the cause of death, but other problems were also seen. Allen's bravery and unwillingness to give in had kept him going.[44]

Curnow had long let it be known that his preference was for the ritual of a formal Anglican funeral service (using the Authorised Version of the Bible) rather than the sometimes awkward and disorganised informalities of various secular services he had encountered, and in deference to these wishes Jeny and the family decided that whatever form a memorial tribute to his life as a poet might take it would be kept separate from the funeral service itself. The funeral service took place on 27 September at St Mary's in Holy Trinity Cathedral in Parnell, with the Right Reverend Sir Paul Reeves officiating. Tim gave the reading from the Psalms (Psalm 121, 'I will lift up mine eyes unto the hills') and Wystan read the lesson, from Revelation 21:1–7 ('And I saw a new heaven and a new earth'). David Griffiths sang J.S. Bach's 'Schlummert ein', and the hymns were W. Chalmers Smith's 'Immortal, invisible, God only wise' and Katharina von Schlegel's 'Be still, my soul'. Lilburn's music for 'Landfall in Unknown Seas' was played at the end. In his address Sir Paul Reeves spoke of the importance of family in Curnow's life, his appetite for life ('My impression is of a man who was very particular, almost precise, whether he was shopping, fishing, keeping accounts or eating or drinking'), his conversational humour 'marked by wit, understatement and, if need be, wickedness', and his contribution to New Zealand poetry. In particular, he recalled a lecture by Pei Te Hurinui Jones ('The Maori as Poet') which 'praised Allen Curnow as the only English speaker to understand and capture the word-magic of moteatea in his re-presentations in the *Penguin Book of New Zealand Verse*'.* Towards the end of his address Reeves turned to Curnow's international stature, and offered his own brief summation of his work:

> Allen's achievement as a poet is international and his reputation continued to grow up to the end. He died at the height of his powers. It seems utterly fitting that the northern hemisphere edition of his last book will be launched in London on this the day of his funeral.

> Allen was one of us yet he wrote of things on the edge of our vision and he made them clearer for us. What can we say in return? We can thank God for the gift of a special

---

* Editor's note: For further discussion of this lecture from the early 1960s and Jones's tribute to Allen Curnow for his re-creations of waiata in English, see Joan Metge, *Tuamaka: The Challenge of Difference in Aotearoa New Zealand*, Auckland University Press, Auckland, 2010, p. 4.

life and a special insight. A Samoan proverb says *Stones rot but words last forever*. Allen's work enriches our lives and will continue to do so.[45]

Other tributes poured in in the aftermath of Curnow's death. The Prime Minister and Minister for Arts, Culture and Heritage, Helen Clark, appeared on television and in a press release described Curnow as 'the elder statesman of New Zealand poetry and a giant of New Zealand literature', with 'a significant international reputation as one of the finest contemporary poets'.[46] Television New Zealand also broadcast *Early Days Yet* by way of tribute. Substantial obituaries appeared in all the major newspapers, and the *New Zealand Herald* devoted an editorial to 'A poetic legacy that will last'.[47] In the United Kingdom, obituary notices featured prominently in *The Times*[48] (reprinted in *The Australian*),[49] in *The Guardian* (by Michael Schmidt),[50] and in *The Independent* (by C.K. Stead).[51] In a rare move, Curnow's long-standing editor at the *London Review of Books*, Mary-Kay Wilmers, reprinted one of his earlier contributions to the magazine, 'Investigations at the Public Baths', as a memorial tribute.

The formal memorial tribute to Curnow's career as a poet was held on 5 April 2002 at the Kenneth Myers Centre at the University of Auckland, and provided the first part of a ceremony which had in fact been in the planning for the previous November, before he died, for the award of an honorary Doctor of Literature from the university. The event included readings of Curnow's poems, and comments and poems in tribute, by literary friends and colleagues – Robert Chapman, Jan Kemp, Bill Manhire, Elizabeth Smither, Karl Stead, Hone Tuwhare and John Pocock. Musical interludes were provided by a performance of Lilburn's *Four Preludes* (1942–44) played by the pianist M-Yeon I, and by David Griffiths's singing of Lilburn's musical settings of Glover's *Sings Harry* cycle, accompanied by the pianist Christine Griffiths. The university's Public Orator, Professor Vivienne Gray, delivered the eulogy, and Wystan accepted the award posthumously on his father's behalf, speaking briefly before introducing two of the recorded readings his father had made for the Poetry Archive, 'A Raised Voice' and 'The Bells of Saint Babel's'. 'The sound of his voice', Wystan commented to his audience, 'will restore him to your company',[52] and this concluding part of the ceremony provided its most moving moments, the voice indeed belying his 90 years and 'sounding positively youthful in his enjoyment of language and the intellectual paradoxes of the poems'.

Pocock had travelled from Baltimore to participate in the tribute, and included in his readings the earlier poem, 'Discovery', which had been so influential on his thinking as a historian, as well as a chorus from *The Axe* and one of Whim Wham's most celebrated historical pieces of the 1950s, 'Pioneer Stock'. Writing to Jeny immediately he heard of Curnow's death, his words spoke movingly and personally for those who in different ways knew Curnow other than simply through his public image:

> He was a great man, and I do mean that. His poetic imagination had an extraordinary effect on my own historical imagination, and began having it in 1942 or 1943; I'm glad I had some opportunity to let him know that. He was a good friend and a splendid correspondent; I have letters which I shall keep. And in his later years he came to be of an extraordinary stature – not just because of his reputation or because he lived so long, but because his powers, as a poet and a person, went on growing. So long as I live, I shan't forget him.[53]

Curnow himself, whatever enduring words he *hoped* he had crafted during a lifetime devoted to such an aim, remained ever-sceptical about the judgement posterity might deliver. He was fond of quoting Yeats:

> As Yeats remarked of the poets one night at the Cheshire Cheese, 'there's only one thing to be said with certainty about us, and that's that there are too many of us'.[54]

The headstone on his grave, gently sloping towards the north-east in Purewa Cemetery, Meadowbank, contains the simplest words he ever wrote, claiming the identity which in the fullest and richest senses it had been his lifetime's goal to achieve:

THOMAS ALLEN MONRO CURNOW ONZ

POET

1911–2001

Editor's note:

The notes to the text were left in an incomplete state at the time of Terry Sturm's death in 2009. Some materials which were available to him courtesy of Allen Curnow's widow Jeny, and cited 'Jeny Curnow Papers, privately held' in the following notes, have since been deposited with the Alexander Turnbull Library. While every effort has been made to ensure accuracy of citation elsewhere by reference to the author's research papers as well as external sources, all instances of uncertainty have been marked [?] for further enquiry. Any errors are regretted.

Abbreviations

AC	Allen Curnow	JGAP	J.G.A. (John) Pocock
AEM	Alan Edward Mulgan	JH	J.W.A. (Joseph) Heenan
APB	A.P. (Pat) Blair	JHES	J.H.E. (John) Schroder
AR	Alan Roddick	JKB	James K. Baxter
ARC	Arthur Rolleston Cant	JT	Jeny Tole
ARDF	A.R.D. Fairburn	JW	Jim Walton
ATAC	Alistair Te Ariki Campbell	KG	Kathleen Goldingham
ATL	Alexander Turnbull Library	KM	Karl Miller
AUP	Auckland University Press	LJ	Louis Johnson
AW	Albion Wright	MH	Michael Hulse
BH	Bruce Harding	MHH	M.H. Holcroft
BK	Bernard Kearns	M-KW	Mary-Kay Wilmers
BTS	Board of Theological Studies, New Zealand	MS	Michael Schmidt
		NM	Ngaio Marsh
CB	Charles Brasch	PS	Peter Simpson
CIP	C.I. Patterson	RAKM	R.A.K. Mason
CKS	C.K. Stead	RB	Roy Basler
DD	Dan Davin	RD	Robin Dudding
DG	Denis Glover	RG	Robert Gormack
DL	Douglas Lilburn	RH	Richard Hollyer
DM	Dennis McEldowney	RL	Robert Lowry
EC	Elizabeth Caffin	RM	Richard Mayne
ED	Eileen Duggan	RMA	R.M. Algie
EF	Eunice Frost	RNMR	R.N.M. Robertson
EM	Eric McCormick	SH	Stephen Hamilton
ER	Eric Ramsden	SM	Sidney Musgrove
GO	Gordon Ogilvie	TS	Terry Sturm
HC	Hocken Collections	TW	Arnold (Ted) Wall
HR	Harry Ricketts	UB	Ursula Bethell
IM	Ian Milner	WC	Wystan Curnow
IW	Iris Wilkinson [Robin Hyde]	WFA	W.F. (Fred) Alexander
JB	Jean Bartlett (née Alison)	WHP	W.H. (Bill) Pearson
JC	Jeny Curnow (née Tole)	WL	William Latham

CHAPTER ONE
FAMILY ANCESTRIES

1 Allen Curnow (AC) to Anthony (Tony) Curnow, 27 April 1977. Anthony Curnow Papers, privately held.

2 AC to Betty Curnow, [Oct.] 1945. Betty Curnow Papers, Alexander Turnbull Library (ATL) 86-101.

3 'Author's Note' to Allen Curnow, *Collected Poems 1933–1973*, A.H. & A.W. Reed, Wellington, 1974, p. xiii.

4 'Conversation with Allen Curnow', AC interviewed by M.P. Jackson, *Islands*, vol. 2, no. 2, Winter 1973, in *Look Back Harder: Critical Writings 1935–1984*, ed. Peter Simpson, Auckland University Press, Auckland, 1987, p. 254.

5 Gravestone, Lyttelton Cemetery.

6 Kathleen Goldingham (KG) to AC, 18 Sept. 1949. Betty Curnow Papers, ATL 86-101.

7 AC to C.K. Stead (CKS), 28 Feb. 1999. C.K. Stead Papers, privately held. Unless otherwise identified, letters from AC to CKS are held in Stead's private papers (copies of which have been deposited at the Alexander Turnbull Library, Wellington, since the writing of this book).

8 Information from Invercargill electoral rolls, 1896 to 1905, where Gambling is listed as an accountant, Rose as a music teacher and Jessie as employed in domestic duties, all living at Deveron Street.

9 Jeny Curnow, Biography of Allen Curnow, Part One. Jeny Curnow Papers, ATL MSDL-0203. This consists of a typescript in two parts totalling 85 pages, written on two separate occasions (ATL MSDL-0203, 0204). The first covers Curnow's life to the time of his arrival in the United States (February 1950) during his first trip overseas, much of it dictated by Curnow himself, or drafted directly from conversation with him, in the years 1998–99. The material in it was also read and cross-checked by Curnow himself. The second part of the typescript was written after Curnow's death, and covers the period after 1950. Written in 2003, it draws on the author's own memory of events from 1954 to 2001, and of things told to her by Curnow, as well as on travel diaries written during overseas trips from the 1960s to the 1990s. The citation 'Part One' refers to the typescript written during Curnow's lifetime; 'Part Two' refers to the additional typescript completed after his death.

10 'Conversation with Allen Curnow', in *Look Back Harder*, p. 254.

11 Jeny Curnow, Biography of Allen Curnow, Part One. Jeny Curnow Papers, ATL MSDL-0203. KG to AC, 18 Sept. 1949. Betty Curnow Papers, ATL 86-101.

12 'New Zealander in Ancestral Norfolk', *London Calling*, 13 April 1950, p. 12.

13 Ibid.

14 Ibid.

15 Jeny Curnow, Biography of Allen Curnow, Part One. Jeny Curnow Papers, ATL MSDL-0203.

16 Arnold (Ted) Wall (TW) to AC, 'Curnoviana', 1994. AC Papers, ATL 6371-16.

17 AC Papers, ATL 6371-19 and 6371-23.

18 AC Papers, ATL 7574-29 and 7574-36.

19 AC to Douglas Lilburn (DL), 12 May 1998. Douglas Lilburn Papers, ATL 7623-140.

20 *English History for Schools*, George Philip & Son, London, 1879; *Elementary Science: Arranged for the Use of Primary Schools in New Zealand*, George Robertson, Melbourne, 1879.

21 *Lyttelton Times*, 29 March 1882.

22 AC to Betty Curnow, 13 Jan. 1950. Betty Curnow Papers, ATL 86-101.

23 Ibid.

24 AC to Tony Curnow, 3 Oct. 1974. Anthony Curnow Papers, privately held. See also A.L. Rowse to AC, 21 Sept. 1966. AC Papers, ATL 2402-30.

25 *Cornish Review*, no. 6, Winter 1950, pp. 23 and 24.

26 See also Chapter 3 ('The Changeling'), p. 46 and Chapter 15 ('Sea Tryst'), pp. 271-74. *Cornish Review*, no. 6, Winter 1950, p. 23; *New Zealand Listener*, 12 January 1951, p. 15.

27 *Cornish Review*, no. 6, Winter 1950, p. 24.

28 'Allen Curnow talks to Peter Simpson', *Landfall* 175, vol. 44, no. 3, Sept. 1990, p. 307.

29 Ibid.

30 AC to CKS, 10 June 1988.

31 'Notes', *Early Days Yet: New and Collected Poems 1941–1997*, Auckland University Press, Auckland, 1997, p. 243.

32 AC to TW, 15 April 1973. AC Papers, ATL 2402-49.

33 Ibid.

34 AC Papers, ATL 6371-23.

35 AC to Dan Davin, 2 Sept. 1973. Dan Davin Papers, ATL 5079-075.

36 Notes by TW. AC Papers, ATL 4650-11.

37 *Long and Happy: An Autobiography*, A.H. & A.W. Reed, Wellington, 1965, pp. 108–9.
38 Ibid.
39 AC to Tony Curnow, 26 Dec. 1980. Anthony Curnow Papers, privately held.
40 Unpublished draft, AC Papers, ATL 4650-05.
41 AC to TW, 31 Oct. 1987. AC Papers, ATL 4650-11.
42 AC to Faith Pinkney, 8 July 1988. AC Papers, ATL 4650-11.
43 Faith Richmond, *Remembrance*, Collins, Sydney, 1988, p. 101ff.
44 See Tony Deverson, 'Wall, Arnold', *Te Ara – the Encyclopedia of New Zealand*, updated 1 April 2014, http://www.TeAra.govt.nz/en/biographies/3w2/wall-arnold.
45 Foreword, *Long and Happy*, pp. 5–6.
46 AC to Michael Schmidt, 26 Feb. 1997. AC Papers, ATL 6371-09.
47 TW to AC, 30 Jan. [?1964]. AC Papers, ATL 2402-07.
48 Tony Curnow, untitled draft autobiography, c. 1990s, p. 8. Anthony Curnow Papers, privately held.
49 Tony Curnow, untitled draft autobiography, c. 1990s, p. 8. Anthony Curnow Papers, privately held.
50 AC to Tony Curnow, 8 July 1975. Anthony Curnow Papers, privately held.

CHAPTER TWO
EARLY CHILDHOOD, 1911–21

1 Allen Curnow (AC), fragment, [?1960s], Jeny Curnow Papers, privately held.
2 *New Zealand Verse*, ed. W.F. Alexander and A.E. Currie, Walter Scott Publishing Company, London, 1906, p. 208.
3 'Conversation with Allen Curnow', AC interviewed by M.P. Jackson, *Islands*, vol. 2, no. 2, Winter 1973, in *Look Back Harder: Critical Writings 1935–1984*, ed. Peter Simpson, Auckland University Press, Auckland, 1987, p. 245.
4 Interview, *The Press*, 13 June 1987.
5 Jeny Curnow, Biography of Allen Curnow, Part One. Jeny Curnow Papers, Alexander Turnbull Library (ATL) MSDL-0203.
6 Tony Curnow to Allen Curnow (AC), 17 Oct. 1949. AC Papers, ATL 2402-02.
7 Obituary, Dunedin *Evening Star*, 2 Nov. 1949. Tony Curnow, 'Worlds Apart', revised draft autobiography, 2007, p. 27. Anthony Curnow Papers, privately held.
8 Alan Mulgan, 'A Notable Volume of Topical Verse – "X.Y.'s" Identity Revealed', unidentified and undated newspaper clipping, Terry Sturm Papers, privately held.
9 'Cheerful Verse', *Southland Times*, undated photocopy of newspaper clipping, Terry Sturm Papers, privately held.
10 *Canta*, 12 July 1933.
11 'Conversation with Allen Curnow', in *Look Back Harder*, p. 246.

12 Jeny Curnow, Biography of Allen Curnow, Part One. Jeny Curnow Papers, ATL MSDL-0203.
13 Tony Curnow, 'Worlds Apart', revised draft autobiography, 2007, p. 32. Anthony Curnow Papers, privately held.
14 Jeny Curnow, Biography of Allen Curnow, Part One. Jeny Curnow Papers, ATL MSDL-0203.
15 Ibid.
16 Jessie Curnow to AC, March 1968. AC Papers, ATL 2402-30.
17 AC, fragment, [?1960s], Jeny Curnow Papers, privately held.
18 Jessie Curnow, 'Reminiscences on 90th birthday', unidentified and undated photocopy of newspaper clipping, Terry Sturm Papers, privately held.
19 AC, 'A Colonial At Home' typescript. Betty Curnow Papers, ATL 86-101. Broadcast on 3YA, 10 May 1937.
20 AC to Donald Davie, 30 April 1986. AC Papers, ATL 90-226-1/1.
21 Preface to *Collected Poems 1933–1973*, A.H. & A.W. Reed, Wellington, 1974.
22 Tony Curnow, 'Worlds Apart', revised draft autobiography, 2007, p. 54. Anthony Curnow Papers, privately held.
23 Ibid., p. 56.
24 Ibid.
25 Lecture, c. 1947. Betty Curnow Papers, ATL 86-101.
26 Betty Curnow Papers, ATL 86-101.
27 Fragment, [?1960s], Jeny Curnow Papers, privately held.
28 See Roy Sinclair, 'Haunting Ballad of Otira Gorge', *The Press*, 23 Dec. 1983.
29 Tim Curnow Papers, ATL 7905.
30 AC to Ted Wall (TW), 21 Sept. 1987. AC Papers, ATL 4650-11.
31 Ibid.
32 TW to AC, 29 Sept. 1987. AC Papers, ATL 4650-11.
33 AC to W.H. (Bill) Pearson (WHP), 26 March 1994. AC Papers, ATL 5428-05.
34 AC to J.G.A. (John) Pocock (JGAP), 11 July 1994. AC Papers, ATL 7574-55.
35 Ibid.
36 AC to Douglas Lilburn (DL), 20 May 1994. AC Papers, ATL 7623-139.
37 AC to DL, 5 July 1994. AC Papers, ATL 7623-139.

CHAPTER THREE
THE LYTTELTON YEARS AND ADOLESCENCE, 1921–30

1 Tony Curnow, 'Worlds Apart', revised draft autobiography, 2007, p. 12. Anthony Curnow Papers, privately held.
2 Jeny Curnow, Biography of Allen Curnow, Part One. Jeny Curnow Papers, Alexander Turnbull Library (ATL) MSDL-0203.

3   Tony Curnow, 'Worlds Apart', revised draft autobiography, 2007, p. 3. Anthony Curnow Papers, privately held.

4   Allen Curnow (AC) to Douglas Lilburn (DL), 1 April 1992. AC Papers, ATL 7623-138.

5   Ibid.

6   AC to Faith Pinkney, [?April] 1991. AC Papers, ATL 4650-11.

7   Jeny Curnow, Biography of Allen Curnow, Part One. Jeny Curnow Papers, ATL MSDL-0203.

8   Karl Miller to AC, 10 May 1991. AC Papers, ATL 4650-10.

9   AC to C.K. Stead (CKS), 30 April 1991. C.K. Stead Papers, privately held. Unless otherwise identified, letters from AC to CKS are held in Stead's private papers (copies of which have been deposited at the Alexander Turnbull Library, Wellington, since the writing of this book).

10   AC to CKS, 18 June 1988.

11   AC to CKS, 2 March 1988.

12   AC to CKS, 5 March 1988.

13   AC to Tony Curnow, 11 Sept. 1990. Anthony Curnow Papers, privately held.

14   'Land of our Birth', fragment for radio talk, 1930s/40s. Betty Curnow Papers, ATL 86-101.

15   Ibid.

16   Ibid.

17   'Notes for an Unwritten Poem', in *The Years Between: Christchurch Boys' High School, 1881–1981*, Christchurch High School Old Boys' Association, Christchurch, 1981, pp. 223–4.

18   Lecture, c. 1947. Betty Curnow Papers, ATL 86-101.

19   'Land of our Birth', fragment for radio talk, 1930s/40s. Betty Curnow Papers, ATL 86-101.

20   'Conversation with Allen Curnow', AC interviewed by M.P. Jackson, *Islands*, vol. 2, no. 2, Winter 1973, in *Look Back Harder: Critical Writings 1935–1984*, ed. Peter Simpson, Auckland University Press, Auckland, 1987, p. 246.

21   Jeny Curnow, Biography of Allen Curnow, Part One. Jeny Curnow Papers, ATL MSDL-0203.

22   J.H.E. (John) Schroder to AC, 14 May 1976. AC Papers, ATL 6371-11.

23   'Notes for an Unwritten Poem', in *The Years Between*, pp. 224–5.

24   Ibid., p. 223.

25   AC, interview with Tony Reid, *New Zealand Listener*, 12 March 1983.

26   'Conversation with Allen Curnow', in *Look Back Harder*, p. 246.

27   AC, interview with Tony Reid, *New Zealand Listener*, 12 March 1983.

28   Jeny Curnow, Biography of Allen Curnow, Part One. Jeny Curnow Papers, ATL MSDL-0203.

29   Rachel McAlpine to AC, 10 Feb. 1977. AC Papers, ATL 6371-11.

30   Jeny Curnow, Biography of Allen Curnow, Part One. Jeny Curnow Papers, ATL MSDL-0203.

31   'Conversation with Allen Curnow', in *Look Back Harder*, p. 247.

32   AC to Terry Sturm, 27 July 1974. Terry Sturm Papers, privately held.

33   'Conversation with Allen Curnow', in *Look Back Harder*, p. 247.

CHAPTER FOUR
STUDENT LIFE IN AUCKLAND, 1931–33

1   'Conversation with Allen Curnow', Allen Curnow interviewed by M.P. Jackson, *Islands*, vol. 2, no. 2, Winter 1973, in *Look Back Harder: Critical Writings 1935–1984*, ed. Peter Simpson, Auckland University Press, Auckland, 1987, p. 250.

2   Jeny Curnow, Biography of Allen Curnow, Part One. Jeny Curnow Papers, Alexander Turnbull Library (ATL) MSDL-0203.

3   Elsie Locke, *Student at the Gates*, Whitcoulls, Christchurch, 1981, p. 128.

4   Rachel Barrowman, *A Popular Vision: The Arts and the Left in New Zealand, 1930–1950*, Victoria University Press, Wellington, 1991, p. 172; Locke, *Student at the Gates*, pp. 122–9.

5   Denys Trussell, *Fairburn*, Auckland University Press and Oxford University Press, Auckland, 1984, p. 172.

6   Locke, *Student at the Gates*, p. 145.

7   Allen Curnow (AC) to Elizabeth (Betty) Le Cren, 26 April 1936. Betty Curnow Papers, ATL 86-101.

8   Hector Monro, *Fortunate Catastrophes: An Anecdotal Autobiography*, Quokka Press, Melbourne, 1991, p. 107. Quoting James Bertram, 'Blackwood Paul, James Bertram: A Note on a War Generation', *Landfall* 74, vol. 19, no. 2, June 1965, p. 139.

9   Jeny Curnow, Biography of Allen Curnow, Part One. Jeny Curnow Papers, ATL MSDL-0203.

10   Allan K. Davidson, *Selwyn's Legacy: The College of St John the Evangelist Te Waimate and Auckland 1843–1992, A History*, The College of Saint John the Evangelist, Auckland, 1993, p. 175.

11   A.P. (Pat) Blair (APB) to Terry Sturm (TS), 16 March 2005. Terry Sturm Papers, privately held.

12   'Conversation with Allen Curnow', in *Look Back Harder*, p. 247.

13   'And Talking of Poetry', *St. John's*, 1932, pp. 17–18.

14   'The Eyes Unseeeing', 'Ye Kronikle' of the College of St. John, 1931, p. 20.

15   Robert Lowry (RL) to Denis Glover (DG), 29 Sept. 1931. Denis Glover Papers, ATL 0418-004.

16   'Conversation with Allen Curnow', in *Look Back Harder*, pp. 247–8.

17   RL to DG, 15 July 1931. Denis Glover Papers, ATL 0418-004. Stephen Derek Hamilton, 'New Zealand English Language Periodicals of Literary Interest Active 1920s–1960s', PhD thesis, University of Auckland, 1996, p. 39.

18   AC to Stephen Hamilton (SH), 23 Oct. 1992. AC Papers, ATL 7574-84.

19   Ibid.

20   RL to DG, 24 July 1932. Denis Glover Papers, ATL 0418-005.

21 AC to SH, 23 Oct. 1992. AC Papers, ATL 7574-84.
22 Jean Bartlett (née Alison) (JB) interview with TS, 25 Aug. 2005. Terry Sturm Papers, privately held.
23 Monro, *Fortunate Catastrophes*, p. 72.
24 Locke, *Student at the Gates*, p. 159.
25 JB interview with TS, 25 Aug. 2005. Terry Sturm Papers, privately held.
26 Jeny Curnow, Biography of Allen Curnow, Part One. Jeny Curnow Papers, ATL MSDL-0203. See also Locke, *Student at the Gates*, p. 113.
27 Jeny Curnow, Biography of Allen Curnow, Part One. Jeny Curnow Papers, ATL MSDL-0203.
28 Ibid.
29 JB interview with TS, 25 Aug. 2005. Terry Sturm Papers, privately held.
30 James and Helen McNeish, *Walking on my Feet: A.R.D. Fairburn 1904–57: A Kind of Biography*, Collins, Auckland, 1983, p. 42.
31 Locke, *Student at the Gates*, p. 146.
32 JB interview with TS, 25 Aug. 2005. Terry Sturm Papers, privately held.
33 RL to DG, 10 Feb. 1933. Denis Glover Papers, ATL 0418-005.
34 Jeny Curnow, Biography of Allen Curnow, Part One. Jeny Curnow Papers, ATL MSDL-0203.
35 AC to DG, [Sept. 1979]. AC Papers, ATL 2402-16.
36 APB to TS, 30 March 2005. Terry Sturm Papers, privately held.
37 W.J. Simkin, *The College of St. John the Evangelist, Auckland, New Zealand*, Coulls Somerville Wilkie, Wellington, 1938, p. 67.
38 Minutes of St John's College Trust Board, 14 Dec. 1932, John Kinder Theological Library.
39 Minutes of St John's College Trust Board, 12 April 1933, John Kinder Theological Library.
40 Locke, *Student at the Gates*, p. 159.
41 Board of Theological Studies (BTS), ANG 057/7/2, John Kinder Theological Library.
42 *Phoenix*, vol. 2, no. 1 (April 1933).
43 *New Zealand Truth*, 31 May 1933.
44 AC to SH, 23 Oct. 1992. AC Papers, ATL 7574-84.
45 *Art in New Zealand*, June 1933.
46 AC to TS, 27 July 1974. Terry Sturm Papers, privately held.
47 Jeny Curnow, Biography of Allen Curnow, Part One. Jeny Curnow Papers, ATL MSDL-0203.
48 E.H. Strong to St John's College Trust Board, 11 Aug. 1933, SJT 001/3/13, John Kinder Theological Library.
49 E.H. Strong to St John's College Trust Board, 20 Aug. 1933, SJT 001/3/13, John Kinder Theological Library.
50 Information supplied by DG, subsequently confirmed by AC.
51 AC to DG, [Aug.] 1933. Denis Glover Papers, ATL 0418-072.
52 AC to TS, 27 July 1974. Terry Sturm Papers, privately held.
53 Ibid.

54 *Phoenix*, vol. 2, no. 2, June 1933.
55 Ronald Holloway, 'Remembering Bob Lowry', *Landfall* 69, vol. 18, no. 1, March 1964, p. 56; Vanya Lowry, *From the Wistaria Bush: A Memoir*, Auckland University Press, 2001, pp. 65–86.
56 Joel 3:14.
57 *The Press*, 20 Jan. 1940.
58 Job 40:15–24.
59 *Art in New Zealand*, March 1934, p. 150.
60 Tremayne Monro Curnow to W.F. Alexander, [?1939]. W.F. Alexander Papers, ATL 0423-02.
61 BTS, ANG 057/7/2, John Kinder Theological Library.
62 Davidson, *Selwyn's Legacy*, p. 186.

CHAPTER FIVE
WIDENING HORIZONS, 1934 TO MID-1936

1 Allen Curnow (AC) to Denis Glover (DG), 20 Nov. 1972. Denis Glover Papers, Alexander Turnbull Library (ATL) 0418-011.
2 Jeny Curnow, Biography of Allen Curnow, Part One. Jeny Curnow Papers, ATL MSDL-0203.
3 AC to Terry Sturm (TS), 27 July 1974. Terry Sturm Papers, privately held.
4 AC to Jane Perry, 13 Aug. 2001. Jane Perry Papers, privately held.
5 Ibid.
6 'Conversation with Allen Curnow', AC interviewed by M.P. Jackson, *Islands*, vol. 2, no. 2, Winter 1973, in *Look Back Harder: Critical Writings 1935–1984*, ed. Peter Simpson, Auckland University Press, Auckland, 1987, p. 250.
7 Iris Wilkinson (IW) to AC, [June/July 1934]. AC Papers, ATL 2402-6A.
8 AC to Tony Curnow, 10 July 1993. Anthony Curnow Papers, privately held.
9 Jeny Curnow, Biography of Allen Curnow, Part One. Jeny Curnow Papers, ATL MSDL-0203.
10 'Without', *The Red Tram*, Auckland University Press, Auckland, 2004, pp. 52–53.
11 'Conversation with Allen Curnow', in *Look Back Harder*, p. 250.
12 AC to TS, 27 July 1974. Terry Sturm Papers, privately held.
13 Jeny Curnow, Biography of Allen Curnow, Part One. Jeny Curnow Papers, ATL MSDL-0203.
14 Ibid.
15 See Gordon Ogilvie, *Denis Glover: His Life*, Godwit, Auckland, 1999, pp. 59–60.
16 AC to TS, 27 July 1974. Terry Sturm Papers, privately held.
17 A.R.D. Fairburn (ARDF) to Denis Glover (DG), 10 Oct. 1934. Denis Glover Papers, ATL 0418-015.
18 '"Obscenity" in Literature', *Tomorrow*, 6 March 1935.
19 *Tomorrow*, 17 Oct. 1934.
20 Iris Wilkinson (IW) to AC, 4 Jan. 1935. AC Papers, ATL 2402-6A.
21 Ibid.

22 AC to TS, 27 July 1974. Terry Sturm Papers, privately held.

23 W.P.D. Wightman, *Science and Monism*, George Allen & Unwin, London, 1934.

24 *The Press*, 2 Feb. 1935.

25 *Canta*, 13 March 1935.

26 *Art in New Zealand*, Sept. 1935.

27 *The Press*, 6 July 1935.

28 *Tomorrow*, 9 Oct. 1935.

29 AC to DG, 31 Oct. 1973. Denis Glover Papers, ATL 0418-012.

30 AC to Gordon Ogilvie, 17 July 1995. Ogilvie, *Denis Glover*, p. 80.

31 ARDF to DG, 8 June 1935. Denis Glover Papers, ATL 0418-015. Ogilvie, *Denis Glover*, pp. 78, 481 n. 4.

32 ARDF to DG, 6 April 1935. Denis Glover Papers, ATL 0418-015.

33 Douglas Lilburn to AC, 11 Jan. 1982. AC Papers, ATL 2402-44.

34 *The Press*, 20 April 1935.

35 *The Press*, 25 May 1935.

36 *The Press*, 5 Oct. 1935.

37 *The Press*, 30 Nov. 1935.

38 *Poetry and Language*, The Caxton Club Press, Christchurch, 1935, p. 9.

39 Ibid., p. 14.

40 *The Press*, 29 Feb. 1936.

41 *Tomorrow*, 15 Jan. 1936, p. 21.

42 ARDF to DG, 6 April 1935. Denis Glover Papers, ATL 0418-015.

43 ARDF to DG, [Feb./March 1936]. Denis Glover Papers, ATL 0418-015.

CHAPTER SIX
MARRIAGE, JOURNALISM AND
ENEMIES, 1936–37

1 Allen Curnow (AC), interview with Tony Reid, *New Zealand Listener*, 12 March 1983.

2 Information about Le Cren family history is taken from 'The Le Cren Family, 1738–1988', written and compiled by Denis Jaumaud Le Cren, a nephew of Betty Curnow. Betty did most of the research for this family history, copies of which were distributed among family members. Belinda Curnow Papers, privately held.

3 Betty Curnow, notes for Terry Sturm, 1974. Terry Sturm Papers, privately held.

4 Tim Curnow, interview with Terry Sturm, 10 Sept. 2004. Terry Sturm Papers, privately held.

5 Wystan Curnow, 'Eulogy for my Mother', funeral service for Betty Curnow, 30 Sept. 2005. Wystan Curnow Papers, privately held.

6 Unidentified newspaper report, [1958]. Belinda Curnow Papers, privately held.

7 Tim Curnow, 'Eulogy for Mum', funeral service for Betty Curnow, 30 Sept. 2005. Tim Curnow Papers, privately held.

8 AC to Elizabeth (Betty) Le Cren, [April] 1936. Betty Curnow Papers, Alexander Turnbull Library (ATL) 86-101.

9 TS, interview with Diana Goldsbrough, 13 Dec. 2005. Terry Sturm Papers, privately held.

10 Ibid.

11 AC to Betty Le Cren, [June] 1936. Betty Curnow Papers, Alexander Turnbull Library (ATL) 86-101.

12 AC to A.R.D. Fairburn (ARDF), 1 June 1936. A.R.D. Fairburn Literary Estate Papers, privately held. Copies of some letters are also held in the University of Auckland and Alexander Turnbull libraries.

13 ARDF to Denis Glover (DG), 11 Sept. 1935. Denis Glover Papers, ATL 0418-015.

14 AC to ARDF, 1 June 1936. A.R.D. Fairburn Literary Estate Papers, privately held.

15 ARDF to AC, 7 July 1936. ARDF Papers, ATL 0214-04.

16 In AC to Betty Le Cren, [July] 1936. Betty Curnow Papers, Alexander Turnbull Library (ATL) 86-101.

17 AC to Betty Le Cren, [Aug.] 1936. Betty Curnow Papers, ATL 86-101.

18 AC to Betty Le Cren, [July] 1936. Betty Curnow Papers, ATL 86-101.

19 *The Press*, 11 April 1936.

20 *The Press*, 18, 24 April and 2 May.

21 AC to Betty Le Cren, [May] 1936. Betty Curnow Papers, ATL 86-101.

22 AC to Betty Le Cren, [June] 1936. Betty Curnow Papers, ATL 86-101.

23 AC to Betty Le Cren, [?June 1936]. Betty Curnow Papers, ATL 86-101.

24 AC to Betty Le Cren, [July] 1936. Betty Curnow Papers, ATL 86-101.

25 *The Press*, 17 July 1936.

26 AC to Betty Le Cren, [July/Aug.] 1936. Betty Curnow Papers, ATL 86-101.

27 *Tomorrow*, 22 July 1936.

28 'Author's Note', *Enemies: Poems 1934–36*, The Caxton Press, Christchurch, 1937.

29 AC to Betty Le Cren, [June] 1936. Betty Curnow Papers, ATL 86-101.

30 AC to Betty Le Cren, [July] 1936. Betty Curnow Papers, ATL 86-101.

31 There is a photograph, including AC, in W.S. Broughton, *A.R.D. Fairburn*, Reed, Wellington, 1968, p. 17.

32 Information in this paragraph all from Betty Curnow's diaries, privately held.

33 AC to W.F. (Fred) Alexander (WFA), 4 March 1937. W.F. Alexander Papers, ATL 0423-02.

34 *Tomorrow*, 20 Jan. 1937.

35 *The Press*, 6 March 1937.

36 AC to ARDF, [June] 1937. A.R.D. Fairburn Literary Estate Papers, privately held.

37 A.R.D. Fairburn, review of *Enemies*, *Tomorrow*, 28 April 1937, pp. 414–16.

38 AC to ARDF, 26 June 1937. A.R.D. Fairburn Literary Estate Papers, privately held.

39 Ibid.

40 A.R.D. Fairburn, review of *Enemies*, *Tomorrow*, 28 April 1937, pp. 415.

41 AC to ARDF, 26 June 1937. A.R.D. Fairburn
Literary Estate Papers, privately held.
42 *Southland Times*, 22 Jan. 1938.
43 Tremayne Curnow to WFA, [1937]. W.F.
Alexander Papers, ATL 0423-02.
44 AC to WFA, 4 March 1937. W.F. Alexander
Papers, ATL 0423-02.

CHAPTER SEVEN
A TURNING POINT IN HISTORY: *NOT IN
NARROW SEAS*, 1937–38

1 Allen Curnow (AC) to Andrew, 21 July 1987. AC
Papers, Alexander Turnbull Library (ATL) 7574-98.
2 *Tomorrow*, 9 June 1937.
3 AC to A.R.D. Fairburn (ARDF), [June] 1937.
A.R.D. Fairburn Literary Estate Papers, privately
held. Copies of some letters are also held in the
University of Auckland and Alexander Turnbull
libraries.
4 ARDF to AC, frag. [June 1937], ARDF Papers,
ATL 0214-04.
5 *Tomorrow*, 4 Aug. 1937.
6 Betty Curnow: Diary, 12 Dec. 1937. Betty Curnow
Papers, ATL 86-101.
7 *Tomorrow*, 18 Aug. 1937.
8 *Tomorrow*, 13 Oct. 1937.
9 *The Press*, 4 Dec. 1937.
10 *The Press*, 11 Dec. 1937.
11 *The Press*, 31 Dec. 1937.
12 Allen Curnow, 'House and Land', *Island and
Time*, The Caxton Press, Christchurch, 1941.
13 Betty Curnow: Diary, 22 March 1938. Betty
Curnow Papers, ATL 86-101.
14 AC to ARDF, 16 Nov. 1938. A.R.D. Fairburn
Literary Estate Papers, privately held.
15 *The Press*, 3 Oct. 1938.
16 Gordon Ogilvie, *Denis Glover: His Life*, Godwit,
Auckland, 1999, p. 98.
17 AC to ARDF, 16 Nov. 1938. A.R.D. Fairburn
Literary Estate Papers, privately held.
18 'Conversation with Allen Curnow', AC
interviewed by M.P. Jackson, *Islands*, vol. 2, no. 2,
Winter 1973, p. 148.
19 *The Press*, 6 March 1937.
20 'Rata Blossom or Reality? New Zealand and a
Significant Contribution', *Tomorrow*, 11 May 1938.
21 Ibid., p. 438.
22 AC to W.F. Alexander (WFA), 28 April [1938].
W.F. Alexander Papers, ATL 0423-02.
23 Ibid.
24 Information provided by Glover, interview with
TS, 1974. Terry Sturm Papers, privately held.
25 *Tomorrow*, 13 Oct. 1937.
26 *Tomorrow*, 8 Dec. 1937.
27 *Tomorrow*, 11 May 1938.
28 *Tomorrow*, 17 Aug. 1938.
29 *Tomorrow*, 28 Sept. 1938.
30 *Tomorrow*, 31 Aug. 1938.
31 *Tomorrow*, 17 Aug. 1938.
32 *A Book of New Zealand Verse 1923–45*, The Caxton
Press, Christchurch, 1945, p. 22.

33 AC to ARDF, 16 Nov. 1938. A.R.D. Fairburn
Literary Estate Papers, privately held.
34 AC to Andrew, 21 July 1987. AC Papers, ATL
574-98.
35 Ezra Pound, 'A Few Don'ts by an Imagiste',
Poetry, vol. 1, no. 6, March 1913.
36 AC to ARDF, 16 Nov. 1938. A.R.D. Fairburn
Literary Estate Papers, privately held.

CHAPTER EIGHT
A CHANGING CHRISTCHURCH,
DEARTH OF POEMS, AND WHIM WHAM,
1939–40

1 Allen Curnow (AC) to Douglas Lilburn
(DL), 15 Aug. [1940]. Douglas Lilburn Papers,
Alexander Turnbull Library (ATL) 7623-127.
2 Betty Curnow: Diary, April 1940. Betty Curnow
Papers, privately held.
3 Betty Curnow: Diary, 22 May. Betty Curnow
Papers, privately held.
4 Tremayne Curnow to W.F. Alexander (WFA),
[May] 1939. W.F. Alexander Papers, ATL 0423-
02. 'R.A.K. Beaglehole' is a joke blending R.A.K.
Mason and J.C. Beaglehole.
5 *The Press*, 6 May 1939.
6 *Tomorrow*, 21 June 1939.
7 *Tomorrow*, 19 July 1939.
8 Eric Gill to AC, 18 Sept. 1939. Betty Curnow
Papers, privately held.
9 AC to Douglas Lilburn (DL), 15 Aug. 1940.
Douglas Lilburn Papers, ATL 7623-127.
10 AC to Terry Sturm, 7 Oct. 1974. Terry Sturm
Papers, privately held.
11 These drafts can be found in Tim Curnow
Papers, ATL 7905.
12 *The Press*, 20 Jan. 1940 – '(By T.A.M.C.)'.
13 AC to DL, 15 Aug. [1940]. Douglas Lilburn
Papers, ATL 7623-127.
14 AC to Joseph Heenan, 1 Oct. 1943. (Sir) Joseph
William Allan Heenan Papers, ATL 1132-042.

CHAPTER NINE
'THE SHOCK OF ANOTHER WAR':
ISLAND AND TIME, 1940–41

1 'In Preparation, *Island and Time* by Allen
Curnow', Allen Curnow et al. [A.R.D. Fairburn,
Denis Glover and R.A.K. Mason], *Recent Poems*,
The Caxton Press, Christchurch, 1941, p. 51.
Author's italics.
2 Betty Curnow: Diary, 1 Sept. 1939. Betty Curnow
Papers, privately held.
3 Norman Macbeth to Edmund Binney Lock,
25 May 1987, read at a function in honour of Allen
Curnow at *The Press*, June 1987. Allen Curnow (AC)
Papers, ATL 7574-81. Macbeth was editor of *The
Press* from 1973 to 1978 and Lock from 1978 to 1990.
4 Tim Curnow Papers, ATL 7905.
5 Originally titled 'No Laughing Matter', *The Press*,
18 March 1939.
6 *The Press*, 20 Jan. 1940.

7 'The Last of Yeats', *The Press*, 15 June 1940.
Author's italics.

8 'Prophets of Their Time: Some Modern Poets',
The Press, 20 Jan. 1940.

9 AC to Douglas Lilburn (DL), 15 Aug. [1940].
Douglas Lilburn Papers, ATL 7623-127.

10 Allen Curnow, *Island and Time*, The Caxton
Press, Christchurch, 1941.

11 'A Job for Poetry: Notes on an Impulse', *Book* 1,
March 1941, in *Look Back Harder: Critical
Writings 1935–1984*, ed. Peter Simpson, Auckland
University Press, Auckland, 1987, p. 24.

12 AC to DL, 2 Sept. 1940. Douglas Lilburn Papers,
ATL 7623-127.

13 'A Job for Poetry: Notes on an Impulse', in *Look
Back Harder*, p. 25.

14 AC to DL, 15 Aug. [1940]. Douglas Lilburn
Papers, ATL 7623-127.

15 'A Job for Poetry: Notes on an Impulse', in *Look
Back Harder*, p. 24.

16 A.R. Lacey on Bergson in *Oxford Companion to
Philosophy*, ed. Ted Honderich, Oxford University
Press, Oxford, 1995, p. 88.

17 Ibid.

18 'In Preparation, *Island and Time* by Allen
Curnow', Allen Curnow et al. [A.R.D. Fairburn,
Denis Glover and R.A.K. Mason], *Recent Poems*,
The Caxton Press, Christchurch, 1941, p. 51.
Author's italics.

19 AC to DL, 2 Sept. 1940. Douglas Lilburn Papers,
ATL 7623-127.

20 'J.G.M.', *New Zealand Listener*, 13 June 1941.

21 D'Arcy Cresswell, *Present without Leave*, Cassell,
London, 1939, p. 6.

22 'Discovery', *Sailing or Drowning*, The Progressive
Publishing Society, Wellington, [1943], p. 7.

23 'A Job for Poetry: Notes on an Impulse', in *Look
Back Harder*, p. 25.

24 AC to DL, 2 Sept. 1940. Douglas Lilburn Papers,
ATL 7623-127.

25 AC to DL, 10 Dec. 1940. Douglas Lilburn Papers,
ATL 7623-127.

26 AC to DL, 31 Dec. 1940. Douglas Lilburn Papers,
ATL 7623-127.

27 *Journal of the Aviation Historical Society of
New Zealand*, Dec. 2003, pp. 46–47.

28 AC to Denis Glover (DG), 30 Oct. 1943. Denis
Glover Papers, ATL 0418-008.

29 See Gordon Ogilvie, *Denis Glover: His Life*,
Godwit, Auckland, 1999, pp. 123, 484 n. 62.

30 See Ogilvie, *Denis Glover*, pp. 123, 484 n. 63.

31 Gordon Ogilvie interview with Denis Glover,
17 July 1995. Ogilvie, *Denis Glover*, p. 121.

32 See Friedrich Voit, 'Karl Wolfskehl', *Out of the
Shadow of War*, ed. James N. Bade and James
Braund, Oxford University Press, Auckland,
1998, p. 109; and AC to Betty Curnow, [Feb.
1941]: 'I revised again the small poem I discussed
with Dr Wolfskehl'. Betty Curnow Papers,
privately held.

33 AC to Terry Sturm, 7 Oct. 1974. Terry Sturm
Papers, privately held.

CHAPTER TEN
PACIFIC OUTREACH, THE MID-WAR
YEARS, 1941–42

1 Allen Curnow, 'Introduction to *A Book of
New Zealand Verse 1923–45*', in *Look Back Harder:
Critical Writings 1935–1984*, ed. Peter Simpson,
Auckland University Press, Auckland, 1987, p. 67.

2 *The Press*, 4 June 1941.

3 *Evening Star*, 3 May 1941.

4 Allen Curnow, 'The Unhistoric Story', *Folios of
New Writing*, Aug. 1941, pp. 62–63.

5 Betty Curnow: Diary, 8 July 1941. Betty Curnow
Papers, privately held.

6 J.G.A. Pocock, 'Landscape as Ithaca: Island and
History in Curnow's Earlier Poems', handwritten
MS, p. 1. J.G.A. Pocock Papers, privately held.
This is an early draft of 'Instant History: Allen
Curnow in Christchurch', *London Magazine*,
Dec./Jan. 1991–92, pp. 44–52.

7 J.G.A. Pocock, 'Instant History: Allen Curnow
in Christchurch', *London Magazine*, Dec./Jan.
1991–92, pp. 44–45.

8 J.G.A. Pocock, 'Historian and Poet in
New Zealand', *The Arts in New Zealand*, vol. 17,
no. 6, Jan./Feb. 1946, p. 38. Author's italics.

9 'Landscape as Ithaca', p. 4.

10 'Instant History', p. 49.

11 'Landscape as Ithaca', pp. 6–7.

12 Ibid., p. 5.

13 J.G.A. Pocock, *The Discovery of Islands: Essays
in British History*, Cambridge University Press,
Cambridge, 2005, p. 11.

14 *The Press*, 20 Jan. 1940; 15 June 1940.

15 *The Press*, 27 April 1940.

16 *The Press*, 27 July 1940.

17 J.H.E. Schroder to Eileen Duggan (ED),
[Dec.] 1940. Eileen Duggan Papers, Catholic
Archdiocesan Archives, Wellington.

18 ED to W.F. Alexander, [1940]. W.F. Alexander
Papers, ATL 0423-06.

19 Allen Curnow, 'The Poetry of R.A.K. Mason',
Book 2, May 1941, in *Look Back Harder*, p. 26.

20 Ibid.

21 Ibid. Author's italics.

22 Allen Curnow (AC) to Denis Glover (DG),
2 Dec. 1943. Denis Glover Papers, ATL 0418-008.

23 Philip Norman, *Douglas Lilburn: His Life
and Music*, Canterbury University Press,
Christchurch, 2006, pp. 98–99.

24 AC to Douglas Lilburn (DL), 17 July 1941.
Douglas Lilburn Papers, ATL 7623-127.

25 Draft letter, Rita Angus to Betty Curnow,
27 Jan. 1969. Betty Curnow Papers, privately held.

26 Jeny Curnow, Biography of Allen Curnow, Part
One. Jeny Curnow Papers, ATL MSDL 0203.

27 AC to DG, 10 Dec. 1942. Betty Curnow Papers,
privately held.

28 AC to DG, 28 May 1942. Denis Glover Papers,
ATL 80-387-002.

29 Ibid.

30 See Janet Paul, 'Ernst Plischke', *Out of the
Shadow of War: The German Connection with*

New Zealand in the Twentieth Century, ed. James
N. Bade and James Braund, Oxford University
Press, Melbourne, 1998, pp. 192–8; Linda Tyler,
'Plischke, Ernst Anton', *Te Ara – the Encyclopedia
of New Zealand*, updated 30 Oct. 2012, http://
www.TeAra.govt.nz/en/biographies/5p31/
plischke-ernst-anton. A photograph of the
interior of Khan's house features in *Yearbook of the
Arts in New Zealand*, no. 4, 1948, p. 13.

31 The editor is grateful to Emeritus Professor of
English at the University of Auckland Macdonald
P. Jackson for assistance in clarifying this passage
of text from the author's draft manuscript.

32 'Introduction to *A Book of New Zealand Verse
1923–45*', in *Look Back Harder*, p. 67. Author's italics.

33 *The Axe: A Verse Tragedy*, The Caxton Press,
Christchurch, 1949, act III, scene 1.

34 'Moro Assassinato', *An Incorrigible Music*,
Auckland University Press/Oxford University
Press, Auckland, 1979, pp. 34–50.

35 AC to DG, 6 March 1942. Denis Glover Papers,
ATL 80-387-002.

CHAPTER ELEVEN
'LANDFALL IN UNKNOWN SEAS':
1942–43

1 Allen Curnow (AC) to Douglas Lilburn (DL),
1 May 1953 [error for 1954]. Douglas Lilburn
Papers, Alexander Turnbull Library (ATL)
7623-128.

2 See Philip Norman, *Douglas Lilburn: His
Life and Music*, Canterbury University Press,
Christchurch, 2006, pp. 64–65.

3 Betty Curnow: Diary, 30 May 1942. Betty
Curnow Papers, privately held.

4 Allen Curnow (AC) to Denis Glover (DG),
30 June 1942. Betty Curnow Papers, privately
held.

5 AC to M.H. Holcroft (MHH), 31 July 1942.
M.H. Holcroft Papers, ATL 1186-05.

6 Ibid.

7 AC to DG, 8 Aug. 1942. Betty Curnow Papers,
privately held.

8 DG to AC, 30–31 May 1942. AC Papers,
ATL 2402-04.

9 DG to AC, 3 Sept. 1942. AC Papers,
ATL 2402-04.

10 AC to DG, 10 Dec. 1942. Betty Curnow Papers,
privately held.

11 AC to DG, 15 Nov. 1942. Denis Glover Papers,
ATL 80-387-026.

12 AC to DG, 28 July 1942. Betty Curnow Papers,
privately held.

13 'Conversation with Allen Curnow', AC
interviewed by M.P. Jackson, *Islands*, vol. 2,
no. 2, Winter 1973, in *Look Back Harder: Critical
Writings 1935–1984*, ed. Peter Simpson, Auckland
University Press, Auckland, 1987, pp. 250–51.

14 Betty Curnow: Diary, 2 April 1942. Betty Curnow
Papers, privately held.

15 Rachel Barrowman, 'Heenan, Joseph William

Allan', *Te Ara – the Encyclopedia of New Zealand*,
updated 30 Oct. 2012, http://www.TeAra.govt.
nz/en/biographies/4h24/heenan-joseph-william-
allan.

16 AC to DG, 28 July 1942. Betty Curnow Papers,
privately held.

17 Jeny Curnow, Biography of Allen Curnow, Part
One. Jeny Curnow Papers, ATL MSDL-0203.

18 Ibid.

19 'Conversation with Allen Curnow', in *Look Back
Harder*, p. 251.

20 AC to MHH, 23 July 1942. M.H. Holcroft
Papers, ATL 1186-05.

21 J.G.A. Pocock, 'Landscape as Ithaca: Island
and History in Curnow's Earlier Poems',
hand-written MS, 10 pp. J.G.A. Pocock Papers,
privately held. This is an early draft of 'Instant
History: Allen Curnow in Christchurch', *London
Magazine*, Dec./Jan. 1991–92, pp. 44–52.

22 Jeny Curnow, Biography of Allen Curnow, Part
One. Jeny Curnow Papers, ATL MSDL-0203.

23 AC to DG, 7 Oct. 1942. Betty Curnow Papers,
privately held.

24 DG to AC, 25 Jan. 1943. AC Papers, ATL 2402-04.

25 Jeny Curnow, Biography of Allen Curnow,
Part One. Jeny Curnow Papers, ATL
MSDL-0203.

26 Quoted in Norman, *Douglas Lilburn*, p. 105, from
Tony Potter, *NZ Star Times*, 10 June 2001.

27 *New Zealand Listener*, 31 Dec. 1942.

28 AC to DG, 27 Jan. 1943, continuation of 10 Dec.
1942. Betty Curnow Papers, privately held.

29 AC to Joseph Heenan, 23 Sept. 1943. J.W.A.
Heenan Papers, ATL 1132-042.

30 *The Press*, 30 Sept. 1943.

31 *New Zealand Listener*, 29 Oct. 1965, p. 8.

32 *New Zealand Listener*, 15 Oct. 1943.

33 AC to DL, 1 May 1953 [error for 1954]. Douglas
Lilburn Papers, ATL 7623-128.

34 'Conversation with Allen Curnow', in *Look Back
Harder*, p. 251.

CHAPTER TWELVE
FAMILY EXPANSION, *SAILING OR
DROWNING*, AND THE CAXTON
ANTHOLOGY, 1943–44

1 Allen Curnow (AC), interview with Tony Reid,
New Zealand Listener, 12 March 1983.

2 AC to Denis Glover (DG), 27 Jan. 1943,
continuation of 10 Dec. 1942. Betty Curnow
Papers, privately held.

3 AC to DG, 7 Oct. 1942. Betty Curnow Papers,
privately held.

4 AC to DG, 15 Nov. 1942. Denis Glover Papers,
ATL 80-387-026.

5 AC to DG, 10 Dec. 1942. Betty Curnow Papers,
privately held.

6 AC to DG, 27 Jan. 1943, continuation of
10 Dec. 1942. Betty Curnow Papers, privately
held.

7 DG to AC, 12 June 1943. AC Papers, ATL 2402-04.

8 *The Press*, 22 Feb. 1941.
9 *The Press*, 29 March 1941.
10 AC to DG, 28 July 1942. Betty Curnow Papers, privately held.
11 *Meanjin Papers*, vol. 2, no. 2, Winter 1943, p. 21.
12 AC to M.H. Holcroft (MHH), 10 Jan. 1944. M.H. Holcroft Papers, ATL 1186-05.
13 Draft, 'Dialogue of Island and Time', [1940]. Tim Curnow Papers, ATL 7905.
14 AC to DG, 15 Nov. 1942. Denis Glover Papers, ATL 80-387-026.
15 Betty Curnow: Diary, 22 Oct. 1942. Betty Curnow Papers, privately held.
16 See preface to *Four Plays: The Axe, The Overseas Expert, The Duke's Miracle, Resident of Nowhere*, A.H. & A.W. Reed, Wellington, 1972, pp. 12–13.
17 *New Zealand Listener*, 20 Aug. 1943.
18 AC to Betty Curnow, [Aug. 1943]. Betty Curnow Papers, privately held.
19 Ann Beaglehole, 'Dronke, Minnie Maria', *Te Ara – the Encyclopedia of New Zealand*, updated 30 Oct. 2012, http://www.TeAra.govt.nz/en/biographies/4d19/dronke-minnie-maria.
20 AC to DG, 27 Jan. 1943, continuation of 10 Dec. 1942. Betty Curnow Papers, privately held.
21 AC to MHH, 24 Aug. 1943. M.H. Holcroft Papers, ATL 1186-05.
22 AC to DG, 13 March [1944], misdated 1943. Betty Curnow Papers, privately held.
23 Jeny Curnow, Biography of Allen Curnow, Part One. Jeny Curnow Papers, ATL MSDL-0203.
24 Ngaio Marsh to AC, [?Aug./Sept. 1944]. Betty Curnow Papers, privately held.
25 AC to DG, 21 Oct. 1943. Denis Glover Papers, ATL 0418-008.
26 James Norgate, 'Challenging Discourses in Allen Curnow's ouevre', PhD dissertation, Massey University, 1997, Appendix III, pp. 215–17.
27 AC to W.F. Alexander (WFA), 8 Nov. 1944. W.F. Alexander Papers, ATL 0423-02.
28 AC to DG, 2 Dec. 1943. Denis Glover Papers, ATL 0418-008.
29 AC to DG, 13 March 1944, misdated 1943. Betty Curnow Papers, privately held.
30 A.R.D. Fairburn (ARDF) to AC, 19 Nov. 1943. *The Letters of A.R.D. Fairburn*, ed. Lauris Edmond, Oxford University Press, Auckland, pp. 130–1.
31 Ibid.
32 AC to WFA, 15 Nov. 1944. W.F. Alexander Papers, ATL 0423-02.
33 Eileen Duggan (ED) to WFA, [1944]. W.F. Alexander Papers, ATL 0423-06.
34 AC to WFA, 15 Nov. 1944. W.F. Alexander Papers, ATL 0423-02.
35 *A Book of New Zealand Verse 1923–45*, ed. Allen Curnow, The Caxton Press, Christchurch, 1945, p. 24.
36 Jeny Curnow, Biography of Allen Curnow, Part One. Jeny Curnow Papers, ATL MSDL-0203.
37 AC to DG, 27 April 1944. Denis Glover Papers, ATL 0418-008.
38 Jeny Curnow, Biography of Allen Curnow, Part One. Jeny Curnow Papers, ATL MSDL-0203.
39 Alex Calder, 'Unsettling Settlement: Poetry and Nationalism in Aotearoa / New Zealand', *REAL: The Yearbook of Research in English and American Literature*, 14, 1998, pp. 169–75.
40 Allen Curnow, 'The Poetry of R.A.K. Mason', *Book 2*, May 1941, in *Look Back Harder: Critical Writings 1935–1984*, ed. Peter Simpson, Auckland University Press, Auckland, 1987, p. 26.
41 Betty Curnow: Diary, 8 Jan. 1944. Betty Curnow Papers, privately held.
42 See reproduction, Philip Norman, *Douglas Lilburn: His Life and Music*, Canterbury University Press, Christchurch, 2006, p. 105.
43 AC to WFA, 8 Nov. 1944. W.F. Alexander Papers, ATL 0423-02.
44 AC to WFA, 15 Nov. 1944. W.F. Alexander Papers, ATL 0423-02.
45 Ursula Bethell (UB) to MHH, 8–10 March 1942. *Vibrant with Words: The Letters of Ursula Bethell*, ed. Peter Whiteford, Victoria University Press, Wellington, 2006, p. 280.
46 UB to Charles Brasch (CB), 29 April 1944. *Vibrant with Words*, pp. 333–4.
47 AC to CB, 27 Aug. 1943. Charles Brasch Papers, Hocken Collections (HC) MS-0996-003/127.
48 CB to AC, 16 Nov. 1943. Charles Brasch Papers, HC MS-0996-003/127.
49 Ibid.
50 DG to AC, 12 June 1944. AC Papers, ATL 2402-04.
51 AC to DG, 15 Nov. 1942. Denis Glover Papers, ATL 80-387-026.
52 Ibid.
53 AC to ARDF, 6 Dec. 1944. A.R.D. Fairburn Papers, ATL 1128-080.
54 ARDF to AC, 4 Oct. 1944. AC Papers, ATL 2402-13. *The Letters of A.R.D. Fairburn*, ed. Lauris Edmond, Oxford University Press, Auckland, 1981, pp. 133–4.
55 AC to ARDF, 4 April 1945. A.R.D. Fairburn Papers, ATL 1128-080.
56 AC to ARDF, 1 June 1945. A.R.D. Fairburn Papers, ATL 1128-080.
57 AC to ARDF, 11 Oct. 1944. A.R.D. Fairburn Papers, ATL 1128-080.
58 ARDF to AC, 20 Nov. 1944. AC Papers, ATL 2402-13.
59 A.R.D. Fairburn, 'New Zealanders You Should Know ... Mr Allen Curnow', *Action*, Dec. 1944, pp. 35–37.
60 Ibid., p. 37.
61 Ibid., p. 36.

CHAPTER THIRTEEN
RESTLESS YEARS, 1945–46

1 Allen Curnow (AC) to Betty Curnow, [Nov.] 1946. Betty Curnow Papers, Alexander Turnbull Library (ATL) 86-101.

2 AC to Betty Curnow, Jan. [1945]. Betty Curnow Papers, ATL 86-101.

3 AC to Betty Curnow, [Oct.] 1945. Betty Curnow Papers, ATL 86-101.

4 Ibid.

5 AC to A.R.D. Fairburn (ARDF), 16 March 1946. A.R.D. Fairburn Papers, ATL 1128-080.

6 *Times Literary Supplement*, 6 Oct. 1945.

7 *Poetry*, no. 4, July 1946.

8 *The Press*, 21 July 1945.

9 AC to M.H. Holcroft (MHH), 21 July 1945. M.H. Holcroft Papers, ATL 1186-05.

10 *The Press*, 21 July 1945.

11 ARDF to AC, 27 Aug. 1945. AC Papers, ATL 2402-13.

12 ARDF to AC, 17 Sept. 1945. AC Papers, ATL 2402-13.

13 James K. Baxter to AC, 7 July 1945. James K. Baxter Papers, Hocken Collections (HC) MS-0975/177. I am indebted to Paul Millar for information about this letter.

14 Ibid.

15 AC to ARDF, 9 Sept. 1945. A.R.D. Fairburn Papers, ATL 1128-080.

16 *A Treasury of New Zealand Verse*, ed. W.F. Alexander and A.E. Currie, Whitcombe & Tombs, Christchurch, 1926, was a revised and enlarged edition of *New Zealand Verse*, ed. W.F. Alexander and A.E. Currie, Walter Scott Publishing Company, London, 1906.

17 *Evening Star*, [July] 1945.

18 AC to W.F. Alexander (WFA), 24 July 1945. W.F. Alexander Papers, ATL 0423-02.

19 Ibid.

20 Betty Curnow: Diary, privately held, 1 Aug. 1945.

21 AC to Betty Curnow, [Sept.] 1945. Betty Curnow Papers, 86-101.

22 AC to Betty Curnow, [Nov.] 1945. Betty Curnow Papers, 86-101.

23 Ibid.

24 AC to Betty Curnow, [Nov. 1945]. Betty Curnow Papers, 86-101.

25 Charles Brasch: Journal, 11 May 1946. Charles Brasch Papers, HC MS-0996-009/011.

26 Charles Brasch: Journal, 23 Oct. 1946. Charles Brasch Papers, HC MS-0996-009/011.

27 Charles Brasch: Journal, 28 Feb. 1946. Charles Brasch Papers, HC MS-0996-009/011.

28 Charles Brasch: Journal, 24 July 1946. Charles Brasch Papers, HC MS-0996-009/011.

29 Charles Brasch: Journal, 15 Feb. 1947. Charles Brasch Papers, HC MS-0996-009/012.

30 Charles Brasch: Journal, 20 March, 1948. Charles Brasch Papers, HC MS-0996-009/012.

31 Charles Brasch: Journal, 15 Feb. 1947. Charles Brasch Papers, HC MS-0996-009/012.

32 Charles Brasch: Journal, 10 Aug. 1949. Charles Brasch Papers, HC MS-0996-009/014.

33 AC to Betty Curnow, Jan. 1946. Betty Curnow Papers, ATL 86-101.

34 *The Press*, 23 Feb. 1946.

35 *The Press*, 2 March 1946.

36 Betty Curnow: Diary, privately held, 23 April 1945.

37 AC to ARDF, 5 April 1946. A.R.D. Fairburn Papers, ATL 1128-080.

38 A.E. Currie to WFA, 29 June 1946. W.F. Alexander Papers, ATL 0423-03.

39 *Otago Daily Times*, [July] 1946.

40 AC to ARDF, 7 Aug. 1946. A.R.D. Fairburn Papers, ATL 1128-080.

41 *Otago Daily Times*, [July] 1946.

42 *The Press*, 5 July 1946.

43 *New Zealand Listener*, 22 June 1946.

44 'D.F.T.', *New Zealand Listener*, 5 July 1946.

45 Betty Curnow: Diary, privately held, 18 March 1947.

46 AC to ARDF, 7 Aug. 1946. A.R.D. Fairburn Papers, ATL 1128-080.

47 AC to Charles Brasch (CB), [23] April 1947. Charles Brasch Papers, HC MS-0996-002/089.

48 'In Time of Pestilence' (1593).

49 *The Axe: A Verse Tragedy*, The Caxton Press, Christchurch, 1949, p. 7.

50 *Four Plays: The Axe, The Overseas Expert, The Duke's Miracle, Resident of Nowhere*, A.H. & A.W. Reed, Wellington, 1972, pp. 7–8.

51 *The Axe* (1949), p. 7.

52 *The Axe*, programme note, April 1948.

53 *The Axe* (1949), act II, scene 3, pp. 54–55.

54 *The Axe* (1949), act II, scene 1, p. 45.

55 *The Axe*, programme note, April 1948.

56 AC, interview with Bruce Harding (BH), 8 Oct. 1984. Bruce Harding Papers, privately held. See also BH to AC, 15 Oct. 1984 and AC to BH, 30 Oct. 1984, AC Papers, ATL 7574-85.

57 AC to CB, 5 April 1946. Charles Brasch Papers, HC MS-0996-003/220.

58 Betty Curnow: Diary, privately held, 17 Aug. 1946.

59 Additional note in Betty Curnow: Diary, privately held, 1946, made in 1974.

60 16 Oct. 1946.

61 AC to Betty Curnow, [Oct. 1946]. Betty Curnow Papers, ATL 86-101.

62 AC to Betty Curnow, [Oct.] 1946. Betty Curnow Papers, ATL 86-101.

63 AC to Betty Curnow, [Nov.] 1946. Betty Curnow Papers, ATL 86-101.

64 Jeny Curnow, Biography of Allen Curnow, Part One. Jeny Curnow Papers, ATL MSDL-0203.

CHAPTER FOURTEEN
LAST YEARS IN CHRISTCHURCH, 1947–49

1 Allen Curnow, 'Introduction to *A Book of New Zealand Verse 1923–45*', in *Look Back Harder: Critical Writings 1935–1984*, ed. Peter Simpson, Auckland University Press, Auckland, 1987, p. 75.

2 *Canta*, 2 April 1947, p. 4.

3 Allen Curnow (AC) to J.H.E. Schroder (JHES), 9 June 1950. J.H.E. Schroder Papers, Alexander Turnbull Library (ATL) 0280-24.

4 AC to A.R.D. Fairburn (ARDF), 1 Nov. 1946. A.R.D. Fairburn Papers, ATL 1128-080.

5 Ibid.

6 'Modern Australian Poetry', in *Look Back Harder*, p. 83.
7 AC to ARDF, 4 May 1947. A.R.D. Fairburn Papers, ATL 1128-080.
8 'Modern Australian Poetry', in *Look Back Harder*, pp. 83–84.
9 Charles Brasch (CB) to AC, 23 April 1947. Charles Brasch Papers, Hocken Collections (HC) MS-0996-002/089.
10 'Modern Australian Poetry', in *Look Back Harder*, p. 89.
11 W.S. Broughton, 'Lawlor, Patrick Anthony', *Te Ara – the Encyclopedia of New Zealand*, updated 30 Oct. 2012, http://www.TeAra.govt.nz/en/biographies/4l6/lawlor-patrick-anthony.
12 A.E. Currie to W.F. Alexander, 18 July 1947. W.F. Alexander Papers, ATL 0423-03.
13 *The Press*, 6 Dec. 1947.
14 *The Press*, 14 Aug. 1948.
15 AC to Alan Edward Mulgan (AEM), 10 Feb. 1948. A.E. Mulgan Papers, ATL 0224-15.
16 AC to AEM, 23 Nov. 1948. A.E. Mulgan Papers, ATL 0224-15.
17 'Introduction to *The Penguin Book of New Zealand Verse*', in *Look Back Harder*, p. 142.
18 *The Press*, 6 Dec. 1947.
19 *The Press*, 14 Aug. 1948.
20 *The Press*, 17 April 1948.
21 *The Press*, 4 Oct. 1947.
22 *The Press*, 31 July 1948. Allen Curnow, 'Three Caxton Poets: Brasch, Baxter, Hart-Smith', in *Look Back Harder*, pp. 94–97.
23 Charles Brasch: Journal, 14 March 1953. Charles Brasch Papers, HC MS-0996-009/022.
24 Review of James K. Baxter, *Blow, Wind of Fruitfulness* (The Caxton Poets No. 2, The Caxton Press, Christchurch, 1948), *Landfall*, no. 7, vol. 2, no. 3, Sept. 1948, pp. 230–3.
25 'James K. Baxter: *Blow, Wind of Fruitfulness*', in *Look Back Harder*, p. 98.
26 Ibid., p. 100.
27 Ibid.
28 AC to CB, [?April 1948, possibly 1947]. Charles Brasch Papers, HC MS-0996-002/089.
29 *Auckland Star*, 20 Aug. 1953.
30 *New Zealand Listener*, 8 Sept. 1950, p. 12.
31 Ibid.
32 Ibid.
33 *Yearbook of the Arts in New Zealand*, no. 4, 1948, pp. 134–5.
34 AC to CB, 3 May 1948. Charles Brasch Papers, HC MS-0996-002/089.
35 AC to Eric Ramsden (ER), 12 July 1948. G.E.O. Ramsden Papers, ATL 0196-203.
36 *The Axe: A Verse Tragedy*, The Caxton Press, Christchurch, 1949 [i.e. 1950], p. 9.
37 AC to ER, 12 July 1948. G.E.O. Ramsden Papers, ATL 0196-203.
38 'Instant History', *London Magazine*, Dec./Jan. 1991–92, pp. 47–49.
39 AC interviewed by Arthur Baysting, *New Zealand Listener*, 7 March 1969.
40 AC to ARDF, 10 Feb. 1948. A.R.D. Fairburn Papers, ATL 1128-080.
41 AC to CB, 3 May 1948. Charles Brasch Papers, HC MS-0996-002/089.
42 AC to Literary Fund Advisory Committee, [July] 1948. P.A. Lawlor Papers, ATL 77-067-2/1.
43 Betty Curnow: Diary, privately held, 22 Oct. 1948.
44 AC to ER, 12 July 1948. G.E.O. Ramsden Papers, ATL 0196-203.
45 Joseph Heenan (JH) to JHES, 9 Feb. 1949. J.W.A. Heenan Papers, ATL 1132-206.
46 JHES to JH, 21 Dec. 1948. J.W.A. Heenan Papers, ATL 1132-206.
47 JHES to JH, 13 Feb. 1949. J.W.A. Heenan Papers, ATL 1132-206.
48 JH to JHES, 4 March 1949. J.W.A. Heenan Papers, ATL 1132-206.
49 AC to CB, 15 Feb. 1949. Charles Brasch Papers, HC MS-0996-002/089.
50 Ibid.
51 AC to ARDF, 7 Feb. 1949. A.R.D. Fairburn Papers, ATL 1128-080.
52 AC to CB, 8 Dec. 1948. Charles Brasch Papers, HC MS-0996-002/089.
53 AC to ARDF, 7 Feb. 1949. A.R.D. Fairburn Papers, ATL 1128-080.
54 AC to Eileen Duggan, 13 Dec. 1948. Eileen Duggan Papers, Catholic Archdiocesan Archives, Wellington.
55 AC to CB, 15 Feb. 1949. Charles Brasch Papers, HC MS-0996-002/089.
56 'Introduction to *A Book of New Zealand Verse 1923–45*', in *Look Back Harder*, p. 74.
57 Ibid., p. 75.
58 *The Press*, 21 March 1949.

CHAPTER FIFTEEN
UNITED KINGDOM, MARCH 1949– JANUARY 1950

1 Allen Curnow (AC) to Betty Curnow, 26 April 1949. Betty Curnow Papers, Alexander Turnbull Library (ATL) 86-101.
2 Ibid.
3 Ibid.
4 J.H.E. Schroder (JHES) to Joseph Heenan (JH), 9 May 1949. J.W.A. Heenan Papers, ATL 1132-206.
5 JHES to JH, 6 June 1949 (enclosing a copy of the letter sent to Fraser). J.W.A. Heenan Papers, ATL 1132-206.
6 JH to JHES, 13 June 1949. J.W.A. Heenan Papers, ATL 1132-206.
7 AC to Betty Curnow, 26 April 1949. Betty Curnow Papers, ATL 86-101.
8 AC to Betty Curnow, 4 July 1949. Betty Curnow Papers, ATL 86-101.
9 AC to Betty Curnow, 25–26 May 1949. Betty Curnow Papers, ATL 86-101.
10 Ibid.
11 Ibid.
12 AC to Betty Curnow, 4 July 1949. Betty Curnow Papers, ATL 86-101.

13 AC to Betty Curnow, 13 June 1949. Betty Curnow Papers, ATL 86-101.
14 *New Zealand Listener*, 18 Dec. 1982, pp. 24–25.
15 AC to Richard Mayne (RM), 9 Feb. 1987. AC Papers, ATL 4650-12.
16 Ibid.
17 William Latham (WL) to AC, 26 May 1967. AC Papers, ATL 7574-02.
18 AC to Evelyn Segal, 24 Oct. 1967. AC Papers, ATL 2402-30.
19 AC to WL, 20 Dec. 1967. AC Papers, ATL 7574-02.
20 AC to WL, 15 Oct. 1967. AC Papers, ATL 7574-02.
21 AC Papers, ATL 2402-02.
22 Draft reminiscences of Dylan Thomas, untitled typescript, [1967], p. 10. AC Papers, ATL 2402-59.
23 Ibid.
24 AC to Betty Curnow, 15 June 1949. Betty Curnow Papers, ATL 86-101.
25 AC, quoting Dylan Thomas, to Betty Curnow, 15 June 1949. Betty Curnow Papers, ATL 86-101.
26 'Introduction to *The Penguin Book of New Zealand Verse*', 1960, in *Look Back Harder: Critical Writings 1935–1984*, ed. Peter Simpson, Auckland University Press, Auckland, 1987, p. 158.
27 AC to Betty Curnow, 15 June 1949. Betty Curnow Papers, ATL 86-101.
28 Draft reminiscences of Dylan Thomas, untitled typescript, [1967], p. 2. AC Papers, ATL 2402-59.
29 Untitled draft for *Encounter* magazine, [1987]. AC Papers, ATL 4650-05.
30 JH to AC, 8 July 1949. J.W.A. Heenan Papers, ATL 1132-042.
31 AC to Betty Curnow, 22 July 1949. Betty Curnow Papers, ATL 86-101.
32 AC to Betty Curnow, 24 June 1949. Betty Curnow Papers, ATL 86-101.
33 'Instant History', *London Magazine*, Dec./Jan. 1991–92, p. 50.
34 AC to Betty Curnow, 4 July 1949. Betty Curnow Papers, ATL 86-101.
35 AC to Betty Curnow, 8 Aug. 1949. Betty Curnow Papers, ATL 86-101.
36 AC to Betty Curnow, 25–26 May 1949. Betty Curnow Papers, ATL 86-101.
37 AC to Betty Curnow, 6 Sept. 1949. Betty Curnow Papers, ATL 86-101.
38 Ibid.
39 AC to Betty Curnow, 19 Sept. 1949. AC Papers, ATL 2402-02.
40 'About Dylan Thomas', in *Look Back Harder*, p. 321.
41 AC to Betty Curnow, 19 Sept. 1949. AC Papers, ATL 2402-02.
42 Ibid.
43 'About Dylan Thomas', in *Look Back Harder*, p. 321.
44 Draft reminiscences of Dylan Thomas, untitled typescript, [1967], p. 6. AC Papers, ATL 2402-59.
45 Ibid.
46 'About Dylan Thomas', in *Look Back Harder*, p. 321.
47 AC to Betty Curnow, 16 Aug. 1949. Betty Curnow Papers, ATL 86-101.
48 AC to Betty Curnow, 18 Aug. 1949. Betty Curnow Papers, ATL 86-101.

49 AC to JHES, 30 Sept. 1949. J.H.E. Schroder Papers, ATL 0280-24.
50 AC to Betty Curnow, 29 Sept. 1949. Betty Curnow Papers, ATL 86-101.
51 Ibid.
52 Quoted by AC, AC to Betty Curnow, 11 Oct. 1949. Betty Curnow Papers, ATL 86-101.
53 Betty Curnow: Diary, privately held, 6 Sept. 1948.
54 AC to Betty Curnow, 11 Oct. 1949. Betty Curnow Papers, ATL 86-101.
55 Ibid.
56 Ibid.
57 Ibid.
58 AC to Betty Curnow, 14 Oct. 1949. Betty Curnow Papers, ATL 86-101.
59 AC to Betty Curnow, 29 Sept. 1949. Betty Curnow Papers, ATL 86-101.
60 AC to Charles Brasch (CB), 22 Dec. 1949. Charles Brasch Papers, Hocken Collections (HC) MS-0996-002/089.
61 AC to Betty Curnow [5 Dec] 1949. Betty Curnow Papers, ATL 86-101.
62 AC to Betty Curnow, 7 Nov. 1949. Betty Curnow Papers, ATL 86-101.
63 AC to Betty Curnow, [5 Dec.] 1949. Betty Curnow Papers, ATL 86-101.
64 AC to Betty Curnow, 18 Aug. 1949. Betty Curnow Papers, ATL 86-101.
65 'New Zealander in Ancestral Norfolk', *London Calling*, 13 April 1950, p. 11.
66 Ibid., p. 12.
67 Jeny Curnow, Biography of Allen Curnow, Part One. Jeny Curnow Papers, ATL MSDL-0203.
68 Ibid.
69 'New Zealander in Ancestral Norfolk', *London Calling*, 13 April 1950, p. 12.
70 Jeny Curnow, Biography of Allen Curnow, Part One. Jeny Curnow Papers, ATL MSDL-0203.
71 'New Zealander in Ancestral Norfolk', *London Calling*, 13 April 1950.
72 Interview with John Arlott for the BBC Overseas Service, [Dec. 1949], re-broadcast in New Zealand on 2YA 'Critically Speaking' series, 27 April 1950.
73 AC to CB, 22 Dec. 1949. Charles Brasch Papers, HC MS-0996-002/089.
74 AC to JHES, 13 Dec. 1949. J.H.E. Schroder Papers, ATL 0280-24.
75 AC to CB, 22 Dec. 1949. Charles Brasch Papers, HC MS-0996-002/089.
76 AC to JHES, 13 Dec. 1949. J.H.E. Schroder Papers, ATL 0280-24.
77 AC to Anthony Thwaite, 19 Aug. 1999. AC Papers, ATL 7574-85.
78 AC to Betty Curnow, 13 Jan. 1950. Betty Curnow Papers, ATL 86-101.
79 AC, diary-like notes on loose leaves covering trip to Cornwall, 10/11 Jan. 1950. Betty Curnow Papers, ATL 86-101.
80 Ibid.
81 Ibid.

82 AC to Betty Curnow, 13 Jan. 1950. Betty Curnow Papers, ATL 86-101.

83 AC, diary-like notes on loose leaves covering trip to Cornwall, 10/11 Jan. 1950. Betty Curnow Papers, ATL 86-101.

84 Sven Berlin to AC, 31 Dec. 1950. AC Papers, ATL 2402-01.

85 Betty Curnow to CB, 28 March [1950]. Charles Brasch Papers, HC MS-0996-002/089.

86 *New Zealand Listener*, 12 Jan. 1951, p. 15.

87 *Cornish Review*, no. 8, Summer 1951.

CHAPTER SIXTEEN
UNITED STATES, FEBRUARY–APRIL 1950

1 Fragment. Allen Curnow (AC) Papers, Alexander Turnbull Library (ATL) 2402-02.

2 AC to Charles Brasch, 23 Jan. 1950. Charles Brasch Papers, Hocken Collections (HC) MS-0996-002/089.

3 AC to J.H.E. Schroder (JHES), 1 Feb. 1950. J.H.E. Schroder Papers, ATL 0280-24.

4 AC to Betty Curnow, 6 Feb. 1950. Betty Curnow Papers, ATL 86-101.

5 Jeny Curnow, Biography of Allen Curnow, Part One. Jeny Curnow Papers, ATL MSDL-0203.

6 J.G.A. Pocock to AC, 4 Oct. [1951]. AC Papers, ATL 2402-05.

7 Betty Curnow: Diary, privately held, 26 May 1950.

8 AC to Betty Curnow, 6 Feb. 1950. Betty Curnow Papers, ATL 86-101.

9 Jeny Curnow, Biography of Allen Curnow, Part One. Jeny Curnow Papers, ATL MSDL-0203.

10 Draft reminiscences of Dylan Thomas, untitled typescript, [1967], p. 7. AC Papers, ATL 2402-59.

11 AC to Betty Curnow, 14 March 1950. AC Papers, ATL 2402-02.

12 AC: Notebook, [?Feb.] 1950. AC Papers, ATL 2402-02.

13 *The Press*, 26 May 1950.

14 AC: Notebook, Feb. 1950. AC Papers, ATL 2402-02.

15 Draft reminiscences of Dylan Thomas, untitled typescript, [1967], pp. 9–13. AC Papers, ATL 2402-59.

16 AC to Betty Curnow, 14 March 1950. AC Papers, ATL 2402-02.

17 AC: Notebook, [?March] 1950. AC Papers, ATL 2402-02.

18 AC to Betty Curnow, 14 March 1950. AC Papers, ATL 2402-02.

19 Ibid.

20 Ibid.

21 Draft reminiscences of Dylan Thomas, untitled typescript, [1967], p. 18. AC Papers, ATL 2402-59.

22 Ibid., p. 19.

23 Ibid., p. 20.

24 Ibid.

25 *New Zealand Listener*, 18 Dec. 1982, p. 25.

26 Ibid.

27 Cid Corman to AC, 28 Jan. 1951. AC Papers, ATL 2402-01.

28 AC to Douglas Lilburn, 1 Aug. 1955. Douglas Lilburn Papers, ATL 7623-128.

29 Ibid.

30 AC to Bill Manhire, 30 June 1982. AC Papers, ATL 2402-45.

31 *New Zealand Listener*, 18 Dec. 1982, p. 25.

32 Draft reminiscences of Dylan Thomas, untitled typescript, [1967], p. 21. AC Papers, ATL 2402-59.

33 AC: Notebook, [April] 1950. AC Papers, ATL 2402-02.

34 AC to Betty Curnow, 19 April 1950. AC Papers, ATL 2402-02.

35 AC to Betty Curnow, 24 April 1950. AC Papers, ATL 2402-02.

36 Fragment. AC Papers, ATL 2402-02.

37 AC: Notebook, 17 Feb. 1950. AC Papers, ATL 2402-02.

38 AC Papers, ATL 2402-02.

39 Fragment. AC Papers, ATL 2402-02.

40 *Poetry*, May 1950, p. 124.

41 Charles Brasch: Journal, 8 June 1950. Charles Brasch Papers, HC MS-0996-009/015.

42 *The Press*, 26 May 1950.

43 *New Zealand Listener*, 2 June 1950, p. 7.

44 Ibid.

CHAPTER SEVENTEEN
MOVING TO AUCKLAND, JUNE 1950–NOVEMBER 1954

1 Allen Curnow (AC) to Douglas Lilburn (DL), 1 April 1954. Douglas Lilburn Papers, Alexander Turnbull Library (ATL) 7623-128.

2 AC to J.H.E. Schroder (JHES), 24 July 1950. J.H.E. Schroder Papers, ATL 0280-24.

3 *The Press*, 19 Aug. 1950.

4 AC to JHES, 24 July 1950. J.H.E. Schroder Papers, ATL 0280-24.

5 AC to A.R.D. Fairburn, 7 Aug. 1950. A.R.D. Fairburn Papers, ATL 1128-080.

6 AC to Joseph Heenan, 5 Oct. 1950. J.W.A. Heenan Papers, ATL 1132-042.

7 'J.E.B.', *New Zealand Listener*, 8 Dec. 1950.

8 AC, 'Painting in Canterbury', *New Zealand Listener*, 8 Dec. 1950.

9 James Bertram to Charles Brasch (CB), 23 Jan. 1951. Charles Brasch Papers, Hocken Collections (HC) MS-0996-003/017.

10 Betty Curnow to CB, 10 Sept. 1951. Charles Brasch Papers, HC MS-0996-002/089.

11 Denis Glover (DG) to AC, 5 April 1951. AC Papers, ATL 2402-04.

12 *The Press*, 12 May 1951.

13 Draft notes in response to Patrick Evans's 'The Curnow-Baxter Feud' (*The Penguin History of New Zealand Literature*, Penguin, Auckland, 1990, pp. 163–6), [c. 1990–91 and 1996]. AC Papers, ATL, 7574-26.

14 AC to Dan Davin, 30 Oct. 1951. Dan Davin Papers, ATL 5079-075.
15 CB to AC, 11 Dec. 1952. Charles Brasch Papers, HC MS-0996-002/089.
16 AC to DL, 30 June 1952. Douglas Lilburn Papers, ATL 7623-128.
17 AC to DL, 8 March 1952. Douglas Lilburn Papers, ATL 7623-128.
18 AC to DL, 27 May 1952. Douglas Lilburn Papers, ATL 7623-128.
19 See Philip Norman, *Douglas Lilburn: His Life and Music*, Canterbury University Press, Christchurch, 2006, pp. 176–7 and 436 n. 29.
20 *Here & Now*, Dec. 1951. 'The *New Zealand Poetry Yearbook*', in *Look Back Harder: Critical Writings 1935–1984*, ed. Peter Simpson, Auckland University Press, Auckland, 1987, pp. 107–8.
21 Ibid., p. 106.
22 AC to DL, 27 May 1952. Douglas Lilburn Papers, ATL 7623-128.
23 CB to AC, 11 Dec. 1952. Charles Brasch Papers, HC MS-0996-002/089.
24 AC to CB, 3 March 1953. Charles Brasch Papers, HC MS-0996-002/089.
25 AC to CB, 29 May 1953. Charles Brasch Papers, HC MS-0996-002/089.
26 CB to AC, 7 June 1953. Charles Brasch Papers, HC MS-0996-002/089.
27 'M. H. Holcroft: *Dance of the Seasons*', in *Look Back Harder*, p. 122.
28 Ibid., p. 124.
29 Ibid.
30 'The *Poetry Yearbook*: a Letter to Louis Johnson', in *Look Back Harder*, p. 110.
31 Ibid., p. 109.
32 Ibid., p. 111.
33 'M. H. Holcroft: *Dance of the Seasons*', in *Look Back Harder*, p. 123.
34 *New Zealand Listener*, 17 April 1953, p. 11.
35 See AC Papers, ATL 7574-84.
36 *New Zealand Listener*, 22 May, 1953, p. 5.
37 AC to CB, 29 May 1953. Charles Brasch Papers, HC MS-0996-002/089.
38 *Craccum*, 14 Aug. 1953.
39 *Auckland Star*, 20 Aug. 1953.
40 *Here & Now*, 11 Sept. 1953; *Parson's Packet*, no. 27, March–April 1954.
41 CB to AC, 29 Nov. 1953. Charles Brasch Papers, HC MS-0996-002/089.
42 AC to CB, 5 Dec. 1953. Charles Brasch Papers, HC MS-0996-002/089.
43 AC to CB, 20 Jan. 1954. Charles Brasch Papers, HC MS-0996-002/089.
44 Ibid.
45 CB to AC, 22 Jan. 1954. Charles Brasch Papers, HC MS-0996-002/089.
46 DG to AC, 28 Jan. 1954. AC Papers, ATL 2402-04.
47 Radio broadcast, 28 April 1954.
48 AC to DL, 1 April 1954. Douglas Lilburn Papers, ATL 7623-128.
49 Ibid.
50 Ibid.
51 AC to DG, 23 Aug. 1954. Denis Glover Papers, ATL 0418-008.
52 AC to DG, 18 Dec. 1954. Denis Glover Papers, ATL 0418-008.
53 Jim Walton to AC, 28 April 1956. AC Papers, ATL 2402-01.
54 AC to DG, 18–20 Dec. 1954. Denis Glover Papers, ATL 0418-008.

CHAPTER EIGHTEEN
A NEW LIFE AND NEW POEMS, 1955–57

1   Jeny Curnow, Biography of Allen Curnow, Part Two. Jeny Curnow Papers, Alexander Turnbull Library (ATL) MSDL-0204.
2   See Jeny Curnow, 'My Early Life', a typescript of her life up to the time she met Curnow, pp. 22–23. J.M. Curnow Papers, ATL MSDL-2038.
3   Jeny Curnow, Biography of Allen Curnow, Part Two. Jeny Curnow Papers, ATL MSDL-0204.
4   Ibid.
5   Ibid.
6   Allen Curnow (AC) to Denis Glover (DG), 17 Jan. 1955. Denis Glover Papers, ATL 0418-008.
7   Ibid.
8   'Olson as Oracle: "Projective Verse" Thirty Years On', in *Look Back Harder*, ed. Peter Simpson, Auckland University Press, Auckland, 1987, p. 315.
9   *W.B. Yeats: Selected Poetry*, ed. A. Norman Jeffares, Pan Books, 1974 (first edition Macmillan, 1962), p. 202.
10 DG to AC, 7 March 1955. AC Papers, ATL 2402-21.
11 AC to DG, 12 Aug. 1955. Denis Glover Papers, ATL 0418-008.
12 *New Zealand Listener*, 11 Nov. 1955.
13 Geoffrey Moore to AC, 24 June 1956. AC Papers, ATL 2402-05.
14 AC to DG, [?mid-1956]. Denis Glover Papers, ATL 0418-008.
15 Ibid.
16 Ibid.
17 AC to M.H. Holcroft, 26 March 1953. M.H. Holcroft Papers, ATL 1186-05.
18 Louis Johnson to AC, [?May] 1956. AC Papers, ATL 2402-03.
19 Ibid.
20 AC to DG, 3 Sept. 1956. Denis Glover Papers, ATL 0418-008.
21 AC to Charles Brasch (CB), 15 Oct. 1956. Charles Brasch Papers, Hocken Collections (HC) MS-0996-002/089.
22 AC to DG, 1 Nov. 1956. Denis Glover Papers, ATL 0418-008.
23 Eunice Frost to AC, 30 Oct. 1956. AC Papers, ATL 2402-23.
24 AC to CB, 20 Nov. 1956. Charles Brasch Papers, HC MS-0996-002/089.
25 CB to AC, 1 Dec. 1956. AC Papers, ATL 2402-28.
26 Brassington, Gough & Clark to Frank Haigh, 3 March 1957. AC Papers, ATL 2402-05.

27 AC to DG, 12 Feb. 1957. Denis Glover Papers, ATL 0418-008.

28 AC to DG, 21 May 1957. Denis Glover Papers, ATL 0418-008.

29 DG to AC, 25 Aug. 1957. AC Papers, ATL 2402-04.

30 AC to DG, 27 Aug. 1957. Denis Glover Papers, ATL 0418-008.

31 DG to AC, 13 Nov. 1957. AC Papers, ATL 2402-04.

32 AC, interview with James McNeish, transcript of reminiscences of A.R.D. Fairburn, [c. 1964–1980], p. 4. James McNeish Papers, ATL 7811-087.

33 Ibid.

34 Ibid.

35 Ibid.

36 AC to A.R.D. Fairburn, 11 March 1957. A.R.D. Fairburn Papers, ATL 1128-100.

37 AC, interview with James McNeish, transcript of reminiscences of A.R.D. Fairburn, [c. 1964–1980], p. 4. James McNeish Papers, ATL 7811-087.

38 Ibid., p. 5.

39 Denys Trussell, *Fairburn*, Auckland University Press and Oxford University Press, Auckland, 1984, p. 277.

40 AC, 'The Art Gallery Controversy: A Precedent to be Avoided', *New Zealand Herald*, [Aug.] 1955.

41 R.M. Algie (RMA) to AC, 25 June 1957. AC Papers, ATL 2402-01.

42 DG to AC, 31 May 1957. AC Papers, ATL 2402-04.

43 Jim Walton to AC, 8 Feb. 1958. AC Papers, ATL 2402-01.

44 Richard Campion to AC, 24 June 1957. AC Papers, ATL 2402-05.

45 AC to DG, 8 July 1958. Denis Glover Papers, ATL 0418-008.

46 RMA to AC, 29 July 1958. AC Papers, ATL 2402-01.

47 *The Press*, 7 Sept. 1957.

48 *The Press*, 31 Aug. 1957.

49 James Bertram to CB, 15 Jan. 1958. Charles Brasch Papers, HC MS-0996-003/017.

50 Charles Brasch: Journal, 7 Sept. 1957. Charles Brasch Papers, HC MS-0996-009/025.

51 AC to DG, 18 Nov. 1957. Denis Glover Papers, ATL 0418-008.

52 AC to DG, 19 Dec. 1957. Denis Glover Papers, ATL 0418-008.

53 AC to DG, 22 Nov. 1957. Denis Glover Papers, ATL 0418-008.

CHAPTER NINETEEN
PENGUIN ANTHOLOGY DELAYS, 1958–60

1 Allen Curnow (AC) to Douglas Lilburn, 19 Nov. 1958. Douglas Lilburn Papers, Alexander Turnbull Library (ATL) 7623-128.

2 Alistair Te Ariki Campbell (ATAC) to Allen Curnow (AC), 19 June 1958. AC Papers, ATL 2402-03.

3 AC to ATAC, 20 June 1958. AC Papers, ATL [?2402-03].

4 ATAC to AC, 23 June 1958. AC Papers, ATL 2402-03.

5 AC to ATAC, 24 June 1958. ATAC Papers, ATL 91-046-1/12.

6 ATAC to AC, 26 June 1958. AC Papers, ATL 2402-03.

7 AC to ATAC, 30 June 1958. AC Papers, ATL 2402-03.

8 Eunice Frost (EF) to AC, 28 June 1958. AC Papers, ATL 2402-03.

9 AC to EF, 30 June 1958. AC Papers, ATL 2402-03.

10 EF to AC, 2 July 1958. AC Papers, ATL 2402-03.

11 AC to Charles Brasch (CB), 9 July 1958. Charles Brasch Papers, Hocken Collections (HC) MS-0996-002/089.

12 Richard Hollyer (RH) to EF, 5 Sept. 1958. AC Papers, ATL 2402-03.

13 AC to Simon Garrett, 4 Aug. 1982. AC Papers, ATL 2402-57.

14 James K. Baxter (JKB) to Penguin, 21 June 1958. AC Papers, ATL 2402-03.

15 AC to CB, 4 July 1958. AC Papers, ATL 2402-03.

16 AC to EF, 3 July 1958. AC Papers, ATL 2402-03.

17 AC to Louis Johnson (LJ), 16 July 1958. AC Papers, ATL 2402-03.

18 LJ to AC, 19 July 1958. AC Papers, ATL 2402-03.

19 Ibid.

20 AC to LJ, 22 July 1958. AC Papers, ATL 2402-03.

21 JKB to AC, 18 July 1958. AC Papers, ATL 2402-03.

22 AC to JKB, 22 July 1958. AC Papers, ATL 2402-03.

23 AC to EF, 28 July 1958. AC Papers, ATL 2402-03.

24 EF to AC, 19 Aug. 1958. AC Papers, ATL 2402-03.

25 AC to EF, 1 Sept. 1958. AC Papers, ATL 2402-03.

26 AC to EF, 28 July 1958. AC Papers, ATL 2402-03.

27 AC to EF, 30 July 1958. AC Papers, ATL 2402-03.

28 AC to ATAC, 11 Aug. 1958. AC Papers, ATL 2402-03.

29 ATAC to AC, 16 Aug. 1958. AC Papers, ATL 2402-03.

30 AC to ATAC, 19 Aug. 1958. AC Papers, ATL 2402-03.

31 EF to LJ, 21 Aug. 1958. AC Papers, ATL 2402-03.

32 EF to JKB, 25 Aug. 1958. AC Papers, ATL 2402-03.

33 LJ to AC, 13 Sept. 1958. AC Papers, ATL 2402-03.

34 AC to CB, 3 Sept. 1958. AC Papers, ATL 2402-03.

35 AC to LJ, 4 Sept. 1958. AC Papers, ATL 2402-03.

36 AC to JKB, 4 Sept. 1958. AC Papers, ATL 2402-03.

37 JKB to AC, 4 Sept. 1958. AC Papers, ATL 2402-03.

38 AC to JKB, 6 Sept. 1958. AC Papers, ATL 2402-03.

39 JKB to AC, 8 Sept. 1958. AC Papers, ATL 2402-03.

40 AC to DG, 10 Sept. 1958. AC Papers, ATL 2402-03.

41 DG to AC, 12 Sept. 1958. AC Papers, ATL 2402-03.

42 AC to EF, 8 Sept. 1958. AC Papers, ATL 2402-08.

43 EF to AC, 18 Sept. 1958. AC Papers, ATL 2402-08.

44 EF to AC, 28 April 1959. AC Papers, ATL
2402–08.

45 C.I. Patterson (CIP) to Penguin, 12 July 1960.
Eileen Duggan Papers, Catholic Archdiocesan
Archives, Wellington.

46 AC to RH, 27 Nov. 1958. AC Papers, ATL
2402–08.

47 AC to Julie Belcher, 25 Feb. 1960. AC Papers,
2402–08.

48 'Introduction to *The Penguin Book of New
Zealand Verse*', 1960, in *Look Back Harder: Critical
Writings 1935–1984*, ed. Peter Simpson, Auckland
University Press, Auckland, 1987, pp. 154–5.

49 CIP to Penguin, 12 July 1960. Eileen Duggan
Papers, Catholic Archdiocesan Archives,
Wellington.

50 CIP to Eileen Duggan, 1 June 1961. Eileen
Duggan Papers, Catholic Archdiocesan Archives,
Wellington.

51 'Letter to Editor', *New Zealand Listener*, 27
March 1999.

CHAPTER TWENTY
MORE PLAYS, 1958–61

1 Allen Curnow (AC) to Jim Walton (JW), 10
Sept. 1960. AC Papers, Alexander Turnbull
Library (ATL) 2402–07.

2 *Landfall* 46, vol. 12, no. 2, June 1958, pp. 181–4.

3 *Poetry*, vol. 94, no. 1, April 1959.

4 *New Zealand Listener*, 7 Feb. 1958.

5 *The Press*, 15 March 1958.

6 Charles Brasch: Journal, 16 Jan. 1958. Charles
Brasch Papers, Hocken Collections (HC) MS-
0996-009/025.

7 Charles Brasch: Journal, 17 March 1958. Charles
Brasch Papers, HC MS-0996-009/025.

8 Archibald MacLeish, 'Ars Poetica' (1926), from
Collected Poems 1917–1952, Houghton Mifflin,
Boston, 1952.

9 Charles Brasch (CB) to AC, 27 May 1958. AC
Papers, ATL 2402–28.

10 AC to J.H.E. Schroder (JHES), 30 May 1958,
continuation of 29 May 1958. J.H.E. Schroder
Papers, ATL 0280-24.

11 JHES to AC, 27 May 1958. AC Papers, ATL
2402–05.

12 Ibid.

13 AC to JHES, 29 May 1958. J.H.E. Schroder
Papers, ATL 0280-24.

14 AC to Denis Glover (DG), 6 Jan. 1958. Denis
Glover Papers, ATL 0418-009.

15 AC to DG, 20 Feb. 1958 and 6 March 1958. Denis
Glover Papers, ATL 0418-009.

16 *Auckland Star*, 17 Oct. 1968.

17 AC to R.N.M. Robertson (RNMR), 19 Feb. 1963.
AC Papers, ATL 2402–27.

18 AC to RNMR, 19 Feb. 1963. AC Papers, ATL
2402–27.

19 AC to CB, 22 May 1958. Charles Brasch Papers,
HC MS-0996-002/089.

20 AC to CB, 3 Sept. 1958. AC Papers, ATL 2402–03.

21 DG to AC, 19 March [1959]. AC Papers, ATL
2402–04.

22 AC to Ngaio Marsh (NM), 13 Feb. 1959. AC
Papers, ATL 2402–06.

23 NM to AC, 9 March 1959. AC Papers, ATL
2402–06.

24 AC to Douglas Lilburn (DL), 17 April 1959.
Douglas Lilburn Papers, ATL 7623-128.

25 AC to James Caffin, 17 June 1959. AC Papers,
ATL 2402–28.

26 NM to AC, 9 March 1959. AC Papers, ATL
2402–06.

27 Interview, *Auckland Star*, Arts section, [?June]
1959.

28 AC to James Caffin, 17 June 1959. AC Papers,
ATL 2402–28.

29 AC to James Caffin, 24 June 1959. AC Papers,
ATL 2402–28.

30 'D.L.' [David Lawson], *Auckland Star*, 10 June
1959.

31 *New Zealand Herald*, 10 June 1959.

32 Bruce Mason, *The Dominion*, [late June] 1959.

33 'E.H.B.', *Evening Standard*, [late June] 1959.

34 Sarah Campion, 'No Caviare to the General',
Moon Section, by Allen Curnow, C.A.S. Players,
July 1959, *Landfall* 51, vol. 13, no. 3, Sept. 1959, pp.
269–71.

35 AC to JW, 10 Sept. 1960. AC Papers, ATL 2402–
07.

36 *Four Plays*, A.H. & A.W. Reed, Wellington, 1972,
p. 14.

37 AC to Peter Harcourt, 13 June 1977. AC Papers,
ATL 6371-11.

38 *Four Plays*, p. 16.

39 AC to CB, 4 Oct. 1959. Charles Brasch Papers,
HC MS-0996-002/089.

40 NM to AC, [possibly 1959]. AC Papers, ATL
2402–06.

41 *Landfall* 53, vol. 14, no. 1, March 1960, pp. 98–102.

42 CB to AC, 2 Oct. 1959. AC Papers, ATL 2402–27
and Charles Brasch Papers, HC MS-0996-
002/089.

43 AC to CB, 4 Oct. 1959. Charles Brasch Papers,
HC MS-0996-002/089 and AC Papers, ATL
2402–27.

44 *Comment*, no. 3, 1960, p. 35.

45 AC to Sidney Musgrove (SM), 17 May 1960. AC
Papers, ATL 2402–06.

46 AC to DG, 13 May 1960. Denis Glover Papers,
ATL 0418-008.

47 AC to SM, 17 May 1960. AC Papers, ATL 2402–
06.

48 Interview with Belinda Curnow, 12 July 2004,
transcript, p. 18. Terry Sturm Papers, privately
held.

49 AC to SM, 17 May 1960. AC Papers, ATL 2402–06.

50 AC to DL, 23 Feb. 1960. Douglas Lilburn Papers,
ATL 7623-129.

51 DL to AC, 25 May 1960. AC Papers, ATL 2402–06.

52 Bernard Kearns (BK) to AC, 25 Aug. 1960. AC
Papers, ATL 2402–27.

53 AC to BK, 9 Sept. 1960. AC Papers, ATL 2402–06.

54 AC to DL, 8 Nov. 1960. Douglas Lilburn Papers, ATL 7623-129.

55 DL to AC, 8 Jan. 1961. AC Papers, ATL 2402-06.

56 Philip Norman, *Douglas Lilburn: His Life and Music*, Canterbury University Press, Christchurch, 2006, p. 210.

57 AC to DL, 1 Oct. 1961. Douglas Lilburn Papers, ATL 7623-129.

58 AC to DL, 23 Feb. 1960. Douglas Lilburn Papers, ATL 7623-129.

59 AC to DL, 31 May 1960. Douglas Lilburn Papers, ATL 7623-129.

60 DL to AC, 25 May 1960. AC Papers, ATL 2402-06.

61 AC to DL, 14 June 1960. Douglas Lilburn Papers, ATL 7623-129.

62 AC to JW, 10 Sept. 1960. AC Papers, ATL 2402-07.

63 Ibid.

64 AC to Dan Davin (DD), 19 June 1959. AC Papers, ATL 2402-27.

65 AC to DD, 13 Sept. 1959. AC Papers, ATL 2402-06.

66 AC to DG, 13 Feb. 1961. AC Papers, ATL 2402-04.

67 DG to AC, 21 Feb. 1961. AC Papers, ATL 2402-04.

68 R.A.K. Mason (RAKM) to AC, 23 May 1962. AC Papers, ATL 2402-06.

69 AC to JW, 10 Sept. 1960. AC Papers, ATL 2402-07.

70 Jeny Curnow, Biography of Allen Curnow, Part Two. Jeny Curnow Papers, ATL MSDL-0204.

71 AC to Tony Curnow, 6 June 1960. AC Papers, ATL 2402-07.

CHAPTER TWENTY-ONE
UNITED STATES, MARCH– SEPTEMBER 1961

1 Allen Curnow (AC), address to the Third International Congress of Artists and Writers, 'Poetry and Knowledge', typescript. AC Papers, Alexander Turnbull Library (ATL) 7573-43.

2 'The Kiwi and Mr Curnow', *Education*, Feb. 1961.

3 Allen Curnow (AC) to Jeny Tole (JT), 10 March 1961. J.M. Curnow Papers, ATL 4652-01.

4 *Education*, April 1961, pp. 91–92.

5 *Education*, Aug. 1961, pp. 221–2.

6 AC to JT, 27 March 1961. J.M. Curnow Papers, ATL 4652-01.

7 AC to JT, 1 April 1961. J.M. Curnow Papers, ATL 4652-02.

8 AC to JT, 3 April 1961. J.M. Curnow Papers, ATL 4652-02.

9 AC to Wystan Curnow (WC), 3 April 1961. Wystan Curnow Papers, privately held.

10 AC to JT, 3 April 1961. J.M. Curnow Papers, ATL 4652-02.

11 AC to C.K. Stead (CKS), 29 April 1961. C.K. Stead Papers, privately held. Unless otherwise identified, letters from AC to CKS are held in Stead's private papers (copies of which have been deposited at the Alexander Turnbull Library, Wellington, since the writing of this book).

12 AC to WC, 5 April 1961. Wystan Curnow Papers, privately held.

13 Eric Sellin to AC, 11 May 1961. AC Papers, ATL 2402-07.

14 AC to JT, 24 April 1961. J.M. Curnow Papers, ATL 4652-02.

15 AC to JT, 26 April 1961. J.M. Curnow Papers, ATL 4652-02.

16 Ibid.

17 Ibid.

18 AC, address to the Third International Congress of Artists and Writers, 'Poetry and Knowledge', typescript. AC Papers, ATL 7573-43.

19 AC to Betty Curnow, 27 April 1961. Betty Curnow Papers, ATL 86-101.

20 AC to JT, 3 May 1961. J.M. Curnow Papers, ATL 4652-03.

21 AC to JT, 29 April 1961. J.M. Curnow Papers, ATL 4652-02.

22 Fragment on Washington, untitled, [May] 1961. AC Papers, ATL 2402-14.

23 Ibid.

24 Ibid.

25 AC to JT, 9 May 1961. J.M. Curnow Papers, ATL 4652-03.

26 AC to JT, 18 May 1961. J.M. Curnow Papers, ATL 4652-03.

27 Ibid.

28 AC to Denis Glover (DG), 13 June 1961. Denis Glover Papers, ATL 0418-009.

29 AC to JT, 22 May 1961. J.M. Curnow Papers, ATL 4652-03.

30 AC to JT, 25 May 1961. J.M. Curnow Papers, ATL 4652-03.

31 AC to JT, 28 May 1961. J.M. Curnow Papers, ATL 4652-03.

32 AC to JT, 29 May 1961. J.M. Curnow Papers, ATL 4652-03.

33 AC to WC, 4 June 1961. Wystan Curnow Papers, privately held.

34 Ibid.

35 AC to WC, 12 June 1961. Wystan Curnow Papers, privately held.

36 AC to JT, 1 July 1961. J.M. Curnow Papers, ATL 4652-05.

37 Ibid.

38 AC to JT, 5 July 1961. J.M. Curnow Papers, ATL 4652-05.

39 Ibid.

40 AC to JT, 27 June 1961. J.M. Curnow Papers, ATL 4652-04.

41 AC to JT, 13 June 1961. J.M. Curnow Papers, ATL 4652-04.

42 AC to Denis Glover (DG), 22 June 1961. Denis Glover Papers, ATL 0418-009.

43 AC to JT, 7 July 1961. J.M. Curnow Papers, ATL 4652-05.

44 AC to JT, 8 July 1961. J.M. Curnow Papers, ATL 4652-05.

45 *New Zealand Herald*, 12 June 1971.

46 AC to JT, 18 July 1961. J.M. Curnow Papers, ATL 4652-05.

47 AC to JT, 24 July 1961. J.M. Curnow Papers, ATL 4652-05.
48 Ibid.
49 AC to JT, 30 July 1961. J.M. Curnow Papers, ATL 4652-05.
50 AC to JT, 5 Aug. 1961. J.M. Curnow Papers, ATL 4652-06.
51 AC to JT, 10 Aug. 1961. J.M. Curnow Papers, ATL 4652-06.
52 AC to JT, 16 Aug. 1961. J.M. Curnow Papers, ATL 4652-06.
53 AC to JT, 31 May 1961. J.M. Curnow Papers, ATL 4652-03. The biblical reference is to John 1:14, 'And the Word was made flesh and dwelt among us'. The Curnow poem is 'A Leaf', in *Poems 1949–57*: 'a syllable / Made flesh before the word'.
54 DG to AC, 27 June 1961. AC Papers, ATL 2402-28.
55 AC to JT, 31 May 1961. J.M. Curnow Papers, ATL 4652-03.
56 AC to JT, 12 May 1961. J.M. Curnow Papers, ATL 4652-03.
57 AC to Belinda Curnow, 27 June 1961. Belinda Curnow Papers, privately held.
58 AC to Betty Curnow, 6 Sept. 1961. Betty Curnow Papers, ATL 86-101.

CHAPTER TWENTY-TWO
SEPARATION AND REMARRIAGE, SEPTEMBER 1961–AUGUST 1965

1 Allen Curnow (AC) to J.H.E. Schroder (JHES), 25 Sept. 1964. J.H.E. Schroder Papers, Alexander Turnbull Library (ATL) 0280-24.
2 Betty Curnow to Douglas Lilburn (DL), 26 Oct. 1961. Douglas Lilburn Papers, ATL 7623-141.
3 AC to Denis Glover (DG), 28 Dec. 1961. Denis Glover Papers, ATL 0418-009.
4 Tim Curnow, interview with Terry Sturm (TS), 10 Sept. 2004, p. 29. Terry Sturm Papers, privately held.
5 Jeny Curnow, conversation with TS, May 2007. Terry Sturm Papers, privately held.
6 Jeny Curnow, Biography of Allen Curnow, Part Two. Jeny Curnow Papers, ATL MSDL-0204.
7 Jeny Curnow, Biography of Allen Curnow, Part Two. Jeny Curnow Papers, ATL MSDL-0204.
8 AC to DG, 27 July 1963. Denis Glover Papers, ATL 0418-009.
9 AC to Wystan Curnow (WC), 4 Nov. 1963. Wystan Curnow Papers, privately held.
10 Charles Brasch to AC, 28 Nov. 1961. Charles Brasch Papers, Hocken Collections (HC) MS-0996-002/089.
11 AC to JHES, 25 June 1962. J.H.E. Schroder Papers, ATL 0280-24.
12 *New Zealand Listener*, 29 Oct. 1965.
13 AC to R.A.K. Mason, 30 April 1963. R.A.K. Mason Papers, HC MS-0990/168.
14 Oxford University Press to AC, 9 April 1964. AC Papers, ATL 7574-80.
15 *Times Literary Supplement*, unsigned, 4 Jan. 1963.
16 James Bertram to AC, 5 Dec. 1962. AC Papers, ATL 2402-27.
17 C.K. Stead, 'Allen Curnow's Poetry', *Landfall 65*, vol. 17, no. 1, March 1963, pp. 26–45, reproduced in C.K. Stead, 'Allen Curnow: Poet of the Real', *In the Glass Case: Essays on New Zealand Literature*, Auckland University Press, Auckland, 1981, pp. 189–206.
18 'New Zealand Literature: the Case for a Working Definition', in *Look Back Harder: Critical Writings 1935–1984*, ed. Peter Simpson, Auckland University Press, Auckland, 1987, p. 205.
19 Ibid., p. 202.
20 Ibid., p. 195.
21 Ibid., p. 201.
22 AC to WC, 16 Dec. 1963. Wystan Curnow Papers, privately held.
23 *Landfall 27*, vol. 7, no. 3, Sept. 1953, pp. 216–24.
24 *Landfall 34*, vol. 9, no. 2, June 1955, pp. 160–5.
25 C.K. Stead to AC, 6 Dec. 1963. AC Papers, ATL 7574-82. Allen Curnow, '*Coal Flat*: The Major Scale, The Fine Excess', *Comment*, vol. 5, no. 1, Oct. 1963, pp. 39–42.
26 AC to WC, 4 Feb. 1964. Wystan Curnow Papers, privately held.
27 AC to Bill Pearson (WHP), 2 Nov. 1964. W.H. Pearson Papers, ATL 4343-004.
28 *Landfall 69*, vol. 18, no. 1, March 1964, pp. 58–62.
29 Information courtesy of Tim Curnow.
30 AC to WC, 15 Sept. 1963. Wystan Curnow Papers, privately held.
31 AC to WC, 14 Oct. 1963. Wystan Curnow Papers, privately held.
32 AC to PEN, 1 Oct. 1963. Tim Curnow Papers, ATL 7905-01.
33 *New Zealand Herald*, 16 March 1963.
34 AC to WC, 27 Feb. 1964. Wystan Curnow Papers, privately held.
35 *New Zealand Herald*, 22 Feb. 1964.
36 Ibid.
37 Ibid.
38 AC to DG, 20 Feb. 1964. Denis Glover Papers, ATL 0418-008.
39 AC to DG, 20 Feb. 1964, postscript. Denis Glover Papers, ATL 0418-008.
40 Arthur Rolleston Cant (ARC) to AC, 20 Sept. 1962. AC Papers, ATL 2402-28.
41 AC to ARC, 25 Sept. 1962. AC Papers, ATL 2402-28.
42 ARC to AC, 28 Sept. 1962. AC Papers, ATL 2402-28.
43 AC to WC, 18 Feb. 1964. Wystan Curnow Papers, privately held.
44 AC to WHP, 2 June 1964. W.H. Pearson Papers, ATL 4343-004.
45 Ronald Barker to AC, 16 April 1963. AC Papers, ATL 2402-27.
46 AC to WC, 4 Nov. 1963. Wystan Curnow Papers, privately held.
47 AC to JHES, 25 Sept. 1964. J.H.E. Schroder Papers, ATL 0280-24.

48 AC to WC, 28 Oct. 1964. Wystan Curnow Papers, privately held.

49 AC to WC, 14 Dec. 1964. Wystan Curnow Papers, privately held.

50 Ibid.

51 WC to AC, 14 Feb. 1965. AC Papers, ATL 7574-83.

52 AC to WC, 19 Feb. 1965. Wystan Curnow Papers, privately held.

53 AC to WC, 26 Feb. 1965. Wystan Curnow Papers, privately held.

54 AC to WHP, 5 Feb. 1965. W.H. Pearson Papers, ATL 4343-004.

55 Ibid.

56 AC to DG, 10 June 1965. Denis Glover Papers, ATL 0418-009.

57 AC to WC, 26 Feb. 1965. Wystan Curnow Papers, privately held.

58 AC to WC, 7 May 1965. Wystan Curnow Papers, privately held.

59 AC to Douglas Cleverdon, Director Poetry Society, 12 Aug. 1965. AC Papers, ATL [?7574-82/83].

60 AC to WC, 8 Sept. 1965. Wystan Curnow Papers, privately held.

61 WC to AC, 5 Oct. 1965. AC Papers, ATL 7574-83.

62 AC to WC, 8 Sept. 1965, continuation of 30 August 1965. Wystan Curnow Papers, privately held.

63 AC to JHES, 26 Oct. 1965. J.H.E. Schroder Papers, ATL 0280-24.

CHAPTER TWENTY–THREE
TRANSITIONS, 1965–71

1 Allen Curnow (AC) to Wystan Curnow (WC), 8 Oct. 1968. Wystan Curnow Papers, privately held.

2 Ezra Pound, 'Canto LIII', *The Pisan Cantos* (1948).

3 Denis Glover (DG) to AC, 25 Jan. 1943. AC Papers, Alexander Turnbull Library (ATL) 2402-04.

4 *New Zealand Listener*, 29 Oct. 1965.

5 Douglas Lilburn (DL) to AC, 26 Oct. 1965. AC Papers, ATL 2402-63.

6 'A Note in Collusion between the Author and his Publisher', *Whim Wham Land*, Blackwood & Janet Paul, Auckland, 1967, p. vii.

7 *New Zealand Herald*, 8 June 1968.

8 AC to WC, 11 June 1968. Wystan Curnow Papers, privately held.

9 *New Zealand Herald*, 9 May 1970.

10 Walter Pollard to AC, [May] 1970. AC Papers, ATL 7574-92.

11 AC to DG, 19 March 1966. Denis Glover Papers, ATL 0418-008.

12 Roy Leywood to AC, 7 June 1966. AC Papers, ATL 2402-41.

13 AC to WC, 4 July 1966. Wystan Curnow Papers, privately held.

14 *Four Plays*, A.H. & A.W. Reed, Wellington, 1972, pp. 17–18.

15 Ibid., p. 18.

16 Edgar Wind, *Pagan Mysteries in the Renaissance*, Faber & Faber, London, 1958.

17 Leave report, 12 April 1967. AC Papers, ATL 2402-38.

18 Allen Curnow (AC) to Tim Curnow, 5 Oct. 1966. Tim Curnow Papers, ATL 7905-01.

19 AC to WC, 27 Sept. 1966. Wystan Curnow Papers, privately held.

20 Ibid.

21 AC to Tim Curnow, 5 Oct. 1966. Tim Curnow Papers, ATL 7905-01.

22 Jeny Curnow, Biography of Allen Curnow, Part Two. Jeny Curnow Papers, ATL MSDL-0204.

23 AC to JHES, 16 Aug. 1967. J.H.E. Schroder Papers, ATL 0280-24.

24 AC to W.H. (Bill) Pearson (WHP), 30 Oct. 1966. W.H. Pearson Papers, ATL 4343-004.

25 AC to WHP, 21 Nov. 1966. W.H. Pearson Papers, ATL 4343-004.

26 Ibid.

27 AC to WC, 23 Nov. 1966. Wystan Curnow Papers, privately held.

28 AC to James Dickey, 26 Feb. 1968. AC Papers, ATL 2402-30.

29 AC to WC, 12 Nov. 1966. Wystan Curnow Papers, privately held.

30 AC to WHP, 21 Nov. 1966. W.H. Pearson Papers, ATL 4343-004.

31 AC to WHP, 30 Oct. and 21 Nov. 1966. W.H. Pearson Papers, ATL 4343-004.

32 AC to WC, 12 Nov. 1966. Wystan Curnow Papers, privately held.

33 AC to WHP, 21 Nov. 1966. W.H. Pearson Papers, ATL 4343-004.

34 AC to WC, 23 Nov. 1966. Wystan Curnow Papers, privately held.

35 AC to WC, 16 Oct. 1968. Wystan Curnow Papers, privately held.

36 'Manuscript Found in a Suitcase', *New Zealand Herald*, 27 Aug. 1966.

37 AC to WC, 6 Aug. 1967. Wystan Curnow Papers, privately held.

38 Eric McCormick (EM) to AC, 29 July 1967. AC Papers, ATL 2402-41.

39 AC to EM, 15 Aug. 1967. E.H. McCormick Papers, ATL 5292-012.

40 AC to Tim Curnow, 21 Aug. 1967. Tim Curnow Papers, ATL 7905-01.

41 Tim Curnow to AC, 30 Nov. 1967, 19 April 1968. AC Papers, ATL 2402-30 and 2402-31.

42 AC to WHP, 8 May 1968. W.H. Pearson Papers, ATL 4343-004.

43 Draft of introduction to 'Origins', 26 April 1968. AC Papers, ATL 7574-41.

44 Ibid.

45 AC to WC, 8 Oct. 1968. Wystan Curnow Papers, privately held.

46 AC to WC, 8 Oct. 1968. Wystan Curnow Papers, privately held.

47 AC to WC, 28 Jan. 1968. Wystan Curnow Papers, privately held.

48 AC to WC, 8 Oct. 1968. Wystan Curnow Papers, privately held.
49 William Austin to AC, 12 June 1968. AC Papers, ATL 7574-52.
50 AC to Arthur Baysting, *New Zealand Listener*, 7 March 1969, p. 9, shortly before the play's first performance.
51 AC to WC, 8 Oct. 1968. Wystan Curnow Papers, privately held.
52 AC to Arthur Baysting, *New Zealand Listener*, 7 March 1969, p. 9.
53 AC to WHP, 23 Oct 1968. W.H. Pearson Papers, ATL 4343-004.
54 *Four Plays*, A.H. & A.W. Reed, Wellington, 1972, p. 217.
55 AC to WC, 21 Jan. 1969. Wystan Curnow Papers, privately held.
56 AC to WC, 14 Oct. 1969. Wystan Curnow Papers, privately held.
57 Denis Glover (DG) to AC, 21 Aug. 1969. AC Papers, ATL 2402-31.
58 AC to Tony Curnow, 26 April 1970. Anthony Curnow Papers, privately held.
59 *New Zealand Herald*, 17 July 1971.
60 Allen Tate to Roy Basler (RB), 29 June 1971. AC Papers, ATL 7574-87.
61 Richard Eberhart to RB, 27 June 1971. AC Papers, ATL 7574-87.
62 AC to RB, 14 July 1971. AC Papers, ATL 2402-47.
63 AC to Tony Curnow, 21 Nov 1971. Anthony Curnow Papers, privately held.
64 Jeny Curnow to Tony Curnow, 22 May 1969. Anthony Curnow Papers, privately held.
65 AC to Tony Curnow, 26 Nov. 1971. Anthony Curnow Papers, privately held.
66 AC to DG, 13 Dec. 1971. Denis Glover Papers, ATL 0418-011.

CHAPTER TWENTY-FOUR
THE MAKING OF A SEQUENCE: *TREES, EFFIGIES, MOVING OBJECTS*, 1972

1 'Conversation with Allen Curnow', Allen Curnow interviewed by M.P. Jackson, *Islands*, vol. 2, no. 2, Winter 1973, in *Look Back Harder: Critical Writings 1935–1984*, ed. Peter Simpson, Auckland University Press, Auckland, 1987, p. 264.
2 Allen Curnow (AC) to Robin Dudding (RD), 15 July 1972. AC Papers, Alexander Turnbull Library (ATL) 2402-43.
3 Ibid.
4 ATL Papers, [?late June/early July] 1972.
5 AC to W.H. (Bill) Pearson (WHP), 2 Feb. 1968. W.H. Pearson Papers, ATL 4343-004.
6 AC to RD, 15 July 1972. AC Papers, ATL 2402-43.
7 'Conversation with Allen Curnow', in *Look Back Harder*, p. 259.
8 Frank Doggett, *Stevens' Poetry of Thought*, Johns Hopkins Press, Baltimore, 1966.
9 Roy Harvey Pearce and J. Hillis Miller (eds), *The Act of the Mind: Essays on the Poetry of Wallace Stevens*, Johns Hopkins Press, Baltimore, 1965.

10 J. Hillis Miller, 'Wallace Stevens's Poetry of Being', in *The Act of the Mind*, p. 144.
11 Ibid., p. 146.
12 Ibid., p. 154.
13 Ibid., p. 153.
14 Ibid., p. 159.
15 Ibid., p. 160.
16 Ibid., pp. 161–2.
17 Jean Seznec, *The Survival of the Pagan Gods: The Mythological Tradition and Its Place in Renaissance Humanism and Art*, trans. Barbara F. Sessions, Harper Torchbooks, New York, 1961.
18 Edgar Wind, *Pagan Mysteries in the Renaissance*, Faber & Faber, London, 1958.
19 G.S. Kirk, *Myth: Its Meaning and Functions in Ancient and Other Cultures*, Cambridge University Press, London, 1970.
20 Ibid., p. 2.
21 Ibid., p. vi.
22 Ibid., p. vii.
23 Ibid., p. vi.
24 *Four Plays*, A.H. & A.W. Reed, Wellington, 1972, p. 10.
25 *Four Plays*, pp. 10–11.
26 Ibid., p. 11.
27 Ibid., p. 12.
28 Ibid., p. 16.
29 Ibid., p. 17.
30 Ibid., p. 17.
31 J. Hillis Miller, 'Wallace Stevens's Poetry of Being', in *The Act of the Mind*, pp. 161–2.
32 Friedrich Nietzsche, *Twilight of the Idols; and, The Anti-Christ*, trans. R.J. Hollingdale, Penguin, Harmondsworth, 1968, p. 53. Nietzsche's italics.
33 Friedrich Nietzsche, *The Gay Science*, trans. Walter Kaufmann, Random House, New York, 1974, p. 140.
34 'Notes toward a Supreme Fiction', *The Collected Poems of Wallace Stevens*, Faber & Faber, London, 1959, pp. 380–408.
35 Sister M. Vianney to AC, 17 Dec. 1971. AC Papers, ATL 2402-68.
36 AC to Denis Glover (DG), 19 April 1972. Denis Glover Papers, ATL 0418-011.
37 DG to AC, 20 May 1972. AC Papers, ATL 2402-43.
38 AC to DG, 24 May 1972. Denis Glover Papers, ATL 0418-011 and AC Papers, ATL 2402-43.
39 DG to AC, 20 May 1972. AC Papers, ATL 2402-43.
40 AC to DG, 24 May 1972. Denis Glover Papers, ATL 0418-011 and AC Papers, ATL 2402-43.
41 AC to DG, 23 June 1972. Denis Glover Papers, ATL 0418-011.
42 DG to Albion Wright (AW), 9 July 1972. Denis Glover Papers, ATL 0418-062.
43 DG to AW, 22 July 1972. Denis Glover Papers, ATL 0418-062.
44 DG to AC, 6 Aug. 1972. AC Papers, [?ATL 2402-43].
45 AC to DG, 11 Aug. 1972. Denis Glover Papers, ATL 0418-011.

46 DG to AC, 11 Nov. 1972. Denis Glover Papers, ATL 0418-011.
47 AC to DG, 13 Nov. 1972. AC Papers, ATL 2402-44.
48 AC to Tim Curnow, 13 Nov. 1972. Tim Curnow Papers, ATL 7905-02.

CHAPTER TWENTY-FIVE
NEW AND COLLECTED POEMS, 1973

1 Allen Curnow (AC) to Denis Glover (DG), 31 Oct. 1973. Denis Glover Papers, Alexander Turnbull Library (ATL), 0418-012.
2 AC to DG, 13 Nov. 1972. AC Papers, ATL 2402-44.
3 AC to Tony Curnow, 21 Nov. 1971. Anthony Curnow Papers, privately held.
4 AC to Tony Curnow, 6 July 1972. Anthony Curnow Papers, privately held.
5 AC to Tim Curnow, 1 Feb. 1973. Tim Curnow Papers, ATL 7905-03.
6 AC to Tony Curnow, 2 Sept. 1972. Anthony Curnow Papers, privately held.
7 AC to Tony Curnow, 18 March 1973. Anthony Curnow Papers, privately held.
8 AC to Tim Curnow, 12 Dec. 1972. Tim Curnow Papers, ATL 7905-02.
9 AC to Tim Curnow, 4 Feb. 1973. Tim Curnow Papers, ATL 7905-03.
10 *Islands*, vol. 2, no. 2, Winter 1973.
11 AC to Tim Curnow, 4 Feb. 1973. Tim Curnow Papers, ATL 7905-03.
12 AC to Ted Wall (TW), 15 April 1973. AC Papers, ATL, 2402-49.
13 AC to DG, 19 Nov. 1973. Denis Glover Papers, ATL 0418-012.
14 AC to DG, 31 Oct. 1973. Denis Glover Papers, ATL 0418-012.
15 AC to Ian Milner (IM), 18–30 Aug. 1974. Ian Milner Papers, ATL 4567-009.
16 'Two Prefaces', in *Look Back Harder: Critical Writings 1935–1984*, ed. Peter Simpson, Auckland University Press, Auckland, 1987, pp. 243–4.
17 Ibid., p. xii.
18 Hugh Roberts, 'An appreciation of Allen Curnow', *New Zealand Books*, issue 22, Winter 1996.
19 Janet Hughes, 'Misconceiving Curnow', Letters, *New Zealand Books*, issue 23, Spring 1996.
20 Allen Curnow, 'Revisions do supersede', Letters, *New Zealand Books*, Summer 1996.
21 Ibid.
22 AC to DG, 31 Oct. 1973. Denis Glover Papers, ATL 0418-012.
23 AC to DG, 19 Nov. 1973. Denis Glover Papers, ATL 0418-012.
24 AC to TW, 7 Aug. 1973. AC Papers, ATL 2402-42.
25 Ibid.
26 AC to TW, 9 Aug. 1973. AC Papers, ATL 2402-42.
27 DG to David Elworthy, 16 Oct. 1974. AC Papers, ATL 2402-15.
28 AC to Wystan Curnow (WC), 2 March 1973. Wystan Curnow Papers, privately held.
29 AC to DG, 28 April 1973. Denis Glover Papers, ATL 0418-012.

30 AC to DG, 13 May 1973. Denis Glover Papers, ATL 0418-012.
31 AC to DG, 24 May 1973. Denis Glover Papers, ATL 0418-012.
32 AC to DG and Robert Gormack (RG), 22 Sept. 1973. Denis Glover Papers, ATL 0418-012.
33 AC to J.G.A. Pocock, 22 July 1991. J.G.A. Pocock Papers, privately held.
34 AC Papers, ATL 2402-68.
35 DG to RG, [Sept.] 1973. AC Papers, ATL 2402-43.
36 DG to RG, 7 Nov. 1973. AC Papers, ATL 2402-42.
37 AC to DG, [Nov.] 1973. AC Papers, ATL 2402-42.
38 AC to DG, 30 July 1973. AC Papers, ATL 2402-42. Curnow's italics.
39 AC to DG, 31 Oct. 1973. Denis Glover Papers, ATL 0418-012.
40 'Conversation with Allen Curnow', AC interviewed by M.P. Jackson, *Islands*, vol. 2, no. 2, Winter 1973, p. 147.
41 Ibid., p. 148.
42 AC to Alan Roddick (AR), 26 May 1973. Alan Roddick Papers, privately held.
43 AR to AC, 7 May 1973. AC Papers, ATL 2402-42.
44 AC to AR, 12 Nov. 1973. Alan Roddick Papers, privately held.
45 AC to IM, 22 Nov. 1973. Ian Milner Papers, ATL 4567-009.

CHAPTER TWENTY-SIX
DISCOVERING EUROPE: LEAVE, 1974

1 Allen Curnow (AC) to C.K. Stead (CKS), 8 Aug. 1974. C.K. Stead Papers, privately held. Unless otherwise identified, letters from AC to CKS are held in Stead's private papers (copies of which have been deposited at the Alexander Turnbull Library, Wellington, since the writing of this book).
2 AC to Wystan Curnow (WC), 23 March 1974. Wystan Curnow Papers, privately held.
3 Ibid.
4 AC to Tony Curnow, 20 March 1974. Anthony Curnow Papers, privately held.
5 Jeny Curnow (JC): Diary, 14 April 1974. J.M. Curnow Papers, Alexander Turnbull Library (ATL) 5483-1.
6 AC to Belinda Curnow, 26 June 1974. Belinda Curnow Papers, privately held.
7 AC to WC, 16 April 1974. Wystan Curnow Papers, privately held.
8 AC to Belinda Curnow, 29 April 1974. Belinda Curnow Papers, privately held.
9 AC to Tony Curnow, 23 April 1974. Anthony Curnow Papers, privately held.
10 AC to Belinda Curnow, 7 May 1974. Belinda Curnow Papers, privately held.
11 AC to WC, 18 May 1974. Wystan Curnow Papers, privately held.
12 AC to Belinda Curnow, 7 May 1974. Belinda Curnow Papers, privately held.
13 JC: Diary, 9 May 1974. J.M. Curnow Papers, ATL 5483-1.

14 AC to Ian Milner (IM), 18 Aug. 1974. Ian Milner Papers, ATL 4567-009.
15 JC to WC, 13 June 1974. Wystan Curnow Papers, privately held.
16 AC to W.H. (Bill) Pearson (WHP), 28 June 1974. W.H. Pearson Papers, ATL 4343-005.
17 AC to WC, 5 June 1974. Wystan Curnow Papers, privately held.
18 Ibid.
19 AC to WC, 8 June 1974. Wystan Curnow Papers, privately held.
20 AC to Belinda Curnow, 26 June 1974. Belinda Curnow Papers, privately held.
21 AC to IM, 18 Aug. 1974. Ian Milner Papers, ATL 4567-009.
22 AC to WC, 12 Aug. 1974. Wystan Curnow Papers, privately held.
23 Ibid.
24 Ibid.
25 AC to WHP, 28 June 1974. W.H. Pearson Papers, ATL 4343-005.
26 'Moro Assassinato', Part IV '16 March 1978', *An Incorrigible Music*, Auckland University Press/Oxford University Press, 1979, p. 39.
27 AC to WC, 19 Nov. 1974. Wystan Curnow Papers, privately held.
28 Ibid.
29 AC to CKS, 14 Nov. 1974.

CHAPTER TWENTY-SEVEN
EUROPE REVISITED, AND *AN INCORRIGIBLE MUSIC*, 1975–78

1   Allen Curnow (AC) to Tony Curnow, 3 March 1976. Anthony Curnow Papers, privately held.
2   AC to Tony Curnow, 7 Dec. 1976. Anthony Curnow Papers, privately held.
3   Ibid.
4   AC to Douglas Lilburn (DL), 7 March 1975. Douglas Lilburn Papers, Alexander Turnbull Library (ATL) 7623-131.
5   AC to C.K. Stead (CKS), 20 April 1974. C.K. Stead Papers, privately held. Unless otherwise identified, letters from AC to CKS are held in Stead's private papers (copies of which have been deposited at the Alexander Turnbull Library, Wellington, since the writing of this book).
6   CKS to AC, 18 July 1974. AC Papers, ATL 2402-26.
7   AC to CKS, 8 Aug. 1975.
8   Ibid.
9   AC to Tim Curnow, 12 Nov. 1975. Tim Curnow Papers, ATL 7905-04.
10 AC to Tim Curnow, 13 June 1975. Tim Curnow Papers, ATL 7905-04.
11 AC to Tim Curnow, 16 June 1975. Tim Curnow Papers, ATL 7905-04.
12 AC to Eric McCormick, 13 Oct.1977. E.H. McCormick Papers, ATL 5292-012.
13 AC to Tony Curnow, 15 March 1977. Anthony Curnow Papers, privately held.
14 AC to Wystan Curnow, 27 May 1977. Wystan Curnow Papers, privately held.

15 AC Papers, ATL 2402-19.
16 Script for 'The Poet's Tongue', broadcast by ABC, Oct. 1982, AC Papers, ATL 2402-61.
17 Ibid.
18 DG to AC, 9 Feb. 1978. AC Papers, ATL 2402-17.
19 AC to DL, 1 Aug. 1977. Douglas Lilburn Papers, ATL 7623-131.
20 AC to Tim Curnow, 7 Sept. 1977. Tim Curnow Papers, ATL 7905-05.
21 AC to CKS, 27 Oct. 1977.
22 CKS to AC [Dec./Jan., 1977/78]. AC Papers, ATL 2402-32.
23 AC to CKS, 21 Dec. 1977.
24 AC to CKS, 18 March 1978.
25 AC to Tim Curnow, 23 March 1978. Tim Curnow Papers, ATL 7905-05.
26 AC to W.H. (Bill) Pearson (WHP), 12 April 1978. W.H. Pearson Papers, ATL 4343-005.
27 Author's note in *An Incorrigible Music*, Auckland University Press/Oxford University Press, Auckland, 1979.
28 AC to CKS, 19 May 1978.
29 AC to Tony Curnow, 11 May 1978. Anthony Curnow Papers, privately held.
30 Ibid.
31 AC, interview with Ted Reynolds, *New Zealand Herald*, Aug. 1979.
32 AC to Tim Curnow, 20 May 1978. Tim Curnow Papers, ATL 7905-05.
33 Ibid.
34 AC to WHP, 16 May 1978. W.H. Pearson Papers, ATL 4343-005.
35 AC to WHP, 29 May 1978. W.H. Pearson Papers, ATL 4343-005.
36 Ibid.
37 Author's note in *An Incorrigible Music*.
38 JC: Diary, 5 July 1978. J.M. Curnow Papers, ATL 5483-2.
39 AC to Tony Curnow, 10 July 1978. Anthony Curnow Papers, privately held.
40 AC to CKS, 4 Sept. 1978.
41 Anthony Thwaite to AC, 13 Sept. 1978. AC Papers, ATL 2402-32.
42 AC to CKS, 18 Sept. 1978.

CHAPTER TWENTY-EIGHT
RETURN TO NEW ZEALAND, 'MORO ASSASSINATO', 1978–79

1   Allen Curnow (AC) to C.K. Stead (CKS), 21 Nov. 1978. C.K. Stead Papers, privately held. Unless otherwise identified, letters from AC to CKS are held in Stead's private papers (copies of which have been deposited at the Alexander Turnbull Library, Wellington, since the writing of this book).
2   AC to Tim Curnow, Election Eve, Nov. 1978. Tim Curnow Papers, Alexander Turnbull Library (ATL) 7905-05.
3   AC to CKS, 23 Feb. 1979.
4   AC to Tim Curnow, 18 Feb. 1979. Tim Curnow Papers, ATL 7905-05.

5 AC to CKS, 23 Feb. 1979.
6 'In the Duomo', Part III 'A Turning Point in History', *An Incorrigible Music*, Auckland University Press/Oxford University Press, 1979, p. 18.
7 AC Papers, ATL 2402-19.
8 Leonardo Sciascia, *The Moro Affair: And, the Mystery of Majorana*, Carcanet, Manchester, 1987, p. 73.
9 AC to Allan Cole, [Aug.] 1979. AC Papers, 2402-61.
10 *New Zealand Herald*, 22 Feb. 1975.
11 *New Zealand Herald*, 13 May 1972.
12 AC to Tony Curnow, 9 April 1976. Anthony Curnow Papers, privately held.
13 *New Zealand Herald*, 10 April 1976.
14 AC to Tony Curnow, 9 April 1976. Anthony Curnow Papers, privately held.
15 *New Zealand Herald*, 26 May 1973.
16 Norman Macbeth to AC, 30 May 1973. AC Papers, ATL 2402-42.
17 *New Zealand Listener*, 29 Sept. 1979, pp. 17–19.
18 *Islands* 27, vol. 7, no. 5, 1979.
19 AC to Desmond Graham, 27 Nov. 1981. AC Papers, ATL 7574-62.
20 AC to Tony Curnow, 12 June 1979. Anthony Curnow Papers, privately held.
21 See report on the conference, with a photograph of Curnow and Lilburn, in the *New Zealand Listener*, 29 Sept. 1979.
22 '"Dichtung und Wahrheit": A Letter to *Landfall*', in *Look Back Harder: Critical Writings 1935–1984*, ed. Peter Simpson, Auckland University Press, Auckland, 1987, p. 326.
23 Ibid., p. 327.
24 AC to Tim Curnow, 28 Oct. 1979. Tim Curnow Papers, ATL 7905-05.

CHAPTER TWENTY-NINE
A GROWING UK REPUTATION, *YOU WILL KNOW WHEN YOU GET THERE*, 1980–81
1 Allen Curnow (AC) to Tim Curnow, 10 March 1980. Tim Curnow Papers, Alexander Turnbull Library (ATL) 7905-06.
2 Jacket note, *You Will Know When You Get There*, Auckland University Press, Auckland, 1982.
3 Chris Wallace-Crabbe, 'That Second Body: An Australian View of Allen Curnow's Progress', *Ariel*, vol. 16, no. 4, Oct. 1985, p. 74.
4 AC to Tim Curnow, 9 April 1980. Tim Curnow Papers, ATL 7905-06.
5 AC to C.K. Stead (CKS), 12 June 1980. C.K. Stead Papers, privately held. Unless otherwise identified, letters from AC to CKS are held in Stead's private papers (copies of which have been deposited at the Alexander Turnbull Library, Wellington, since the writing of this book).
6 Chris Miller, 'Allen Curnow as Post-Modern Metaphysical', *PN Review* 105, vol. 22, no. 1, Sept.–Oct. 1995, p. 35.

7 AC to Tim Curnow, 10 March 1980. Tim Curnow Papers, ATL 7905-06.
8 CKS to AC, 10 June 1980. AC Papers, ATL 2402-44 and C.K. Stead Papers, privately held.
9 AC to Tony Curnow, 6 Oct. 1980. Anthony Curnow Papers, privately held.
10 AC to Tim Curnow, 9 April 1980. Tim Curnow Papers, ATL 7905-06.
11 *Islands* 27, vol. 7, no. 5, 1979, pp. 467–86.
12 C.K. Stead, 'Preliminary: From Wystan to Carlos: Modern and Modernism in Recent New Zealand Poetry', in *In the Glass Case: Essays on New Zealand Literature*, Auckland University Press, Auckland, 1981, p. 145.
13 Ibid., p. 146.
14 Ibid., p. 147.
15 Ibid., pp. 145, 154.
16 Ibid., p. 145.
17 Ibid., p. 155.
18 AC to Tim Curnow, 9 April 1980. Tim Curnow Papers, ATL 7905-06.
19 AC Papers, ATL 7574-59.
20 C.K. Stead, 'From Wystan to Carlos', p. 148.
21 Ibid., p. 149.
22 Ibid., p. 146.
23 AC Papers, ATL 7574-59.
24 C.K. Stead, *In the Glass Case*, p. 284.
25 *Islands* 29, vol. 8, no. 2, 1980, p. 164.
26 Ibid., p. 165.
27 Ibid.
28 AC to CKS, 26 April 1980.
29 CKS to AC, 30 April 1980. AC Papers, ATL 2402-44 and C.K. Stead Papers, privately held.
30 AC to CKS, 6 May 1980.
31 AC to CKS, 15 July 1980.
32 CKS to AC, 9 May 1980. AC Papers, ATL 7574-78.
33 Ibid.
34 Ibid.
35 AC to CKS, 23 May 1980.
36 Ibid.
37 AC to CKS, 15 July 1980.
38 Alistair Paterson, ed., *15 Contemporary New Zealand Poets*, Pilgrims South Press, Dunedin, 1980, pp. xxii, xv.
39 AC to Tim Curnow, 30 May 1980. Tim Curnow Papers, ATL 7905-06.
40 'Olson as Oracle: 'Projective Verse' Thirty Years On', *The Turnbull Library Record*, vol. 15, no. 1, May 1982, pp. 31–44, and in *Look Back Harder*, ed. Peter Simpson, Auckland University Press, Auckland, 1987, p. 305.
41 AC to CKS, 18 Aug. 1980.
42 *New Zealand Listener*, 6 Sept. 1980, p. 22.
43 CKS to AC, 27 Aug. [1980]. AC Papers, ATL 2402-44 and C.K. Stead Papers, privately held.
44 AC to CKS, 29 Aug. 1980.
45 AC to Denis Glover (DG), 2 Dec. 1943. Denis Glover Papers, ATL 0418-008.
46 Douglas Lilburn (DL) to AC, 21 Sept. 1981. AC Papers, ATL 2402-60.

47 Denis Glover (DG) to AC, 18 July 1980. AC Papers, ATL 2402-44.
48 AC to CKS, 15 July 1980.
49 AC to Tony Curnow, 6 Oct. 1980. Anthony Curnow Papers, privately held.
50 AC to CKS, 31 Oct. 1980.
51 AC to DG, 29 Aug. 1978. Denis Glover Papers, ATL 80-387-001.
52 AC to Dennis McEldowney (DM), 22 July 1981, Auckland University Press (AUP) Correspondence Files.
53 AC Papers, ATL 2402-68.
54 Eliot R. Davis, *A Link With the Past*, Auckland, Oswald-Sealy, 1949.
55 Dick Scott, *Fire on the Clay: The Pakeha Comes to West Auckland*, Auckland, Southern Cross Books, 1979.
56 AC to W.H. (Bill) Pearson (WHP), 27 Feb. 1981. W.H. Pearson Papers, ATL 4343-005.
57 AC to CKS, 24 April 1981.
58 CKS to AC, 24 April 1981. AC Papers, ATL 2402-48 and C.K. Stead Papers, privately held.
59 Draft in C.K. Stead Papers, privately held.
60 CKS to AC, 8 July 1981. AC Papers, ATL 2402-48.
61 AC to WHP, 31 Oct. 1981. W.H. Pearson Papers, ATL 4343-005.
62 AC to Elizabeth Alley, 11 June 1982. Elizabeth Alley, private papers.
63 AC to DL, 4 June 1982. Douglas Lilburn Papers, ATL 7623-133.
64 AC to CKS, [July] 1981.
65 Arthur Schopenhauer, *Essays and Aphorisms*, trans. R.J. Hollingdale, Penguin, 1970, p. 73. Schopenhauer's italics.
66 Donald Davie to AC, 1 Aug. 1981. AC Papers, ATL 2402-56.
67 Michael Schmidt to AC, 22 Oct. 1981. AC Papers, ATL 2402-56.
68 AC to Tony Curnow, 8 March 1982. Anthony Curnow Papers, privately held.
69 AC to DM, 6 Dec. 1981. AUP Correspondence Files.

CHAPTER THIRTY
CURNOW AND THE THEORY OF 'OPEN FORM', APARTHEID, BRISBANE WRITERS' WEEK, 1981–82

1 Allen Curnow (AC) Papers, Alexander Turnbull Library (ATL) 2402-40.
2 AC to Douglas Lilburn (DL), 31 May 1981. Douglas Lilburn Papers, ATL 7623-133.
3 AC to C.K. Stead (CKS), 19 July 1981. C.K. Stead Papers, privately held. Unless otherwise identified, letters from AC to CKS are held in Stead's private papers (copies of which have been deposited at the Alexander Turnbull Library, Wellington, since the writing of this book).
4 *Islands* 30, vol. 8, no. 3, 1981. C.K. Stead, *Walking Westward*, The Shed, Auckland, 1979.
5 AC to Tim Curnow, 9 April 1980. Tim Curnow Papers, ATL 7905-06.
6 Alistair Paterson, ed., *15 Contemporary New Zealand Poets*, Pilgrims South Press, Dunedin, 1980.
7 AC to W.H. (Bill) Pearson (WHP), 10 June 1981. W.H. Pearson Papers, ATL 4343-005.
8 AC, 'Olson as Oracle: "Projective Verse" Thirty Years On', in *Look Back Harder: Critical Writings 1935–1984*, ed. Peter Simpson, Auckland University Press, Auckland, 1987, pp. 307, 316.
9 Ibid., p. 313.
10 Ibid., p. 314.
11 Ibid, p. 315.
12 C.K. Stead, 'Preliminary: From Wystan to Carlos: Modern and Modernism in Recent New Zealand Poetry', in *In the Glass Case: Essays on New Zealand Literature*, Auckland University Press, Auckland, 1981, p. 149.
13 AC Papers, ATL 2402-40.
14 CKS to AC, 27 July 1981. AC Papers, ATL 2402-48.
15 AC to CKS, 30 July 1981.
16 Michael Schmidt (MS) to AC, 3 Aug. 1982. AC Papers, ATL 2402-56.
17 AC to Michael Schmidt, 4 Aug. 1982. AC Papers, ATL 2402-56.
18 AC to Tony Curnow, 8 March 1982. Anthony Curnow Papers, privately held.
19 AC to Tim Curnow, 27 Feb. 1982. Tim Curnow Papers, ATL 7905-06.
20 See introduction to *Whim Wham's New Zealand: The Best of Whim Wham 1937–1988*, ed. Terry Sturm, Vintage, Auckland, 2005, p. 17.
21 AC to WHP, 3 April 1981. W.H. Pearson Papers, ATL 4343-005.
22 *New Zealand Herald*, 27 June 1981.
23 AC to Tony Curnow, 5 Aug. 1981. Anthony Curnow Papers, privately held.
24 AC Papers, ATL 2402-64.
25 AC to Tim Curnow, 14 Sept. 1981. Tim Curnow Papers, ATL 7905-06.
26 AC to WHP, 17 Oct. 1981. W.H. Pearson Papers, ATL 4343-005.
27 AC to CKS, 12 Aug. 1981.
28 AC to CKS, [?14 Aug. 1981].
29 Alan Roddick, *New Zealand Writers and their Work: Allen Curnow*, Oxford University Press, Wellington, 1980.
30 *The Letters of A.R.D. Fairburn*, ed. Lauris Edmond, Oxford University Press, Auckland, 1981.
31 AC to WHP, 29 Nov. 1981. W.H. Pearson Papers, ATL 4343-005.
32 AC to Tim Curnow, 14 April 1982. Tim Curnow Papers, ATL 7905-06.
33 AC to CKS, 15 May 1982.
34 AC to Tim Curnow, 4 Sept. 1982. AC Papers, ATL 2402-61 and Tim Curnow Papers, ATL 7905-10.
35 AC to CKS, 25 Oct. 1982.
36 AC to DL, 23 Oct. 1982. AC Papers, ATL 2402-45 and Douglas Lilburn Papers, ATL 7623-133.
37 AC to Secretary, Katherine Mansfield Memorial Fellowship, 14 July 1982. AC Papers, ATL 2402-70.

38 AC to W.H. Oliver, 6 Dec. 1982. AC Papers, ATL 2402-57.

39 AC Papers, ATL 2402-59.

40 AC to CKS, 18 Dec. 1982.

41 *New Zealand Listener*, 12 March 1983.

CHAPTER THIRTY-ONE
MENTON, LONDON AND TORONTO,
THE LOOP IN LONE KAURI ROAD, 1983–86

1 'Creeley / Paterson: A Conversation', Albuquerque, New Mexico, 11 Nov. 1982, *Buff* No. 3½, State University of New York at Buffalo, 1983, p. 45.

2 Jeny Curnow (JC) to W.H. (Bill) Pearson (WHP), 17 April 1983. W.H. Pearson Papers, Alexander Turnbull Library (ATL) 4343-006.

3 Allen Curnow (AC) to Tony Curnow, 12 April 1983. Anthony Curnow Papers, privately held.

4 Ibid. Antony Alpers, *The Life of Katherine Mansfield*, Jonathan Cape, London, 1980.

5 AC to Tim Curnow, 19 May 1983. Tim Curnow Papers, ATL 7905-07.

6 Jeny Curnow, Biography of Allen Curnow, Part Two. Jeny Curnow Papers, ATL MSDL-0204.

7 AC to WHP, 16 June 1983. W.H. Pearson Papers, ATL 4343-006.

8 AC to Secretary, Katherine Mansfield Memorial Fellowship, 14 July 1982. AC Papers, ATL 2402-70.

9 JC to WHP, with postscript by AC, 29 Aug. 1983. W.H. Pearson Papers, ATL 4343-006.

10 JC: Diary, 20 July 1983. J.M. Curnow Papers, ATL 5483-3.

11 AC to WHP, 24 July 1983. W.H. Pearson Papers, ATL 4343-006.

12 AC to C.K. Stead (CKS), 24 Aug. 1983. C.K. Stead Papers, privately held. Unless otherwise identified, letters from AC to CKS are held in Stead's private papers (copies of which have been deposited at the Alexander Turnbull Library, Wellington, since the writing of this book).

13 AC to CKS, 24 Aug. 1983.

14 AC to Douglas Lilburn (DL), 24 March 1984. Douglas Lilburn Papers, ATL 7623-134.

15 See AC to CKS, 6 May 1980 and AC letter, *Islands* 29, vol. 8, no. 2, 1980, p. 164, discussed in Chapter 29 beneath 'Brand-name poetics': Stead's 'From Wystan to Carlos' and 'open form', pp. 535-42.

16 Jeny Curnow to WHP, with postscript by AC, 29 Aug. 1983. W.H. Pearson Papers, ATL 4343-006.

17 AC to CKS, 15 Sept. 1983.

18 'Creeley / Paterson: A Conversation', Albuquerque, New Mexico, 11 Nov. 1982, p. 45.

19 *Observer*, 16 Oct. 1983.

20 AC to Tim Curnow, 25 Oct. 1983. Tim Curnow Papers, ATL 7905-07.

21 'Allen Curnow: A Loop in Lone Kauri Road', *The Loop in Lone Kauri Road*, Lopdell House Gallery, Waitakere, 1995, p. 10.

22 'Allen Curnow talks to Peter Simpson', *Landfall* 175, vol. 44, no. 3, Sept. 1990, p. 306; reprinted in *In the Same Room: Conversations with New Zealand Writers*, ed. Elizabeth Alley and Mark Williams, Auckland University Press, Auckland, 1992, p. 90.

23 Ibid., pp. 306, 90.

24 AC to CKS, 9 June 1984.

25 AC to DL, 17 July 1984. Douglas Lilburn Papers, ATL 7623-134.

26 *The Loop in Lone Kauri Road: Poems 1983–1985*, Auckland University Press/Oxford University Press, Auckland, 1986, p. 37.

27 CKS to AC, 28 Oct. 1984. AC Papers, ATL 4650-06.

28 AC to Tony Curnow, 11 July 1984. Anthony Curnow Papers, privately held.

29 AC to CKS, 7 Nov. 1984. AC Papers, ATL 4650-06 and C.K. Stead Papers, privately held.

30 AC Papers, ATL 2402-71.

31 AC to CKS, 7 Nov. 1984. AC Papers, ATL 4650-06 and C.K. Stead Papers, privately held.

32 AC to Dennis McEldowney (DM), 29 Nov. 1984. Auckland University Press (AUP) Correspondence Files.

33 AC to CKS, 12 Dec. 1984. AC Papers, ATL 4650-06 and C.K. Stead Papers, privately held (copies of which have been deposited at the Alexander Turnbull Library, Wellington, since the writing of this book).

34 AC to DM, 9 Jan. 1985. AUP Correspondence Files.

35 AC to CKS, 3 April 1985.

36 AC to Tony Curnow, 15 Sept. 1984. Anthony Curnow Papers, privately held.

37 *Landfall* 151, vol. 38, no. 3, Sept. 1984, pp. 375-7.

38 'Author's Note', in *Look Back Harder: Critical Writings 1935–1984*, ed. Peter Simpson, Auckland University Press, Auckland, 1987, p. viii.

39 AC to Peter Simpson (PS), 14 April 1984. AC Papers, ATL 2402-58.

40 AC to PS, 22 Dec. 1985. Peter Simpson Papers, privately held.

41 AC to PS, 30 Jan. 1986. AC Papers, ATL 90-226-1/1.

42 AC to PS, 10 Oct. 1986. AC Papers, ATL 90-226-1/1.

43 C.K. Stead, 'Preliminary: From Wystan to Carlos: Modern and Modernism in Recent New Zealand Poetry', in *In the Glass Case: Essays on New Zealand Literature*, Auckland University Press, Auckland, 1981, pp. 139–59; originally published in *Islands* 27, vol. 7, no. 5, 1979, pp. 467–86. Alistair Paterson, ed., *15 Contemporary New Zealand Poets*, Pilgrims South Press, Dunedin, 1980.

44 *Talking About Ourselves: Twelve New Zealand Poets in conversation with Harry Ricketts*, Mallinson Rendel, Wellington, 1986.

45 AC to Harry Ricketts (HR), 7 March 1985. AC Papers, ATL 7574-91.

46 AC to Tim Curnow, 21 Nov. 1984. AC Papers, ATL 4650-11 and Tim Curnow Papers, ATL 7905-07.

47 AC to Tim Curnow, 9 Nov. 1984. AC Papers, ATL 4650-11 and Tim Curnow Papers, ATL 7905-07.
48 AC to Tim Curnow, 15 Sept. 1984. Tim Curnow Papers, ATL 7905-07.
49 AC to HR, 7 March 1985. AC Papers, ATL 7574-91.
50 AC, interview with Bruce Harding (BH), 8 Oct. 1984. Bruce Harding Papers, privately held.
51 AC to Robyn Marsack, 16 Jan. 1985. AC Papers, ATL 90-226-1/2.
52 Robyn Marsack, 'A Home in Thought: Three New Zealand Poets', PN Review 46, vol. 12, no. 2, Nov.–Dec. 1985.
53 AC to CKS, 2 June 1985.
54 AC to DL, 3 July 1985. Douglas Lilburn Papers, ATL 7623-135.
55 AC to WHP, 26 June 1985. W.H. Pearson Papers, ATL 4343-006.
56 AC to New Zealand Literary Fund, 24 July 1985. AC Papers, ATL 90-226-1/2.
57 AC to CKS, 18 June 1985.
58 AC to WHP, 26 June 1985. W.H. Pearson Papers, ATL 4343-006.
59 Ibid.
60 AC to CKS, 29 June 1985.
61 AC to WHP, 26 June 1985. W.H. Pearson Papers, ATL 4343-006.
62 AC to DL, [Nov.] 1985. AC Papers, ATL 4650-08.
63 Ibid.
64 Michael Hulse, interview with TS, 9 Sept. 2003. Terry Sturm Papers, privately held.
65 Ibid.
66 David Lange to AC, 15 Nov. 1985. AC Papers, ATL 7574-15.
67 AC to DL, 25 Sept. 1985. Douglas Lilburn Papers, ATL 7623-135.
68 AC to CKS, 11 Aug. 1985.
69 Ibid.

CHAPTER THIRTY-TWO
INTERNATIONAL RECOGNITION,
CONTINUUM AND *SELECTED POEMS*
(VIKING), 1986–90

1 Allen Curnow (AC) to Richard Mayne (RM), 19 Oct. 1986. AC Papers, Alexander Turnbull Library (ATL) 4650-10.
2 RM to AC, 22 April 1986. AC Papers, ATL 4650-10.
3 Bernard O'Donoghue, 'Privileged Happyland?', Poetry Review, vol. 78, no. 1, Spring 1988.
4 Michael Hulse, 'The Mirrored Map', PN Review 59, vol. 14, no. 3, Jan.–Feb. 1988, p. 67.
5 Ibid.
6 AC to C.K. Stead (CKS), 25 April 1986. C.K. Stead Papers, privately held. Unless otherwise identified, letters from AC to CKS are held in Stead's private papers.
7 AC to Tony Curnow, 29 Sept. 1986. Anthony Curnow Papers, privately held.
8 AC to Tim Curnow, 14 June 1986. Tim Curnow Papers, ATL 7905-07.
9 DL to AC, 19 March 1986. AC Papers, ATL 4650-08.
10 AC to CKS, 8 Aug. 1986.
11 RM to AC, 8 Nov. 1986. AC Papers, ATL 4650-10.
12 AC to Tim Curnow, 5 Jan. 1987. Tim Curnow Papers, ATL 7905-07.
13 'Author's Note and Acknowledgements', Continuum: New and Later Poems 1972–1988, Auckland University Press, 1988, p. 10.
14 Epigraph, Continuum.
15 AC to Elizabeth Caffin (EC), 21 Oct. 1987. AC Papers ATL, 7574-10.
16 Norman Macbeth to Binney Lock, 25 May 1987. AC Papers, ATL 7574-81.
17 New Zealand Herald, 29 July 1987.
18 AC, quoted in The Press, 13 June 1987.
19 Ibid.
20 AC to CKS, 16 June 1987.
21 AC to Ian Milner (IM), 15 June 1987. AC Papers, ATL 6371-14 and Ian Milner Papers, ATL 4567-015.
22 AC to Elizabeth Alley, 25 Nov. 1987. Elizabeth Alley, private papers.
23 AC to CKS, 7 April 1987. AC Papers, ATL 4650-06 and C.K. Stead Papers, privately held.
24 Transcript of interview with Shirley Horrocks for documentary Early Days Yet (Point of View Productions, 2001). Shirley Horrocks, private papers.
25 AC to Ted Wall (TW), 2 Oct. 1987. AC Papers, ATL 4650-11.
26 AC to IM, [June] 1987. AC Papers, ATL 4650-10.
27 AC to CKS, 19 June 1987.
28 Ibid.
29 Sydney Morning Herald, 23 Dec. 1989.
30 Transcript of interview with Shirley Horrocks for documentary Early Days Yet (Point of View Productions, 2001). Shirley Horrocks, private papers.
31 Encounter, June 1988, p. 15.
32 Jeny Curnow (JC) to Tony Curnow, 14 Feb. 1988. Anthony Curnow Papers, privately held.
33 AC to Tim Curnow, 30 March 1988. Tim Curnow Papers, ATL 7905-08.
34 Paul Keegan to AC, 25 Aug. 1988. AC Papers, ATL 4650-15.
35 AC to Tim Curnow, 2 Nov. 1988. AC Papers, ATL 4650-11 and Tim Curnow Papers, ATL 7905-08.
36 JC to W.H. (Bill) Pearson, 15 Sept. 1988. W.H. Pearson Papers, ATL 4343-006.
37 AC to Tim Curnow, 2 Nov. 1988. AC Papers, ATL 4650-11 and Tim Curnow Papers, ATL 7905-08.
38 Mac Jackson, 'Still Reflecting: Curnow's Continuum', Landfall 171, vol. 43, no. 3, September 1989, pp. 360–367; Mark Williams, 'Twilight of the gods?', New Zealand Listener, 17 June 1989, p. 66.
39 'Forms and their spurning', Times Literary Supplement, 26 May–1 June 1989.
40 Michael Hulse, 'A Vaster Air', PN Review 73, vol. 16, no. 5, May–June 1990, p. 52.

41 CKS, 'Second Wind', *London Review of Books*, vol. 11, no. 4, 16 Feb. 1989, p. 19. C.K. Stead, 'Allen Curnow's Poetry', *Landfall* 65, vol. 17, no. 1, March 1963, pp. 26–45, reproduced in C.K. Stead, 'Allen Curnow: Poet of the Real', *In the Glass Case: Essays on New Zealand Literature*, Auckland University Press, Auckland, 1981, pp. 189–206.

42 AC to Tim Curnow, 2 Nov. 1988. AC Papers, ATL 4650-11 and Tim Curnow Papers, ATL 7905-08.

43 *Selected Poems 1940–1989*, Viking, London, 1990, p. xi.

44 'Allen Curnow talks to Peter Simpson', *Landfall* 175, vol. 44, no. 3, Sept. 1990, p. 297.

45 Ibid., p. 300.

46 CKS to AC, 13 Feb. 1989. AC Papers, ATL 4650-06 and C.K. Stead Papers, privately held.

47 Quoted in AC to CKS, 13 Feb. 1989.

48 AC to Tim Curnow, [June] 1989. Tim Curnow Papers, ATL 7905-08.

49 Ibid.

50 AC to Peter Scherer, 15 June 1989. AC Papers, ATL 6371-14.

51 AC to Tony Curnow, 19 July 1989. Anthony Curnow Papers, privately held.

52 AC Papers, ATL 4650-19.

53 AC to TW, 2 Aug. 1989. AC Papers, ATL 4650-11.

54 AC to Terry Sturm, 21 Nov. 1989. Terry Sturm Papers, privately held.

55 Ted Hughes to AC, 17 Aug. 1989. AC Papers, ATL 4650-17.

56 AC to Tony Curnow, 12 Dec. 1989. Anthony Curnow Papers, privately held.

57 AC to Tim Curnow, 8 Jan. 1990. Tim Curnow Papers, ATL 7905-08.

58 AC to Michael Hulse, 24 March 1990. AC Papers, ATL 6371-04.

59 'Lean Time Coming?', *New Zealand Herald*, 6 Aug. 1988.

60 *New Zealand Herald*, 7 April 1984.

61 'Showing us Howe', *New Zealand Herald*, 2 May 1987.

62 'Rating Our Chances', *New Zealand Herald*, 2 May 1986.

63 *New Zealand Herald*, 10 Nov. 1984.

64 *New Zealand Herald*, 29 Nov. 1986.

65 *New Zealand Herald*, 12 March 1988.

66 *New Zealand Herald*, 7 Feb. 1987.

67 *New Zealand Herald*, 18 July 1987.

68 *New Zealand Herald*, 29 Feb. 1988.

69 *New Zealand Herald*, 15 Jan. 1983.

CHAPTER THIRTY-THREE
EXPANDING CRITICAL INTEREST IN CURNOW, 1990–93

1 'Über die Lyrik Allen Curnows', *Bäume, Bildnisse, bewegliche Dinge* [*Trees, Effigies, Moving Objects*], Steidl Verlag, Göttingen, 1994, p. 66. Translated by Michael Hulse. Hulse Papers, ATL.

2 'Allen Curnow talks to Peter Simpson', *Landfall* 175, vol. 44, no. 3, Sept. 1990, p. 301.

3 Allen Curnow (AC) to Tony Curnow, 10 June 1990. Anthony Curnow Papers, privately held.

4 Richard Mayne (RM) to AC, 15 Jan. 1991. AC Papers, Alexander Turnbull Library (ATL) 4650-14.

5 *Span* 33, May 1992, p. 170.

6 'Out from Auden's shadow, a "musical" marvel', *Sydney Morning Herald*, 13 Oct. 1990.

7 Ibid.

8 'Ripened Kiwi fruits', *The Independent on Sunday*, 8 July 1990.

9 *Times Literary Supplement*, 14 Sept. 1990.

10 Donald Davie, 'Postmodernism and Allen Curnow', *PN Review* 77, vol. 17, no. 3, Jan.–Feb. 1991, pp. 32, 33.

11 AC to Michael Hulse (MH), 2 Oct. 1990. MH Papers, ATL 8361.

12 'Postmodernism and Allen Curnow', p. 33.

13 AC to Lawrence Dale, 31 July 1990. AC Papers, ATL 4650-09.

14 Transcript of interview with Shirley Horrocks for documentary *Early Days Yet* (Point of View Productions, 2001). Shirley Horrocks, private papers.

15 AC to Geoff Walker, 10 Aug. 1990. AC Papers, ATL 4650-15.

16 *Verse*, vol. 8, no. 2, Summer 1991.

17 Chris Miller, 'Allen Curnow as Post-Modern Metaphysical', *PN Review* 105, vol. 22, no. 1, Sept.–Oct. 1995.

18 Terry Sturm Papers, privately held. AC to Tim Curnow, 8 March 1991. Tim Curnow Papers, ATL 7905-08.

19 AC to W.H. (Bill) Pearson (WHP), 26 Aug. 1990. AC Papers, ATL 4650-09 and W.H. Pearson Papers, ATL 4343-006.

20 AC to C.K. Stead (CKS), 16 Feb. 1993. C.K. Stead Papers, privately held. Unless otherwise identified, letters from AC to CKS are held in Stead's private papers.

21 AC to MH, 27 July 1990. AC Papers, ATL 6371-04.

22 *Verse*, vol. 8, no. 2, Summer 1991, pp. 5–6.

23 *Sport* 7, Winter 1991, pp. 3–4.

24 Fergus Barrowman to AC, 17 April 1991. AC Papers, ATL 4650-09.

25 AC to Denis Glover, 24 July 1978. Denis Glover Papers, ATL 80-387-001.

26 CKS to AC, 25 Dec. 1990. AC Papers, ATL 4650-07.

27 AC to CKS, 14 March 1991.

28 AC to CKS, 30 April 1991.

29 Ibid.

30 'A Four Letter Word', *Trees, Effigies, Moving Objects: A Sequence of 18 Poems*, The Catspaw Press, Wellington, 1972, n.p.

31 Karl Miller (KM) to AC, 10 May 1991. AC Papers, ATL 4650-10.

32 AC to J.G.A. (John) Pocock (JGAP), 1 Feb. 1992. J.G.A. Pocock Papers, privately held.

33 AC Papers, ATL 6371-13.

34 AC to Peter Bland, 12 Sept. 1991. AC Papers, ATL 4650-10.

35 KM to AC, 30 Sept. 1991. AC Papers, ATL 4650-10.
36 AC to Douglas Lilburn (DL), 1 April 1992. AC Papers, ATL 7623-138.
37 'An Appreciation of Allen Curnow', *The Spectator*, 11 July 1992.
38 Jeny Curnow to Belinda Curnow, 20 June 1992. Belinda Curnow Papers, privately held.
39 AC Papers, ATL 6371-06.
40 AC to RM, 12 June 1993. AC Papers, ATL 6371-02.
41 Donald Davie to AC, 10 Oct. and 9 Dec. 1992. AC Papers, ATL 6371-02. AC to Donald Davie, 10 Nov. 1992. AC Papers, ATL 7574-89.
42 AC to RM, 12 June 1993. AC Papers, ATL 6371-02.
43 'Über die Lyrik Allen Curnows', *Bäume, Bildnisse, bewegliche Dinge*, Steidl Verlag, Göttingen, 1994, p. 66. Translated by Michael Hulse. Hulse Papers, ATL.
44 Joachim Sartorius to AC, 2 June 1994. AC Papers, ATL 7574-47.
45 *Frankfurter Allgemeine Zeitung*, 20 Aug. 1994. English translations by Alan Kirkness.

CHAPTER THIRTY-FOUR
EARLY DAYS YET, 1993–96

1 Allen Curnow (AC) to C.K. Stead (CKS), 17 Sept. 1993. CKS Papers, privately held. Unless otherwise identified, letters from AC to CKS are held in Stead's private papers (copies of which have been deposited at the Alexander Turnball Library, Wellington, since the writing of this book).
2 AC to CKS, 4 Feb. 1993.
3 AC to Michael Hulse (MH), 31 May 1993. AC Papers, Alexander Turnbull Library (ATL) 7574-25.
4 Ibid.
5 AC to CKS, 8 April 1993.
6 AC to Tim Curnow, 13 June 1993. Tim Curnow Papers, ATL 7905-09.
7 AC to CKS, 8 April 1993.
8 AC to CKS, 7 May 1993.
9 AC to CKS, 17 Sept. 1993.
10 AC to W.H. (Bill) Pearson (WHP), 25 Nov. 1993. W.H. Pearson Papers, ATL 5428-05.
11 AC to J.G.A. (John) Pocock (JGAP), 7 Dec. 1993. AC Papers, ATL 7574-55.
12 AC Papers, ATL 6371-23.
13 AC to JGAP, 27 March 1994. J.G.A. Pocock Papers, privately held.
14 AC Papers, ATL 6371-19.
15 Ibid.
16 AC to Douglas Lilburn (DL), 2 Sept. 1994. Douglas Lilburn Papers, ATL 7623-139.
17 AC to WHP, 26 March 1994. W.H. Pearson Papers, ATL 5428-05.
18 Ibid.
19 AC to Tim Curnow, 4 July 1994. Tim Curnow Papers, ATL 7905-09.

20 AC to DL, 2 Sept. 1994. Douglas Lilburn Papers, ATL 7623-139.
21 AC to Tim Curnow, 23 Nov. 1994. Tim Curnow Papers, ATL 7905-[?09].
22 AC to DL, 21 Oct. 1994. Douglas Lilburn Papers, ATL 7623-139.
23 Tim Bates to AC, 19 July 1995. AC Papers, ATL 6371-02.
24 Michael Schmidt (MS) to Tim Curnow, 4 Aug. 1995. Tim Curnow Papers, ATL 7905-14 and AC Papers, ATL 6371-07.
25 AC to JGAP, 7 Jan. 1996. J.G.A. Pocock Papers, privately held.
26 AC to MS, 20 Sept. 1995. AC Papers, ATL 6371-07 and Tim Curnow Papers, ATL 7905-14.
27 AC to JGAP, 7 Jan. 1996. J.G.A. Pocock Papers, privately held.
28 AC to Tony Curnow, 29 Nov. 1982. Anthony Curnow Papers, privately held.
29 Gordon Ogilvie (GO) to AC, 9 March 1998. AC Papers, ATL 7574-64.
30 AC to GO, 25 March 1998. AC Papers, ATL 7574-64.
31 AC to Tony Curnow, 17 June 1995. AC Papers, ATL 6371-16.
32 *The Loop in Lone Kauri Road*, catalogue, June 1995, preface.
33 AC to MH, 26 June 1995. AC Papers, ATL 7574-25.
34 *The Scrap-book*, limited edition, Wai-te-ata Press, Wellington, 1996; poem first published in *London Review of Books*, vol. 11, no. 23, 7 Dec. 1989 and in *Landfall* 175, vol. 44, no. 3, Sept. 1990 (as 'A Scrap-Book').
35 *Landfall* 191, Autumn 1996, pp. 13–19.
36 AC to MH, 21 May 1996. AC Papers, ATL 7574-25.
37 AC to *New Zealand Herald*, 27 May 1996.
38 Janet Wilson to Terry Sturm, 23 Nov. 1995. Terry Sturm Papers, privately held.
39 *Journal of New Zealand Literature*, no. 15, 1997 and no. 17, 1999.
40 MS to authors et al., 22 June 1996. AC Papers, ATL 6371-20.
41 *Poets on Poets*, ed. Nick Rennison and Michael Schmidt, Carcanet Press, Manchester, 1997, p. 461.
42 MS to AC, 28 Feb. 1997. AC Papers, ATL 6371-09.
43 Mary-Kay Wilmers to AC, 3 June 1997. AC Papers, ATL 6371-21.

CHAPTER THIRTY-FIVE
LAST POEMS, THE BELLS OF SAINT BABEL'S, 1997–2001

1 *The Collected Works of W.B. Yeats, Volume III: Autobiographies*, ed. W.H. O'Donnell and D.N. Archibald, Scribner, New York, 1999, p. 151.
2 Gordon McLauchlan, 'Another from the laureate', *New Zealand Herald*, 23 Aug. 1997.
3 Interview with Brian Edwards, 'Top o' the Morning', National Radio, Saturday 30 Aug. 1997.

4   David Eggleton, 'Curnow's progress: One poet's journey from faith to scepticism', *New Zealand Listener*, 25 Oct. 1997.

5   AC to Tim Curnow, 3 Nov. 1997. Tim Curnow Papers, Alexander Turnbull Library (ATL) 7905-09.

6   *Sydney Morning Herald*, 4 July 1998.

7   Elizabeth Lowry, 'Belonging down there', *Times Literary Supplement*, 19 Sept. 1997.

8   *Sunday Times*, 9 Nov. 1997.

9   Allen Curnow (AC) to Peter Simpson, 29 June 1997. AC Papers, ATL 7574-86.

10 AC, 'The Kindest Thing', *London Review of Books*, vol. 19, no. 13, 3 July 1997.

11 Mary-Kay Wilmers (M-KW) to AC, 19 Nov. 1997. AC Papers, ATL 6371-21. 'Ten Steps to the Sea', *London Review of Books*, vol. 20, no. 1, 1 January 1998, p. 6.

12 *Paeans for Peter Porter: A celebration for Peter Porter on his seventieth birthday by twenty of his friends, 16 February 1999*, ed. Anthony Thwaite, London, Bridgewater Press, 1999.

13 Anthony Thwaite to AC, 3 April 1998. AC Papers, ATL 7574-79 and 7574-88.

14 Peter Porter to AC, 16 March 1999. AC Papers, ATL 7574-85.

15 AC to Elaine Feinstein, 19 April 1998. AC Papers, ATL 7574-28.

16 C.K. Stead (CKS) to AC, 4 Jan. 2000. AC Papers, ATL 7574-79.

17 *Time Literary Supplement*, 15 Oct. 1999.

18 AC to CKS, 8 Oct. 1998. CKS Papers, privately held. Unless otherwise identified, letters from AC to CKS are held in Stead's private papers (copies of which have been deposited at the Alexander Turnbull Library, Wellington, since the writing of this book).

19 Jeny Curnow: Diary, 20 Nov. 1998. J.M. Curnow Papers, ATL 5483-[?].

20 AC to W.H. (Bill) Pearson (WHP), 27 March 1999. W.H. Pearson Papers, ATL 7628-07.

21 AC fax to M-KW, 26 March 1999. AC Papers, ATL [?7574-85].

22 AC to CKS, 30 March 1999.

23 CKS to AC, 2 April 1999. AC Papers, ATL 7574-79.

24 'The Bells of Saint Babel's', *London Review of Books*, vol. 21, no. 12, 10 June 1999, p. 19.

25 AC to CKS, 25 April 1999.

26 AC to Elizabeth Caffin (EC), 21 May 1999. Auckland University Press (AUP) Correspondence Files.

27 Editorial, *Sunday Star-Times* supplement, p. 3.

28 AC, 'The Cake Uncut', *London Review of Books*, vol. 22, no. 4, 17 Feb. 2000.

29 AC to EC, 27 Jan. 2000. AUP Correspondence Files.

30 *New Zealand Verse*, ed. W.F. Alexander and A.E. Currie, Walter Scott Publishing Company, London, 1906, p. 208.

31 Ibid., p. 185.

32 M-KW to AC, 24 May 2000. AC Papers, ATL 7574-85.

33 'Fantasia and Fugue for Pan-pipe', *London Review of Books*, vol. 22, no. 13, 6 June 2000, p. 6.

34 AC to CKS, 14 Sept. 2000. AC Papers, ATL 7574-79 and C.K. Stead Papers, privately held.

35 Ibid.

36 AC to CKS, 28 November 2000.

37 'A Nice Place on the Riviera', *London Review of Books*, vol. 23, no. 4, 22 February 2001, p. 23.

38 AC to CKS, 17 Jan. 2001.

39 Blaise Pascal, *Pensées*, tr. A.J. Krailsheimer, Penguin, Harmondsworth, 1966, XII.210.

40 Katherine Mansfield to John Middleton Murry, 18 Oct. 1920. *The Collected Letters of Katherine Mansfield, Volume 4: 1920–1921*, ed. Vincent O'Sullivan and Margaret Scott, Clarendon Press, Oxford, 1996, p. 75.

41 AC to Tony Curnow, 3 July 2001. Anthony Curnow Papers, privately held.

42 AC to CKS, 3 Aug. 2001.

43 Richard Carrington to Tim Curnow, 1 Sept. 2001. Tim Curnow Papers, ATL 7905-[?].

44 Jeny Curnow, Biography of Allen Curnow, Part Two. Jeny Curnow Papers, ATL MSDL-0204.

45 Address delivered by the Rt Rev. Sir Paul Reeves at the funeral of Allen Curnow, St Mary's in Holy Trinity Cathedral, Parnell, Auckland, 27 September 2001. Copy enclosed with Jeny Curnow to WHP, 11 Oct. 2001, W.H. Pearson Papers, ATL 7628-07.

46 Press release, Prime Minister and Minister for Arts, Culture and Heritage, Helen Clark, 24 Sept. 2001.

47 *New Zealand Herald*, 25 Sept. 2001.

48 *The Times*, 26 Sept. 2001.

49 *The Australian*, 9 Oct. 2001.

50 *The Guardian*, 28 Sept. 2001.

51 *The Independent*, 30 Sept. 2001.

52 *University of Auckland News*, May 2002.

53 J.G.A. Pocock to Jeny Curnow, 25 Sept. 2001. AC Papers, ATL 7574-22.

54 AC to Denis Glover, 11 May 1980. Denis Glover Papers, ATL 80-387-002.

POETRY

Valley of Decision: Poems by Allen Curnow, Phoenix Miscellany: 1, Auckland University College Students' Association Press, Auckland, 1933
Three Poems, The Caxton Club Press, Christchurch, [1935]
Enemies: Poems 1934–36, The Caxton Press, Christchurch, 1937
Not in Narrow Seas: Poems with Prose, The Caxton Press, Christchurch, 1939
Island and Time, The Caxton Press, Christchurch, 1941
Recent Poems (with A.R.D. Fairburn, Denis Glover and R.A.K. Mason), The Caxton Press, Christchurch, 1941
Sailing or Drowning: Poems, The Progressive Publishing Society, Wellington, [1943]
Jack without Magic: Poems, The Caxton Press, Christchurch, 1946
At Dead Low Water and Sonnets, The Caxton Poets No. 5, The Caxton Press, Christchurch, 1949
Poems, 1949–57, A Glover Book from The Mermaid Press, Wellington, 1957
A Small Room with Large Windows: Selected Poems, Oxford University Press, London, 1962
Trees, Effigies, Moving Objects: A Sequence of 18 Poems, The Catspaw Press, Wellington, 1972
An Abominable Temper and Other Poems, The Catspaw Press, Wellington, 1973
Collected Poems 1933–1973, A.H. & A.W. Reed, Wellington, 1974
An Incorrigible Music: A Sequence of Poems, Auckland University Press/Oxford University Press, Auckland, 1979
Selected Poems, Penguin, Auckland, 1982
You Will Know When You Get There: Poems 1979–81, Auckland University Press/Oxford University Press, Auckland, 1982
The Loop in Lone Kauri Road: Poems 1983–1985, Auckland University Press/Oxford University Press, Auckland, 1986
Continuum: New and Later Poems 1972–1988, Auckland University Press, Auckland, 1988
Selected Poems 1940–1989, Penguin, London and Viking, New York, 1990
Looking West, Late Afternoon, Low Water, Holloway Press, Auckland, 1994
The Scrap-book, Wai-te-ata Press, Wellington, 1996
Early Days Yet: New and Collected Poems 1941–1997, Auckland University Press, Auckland and Carcanet Press, Manchester, 1997
The Bells of Saint Babel's: Poems 1997–2001, Auckland University Press, Auckland and Carcanet Press, Manchester, 2001

PROSE

Poetry and Language, The Caxton Club Press, Christchurch, 1935
Look Back Harder: Critical Writings 1935–1984, ed. Peter Simpson, Auckland University Press, Auckland, 1987

PLAYS

The Axe: A Verse Tragedy, The Caxton Press, Christchurch, 1949
Four Plays: The Axe, The Overseas Expert, The Duke's Miracle, Resident of Nowhere, A.H. & A.W. Reed, Wellington, 1972

ANTHOLOGIES

A Book of New Zealand Verse 1923–45, ed. Allen Curnow, The Caxton Press, Christchurch, 1945
A Book of New Zealand Verse 1923–1950, ed. Allen Curnow, The Caxton Press, Christchurch, 1951
The Penguin Book of New Zealand Verse, ed. Allen Curnow, Penguin, Harmondsworth, 1960; reprinted Blackwood & Janet Paul, Auckland, 1966

BROADSHEET POEMS

The Hucksters & The University or Out of Site, Out of Mind or Up Queen Street Without a Paddle!, The Pilgrim
  Press, Auckland, 1957
Mr Huckster of 1958, The Pilgrim Press, Auckland, 1958
On The Tour: Verwoerd be our Vatchwoerd!, or God Amend New Zealand, The Pilgrim Press, Auckland, 1960

TRANSLATIONS

Bäume, Bildnisse, bewegliche Dinge [*Trees, Effigies, Moving Objects*], trans. Karin Graf and Joachim Sartorius,
  Steidl Verlag, Göttingen, 1994
Il Miraculo del Duca [*The Duke's Miracle*], trans. Italo Verri, Dr Lucio Scardino's Liberty House imprint,
  Ferrara, 1993

FILM

Early Days Yet: A documentary about the great poet Allen Curnow, directed and produced by Shirley Horrocks,
  Point of View Productions, Auckland, 2001

WHIM WHAM

A Present for Hitler & Other Verses, The Caxton Press, Christchurch, 1940
Whim Wham: Verses 1941–1942, The Caxton Press, Christchurch, 1942
Whim Wham 1943, The Progressive Publishing Society, Wellington, 1943
The Best of Whim Wham, Paul's Book Arcade, Hamilton and Auckland, 1959
Whim Wham Land, Blackwood & Janet Paul, Auckland, 1967
Whim Wham's New Zealand: The Best of Whim Wham 1937–1988, ed. Terry Sturm, Vintage Auckland, 2005

and politics, 60, 67, 69, 73–74, 87, 90, 132, 591; New
Zealand after Britain joins EEC, 399–400,
410; nuclear arms race, 359, 446, 524–25, 583,
591, 613, 646; pacifist sympathies, 137, 159;
'Rogernomics', 613–15; rugby and South
Africa, 360–61, 400, 410–11, 480, 524, 559–62;
in USA (1961), 378–80, 383; Vietnam War,
411–13, 446, 450–51, 524–25
pseudonyms: 'Amen', 119; 'Julian', 67, 82–84, 86–87,
91, 103, 106, 110, 112, 118–19, 124; 'Philo', 71–72.
See also Whim Wham
public addresses and lectures, 423–24;
'New Zealand Literature: The Case for a
Working Definition' (1963), 394–95; 'Olsen
as Oracle: Projective Verse Thirty Years
On' (1981), 541–42, 556–59; 'Poetry and
Knowledge' paper (1961), 372–76
radio and television programmes, 34–35, 104–05,
111, 240, 467, 504, 565, 601; in Britain and
USA, 275–76, 282, 381, 586, 588–90; current
affairs programme (1964), 400; drama,
361–63, 413–15, 421–22, 424–26, 500–501, 516;
Louis MacNeice memorial address, 396;
poetry and music, 177–80; poetry readings,
293, 393, 478, 665; television appearances, 378,
497, 648
and religious vocation, 29–30, 58–59, 61, 64, 69,
77–79; abandonment of, 81–82
satire in work, 82–84, 90, 133–35, 328–30, 401–02,
410–13, 477, 524–25
and theatre, 125–26, 189–92, 259, 355–57, 381, 392, 573,
610
travel overseas: 1949–50: Britain, 6–7, 12–13, 230,
239–42, 251–74; 1950: USA, 277–85; 1961: USA,
365–66, 368–86, 415–19; 1966–67: USA, 415–19;
1974: Europe, 480–97; 1974: USA, 497–98;
1983: France, Italy, England, 569–74; 1985:
England, Canada, 587–91; 1988: England,
Italy, 605–06; 1989: England, 609; 1992: Italy,
Spain, England, USA, 632–33; 1998: England,
657–58. See also Australia, visits to
university positions. See under Auckland
University College/University of Auckland
university student years, 58–77; part-time at
Canterbury, 57; theological studies, 59, 66,
68–70, 76–77; completes BA degree, 111,
182
views: on 1930s poets, 107, 137–39, 140n, 153; on the
artist in New Zealand, 121–22; on censorship,
396–400; on church as institution, 69, 71–74,
81–83; on colonialisation, 35, 122–23, 355; on
dogmatic theology, 156–57; on Englishness/
Britishness, 5, 7, 11, 35, 401, 443, 490, 659;
on language in poetry, 93–95, 116, 558; on
national identity, 13, 138–39, 142–43, 176, 182,
184, 238, 595; on national literary concepts,
106–07, 116–17, 139, 584; on New Zealand
historians, 169; on New Zealand poetry,
92, 117, 122, 153, 182–83, 184, 195–96, 235–36,
244–45, 288–89; on New Zealand society, 196,
355, 358–59, 602; on 'open form' poetry, 537–42,
545, 556–58; on phenomenology, 557–58, 585;

on revisionist interpretations, 597–98, 621; on
USA in atomic era, 284–85
Curnow, Allen: critical writing, 92–95, 153, 300–302,
407, 422
anthology introductions, 122, 194–96, 244–45,
323–24, 537
'Aspects of New Zealand Poetry' (1942), 153, 194–95
on Australian poetry, 231–32
credo in letter to Lilburn (1952), 299–300
'critical nationalism' perception, 195, 584
'A Job for Poetry' (1941), 139–42, 144
Look Back Harder (1987), 422, 478, 584–85, 597
modernist aesthetic principles in, 196, 231
'Painting in Canterbury', 293
Poetry and Language (1935), 87, 93–95, 118
'Poets in New Zealand' (1937), 116–17
'Pricking Some Intellectual Bubbles' (1935), 87,
89–90
private reaction to Stead's 1979 article, 537–41
reviewing practice, 331
Curnow, Allen: journalism
proofreading, 56–58
on staff of The Press: in 1930s, 81, 82–83, 86, 95, 96,
98–102, 111–13, 126; literary page articles and
reviews, 87, 92–93, 116–17, 137–38, 153, 234–35,
291; in wartime, 136–37, 159–60, 182, 185, 196,
204; post-war, 240, 287–88, 290–92
as sub-editor in London, 254–55, 259, 262–64
passim
Curnow, Allen: plays, 238–39, 421
The Axe (1949), 152, 163, 189–92, 217–23, 268, 443;
publication, 243, 291; on radio, 361–63, 392;
stage productions, 236–39, 303–04
Dr Pom (1964), 400–403, 566
The Duke's Miracle (radio play, 1966), 407, 409,
413–15, 421–22, 442, 444, 500–501, 516; Italian
translation, 622–23
Four Plays (1972), 219, 358, 403, 426, 442–43, 446,
470
Moon Section (Out of the Bright Sky) (1959), 268,
306–07, 331–32, 348, 351–59, 444, 566
The Overseas Expert (Fool's Gold) (1960), 352,
357–59, 392, 401, 443
Resident of Nowhere (radio play, 1968), 421, 424–26,
444
Curnow, Allen: poems. For individual titles, see end
of index
Curnow, Allen: poems – collections
An Abominable Temper (1973), 33, 461, 467, 472–76
At Dead Low Water and Sonnets (1949), 4, 229,
242–43, 268
Bäume, Bildnisse, bewegliche Dinge (1994), 635–36
The Bells of Saint Babel's (2001), 4, 651, 654, 659–60,
664–67, 669
Collected Poems (1974), 57, 62, 466–72, 497–98,
501–02, 559; revision of early poems, 467–69
Continuum: New and Later Poems 1972–1988 (1988),
598–99, 601–05, 607, 609
Early Days Yet: New and Collected Poems (1997),
645n, 646, 649–52
Enemies (1937), 85, 90, 91, 102–03, 105, 106–10,
467–68

CURNOW, ALLEN: POEMS